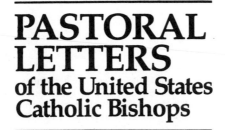

PASTORAL LETTERS
of the United States Catholic Bishops

Hugh J. Nolan, Editor

VOLUME V
1983-1988

National Conference of Catholic Bishops
United States Catholic Conference

The bishops of the United States have provided religious and moral guidance and leadership to American Catholics since the establishment of the Church in the United States. *Pastoral Letters of the United States Catholic Bishops, 1983-1988,* Volume V, is a collection of statements issued by the Catholic hierarchy of the United States during the five-year period of 1983 to 1988. This collection was initiated by the USCC Office for Publishing and Promotion Services and is authorized for publication by the undersigned.

Reverend Robert N. Lynch
General Secretary
NCCB/USCC

June 27, 1989

Excerpts from *The Documents of Vatican II,* Walter M. Abbott, SJ, General Editor, Copyright © 1966, America Press, Inc., 106 West 56th Street, New York, N.Y. are reprinted with permission. All rights reserved.

Excerpts from *Vatican Council II: The Conciliar and Post Conciliar Documents,* Austin P. Flannery, ed. (Collegeville, Minn.: Liturgical Press, 1975) are reprinted with permission. All rights reserved.

Unless otherwise noted, Old Testament scriptural excerpts in this volume are from *The New American Bible,* copyright © 1970, Confraternity of Christian Doctrine, Washington, D.C.; New Testament scriptural excerpts are from *The New American Bible,* copyright © 1970 and 1986, Confraternity of Christian Doctrine, Washington, D.C. Both are used with the permission of the copyright owner.

ISBN 1-55586-200-4

I am the good shepherd.
I know my sheep
and my sheep know me
in the same way that the Father knows me
and I know the Father;
for these sheep I will give my life.
I have other sheep
that do not belong to the fold.
I must lead them, too,
and they shall hear my voice.

John 10:14-16

Contents

Appendix

Foreword

This fifth and latest volume of the *Pastoral Letters of the United States Catholic Bishops* contains the statements and resolutions made collectively by the bishops from 1983 to 1988. While these vital years are marred by a deterioration of moral and ethical standards, they are also filled with hope, which is reflected in the statements and which points to a joyous and successful entry by the Catholic Church in the United States into her next centennial.

There is scarcely a serious international or domestic problem involving the United States during these years that the National Conference of Catholic Bishops and the United States Catholic Conference have not touched with a thoughtful statement. Of particular concern to the bishops has been the need for greater social justice to correct many of the evils affecting people throughout the world.

The bishops made a Christmas 1988 *Statement on Religious Freedom in Eastern Europe and the Soviet Union.* They called at this particular time for the God-given right of religious freedom because many countries persecuted by the Soviets were celebrating significant anniversaries. Just as Christ cares for all human beings, so too do the bishops:

> The difficulties faced by non-Catholics in Eastern Europe and the Soviet Union and by some religions in Vietnam, Cambodia, Cuba, Iran, Turkey, Sudan, and elsewhere also demand serious attention. . . . We share their sufferings just as we share the duty to protect and promote through our words and actions religious freedom and tolerance wherever and whenever they are lacking.

The American prelates close by quoting Pope John Paul II's prayer that

> . . . these brothers and sisters of ours will feel our spiritual closeness, our solidarity, and the comfort of our prayer. We know that their sacrifice, to the extent that it is joined to Christ's, bears fruits of true peace.

In 1983, the bishops passed a *Resolution on Central America* requesting a political rather than military solution to the problems in those countries. This was followed in 1987 by a carefully reasoned *Statement on Central America,* which also strongly supports the episcopate in Central America.

To voice their opposition to racial injustice, the bishops issued a *Statement on South Africa* (1985). It was followed by *Divestment, Disinvestment, and South Africa* (1986).

Throughout this same period, the bishops of the United States issued several resolutions seeking liberation for persecuted countries such as Lithuania and the Ukraine. These resolutions demonstrate the sensitivity of the Church in the United States to sufferers abroad.

Additional interest for the welfare of the foreign-born seeking to come to the United States prompted the bishops' conference to pass a *Resolution on Immigration Reform* (1985). This, in turn, led to the document entitled, *Together, A New People: Pastoral Statement on Migrants and Refugees* (1986).

Much of the success of the Church's teachings depended on the thinking of government officials. In 1984, the bishops twice wrote on the role of *Religion and Politics* and also authored a document entitled, *Political Responsibility: Choices for the 1980s*. In the presidential election year of 1988, the conference produced the unbiased *Testimony to Democratic and Republican Platform Committees*.

Each decade for the last half century, the bishops have begged for relief from the double taxation borne by parents who exercise their God-given right to send their children to the school of their choice. In 1983, the bishops entitled their honest request, *Broadening Tuition Tax Credit Proposals*.

Value and Virtue: Moral Education in the Public School (1987) resists the onslaught by secular humanists on the morality of public school students. This statement was followed by the *Statement on School-based Clinics* (1987), in which the National Conference of Catholic Bishops denounced the distribution of contraceptives in school clinics as a preventative for AIDS. And on March 23, 1988, the Administrative Board asked our young people to ignore instructions about so-called safe sex and to understand the great worth and benefits of chastity in the *Statement to Youth on School-based Clinics*.

In their unending battle against the scourge of legalized abortion, the American prelates published in 1985 a well-thought-out *Pastoral Plan for Pro-Life Activities*. This was followed in 1988 with a pointed protest entitled, *Statement on Federal Funding of "in vitro" Fertilization Experiments*. While pro-abortionists alleged that it was discriminatory not to make abortions available to the poor, the bishops demonstrated that it was a violation of religious liberty to use the taxes of citizens opposed to abortions in order to pay for them.

To help the poor, the bishops took practical steps with *Tax Reform and the Poor* (1985), *Statement on Food and Agriculture* (1985), and the powerful *Homelessness and Housing: A Human Tragedy, a Moral Challenge* (1988). *The Report of the Ad Hoc Task Force on Food, Agriculture, and Rural Concerns* (1988) asks for an extension of federal loans for farmers suffering from a series of droughts.

Answering the Holy Father's plea for increased evangelization throughout the world, the U.S. bishops wrote the pastoral statement *A Vision of Evangelization* (1985), which provides methods of ministry for all levels of society. To show special care for our college students, the bishops published a special pastoral letter, *Empowered by the Spirit: Campus Ministry Faces the Future* (1985).

A high point of the many pronouncements by the bishops is the monumental work, *Economic Justice for All* (1986). Based on Sacred Scripture, it offers principles and concrete options to combat one of the world's worst evils—economic injustice. This pastoral has received wide attention in our colleges and universities. A companion to this economic pastoral is *To the Ends of the Earth: A Pastoral Statement on World Mission* (1986). This work hopes in its worldwide missionary effort to proclaim the teachings of a just economy. This triumvirate of outstanding statements is completed by *Building Peace: A Pastoral Reflection on the Response to "The Challenge of Peace"* (1988). This statement is both a study and a promotion of the implementation of the highly publicized peace pastoral.

All of these statements collected here have been edited in order to make them as meaningful and as useful as possible for the reader. The sectional introductions succinctly place the documents in their historical setting and also trace, where necessary, their development from the actual dialogue that took place on the floor. The editor, Father Hugh J. Nolan, does an excellent job in utilizing primary sources and the minutes of the general meetings—all of which he attended.

Not to know and study these documents would be to miss a critical ingredient of the history of Catholicism in the United States during these significant years. I hope that all people will give a careful reading to these documents and thereby reap the benefits of knowledge and insight that they offer.

Most Reverend Anthony J. Bevilacqua
Archbishop of Philadelphia

Preface

The pastoral letters and statements that comprise this fifth and latest volume in the *Pastoral Letters of the United States Catholic Bishops* are the official messages issued during the years 1983-1988 to the nation's Catholic clergy and faithful by the Catholic bishops of the United States, organized as the National Conference of Catholic Bishops (NCCB). The term "pastoral letters" is used here in a broad sense. It is not always possible to draw a distinct line between the pastorals and the statements made collectively by the American bishops, so for the sake of completeness, the statements are also included, as are the significant accompanying resolutions and the occasional testimonies presented to various governmental bodies. To facilitate the use of these documents, paragraphs have been numbered, and the documents have been arranged chronologically. For the most part, they have emerged from the general meetings of the entire body of bishops. On occasion—usually an emergency that would not wait for a general meeting—statements have been issued either by the president of the National Conference of Catholic Bishops/United States Catholic Conference or by the Administrative Board (USCC) or the Administrative Committee (NCCB), with the proper approval and utilizing as much consultation as time permits. These emergency statements, too, have been included in this volume.

The two sectional Introductions trace the historical origin of each document, following its development from the meeting floor discussions through to its approval and subsequent publication. Some insight is also provided as to the effectiveness of each statement. Because of its greater importance, the commentary on *Economic Justice for All* is much lengthier than the usually briefer comments on the other statements.

The documents in this volume should be read in the context of Pope John Paul II's March 11, 1989, admonition to the American heirarchy during their meeting with the Holy Father: "The central theme of our discussions in the general context of evangelization has been 'Bishop as Teacher of the Faith.'" Addressing the problem of erroneous teachings, the pope on the same occasion asserted: "As Peter in your midst, I must encourage and confirm you and your suffragans and the auxiliary bishops, and the particular churches over which you preside, in this consecration to the truth that is the Word of God, that is the Son of God made flesh for the salvation of all." These national teachings fulfill Pope John Paul II's encouraging hope: "You have expressed your determination to pursue with responsibility and sensitivity your pastoral service in this regard."

More and more, the hierarchy of the United States, as one of the first established and most significant national episcopal conferences in the universal Church, has accepted this challenge in a nation recognized as one of the two superpowers of the world. From 1983 to 1988, there was, on the whole, a remarkable advance in the thought and the actions of the NCCB, especially in the field of social justice. The prelates have also made greater efforts to publicize their statements throughout the nation from the pulpit and in all forms of modern media.

The allegation that the bishops sometimes operate in areas of limited competence — even going beyond that competence — is answered more clearly in recent statements, which have benefited from an ever-expanding consultation process. *Economic Justice for All*, with its incredibly vast consultation of worldwide ecclesiastical authorities, economists, and high government officials, is a prime example of this increased scope.

Each individual has a significant role in the implementation and dissemination of these statements. He must in accordance with his vocation not only live the message of these episcopal teachings but also spread the "good news" to the best of his ability. The bishops indicate this in nearly all of their documents, but most specifically in *To the Ends of the Earth: A Pastoral Statement on World Mission*, which tells us we are our brother's keeper and that we are to provide for him spiritually and materially to the very best of our ability. Yes, the prime obligation is the spiritual help, but the material needs are to be met even unto the point of deep sacrifice.

Moreover, in this series of documents dealing principally with social justice as the proper pathway for the American Church's next centennial, there is a clearer *Vision of Evangelization* (1985) based on Pope John Paul II's vision. These social justice statements, in particular, are written to encourage and assist not only Catholic Americans in assuming their proper roles on the political, social, and economic levels but all other readers of the documents, regardless of their religious beliefs. The statements asking Americans to assume proper political responsibility are addressed to all Americans. On the social level, the bishops beg for the God-given human rights for every member of the human race — especially the right to migrate and to worship God according to conscience.

Highlighting this period (1983-1988) is the 1986 *Economic Justice for All: Pastoral Letter on Catholic Social Teaching and the U.S. Economy*, which almost instantly received worldwide notice. From Brazil, the famed liberation theologians Fathers Clodovis and Boff proclaimed: "It cannot be denied: The American episcopate has shown true evangelical boldness and prophetic courage . . . the American bishops give the distinct impression that they are truly friends of all the world's poor — not only those of their own country but in a special way, of the poor from the Third World. . . . The bishops note that rather than diminishing, poverty is actually increasing in the United States just as in Brazil; the rich in the United States are becoming even richer while the poor grow poorer." This letter shows how such excessive poverty can paralyze even the spiritual growth of its victims. The pastoral opens with a rock-solid scriptural basis: love of the poor without exception and of justice without limitation. And while disclaiming to have all the answers, it does offer some sound scientifically based, widely consulted solutions that at least offer some admission of and approach to this devastating, worldwide problem. Unfortunately, this evil is steadily worsening even in the United States, the bishops warn. "Since 1973, the poverty rate has increased by nearly a third." Most disturbing, "today, children are the largest single group among the poor." Today, one in every four white American children under the age of six and one in every two black children under the age of six are poor. In less than a year, 130,000 copies of the pastoral had been mailed, including 28,000 in Spanish. This pastoral contacted more institutions and individuals than the pastoral on peace. Labor unions, educators, politicians, local business people—all identify with economic problems.

Furthermore, after six years of social cutbacks, rising homelessness, low-income housing shortages, and other attacks on the poor, this pastoral was most timely. It offered guidelines to our leaders who were looking for antipoverty remedies such as minimum wage, job retraining, child care, educational subsidies, and raising benefits above the poverty level. It is safe to write that at the time of its publication no statement of any religious body was so desperately needed throughout the world.

The editor of this volume wishes to thank His Excellency Anthony J. Bevilacqua, archbishop of Philadelphia, for his Foreword; and to express his gratitude to the Office for Publishing and Promotion Services of the United States Catholic Conference, especially Ann Zimmerman and Linda D. Hersey for their constant encouragement.

Hugh J. Nolan
Editor

I. Greater Social Justice
1983-1985

Introduction

In a statement issued at their September 15, 1983 meeting, the forty-seven member Administrative Board of the United States Catholic Conference, praising the June 29, 1983 Supreme Court's decision providing tuition tax deductions for public and nonpublic school parents, asked that the tax credit legislation pending in the U.S. Congress be revised to include public as well as nonpublic school parents. In view of the long wait by the nonpublic education community, the bishops urged Congress to act promptly to broaden the proposed legislation "along the lines we have described and then enact it without further delay."

In October of that same year, testimony was given before the National Commission on U.S. Policy in Central America, on behalf of the U.S. bishops. During the previous decade, the concern of the U.S. bishops for Central America had heightened. On October 21, Archbishop James Hickey of Washington, D.C., representing the USCC, testified to the bipartisan panel known as the Kissinger Commission. His Excellency assured the commission that as American citizens the bishops "want to see our vital national interests protected and our government's policies reflect our national values and ideals."

Stating that the internal conflicts in Central America existed long before any outside intervention, the Washington prelate quoted the Central American bishops regarding the cessation of all intervention now and in the future: "If not, the intervention of one will automatically generate the intervention of the other and thus the establishment of peace will become progressively more difficult."

Archbishop Hickey asserted that we need a consistent policy that sees human rights as a principal force of the U.S. concern. He then offered eight criteria for the protection of human rights. In El Salvador, he identified the U.S. policy process as a determination to pursue the road of military force with a diplomatic facade, rather than as a political policy with a military component. Referring to Nicaragua, the archbishop affirmed: "As an American citizen and as a Catholic bishop, I find the use of U.S. tax dollars for the purpose of destabilization of a recognized government to be unwise, unjustified, and destructive of the very values that a democratic nation should support in the world." A sound realist, he further noted that direct Soviet intervention in Central America is no more welcome than direct U.S. intervention in Eastern Europe and that this point should be made clear to the Soviets.

After presenting the bishops' concerns about the current U.S. policy and their proposals for peace in Central America, he concluded: "We are convinced these proposals lay the foundation for a new relationship between the United States and Central America which will protect our national interests, help meet the needs of this troubled region, and serve also to curb Soviet and Marxist inroads in this hemisphere."

At its November 1982 plenary assembly, the National Conference of Catholic Bishops, mindful that the U.S. Hispanic population numbered at least 20 million, authorized the preparation of a pastoral letter on the Hispanic ministry. The final draft of *The Hispanic Presence: Challenge and Commitment* was approved at the plenary assembly of the National Conference of Catholic Bishops on November 12, 1983.

The need for this pastoral letter is obvious from this statistic: In fifteen years, nearly 1 million Hispanic men and women in the United States have left the Catholic Church. In ten years, Hispanic Catholics have had a defection rate of 8 percent. In contrast, the Protestant segment of Americans of Hispanic origin is large and rapidly growing larger.[1]

The bishops entitled their first chapter "A Call to Hispanic Ministry," warning that focusing primarily on numbers could easily lead one to see Hispanics simply as a large pastoral problem, while overlooking the even more important unique pastoral opportunity they offer. "Hispanic Catholicism is an outstanding example of how the Gospel can permeate a culture to its very roots." But no culture is without its defects. "Hispanic culture, like any other, must be challenged by the Gospel." Socioeconomic conditions are not favorable for this ministry, however, as most Hispanics in the United States live near or below the poverty level. This makes them more susceptible to "rice" proselytizing. Their lack of education aggravates the situation.

After praising in chapter II the "Achievements in Hispanic Ministry in the United States," the prelates considered in chapter III "Urgent Pastoral Implications." Under this heading they examined every aspect of pastoral ministry from Hispanic youth to family, from social justice to prejudice, from migrant farm workers to ties with Latin America. The liturgy, preaching, catechizing, Catholic education, and religious vocations are also considered in this, the lengthiest chapter.

Chapter IV, "Statement of Commitment," studies the various commitments necessary for the Hispanic ministry and concludes with the promise of a national pastoral plan for Hispanic ministry "at the earliest possible date." That promise was fulfilled in November 1987 when the general meeting of the NCCB approved the *National Pastoral Plan for Hispanic Ministry*.

Also at the November 1983 general meeting of the NCCB, the

---

[1]Andrew M. Greeley, "Defection among Hispanics" *America* (July 30, 1988).

bishops passed a *Resolution on Central America* to express their sense of solidarity with the Catholic Church of that region. In their resolution, the U.S. prelates quoted from their Central American confreres' statement a most pertinent passage supportive of Archbishop Hickey's October testimony to the Kissinger Commission: "Our people equally suffer because of the meddling of foreign powers, come to support those in the countries who fit their own interests, which are generally far from, even opposed to, those of the great majority."

The Resolution on Central America stresses the need for "an honorable and civilized dialogue" among the contending parties and the withdrawal of all "outside powers and ideological forces that are interfering politically and militarily in Central America." Promising their continual effort to do all they could to promote peace, the bishops of the United States closed their resolution with a prayer that from Panama to Guatemala there be built among us "a civilization of love."

The previous year, at its November 1982 plenary assembly, the National Conference of Catholic Bishops authorized the preparation of a pastoral statement on prayer and worship commemorating the twentieth anniversary of the promulgation of *Sacrosanctum Concilium*, the *Constitution on the Sacred Liturgy*. The twentieth anniversary offered the bishops an opportunity to commemorate this significant event in the life of our faith, to evaluate its effect, and to foster its continued importance for the future of the Church in the United States of America. No other work can be more important. The plenary assembly of the National Conference of Catholic Bishops approved the third and final draft of *The Church at Prayer: A Holy Temple of the Lord* on November 17, 1983.

This document opens with a rather complete presentation of "General Liturgical Principles." Liturgical renewal implies an ever deeper involvement of the whole Christian community in the paschal mystery of Jesus Christ. Chapter two, "The Eucharistic Mystery," is perhaps the most important and helpful of all chapters. The Eucharist teaches us especially the meaning of God's peace and justice. Chapter three, "The Sacraments and Sacramentals," offers many new insights stressing that confirmation with baptism is a sacrament of initiation. The statement encourages the use of sacramentals. The fourth chapter, "Liturgical Prayer," advises that the laity should learn liturgical prayer; that liturgical formation is as necessary for the laity as it is for the clergy, and that liturgy must be the primary school for Christian prayer and spirituality. "Liturgical Time" has to do mostly with the special sessions on the Church's calendar. "Liturgical Music, Art, and Architecture," gives guidelines in these various fields.

Carefully, these bishops explained that the Church, always a community of penitents, recognizes the mystery of the Father's love entrusted to "vessels of clay." All lives should manifest what the liturgy expresses. "We do not worship God primarily to become better people; the very nature and excellence of God demand worship." In the worship of the Church, however, Christians are formed as moral persons. Special effort must be made to ensure that the spirituality of individual Catholics is both Christian and liturgical. The goal is to enrich the Church's life of worship and prayer, for the individual and for the community.

In our own country, special care must be taken to adapt the liturgy so that it includes women and responds to the needs of persons of all ages, races, and ethnic groups. "Liturgical adaptation is not simply a concession granted by the *Constitution on the Sacred Liturgy*; it is rather a theological imperative of liturgical renewal."

With great hope, the document noted that recent liturgical reforms in many churches of North America, especially those related to the Eucharist, already point to an evolving ecumenical unity of liturgical prayer that gives hope for eventual doctrinal agreement. Liturgical reform, the bishops pointed out, has helped the Church to come into the presence of the all-holy God in languages, signs, and gestures spoken and made by contemporary Catholics without the loss of its tradition—truly a gift of the Holy Spirit. However, there remain many areas of unfinished liturgical business.

"Mindful of our own responsibilities . . . to carry out the office of sanctification in the Church, "the bishops concluded, "we pledge renewed efforts to continue the great work of the Council in liturgical renewal." This statement has been very well received and implemented on the diocesan level.

Toward the beginning of 1984, at the March NCCB Administrative Committee meeting, the *Pastoral Statement on the Catholic Charismatic Renewal* of the Bishops' Liaison Committee was approved. This statement updates a 1975 statement on the same subject. Bishop Kenneth J. Povish, chairman of the committee, was assisted by Archbishop Charles Salatka, Bishops Joseph Ferrario, Francisco Garmendia, Edward Hughes, Raymond Lucker, Joseph McKinney, and Fathers Kilian McDonnell and Robert Sherry in the document's preparation.

Addressed primarily to the bishops, *Catholic Charismatic Renewal* is composed of eleven Pastoral Observations and eleven Pastoral Orientations "concerning the great things Catholic charismatics are convinced the Lord Jesus is doing in our day." This episcopal committee cited that two popes— Paul VI and John Paul II—have spoken encouragingly about the movement. "Since our last two statements (1969 and 1975), we have seen the charismatic renewal mature in its grasp of the core of the Gospel and those realities which belong constitutively to the inner nature of the Church." These bishops explained that the call to discipleship and to baptism is an invitation to enter into a personal relationship with Jesus Christ as Lord and Savior. "It is also an invitation to enter into personal bonds with the whole People of God."

Charismatics seek to be completely open to the Holy Spirit as they contribute to the ongoing effort to renew the whole Church. Charisms are given to individual members for the blessing of the whole community, which as a body is entirely ministerial to its individuals, families, parishes, and the Church in general.

The committee concludes its report by assuring those in the charismatic renewal of the support they enjoy from the bishops of the United States, and "we encourage them in their efforts to renew the life of the Church."

Nearly a decade ago, on February 12, 1976, the USCC Administrative Board issued the statement, *Political Responsibility: Reflections on an Election Year*. Then, on October 26, 1979, they issued a second statement, *Political Responsibility: Choices for the 1980s*. In its planning document, as approved by the general membership of the United States Catholic Conference in November 1983, the Department of Social Development and World Peace was authorized to prepare an update of the 1979 statement on *Political Responsibility* in the name of the USCC Administrative Board. This statement was approved by the board in March 1984.

In this document, the bishops began their teaching by insisting that the election year necessitated emphasis on the importance of responsible political participation. Previously, in 1976 and in 1979, they had issued statements calling for "a committed, informed citizenry to revitalize our political life." The prelates were encouraged by the improvement in voter participation rates demonstrated in the 1982 Congressional elections, yet the level of participation in the political process by American voters was still a matter of serious concern to them. They noted that among the poor only about one of every four eligible voters had gone to the polls in the previous national election. All Christians, however, have a call to citizenship and political life. As Pope John Paul II observed, "An important challenge for the Christian is that of political life. In the state citizens have a right and duty to share in the political life."

Christian responsibility in the area of human rights includes two complementary pastoral actions: (1) the affirmation and promotion of human rights and (2) the denunciation and condemnation of violations of these rights. The Church, as a community of faith, must call attention to the moral and religious dimension of secular issues, keep alive the value of the Gospel as a norm for social and political life, and point out the demands of the Christian faith for a just transformation of society. The Church's responsibility in this area falls on all its members.

The bishops presented the Church's role in the political order on the following issues:

- education regarding the teachings of the Church and the responsibilities of the faithful;

- analysis of issues for their social and moral dimensions;
- measurement of public policy against gospel values;
- participation with other concerned parties in debate over public policy; and
- discussion with courage, skill, and concern of public issues involving human rights, social justice, and the life of the Church in society.

The document treats fourteen current issues starting with "Abortion." Under "Economy," for example, the bishops commented, "Efforts to achieve responsible fiscal policies and to stimulate economic growth and security are important and necessary tasks, but they should be governed by a fundamental concern for equity and fairness. Our nation's economic ills must not be solved at the expense of the poor and most vulnerable members of society."

This is not, of course, a complete listing of the political issues of concern to the Church. As Pope John Paul II has said, "The Church cannot remain insensible to whatever serves true human welfare any more than she can remain indifferent to whatever threatens it." In the world of American politics, as in all human communities, "What is in question . . . is the human person. We are not dealing with the abstract human person but the real, concrete, historical person. . . . Every person coming into the world on account of the mystery of the redemption is entrusted to the solicitude of the Church."

The bishops concluded with a prayer that Christians will provide courageous leadership in promoting a spirit of responsible political involvement: "May they follow the example of Jesus in giving special concern for the poor, and may all their actions be guided by a deep love of God and neighbor."

This statement put the American bishops on record as to just why the Church was interested in the realm of politics: because she is interested in and will work tirelessly to obtain total gospel justice for all in every realm.

On June 26, 1984, Cardinal Joseph Bernardin of Chicago and Archbishop John O'Connor of New York presented testimony *Concerning Arms Control* to the House Foreign Relations Committee on behalf of the United States Catholic Conference. Their statement criticized several U.S. arms decisions. Using the principles of the pastoral letter *The Challenge of Peace*, they offered two criteria for assessing the new weapons systems: (1) their influence on the arms race and their worth for deterrence and (2) financial cost. Applying the principles of their pastoral on peace, the prelates cautioned: "Much of the history of the arms race is technology moving ahead of both political and moral reflection or restraint." As an example, they pointed to the MIRVing (multiple independent reentry vehicle) of nuclear weapons "without the kind of public debate we believe such a revolutionary change in the arms race called for." They opposed the deployment of U.S. Pershing and cruise missiles in Western Europe and asked for further study in the deployment of the MX missile. They also expressed doubts about the proposed space-based defense system. The bishops advised "a new effort of political will and creative diplomacy on behalf of a new round of superpower negotiations to reverse the arms race."

Pursuant of this request, quoting the pope's call for new international institutions capable of building peace among nations, the bishops specifically pleaded for a presently unpopular cause: renewed support for the United Nations. "A creative U.S. initiative should be both critical and constructive; it need not be silent about needed reforms, but these can be proposed in a manner which all can recognize as fundamentally in support of the United Nations."

In their offering of possible solutions, the American prelates proposed a conscious U.S. policy of independent initiatives to restrain the arms race, a convincingly articulated U.S. policy aimed at reconstituting negotiations with the Soviet Union, and a long-needed reaffirmation of U.S. support for the objectives and the institutions of the United Nations.

It would be difficult to estimate how much influence this testimony had on the national policy. However, President Reagan did take an independent initiative to restrain the arms race in his negotiations with the Soviet Union to destroy certain nuclear weapons on both sides. This testimony also put the American Catholic Church on record once again for its efforts to promote international peace.

That same summer, on August 9, 1984, the president of the United States Catholic Conference, along with the USCC Executive Committee, consisting of Bishop James Malone, chairman (Youngstown, Ohio), Archbishops John May (St. Louis), Thomas Kelly (Louisville), Bernard Law (Boston), and Edmund Szoka (Detroit), issued a statement on *Religion and Politics*.

After explaining that the United States Catholic Conference, as an agency of the U.S. Catholic bishops, speaks on public policy issues but does not take positions for or against political candidates, the committee clarified: "In regard to public issues, the bishops exercise their teaching role by defining the content of moral principles and indicating how they apply to specific problems." By presenting positions on such issues, the USCC hopes to offer moral guidance to Catholics and other persons of good will in making their decisions on political candidates and parties.

Opposing those who claim that personally they do not believe in abortion but will not impose their personal beliefs on others, the bishops rejected the idea that candidates satisfy the requirements of rational analysis in saying their personal views should not influence their policy decisions; "the implied dichotomy—between personal morality and public policy—is simply not logically tenable in any adequate view of both."

The statement concludes with the teaching that policy proposals should be evaluated from a moral persective; "we have done this and will continue to do so. We encourage others to do the same." Despite the bishops' explanation, the statement was interpreted by many as being anti-Democratic.

On October 14, 1984, as the national presidential election approached, the USCC Administrative Board requested that Bishop James Malone, conference president (Youngstown, Ohio), issue another statement on *Religion and Politics* to correct any misunderstandings ensuing from the previous statement. "As a nation we are constitutionally committed to the separation of church and state . . . but not at the price of excluding religious and moral content from discussions of domestic and foreign policy," the bishop began. He explained that the bishops neither seek the formation of a voting bloc nor preempt the right and duty of individuals to decide conscientiously whom they will support for public office.

Referring to the USCC's statement of August 9, 1984, Bishop Malone noted that current concerns range from abortion to safeguarding human life from the devastation of nuclear war. They extend to the enhancement of life through promoting human rights in all areas. He admitted that none of these issues would be resolved quickly for they will extend far beyond the present political campaign. "Let us conduct our immediate dialogue with reason and civility so that the resources of religious and moral vision and the method of rational public debate will be sustained and enhanced in our public life."

Although the November 1984 meeting issued no pastoral letter or statement, it did have a lengthy presentation by Archbishop Rembert Weakland, OSB, on the first draft of the economic pastoral, then entitled *Catholic Social Teaching and the U.S. Economy*, later called *Economic Justice for All*, and a limited discussion of that document. In addition, the bishops approved the publication of a document on the continuing formation of priests, which updated the 1972 *Program of Continuing Education of Priests.*

In his presidential address, the articulate Bishop James Malone explained:

> The episcopal conference is a significant theological development within the Church; it is also significant as a social institution through which the Church addresses society. Theologically, the conciliar vision of the Church has provided a foundation, rationale, and legitimation for the meeting we are now having. Although the U.S. bishops have met and acted in a corporate fashion for many years, our activity took on new theological meaning in light of the Council. The full ecclesial significance of the episcopal conference is yet to be determined, but there is no question that our efforts to work as a conference of bishops here in the United States has had a substantial impact on the way we interpret our pastoral ministry.

The purpose of the episcopal conference is to provide a structure of cooperation within which a pastoral consensus can be formed in approaching issues of national significance. The conference exists to enhance the ministry of each bishop not to constrain it. A precise example of how the conference adds to an individual bishop's role is the ability to project through the conference a position on questions of national scope and substance.

With their approval of *The Continuing Formation of Priests: Growing in Wisdom, Age and Grace*, the members of the National Conference of Catholic brought to fruition a three-year project of the ad hoc Bishops' Committee on Priestly Life and Ministry, first chaired by Bishop William Hughes and later by Bishop Richard J. Sklba. This timely document was written principally by Father Edward J. Mahoney.

The NCCB felt that the 1972 *Program of Continuing Education of Priests* needed updating because of the manifold changes—cultural, social, ecclesial, and ministerial—that had taken place in those twelve years. Praising the great contribution of *The Program of Continuing Education*, the committee decided to use the word *formation* in place of *education* to convey "the notion of growth as a lifelong dialogue-journey through which a priest comes to greater awareness of self, others and God."

The first chapter places the priest in the many contexts of his everyday ministry. Chapter II treats "Motivation, Assessment, and Responsible Persons" extending from the "bishop or religious superior" to the "staff members." Possibly, the chapter's greatest contribution can be found in the sections on the presbyteral and diocesan pastoral councils. Chapter III, "Programs and Resources," seems the most practical. Many priests will be delighted to read the section on "sabbaticals." The final chapter, "The Future," challenges the priest, reminding him: "All this requires a continued willingness to be stretched by the Word of God as Mary was." In its conclusion, the document encourages all priests: "As the priest approaches the third millenium he looks to the future with hope. He does not see the responsibility of conversion as a task or a burden, but a wonderful opportunity for his personal life and for his ministry."

The document was well received and implemented in most dioceses with the possible exception of "sabbaticals" because of the pressing shortage of priests.

Also appearing on the agenda of the November 1984 meeting was a discussion of the scheduling of general meetings. It was agreed that the bishops would return to two meetings a year, one in the fall and the other in the spring, beginning in 1985.

Occasionally, when a matter too urgent to await a general meeting of the United States Catholic Conference arises, the president *ex officio* will issue a statement. Such was the case when the U.S. Congress planned to vote on the MX Missile on March 19, 1985.

In a letter to each member of Congress, dated March 15, 1984, President Bishop Malone, in the name of the conference protested the USCC's opposition to the MX for its "potentially destabilizing impact on the nuclear arms race and its cost in light of pressing human needs here and elsewhere in the world." Calling the MX system of dubious value, the bishop identified the tremendous cost as "perhaps more important for us as bishops and pastors." In this period of budgetary constraints, it behooves us "to scrutinize expenditures with great care." In light of the great basic human needs here and abroad, "I am compelled as president of the USCC to urge you to vote against funding the MX Missile."

Another letter, dated April 19, 1985, from Bishop Malone, as president of the USCC, to President Ronald Reagan was occasioned by the U.S. Department of the Treasury's proposed reforms, which would end or reduce tax consideration for charitable contributions. Bishop Malone cited a study showing that the proposal would reduce contributions to charity by $13 billion, or 20 percent.

In the same letter, His Excellency praised the Treasury proposal to eliminate federal taxes on those living in poverty and assured President Reagan of its total support by the Catholic bishops.

On August 15 of that same year, Monsignor Daniel Hoye, in his capacity as general secretary of the U.S. Catholic Conference, presented this USCC statement on *Tax Reform and the Poor* to the House Ways and Means Committee. The statement voiced the fear that "the tax system is actually making the poor poorer." Since inflation eroded the protection from taxes that the poor once had, the conference felt that Congress should repair the damage by exempting the poor from federal income taxes. The conference judged a proposal to tax health-insurance benefits "unwise and unfair." In addition, it opposed a flatrate income tax and asked for "significantly more progressivity" in the tax system. The conference urged retention of the charitable-giving deduction for taxpayers who do not itemize.

The bishops made their strongest plea for tuition tax credits. "We want to state our strong conviction that these proposals would be incomplete without adequate provisions for tuition tax credits for those low- and middle-income families who exercise their natural right as parents by sending their children to private and parochial schools." Citing the president of the United States, the prelates pleaded that now is an appropriate time to enact tuition tax credits by integrating them into the comprehensive tax-reform legislation. "We urge the Ways and Means Committee to give serious consideration to tuition tax credits."

Later that fall, the USCC decided it could no longer keep silent about the abuses in South Africa after the white-supremacy government there declared a state of emergency in thirty-six black townships on July 21, 1985, and apartheid abuses steadily worsened. About a month prior to the issuance of the bishops' statement, on August 7, 1985, Pope John Paul II stated at the end of a weekly general audience: "Our repudiation of every form of racial discrimination is firmly believed and total." Consequently, in view of the deteriorating situation, and as a support to the Holy Father's opposition to apartheid, the USCC Committee on Social Development and World Peace recommended a *Statement on South Africa* to the Administrative Board. After carefully reviewing and discussing the document, the board decided to issue the statement in its own name on September 11, 1985, along with an extensive Background Paper.

The statement addresses the South African situation from three different segments of society: "The Church"; "The U.S. Government"; and "The Private Sector." Stating that the central question posed by apartheid is a direct attack on the dignity of the human person, the bishops assert: "Christian teaching demands that the unique dignity of every person should find expression in the protection and promotion of the human rights the person; apartheid is a systematic assault on the basic rights of black and coloured races in South Africa."

Proclaiming that different segments of U.S. society—our government, churches, corporations, foundations—have a direct influence on South Africa and, consequently, affect the opinion that South Africans have of the United States, the bishops recommend five practical policy actions to the U.S. government. The first action sets the tone for those to follow: "an unambiguous U.S. policy of commitment to human rights in South Africa."

The statement did alert many Americans, especially Catholics, to the great evils of South Africa's apartheid policy. Also, many Catholic colleges incorporated discussion of the document into their classes.

Also during its fall meeting, the Administrative Board addressed the growing importance of communications in the area of evangelization. Recognizing the prominent role that the media plays in reaching the faithful, the NCCB authorized the USCC Department of Communications to formulate a document on the utilization of the media for the promotion of Catholicism in the United States. *In the Sight of All, Communications: A Vision All Can Share* was promulgated by the board in September 1985, "to build up one community of faith that gives witness to Christ . . . to proclaim the gospel to all peoples, believers and unbelievers . . . to promote dialogue among all people, especially on religious values and issues."

The statement stressed the importance of communication work as a ministry today and literally begged all ordinaries to utilize fully the communication of this pastoral task. They quoted Pope Paul VI in *Evangelii Nuntiandi*: "The Church would feel guilty before the Lord if she did not utilize the powerful means that human skill is daily rendering more perfect. It is through them that she proclaims 'from the housetops' the message of which she is the depository."

Regretting that existing channels of church communication do not reach everyone, the bishops thought that through these newer means of communication, the Church in the United States today has the opportunity to touch the life of every citizen, and they cited the example of a 1985 television drama with a religious theme that reached an audience of approximately 40 million people.

In a competent yet compact manner, *In the Sight of All* discusses such issues as "The Style of Church Communication"; "Communication as Ministry"; and "Church Use of Communication Resources." In addition, it lists options for the church use of communication resources, an impressive series of maps showing, for example, "Television Markets in the Continental U.S.," and a helpful "Summary."

At the general meeting of the U.S. hierarchy on November 14, 1985, Archbishop Stephen Sulyk of the Ukrainian-Rite Archeparcy of Philadelphia urged the passage of a *Statement on the Ukraine*, protesting the increasing oppression of the Church in the Ukraine. Cardinal O'Connor (New York), chairman of the Committee on Social Development and World Peace, was asked if he concurred with the archbishop's resolution. His Eminence responded affirmatively. The resolution was approved unanimously.

A decade ago, at the November 1975 annual meeting, the NCCB approved for publication the *Pastoral Plan for Pro-Life Activities*. In 1985, the NCCB Committee for Pro-Life Activities updated the document on behalf of the bishops. In September, the USCC Administrative Board submitted the document to the general membership and the *Pastoral Plan for Pro-Life Activities: A Reaffirmation* was adopted at the fall 1985 general meeting.

With the 1973 decisions of the Supreme Court removing any effective legal protection for unborn children (and the efforts to justify euthanasia, stimulated by those decisions), the prelates perceived that respect for human life was declining in our society when the 1975 *Pastoral Plan for Pro-Life Activities* was issued. A decade later, the bishops observed that these destructive trends continue to exert their evil effects, though resistance to them is stronger than it was ten years ago. Accordingly, the bishops decided that it was appropriate not only to revise the original pastoral plan in light of their contemporary situation, but also to reaffirm its central message regarding the dignity of human life while urging intensified efforts to implement the plan.

The bishops did not underestimate the problem. As a result of the judicial and legislative endorsement of abortion, American society today faces enormous challenges. So do the Church and individual Catholics. The Plan ends on an optimistic note, however, asserting that much progress has been made. After pleading for prayer and sacrifice, the prelates entrusted their Plan to the Mother of Jesus Christ and of all who have life through him. The bishops concluded by asking all the faithful to pray the "Hail Mary" daily for the success of the Plan. Fortunately, the pro-life movement is gaining much ground, especially through a coordinated national effort known as Operation Rescue.

The *Pastoral Plan for Pro-Life Activities: A Reaffirmation* calls into action the resources of the Church in three major areas:

1. *a public information and education effort* to deepen understanding of the humanity of the unborn, the sanctity of human life, the moral evil of abortion, and the consistent efforts of the Church to witness on behalf of all human life;
2. *a pastoral effort* addressed to the special needs of women with problems related to pregnancy, of men and women struggling to accept responsibility for their power to generate human life, and of all persons who have had or have taken part in an abortion; and
3. *a public policy effort* directed to ensuring effective legal protection for the right to life of the unborn.

Three facets of the Church's program of pastoral care deserve particular attention:

1. *Prayer and Worship.* Responsibility for the least among us transcends all social theories and finds its roots in the teaching of Jesus Christ.
2. *Service and Care.* Respect for human life leads individuals and groups to reach out to those with special needs, with the support of the Catholic community. Many of these services, involving the dedicated efforts of professionals and volunteers, have been and will continue to be provided by church-sponsored health care and social service agencies.
3. *Reconciliation.* Christ's redeeming act, the paschal mystery of his death and resurrection, is the cause of human reconciliation in its twofold aspect: liberation from sin and communion with God.

Priests have a privileged opportunity to serve others by offering the unconditional and efficacious love of Christ in the sacrament of penance. This relationship between morality and law is highlighted in the case of abortion. The abortion decisions of the United States Supreme Court violate the moral order and have disrupted the legal process, which previously attempted to safeguard the rights of unborn children. While at any given time human law may not articulate fully the moral imperative, our legal system can and must be reformed continually so that it fulfills increasingly its proper task.

Implementing this aspect of the pastoral plan will undoubtedly require well-planned and coordinated advocacy by citizens at the national, state, and local levels. Restoring respect for human life in our society is an essential task of the Church that extends through all its institutions, agencies, and organization and embraces diverse tasks and goals. The state Catholic conference or its equivalent should provide overall coordination in each state. The general purpose of the committee is to coordinate activities within the diocese to implement this pastoral plan. The general purpose of the parish pro-life committee is to make parishioners more aware of the pro-life issues and needs and to recruit volunteers to help meet those needs. The parish committee should rely on the diocesan pro-life director for information and guidance.

Also at the November 1985 meeting, the assembled prelates unanimously passed a *Resolution on Immigration Reform*, requesting among other things an opportunity for the legalization of undocumented aliens. This resolution stressed the need for a specialized ministry to immigrants. The U.S. government did pass such reform laws shortly thereafter, and the Church has been doing heroic work for all immigrants but especially the undocumented.

The Catholic Church has always had a strong interest in immigration-related legislation. The bishops expressed their specific concern for "legislative proposals pertaining to undocumented immigration and foreign agricultural workers," giving their principal reason for this resolution: "We believe the approaches now being most actively pursued are neither workable nor morally acceptable." The prelates then presented an acceptable, thoroughly written program containing seven points, starting with legislation and ending with protection and benefits for all resident aliens.

Affirming that only when legalization is treated as the center of immigration reform would they judge employer sanctions tolerable, the bishops turned their attention to foreign temporary agricultural worker programs, asserting that they could not accept any large-scale new program, or "reforms" of existing programs, that eroded protections offered U.S. farm workers and adversely affected wages, as well as living and working conditions, of all farm workers.

The resolution concluded with the observation that this might be a useful time for Congress and the nation to pause and evaluate the model on which current proposals for immigration reform are based and separate the legalization/sanctions reforms from the issue of temporary agricultural workers. Then the bishops committed themselves to help devise legislation that would reflect the American commitment to social and economic justice for all.

Another piece of business that took place at the November 1985 meeting was the adoption of a *Statement on Lithuania*, urging the Soviets to respect religious freedom in Lithuania, where the Church is so harshly repressed. In the U.S.S.R., little or no attention was paid to the bishops' statement, so another resolution on Lithuania would be passed in November 1986, requesting some specific acts of justice and freedom for the Church in Lithuania.

Last summer, at the June 1985 meeting in Collegeville, Minnesota, Bishop Hughes reminded the assembly of bishops that on November 18, 1981, the plenary meeting of bishops authorized the publication of a pastoral letter entitled *Catholic Higher Education and the Pastoral Mission of the Church*—a title eventually changed to *Empowered by the Spirit: Campus Ministry Faces the Future.* On September 12, 1981, the National Advisory Council had hoped that the bishops might affirm, support, and challenge campus ministers in their profoundly important task of maintaining a strongly Catholic, effectively pastoral presence in public higher education. Bishop Hughes remarked that the Advisory Council's recommendation was forwarded to the Committee on Education, which unanimously approved the project. At the November 1982 annual meeting, the body of bishops authorized the Committee on Education to draft such a pastoral letter on campus ministry. A writing committee was appointed, and Bishop William Friend (Shreveport) accepted the role of chairman. The committee met for the first time in June 1983 and engaged in a two-year process of extensive consultation and writing. Bishop Hughes closed his remarks by asserting that the draft before the bishops had the support of the Committee on Education, but the input of the bishops was being sought for an even better document.

Bishop Hughes then introduced Bishop Friend, who first described the process that has been followed to date, pointing out that the committee consisted of three bishops; three women religious (themselves campus ministers); one male religious (a campus minister); one diocesan priest (a campus minister); and one layman (director of a pastoral institute at a Catholic university); plus Father Joseph Kenna (USCC staff) and Father James J. Bacik (a campus minister from Toledo, Ohio, who served as principal writer).

Bishop Friend continued by pointing out that the committee approached the task in two complementary sets of actions: (1) document, research, and writing and (2) consultations. The committee felt strongly that it should follow the process established in the writing of the peace pastoral and also in the economic pastoral. The consultations were broad-based and thorough. The Administrative Board, at its March 1985 meeting, approved the distribution of the draft to all the bishops of the United States and encouraged consultation as each bishop saw fit.

Bishop Friend then introduced Father Bacik, who pointed out that the committee began with the intention of discussing campus ministry on non-Catholic campuses. As time went on, they made two changes: (1) the committee decided to deal with higher education as a whole to address the impact campus ministry could have on the campus environment; and (2) they decided to say something about Catholic as well as non-Catholic institutions.

The committee adopted "The Quest for Wisdom" as a theme to bind together higher education and the Church's contribution to higher education. The search for wisdom, it was felt, leads students to a richer personal synthesis by combining the theoretical and the practical. Additionally, the committee wanted to give the draft a dialogical tone, combining vision and practicality, including some practical suggestions for improving campus ministry. A further purpose of the draft was to contribute to the public debate in higher education, while still another purpose was to affirm campus ministers and encourage them in carrying out and enhancing their ministry.

In his presentation to the bishops, Father Bacik noted that the first part of this first draft was addressed to everyone concerned with higher education. This constituted the major objection of the bishops at Collegeville because it was not specific enough. They had less trouble accepting the second part addressed to campus ministers, which stressed the formation of faith communities and the spiritual development of the students. Following the suggestion of many of the bishops at the Collegeville meeting, the pastoral was recast, placing the primary focus on campus ministry not on higher education in general as the first draft had done.

The second draft, *Empowered by the Spirit*, offered to the November 1985 meeting, emphasized that the campus minister's role involves cooperating with the ministry of the diocese in which the campus is located. Another significant change came from the acceptance of Archbishop John F. Whealon's motion dealing with the substitution of the word *Catholic* in several instances where the word *Christian* initially appeared. For example, he observed that formation of a "Catholic" conscience, differs from a "Christian" conscience because it must take into account the teaching of the magisterium.

Just before the final vote, Bishop Edward Hughes, chairman of the Committee on Education at the time of the initiation of the campus ministry pastoral project, asked for overwhelming approval of this pastoral. His request was heard. On November 15, 1985, the final vote was 237 to 4.

At the same meeting, because of the then pressing farm crisis, the bishops unanimously approved a message to President Reagan and members of Congress in the form of the *Statement on Food and Agriculture*. Archbishop Ignatius Strecker (Kansas City, Kansas) suggested in his own name and in the names of fifty other bishops that a statement such as this be added to the agenda: "Our concern for these matters has been expressed as early as 1972 when we issued the statement *Where Shall the People Live?* and again in 1979 in the statement *The Family Farm.* Our concerns and our position remain the same."

The U.S. hierarchy supported emergency and long-term federal legislation in favor of mid-sized and family farms. They pleaded for a just return to the farmers and for a just wage for the farm workers, many of whom were impoverished migrant families. Mindful of the future food welfare of the nation, the American bishops advocated more rather than fewer owner-operator farms. They also asked incentives for regeneration agriculture through soil conservation and other means. The statement warned: "The success or failure of our efforts to address this problem will have serious effects on every consumer and thus every citizen of the land."

Adopted by a voice vote, this statement had only a limited success. Consequently, at their general meeting in November 1988, the bishops issued a much more comprehensive *Report of the Ad Hoc Task Force on Food, Agriculture, and Rural Concerns.*

On November 15, 1985, Bishop Edward Hughes (Philadelphia) made an eloquent protest against the Supreme Court ruling in the *Aguilar* vs. *Felton* case that struck down publicly funded remedial aid on private school premises. His plea for a "sustained protest" received resounding acceptance by the body of bishops, which unanimously passed a *Resolution on the Supreme Court's Aguilar Decision* denouncing the "unjust, discriminatory, and narrow decision." Cardinal John Krol called upon the bishops not to let the matter go with only a protest, but to keep "constant pressure" on until this wrong is corrected.

A Vision of Evangelization was introduced at the general meeting of the bishops—also on November 15, 1985—by Bishop William R. Houck (Jackson, Mississippi), chairman of the ad hoc Bishops' Committee on Evangelization. Bishop Houck explained that the statement is meant neither as a pastoral letter nor as a teaching document "but as an internal paper on what the [bishops'] conference means by evangelization. The statement is patterned after Pope Paul VI's *Evangelii Nuntiandi*. The essence of evangelization is the proclamation of salvation in Jesus Christ and the person's response in faith."

Broadening Tuition Tax Credit Proposals

A Statement Issued by the
Administrative Board of the
United States Catholic Conference

September 15, 1983

1. The Supreme Court's decision June 29 upholding a Minnesota statute which provides tuition tax deductions for public and nonpublic school parents is an important step in the development of constitutional law in this area. Moreover, on the practical level the decision in *Mueller* v. *Allen* has significant positive implications for federal tuition tax credit legislation.

2. Since June 29 a number of questions have been raised relative to tuition tax credits and the *Mueller* decision. Among these is whether the tax credit legislation pending in Congress should be revised to include benefits for public as well as nonpublic school parents, as the Minnesota statute at issue in *Mueller* does.

3. It can, of course, be argued that nothing in the Supreme Court's recent decision clearly requires that this be done for constitutional reasons. Although that may be the case, we nevertheless conclude that the legislation should in fact be revised to conform more closely to the statute sustained in *Mueller*. For similar reasons, we also strongly recommend that the legislation be broadened to include benefits for certain public and nonpublic education expenses covered in the Minnesota statute.

4. The nonpublic education community has waited patiently for many years for Congress to act on tuition tax credits. An overwhelmingly favorable case has been made for the legislation on educational and other grounds. The *Mueller* decision has alleviated constitutional concerns. In view of this, we urge Congress to act promptly to broaden the legislation along the lines we have described and then enact it without further delay.

Testimony to the National Commission on U.S. Policy in Central America

Testimony Presented by
Archbishop James Hickey on Behalf of the
United States Catholic Conference

October 21, 1983

Mr. Chairman and Members of the Commission:

1. On behalf of the Catholic bishops of the United States and our president, Archbishop John R. Roach, I thank you for the opportunity to appear before this National Commission on U.S. Policy in Central America.

I. Our Perspective

2. As you know, the American Catholic bishops are not new to this discussion. For more than four years, the bishops' conference has been consistently raising questions about U.S. policy in Central America. I include for the record the *Statement on Central America* overwhelmingly adopted by the U.S. bishops in November of 1981, which is the foundation of our frequent testimony. Speaking personally, I have been visiting and observing Central America for more than eight years as I sought to support our missionary efforts there and understand the forces at work in the region.

3. The American Catholic bishops come to this discussion with several perspectives. As Americans, we want to see our vital national interests protected and our government's policies reflect our national values and ideals.

4. As citizens, we want U.S. policies to help bring about greater justice, democracy, and stability in this hemisphere and to limit communist influence in the region.

5. As Catholics, we start with the social teaching of our Church which calls us to defend human dignity and human rights and to work for social justice and peace as an integral part of our faith. Our views have been shaped and our hearts moved by the inspiring witness of the Church in Central America as it seeks to defend the poor, work for justice, and search for peace and reconciliation in the face of brutal violence, continuing conflict, and frequent repression from regimes of both right and left. As Catholics, we are not naive about Marxist influence or activity. We emphatically reject any innuendo that the Church's defense of the poor and advocacy of social justice serve Marxist interests. The Church's mission requires it to defend human rights whenever they are threatened, whether by dehumanizing ideologies or economic exploitation. Let me cite the activities of the Church in both El Salvador and Nicaragua, in both Poland and the Philippines, as examples of this consistency.

6.   As bishops in the United States, we are not experts or specialists, but as pastors and religious leaders, we have the right and responsibility to judge policies of our government by the values articulated in our teaching. We have developed our position in dialogue with our brother bishops in Central America, but we speak as U.S. pastors to the U.S. government about U.S. policies in the region.

II. Our Concerns

7.   For that reason and on that basis, we welcome this opportunity to share our deep concerns about the future course of U.S. policy and activity. We fear that future U.S. policy may be based on a number of misconceptions regarding the basic issues and choices in Central America.

Roots of the Conflict

8.   One concern is that the conflict in Central America is too often seen as primarily a geopolitical battle—a struggle between East and West, between the United States and the Soviet Union. We have repeatedly pointed out that long before there was outside intervention there was a legitimate struggle in El Salvador and other parts of the region for social, political, and economic justice. The conflict has been over land, wages, the right to organize, and the issue of political participation. To ignore this long struggle of people for justice, dignity, and freedom is fundamentally to misunderstand the nature of the conflict today in Central America.

9.   Because the conflicts in Central America are fundamentally rooted in questions of social injustice and the persistent denial of basic human rights for large sectors of the population, the USCC has always opposed interpretations of the Salvadoran and Central American conflict which place primary emphasis on the superpower or East-West rivalry. This is not to ignore the international implications and dimensions of the conflict. Nor to deny the willingness of outside actors such as the Soviet Union to take full advantage of the crisis. But we urge the commission to reject the notion that the geopolitical struggle is at the core of the problem in Central America.

The Search for a Military Solution

10. A second concern is the continuing pursuit of a military solution for Central America. U.S. statements move back and forth on this question, but our actions speak more clearly—U.S. policy still has hopes that military force can solve the problems.

11. In El Salvador, victory by either side, which could only mean abject surrender and bitter defeat for a large number of Salvadorans on one side or the other, would not serve the interest of either El Salvador or the United States. A society divided into victors and vanquished is unlikely to result in either stable peace or justice. Likewise, if the U.S.-backed *contras* were to somehow topple the government of the Sandinistas, do U.S. policymakers really believe that would bring peace and stability to Nicaragua or the region? We hope the commission will make clear that a continuing military struggle in an already devastated region is not in our interests or Central America's.

A Wider War

12. A major concern of ours and of the bishops of Latin America is the imminent possibility of a wider war which will plunge the entire region into armed conflict. The heightened tensions, strident language, and increased military activity make this threat a real danger. Last August the bishops of Latin America spoke of:

> The possibility of unleashing an open war covering the whole subregion with sorrow and destruction. Militarization is increasing; nations are feverishly readying for war, leading to serious deterioration of productive activities; tensions grow, accusations are hurled back and forth, border incidents multiply while, as a result, misery grows and with it the risk of outside interventions (CELAM, August 1983).

13. We hope the commission will seek a way to help Central America step back from the brink of regional war. We need to find ways to reduce the tensions in the region which are turning nations into armed camps with unfortunate consequences for the domestic life as well as the region.

Intervention

14. When U.S. policymakers talk about the dangers of outside interference in Central America, they refer to the Soviet Union and its proxies. When Central Americans talk about outside interference they are talking about the Soviets to be sure, but they are also talking about the United States. There is no need to recite the sad history of U.S. intervention in the region—a living memory for the people and leaders of Central America. The present and past experience of intervention has led to the unified opposition by the Latin American hierarchies to all outside intervention without exception. By outside intervention they do not refer to the efforts of other Latin American states to facilitate political dialogue; such efforts the bishops specifically endorse. 15. Rather, the unacceptable interference is that of the "foreign powers," essentially the Soviet Union and the United States. Latin America does not expect, nor desire, the United States simply to forfeit any active role in the Latin American quest for peace and development. Still less do they welcome expanded Soviet influence in any area of the hemisphere. What they oppose now more strongly than ever in the past, is in the words of the Central American bishops: "the meddling of foreign powers who come to support those in the countries who fit their own interests which are generally far from, even opposed to, those of the great majority."

16. To give a clearer sense of this nearly universal Latin American episcopal concern, let me cite the relevant paragraphs from the recent statements of the bishops of Central and Latin America.

17. The bishops of Latin America stated in July:

> We desire that neither the governments nor opposition groups invite foreign powers to intervene in this conflict, and that those foreign powers, if already present, leave; and if not present refrain from planning to do so. In this way both will avoid the repeated calamity of other historical experiences that have demonstrated the futility of such interventions (CELAM, July 1983).

18. Even more strongly the Central American bishops wrote in August:

> To the outside powers and ideological forces that are interfering politically and militarily in Central America contrary to our cultural values, we demand that they do not do so, so that our people and only they can end their conflicts, overcome their differences and plot their course toward the longed-for goal of peace.
>
> There must be absolute guarantees now and for the future that all of them leave. If not, the intervention of one will automatically guarantee the intervention of the other and thus the establishment of peace will become progressively more difficult (SEDAC, August 1983).

19. The commission must take into account the long history of outside interference in Central America and our role in it.

Human Rights

20. One inconsistent aspect of the debate over Central America is the use of human rights criteria for tactical advantage or propaganda points rather than as a steady and consistent benchmark for governments in the region and our relationships with them. Selective application of human rights standards depending on our ideological preferences erodes our credibility both at home and abroad. Human rights are being violated throughout the region.

21. The people of Central America are assaulted by death squads, arbitrary imprisonment, uninvestigated murders, harassment of land reform efforts, restrictions on free union activity, interference in education and journalism, and other threats to life and freedom. While life itself is threatened in some parts of the region, human freedom and social justice are too often violated by powerful interests and governments across Central America. We need a consistent policy which sees human rights as a principal focus of U.S. concern, not as debater's points in our policy discussions. We hope this commission will make respect for human rights a fundamental criterion for U.S. policy for all nations in the region.

III. Criteria

22. In dealing with these concerns, we need a clear vision of our goals and a way to judge which policies hold the best chance of achieving them. Permit me to suggest some basic criteria for evaluating both present and future policies:

- Do they move the parties toward diplomatic rather than military options, toward ceasefire, dialogue, and negotiations? Toward free and open elections where all can participate without the threat of violence or coercion?
- Do they increase respect for human rights and basic freedoms? Do they make respect for human rights a consistent standard for governments in the region?
- Do they address basic issues of social justice, genuine land reform, broad participation in development, and economic justice? Do they in fact offer hope of a better life for the poor and dispossessed in the region?
- Do they build the capacity of people and their governments in the region to deal with their own problems? Do they promote self-determination and self-sufficiency?
- Do they respect and respond to the cultural, ethical, and religious values of the people of Central America or impose answers from a distance?
- Do they respect and support the positive role of nongovernmental and local institutions (churches, small business, trade unions, cooperatives, etc.)?
- Do they strengthen the hand of moderate and democratic forces or, by further polarization, help the extremes of both right and left? Do they combat communism by offering alternatives to Marxism as vehicles for needed reform?
- Do they support effective civilian control of the military, the rule of law, and an effective criminal justice system?

IV. Critique of Current Policy

23. In applying these criteria, we remain deeply disturbed by the direction of current U.S. policy in Central America. Let me cite policy toward El Salvador and Nicaragua as the two examples I am most familiar with. This is not to minimize the serious problems in Guatemala and Honduras.

El Salvador

24. The United States should use its influence to help bring about a ceasefire and dialogue among the relevant parties leading to serious negotiations aimed at elections and a stable government in El Salvador, as well as to begin the political, social, and economic reconstruction of the country. These three elements have been stressed by the Salvadoran bishops and by John Paul II in his visit to El Salvador.
25. These steps are, if anything, more necessary today than ever before. The violence has already taken the lives of 30,000-40,000 civilians, the majority killed by death squads or the security forces. Thousands of Salvadorans have been driven into exile. The tactics of the leftist opposition become more and more destructive as the war drags on. The U.S. role in El Salvador continues primarily in a military direction. A continuation of the present course is exceedingly dangerous for both the United States and for El Salvador. Archbishop Rivera Damas has described the conflict as a war that cannot and should not be won. The political option, a negotiated settlement, is the humane and wise way to end this brutal conflict.
26. It is not clear to me, however, either from the content of U.S. policy or from recent statements explaining it, that there is a real determination in the U.S. policy process to pursue the road of military force with a diplomatic facade, rather than a political policy with a military component.

Nicaragua

27. U.S. policy gives the appearance of encouraging war in Nicaragua. It seems clear that intensified military pressure, through both overt measures and covert support of the *contras*, is the principal element of U.S. policy.
28. Let me make clear that I am deeply disturbed by the trends inside Nicaragua. During my Nicaraguan visit last February, much in the direction of the country disturbed me and the two other archibishops accompanying me. I have shared my concerns before the Congress: the expanding control of key sectors of social life by the Nicaraguan government; the visits we had with journalists, labor leaders, and

businessmen who described restrictions on their activities and the imprisonment of some colleagues; and the harassment of church leaders, including even the Holy Father during his visit there.

29. My concerns also include the lack of positive commitment on the part of the Nicaraguan government to the promises for early and free elections together with genuine political and economic pluralism. I still have these same concerns; nothing in the intervening months has alleviated them. Violations of human rights must be brought to light and opposed. We have and are doing that.

30. I fear U.S. policy is contributing to the deteriorating internal situation in Nicaragua. It provides precisely the pretext for increased government control and surveillance. The public rhetoric of our government toward Nicaragua, the cutoff of bilateral economic aid, U.S. support for a military buildup on the Honduran border, and covert efforts to destabilize the government employing even members of discredited Somosista elements, all contribute to a state-of-seige mentality which reinforces misguided policies. U.S. actions do not determine internal Nicaraguan policy, but they exaggerate some of its most troubling aspects. The forces of political moderation in Nicaragua are being diminished by counterproductive U.S. policy.

31. Instead of a policy that isolates and provides an excuse for the Sandinistas to consolidate their power, the USCC has advocated that U.S. policy engage Nicaragua diplomatically. Our policy should include the provision of economic assistance under the same conditions we give aid to other countries. I refer especially to their human-rights performance. We see no reason to change this advice nor do we see reason to change our opposition to further funding of covert activity against Nicaragua. Let me state personally that as an American citizen and as a Catholic bishop, I find use of U.S. tax dollars for the purpose of covert destabilization of a recognized government to be unwise, unjustified, and destructive of the very values that a democratic nation should support in the world. Such actions seem to be in violation of our treaty pledges and our commitments under the UN Charter.

32. In these two cases, and in other parts of the region, U.S. policy fails to respond to the criteria that we have laid out. It neglects the root causes of the problems, strengthens the extremists of both right and left, relies on military force rather than diplomatic creativity, and applies human-rights standards only selectively. In ignoring these criteria, I fear our policies isolate us from our allies in the region and around the world, erode our credibility at home, and undermine our future role and influence in the region.

V. Choices for the Future

Peace: The Primary Goal

33. The first requirement for future U.S. policy in Central America is to change the basic thrust of present policy and stop the drift toward a regional war in Central America. Among our goals in Central America should be a group of states developing and maturing under viable political systems, enjoying good relations with one another and with us. Therefore, our policy should foster regional stability through efforts which encourage the individual nations to reach an accommodation with one another and settle their differences without outside intervention or arms.

34. In Central America, there are some tasks the United States is well-suited to fulfill and other tasks that we should leave to other actors. I believe the United States can set a tone and an atmosphere in Central America that is conducive to diminishing the military elements of the struggle and encouraging the opportunity for diplomatic dialogue. There are three dimensions to this role for U.S. policy.

35. First, there is a superpower or geopolitical dimension. I have argued throughout this testimony that this is not the way the problem in Central America should be defined, nor is it the principal aspect of the diplomatic agenda. But there is need for a direct approach by the United States to the Soviet Union to address Soviet intervention directly or by proxy in the Central American region. This aspect of U.S. policy has its greatest relevance in terms of Nicaragua, but it is a mistake to focus U.S. pressure only on Nicaragua. This puts us in the position of a superpower squaring off against a small state; it raises all the old memories of U.S. intervention, and it fails to address the key issue: the Soviet Union's conception of where its primary interests are in its relationship with the United States.

36. The overall state of U.S.-Soviet relations has deteriorated in recent months, but it is still possible to recognize different levels of the relationship. Direct Soviet intervention in Central America is no more welcome, legitimate, or tolerable than direct U.S. intervention in Eastern Europe. The point should be made clearly to the Soviets. Save for this direct approach on a superpower basis to the Soviets, the geopolitical dimension of the problem should not be given a more expansive role in our policy.

37. Second, the principal focus of U.S. efforts to achieve peace in the region should be a regional approach. U.S. efforts should be primarily aimed at supporting the activity of the Contadora Group or a similar regional effort. The United States is not in a position to play a mediator's role in Central America. We are looked upon as partisans. The Contadora Group is a Latin American initiative aimed at solving the

Central American crisis precisely because it has grave consequences for all of Latin America. The Contadora formula is aimed at disengaging the superpowers from the conflict, withdrawing all foreign military forces and assitance, and then proceeding to a multidimensional diplomatic dialogue.

38. Contadora nations can say and do things that the United States would be either unable or unwilling to say or do. But the Contadora initiative cannot succeed without strong, explicit, consistent U.S. support. I realize that the U.S. government has often said that it supports the Contadora activity, but U.S. warships in Central America and support for the *contras* do not provide a convincing picture of support to anyone.

39. Present U.S. policy follows an independent course in El Salvador, toward Nicaragua and in the region as a whole, while still giving verbal support to Contadora. The recommendation of this testimony is that the United States endorse the Contadora effort, subscribe to its component elements, and then shape U.S. policy so that it supports at each stage the Contadora effort. Real progress requires a belief in Central America that the United States is truly supporting Contadora, not just tolerating it.

40. Third, if the United States did move fully in support of the Contadora process our policy toward individual countries in the region would have to shift. As I have argued above, we should seek genuine dialogue, ceasefire, and negotiations in El Salvador as part of our support for Contadora. Such an approach would require pressure by the United States on the Salvadoran military and pressure by the Contadora countries on the FDR-FMLN. In relation to Nicaragua, genuine U.S. support for Contadora would mean first the stopping of covert support for the *contras* and, second, the willingness to open serious high-level diplomatic dialogue designed to recast the U.S.-Nicaragua relationship. Such a reorientation would not signify U.S. support for Nicaraguan policy, but it would be aimed at conducting diplomatic relations based on the recognition of the right of self-determination and respect for the principle of nonintervention by the Nicaraguans toward their neighbors, and by us toward the Nicaraguans.

41. A halt in the drift toward a regional war should be the first priority for U.S. policy. It must be clearly understood that no significant economic program for the region can be implemented when war rages in some countries and threatens others. A political solution must precede large-scale and lasting economic programs. Likewise, a proposed economic effort should not be used to justify more military aid for the region. The need is not for a military policy to protect economic development, but for a comprehensive policy that brings peace to Central America and with it a real chance for economic reconstruction and development.

Social Justice and Democracy

42. A second essential choice for the future is the acceptance, and more than that, the welcoming of dramatic social change to achieve social justice and human rights in the region. We need to define U.S. interest in a way that recognizes and supports substantial political and economic change in countries needing both. If we fail to define our interests to accommodate change, we are fated to oppose it. This will place the United States in opposition to the majority of the people in a region that cries out for change, and in opposition to the Catholic Church there, which supports change. We must support genuine land reform and other efforts to eliminate the enormous inequities in the region.

43. In addition, our long-term choices should reflect the best of our own political tradition. Not that we seek to impose it on others but that we are committed to abide by our deepest values in our policy toward others. We should strive to be seen as a mature, democratic, stabilizing force in the region, not a destabilizing bully. We should be confident enough of democratic values and virtues that we support moderate democratic regimes and that we use only democratic means in our support. Let us be known in Central America by the finest line of our heritage: liberty and justice for all.

Fund for Central American Development
A Long-Term Policy

44. I realize the bipartisan commission is examining ideas for a long-term approach to economic development in the Central American region. I am convinced that such an approach is absolutely necessary, and I am equally convinced that it cannot succeed unless it is linked to peace in the region. The United States should not repeat the mistake of the Mekong Delta proposal during the Vietnam era; it is not possible to carry out a large-scale, well-planned development effort while a war is going on.

45. I am sure that a serious long-term development effort on the part of the United States would receive the support of the Church in our country, if it were shaped in accord with some key principles. My concern here is not to design a development program but to specify the importance of these principles.

46. The first principle is that the short-range objective of such economic assistance should be targeted to meet basic human needs. Existing U.S. law as well as the approach of multilateral agencies are presently geared toward a basic human needs approach. The people throughout Central America are in dire need of help in areas such as food, nutrition, health, and housing.

47. Given the historic problem of institutionalized structures of inequity in many countries of the region, a second principle for a development effort should be a system of monitoring how both short-term and long-term economic assistance are being used. Such a system of monitoring would have to be carefully and cooperatively designed with each country to protect both cultural autonomy and political self-determination, but some oversight is needed to assure that funds go to those most in need.

48. Third, a long-term effort should seek to build and preserve the human capital of the region through support for education, training, cultural development, as well as much needed assistance for the reform of legal and justice systems. These efforts should make extensive use of multilateral agencies like the Inter-American Development Bank, the World Bank, or other regional efforts. No one expects an enlargement of the activities of these institutions without significant new U.S. support, but they can act as mediating institutions which do not carry all the historic baggage the United States brings to any Central American policy.

49. Fourth, a long-term economic strategy should be aimed at complementing our support for political self-determination with effective action to enhance economic self-determination for the countries of Central America. In an interdependent world, nations do not achieve total independence, but they should be forced to face a permanent state of dependence, a condition which epitomizes exploitation for Latin Americans. It is crucial that the economic reconstruction and development of the region be controlled by the Central Americans themselves, not by powerful outside interests or by the remnants of an oligarchy.

50. Fifth, long-term economic planning should be respectful and supportive of local institutions in Central America. These institutions which are social, educational, economic, and religious often embody key cultural and ethical values that must be preserved. I know from my contact with El Salvador that key institutions of higher education, for example, are already in place and should be supported and not displaced. These efforts should involve and build upon the strengths of local institutions, cooperatives, trade unions, churches, and non-governmental organizations. North American models and structures cannot substitute for the development of local efforts respectful of the values and beliefs of the people of the region.

Refugees and Displaced Persons: A Special Crisis

51. An urgent concern for both the Church in Central America and the Church in the United States is the question of refugees and displaced persons.

52. A first recommendation applies to the United States. The USCC has long advocated a policy of Extended Voluntary Departure for

Salvadoran refugees in the United States. We find no good reason why this status is applied to other groups in similar situations and denied to Salvadorans. We hope the commission will add its weight to this just and humane proposal in your final report.

53. A second tremendous tragedy and need is the situation of the more than 1 million displaced persons and refugees. These victims of the Central American crisis are throughout the region, but concentrated in Southern Mexico, El Salvador, and Honduras. A major commitment is needed to meet the immediate needs of these people and offer training and relocation to them as they seek to cope with the enormous trauma of displacement. Our own Catholic Relief Services is already working to develop effective assistance for these people. But our private efforts are not enough. Refugees are at least theoretically eligible for some assistance through the United Nations, but there is virtually no adequate help for people displaced within our own country.

54. In short, for a seed to grow and develop one needs to prepare the soil. The weeds and stones of past neglect, injustice, and violence in Central America must be removed so as to permit the growth of those spiritual and social values on which true democracy thrives.

Conclusion

55. In this testimony, we have outlined our concerns about current policy, criteria for future choices, and our own proposals for peace and development in Central America. We are convinced they lay the foundation for a new relationship between the United States and Central America which will protect our national interests, help meet the needs of this troubled region, and serve also to curb Soviet and Marxist inroads in this hemisphere.

56. In the past, U.S. policy toward Central America has too often been seen as defending the status quo and authoritarian regimes. Future policies cannot ask people to choose between the status quo and revolutionary violence, between continued injustice and Marxism. U.S. policy, given our history and traditional values, should stand as a beacon of hope, a force for justice, and a defender of human rights.

57. Years ago the Catholic Church was perceived by some as distant from the struggles of ordinary people for justice, too closely linked to the status quo and authoritarian regimes. By reflecting on the Gospel and the situation in Latin America and by applying the Church's teaching on justice and peace to their own lands, the Church has renewed itself and become a leading advocate for nonviolent social change, a defender of human rights.

58. The Church and its leaders are a powerful force for justice and reconciliation in Central America. As a Catholic, I am proud and deeply impressed by the witness of my Church. As an American, I want to be equally proud of my country's contributions to justice and peace in that region and in all the world.

The Hispanic Presence
Challenge and Commitment

*A Pastoral Letter on Hispanic Ministry
Issued by the National Conference of
Catholic Bishops*

November 12, 1983

I. A Call to Hispanic Ministry

1. At this moment of grace we recognize the Hispanic community among us as a blessing from God. We call upon all persons of good faith to share our vision of the special gifts which Hispanics bring to the Body of Christ, His Pilgrim Church on earth (1 Cor 12:12-13).

Invoking the guidance of the Blessed Virgin Mary, we desire especially to share our reflections on the Hispanic presence in the United States with the Catholic laity, religious, deacons, and priests of our country. We ask Catholics, as members of the Body of Christ, to give our words serious attention in performing the tasks assigned to them. This Hispanic presence challenges us all to be more *catholic*, more open to the diversity of religious expression.

2. Although many pastoral challenges face the Church as a result of this presence, we are pleased to hear Hispanic Catholics voicing their desire for more opportunities to share their historical, cultural, and religious gifts with the Church they see as their home and heritage. Let us hear their voices; let us make all feel equally at home in the Church (Pastoral Letter of the Hispanic Bishops of the United States: *The Bishops Speak with the Virgin*, 1982 [PHB], I.b & III.c); let us be a Church which is in truth universal, a Church with open arms, welcoming different gifts and expressions of our "one Lord, one faith, one baptism, one God and Father of all" (Eph 4:5-6).

3. Hispanics exemplify and cherish values central to the service of Church and society. Among these are

    a) profound respect for the dignity of each *person*, reflecting the example of Christ in the Gospels;

    b) deep and reverential love for *family life*, where the entire extended family discovers its roots, its identity, and its strength;

    c) a marvelous sense of *community* that celebrates life through "fiesta";

    d) loving appreciation for God's gift of *life*, and an understanding of time which allows one to savor that gift;

    e) authentic and consistent devotion to Mary, the Mother of God.

4.   We are *all* called to appreciate our own histories and to reflect upon the ethnic, racial, and cultural origins which make us a nation of immigrants. Historically, the Church in the United States has been an "immigrant Church" whose outstanding record of care for countless European immigrants remains unmatched. Today that same tradition must inspire in the Church's approach to recent Hispanic immigrants and migrants a similar authority, compassion, and decisiveness.

Although the number of Hispanics is increasing in our country, it would be misleading to place too much emphasis on numerical growth only. Focusing primarily on the numbers could very easily lead us to see Hispanics simply as a large pastoral problem, while overlooking the even more important fact that they present a unique pastoral opportunity.

The pastoral needs of Hispanic Catholics are indeed great; although their faith is deep and strong, it is being challenged and eroded by steady social pressures to assimilate. Yet the history, culture, and spirituality animating their lively faith deserve to be known, shared, and reinforced by us all. Their past and present contributions to the faith life of the Church deserve appreciation and recognition.

Let us work closely together in creating pastoral visions and strategies which, drawing upon a memorable past, are made anew by the creative hands of the present.

5.   The Church has a vast body of teaching on culture and its intimate link with faith. "In his self-revelation to his people culminating in the fullness of manifestation in his incarnate Son, God spoke according to the culture proper to each age. Similarly the Church has existed through the centuries in varying circumstances and has utilized the resources of different cultures in its preaching to spread and explain the message of Christ, to examine and understand it more deeply, and to express it more perfectly in the liturgy and in various aspects of the life of the faithful" (*Gaudium et Spes* [GS], 58).

As with many nationalities with a strong Catholic tradition, religion, and culture, faith and life are inseparable for Hispanics. Hispanic Catholicism is an outstanding example of how the Gospel can permeate a culture to its very roots (*Evangelii Nuntiandi* [EN], 20). But it also reminds us that no culture is without defects and sins. Hispanic culture, like any other, must be challenged by the Gospel.

Respect for culture is rooted in the dignity of people made in God's image. The Church shows its esteem for this dignity by working to ensure that pluralism, not assimilation and uniformity, is the guiding principle in the life of communities in both the ecclesial and secular societies. All of us in the Church should broaden the embrace with which we greet our Hispanic brothers and sisters and deepen our commitment to them.

Hispanic Reality

6.   No other European culture has been in this country longer than the Hispanic. Spaniards and their descendants were already in the Southeast and Southwest by the late sixteenth century. In other regions of our country a steady influx of Hispanic immigrants has increased their visibility in more recent times. Plainly, the Hispanic population will loom larger in the future of both the wider society and the Church in the United States.

Only 30 years ago the U.S. census estimated there were 6 million Hispanics in the country. The 1980 census counted almost 15 million — a figure which does not include the population on the island of Puerto Rico, many undocumented workers, recent Cuban refugees, those who have fled spiraling violence in Central and South America, nor countless other Hispanics missed in the census. A number of experts estimate a total U.S. Hispanic population of at least 20 million.[1]

The United States today ranks fifth among the world's Spanish-speaking countries; only Mexico, Spain, Argentina, and Colombia have more Hispanics.[2]

Hispanic Catholics are extremely diverse. They come from 19 different Latin American republics, Puerto Rico, and Spain. The largest group, comprising 60 percent, is Mexican-American. They are followed by Puerto Ricans, 17 percent, and Cubans, 8 percent. The Dominican Republic, Peru, Ecuador, Chile, and increasingly Central America, especially El Salvador, as well as other Latin American countries, are amply represented.

Hispanics vary in their racial origins, color, history, achievements, expressions of faith, and degree of disadvantage. But they share many elements of culture, including a deeply rooted Catholicism, values such as commitment to the extended family, and a common language, Spanish, spoken with different accents.

They are found in every state of the Union and nearly every diocese. Although many, especially in the Southwest, live in rural areas, over 85 percent are found in large urban centers like New York, Chicago, Miami, Los Angeles, San Antonio, and San Francisco. In places like Hartford, Washington, D.C., and Atlanta, a growing num-

---

[1] An accurate count of Hispanics has not yet taken place. As established successfully in court, the 1970 census undercounted Hispanics. Similar claims have been made regarding the 1980 figure. Estimates that include all of the populations cited in the text vary from 15 to 17 million. Our preference for 20 million accepts as likely the following: 14.6 million (1980 census) plus 3.2 million (population of Puerto Rico), plus 126,000 (Mariel boat-lift per USCC estimate), plus 1.9 million (1978 estimate of undocumented Hispanics), plus undercount for improperly identified non-Hispanics. See *Hispanic Catholics in the United States,* Rev. Frank Ponce, Pro-Mundi Vita, Brussels, 1981.

[2] The Spanish-speaking populations mentioned are as follows: Mexico 71.9 million; Spain 37.5 million; Colombia 27.6 million; Argentina 27 million (United Nations, 1980).

ber of advertisements in Spanish and English, as well as large Hispanic barrios,[3] are evidence of their increasing presence.

It is significant that Hispanics are the youngest population in our country. Their median age, 23.2, is lower than that of any other group; 54 percent are age 25 or less.

Socioeconomic Conditions

7. In general, most Hispanics in our country live near or below the poverty level. While limited improvements in their social and economic status have occurred in the last generation, the Hispanic community as a whole has yet to share equitably in this country's wealth — wealth they have helped produce. Despite rising expectations, Hispanic political participation in the political process is limited by economic and social underdevelopment. Thus Hispanics are severely underrepresented at decision-making levels in Church and society.

The annual median income for non-Hispanic families is $5,000 higher than the median for Hispanic families; 22.1 percent of Hispanics live below the poverty level, compared with 15 percent of the general population.[4]

Historically, unemployment has been higher among Hispanics than other nationalities. The Puerto Ricans are the hardest hit, with unemployment rates generally a third higher than other Hispanics.[5] In times of crisis, such as in the economic downturn of the early 1980s, Hispanics are among the last hired and the first fired.

Well over half the employed Hispanics work at nonprofessional, nonmanagerial jobs, chiefly in agricultural labor and urban service occupations. In both occupational areas, the courageous struggle of workers to obtain adequate means of negotiation for just compensation has yet to succeed.

Lack of education is an important factor keeping Hispanics poor. While more Hispanics now finish high school and college than did ten years ago, only 40 percent graduate from high school, compared with 66 percent of the general population. Hispanics are underrepresented even within the Catholic school system, where they account for only 9 percent of the student population.

Educational opportunities are often below standard in areas of high Hispanic concentration. Early frustration in school leads many young Hispanics to drop out without the skills they need, while many

---

[3]*Barrios:* literally, neighborhoods. In the United States, the Spanish word has come to mean the Hispanic, generally poor, ethnic neighborhoods in a number of major cities.

[4]See *Money, Income and Poverty Status of Families and Persons in the United States: 1981,* Series p-60, No. 134, Bureau of the Census, Washington, D.C., July 1982.

[5]U.S. Government figures for 1981 held overall Hispanic unemployment at 9.8 percent, Mexican-American at 9.4, Cubans at 7.8, and Puerto Ricans at 13.4.

of those who stay find themselves in an educational system which is not always supportive. Often Hispanic students are caught in a cultural cross fire—living their Hispanic culture at home, while feeling pressured at school and at work to assimilate and foresake their heritage.

Impersonal data tells us that Hispanics are numerous, rapidly increasing, of varied national origins, found everywhere in the United States, socioeconomically disadvantaged, and in need of greater access to education and the decision-making processes. But there is a human reality behind the dry, sometimes discouraging data. We see in the faces of Hispanics a profound serenity, a steadfast hope, and a vibrant joy; in many we recognize an evangelical sense of the blessing and prophetic nature of poverty.

II. Achievements in Hispanic Ministry in the United States

8.   In responding to the pastoral needs of Hispanics, we are building on work begun many years ago. We recognize with gratitude what was done by farsighted men and women, Hispanic and non-Hispanic, who, pioneers in this apostolate, helped maintain and develop the faith of hundreds of thousands. They deserve credit for their courageous efforts.

9.   In many respects the survival of faith among Hispanics seems little less than a miracle. Even at times when the institutional Church could not be present to them, their faith remained for their family-oriented tradition of faith provided a momentum and dynamism accounting for faith's preservation. But let us not depend only on that tradition today; every generation of every culture stands in need of being evangelized (EN, 54).

One of the glories of Hispanic women, lay and religious, has been their role in nurturing the faith and keeping it alive in their families and communities. Traditionally, they have been the basic leaders of prayer, catechists, and often excellent models of Christian discipleship.

The increasing number of lay leaders and permanent deacons (20 percent of the U.S. total) is a sign that lay leadership from the grass roots has been fostered and called to service in the Church.

Also noteworthy are the various apostolic *movimientos* (movements) which have helped ensure the survival of the faith for many Hispanic Catholics. For example, *Cursillos de Cristiandad, Encuentros Conyugales, Encuentros de Promocion Juvenil, Movimiento Familiar Cristiano, Communidades Eclesiales de Base,* and the Charismatic Renewal as well as others, have been instrumental in bringing out the apostolic potential in many Hispanic individuals, married couples, and communities. A number of associations, such as PADRES and HERMANAS, have provided support networks to priests and women in the Hispanic movement.

Religious congregations of men and women are among those who have responded generously to the challenge. That a substantial percentage of Hispanic priests are religious is a sign of their expenditure of resources, personnel, and energy. In a special way religious congregations of women have contributed to meeting the spiritual and material needs of migrant farm workers, the inner-city poor, refugees from Latin America, and the undocumented. North American missionaries returning from Latin America have likewise brought with them a strong attraction and dedication to Hispanics.

As far back as the 1940s, the bishops showed genuine concern for Hispanic Catholics by establishing, at the prompting of Archbishop Robert E. Lucey of San Antonio, a committee for the Spanish-speaking to work with Hispanics of the Southwest. In 1912, Philadelphia began its Spanish apostolate. New York and Boston established diocesan offices for the Spanish-speaking in the 1950s. Early efforts to minister to Hispanics were made in other areas as well.

Later, persistent efforts by bishops who recognized the need for a Hispanic presence at the national church leadership level culminated in 1970 with the establishment of the USCC Division for the Spanish-speaking as part of the USCC Department of Social Development. In 1974, the division became the NCCB/USCC Secretariat for Hispanic Affairs.

Under the leadership of the bishops, and with the support of the NCCB/USCC Secretariat for Hispanic Affairs, Hispanic Catholics have been responsible for two national pastoral *Encuentros*. In 1972 and 1977, these gatherings of lay men and women dedicated to their own local communities concluded with prophetic calls to the Church at large. Also, as a result of the *II Encuentro Nacional Hispano de Pastoral* in 1977, ministry with Hispanic youth was encouraged at the regional, diocesan, and parish levels through the National Youth Task Force, now renamed *Comité Nacional Hispano de Pastoral Juvenil* (National Hispanic Committee for Youth Ministry).[6]

The appointment of Hispanic bishops and archbishops since 1970 has greatly enhanced this apostolate. We rejoice with all the Hispanic Catholics who see in these new bishops a visible and clear sign that the Holy See is recognizing their presence and the contribution they are capable of making to the life to the Church in the United States. Recent apostolic delegates have voiced their concern for ethnic and minority groups in the Church in this country and have urged the leadership of the Church to address their needs.

---

[6]See *Conclusions of the II Encuentro*, NCCB Secretariat for Hispanic Affairs, 1977.

The past decade has also seen the emergence of regional offices, pastoral institutes, diocesan commissions and offices, and *centros pastorales* (pastoral centers), all of which have become effective pastoral instruments working with Hispanics.

III. Urgent Pastoral Implications

10. We urge all U.S. Catholics to explore creative possibilities for responding innovatively, flexibly, and immediately to the Hispanic presence. Hispanics and non-Hispanics should work together, teach and learn from one another, and together evangelize in the fullest and broadest sense. Non-Hispanic clergy, especially religious, priests, and bishops who have been at the forefront of the Hispanic apostolates, are needed more than ever today to serve with the Hispanic people.

The Church's Mission and the Hispanic Presence

11. From an ecclesial perspective, evangelization, which is the Church's central mission and purpose, consists not just in isolated calls to individual conversion but in an invitation to join the People of God (EN, 15). This is reflected in the Hispanic experience of evangelization, which includes an important communitarian element expressed in an integral or "holistic" vision of faith and pastoral activity carried out in community (*II Encuentro Nacional Hispano de Pastoral* [II ENHP], I.4.c).

This experience is summed up in the concept of the *pastoral de conjunto*, a pastoral focus and approach to action arising from shared reflection among the agents of evangelization (Final Documents of III General Conference of CELAM, 1979 [Puebla], 650, 122 and 1307). Implicit in a *pastoral de conjunto* is the recognition that both the sense of the faithful and hierarchical teaching are essential elements in the articulation of the faith. This pastoral approach also recognizes that the Church's essential mission is best exercised in a spirit of concord and in group apostolate (*Apostolicam Actuositatem* [AA], 18.)

An effective Hispanic apostolate includes the application of this experience, which can benefit the Church in *all* its efforts to fulfill its mission. Essential to this is an integral vision, forged in community, which encompasses the totality of human challenges and opportunities as religious concerns.

Creative Possibilities

12. We therefore invite all our priests, deacons, and religious and lay leaders to consider the following creative opportunities.

a. Liturgy

Universal in form, our Church "respects and fosters the spiritual adornments and gifts of the various races and peoples" in its liturgical life (*Sacrosanctum Concilium* [SC], 37). As applied to the Hispanic presence, this requires making provision for Spanish and bilingual worship according to the traditions and customs of the people being served. We are thus challenged to greater study of Hispanic prayer forms. It is encouraging in this regard that Hispanic Catholic artists and musicians are already contributing to the liturgy in our country.

The presence of Hispanic liturgists on parish and diocesan commissions is essential. Every effort should be made to bring this about.

As their homes have been true "domestic churches" for many Hispanic Catholics, so the home has traditionally been for them the center of faith and worship. The celebration of traditional feasts and special occasions in the home should therefore be valued and encouraged.

The choice of liturgical art, gestures, and music, combined with the spirit of hospitality, can refashion our churches and altars into spiritual homes and create in our communities an inviting environment of family *fiesta*.

b. Renewal of Preaching

The recasting and proclamation of the Word in powerful, new, liberating images are unavoidable challenges for Hispanic ministry. As the Apostle Paul asked, "How can they believe unless they have heard of him? And how can they hear unless there is someone to preach?" (Rom 10:14).

Those who preach should always bear in mind that the ability to hear is linked to the hearer's language, culture, and real-life situation. In proclaiming the gospel message, they should strive to make these characteristics and realities their own, so that their words will transmit the Gospel's truly liberating content.

Thirsting for God's Word, Hispanics want clear and simple preaching on its message and its application to their lives. They respond to effective preaching, and they often express a keen desire for better, more powerful preaching which expresses the gospel message in terms they can understand.

We strongly recommend that priests engaged in ministry with Hispanics, such as parish priests and chaplains, enroll in Spanish courses so that they can readily speak with and listen to Hispanics. Similarly, we urge Hispanic permanent deacons to develop their preaching skills. We ask that these men be called on more often to exercise the ministry of the Word. The continuing education of permanent deacons and periodic evaluation of their ministry are necessary in this regard.

c. Catechesis

Like initial evangelization, catechesis must start where the hearer of the Gospel is (EN, 44). In the case of Hispanics, this suggests not merely the use of Spanish but also an active dialogue with their culture and their needs (*National Catechetical Directory* [NCD], 229). Since religious education is a lifelong process for the individual (NCD, 32), parishes should provide an atmosphere for catechesis which in every respect encourages the ongoing information of adults as well as children. Such efforts will match the effectiveness of grade-level programs for children among the English-speaking and explore new methods in adult catechesis.

It is essential, too, that dioceses sponsor catechist formation courses in Spanish for Hispanics. They should be assured of having appropriate, effective materials and programs in Spanish (NCD, 194, 195). Catechists should take advantage of every "teachable moment" to present the Church's doctrine to Hispanic Catholics. Hispanic family celebrations[7] like baptisms, *quinceañeras*, weddings, anniversaries, *fiestas patrias*, *novenarios*, *velorios*, and funerals often provide excellent teachable moments which are also "moments of grace" enabling the catechist to build upon the people's traditions and use them as living examples of gospel truths (Puebla, 59 and *Catechesi Tradendae* [CT], 53).

Throughout our country there is deep yearning and hunger, "not a famine for bread, or a thirst for water, but for hearing the word of the Lord" (Am 8:11). We urge continuing efforts to begin bible study

---

[7]The salient Hispanic family celebrations in the United States described in the text can be defined as follows:

a) *Quinceañeras:* a young woman's fifteenth birthday celebration (*quince años* — fifteen years) usually celebrated by the Hispanic family as a rite of passage into adulthood. Sister Angela Erevia, at the Mexican American Cultural Center in San Antonio, Texas, has called this celebration a "teachable moment" since it traditionally includes as a central moment a *Quinceañera* Mass which expresses thanksgiving to God for the young woman's fifteen years.

b) *Fiestas Patrias:* (literally, "patriotic holidays") reference is made to the main national day of each Latin American country, usually but not always the day of independence, which is a special moment in the life of many U.S. Hispanic communities.

c) *Novenarios:* devotion to the saints and to the Blessed Virgin Mary through a variety of novenas. These traditionally occur in the home and gather the entire family in prayers and special readings of devotional materials, often following an important family event. One notable example is the *Novenario de Difuntos* (*difuntos* — the dead), which takes place following the death of a family member.

d) *Velorios:* wakes. In the traditional Hispanic family practice, these are often more than social occasions which gather far-flung relatives. They also include moments of prayer. Many Hispanic families still see the rosary as an essential form of prayer complementary to Christian mourning.

groups in Hispanic communities, and to call forth Hispanic leaders to guide and direct such programs.

d. Vocation and Formation of Lay Ministers

Adequate training must have a high priority in Hispanic ministry. In planning such training, the goals of enhancing pluralism and catholicity will suggest the means. Formation should aim to incorporate the knowledge and practical experience necessary to minister effectively, while also fostering a serious commitment of service.

Although Hispanics lack sufficient clergy trained to minister with them, there are among them many lay people who are well disposed to respond to the call to be apostles (AA, 3). From this we conclude that fostering vocations and training for lay ministries will help provide the much needed laborers in the vineyard.

One model in this direction is the *escuela de ministerios*,[8] which helps train lay leaders, calls youths to greater participation in the Church, and is likely to serve as a place of election for priestly and religious vocations.

e. Vocations to Priestly, Religous Ministries

The scarcity of Hispanic priests, religious sisters and brothers, and permanent deacons is one of the most serious problems facing the Church in the United States. There are historical reasons, among them neglect, for the unfortunate lack of Hispanic vocations. In the past, too, a major reason for the failure of many Hispanic young people to persevere in pursuing vocations has been the presence in seminaries and convents of cultural expressions, traditions, language, family relationships, and religious experiences which conflicted with their own. Today, however, we are pleased to note that these conflicts are fewer and the situation is vastly improved. In recent years many, if not most, seminaries and convents have made significant strides in meeting the needs of Hispanics. We congratulate these institutions

---

[8]*Escuelas de Ministerios*. In the past decade, a number of dioceses have established centers for the formation of lay leaders known generically by this name. Although they vary from place to place, these schools of ministries generally provide a core program of catechetics, basic biblical study, ecclesiology, and adult education in social sciences and humanities. In addition, they train students in a variety of specialized ministries according to aptitude and preference of the student and the needs of the diocese. The essential goal of the schools is to promote talented and committed individuals as leaders at the service of their communities. Those who complete the programs and show growth in the desire to serve are then commissioned to serve as lay movement leaders, catechists, lectors, extraordinary ministers of the Eucharist, and small community and study group leaders. See *Hispanic Portrait of Evangelization No. 10* by Cecilio J. Morales, Jr., NCCB Committee on Evangelization, 1981.

and encourage them to continue improving their programs for Hispanic ministry.

We also encourage seminaries to provide courses in Spanish, Hispanic culture and religiosity, and Hispanic pastoral ministry for
seminarians, priests, religious, permanent deacons, and all pastoral
ministers.

In light of the present situation, we commit ourselves to fostering
Hispanic vocations. Bishops, priests, religious, and laity now must
aggressively encourage Hispanic youth to consider the priestly or
religious vocation. We call upon Hispanic parents to present the life
and work of a priest or religious as a highly desirable vocation for
their children and to take rightful pride in having a son or daughter
serve the Church in this way. Without their strong support, the Church
will not have the number of Hispanic priests and religious needed to
serve their communities.

This requires encouraging a more positive image of priests and
religious than presently exists in many Hispanic families. The Church's
presence in Hispanic communities must be one which makes it possible for people to experience the reality of its love and care. Priests
and religious have a serious responsibility to give Hispanic youth a
positive, joyful experience of the Church and to invite them to consider the priesthood or religious life as they make decisions about
their future. Diocesan vocation offices are urged to make special efforts
to reach Hispanic youth with the invitation to follow Jesus in a priestly
or religious vocation.

Above all, the Church in the United States must pray to the Lord
of the harvest to send the Hispanic vocations that are sorely needed.
We urge special, unceasing prayer in Hispanic parishes for this purpose, and we call upon parents to pray that one or more of their
children will be given the grace of a vocation to the priesthood or
religious life.

f. Catholic Education

Catholic educators in the United States have a long record of
excellence and dedication to the instruction and formation of millions
of the Catholic faithful. Now they must turn their skills to responding
to the educational needs of Hispanics. Education is an inalienable
right; and in nurturing the intellect, Catholic schools and institutes
of learning must also foster the values and culture of their pupils
(*Gravissimum Educationis* [GE], 178).

We therefore urge Catholic schools and other Catholic educational institutions to offer additional opportunities, including scholarships and financial aid, to Hispanics who cannot now afford to
attend them.

We also recommend adaptations which respond adequately to

the Hispanic presence in our schools. Curricula should provide opportunities for bilingual education; teachers should be familiar with the Spanish language, and should respect and understand Hispanic culture and religious expression. At the same time, care must be taken to ensure that bilingual education does not impede or unduly delay entrance into the political, socioeconomic, and religious mainstream because of inability to communicate well in the prevalent language.

It is important not only to affirm to Hispanic youths the inherent value of their heritage, but also to offer instruction in Hispanic history and culture. Society often tells them that their parents' culture, so deeply steeped in Catholicism, is valueless and irrelevant. The Church can teach them otherwise.

The Church must also become an advocate for the many young Hispanics who attend public schools, doing all it can to ensure that provision is made for their needs. Particular attention should be given to those who have dropped out of school, whether Catholic or public, and who need remedial education or assistance in developing technical skills.

g. Communications

Ours is an era in which "the medium is the message." The Church has recognized this fact by supporting the modernization of the means of communications at its disposal. For the most part, however, the church press and electronic media lag in the area of Hispanic ministry. While a few worthy publications in Spanish have been begun in the past decade, the Catholic press largely ignores coverage of Hispanic news. Similarly, the Church lacks a solid body of television and radio programming that addresses the needs of the Hispanic community, although some fine first efforts have been launched through the Catholic Communication Campaign and the Catholic Telecommunications Network of America.

This suggests the need for greater efforts toward planned and systematic programming and regular coverage of issues relevant to the Hispanic community. Training and hiring of talented Hispanics in communications and journalism are required to produce fresh and lively material. Materials and programming imported from Latin America may also help in the short term to bridge our communications gap.

h. Effective Ecumenism

The Lord Jesus prayed for the unity of His followers (Jn 17:21), yet the division of the churches is a major obstacle to evangelization. This is underlined in the United States by instances of active proselytizing among Hispanics carried on in an anti-ecumenical manner by Protestant sects. A variety of fundamentalist groups divide Hispanics and their families with their preaching, which reflects an anti-Catholic spirit hardly emanating from the Gospel of Jesus Christ (PHB, II.c.).

Our response as Catholics is not to attack or disparage brothers and sisters of other Christian traditions, but to live the Gospel more authentically in order to present the Catholic Church as the fullness of Christianity (*Lumen Gentium* [LG], 14) and thus nourish the faith of our Hispanic peoples. Other Christian churches have been part of the history of salvation. Prayer, dialogue, and partnership in efforts of common concern remain high on the Catholic agenda. In the Hispanic context, however, the Catholic Church and its tradition has played the major historical role of inculturation of the Gospel; the Church is committed to continuing this mission.

i. Hispanic Youth

Desiring to be the light of the world and salt of the earth, many Hispanic young people dedicate their energies and talents to the mission of the Church. Their values are deeply Christian. Whatever their circumstances, they feel themselves members of a spiritual family led by their Mother Mary. This is evident in their art, poetry, and other forms of expression. Yet pressures on Hispanic youth to adapt and live by self-seeking values have led many away from the Church.

Like youths of other backgrounds, Hispanic young people have a spirit of generosity toward the disadvantaged. In their case, however, this is often more than sensitivity toward the poor; it is of solidarity with people who have as little as they or less. If they are not to fall prey to dreams of success at any price in order to escape poverty, they need to see their talents and potential valued by the Church.

In responding to their needs, the wise pastoral minister will note the marvelous potential for their abundant energies and their ability to speak the language of youth. Committed Hispanic youths grasp with the immediacy of their own experience how to share their Christian vision with their peers through means such as modern and traditional Hispanic music and art.

Hispanic youths and young adults with leadership qualities must be offered opportunities for religious education, biblical studies, catechesis, and special training, so that their vocations to serve the Church will flourish. Such programs should take into account the fact that these youths will develop best in familiar, warm environments.

j. Family

The tradition of commitment to family is one of the distinguishing marks of Hispanic culture. Although there are variations among Mexican-Americans, Puerto Ricans, Cubans, and other Hispanics, there are shared family values and cultural attributes among all Hispanics.[9]

Whether *nuclear* or *extended*, the family unit has been the privileged place where Christian principles have been nurtured and expressed and evangelization and the development of spirituality have occurred. The Hispanic family often exemplifies Pope John Paul II's description of family prayer: "Joys and sorrows, hopes and disappointments, births and birthday celebrations, wedding anniversaries of parents, departures, separations and homecomings, important and far-reaching decisions, and the death of those who are dear, etc.— all of these mark God's loving intervention in the family history. They should be seen as suitable moments for thanksgiving, for petition, for trusting abandonment of the family into the hands of the common Father in heaven" (*Familiaris Consortio* [FC], 59).

In our pastoral planning, however, we must not take for granted the continued strength and unity of the Catholic Hispanic family. Hispanic nuclear families are already experiencing the same social pressures faced by other groups. The unity of the Hispanic family is threatened in particular by the uprooting caused by mobility, especially from a rural to an urban life style and from Latin American countries to our own; by poverty, which a high proportion of Hispanic families endure; and by pressures engendered by the process of assimilation, which often leads to generation gaps within the family and identity crises in young people.

There is an urgent need for pastoral ministries that will prepare our people well for married life, for parenthood, and for family counseling and religious education. We make a special plea for measures to assist Hispanic families which are "hurting" as well as the divorced, the separated, single parents, and victims of parental or spousal abuse.

Because of their unique family ties, we invite Hispanic families, along with those from other cultural groups with strong family traditions, to contribute to the gradual unfolding of the richness of Christ's truth. "In conformity with her constant tradition, the Church receives from the various cultures everything that is able to express better the unsearchable riches of Christ. Only with the help of all the cultures will it be possible for these riches to be manifested ever more clearly and for the Church to progress towards a daily, more complete, and profound awareness of the truth which has already been given her in its entirety by the Lord" (FC, 10).

---

[9]A 1974 report by the Illinois State Advisory Committee to the U.S. Commission on Civil Rights suggests that the following characteristics are generally found among Hispanics: orientation towards the person rather than towards ideas or abstractions; commitment to individual autonomy within the context of familial and traditional Hispanic values; emphasis on the central importance of the family; emphasis on being rather than doing; emphasis on the father as the main authority figure.

k. Migrant Farm Workers

As noted, Hispanics are highly mobile and are found in both urban and rural settings. As a result, they tend to escape the attention and care of the urban Church. This underlines the need for adaptations in pastoral care, particularly in the case of migrant workers.

There are three major migrant streams in the United States. In the East, farm workers migrate from Mexico, South America, and Florida north to New York and New England, working on sugar cane, cotton, tobacco, apple, and grape crops. In the Central Plains, migrants go north from Texas to the Great Lakes to harvest fruits, vegetables, and grains. There is also a substantial number of Puerto Rican seasonal laborers, most of them young and single, who work mainly in the Northeast. In the West, migrants move northward through California, Nevada, and Idaho up to the Northwest; some even go as far as Alaska in search of seasonal jobs. Migration usually begins in the spring and ends in late fall, when the migrants return to their southern home bases.[10]

Abuses of farm workers are notorious, yet they continue to go unrelieved. Conditions are worsening in many regions. Men and women are demoralized to the point where the riches of Hispanic culture, strong family ties and the profound faith life, are sometimes lost. We denounce the treatment of migrants as commodities, cheap labor, rather than persons. We urge others to do the same. Economic conditions often require children to be part of the labor force. Along with the other problems associated with mobility, their education suffers. In the same vein, we find deplorable the abuse of the rights of undocumented workers. All this makes it imperative for the Church to support the right of migrant farm workers to organize for the purpose of collective bargaining.

Experience in the Hispanic apostolate suggests the need for mobile missionary teams and various forms of itinerant ministries. Dioceses and parishes in the path of migrant streams also have a responsibility to support this work and coordinate the efforts of sending and receiving dioceses.

Undoubtedly, too, Hispanic migrants themselves, whose agricultural understanding of life so closely resembles that of Jesus the Galilean,[11] have much to contribute to meeting the challenge.

---

[10]See *Farmworkers in the U.S.*, USCC, 1978.

[11]Reference is made to the human characteristics of Jesus and their link to the setting and circumstance of migrant workers. In *The Galilean Journey* and *Jesus the Galilean*, both published by Orbis Books, Rev. Virgilio Elizondo reflects on this theme. Jesus' outlook is seen as conditioned by his nationality, language, the political context, and the religious understanding of his time. Elizondo picks up the pastoral experience of the Hispanic apostolate to establish parallels between the inhabitants of the conquered border province of Galilee in Roman times and the marginality of the Mexican-American in the

l. Social Justice and Social Action

The integral evangelization described earlier as the central focus of the pastoral strategy we envisage will be incomplete without an active component of social doctrine and action. As we said in our pastoral letter on war and peace, "at the center of all Catholic social teaching are the transcendence of God and the dignity of the human person. The human person is the clearest reflection of God's presence in the world" (*The Challenge of Peace: God's Promise and Our Response* [CP], I, 15). This thought must be applied specifically to the reality of the Hispanic presence and the ministry which responds to it.

In the past twenty years Catholic teaching has become increasingly specific about the meaning of social justice. From Pope John XXIII's encyclical *Pacem In Terris* to Pope John Paul II's *Laborem Excercens*, we have seen social teaching define as human rights such things as good governance, nutrition, health, housing, employment, and education. In the United States we have applied these teachings to the problems of our time and nation.

Now we call attention to those social concerns which most directly affect the Hispanic community, among them voting rights, discrimination, immigration rights, the status of farm workers, bilingualism, and pluralism. These are social justice issues of paramount importance to ministry with Hispanics and to the entire Church.

As it engages in social teaching, the Church embraces the quest for justice as an eminently religious task. Persons engaged in this endeavor must be involved with, informed by, and increasingly led by those who know from experience the paradoxical blessings of poverty, prejudice, and unfairness (Mt 5:3). Accordingly, we urge Hispanics to increase their role in social action, and non-Hispanics increasingly to seek out Hispanics in a true partnership.

m. Prejudice and Racism

Within our memory, Hispanics in this country have experienced cruel prejudice. So extensive has it been in some areas that they have been denied basic human and civil rights. Even today Hispanics, blacks, the recent Southeast Asian refugees, and Native Americans continue to suffer from such dehumanizing treatment, treatment which makes us aware that the sin of racism lingers in our society. Despite great strides in eliminating racial prejudice, both in our country and in our Church, there remains an urgent need for continued purification and reconciliation. It is particularly disheartening to know that

---

United States. In *Journeying Together Toward the Lord* (USCC Department of Education and Secretariat for Hispanic Affairs, 1982), a manual for migrant catechists, this idea is used quite effectively as the vehicle for reflection on the faith.

some Catholics hold strong prejudices against Hispanics and others and deny them the respect and love due their God-given human dignity.

This is evident even in some parish communities where one finds a reluctance among some non-Hispanics to serve with Hispanics or to socialize with them at parochial events. We appeal to those with this unchristian attitude to examine their behavior in the light of Jesus' commandment of love and to accept their Hispanic brothers and sisters as full partners in the work and life of their parishes. Our words in our pastoral letter on racism deserve repeating: "Racism is not merely one sin among many, it is a radical evil dividing the human family and denying the new creation of a redeemed world. To struggle against it demands an equally radical transformation in our own minds and hearts as well as the structure of our society" (*Brothers and Sisters to Us* [BSU], p. 10).

We urge those who employ Hispanics to provide them with safe and decent working conditions and to pay them salaries which enable them to provide adequately for their families. The inhuman condition of pervasive poverty forced on many Hispanics is at the root of many social problems in their lives. Decent working conditions and adequate salaries are required by justice and basic fairness.

n. Ties with Latin America

Hispanics in our midst are an as yet untapped resource as a cultural bridge between North and South in the Americas. The wellspring of Hispanic culture and faith is historically and geographically located in Latin America. For this reason, a dynamic response to the Hispanic presence in the United States will necessarily entail an ever greater understanding of and linkage with Latin American society and Church.

Latin America, the home of 350 million Catholics, continues to experience grave socioeconomic injustice, and, in many nations, a severe deprivation of the most basic human rights. These conditions are oppressive and dehumanizing; they foster violence, poverty, hatred, and deep divisions in the social fabric; they are fundamentally at variance with gospel values.[12] And yet our fellow Catholics in Latin

---

[12]Socioeconomic injustice and violations of human rights in a number of Latin American countries are the principal themes of concern expressed repeatedly by the U.S. Catholic Conference with reference to U.S. policy in the region. See *Quest for Justice: A Compendium of Statements of the United States Catholic Bishops on the Political and Social Order 1966-1980,* J. Brian Benestad and Francis J. Butler, NCCB/USCC, 1981, pp. 123-129; also see pp. 433-439 for a list of statements and testimony offered in that period; see also *Statement of the U.S. Catholic Conference on Central America,* Archbishop John R. Roach, July 22, 1983. The same analysis is found in major statements by the Latin American Episcopal Council (CELAM). See *Declaration of Medellin,* CELAM, 1968; and *Message to the Peoples of Latin America,* CELAM, 1979.

America, especially the poor, are often vibrant witnesses to the liberating quality of the Gospel, as they strive to build a "civilization of Love" (Puebla, 9).

We shall continue to support and assist the Church in Latin America. We also look forward to a continuing exchange of missionaries, since the cooperation we envision is not one-sided. For our part, we shall continue to send those most prepared to evangelize in Latin America, including our Hispanic personnel as they grow in numbers. With careful regard to circumstances in the areas from which they come, we welcome Latin American and other priests and religious who come to serve Hispanics in the United States. We recommend that upon arrival they receive special language and cultural preparation for pastoral activity. The Church in the United States has much to learn from the Latin American pastoral experience; it is fortunate to have in the Hispanic presence a precious human link to that experience.

o. Popular Catholicism

Hispanic spirituality is an example of how deeply Christianity can permeate the roots of a culture. In the course of almost 500 years in the Americas, Hispanic people have learned to express their faith in prayer forms and traditions that were begun and encouraged by missionaries and passed from one generation to the next.

Paul VI recognized the value inherent in popular Catholicism. While warning against the possible excesses of popular religiosity, he nonetheless enumerated values that often accompany these prayer forms. If well-oriented, he pointed out, popular piety manifests a thirst for God, makes people generous, and imbues them with a spirit of sacrifice. It can lead to an acute awareness of God's attributes, such as his fatherhood, his providence, and his loving and constant presence (EN, 48).

Hispanic spirituality places strong emphasis on the humanity of Jesus, especially when he appears weak and suffering, as in the crib and in his passion and death. This spirituality relates well to all that is symbolic in Catholicism: to ritual, statues and images, holy places, and gestures. It is also a strongly devotional spirituality. The Blessed Virgin Mary, especially under the titles of Our Lady of Guadalupe (Mexico), Our Lady of Providence (Puerto Rico), and Our Lady of Charity (Cuba), occupies a privileged place in Hispanic popular piety.

A closer dialogue is needed between popular and official practice, lest the former lose the guidance of the Gospel and the latter lose the active participation of the unsophisticated and the poorest among the faithful (Final Documents of the II General Conference of CELAM [Medellín], 3). An ecclesial life vibrant with a profound sense of the transcendent, such as is found in Hispanic popular Catholicism, can also be a remarkable witness to the more secularized members of our society.

p. *Comunidades Eclesiales de Base*

Hispanics in the Americas have made few contributions to the Church more significant than the *comunidades eclesiales de base* (Basic Ecclesial Communities). The small community has appeared on the scene as a ray of hope in dealing with dehumanizing situations that can destroy people and weaken faith. A revitalized sense of fellowship fills the Church in Latin America, Africa, Europe, and Asia with pastoral joy and hope. The Synod of Bishops in 1974 witnessed an outpouring of such hope from Latin American pastors, who saw in *comunidades eclesiales de base* a source of renewal in the Church. Since these communities are of proven benefit to the Church (EN, 58), we highly encourage their development.

The *comunidad eclesial de base* is neither a discussion or study group nor a parish. It is "the first and fundamental ecclesiastical nucleus, which on its own level must make itself responsible for the richness and expansion of the faith, as well as of the worship of which it is an expression" (*Joint Pastoral Planning*, Medellín 1968 [JPP], 10). It should be an expression of a Church that liberates from personal and structural sin; it should be a small community with personal relationships; it should form part of a process of integral evangelization; and it should be in communion with other levels of the Church. The role of the parish, in particular, is to facilitate, coordinate, and multiply the *comunidades eclesiales de base* within its boundaries and territories. The parish should be a community of communities. The ideal *comunidad eclesial de base* is a living community of Christians whose active involvement in every aspect of life is nourished by profound commitment to the Gospel.

q. Other Possibilities

We urge U.S. Catholics to use their best creative talents to go boldly beyond these first steps, which are merely prerequisites for effective action.

One opportunity for creative action arises from the presence of Hispanics in the U.S. military. We encourage the Military Vicariate to explore new means of integral evangelization, with particular attention to this Hispanic presence.

Similarly, as those in prison ministry know, incarcerated Hispanics are in dire need of attention. There is a need for pastoral ministers to assist in this area.

Among Hispanics there are also handicapped persons whose special needs are compounded by many of the problems we have described.

According to estimates nearly 2 million Hispanic Catholics have one or more disabling conditions, including blindness, deafness, mental retardation, learning disabilities, and orthopedic impairments. There is a serious need for programs of ministry which encourage participation by disabled Hispanic Catholics.

This is only a partial list. As throughout this document, our intent here has been to encourage further reflection, dialogue, and action, not limit them.

IV. Statement of Commitment

13. While conscious of the many ethnic and racial groups who call legitimately upon our services and resources, and grateful for the present significant, if limited, outreach to the Hispanic people of the United States, we commit ourselves and our pastoral associates to respond to the call to Hispanic ministry. Awareness of the good works of the past and present must not make us slow to read the signs of the times. Our preparations today will make it easier to carry out tomorrow's task.

We recognize the realities of the U.S. Hispanic presence, the past efforts of those involved in the Hispanic apostolate, and the urgent need to launch new and creative efforts. To inaugurate this new era in the Church considerable adjustments will be required on the part of Hispanics and non-Hispanics alike. Yet we are hopeful that commitment to minister with Hispanics will lead to a reaffirmation of catholicity and a revitalization of all efforts to fulfill the Church's essential mission.

Commitment to Catholicity

14. The universal character of the Church involves both pluralism and unity. Humanity, in its cultures and peoples, is so various that it could only have been crafted by the hand of God. The Church recognizes this in saying that "each individual part contributes through its special gifts" (LG, 13), Yet the Church transcends all limits of time and race; humanity as a whole is called to become a People of God in peace and unity.

The gospel teaching that no one is a stranger in the Church is timeless. As the Apostle Paul says, "there does not exist among you Jew or Greek, slave or freeman, male or female. All are one in Christ Jesus" (Gal 3:28).

Our commitment to Hispanic ministry therefore leads us, as teachers, to invite *all* Catholics to adopt a more welcoming attitude toward others. Hispanics, whose presence in this land is antedated only by that of Native Americans, are called to welcome their brothers and sisters, the descendants of other European immigrants. Similarly, the latter are called to embrace Hispanic newcomers from Latin America. Where all are freed from attitudes of cultural or ethnic dominance, the gifts of all will enrich the Church and give witness to the Gospel of Jesus Christ.

Commitment to Respond to Temporal Needs

15. Evangelization is a spiritual work which also extends to all that is human and seeks to bring it to fulfillment. Pope John Paul II reminded us of this when he said, "The Church will never abandon man, nor his temporal needs, as she leads humanity to salvation" (*Address to the Bishops of the United States,* John Paul II, October 1979).

Our Hispanic faithful proclaimed this same reality in their *II Encuentro;* there they make a commitment to integral evangelization, "with the testimony of a life of service to one's neighbor for the transformation of the world" (II ENHP, Evangelization, 1).

We, in our turn, pledge to raise our voices and go on raising them as leaders in defense of the human dignity of Hispanics. We remind our pastoral associates that their work includes the effort to gain for Hispanics participation in the benefits of our society. We call all U.S. Catholics to work not just *for* Hispanics but *with* them, in order to secure their empowerment in our democracy and the political participation which is their right and duty. In this way we deepen our preferential option for the poor which, according to Jesus' example and the Church's tradition, must always be a hallmark of our apostolate (Puebla, 1134).

Call to Recognize the Hispanic Reality

16. In committing ourselves to work *with* Hispanics and not simply *for* them, we accept the responsibility of acknowledging, respecting, and valuing their presence as a gift. This presence represents more than just potential; it now performs a valuable service for our Church and our society although this service is often overlooked; it is a prophetic presence, one to be encouraged and needed.

Commitment of Resources

17. Also part of our commitment, as shepherds and stewards of the common resources of the Church, is the pledge to harness these resources for Hispanic ministry. We make this explicit when we keep in mind and take steps to make visible the spirit of the early Christian community (Acts 2:44).

More than an expression of sentiment, this declaration of commitment includes the recognition that we must secure the financial and material resources necessary to reach our goals.

We see the need to continue to support, on a more permanent basis, the existing national, regional, and diocesan entities of the Hispanic apostolate. Given the obvious limitations of resources, it is also necessary to supervise and evaluate current efforts more thoroughly, so as to encourage the best use of personnel, monies, and physical plants. In addition, it is imperative to call to the attention of the appropriate administrators the need to seek more qualified Hispanics to serve their communities. More Hispanics are also needed in the offices of the National Conference of Catholic Bishops and the United States Catholic Conference, in our regional and diocesan offices, our schools, our hospitals, and in the many other agencies of the Church.

What now exists is not sufficient to meet all the needs and challenges. Serious efforts to assess these needs more carefully and earmark resources for Hispanic ministry must take place at every level. The Church in the United States is fortunate in having at its disposal a variety of institutions and ministries whose energies can and should be applied to the task. Schools, parishes, pastoral institutes, communication media, and a variety of specialized ministries must all be encouraged to make this commitment their own.

In the face of very real financial constraints we pledge to explore new possibilities for funding. We are aware of creative budgeting formulas which encourage all ministries and agencies to respond to the Church's priorities; we shall study these as we strive to respond to this clear pastoral need.

Convocation for the III Encuentro

18. We ask our Hispanic peoples to raise their prophetic voices to us once again, as they did in 1972 and 1977, in a *III Encuentro Nacional Hispano de Pastoral,* so that together we can face our responsibilities well. We call for the launching of an *Encuentro* process, from *comunidades eclesiales de base* and parishes, to dioceses and regions, and to the national level, culminating in a gathering of representatives in Washington, D.C., in August 1985.

Towards a Pastoral Plan

19. Beyond the *Encuentro* process, in which we shall take part, we recognize that integral pastoral planning must avoid merely superficial adaptations of existing ministries. We look forward to reviewing the conclusions of the *III Encuentro* as a basis for drafting a National Pastoral Plan for Hispanic Ministry to be considered in our general meeting at the earliest possible date after the *Encuentro.*

Conclusion

20. As we continue our pilgrimage together with our Hispanic brothers and sisters, we frame our commitment in the same spirit as our brother bishops of Latin America gathered at Puebla (*Message to the Peoples of Latin America,* Puebla 1979, 9):

a) We call upon the entire Catholic Church in the United States — laity, religious, deacons, and priests — to join us in our pledge to respond to the presence of our Hispanic brothers and sisters;

b) We honor and rejoice in the work that has taken place before us, and we pledge our best efforts to do even better henceforth;

c) We envisage a new era of ministry with Hispanics, enriched by the gifts of creativity placed providentially before us and by the Spirit of Pentecost who calls us to unity, to renewal, and to meeting the prophetic challenge posed by the Hispanic presence;

d) We commit ourselves to engage in a thorough, conscientious, and continuing pastoral effort to enhance the catholicity of the Church and the dignity of all its members;

e) We look hopefully to the greater blessings Hispanics can bring to our local churches.

May this commitment receive the blessing, the encouragement, and the inspiration of Our Lord. May his Blessed Mother, Patroness of the Americas, accompany us in our journey. Amen.

Resolution of the
U.S. Catholic Conference
on Central America

A Resolution Passed by the
United States Catholic Conference

November 17, 1983

1. In this Holy Year marked by the extraordinary pastoral visit of Pope John Paul II to Central America and the Roman Synod on Reconciliation, we bishops of the United States wish to express our deep sense of solidarity with our brother bishops of Central America and, through them, with all the priests, religious, and laity of that region.

2. In their joint communiqué three months ago, the archbishops and bishops of the countries of Central America and Panama, meeting in regular session of the SEDAC Council of the Presidency, described the reality of their countries as typified by a "virtual state of civil war, grave political, economic, and social disturbances, the result more often than not of long-standing and flagrant injustices and of differing ideologies that, while diverse, are equally inhuman and dehumanizing."

3. "Our people," they continued, "equally suffer because of the meddling of foreign powers, come to support those in the countries who fit their own interests which are generally far from, even opposed to, those of the great majority.

4. "The consequences of this are the cold-blooded killings, an endless chain of vengeance, absolute disregard for life and the dignity of the human person, huge numbers of displaced persons and refugees, prisoners and disappeared. Irreconcilable hatreds are being fomented, deep divisions, arbitrary suppression of individual freedoms and guarantees, disinformation, merciless destruction of goods and services and the resultant general impoverishment."

5. These bishops stressed the Church's oft-repeated insistance on the need for "an honorable and civilized dialogue" between and among the contending parties; elections "absolutely free of all coercion or manipulation" representing the people's "sacred right to give themselves the kind of government they desire"; and the withdrawal of all "outside powers and ideological forces that are interfering politically and militarily in Central America, contrary to our cultural values."

6. We join with our brother bishops in affirming these goals. Indeed these objectives have been central themes in the positions we have taken on U.S. policy in Central America. We promise our continued effort to do what we can to further them, and we express once again our support and admiration for the suffering Church and people of Central America. Continued instances of violence directed against the bishops, priests, and laity, most recently in Nicaragua and El Salvador, only heighten our concern.

7.   With these bishops we make our own the prayer that "Christ Jesus make us effective instruments of his peace" and that "Mary, God's Mother and ours, make possible that, from Panama to Guatemala, there be built among us a civilization of love."

The Church at Prayer
A Holy Temple
of the Lord

*A Pastoral Statement Commemorating the
Twentieth Anniversary of the*
Constitution on the Sacred Liturgy
*Issued by the
National Conference of Catholic Bishops*

December 4, 1983

Introduction

1. Twenty years have passed since the Second Vatican Council solemnly promulgated the *Constitution on the Sacred Liturgy (Sacrosanctum Concilium)* on December 4, 1963. Responding to a deeply felt duty to provide for the renewal and fostering of the liturgy, the Council fathers issued this Constitution as an altogether necessary step in its stated goal "to impart an ever increasing vigor to the Christian life of the faithful" (art. 1). The passage of a score of years now offers us an opportunity not only to commemorate so significant an event in the pilgrim life of our family of faith, but also to evaluate its effect, and to foster its continued importance for the future of the Church in the United States of America.

2. For us as bishops, no work can be more important. As the Council explained, "It is the liturgy through which, especially in the divine sacrifice of the Eucharist, 'the work of our redemption is accomplished'" (art. 2). In this *"Year that is truly Holy,"* this extraordinary Jubilee of the Redemption which coincides with the anniversary we celebrate, we are reminded by Pope John Paul II that the redemption is communicated

> through the proclamation of the Word of God and through the sacraments, in that divine economy whereby the Church is constituted as the Body of Christ, "as the universal sacrament of salvation" . . . (*Open the Doors to the Redeemer, 3*).

3. The generation after the Council is challenged anew to reaffirm God's close and intimate contact with each human life, to stress the importance of prayer, and especially liturgical prayer, as the principal means by which God interacts with his people, to recall the goals of the liturgical reforms mandated by the Council, to assess the strengths and the weaknesses inherent in the implementation of reform measures, to derive encouragement from liturgical achievements, and to specify the paths that lie before us in the vital work yet to be done in promoting the renewal of Catholic life and worship.

4. At the same time we are mindful of liturgical abuses that have occurred, sometimes through unbridled zeal without theological information, sometimes through personal whim or neglect. While lamenting these unhappy instances, we are hopeful that they will not prevent us from seeking with zeal and courage an authentic renewal of our liturgical life. What Pope Paul VI said in 1975 still applies today:

> In the course of our eagerness to rekindle the vitality and authenticity of religion in the life of individuals, but especially in the life of the people of God, we must revere and promote the liturgy in our times, in ecclesial and collective life. . . . For us it suffices here to confirm the liturgical program that the Church has set before itself, to make stable and fruitful the idea and therefore the practice of liturgy. In that program lies the secret of a new vitality for the Church's tradition, the face of the Church's beauty, the expression of the Church's interior and universal unity . . . (*Address to a General Audience*, August 6, 1975).

This *"liturgical program" continues to be our program for the Church in the United States of America,* for its growth and vitality, for its participation in the great work of the redemption and reconciliation accomplished in Jesus Christ.

General Liturgical Principles

Christ is always present in his Church, especially in her liturgical celebrations (Article 7).

5. One of the primary concerns of the Second Vatican Council was to affirm the incarnational and the sacramental character of the Church. The Word of God who took flesh of the virgin of Nazareth continues to dwell in the world through the Church. Thus what is central to the life and work of the Church is to build up that union with God made visible in Jesus Christ, a relationship made possible by his life, death, and resurrection. The paschal mystery is at the heart of the life of the Church. It is this mystery that the Church proclaims and shares with her members who are formed into the People of God through the outpouring of the Holy Spirit. The experience of this mystery is made possible through personal prayer but above all in and through the celebration of the liturgy.

6. The liturgy is a principal means by which God acts upon the Church to make it holy. That sanctification takes place through the presence of Christ in the power of the Holy Spirit, a presence manifested through the word of Sacred Scripture, through the community itself gathered in prayer and song, and above all through the sacraments, especially the Eucharist. The sanctification of the Church results in the creation of a community capable of continuing the saving work of Jesus Christ in the world.

7.   The liturgy is the chief means by which the Church, through Jesus Christ and in the unity of the Holy Spirit, responds to God's saving presence in thanksgiving, praise, petition, and longing. In the liturgy the members of the worshiping community are united both inwardly and outwardly with Christ: inwardly by being conformed to Christ in his disposition of humble, self-giving service of the Father and his people; outwardly by expressing both in word and action that interior conformity with the attitude of Christ. In responding to God's gift of his life offered in Christ, the Church recognizes the mystery of the Father's love entrusted to "vessels of clay." It is our challenge in faith to live the paradox of this human element which leaves the People of God in his world always an imperfect community, always inadequate in its acceptance of God's love, thus always in need of reform and renewal. In this sense the Church is always a community of penitents.

8.   The primary purpose of the liturgical reforms in which we have been engaged in a special way for the past twenty years has not been simply a change in sacramental rites. Rather the reform of the rites has been distinguished by a noble simplicity which both protects and proclaims the core of our Christian tradition so that authentic tradition might grow in the lives of present-day Catholics and bear fruit in the future. The goal is above all to enrich the Church's life of prayer and worship so that those who believe in Christ and are members of his Church might be empowered and motivated to proclaim the good news that God has offered salvation to all in his Son Jesus Christ.

9.   The worship that is given to God does not consist simply in the externals of liturgical rites but rather includes the very lives of those who celebrate the liturgy — lives which should manifest what the liturgy expresses, which reveal the life and love of Christ to others, and which call them to share in the Spirit of God and in the work of building up God's kingdom on earth. For as we noted in our reflections commemorating the fifteenth anniversary of the *Decree on the Apostolate of the Laity* in 1980,

> the quality of worship depends in great measure on the spiritual life of all present. As lay women and men cultivate their own proper response to God's call to holiness, this should come to expression in the communal worship of the Church (*Called and Gifted: The American Catholic Laity*, p. 3).

10.   Liturgical renewal, then, implies an ever deeper involvement of the whole Christian community in the paschal mystery of Jesus Christ. The primary means to achieve renewal is that liturgical formation which enables all those who take part in the liturgy to become more

and more imbued with its spirit and power. Liturgical formation is as necessary for the laity as it is for the clergy. For

> as lay persons assume their roles in liturgical celebration according to the gifts of the Spirit bestowed on them for that purpose, the ordained celebrant will be more clearly seen as the one who presides over the community, bringing together the diverse talents of the community as gift to the Father (*Called and Gifted: The American Catholic Laity*, p. 4).

The secondary means is an ongoing reform of the liturgical rites themselves to ensure that the words and actions of the liturgy express more and more adequately the holy realities which these words and actions signify. Liturgical formation and the continued reform of the rites therefore bring about that complete, active, and conscious participation in the liturgy required of the assembly and its ministers.

11. Properly trained ministers and programs for such training must be available for liturgical formation. To provide for the future, seminarians and those beginning their lives as religious must be properly formed both academically and spiritually in the spirit of the liturgy. In this regard we direct the attention of those responsible to the norms and guidelines set forth in the *Instruction on Liturgical Formation in Seminaries* issued by the Sacred Congregation for Catholic Education in 1979. Bishops, priests, and deacons must be helped also to understand better what they are doing when they celebrate the liturgy, to live the liturgical life more profoundly, and to share it effectively with others. They have a special responsibility to be formed in the spirit of the liturgy. As leaders in the Christian community and in the liturgical assemblies, bishops and priests have as one of their principal tasks to preside at worship in such a manner that the other members of the assembly are led to pray. In a sense they should be transparent images of what it means for a Christian to die and rise with Jesus.

12. Deacons and other liturgical ministers likewise require a formation that is at once personally profound and directed toward their service within the assembly. The laity must not only be helped to participate fully both internally and externally in the liturgy, but they must also be encouraged to use and develop their various ministerial gifts in the liturgical celebration.

13. In recent years we have seen a renewed interest in traditional and newer forms of prayer, but special effort must be made to assure that the spirituality of individual Catholics is both Christian and liturgical. The way the Church prays and worships should be the way individual Christians pray and worship. In that sense the liturgy is normative for Christian spirituality. The personal prayer of individual Christians is important because it ensures that they will come to the liturgy with the proper dispositions. In liturgical celebrations their minds and hearts will be in tune with what they say and do. Personal prayer, however, does not displace the liturgy nor is it a substitute for it;

rather it should lead Christians to the celebration of the paschal mystery and, in turn, be nourished by that mystery.

14. We do not worship God primarily to become better people; the very nature and excellence of God demand worship. But when we worship, by the grace of the redemption, we can be transformed into better people. And so the worship of the Church is a monument in which Christians are formed as moral persons. The liturgy helps to form Christian character, and, as a result, those who celebrate the liturgy are empowered to relate to one another in justice and peace and to involve themselves in the establishment of God's kingdom on earth.

15. The Eucharist especially teaches us the meaning of God's peace and justice. For as we have said in another pastoral letter, the Mass is

> a unique means of seeking God's help to create the conditions essential for true peace in ourselves and in the world. In the Eucharist we encounter the risen Lord, who gave us His peace. He shares with us the grace of the redemption, which helps us to preserve and nourish this precious gift (*The Challenge of Peace: God's Promise and Our Response*, 295).

God's gifts of justice and peace, indeed all those gifts which strengthen our moral life, are summed up in the liturgy, especially in the Eucharist as a sacrament of reconciliation. As God loves us and shares this new life with us, so we are enabled to love and serve one another. In the liturgy the divine story of creation and redemption is told and retold; that revelation is reinforced by ritual patterns which communicate Christian meaning and values in verbal and nonverbal ways. As a result a Christian vision of life is shared. It is a vision framed and permeated by faith. In celebrating the liturgy, Christians do not leave their everyday world and responsibilities behind; rather they enter into God's real world and see it as it actually is in Jesus—a place where God's providence and love are indeed at work.

16. In order that the Christian vision may be available to all members of the Church, efforts have been made in the past twenty years to adapt the liturgical rites and symbols to the diverse cultures of the world. If the Church is to become incarnate in every culture, the liturgy must express the paschal mystery, which lies at the heart of the Church, in some symbols derived from these diverse cultures. In our own country, special care must be taken to adapt the liturgy so that it is perceived as inclusive of women and responsive to the needs of persons of diverse ages, races, and ethnic groups. Liturgical adaptation is not simply a concession granted by the *Constitution on the Sacred Liturgy*; it is rather a theological imperative of liturgical renewal that the paschal mystery may be celebrated for all people and that all may be able to bring their talents to the service of the liturgy.

17. A renewed appreciation of the centrality of worship in the life of the Church with its emphasis on God's initiative in offering unity and peace to his people through his Son has increased our sensitivity to the need for greater ecumenical activity among all Christians. While working to overcome doctrinal and structural differences, Christians have been encouraged to pray together and to celebrate those rites which have been authorized for common celebration, especially celebrations of the Word of God, so that Christian unity might be more readily and effectively achieved.

18. In our own country the rediscovery by other churches and ecclesial communities of liturgical sources and traditions common to our Christian heritage encourages all Christians. Recent liturgical reforms in many churches of North America, especially in the rites of the Eucharist, already point to a convergence and unity of liturgical prayer that gives hope for eventual doctrinal agreement. That many churches now use a similar three-year cycle of scripture readings for the Eucharist based on *The Roman Lectionary* means that the majority of American Christians hear the same Word proclaimed each Sunday. The liturgy has already become a source of unity and a sign of hope for even greater unity.

The Eucharistic Mystery

At the Last Supper, on the night he was betrayed, our Savior instituted the eucharistic sacrifice of his Body and Blood. This he did in order to perpetuate the sacrifice of the Cross throughout the ages until he should come again, and so to entrust to his beloved Spouse, the Church, a memorial of his death and resurrection: a sacrament of love, a sign of unity, a bond of charity, a paschal banquet in which Christ is consumed, the mind is filled with grace, and a pledge of future glory is given to us (Article 47).

19. It is by means of the liturgy that the Church touches its members at the principal moments in their lives. Baptism and confirmation, penance and anointing, orders and marriage each reveal and reflect for Catholic Christians a particular facet of the paschal mystery of Christ and make possible a vital transforming relationship with Christ in his Church. However, it is the Eucharist which is the preeminent celebration of the paschal mystery. In the Eucharist the victory of Christ over death is made manifest, enabling the community to be one with Christ and to give to the Father, in the unity of the Holy Spirit, all honor and glory.

20. The revised liturgical books, along with numerous decrees relating to the Eucharist have been issued in the past twenty years. These documents have resulted in a renewed appreciation of all aspects of eucharistic theology and spirituality: the celebration of the sacrifice of the Mass, the reception of Holy Communion, and the reservation of the Blessed Sacrament whether for the communion of the sick and dying or for devotion on the part of the faithful. Just as there has been a renewed appreciation of the Eucharist as both sacrifice and meal, so too the Eucharist is the "school of active love for neighbor," as Pope John Paul II stated in his letter *On the Mystery and Worship of the Eucharist*: "The Eucharist educates us to this love in a deeper way; it shows us, in fact, what value each person, our brother or sister, has in God's eyes, if Christ offers himself equally to each one, under the species of bread and wine" (no. 6). The Eucharist is therefore the bond of charity and unity which unites Christians in God's love.

21. The revised *Order of Mass* sets out a rite that is simple and uncluttered, a rite which underscores the unity and bond of the assembly. This enables the symbols to speak with clarity but also necessitates great care on the part of the ministers so that the celebrating community will be drawn to a reverent experience of the mysterious presence of Christ in word and sacrament. A recent evaluation project, centered on the structural elements of the *Order of Mass*, was sponsored by our Committee on the Liturgy and the Federation of Diocesan Liturgical Commissions. It provided an excellent opportunity both for liturgical formation concerning the Eucharist and for suggesting ways to improve the celebration.

22. Certainly for Roman Catholics one of the most significant achievements of the contemporary liturgical reform has been a retrieval of the riches of Sacred Scripture and the breadth of exposure to the Word of God set out in the new lectionary. The importance of the homily as an effective way of relating that Word to the contemporary lives of the community has been stressed by our Committee on Priestly Life and Ministry in its document, *Fulfilled in Your Hearing: The Homily in the Sunday Assembly*. We urge those charged with the ministry of preaching the homily to study that document carefully and to make even greater efforts to preach a well-prepared homily at both Sunday and daily celebrations. Likewise the restoration of the general intercessions has offered an opportunity to relate the Eucharist to the universal Church and the world.

23. The introduction of vernacular languages into the liturgy has enabled the faithful to make the liturgy truly their own through greater understanding of the rites. We must also continue our efforts to preserve the treasures of our liturgical patrimony in Latin. Regular reception of Holy Communion as an integral part of the eucharistic celebration, a more frequent availability of Communion under both kinds, and the extension of the practice of concelebration have also contributed to the desired effect of greater participation in the eucharistic liturgy. Nevertheless, as bishops charged with the promotion and custody of the liturgy, we urge priests, deacons, and lay people to give more of their energy to an even greater and more profound participation in the Church's eucharistic mystery.

The Sacraments and Sacramentals

For well-disposed members of the faithful the liturgy of the sacraments and sacramentals sanctifies almost every event of their lives with the divine grace which flows from the paschal mystery of the passion, death, and resurrection of Christ. From this source all sacraments and sacramentals draw their power. There is scarcely any proper use of material things which cannot thus be directed toward the sanctification of men and the praise of God (Article 61).

24. In revising other aspects of the liturgy, efforts have been made to help the faithful develop an integral view of the sacraments and sacramentals as related components of Christian liturgy and as manifestations of the Church which is itself a sacramental community. The rites have been carefully related to the paschal mystery of Christ, to the Eucharist as the principal celebration of that mystery, and to the critical experiences of individual Christians and communities. The Liturgy of the Word has been restored as an integral component in all sacramental celebrations and other liturgical rites.

25. The *Rite of Christian Initiation of Adults* is only gradually being implemented and appreciated in our country, but already many parishes have discovered the benefits that are available not only to the newly initiated members of the Church but also to the parish community as a whole. Above all, the rites of initiation have affirmed the importance of a vital ecclesial community in the life of Christians and have shown the essential relationship among the doctrines Christians believe, the worship they carry out, and the responsible moral lives they live. The *Rite of Baptism for Children* also has stressed the importance of the faith community as the essential environment in which the infant grows toward a personal faith commitment as well as the primary responsibility of both parents and godparents for nurturing that faith in the life of the child.

26. Although pastoral, liturgical, and theological questions continue to be raised about the sacrament of confirmation, the introduction of a new rite for this sacrament of initiation has contributed to a renewed appreciation of the role of the Holy Spirit in Christian life. As pastors and theologians continue to study the sacrament, it should be stressed that although the sacrament of confirmation may be an occasion for giving testimony to a religious commitment, it is above all the outpouring of the Holy Spirit, "the seal of the gift of the Holy Spirit," who operates in a powerful transforming way in the life of the baptized Christian.

27. Although intensive study and discussion preceded formulation of the revised *Rite of Penance*, pastoral problems continue to surround the sacrament. The new rites of reconciliation emphasize the reality of both personal and social sin in the Christian community and affirm that Christians are reconciled with God through the ministry of the

Church. The fact is, however, that the importance of this sacrament has declined in the lives of many Christians, who are not likely to recover appreciation for it unless they are once again convinced of its role in their lives. In spite of the evil so obviously rampant in our world, a genuine sense of sin in our lives is often absent. Greater pastoral efforts must be directed toward a recovery of that sense of sin joined to a more profound understanding of the merciful forgiveness and reconciliation offered to us in Christ Jesus.

28. We urge our priests and those who have charge of catechesis to greater efforts in leading all of us toward a deeper faith in the healing power of God who, in his Son Jesus Christ, has reconciled us. That faith can only be deepened if we understand the existence of sin in our lives, "for the members of the Church . . . are exposed to temptation and often fall into the wretchedness of sin" (*Rite of Penance*, 3). As individuals and as a people we must come before God seeking pardon and reconciliation. As individuals we need to experience healing, reconciliation, and forgiveness, an experience that comes preeminently through the ministry of the Church. And as a people we must experience this same forgiveness:

> In fact, people frequently join together to commit injustice. But it is also true that they help each other in doing penance; freed from sin by the grace of Christ, they become, with all persons of good will, agents of justice and peace in the world (*Rite of Penance*, 5).

Therefore, not only should great attention be given to celebrations of the sacrament with individuals, but pastors should also assure communal celebrations of penance, especially in Advent and Lent, according to the norms of the rite, remembering that inner conversion embraces sorrow for sin and the intent to lead a new life.

29. The revised rites for the sick and the dying, known as *Pastoral Care of the Sick: Rites of Anointing and Viaticum*, convey with sensitivity and power the Lord's healing love. These rites have been deeply appreciated because of their pastoral sensitivity and the consolation and strength they have brought not only to the sick and dying but also to their families and friends in time of crisis. In keeping with the revised ritual, priests, deacons, other ministers, and those engaged in any ministry to the sick in homes, hospitals, and hospices should avail themselves of the riches and variety of these liturgical texts and rites, never contenting themselves with brief or "emergency" forms unless absolutely necessary. The sick and the dying are members of the Body of Christ, greatly in need of the Church's pastoral care.

30. That same consolation has been experienced through the revised *Rite of Funerals* which carefully relates the death of Christians to the death and resurrection of Christ. Although the funeral rites honestly acknowledge the dread of death as a result of sin and evil in the world, above all they stress the right of Christians to hope for triumph over death because of Christ's resurrection. In that trust we wish to make clear our responsibility to pray for the deceased so that freed fully from their sins they may experience the joy of God's light and love. At the same time we urge continued effort by pastors, deacons, musicians, and other ministers toward better celebrations of the funeral rites so that these will console the living and demonstrate the community's faith in the saving death and resurrection of Christ.

31. In the revised rites of ordination emphasis has been clearly placed on the candidate's responsibility for proclaiming the Word of God, presiding over the liturgy, and ministering the sacraments. An unclouded understanding of these basic ministries sets a firm foundation for other pastoral and liturgical services, fosters commitment on the part of the laity, and cultivates the development of Christian community. Of special significance has been the restoration of the permanent diaconate and the emergence of lay involvement in a number of ministries which were until recently performed only by the ordained clergy. Continuing education and formation in the liturgy is therefore all the more important for priests, deacons, and lay ministers. Liturgical renewal and spiritual growth need "mystagogues," men and women themselves well versed in the ways of the Lord, to lead others to drink more deeply from the refreshing waters of divine life, always eager to live the Christian life as though newly baptized.

32. The revised rites for the sacrament of marriage acknowledge human friendship as one of the most basic symbols of God's loving presence to human life. In marriage Christian men and women sacramentalize the covenant relationship of commitment between Christ and his Church, between God and humankind. Their love is expressed in their self-gift to each other, in children who manifest the creative nature of love, and in their witness of fidelity in a world where lifetime commitments are increasingly rare. The revised rites and liturgical texts for Christian marriage underscore the totality of the mutual gift involved in this sacrament which St. Paul calls a "great mystery" and Pope John Paul II recently called a "memorial," for marriage calls to mind the great works of God in creation. Likewise marriage is a communion which specifically represents Christ's incarnation and the mystery of the covenant. For all that is human in marital love signifies the intimacy of our relationship with God (*Address to a General Audience*, November 3, 1979). When couples are preparing for marriage, their attention should be directed toward the proper choice of liturgical texts, music, and rites. They should also be shown how the *Rite of Marriage* itself expresses the bond and covenant into which they are about to enter.

33. In the Church, the vocation to Christian marriage is complemented and strengthened by the vocation to celibacy ratified in the revised *Rites of Religious Profession* and the *Rites of Consecration to a Life of*

Virginity. These rites, so little known to most Catholics, reflect the positive value of celibate love.

Liturgical Prayer

The Church, by celebrating the Eucharist and by other means, especially the celebration of the divine office, is ceaselessly engaged in praising the Lord and interceding for the salvation of the entire world (Article 83).

34. By both word and example, the Lord Jesus taught his disciples that prayer is necessary for Christian believers. Like the prayer of Jesus himself, it should flow from the experience of living intimately in the presence of God. Such a communion is one in which we, as God's people, share in the divine life and love and, in turn, respond to these gifts with praise and thanksgiving, petition and longing. To foster that spirit of prayer the Liturgy of the Hours or Divine Office has been reformed. Although a special mandate has been given to bishops, priests, and deacons to celebrate the Liturgy of the Hours, it is also clearly desired that all the faithful take part in this liturgical prayer of the Church, especially Morning and Evening Prayer. The theological and liturgical thrust of the Liturgy of the Hours should be a model and an ideal for the way in which all Catholic Christians pray.

35. This communal experience of liturgical prayer will be new for many; its effectiveness will depend to a great extent on liturgical formation and the experience of well-structured and prayerfully executed celebrations. Unfortunately it must be acknowledged that the revised Liturgy of the Hours, which has been designed especially for communal celebration, has not yet become a vital prayer form for many priests and religious who do not reside in liturgically structured communities. In order that extended psalmody and patristic readings be experienced as inspiring sources of strength for ministry, it is necessary to provide adequate scriptual, theological, and liturgical background. Similarly, more realistic efforts must be made to adapt the Liturgy of the Hours to the actual situations which prevail in parishes. Where the responsibility to pray in the spirit of the Church has been taken seriously and time and effort have been put into the preparation and celebration of the Liturgy of the Hours, the experience has been very rewarding. This is an area which calls for much more attention on the part of pastors and prayer leaders in our Catholic communities.

Liturgical Time

Once each week, on the day which she has called the Lord's Day, Holy Mother Church keeps the memory of the Lord's resurrection. She also celebrates it once every year, together with his blessed passion, at Easter, that most solemn of all feasts.

In the course of the year, moreover, she unfolds the whole mystery of Christ from the incarnation and nativity to the ascension, to Pentecost and the expectation of the blessed hope of the coming of the Lord. Thus recalling the mysteries of the redemption, she opens up to the faithful the riches of her Lord's powers and merits (Article 102).

36. The life of the Church is sanctified not only by the Liturgy of the Hours but also by the celebration of the liturgical year. In revising the liturgical calendar, each liturgical season is focused on the paschal mystery of Christ as the center of all liturgical worship. Hence the feasts of the Lord, especially the celebration of his death and resurrection, have been given preference. These mysteries are celebrated in a special way during the Paschal Triduum but also on Sunday which, since early centuries, has been observed as the "Lord's Day."

37. Lent has been restored to its proper observance as a preparation for the celebration of the paschal mystery. The primary features of this season are the purification and enlightenment of catechumens and works of prayer, almsgiving or service to others, and penance, especially fasting and abstinence. Through the celebration of the forty days of Lent and the fifty days of Easter, the main lines of the Church's Year of the Lord are clearly established; it is essentially a celebration of the saving work of Christ.

38. Throughout the rest of the year the various aspects of that saving mystery unfold. Of special importance is the celebration of Christmas. During the Christmas season the mysteries highlighted in the gospel infancy narratives are celebrated. The solemnity of the Epiphany of the Lord reveals the universal saving mission of Christ the Messiah. The feast of the Baptism of the Lord, which marks the beginning of Christ's public ministry, brings the Christmas season to an end. The season of Advent is celebrated with joyful expectancy as a reminder of God's fidelity and care culminating in the first coming of Christ, and as preparation for his second coming at the end of time.

39. The Sundays of the Year ("Ordinary Time") and the feasts and solemnities of the Lord are always celebrations of the same paschal mystery commemorated in the "great seasons." Yet all too often little attention is given to these "ordinary times." In view of the increasing secularization of the Lord's Day, we suggest that full celebration of the Sundays of the Year be promoted, since they are essential and crucial to the development and deepening of the Christian life. In addition, we urge our people and pastors to make greater efforts in planning the whole liturgical year in such a way that each season, memorial, feast, and solemnity is given its proper significance and importance. Furthermore, we must all be reminded of the close link between liturgy and devotion, liturgy and popular piety. The devotion which surrounds the solemnity of Corpus Christi, for example, is a model of the proper relationship between liturgy and popular piety in the liturgical year. True and authentic piety can only help us to be more devoted to the liturgy.

40. Special care has been taken to stress the role of Mary, the Mother of God, in the life of the Church, as we have stated many times, especially in our pastoral letter on the Blessed Virgin Mary (*Behold Your Mother: Woman of Faith*, November 21, 1973). The great Marian feasts and solemnities of the revised calendar relate the life of Mary to the mystery of her Son; in this way she is honored both as the Mother of the Church and as a model for Christian discipleship.

41. The new calendar significantly reduces the number of saints' days so that the mystery of Christ may not be overshadowed. The *Constitution on the Sacred Liturgy* prescribed that only saints of universal importance should be proposed to the whole Church for obligatory commemoration. Every nation, indeed every diocese, has its own particular and proper calendar celebrating certain mysteries, saints, and days of prayer.

42. In the United States, for example, the Church honors Mary in a special way under the title of the Immaculate Conception as patroness of the United States and under the title of Our Lady of Guadalupe as patroness of the Americas. American holy men and women such as Isaac Jogues and companions, Kateri Tekakwitha, Elizabeth Ann Seton, John Neumann, Frances Cabrini, and others testify to holiness in America. Thanksgiving Day, while not a liturgical feast, nevertheless is celebrated liturgically by American Catholics as a day of prayer and thanksgiving for the gifts God has bestowed upon us.

43. Efforts must also be made to relate the liturgical year to the secular calendar so that the ordinary lives of Christians may be sanctified. Ecumenical discussions have raised a number of important questions concerning the possibility of a fixed date for Easter and a common calendar shared by various churches and ecclesial communities; these are questions that require and deserve further study by the whole Church.

Liturgical Music, Art, and Architecture

Holy Mother Church has always been the patron of the fine arts and has ever sought their noble ministry, to the end especially that all things set apart for use in divine worship should be worthy, becoming, and beautiful, signs and symbols of things supernatural (Article 122).

44. In matters of liturgical music, art, and architecture, only directives of a very general nature have been issued in the past twenty years, and rightly so, for the creation of art is something that can be neither clearly defined nor readily mandated. In this regard, our Committee on the Liturgy has issued statements which have been well received and proven very useful, especially *Music in Catholic Worship, Liturgical Music Today* and *Environment and Art in Catholic Worship*. The norms and guidelines of these documents should be followed by pastors and all those engaged in the liturgical arts. Our churches must be homes for the arts and houses pleasing to the Lord.

45. Artists, architects, artisans, and musicians who work for the Church should be competent in their own right and should have a clear understanding of the theology of the liturgy and the role of their proper arts in liturgical celebrations. We must continue to search for appropriate ways to enrich our liturgies both by retrieving our artistic tradition and using it appropriately, being open to new forms of the artistic imagination, and by utilizing the cultural heritage of the diverse ethnic and racial groups of the Church in America. While we continue to make efforts to alleviate world poverty, it is important that some of the Church's material resources, even in the case of financially impoverished communities, be allocated to the development of the liturgical arts because they nourish the human spirit and bear witness to the preeminence of the sacred in human life. They enable Christians to grow more and more into that holy temple wherein God can dwell and empower people to transform the world in his name.

Conclusions

Mother Church earnestly desires that all the faithful should be led to that full, conscious, and active participation in liturgical celebrations which is demanded by the very nature of the liturgy, and to which the Christian people, "a chosen race, a royal priesthood, a holy nation, a redeemed people" (I Pt 2:9,4-5) have a right and obligation by reason of their baptism (Article 14).

46. There have been many significant liturgical gains in the past twenty years, but there remain many areas of unfinished liturgical business. Liturgical reform must move more and more toward genuine Christian renewal. That means above all that we must continue to make efforts to appreciate and open our hearts to the spiritual and prayerful dimensions of the liturgy.

47. Much progress has been made over the past generation through great personal and pastoral effort to help people develop a sense of communal prayer. Yet, in many cases, piety continues to be individualistic and untouched by the richness and treasures of the liturgy. Even specialized programs in spiritual renewal are at times only minimally related to experience of Christian worship and sacraments.

48. The liturgy should be the primary school for Christian prayer and spirituality, enabling Christians to live justly, peacefully, and charitably in the world. Often we fail to understand that the celebration of the liturgy is the Church's ministry of worship and prayer, calling people to conversion and contemplation, inviting them into communion with God and with each other. And the more professional we become in the area of liturgy, the more we may be tempted to become preoccupied with external forms and aesthetic experiences. The end result may simply be a new form of ritualism.

49. Liturgical ministers themselves must be people of prayer. If sometimes there is a gap between liturgical ministers and the larger Christian community, it may be because the ministers may not appear to be praying people. Liturgical ministers must be spiritually and personally involved in the mystery of Christ, and they must show outwardly this involvement if they are to lead people into that same experience.

50. If in the last analysis a great part of the responsibility for liturgical formation and renewal falls on the individual Christian, there is nevertheless a need for help from others in this regard. Parish liturgy committees, diocesan liturgical commissions, and offices of worship also have a great task before them to continue the work begun twenty years ago when the *Constitution on the Sacred Liturgy* was first promulgated. Parish liturgy committees should assist priests, deacons, and other liturgical ministers such as readers and ministers of communion in fulfilling their roles. At the same time, through planning and careful attention to the norms of each of the rites, they will help lead the assembly toward a more profound worship of God and communion with Christ and one another.

51. The diocesan liturgical commission or office of worship must assist the bishop in carrying out his functions as promoter and guardian of the liturgical life of the diocese. First convened by our Committee on the Liturgy in 1968, the Federation of Diocesan Liturgical Commissions, especially through the annual national meeting of liturgical commissions and worship office personnel, should continue to assist us on a national level. In this way, all those engaged in the great work of liturgical renewal will ensure not only the continuation of "that full, conscious, and active participation in liturgical celebrations," but also help the Church always to be a Church of pilgrims, ever renewed and ever being renewed in its life and worship.

52. We must continue to struggle to overcome our selfishness, our closed-mindedness, our indifference, our timidity, and our lack of trust in God and one another. Both Christian life and worship presuppose community—a willingness to learn from others and to be open to others in generosity and love. Only on such a base can liturgy really be said to affect and deepen the sense of community. In its language, symbol, style, and spirit today's liturgy is a growing sign and instrument of community, people at one with each other and with God.

53. This score of years has witnessed the most sweeping changes in liturgical life that the Catholic Church has known in centuries. When we observe similar shifts in culture, values, and attitudes elsewhere throughout the world, we can have no doubt that the Council acted under the guidance of the Holy Spirit. Liturgical flexibility and adaptation have made it possible for the Church's proclamation of the good news to challenge our times with a realistic chance for a hearing and an impact. Above all, the liturgical reform has helped the Church to come into the presence of the all-holy God in languages, signs, and gestures spoken and made by contemporary Catholics without loss of its tradition—truly a gift of the Holy Spirit.

54. For older generations acceptance of liturgical changes has been a true venture in faith; it is a sign of the Church's vitality that the vast majority has endorsed and taken to heart the reforms initiated by the Council. For a newer generation the provisions of the *Constitution on the Sacred Liturgy* have offered hope that worship and world, liturgy and life can be harmonized and truly become the gift of the Father, who has loved us through the Son and empowers us to return that love in the Spirit.

55. Mindful of our own responsibilities as bishops to carry out the office of sanctification in the Church, we pledge renewed efforts to continue the great work of the Council in liturgical renewal and in the renewal of prayer, penance, and worship in the life of the Church. This anniversary and this Holy Year of the Redemption must lead us all to a "renewed and deepened *Spirit of Advent*," a prayerful spirit of expectation, as our Holy Father John Paul II reminds us (*Open the Doors to the Redeemer*, 9). We urge, therefore, our helpers in the ministry, priests and deacons, our lay ministers in the liturgy, our liturgists, but above all our liturgical assemblies to engage themselves continually with faith and trust in that holy work which is the liturgy, and always to remember these words of the *Constitution on the Sacred Liturgy* as we await the coming of the Lord:

> In the earthly liturgy we take part in a foretaste of that heavenly liturgy which is celebrated in the holy city of Jerusalem toward which we journey as pilgrims, where Christ is sitting at the right hand of God, minister of the holies and of the true tabernacle. With all the warriors of the heavenly army we sing a hymn of glory to the Lord; venerating the memory of the saints, we hope for some part and fellowship with them; we eagerly await the Savior, our Lord Jesus Christ, until he our life shall appear and we too will appear with him in glory (Article 8).

A Pastoral Statement on the Catholic Charismatic Renewal

A Statement of the
Bishops' Liaison Committee with the
Catholic Charismatic Renewal
Approved by the Administrative Committee of
the National Conference of Catholic Bishops

March 1984

Introduction

In line with its mandate to keep the bishops informed and to relate to the movement in their name, the Bishops' Liaison Committee with the Catholic Charismatic Renewal thinks it timely to update its 1975 statement. As with *A Glossary of Charismatic Terms*, which we published in 1980, we address this statement primarily to the bishops, but we are aware that many others working with the renewal will be interested in it. The statement is divided into eleven Pastoral Observations and eleven Pastoral Orientations concerning the great things Catholic charismatics are convinced the Lord Jesus is doing in our day.

The Bishop's Liaison Committee with the Catholic Charismatic Renewal approved this final edition for distribution in its own name.

I. Pastoral Observations

1. As a movement within the Church, the charismatic renewal is rooted in the witness of the gospel tradition: Jesus is Lord by the power of the Spirit to the glory of the Father. As the renewal continues its attempt to make its own that gospel witness, the Bishops' Liaison Committee with the Catholic Charismatic Renewal, after wide consultation, wishes to inform the bishops of the changed situation since its last statement.

Papal Encouragement

2. This episcopal committee endeavors to assist each bishop in his pastoral responsibility "not to extinguish the Spirit, but to test all things and hold fast to that which is good" (1 Tm 5:19; *Lumen Gentium*, 12.) Since our statements about the charismatic renewal in 1969 and 1975, we note with joy that two popes have spoken encouragingly about it. Pope Paul VI said, "How would it be possible that this 'spiritual renewal' not be a chance for the Church and the world?" (Address of May 19, 1975). Pope John Paul II said that he sees the future of the Church lying in spiritual renewal movements and groups. Speaking specifically of the charismatic renewal, he said he made his own the words of St. Paul to the Philippians: "I give thanks to God every time I think of you" (Phil 1:3). Referring to the words of Pope Paul VI concerning what the renewal offers for the Church and the world, John Paul II said that the six years which have passed since his predecessor uttered those words "have borne out the hope that inspired his vision" (May 7, 1981). The pope has himself taken the initiative, both privately and publicly, to meet with leaders of the charismatic renewal. In doing so he has provided a model. Bishops and pastors who exercise the same kind of initiative find such meetings with leaders in the renewal fruitful for the local Church.

Central Elements and Optional Means

3.   All renewal movements in the Church—and there are more than one—truly make new again by returning to the words and deeds of Jesus Christ which form the fundamental reality of the Gospel. Insofar as the charismatic renewal makes its own this primary reality of the Gospel, it witnesses to elements of the good news which are central, not optional: the covenant love of the Father, the Lordship of Jesus, the power of the Spirit, sacramental and community life, prayer, charisms, and the necessity of evangelization. However the concrete manner, the historic forms in which the charismatic renewal incarnates these necessary elements of the Gospel are optional for all Christians. These "forms" include prayer groups, covenant communities, publications, conferences, and seminars. This distinction—between the central elements and their optional expression—is helpful. Insofar as the renewal makes its own what is central to the enduring reality of the Gospel, it cannot be dismissed as peripheral to the life of the Church. Clearly the charismatic renewal is in and for the Church, not alongside the Church. It has repeatedly shown its commitment to the Church, asking the bishops and the pope for pastoral guidance and supporting them by their prayers.

Personal Relation to the Triune God

4.   Since our last two statements, we have seen the charismatic renewal mature in its grasp of the core of the Gospel and those realities which belong constitutively to the inner nature of the Church. The *Constitution on the Church in the Modern World* (7) spoke of those who attain "a more personal and explicit adherence to faith" and "a more vivid sense of God." The call to discipleship and to baptism (Mt 28:19) is an invitation to enter into a personal relationship with Jesus Christ, as Lord and Savior, and with the Holy Spirit as the power of God who gives us access through Christ to the Father, who dwells in inaccessible light (1 Tm 6:16). It is also an invitation to enter into personal bonds with the whole People of God.

5.   Many lives have been touched at this personal level, have undergone a deep conversion, and have radically reoriented themselves toward God and have been able to nourish themselves on the bread of true doctrine, which the Church offers to them in the name of Christ. For many people, rediscovering the personal dimensions of the faith has meant rediscovering the experience of Church, eucharistic life, the sacrament of penance, Mary's role, and the ancient discipline of fasting. From this has come a new depth of personal prayer, nourished by the two tables of the Lord, the table of his Body and the table of his Word (*Imitation of Christ*, Book IV, chapter 11). Many, too, have rediscovered the centrality of the cross, which remains at the heart of Christian discipleship even after the glory of the resurrection and the outpouring of the Spirit. From an intensified relationship to the triune God comes new growth in love for all the members of the human family.

6.   This recovery of the personal (not private) dimension is especially important in the evangelization of persons immersed in the youth culture for whom what is primary is neither inherited theological formulation nor ritual, but personal relationship.

The Experience of the Holy Spirit and Spiritual Gifts

7.   Past statements of the United States bishops' committees, as well as statements of Pope Paul VI and Pope John Paul II, have commended the Catholic charismatic renewal for the fruit of holiness and good works born in the lives of those who become involved in this movement. These people say the transformation in their lives is a result of repentance, turning to Jesus Christ and receiving an influx of the Holy Spirit. They generally term this experience of the Holy Spirit being baptised in the Holy Spirit and say it usually results in the receiving of such spiritual gifts as prayer in tongues, prophecy, and healing. In fact it must be recognized that these spiritual realities do occur in the Catholic charismatic renewal, however they may be labeled or theologically analyzed. As the United States Bishops' Committee on Doctrine observed in 1969, "It would be difficult to inhibit the working of the Spirit which manifested itself so abundantly in the early Church." We should be grateful to God for pouring out in our time those gifts and graces with which he blessed the Church at its very beginning.

Mature Lay Life

8.   The charismatic renewal is a movement which seeks to be completely open to the Holy Spirit as it contributes to the ongoing effort to renew the whole Church. Though the Catholic charismatic renewal has influenced many bishops, priests, and religious personally, it has contributed in an even more profound way to the realization of the role of the laity in the mission of the Church. From its beginnings on university campuses, to the formation of thousands of parish prayer groups, it has been largely led, taught, discerned, and participated in by lay people. In a way not known in recent history, lay men and women are engaged in evangelization and the proclamation of the Lordship of Jesus in programs of spiritual formation and spiritual direction. Clearly the charismatic renewal has as its goal the transformation of all the members of the People of God.

Charisms as Ministry

9.   In the charismatic renewal, the charisms have had, and will continue to have, an important role. As it matures, this movement sees the charisms not as isolated gifts given to certain individuals, but rather as gifts given for the community. The community is seen as entirely ministerial (1 Cor 12), with no members who are merely ministered to. Every member is called to build up the Body of Christ through the particular charism which he or she has received. Thus the community constitutes a web of mutually supporting ministries (1 Cor 12). New appreciation of the role of the prophetic charisms does not signal undue attention to what is peripheral. Rather, it represents due attention to what is foundational. Speaking of the apostles and New Testament prophets, St. Paul refers to the Church as "built upon the foundation of the apostles and prophets, Christ Jesus himself being the cornerstone" (Eph 2:20). It is recognized that all charisms are not equally important; on the contrary, their dignity is determined by how immediately they are related to the common good of the body. The gifts are charisms of ministry and are not to be confused with ecclesiastical office. Nor is their exercise to be seen as expressing only emotional content.

Renewal of Family

10.   All renewal begins at the sources of the Church's life. In that context the charismatic renewal lays particular stress on personal conversion, a gift which quickly touches relationships, primarily the family. At this time, when handing on the faith to children presents special problems to all, many parents in the renewal, especially in covenant communities which have especially rich spiritual resources, have had success in this area. The building up of family life assumes greater importance when other primary groups are fragmenting.

Community and the Credibility of the Gospel

11. If some people judge that God is no longer relevant to their lives, one reason is the lack of a vital Christian community in which they can experience his presence and power and can see and hear the Gospel preached and lived authentically. The charismatic renewal has grasped the communitarian dimension of the good news. The return to different forms of community is prompted by the deepest Christian instinct. The first reaction of the early Church to the presence of the risen Christ and the power of the Spirit was the formation of community, which constituted the historic nucleus of Church (Acts 2:44-47; 4:32-35). Within the context of today's Church, committed Christians have come together to find spiritual nourishment, to pray and praise, to evangelize, to serve others. A variety of communities arise in this way. There are interparochial prayer groups, parish prayer groups, and covenant communities. Some are wholly Catholic in membership; some are ecumenical. In all of the various community forms there is evidence of a great spiritual hunger for God, his presence and his Word.

Parish Prayer Groups

12. Because the charismatic renewal is at the heart of the Church, it also has a role in parish renewal. As one of many forms of new yeast giving leaven to the whole mass, the prayer group, parochial and interparochial, has contributed significantly to the revitalization of parish life in the areas of liturgy, music, evangelization, Scripture, prayer, and youth outreach. It also provides the kind of Christian environment in which many are hearing the call of the Lord to serve the Church as servant leaders. The broad charismatic renewal sees itself as intimately bound to diocesan and parish goals and subject to the authority of the diocesan bishop. Diocesan and city-wide charismatic offices have in some instances become centers of spirituality as well as outreach to the marginalized and destitute by feeding the hungry, counseling the poor, visiting prisons, teaching domestic crafts.

Covenant Communities

13. The emergence of covenant communities is a development of major importance. By providing leadership resources, formation programs, growth seminars, and sharing across a large spectrum of human and spiritual needs, they have become a significant sign of the kingdom of God present in power. Every state and stage of life is there represented: married, single, widowed, old, and young. Through collaboration with the local bishop, these communities have developed new approaches to the pursuit of full Catholic life.

14. Within some of these covenant communities are households of men and households of women who are "single for the Lord," that is, living a life of committed celibacy, evangelical simplicity, and poverty, developing profoundly human and graced bonds of friendship and fellowship, which make these celibate communities effective tools of evangelization, especially among the youth. Some of these brotherhoods and sisterhoods, existing within the structure of a covenant community, have an ecumenical character.

The Liaison to the Renewal

15. A movement in the Church should be able to act with some freedom and take initiatives. While safeguarding this liberty of action there is a mutuality of responsibility. Those in the renewal should look to the bishop for guidance, keeping him informed, asking his suggestions, maintaining contact with his diocesan liaison. On the other hand, bishops need to take personal pastoral responsibility for the renewal, especially for the formation of leaders. Much of this can be delegated, but not all. Responsibilities which can be delegated out are typically delegated to the diocesan liaison, a person familiar with the renewal and respected by the participants. Such a person is an effective link between the renewal and the bishop.

II. Pastoral Orientations

16. Participants in the renewal have often expressed the wish that the bishops exercise a more active pastoral role in its regard. In response we offer the following pastoral orientations.

Focus and Breadth of Evangelization

17. In his encyclical *On Evangelization in the Modern World,* Pope Paul VI recalled the central role of the explicit proclamation of the Lordship of Jesus: "There is no true evangelization if the name, the teaching, the life, the promises, the kingdom and the mystery of Jesus of Nazareth, the Son of God, are not proclaimed" (art. 22). At the same time, the struggle against the injustice which condemns people to live on the margin of life in poverty, hunger, and disease is not foreign to evangelization. In short, evangelization should touch the whole of human existence, both personal and social (cf. arts. 29 and 30); evangelization speaks even to issues such as nuclear armaments.

The Social Imperative

18. In addressing an international meeting of charismatic leaders in Rome in May 1981, Pope John Paul II repeated the words of Pope Paul VI to an earlier charismatic congress: "The poor and the needy and afflicted and suffering across the world and near at hand all cry out to you, as brothers and sisters of Christ, asking for the proof of your love, asking for the Word of God, asking for bread, asking for life." Speaking in Harlem (October 2, 1979), during his United States visit, Pope John Paul II also said:

> If we are silent about the joy that comes from knowing Jesus, the very stones of our cities will cry out! . . . But how many people have never known this joy? . . . And we need not look to the far ends of the earth for them. They live in our neighborhoods, they walk down our streets. . . . They live without hope because they never heard, really heard the good news of Jesus Christ. . . . We must bring to them the witness of true joy. We must pledge to them our commitment to work for a just society and city, where they feel respected and loved.

To restrict Christianity to the purely spiritual and "religious" is to truncate the Gospel. We would want the renewal to embrace a Christianity which is incarnated in response to the misery of the world and a Christianity which provides an environment for lives at once authentically human and fully Christian. The imperative to be involved in the great problems of humanity is not a moral dimension which is supplementary to the Gospel; it is integral to Christian existence. The call to evangelize is a call to make the world come of age, touching and transforming the whole of human existence, including the social and political domains, and restoring all things in Christ. As the charismatic renewal grows, we encourage all members to participate in the Church's mission to serve the poor and to learn from those who emphasize the need to transform the world through the pursuit of justice and peace.

Formation Programs

19. Large numbers have benefited from Life in the Spirit seminars and other formation programs which are regularly offered in most charismatic groups. We would encourage those who present programs for a fuller life in the Spirit not to be discouraged but to persist in their apostolic ministry, even though many who have been through these seminars, whose lives have been touched and changed, do not remain in formal contact with the charismatic renewal. Seeds have been sown and lives have been redirected. Many are thus enabled to serve the Church and pursue the full Christian life in the Church. These instructional programs are very helpful in the preparation for the sacraments of initiation where the young discover with a sense of expectancy the meaning of a full life in the Spirit, and adults, some for the first time, experience the joy of living out their sacramental commitments.

Leaving the Catholic Church

20. Discovering in the charismatic renewal that the faith is not found principally and first of all in exterior forms but in a personal relationship with God and with their brothers and sisters, many have had awakened in them a new spiritual awareness and hunger. It may happen that such people judge that they cannot find in their parishes the food and fellowship for which they have an authentic need. Turning to sources they believe will satisfy them, some then leave the Church. At times no theological judgment on the Church is involved in this step, nor even necessarily a rejection of it. What is involved, rather, is a pragmatic judgment: these people want food and fellowship to meet the needs as they perceive them, and they go where they can get them. In other cases, however, there is a rejection of the Catholic Church and a harsh judgment upon it. Unfortunately, some even attempt to proselytize other Catholics.

21. This problem emphasizes the need for strong leadership and well-developed formation programs. Sound formation, sensitive pastoral leadership (including that of the parish priest), and genuine fellowship will call people closer to the Church, not lead them away. Authentic renewal does not divide God's people but makes them truly one flock under one shepherd.

Ecumenism

22. We see in the charismatic renewal an ecumenical force in which we rejoice. We make our own the words of Pope Paul VI, repeated by Pope John Paul II during his visit to the United States (October 5, 1979): "Let the work of drawing near to our separated brethren go on, with much understanding, with much patience, with great love; but without deviating from the true Catholic doctrine." Included in this are a balance between Word and sacraments as channels of grace; the recognition of the liturgy as the "indispensable source of the true Christian spirit"; traditional devotion to Mary, the Mother of God; and our obedience to the Holy Father, the successor of St. Peter. Authentic ecumenism maintains loyalty to the life and broad experience of the Church.

23. In speaking even briefly of ecumenism, we see the need to stress the centrality of sacramental life. If the Catholic charismatic renewal is genuinely to be in and of the Church, the gift and presence of Jesus in the sacraments must be central to all spiritual growth and activity.

Openness to the Holy Spirit leads to a deeper appreciation of the sacramental life of the Church. Through the eucharistic sacrifice and the other sacraments, Catholics share in the very life of the Lord: they become members of God's family, are strengthened in their faith, nourished by his body and blood, pardoned by his forgiveness, and comforted by his holy anointing. Through sacraments the Christian community is enriched and sustained, enlivened and perpetuated. We call on all those in the renewal to live fully the sacramental life of the Church.

24. Finally, liaisons and leaders in the charismatic renewal must be aware that the movement crosses all lines and embraces both the sophisticated and the simple in faith. For the latter, experience indicates that careless exposure to non-Catholic teachers and evangelists poses real problems and should be discouraged.

Healing

25. It is clear from the Gospels that healing the sick was an important and integral part of the ministry of Jesus. He gave his apostles specific instructions "to preach the kingdom of God and to heal" (Lk 9:2). To restrict healing to the physical order would be to limit God's sovereignty. Healings may be spiritual, psychological, or physical, or a combination of these, and often occur in conjunction with natural means, such as the work of physicians or rehabilitative groups; healing can extend even to memories anchored in traumatic experiences which keep one from full freedom and maturity.

26. The Church recognized the charism of healing (1 Cor 12:28,30) as one of those gifts which serve as a sign that the kingdom of God is present. Healings constitute an invitation to enter that kingdom. Both sacramentally in the anointing of the sick and in places of pilgrimage (such as Lourdes and Fatima) the Church has continued this healing ministry.

27. While healings have a public dimension which can be used in the service of evangelization, care should be taken that they not be exploited. Healings should not be seen in isolation but as a sovereign act of God which enables a person to return to wholeness. Healing is a call to a full Christian life lived in the milieu of a loving, supportive community.

28. While the healing ministry is to be affirmed, cautions seem necessary in two areas. First, even to suggest that failure to secure healing is due to the afflicted person's sinfulness or lack of faith is theologically untenable. Second, nonsacramental anointings sometimes employed in healing services should be very carefully distinguished from the Sacrament of the Anointing of the Sick, and among people apt to be confused by this distinction, nonsacramental anointing should be avoided.

Deliverance Ministries

29. In the biblical witness, deliverance ministries are part of the healing ministry (Lk 9:1) of which the ministry of inner healing is a part. On occasion when prayers for spiritual healing are being offered, deliverance prayer is sometimes needed. Here both wise pastoral guidance and discernment of spirits are absolute requirements. Prayers of deliverance and exorcism should not be confused. Deliverance addresses some form of inordinate control being exercised over a specific aspect of a person's life; it concerns something more than ordinary temptation and less than the total control found in full possession. (The latter is full possession which is the proper object of exorcism.)

30. Silent prayers of deliverance can be offered by every Christian. If there is to be vocal prayer for deliverance, this should be done by a team whose ministry is recognized by the local community and its pastoral authority. Exorcism in the strict sense should be done only by those explicitly appointed by the bishops, as an exercise of the power received through ordination. Excessive preoccupation with the demonic and an indiscriminate exercise of deliverance ministries are based upon a distortion of biblical evidence and are pastorally harmful.

31. As in the ministry commissioned by Jesus, prayer for deliverance is an aspect of the healing ministry (Mk 6:12,13; Mt 10:1). So attention should not be centered merely on deliverance from evil spirits, but, more positively, on total healing (medical, psychological, social, spiritual) and a life in Jesus Christ. Prayer for inner healing is part of that wider ministry. Various approaches to the deliverance ministries are still evolving and publications are available representing the different perspectives.

Fundamentalism

32. One of the most frequent criticisms of the charismatic renewal is the fundamentalism sometimes found in its ranks. (Fundamentalism here means a false literalism in interpreting the Bible.) Careful observation establishes that fundamentalism is found also in the general Catholic population and is not a problem restricted to the charismatic renewal. It surfaces within the charismatic renewal with greater frequency because of the diligence with which those in the renewal read the Scriptures, and because of the availability of fundamentalist preaching on television and by traveling evangelists.

33. Not everything which is called fundamentalism merits that label. Those who believe that Christ really worked miracles, performed exorcisms, and was himself raised from the dead are not guilty of fundamentalism. Nor is taking the scriptural message seriously fundamentalism. We encourage all efforts made to ensure a correct interpretation through scriptural magazines, columns, seminars, and workshops. We encourage reading the Vatican II document *Dogmatic Constitution on Divine Revelation*, especially section 10. Here we are told that sacred tradition and Sacred Scripture form one sacred deposit of the Word of God which is committed to the Church. The entire holy people united with their shepherds remain always steadfast in the teaching of the apostles. The teaching office of the Church serves the Word of God by ". . . teaching only what has been handed on, listening to it devoutly, guarding it scrupulously, and explaining it faithfully. . . ." Thus sacred tradition, Sacred Scripture, and the teaching authority of the Church are joined together to help us correctly interpret the Word of God.

Leadership as a Central Issue

34. To a great extent the success of the renewal depends on an informed, balanced, mature, doctrinally sound leadership, especially at the local and diocesan levels. Indeed, the leadership issue is the most pressing problem facing the renewal. In smaller prayer groups with fewer numbers and smaller resources, the lack of leadership can be acute. Some who have risen to leadership roles in these smaller groups do not have the doctrinal and scriptural formation which would give them a firm hold on their Catholic identity. Some lack the basic skills of leading a prayer meeting, even though there is printed material available distilling the common wisdom acquired over the years. Larger prayer groups and covenant communities should continue to offer their services to these groups.

Overcontrol

35. One of the strengths of the charismatic renewal has been a sense of discipline, accountability, and an appreciation of the role of authority in Christian formation. In some cases these strengths have developed into overcontrol. We note the need to strike a balance between accountability on the one hand, and mature Christian freedom and individual responsibility on the other.

Bishops and Priests as Participants

36. Not all bishops share the prayer forms or the community life which are so much a part of the renewal, but will identify with the emphasis upon personal and ecclesial transformation, as Pope John Paul II noted (May 7, 1981). He called attention to the service many bishops have rendered the Church through their efforts "to ensure for the renewal a pattern of growth and development fully open to all the riches of the love of God in his Church."

37. Echoing the words of Pope John Paul II, we commend the charismatic renewal to the priests of the United States: "The priest, for his part, cannot exercise his service on behalf of the renewal unless and until he adopts a welcoming attitude toward it, based on the desire he shares with every Christian by baptism to grow in the gifts of the Holy Spirit" (May 7, 1981). The priest's responsibility to give pastoral guidance remains, even though an individual priest may not be a participant in the renewal.

Conclusion: Commendation of the Charismatic Renewal

38. We especially rejoice in the efforts to foster the pursuit of holiness, to encourage Catholics to a fuller participation in the Mass and sacraments, to develop ministries to serve the parish and local Church, to foster ecumenical bonds of unity with other Christians, to participate in evangelization, and to assist the development of this renewal in other countries. While this renewal pursues the gospel priority of giving first emphasis to the praise, thanks, worship, and love of God, we remind all that such love is not complete if it does not reach out to all our neighbors, especially the poor.

39. We wish those in the charismatic renewal to know that we make our own the view of Yves Congar: "The charismatic renewal is a grace for the Church." We assure those in the charismatic renewal of the support they enjoy from the bishops of the United States, and we encourage them in their efforts to renew the life of the Church.

Political Responsibility
Choices for the 1980s

A Statement Issued by the
Administrative Board of the
United States Catholic Conference

March 1984

I. Introduction

1. The hallmark of a democratic nation is its ability to engage the voice of its people in a broad range of public decisions. It is important on the occasion of this election year to emphasize the importance of responsible political participation. In 1976 and in 1979, we issued statements calling for "a committed, informed citizenry to revitalize our political life."[1] We now reiterate that call and ask all citizens to ensure that our elections become the vital and popular forum they can and must be if our nation is to address democratically the crucial issues that face us in the years ahead.

2. We are encouraged by the improvement in voter participation rates that was demonstrated in the 1982 congressional elections. Yet the level of participation in the political process by American voters is still a matter of serious concern. Voter participation rates in the United States continue to be among the lowest in industrialized democracies in the world. Almost half of all eligible voters did not participate in the most recent presidential election.[2] Clearly there is need for ongoing improvement in this most essential element of our democratic life.

3. Of special concern is the fact that some segments of the population, such as racial minorities, low-income people, youth, and women, have traditionally had inadequate access to the political process. Among the poor only about one of every four eligible voters went to the polls in the last national election. Likewise the voting participation rates for minorities and youth are far below the national average. While the participation rates for women are near the national average, women still lag far behind in terms of holding elective office.

4. In each of these cases some progress has been made in recent years. Civil rights organizations, human service and religious groups,

---

[1]*Political Responsibility: Reflections on an Election Year*, February 12, 1976; *Political Responsibility: Choices for the 1980s*, October 26, 1979.

[2]In the 1982 Congressional elections 41 percent of those eligible to vote actually did so. In the 1980 Presidential elections 54 percent of eligible voters turned out.

and other voluntary organizations have initiated aggressive voter registration campaigns in order to promote full participation in the electoral and political processes. We commend these efforts and hope that they will be extended in the future.

5.   It is important for all Americans to realize the extent to which we are all interdependent members of a national community. Increasingly, our problems are social in nature, demanding solutions that are likewise social. To fashion these solutions in a just and humane way requires the active and creative participation of all. It requires a renewed faith in the ability of the human community to cooperate in governmental structures that work for the common good. It requires, above all, a willingness to attack the root causes of the powerlessness and alienation that threaten our democracy.

6.   If as a nation we are to address effectively the complex social and economic issues that confront us, then we must have broad democratic participation in the political process from all segments of society. We cannot afford to abandon citizenship ourselves, nor can we permit major segments of society to be shut out from the mainstream of American political life. Rather, we must breathe new life into the practice of citizenship, and we must dedicate ourselves to strengthening the great democratic experiment that we proudly call the United States of America.

7.   All Christians have a call to citizenship and political life. In the words of Pope John Paul II: "An important challenge for the Christian is that of political life. In the state citizens have a right and duty to share in the political life. For a nation can ensure the common good of all and the dreams and aspirations of its different members only to the extent that all citizens in full liberty and with complete responsibility make their contributions willingly and selflessly for the good of all."[3] Accordingly, we urge all citizens to use their franchise by registering to vote and going to the polls. Demand information from the campaigns themselves and from the media coverage of those campaigns. Make candidates declare their values, so you can compare those values with your own. Take stands on the candidates and the issues. If the campaign year is to engage the values of the American people, the campaigners and voters alike must share the responsibility for making it happen. Become involved in the campaign or party of your choice. Finally, use the coming months to better understand the issues and inform your conscience.

---

[3]Papal Address in Nairobi, Kenya, May 7, 1980. *Origins*, vol. 10, no. 2.

II. The Church and the
Political Order

8. It is appropriate in this context to offer our own reflections on the role of the Church in the political order. Christians believe that Jesus' commandment to love one's neighbor should extend beyond individual relationships to infuse and transform all human relations from the family to the entire human community. Jesus came to "bring good news to the poor, to proclaim liberty to captives, new sight to the blind and to set the downtrodden free" (Lk 4:18). He called us to feed the hungry, clothe the naked, care for the sick and afflicted, and to comfort the victims of injustice (Mt 25). His example and words require individual acts of charity and concern from each of us. Yet they also require understanding and action on a broader scale in pursuit of peace and in opposition to poverty, hunger, and injustice. Such action necessarily involves the institutions and structures of society, the economy, and politics.

9. The Church, the People of God, is itself an expression of this love, and is required by the Gospel and its long tradition to promote and defend human rights and human dignity.[4] In his encyclical *Redemptor Hominis*, Pope John Paul II declares that the Church "must be aware of the threats to [humanity] and of all that seems to oppose the endeavor 'to make human life ever more human' and make every element of life correspond to humanity's true dignity—in a word, [the Church] must be aware of all that is opposed to that process."[5] This view of the Church's ministry and mission requires it to relate positively to the political order, since social injustice and the denial of human rights can often be remedied only through governmental action. In today's world, concern for social justice and human development necessarily requires persons and organizations to participate in the political process in accordance with their own responsibilities and roles.

10. Christian responsibility in the area of human rights includes two complementary pastoral actions: the affirmation and promotion of human rights and the denunciation and condemnation of violations of these rights. In addition, it is the Church's role as a community of faith to call attention to the moral and religious dimension of secular issues, to keep alive the values of the Gospel as a norm for social and political life, and to point out the demands of the Christian faith for a just transformation of society. Such a ministry on the part of every individual as well as the organizational Church inevitably involves political consequences and touches upon public affairs.

---

[4]*Human Rights and Reconciliation*, Synod of Bishops, 1974.
[5]*Redemptor Hominis*, 14, Pope John Paul II, March 4, 1979.

The Responsibility of All Members of the Church

11. The Church's responsibility in this area falls on all its members. As citizens we are all called to become informed, active, and responsible participants in the political process. It is the laity who are primarily responsible for activity in political affairs, for it is they who have the major responsibility for renewal of the temporal order. In the words of the Second Vatican Council:

> The laity, by their special vocation, seek the kingdom of God by engaging in temporal affairs and by ordering them according to the plan of God. They live in the ordinary circumstances of family and social life, from which the very web of their existence is woven. Today they are called by God, that by exercising their proper function and led by the spirit of the Gospel, they may work for the sanctification of the world from within as a leaven.[6]

12. The hierarchy also has a distinct and weighty responsibility in this area. As teachers and pastors, they must provide norms for the formation of conscience of the faithful, support efforts to gain greater peace and justice, and provide guidance and even leadership on occasions when human rights are in jeopardy. Drawing on their own experience and exercising their distinctive roles within the Christian community, bishops, clergy, religious, and laity should join together in common witness and effective action to bring about Pope John Paul II's vision of a well-ordered society based on truth, justice, charity, and freedom.[7]

The Distinct Role of the Church

13. The Church's role in the political order includes the following:

- education regarding the teachings of the Church and the responsibilities of the faithful;
- analysis of issues for their social and moral dimensions;
- measuring public policy against gospel values;
- participating with other concerned parties in debate over public policy; and
- speaking out with courage, skill, and concern on public issues involving human rights, social justice, and the life of the Church in society.

14. Unfortunately, our efforts in this area are sometimes misunderstood. The Church's participation in public affairs is not a threat to

---

[6]*Lumen Gentium*, 31.
[7]Pope John Paul, Papal Address, *Origins*, vol. 11, no. 29, 1982.

the political process or to genuine pluralism, but an affirmation of their importance. The Church recognizes the legitimate autonomy of government and the right of all, including the Church itself, to be heard in the formulation of public policy. As Vatican II declared:

> By preaching the truth of the Gospel and shedding light on all areas of human activity through her teaching and the example of the faithful, she [the Church] shows respect for the political freedom and responsibility of citizens and fosters these values. She also has the right to pass moral judgments, even on matters touching the political order, whenever basic personal rights or the salvation of souls makes such judgments necessary.[8]

15. A proper understanding of the role of the Church will not confuse its mission with that of government, but rather see its ministry as advocating the critical values of human rights and social justice.

16. It is the role of Christian communities to analyze the situation in their own country, to reflect upon the meaning of the Gospel, and to draw norms of judgment and plans of action from the teaching of the Church and their own experience.[9] In carrying out this pastoral activity in the social arena we are confronted with complexity. As the 1971 Synod of Bishops pointed out: "It does not belong to the Church, insofar as she is a religious and hierarchical community, to offer concrete solutions in the social, economic and political spheres for justice in the world."[10] At the same time it is essential to recall the words of Pope John XXIII:

> It must not be forgotten that the Church has the right and duty not only to safeguard the principles of ethics and religion, but also to intervene authoritatively with her children in the temporal sphere when there is a question of judging the application of these principles to concrete cases.[11]

17. The application of gospel values to real situations is an essential work of the Christian community. Christians believe the Gospel is the measure of human realities. However, specific political proposals do not in themselves constitute the Gospel. Christians and Christian organizations must certainly participate in public debate over alternative policies and legislative proposals, yet it is critical that the nature of their participation not be misunderstood.

18. We specifically do not seek the formation of a religious voting bloc; nor do we wish to instruct persons on how they should vote by endorsing candidates. We urge citizens to avoid choosing candidates simply on the basis of personal self-interest. Rather, we hope that

---

[8]The *Church in the Modern World*, 76.

[9]*A Call to Action*, 4.

[10]*Justice in the World*, 37.

[11]*Pacem in Terris*, 160, Pope John XXIII, 1963.

voters will examine the positions of candidates on the full range of issues as well as their integrity, philosophy, and performance. We seek to promote a greater understanding of the important link between faith and politics and to express our belief that our nation is enriched when its citizens and social groups approach public affairs from positions grounded in moral conviction and religious belief. Our view is expressed very well by Pope John Paul II when he said:

> Christians know from the Church's luminous teachings that without any need to follow a one-sided or partisan political formula, they ought to contribute to forming a more worthy society, one more respectful of the rights of man, based on the principles of justice and peace.[12]

19. As religious leaders and pastors, our intention is to reflect our concern that politics receive its rightful importance and attention and that it become an effective forum for the achievement of the common good. For, in the words of John Paul II, "[Humanity's] situation in the modern world seems indeed to be far removed from the objective demands of the moral order, from the requirements of justice, and even more of social love. . . . We have before us here a great drama that can leave nobody indifferent."[13]

III. Issues

20. Without reference to political candidates, parties, or platforms, we wish to offer a listing of some issues which we believe are important in the national debate during 1984. These brief summaries are not intended to indicate in any depth the details of our positions in these matters. We refer the reader to fuller discussions of our point of view in the documents listed in the summary which appears below. We wish to point out that these issues are not the concerns of Catholics alone; in every case we have joined with others to advocate these positions. They represent a broad range of topics on which the bishops of the United States have already expressed themselves and are recalled here in alphabetical order to emphasize their relevance in a period of national debate and decision.

A. Abortion

21. The right to life is the most basic human right, and it demands the protection of law. Abortion is the deliberate destruction of an unborn human being and therefore violates this right. We do not

---

[12]Pope John XXIII, Papal Address in Spain. Cf. *Origins*, vol. 11, no. 29, pp. 389ff.
[13]*Redemptor Hominis*, 16.

accept the concept that anyone has the right to choose an abortion. We reject the 1973 Supreme Court decisions on abortion which refuse appropriate legal protection to the unborn child. We support the passage of a constitutional amendment to restore the basic constitutional protection of the right to life for the unborn child. We reject the public funding of abortion. (*Documentation on the Right to Life and Abortion,* 1974, 1976, 1981; *Pastoral Plan for Pro-Life Activities,* 1975.)

B. Arms Control and Disarmament

22. The National Conference of Catholic Bishops (NCCB) has now addressed a broad range of national security policies that depend on the possession and planned use of nuclear weapons. The process began with the NCCB/USCC general meeting in November of 1980 and involved extensive consultations with military experts, strategic planners, arms control negotiators, moral theologians, political scientists, and biblical scholars. The result is a pastoral statement which (1) condemns the counter-city or counter-population use of nuclear weapons, (2) rejects the notion of waging limited nuclear wars (because of the risk of escalation to all-out nuclear war), and (3) questions the moral acceptability of policies that contemplate the initiation of nuclear war to repel a conventional attack, as is the case in NATO strategy.
23. The NCCB statement did not, however, rule out the reliance on possession and deployment of strategic (long-range) nuclear weapons for the purpose of deterring an enemy nuclear first strike. The bishops joined with Pope John Paul II in affirming that such a policy was morally acceptable under current conditions. The U.S. bishops' judgment of "strictly conditional moral acceptance of nuclear deterrence" means that the deployment of certain kinds of new weapon systems that are not clearly essential to deterrence should be avoided; moreover they recommended a bilateral, verifiable, and negotiated halt to all new nuclear weapons deployment and called for intensified negotiations to achieve real reductions in the nuclear arsenals of the superpowers and a comprehensive test ban treaty.
24. We urge those who wish their votes to reflect their concerns about the dangers and the moral evil of preparations for nuclear war to read and reflect on the NCCB statement and to become involved in study and action groups in their local dioceses and parishes. (*The Challenge of Peace: God's Promise and Our Response,* 1983.)

C. Capital Punishment

25. In view of our commitment to the value and dignity of human life, we oppose capital punishment. We believe that a return to the use of the death penalty is leading to, indeed can only lead to, further erosion of respect for life in our society. We do not question society's right to punish the offender, but we believe that there are better approaches to protecting our people from violent crimes than resorting to executions. In its application, the death penalty has been discriminatory toward the poor, the indigent, and racial minorities. Our society should reject the death penalty and seek methods of dealing with violent crime which are more consistent with the gospel vision of respect for life and Christ's message of healing love. (*Community and Crime*, 1978; *U.S. Bishops' Statement on Capital Punishment*, 1980.)

D. Civil Rights

26. Discrimination based on sex, race, ethnicity, or age continues to exist in our nation. Such discrimination constitutes a grave injustice and an affront to human dignity. It must be aggressively resisted by every individual and rooted out of every social institution and structure.

27. Racism is a particularly serious form of discrimination. Despite significant strides in eliminating racial prejudices in our country, there remains an urgent need for continued reconciliation in this area. Racism is not merely one sin among many. It is a radical evil dividing the human family. The struggle against it demands an equally radical transformation in our own minds and hearts as well as in the structures of our society. (*Brothers and Sisters to Us: A Pastoral Letter on Racism in Our Day*, 1979; *The Hispanic Presence: Challenge and Commitment*, 1983.)

E. The Economy

28. Our national economic life must reflect broad values of social justice and human rights. Above all, the economy must serve the human needs of our people. While the economy has improved for many citizens, it is important to call attention to the fact that millions of Americans are still poor, jobless, hungry, and inadequately housed and that vast disparities of income and wealth remain within our nation. These conditions are intolerable and must be persistently challenged so that the economy will reflect a fundamental respect for the human dignity and basic needs of all.

29. Current levels of unemployment and the tremendous human costs which they represent are unnecessary and should not be tolerated. We support an effective national commitment to genuine full employment as the foundation of a just and responsible economic policy. We believe that all Americans who are willing and able to work have a right to useful and productive employment at fair wages. We also call for a decent income policy for those who cannot work and adequate assistance to those in need.

30. Efforts to achieve responsible fiscal policies and to stimulate economic growth and security are important and necessary tasks, but they should be governed by a fundamental concern for equity and fairness. Our nation's economic ills must not be solved at the expense of the poor and most vulnerable members of society. (*The Economy: Human Dimensions*, 1975.)

F. Education

31. All persons of whatever race, sex, condition, or age, by virtue of their dignity as human beings, have an inalienable right to education. We advocate:

- sufficient public and private funding to make an adequate education available for all citizens and residents of the United States of America and to provide assistance for education in our nation's program of foreign aid;
- governmental and voluntary action to reduce inequalities of educational opportunity by improving the opportunities available to economically disadvantaged persons;
- orderly compliance with legal requirements for racially integrated schools;
- voluntary efforts to increase racial/ethnic integration in public and nonpublic schools; and
- equitable tax support for the education of pupils in public and nonpublic schools to implement parental freedom in the education of their children.

(*Sharing the Light of Faith*, 1979; *To Teach as Jesus Did*, 1972.)

G. Energy

32. Energy issues have a wide-ranging impact on the economic and social well-being of our nation. As society undergoes a major transition from reliance on petroleum to alternative energy resources, certain moral principles should guide public decision-making in this field. We seek policies which would:

- promote conservation and responsible stewardship of our limited energy resources;
- commit energy development to improving safety for the workforce and the community;
- promote international cooperation in developing and distributing energy, thus reducing the tensions which may lead to international conflict;
- provide for equitable access to energy resources and benefits, particularly for low-income people; and
- promote the development of renewable energy sources.

(*Reflections on the Energy Crisis*, A Statement by the Committee on Social Development and World Peace, USCC, April 2, 1981.)

H. Family Life

33. The test of how we value the family is whether we are willing to foster, in government and business, in urban planning and farm policy, in education, in health care, in the arts and sciences, in our total social and cultural environment, moral values which nourish the primary relationships of husbands, wives, and children and make authentic family life possible.

34. Implicit government policy and explicit government planning and programs can contribute to an erosion of the health and vitality of the family. Comprehensive decisions of a national or regional scope must take into account their impact on family life. Families, especially those whose influence is lessened by poverty or social status, must be allowed their rightful input in those decisions which affect their daily lives. (*Vision and Strategy: The Plan of Pastoral Action for Family Ministry*, 1978.)

I. Food and Agricultural Policy

35. The right to eat flows directly from the right to life. We support a national policy aimed at securing the right to eat for all the world's people.

36. Internationally, U.S. food aid should effectively combat global hunger and malnutrition and be aimed primarily at the poorest countries and neediest people without regard to political considerations. In order to help establish adequate supplies, the U.S. should help to develop a world grain reserve fair to both producers and consumers. Development assistance should emphasize equitable distribution of benefits and help other nations move toward food self-reliance.

37. Domestically, nutrition programs should help meet the needs of hungry and malnourished Americans, especially children, the poor, the unemployed, and the elderly. It is essential that the food stamp program and child nutrition programs be funded at adequate levels. (*Food Policy and the Church: Specific Proposals*, 1975.)

38. Through its income support programs, its credit and research programs, its tax policies, its strategies for rural development, and its foreign aid, the U.S. should support the maintenance of an agricultural system based on small- and moderate-sized family farms both at home and abroad. (*The Family Farm*, 1979.)

39. We support legislation to protect the rights of farm workers and we call for measures to improve the working conditions and the general welfare of farm-worker families. We reaffirm the Church's traditional teaching in support of the right of all workers to organize and bargain collectively.

J. Health

40. Adequate health care is a basic human right. Access to appropriate health care must be guaranteed for all people without regard to economic, social, or legal status. Special efforts should be made to remove barriers to prompt, personalized, and comprehensive care for the poor.

41. Government also has a responsibility to remove or alleviate environmental, social, and economic conditions that cause much ill health and suffering for its citizens. Greater emphasis is required on programs of health promotion and disease prevention.

42. We support the adoption of a national health insurance program as the best means of ensuring access to high quality health care for all. Until a comprehensive and universal program can be enacted, we urge the following:

- strengthening existing programs for the poor, the elderly, and disabled people;
- development and enhancement of alternative delivery systems;
- broad consumer participation in health planning decisions at all levels; and
- a vigorous national cost-containment program.

(*Health and Health Care: A Pastoral of the American Catholic Bishops*, 1981.)

K. Housing

43. Decent housing is a basic human right. A greater commitment of will and resources is required to meet our national housing goal of a decent home for every American family. To meet this housing need, the government must continue to fund adequately housing assistance programs that will assist people to obtain affordable housing. Continuation of housing production and preservation programs is vital to maintaining the stock of affordable housing. Housing policy must better meet the needs of low- and middle-income families, the elderly, rural families, and minorities. It should also promote reinvestment in central cities and equal housing opportunity. Preservation of existing housing stock and a renewed concern for neighborhoods are required. (*The Right to a Decent Home*, 1975.)

L. Human Rights

44. Human dignity requires the defense and promotion of human rights in global and domestic affairs. With respect to international human rights, there is a pressing need for the U.S. to pursue a double task: (1) to strengthen and expand international mechanisms by which human rights can be protected and promoted; and (2) to take seriously the human rights dimensions of U.S. foreign policy. Therefore, we support U.S. ratification of the International Covenants on Civil and Political Rights and on Economic, Social and Cultural Rights. Further, we support a policy which gives greater weight to the protection of human rights in the conduct of U.S. affairs. The pervasive presence of U.S. power creates a responsibility to use that power in the service of human rights. (*U.S. Foreign Policy: A Critique from Catholic Traditions*, 1976.)

M. Mass Media

45. We are concerned that the communications media be truly responsive to the public interest and that future laws governing the electronic media make the benefits that the new communication technologies have created available to all our citizens. We reject any philosophy of marketplace economics as applied to the telecommunication industries which have the effect of widening the gap between the information rich and the information poor in our society. Specifically, we oppose those legislative initiatives in the Congress which would remove the accountability of broadcasters and the owners of cable systems to the communities they are licensed or franchised to serve.

46. We support the concept of universal telephone service at a cost affordable to all Americans. While we oppose government control of the content of the mass media of communication, we support reasonable and legitimate common carrier regulations to restrict the use of these vehicles in making available to the young, in particular, indecent or pornographic materials, many of which violate every rational standard of decency and are an affront to Christian values. (Statements and Testimony by the USCC Department of Communication before the Congress and the FCC.)

N. Regional Conflict in the World

47. Three situations of regional conflict which are of significance for the whole international system, and where U.S. policy has a substantial, indeed a decisive influence, are Central America, the Middle East, and Southern Africa.

48. Central America has come to be the most visible focus of our attention to regional conflicts. Our position concerning the indigenous roots of the conflicts, the imperative need for fundamental social change, and the futility, not to say immorality, of proposed military solutions has been stated often and is well known. As the dominant external actor, our government must play the creative diplomatic role that it uniquely has in supporting the goals of dialogue leading to cessation of hostilities, resulting in a negotiated end to the conflicts and an internationally guaranteed process of political and social reform and of economic reconstruction. Under no reasonably foreseeable circumstances can direct intervention of military personnel in the region, on the part of the United States or any other outside power, be justified. We have constantly supported substantial economic assistance for the countries of Central America; while recognizing that military assistance will be a dimension of the United States presence in Central America, we continue to reaffirm that our principal contribution to peace in the region should be through our diplomatic role. With bishops of the region we continue to express our alarm over the growing militarization of the Central American countries, the danger of a more generalized war, violations of fundamental human rights and lack of progress in judicial redress, and the wrenching tragedy of so many refugees and displaced persons. We have asked the United States government to institute a policy of Extended Voluntary Departure for nationals of El Salvador in the United States and to make a major commitment to meet the immediate human needs of the refugees and displaced persons in Central America. (USCC Testimony on Central America, 1983, 1984.)

49. In the Middle East the quest for peace continues and the relevant parties bear distinct yet interdependent responsibilities. First, the international community, especially its principal diplomatic actors, inevitably influences the future of the Middle East. Second, the United Nations is a vital element in any Middle East negotiations, and its diplomatic and peace-keeping role will undoubtedly be crucial to a long-term resolution of the conflict. Third, the regional parties, whose conflicting claims of justice are the essence of the political and moral problem in the Middle East, are the key to peace. Finally, the religious communities with roots in the Middle East must reflect the best of our traditions in supporting the movement for peace with justice for all the people of the region. We have a continuing concern for the protection of the basic rights, both civil and religious, of the Christian minorities in the Middle East, and we encourage the local churches there to continue their steadfast witness to the faith. (*The Middle East: The Pursuit of Peace with Justice*, 1978.)

50. The position of South Africa has long been of grave moral concern to the world because of its internal racial policies and its occupation of Namibia/South West Africa. In recent years it has become a threat to the entire area of Southern Africa because of its military incursions into the territories of several of its neighbors; indeed, it has virtually occupied a large portion of Angola. The United States is South Africa's largest trading partner and second largest foreign investor. U.S. foreign policy and its influence on corporate activity in South Africa should be directed in effective ways toward needed change in South Africa and in its relations with neighboring states. (*USCC Administrative Board Statement on Namibia*, 1983.)

51. This is not an exclusive listing of the issues that concern us. As Pope John Paul II has said, "The Church cannot remain insensible to whatever serves true human welfare any more than she can remain indifferent to whatever threatens it. . . ."[14] Thus we are also advocates for the civil and political rights of the elderly, the handicapped, immigrants, and aliens. We oppose excessive government interference in religious affairs as well as any unjust bias of government against religious institutions. We support measures to reform our criminal justice system. We are concerned about protection of the land and the environment as well as the monumental question of peace with justice in the world.

IV. Conclusion

52. In summary, we believe that the Church has a proper role and responsibility in public affairs flowing from its gospel mandate and its respect for the dignity of the human person. We hope these reflections will contribute to a renewed political vitality in our land, both in terms of citizen participation in the electoral process and the integrity and accountability of those who seek and hold public office.
53. We pray that Christians will provide courageous leadership in promoting a spirit of responsible political involvement. May they follow the example of Jesus in giving special concern for the poor, and may all their actions be guided by a deep love of God and neighbor.
54. For in the world of American politics, as in all human communities, the words of Pope John Paul II apply:

> What is in question here is the human person. We are not dealing with the abstract human person but the real, concrete, historical person. . . . Every person coming into the world on account of the mystery of the redemption is entrusted to the solicitude of the Church. . . . The object of her care is human persons in their unique, unrepeatable human reality, which keeps intact the image and likeness of God himself. . . ."[15]

---

[14]*Redemptor Hominis*, 13.
[15]Ibid., 13.

Concerning Arms Control

A Statement Presented to the
House Foreign Relations Committee
by Cardinal Joseph Bernardin of Chicago and
Archbishop John O'Connor of New York on
Behalf of the United States Catholic Conference

June 26, 1984

1. We testify today on behalf of the U.S. Catholic Conference, the public policy agency of the Catholic bishops of the United States. We wish to express, on behalf of the USCC, the appreciation of the Catholic bishops for this opportunity to present our perspective on the moral dimensions of war and peace in the nuclear age. It is now one year since the bishops issued their pastoral letter *The Challenge of Peace: God's Promise and Our Response*. The serious attention given to the letter in the Catholic Church, by other religious communities and by the wider American society has been a very encouraging sign for the bishops.

2. Our purpose in appearing today before this committee is not so much to address specific issues as to invite attention to the growing concern of leaders of the Catholic community in the United States about the dangers of nuclear war and, to their view, that the means employed either to fight nuclear wars or to deter them are subject to rather definite moral limitations. Indeed, in the nuclear age there is a need to reinforce moral limits on all forms of warfare.

3. This is a view which many Americans find difficult to assimilate because, as Einstein remarked, everything has changed except our way of thinking. But there is also in the general public a pervasive fear that nuclear war will occur, with disastrous consequences for all. The Catholic bishops seek to help move the state of public and policy debate beyond fear to a creative response to our common danger.

The Challenge of Peace
Its Nature and Purpose

4. The pastoral letter is a lengthy statement, too long and complex to expect most members of Congress to read in its entirety. One reason we are here today is to set forth its main tenets in shortened but still comprehensive form. We believe that the message of the statement is relevant to the most difficult issues in U.S. foreign and security policies; we are engaged in teaching and expounding the message in parishes and schools and discussion groups all across America in the hope that citizens will make moral judgments a part of the process by which they try to influence political decisions.

5.   As bishops, we do not approach this testimony from a political perspective, but because never before has war, as a "continuation of policy by other means," posed such stark moral alternatives: Does the communist threat to the preservation of Western values justify the deployment and conditional intention to use weapons that threaten civilization as we know it and possibly the survival of the human race? The costs of continuing to pursue the age-old approach of arming to prevent war have steadily mounted in the nuclear age to threaten the potential extinction of the human species. To quote Pope John Paul II at Hiroshima: "In the past it was possible to destroy a village, a town, a region, even a country. Now it is the whole planet that has come under threat."

6.   Some argue in this situation that the threat of communist domination is so repugnant that the United States is justified in possessing and using whatever means necessary to deter or frustrate communist aggression, to do unto the communists, if they attack, what they would do unto us. We agree completely concerning the repugnance of communist domination and the need to frustrate it, but Christian ethics rejects this eye-for-an-eye, tooth-for-a-tooth morality. We cannot find justification for policy solely in the actions or intentions of an adversary.

7.   In searching for a way out of this awful dilemma, we have consulted the accepted sources of Catholic morality: Scripture, the 2,000-year-old development of moral teaching of the Catholic Church, and recent papal and conciliar statements. In this latter category we found especially useful the encyclical *Pacem in Terris* of the late John XXIII, the statements of Pope John Paul II, and one of the major documents of the Second Vatican Council, The *Pastoral Constitution on the Church in the Modern World* (1965).

8.   Concentration on the gospel message inclines some believers to pacifism, the search for nonviolent alternatives. Yet, the conflict of values experienced in a world marked by sin and limitation and the need to protect the innocent from attack brought the Catholic tradition, particularly following St. Augustine, to a position that recognized a limited use of force to protect one's neighbors and one's society. This position was elaborated over the centuries to become a rather extensive body of rules or criteria governing both the resort to war and the conduct of military operations once war is resorted to.

9.   Since the Middle Ages, this body of principles has been known as the just-war doctrine. It is summarized at some length in *The Challenge of Peace*; suffice it here to say that under the just-war doctrine, recourse to war is permissible only in a just cause, by a competent authority (e.g., by the Congress of the United States), with a right

intention (to restore peace), as a last resort, with a reasonable prospect of success and without the collateral suffering and death being disproportionate to the good to be accomplished. These criteria together constitute the *jus ad bellum*.

10. The just-war doctrine also specifies that certain actions are to be avoided in the conduct of a war (e.g., intentional killing of noncombatants) and that actions that are intended to achieve reasonable military or political objectives not entail collateral suffering and death disproportionate to the importance of the objective. These criteria are collectively referred to as the *jus in bello*.

11. It is the *jus in bello* criteria that are especially relevant to war today, at least to nuclear war, because for the first time in history the weapons available include many which by their design and destructive power cannot be used with discrimination and proportionality. The awful nature of these weapons and their effects have caused some Christians to reject the just-war doctrine as irrelevant, to believe that proportionality will always be asserted to justify use; and they have therefore returned to the absolute rejection of killing of the early Christians.

12. But the Church does not embrace pacifism as a public position; it believes that some uses of force are justified in the defense of freedom, independence, and human dignity. The Church continues to employ the just-war criteria to establish limits to the permissible use of force. The problem is simplified if one accepts the proposition that the United States would not undertake a major war except in defense of its territory and its close allies, and that undertaking such a defensive war would be justified in terms of just-war theory. It was thus possible to make much of the major focus of the pastoral letter the question of legitimate means.

Questions of Strategy and Morality
Shaping an Ethic of Means

13. The pastoral letter addresses four specific issues of contemporary nuclear strategy: (1) countercity (or countervalue) attacks; (2) limited use of nuclear weapons; (3) first use of nuclear weapons; (4) possession of nuclear weapons for purposes of deterrence.

14. *Countercity Attacks:* In theory at least this question is relatively simple, and the Catholic moral judgment had already been articulated in the Second Vatican Council's *Pastoral Constitution on the Church in the Modern World:* "Any act of war aimed indiscriminately at the destruction of entire cities or of extensive areas along with their population is a crime against God and man itself; it merits unequivocal and unhesitating condemnation" (no. 81).

15. This language expresses in pure form the traditional principle of discrimination, that the lives of noncombatants must be protected as far as possible, not deliberately and intentionally taken or threatened. It was necessary to repeat this warning because, at times in the nuclear age, attacks on cities have been advocated as part of a strategy of deterrence.

16. *Limited Nuclear War:* Over the course of the years, through successive administrations, there has been much official talk about waging nuclear war as opposed to deterring it. It was reliably reported in 1982 that official defense-guidance policy included plans for waging a protracted but limited nuclear war that would enable the U.S. forces to "prevail."

17. The bishops felt obliged to consider whether such policy could be regarded as morally responsible. There was no question that theoretically some nuclear weapons could be employed without unjustifiably devastating effects, but the majority of experts consulted by the drafting committee of the bishops thought that once nuclear war had begun, it would be difficult if not impossible to prevent escalation to unacceptable levels of destruction. This led the bishops to conclude that it is imperative "to prevent any use of nuclear weapons and to hope that our leaders will resist the notion that nuclear conflict can be limited, contained, or won in any traditional sense" (no. 161).

18. We were gratified to read President Reagan's assurance in his most recent State of the Union message to Congress that "a nuclear war cannot be won and must never be fought. The only value in possessing nuclear weapons is to make sure they will never be used." This is our position also, and we trust it has become official policy.

19. *Initiation of Nuclear War:* The bishops felt equally obliged to consider the "first use" of nuclear weapons by the United States because it is an essential part of the NATO "flexible-response" strategy to deploy nuclear weapons on the soil of our NATO allies to be used if the NATO forces are unable to repel a Warsaw-Pact invasion with conventional (nonnuclear) forces. This doctrine has for years applied to the use of so-called tactical or battlefield nuclear weapons that would be used against the military forces of the invading armies, with predictably grave consequences for the densely populated areas that would be part of the battlefield.

20. With the deployment of U.S. Pershing 2 and cruise missiles in Europe, any escalation from the use of tactical weapons almost certainly risks escalation to the strategic, intercontinental level. While they recognized that this strategy is by intention a deterrent strategy to prevent any war in Europe, the bishops concluded that the same moral logic applied to this policy as to the doctrine that limited nuclear wars can be fought in a controlled, limited way without unacceptable collateral loss of life. Hence, they urged and continue to urge that the NATO allies progressively improve their conventional forces to raise the nuclear threshold and eventually rely entirely on such weapons for defense and on the U.S. commitment of its strategic nuclear forces to deter any Warsaw-Pact nuclear threat to Western Europe.

21. The bishops are quite aware that another European war would be a catastrophe even if fought with conventional weapons, but at least the possibility of a fatal nuclear holocaust would be precluded.

22. *Nuclear Deterrence:* The question of the morality of deterrence policy was perhaps the most complex of the entire pastoral letter. The judgment of the U.S. bishops on deterrence builds upon the statement of Pope John Paul II at the United Nations in 1982:

> In current conditions deterrence based on balance, certainly not as an end in itself but as a step on the way toward a progressive disarmament, may still be judged morally acceptable. Nonetheless, in order to ensure peace, it is indispensable not to be satisfied with this minimum, which is always susceptible to the real danger of explosion (Message to the UN Special Session on Disarmament).

23. The U.S. bishops reflect both dimensions of the papal message in our pastoral letter: We acknowledge the dilemma and the danger of basing the peace of the world on the deterrence relationship. The judgment of the pastoral letter is one of "strictly conditioned moral acceptance of nuclear deterrence" (no. 186). On the one hand, in spite of the pervasive skepticism of the pastoral concerning the possibility of a "limited" use of nuclear weapons, the letter does not condemn deterrence. On the other hand, the acceptance of deterrance is strictly conditioned; the pastoral letter sets forth a series of criteria, prudential judgments by which the U.S. bishops seek to make clear the meaning of "strictly conditioned acceptance." To quote the pastoral:

> Clearly these criteria demonstrate that we cannot approve of every weapons system, strategic doctrine or policy initiative advanced in the name of strengthening deterrence. On the contrary, these criteria require continual public scrutiny of what our government proposes to do with the deterrent" (no. 187).

24. It is the responsibility we feel for continued assessment of the meaning, morality, and direction of defense policy that brings us here to the Congress today. A "strictly conditioned acceptance" of deterrence requires continued participation in the public debate. Several commentators on the pastoral letter have made the point that the bishops drove the public analysis of deterrence back to "first principles," calling for an assessment of the very concept of deterrence. The strategy of deterrence is judged in the pastoral letter as not "adequate as a long-term basis for peace" (no. 186). Deterrence policy is seen as a transitional imperative, providing time and space during which steps should be taken to halt the arms race, reverse its course, and move toward not only arms control but nuclear disarmament. In the spirit of this view of deterrence, we now turn to the question of arms control and disarmament policy.

Arms Control and Disarmament Policy
Politics, Strategy, and Ethics

25. A crucially important characteristic of the pastoral letter is that it sets forth universally binding moral principles, official Catholic teaching, and also a series of specific prudential judgments which the bishops made about several policy issues. The bishops went to some length to highlight the different moral authority of these three parts of the pastoral letter. The moral principles and the elements of Catholic teaching have a binding force; the prudential judgments which apply principles to specific cases or issues deserve serious consideration, but they are by definition open to debate and to other conclusions than the ones drawn by the bishops.

26. The purpose of joining moral principles with specific prudential judgments in the pastoral was not to have the bishops pose as experts on politics and strategy, but to illustrate that the key principles involved can make a substantial difference in the practical order when they are carefully used to shape the direction of concrete policy choices.

27. In this testimony, we continue to be interested in the way specific choices are made in the political and strategic arena which shape the direction of the arms race and influence the collective destiny of the human family. Our interest in specific choices reflects the concern of Pope John Paul II expressed in his address to scientists and scholars at Hiroshima in 1981: "From now on, it is only through a conscious choice and through a deliberate policy that humanity can survive."

28. It is a fundamental conviction of our pastoral letter and of this testimony that moral principles can inform, guide, and illuminate concrete policy choices. We recognize that it is not the province of religious leaders to make the final policy choices in these matters, but we do have an obligation as moral teachers to set forth criteria for choices and illustrate the implications of these criteria. Precisely because we gave "conditional acceptance" to a policy of deterrence we said:

> Nuclear deterrence should be used as a step on the way toward progressive disarmament. Each proposed addition to our strategic systems or change in strategic doctrine must be assessed precisely in light of whether it will render steps toward "progressive disarmament" more or less likely (no. 188).

29. In assessing the impact of new weapons systems on the dynamic of the arms race or the prospects for deterrence, we believe two criteria should be used in tandem. Both of the criteria are found in the statements of Pope John Paul II; we seek to elaborate them here because together they create a framework for assessing specific choices which the Congress faces.

30. The *first criterion* concerns the relationship of technology, politics, and ethics. The relevance of these terms to decisions on defense policy is direct and constant. The technological dynamic of the arms race often drives the political process: because we can build a new system or because someone else has produced it, there emerges an often unspoken imperative that we must build it. A persistent concern of John Paul II is that technological decisions must be governed by political choices, which in turn should be guided by a moral vision. Much of the history of the arms race is technology moving ahead of both political and moral reflection or restraint.

31. The most evident recent case involved the decision by the United States, followed by the Soviet Union, to proceed with the MIRVing of nuclear missiles. The technology of MIRVing (multiple independent reentry vehicle) moved from the research and development stage to deployment without the kind of public debate we believe such a revolutionary change in the arms race called for. The effect of MIRVing has made every step in arms control (and therefore in "progressive disarmament") much more difficult. It may not be too strong to say that we mortgaged the future of arms control by a technological decision taken without adequate citizen or congressional scrutiny.

32. A *second criterion* relates to the cost of the nuclear arms race. Like his predecessors since Pius XII, Pope John Paul II has protested and indeed condemned the diversion of resources on a global basis from spending for human needs to spending on the arms race. In his Christmas message last December, the pope spoke of "the men and women who are dying of hunger, while enormous sums are being spent on weapons" (Christmas Message, 1983, no. 4).

33. We recognize that the problem of spending is a complex one. The cheapest defense might be an increasingly nuclear arsenal. We certainly would oppose such a move. At the same time, we cannot avoid addressing the major increases in the proposed fiscal year 1985 budget for strategic nuclear systems. From the perspective of both arms control and the use of scarce resources, we find these major increases profoundly disturbing. We must ask whether adequate justification has been offered thus far to make the case for proceeding with all these programs.

34. Specifically, we propose two criteria for making the conscious choices that the Congress has the ability and the responsibility to make. First, the impact of each new strategic system on the dynamic of the arms race should be evaluated: technological advance should be scrupulously measured by political and moral criteria. The MIRVing experience should not be repeated. Second, the cost of specific systems should be assessed along with the impact of the weapons system. If a particular system is found to be of dubious strategic value (i.e., not absolutely necessary to preserve our deterrence posture) and yet is certain to cost large sums of money, then these two criteria lead us to recommend against the system in question.

35. Human needs in our own country and in the developing world are so great today that they constitute a radical claim on our personal and national consciences; we should not expend scarce funds on strategic systems that may simply intensify the danger of the arms race rather than enhance the narrow purpose of deterrence: to prevent nuclear war on those actions which could lead to nuclear war.

36. The relevance of these two criteria to existing policy proposals can be illustrated by examples. Perhaps the single most controversial decision in nuclear policy before the Congress is the MX missile. While the House has acted on it for fiscal year 1985, the future of the MX is still unresolved. In the pastoral letter, a year ago, the bishops called attention to the MX as the kind of technological decision that requires intense political and moral assessment. We believe the same kind of assessment is still needed.

37. If anything, the number of knowledgeable analysts who have expressed reservations or outright opposition to the MX has increased since publication of our pastoral letter. They argue that the MX is vulnerable to attack, yet powerful enough to appear threatening to the Soviets as a potential first-strike weapon. Even a citizen's review of the technical debate leads many to conclude that the impact of the MX on the arms race contains very severe risks of moving both superpowers toward an even more unstable relationship than presently prevails. At the same time, we know the MX will cost several billion dollars. The continued questioning of its strategic value, as well as its assured cost, should be sufficient to require a reconsideration of MX deployment.

38. A different but analogous case is provided by proposals to move toward some form of space-based defense for the United States. The history of the strategic debate about defensive as opposed to offensive systems is older than the MX debate. The objectives of defensive systems have always been desirable: to target weapons, not people, and to reduce the incentive to use nuclear weapons at all.

39. The problem has always been the impact of defensive systems on the arms race as a whole. The fear of many experts is that rather than displacing offensive strategies we will produce both an offensive and a defensive race. The impact of space-based defense, like the MX, on the stability of the arms race is precisely why it is under severe questioning as it has been in the past. Yet, the expenditure for moving in a major way toward such a defensive system will be enormous. The Congress does not face an immediate choice comparable to the MX on space defense. But now is the time, in our judgment, to apply the criteria we are proposing to assess the space-defense initiative in terms of its strategic impact and its cost before major commitments are made.

40. The measures we have discussed thus far involve steps that the United States can take independently as it makes "conscious choices" about the configuration of our deterrence posture. Because of the complex and crucial link between technology, politics, and strategy, such individual initiatives are required of both superpowers as a means of restraint. But the essential method for controlling and reversing the dynamic of the arms race is bilateral or multilateral forms of negotiation. Pope John Paul II has been unequivocal on this point; in his address to the UN special session (1982) he said: "Today once again before you all I reaffirm my confidence in the power of true negotiations to arrive at just and equitable solutions" (no. 8). The pope has since then appealed directly to the heads of state of the United States and the Soviet Union to resume the stalled negotiations on strategic and intermediate nuclear forces. The urgency he feels on this question was reflected in Pope John Paul II's statement to the diplomatic corps (January 14, 1984) that "there is not a moment to lose."

41. We use this public opportunity of congressional testimony to reinforce the papal appeal for a new effort of political will and creative diplomacy on behalf of a new round of superpower negotiations to reverse the arms race. Negotiated restraint in the arms race has never been easy to achieve. Small political steps are often outdistanced by major technological advances. It was with this history in mind that the American bishops, in *The Challenge of Peace*, called for "negotiations to halt the testing, production, and deployment of new nuclear systems" (no. 204). This objective—to cap the arms race now—should be vigorously pursued. At the same time, we need to recognize and protect the more modest accomplishments which negotiations have thus far achieved. These include the Limited Test Ban Treaty (1963); the Outer Space Treaty (1967); the Nonproliferation Treaty (1970); the ABM Treaty (1972) and the SALT I agreement (1972). These measures are the legacy of a bipartisan effort of two decades; they provide a limited but firm foundation for future steps in the 1980s. They deserve to be sustained and supported.

42. In addition, we note that our pastoral letter urged the renewal of negotiations for a comprehensive test ban treaty; such a measure would consolidate the achivements of the limited test ban. We believe a renewed effort by the United States to achieve a well-designed treaty would meet with significant public support and could serve as a substantial moral and political restraint on destructive types of technological innovation. Second, we believe that the recently expressed interest by both superpowers in limiting deployment of anti-satellite weapons deserves serious public and congressional attention. From the perspective of our pastoral letter, we support efforts to prevent the initiation of a nuclear race on yet another frontier—outer space.

43. On the nonnuclear front, two topics are of particular interest from a moral perspective. First, we applaud the resumption of the Mutual Balanced-Force Reduction Talks. Our pastoral letter urges steps toward a "no first-use" policy on nuclear weapons. Serious MBFR negotiations could provide the confidence about conventional force levels and capabilities which both sides need to move toward reduced reliance on nuclear weapons in the European theater. Second, we support the recent U.S. initiative on chemical warfare; we urge the administration and the Congress to shape U.S. policy and preparations on chemical war so that our actual policy will support our diplomatic initiative to place chemical warfare beyond the pale of all states.

44. This is not a comprehensive but simply an illustrative agenda of the steps that we feel would help assure political and moral control of strategic policy in the nuclear age.

Positive Steps for Peace

45. The "conscious choices" we have been proposing for consideration are all pertinent to the short-term effort to control the danger of the nuclear age. But we also wish to highlight the broader perspective on principles and policy found in *The Challenge of Peace*.

46. Following the direction of papal and conciliar teaching, our letter looked beyond the necessarily limited steps of daily diplomacy to a basic transformation of political and legal structures, a step which may appear as unlikely today as the emergence of the nation-state did in the Middle Ages.

47. Yet, we live in a world that is not only threatened by nuclear conflict but increasingly interdependent in its structure and substance. Both the danger of the arms race and the positive possibilities of interdependence have led the popes from Pius XII through John Paul II to call for new international institutions capable of building the peace among nations. The U.S. bishops reaffirmed this papal teaching, and we addressed specific measures that the United States could undertake to play a leadership role, politically, legally, and economically in pursuit of a just and peaceful interdependent world.

48. Precisely because new international institutions are needed to build the peace, we specifically make a plea here for a presently unpopular cause: renewed support by the United States for the United Nations. The Catholic Church has supported the United Nations since its inception, not because it is perfect, but precisely because it is necessary in spite of its limitations. A creative U.S. initiative should be both critical and constructive; it need not be silent about needed reforms, but these can be proposed in a manner which all can recognize as fundamentally in support of the United Nations.

49. A conscious U.S. policy of independent initiatives to restrain the arms race, a convincingly articulated U.S. policy aimed at reconstituting negotiations with the Soviet Union and a long-needed reaffirmation of U.S. support for the objectives and institutions of the United Nations would be a source of hope and inspiration to people in our own nation and in other nations of the world. It would say we are determined to build and secure the peace not only for our generation and our country, but also for the children who represent the future of this planet.

Religion and Politics

*A Statement Issued by the President of the
United States Catholic Conference and
Authorized by the Executive Committee of the
United States Catholic Conference*

August 9, 1984

1. As an agency of the Catholic bishops of the United States, the U.S. Catholic Conference speaks on public-policy issues, but it does not take positions for or against political candidates. This point needs emphasizing lest, in the present political context, even what we say about issues be perceived as an expression of political partisanship.

2. Bishops are teachers. In regard to public issues, they exercise their teaching role by defining the content of moral principles and indicating how they apply to specific problems. The bishops' principal role in the public arena is described in this statement of the Second Vatican Council:

> By preaching the truth of the Gospel and shedding light on all areas of human activity through her teaching and the example of the faithful, the Church shows respect for the political freedom and responsibility to citizens to foster these values. She also has the right to pass moral judgments, even on matters touching the political order, whenever basic personal rights or the salvation of souls makes such judgments necessary (*Gaudium et Spes,* 76).

3. In view of the bishops' teaching role, the Catholic Conference focuses its attention on policy issues involving significant moral dimensions. By analyzing and taking positions on such issues, the conference seeks to establish a framework of moral guidance for use by Catholics and other persons of good will in making their decisions on political candidates and parties.

4. The conference's views on many current issues are spelled out in such documents as the statement on *Political Responsibility* issued earlier this year by the USCC Administrative Board and the USCC's testimony to the platform committees of the two major parties. These are public documents, which I commend to the attention of anyone who wishes to know where we stand.

5. The political responsibility statement urges Catholics and others to involve themselves in the political process. It also sets forth specific positions that the bishops have taken on issues. These range from protecting human life from the attack of abortion, to safeguarding human life from the devastation of nuclear war; they extend to the enhancement of life through promoting human rights and satisfying human needs like nutrition, education, housing, and health care for the poor. The platform testimony explains our view of the interdependence of these issues and why belief in the unique dignity of the human person leads the bishops to take positions on them all, with particular emphasis upon abortion and nuclear war.

6.   The Catholic Conference's policy positions express the Catholic moral tradition. With regard to many issues, of course, there is room for sincere disagreement by Catholics and others who share our moral convictions over how moral principles should be applied to the current facts in the public-policy debate. But with regard to the immorality of the direct taking of innocent human life (e.g., by abortion or by direct attacks on noncombatants in war), our views are not simply policy statements of a particular Catholic organization, the U.S. Catholic Conference. They are a direct affirmation of the constant moral teaching of the Catholic Church, enunciated repeatedly over the centuries, as in our day, by the highest teaching authority of the Church.

7.   We seek, however, not only to address Catholics and others who share our moral convictions, but to make a religiously informed contribution to the public-policy debate in our pluralistic society. When we oppose abortion in that forum, we do so because a fundamental human right is at stake—the right to life of the unborn child. When we oppose any such deterrence policies as would directly target civilian centers or inflict catastrophic damage, we do so because human values would be violated in such an attack. When we support civil rights at home and measure foreign policy by human rights criteria, we seek to do so in terms all people can grasp and support.

8.   In proclaiming authentic Catholic moral teaching, therefore, we recognize at the same time the need to join the public-policy debate in a way that attempts to convince others of the rightness of our positions. As the Catholic Conference seeks to observe this prescription itself, so it urges other participants in the policy debate to do the same. It would be regrettable if religion as such were injected into a political campaign through appeals to candidates' religious affiliations and commitments. We reject the idea that candidates satisfy the requirements of rational analysis in saying their personal views should not influence their policy decisions; the implied dichotomy—between personal morality and public policy—is simply not logically tenable in any adequate view of both. This position would be as unacceptable as would be the approach of a candidate or officeholder who pointed to his or her personal commitments as qualification for public office without proposing to take practical steps to translate these into policies and practical programs. This is true of all candidates of all parties.

9.   It is our hope, in short, that the political debate in the months ahead will illuminate policy approaches. Policy proposals should be evaluated from a moral perspective; we have done this and will continue to do so. We encourage others to do the same.

Religion and Politics

A Statement Issued by the President of the United States Catholic Conference at the Request of the Administrative Board of the United States Catholic Conference

October 14, 1984

1.   The Administrative Board of the United States Catholic Conference, meeting September 11-13, asked that I issue a statement reaffirming the conference's position on the question of religion and politics. I am pleased to do so, since our pluralistic society should welcome discussion of the moral dimensions of public policy and thoughtful examination of the relationship of religious bodies to the political order.

2.   As a nation we are constitutionally committed to the separation of church and state, but not to the separation of religious and moral values from public life. The genius of the American political tradition lies in preserving religious freedom for all—but not at the price of excluding religious and moral content from discussions of domestic and foreign policy.

3.   The question therefore is not whether we should discuss the relationship of religion, morality, and politics, but how to discuss the relationship. While responsibility for the quality and character of this discussion rests with all citizens, it rests especially with religious leaders, political leaders, and the media.

4.   The Catholic Conference's statement on political responsibility last March, its testimony to the platform committees of the two major parties in June and August, and my own statement of August 9 express the views of the Catholic bishops concerning the Church's engagement in the political process. I repeat here a basic principle of these documents: We do not take positions for or against particular parties or individual candidates.

5.   Bishops are teachers in the Catholic Church entrusted with the responsibility of communicating the content of Catholic moral teaching and illustrating its relevance to social and political issues. We do not seek the formation of a voting bloc nor do we preempt the right and duty of individuals to decide conscientiously whom they will support for public office. Rather, having stated our positions, we encourage members of our own Church and all citizens to examine the positions of candidates on issues and decide who will best contribute to the common good of society.

6.   The content of Catholic teaching leads us to take positions on

many public issues; we are not a one-issue Church. Many of our positions are reflected in the statement on political responsibility and our platform testimony.

7.   As I said August 9, these concerns range from protecting human life from the attack of abortion to safeguarding human life from the devastation of nuclear war; they extend to the enhancement of life through promoting human rights and satisfying human needs like nutrition, education, housing, and health care, especially for the poor. We emphasize that the needs of the poor must be adequately addressed if we are to be considered a just and compassionate society. Attention to the least among us is the test of our moral vision, and it should be applied to candidates at every level of our government.

8.   Our platform testimony points out that, in speaking of human dignity and the sanctity of life, we give special emphasis to two issues today. They are the prevention of nuclear war and the protection of unborn human life.

9.   These issues pertaining to the sanctity of human life itself are and cannot help but be matters of public morality. Evident in the case of war and peace, this is no less true in the case of abortion, where the human right to life of the unborn and society's interest in protecting it necessarily make this a matter of public, not merely private, morality.

10.   On questions such as these, we realize that citizens and public officials may agree with our moral arguments while disagreeing with us and among themselves on the most effective legal and policy remedies. The search for political and public-policy solutions to such problems as war and peace and abortion may well be long and difficult, but a prudential judgment that political solutions are not now feasible does not justify failure to undertake the effort.

11.   Whether the issue be the control, reduction, and elimination of nuclear arms or the legal protection of the unborn, the task is to work for the feasibility of what may now be deemed unfeasible. The pursuit of complex objectives like these ought not to be set aside because the goals may not be immediately reachable. In debating such matters there is much room for dialogue about what constitutes effective, workable responses, but the debate should not be about whether a response in the political order is needed.

12.   None of these issues will be resolved quickly. All will extend far beyond the present political campaign. The discussion of religion and politics will also be pursued long after the campaign. Let us conduct our immediate dialogue with reason and civility, so that the resources of religious and moral vision and the method of rational political debate will be sustained and enhanced in our public life.

The Continuing Formation of Priests
Growing in Wisdom, Age and Grace

A Statement Prepared by the
Bishops' Committee on Priestly Life and Ministry of
the National Conference of Catholic Bishops

November 15, 1984

Foreword

1. The Purpose of the Document

1. In 1972, the bishops of the United States, in *The Program of Continuing Education of Priests*, addressed the issue of the growth and development of the priest in light of a new understanding of ministry. This was an outgrowth of the Second Vatican Council's call for a "contemporary and truly pastoral image of the priest."[1]

2. *The Program of Continuing Education of Priests* set the stage for a positive evaluation of new structures and policies aimed at the growth and development of priests. It did not lay down hard and fast rules. Rather, it encouraged a flexibility whereby individual dioceses and religious communities might set their own priorities and directions for renewal of priests.

3. Encouragement for this document came from the grass roots as well as from sources such as the *Decree on Priestly Formation* of the Second Vatican Council and *The Ministerial Priesthood* of the 1971 Synod of Bishops. NCCB studies and other published reports indicated that the priest often did not meet his potential for leadership. The shape of the Church to come would not unfold unless serious efforts were undertaken to address the continuing development of the priest.

4. In many respects *The Program of Continuing Education of Priests* was a watershed. It provided a common ground to begin to address the educational and growth needs of the priest and was addressed mainly to directors of continuing education. This revised document, however, addresses itself to all priests ministering in the United States.

5. The last twelve years have been marked by many changes in the world, in the Church, and in the awareness of the priest himself. These years of development in continuing education have underscored the fact that not only are there new *directions* in education which can enhance priestly ministry, but there are also new *ways* of learning. Today the priest is much more conscious of the plurality found in all aspects of life, including his own ministry. All of this

---

[1] *Decree on the Ministry and Life of Priests*, 8.

challenges the Church, and the priest in particular, to look again at *The Program of Continuing Education of Priests*.

6. Directors of continuing education throughout the country have suggested that changes in our society and in the Church call for a new statement that reflects the current social and ecclesial situation.[2]

7. What are some of these changes? First, there is the experience of priesthood within the context of continuing social and cultural shifts. Second, there is the growing expectation within our society that all professional persons are accountable for professional updating. The Church, too, identifies this as an important element in the life of the priest. Third, lay persons are now in more active roles in the Church; the phenomenon of shared ministry raises new questions for continuing education of the priest.

2. The Experience of Continuing Education

8. The vision and the experience of continuing education have greatly expanded over the last twelve years. Directors of continuing education have become more sophisticated in their understanding of how adults learn, and, as a result, they have set new goals and priorities.

9. Programs for the priest conducted a decade ago were frequently styled in a rather didactic manner. While valuing the lecture method, directors came to understand that more involvement by participants is also valuable. New questions and issues arose which could not adequately be handled simply by the relaying of new information. Thus, continuing education directors began to place a greater emphasis on a process approach whereby the priest could engage in critical reflection and dialogue within himself and also be in dialogue with the theological or technical expertise offered by a presenter.

10. Other factors have influenced changes in continuing education for the priest. Studies of the psychological and emotional maturity of the priest suggested that greater attention is needed in these areas of a priest's life. Furthermore, renewed interest in prayer and spirituality has influenced the style of a priest's retreat and other spiritual programs and has spurred the development of programs to train spiritual directors.

11. The publication of other studies on priestly life and ministry also has had an effect on the continuing education of the priest.[3] Recent findings on the causes of stress and its effects on ministry prompted directors of continuing education to develop programs to assist the

---

[2]See unpublished survey conducted by the National Organization for Continuing Education of Roman Catholic Clergy, Inc. (NOCERCC), Chicago, 1982.

[3]See *As One Who Serves: Reflections on the Pastoral Ministry of Priests in the United States* (Washington, D.C.: USCC Office of Publishing and Promotion Services, 1977).

priest in dealing experientially with stress, rather than simply to provide information about stress.[4]

12. In a similar way, continuing education directors have established preaching institutes with the encouragement of the United States bishops.[5] The growing realization of the importance of quality preaching has produced a type of institute or workshop which provides the opportunity for the preacher to pray, reflect, and develop creatively a homily together with his peers.

13. The growing interest in sabbaticals over the last ten years reflects the priest's need to experience extended periods of learning in an environment apart from his day-to-day ministry. More and more, dioceses and religious communities now encourage the priest to take sabbatical leave on a regular basis.

14. During these past twelve years, a variety of support groups has fostered the growth and development of priests. These formal and informal groups allow priests to gather in dialogue, prayer, mutual support, and challenge for ministry. Several dioceses and communities require the priest to establish personal and ministerial goals for himself. Continuing education means accountability, and the Church has attempted to respond accordingly.

15. The diversification and specialization of ministry over the last several years have called for the formation of programs and training systems for priests in special areas of ministry. Dioceses and religious communities have also initiated programs for priests at various points sensitive in life and ministry, for example, first assignment, first pastorate, and retirement.

16. A new awareness of learning as a lifelong dynamic has been at the root of many of the changes in style, method, and direction of continuing education programs. The twelve years since the publication of *The Program of Continuing Education of Priests* have been productive indeed. Certainly some priests remain uninterested in their continuing growth and renewal, but overall, priests have taken an active interest. Having learned much in these years, it is now time to chart a program that reflects this particular moment in the history of our culture and Church, where today's priest lives and ministers.

17. Language changes, as do culture, life styles, and needs. *The Program of Continuing Education of Priests* used the term *continuing education* to refer to any learning after ordination, including growth both internal (spiritual, social, psychological) and external (cultural changes, theological disciplines, and pastoral skills). *Continuing education* also referred

---

[4]See *The Priest and Stress* (Washington, D.C.: USCC Office of Publishing and Promotion Services, 1982).

[5]See *Fulfilled in Your Hearing: The Homily in the Sunday Assembly* (Washington, D.C.: USCC Office of Publishing and Promotion Services, 1982).

to the growth of the whole person in various situations apart from the academic setting.

18. In recent years, terms like *ongoing formation* and *continuing growth and learning* have replaced the phrase *continuing education*. The use of new terminology is more than a bow to the latest trends. Instead, this new language reflects a new awareness. Continuing formation conveys the notion of growth as a lifelong dialogue-journey through which a priest comes to greater awareness of self, others, and God. Therefore, in what follows, the overarching concept of continuing formation will be used to convey the many faceted dimensions of the priest's ongoing development.

Chapter I
The Priest Today: Many Contexts

Do not conform yourselves to this age but be transformed by the renewal of your mind, so that you may judge what is God's will, what is good, pleasing and perfect (Rom 12:2).

1. Preliminary Remarks

19. The reality of growth in the Christian life cannot be denied; it is fundamental to the Gospel and preaching of Jesus. The priest, as every Christian, is on a journey and is called to a greater openness to God's graciousness and love. Any discussion of continuing formation and education of priests needs to be grounded in an understanding of conversion as an ongoing process both personal and communal. Though conversion takes place within the inner life of each person, it is never a private affair and conversion occurs in every facet of one's life — intellectual, affective, social, spiritual, moral, and ecclesial.[6]

20. The priest is called to that same conversion he proclaims and professes as a part of his own ministry. With the people he serves, he will find that conversion always consists in discovering God's mercy and experiencing his kind and patient love. In this knowledge of God as the God of mercy, he will find the source of a conversion that is not merely a momentary, interior act but a permanent state of mind.[7] This continuing conversion is often accelerated by a word, an event, or a personal witness that calls him to assess his present style

---

[6]The process of conversion and transformation is key in the theology of Bernard J. F. Lonergan. See for example Lonergan, "Theology in Its New Context" in *Theology of Renewal*, L. K. Shook, ed. (New York: Herder and Herder, 1968), pp. 34-68. See also Edward K. Braxton, *The Wisdom Community* (New York: Paulist Press, 1980), pp. 71-100.

[7]See *Dives in Misericordia* (Washington, D.C.: USCC Office of Publishing and Promotion Services, 1981), no. 13.

of life and consider another. When confronted with a new perspective, one may choose to enter into dialogue and undertake an uncertain journey, or one may choose to retreat. Those who choose the dialogue-journey are open to the possibility of deeper freedom and richer life.[8]

21. It is in the context of this journey of deepening conversion that the priest is invited to discern new paths for growth and development, new ways to improve his life and ministry. He is encouraged to be a healthy, maturing, and curious person, open to learning. Why? Because he, like the One he follows, is called to serve.[9]

22. The bishops of the United States underscored this when they stated:

> Every priest has a right and an obligation to continue his spiritual growth and education. He has a right to strong support from his superiors, peers and the people he serves. He also has an obligation to his superiors and peers, but above all to his people to continue to grow in grace and knowledge.[10]

23. This journey is a lifelong endeavor. Personal growth, continuing formation, theological education, and human development, all of which lead to greater service to the People of God, are woven throughout the priest's entire life and ministry. A priest who takes advantage of these opportunities enhances his personal life and, more important, ministers to others with renewed vision and imagination.

2. The Context of Priestly Ministry

24. An understanding of the content and context of priesthood in the United States today is essential in order to focus on future directions for continuing formation. What are the pressures a priest faces today? What are the possibilities offered by contemporary society and by the Church? How does ministry itself affect the development of the priest?

25. A look at our culture and society reveals exciting possibilities for the future and real challenges for the present. Over the last twenty-five years our society has evolved more rapidly and in more diverse ways than ever before. While cultural shifts often raise to consciousness previously unknown values, cultural changes can also undermine traditional, deeply held values.

26. For example, our contemporary society has helped us realize the importance of affirming the gifts of all people in terms of their uniqueness. It has also brought us to a greater recognition of the place of

---

[8]See Robert E. Lauder, *The Priest as Person* (Whitinsville, Mass.: Affirmation Books, 1981), pp. 77ff.

[9]See Eugene H. Maly, ed., *The Priest and Sacred Scripture* (Washington, D.C.: USCC Office of Publishing and Promotion Services, 1971), pp. 6ff.

[10]*The Program of Continuing Education of Priests* (Washington, D.C.: USCC Office of Publishing and Promotion Services, 1972), p. 5.

women in society. These positive changes have affected the life and ministry of the priest.

27. On the other hand, the increasing stress on individuality, growing materialism, a new secularism, and an uncritical use of media in our culture have had a negative effect on the life of the Church and the ministry of the priest. It is in this shifting cultural context that the priest ministers and proclaims the Word of God.

28. The growth of the Hispanic, Asian, and other cultural populations in the United States presents a special challenge and a wonderful opportunity for the Church. As a priest encounters a new culture or social group, his vision and imagination are challenged; his intellect is opened to new horizons; his spirit is invited to dialogue. Certainly the Hispanic and other cultures present in our society offer the priest and the Church a rich heritage. However, if he is to minister effectively to these respective ethnic groups, he will need to study their language and try to understand their culture. This presence thus calls the priest and the Church to adopt new styles of ministry and to be more responsive to social and cultural needs and, especially in the case of refugees and minorities, the demands of justice.[11]

29. Within the sphere of the Church, one also finds new pressures and possibilities. The Church in which many priests were ordained no longer exists as it once did. The Second Vatican Council gave assent to a new theology and understanding of the Church, and church structures have been changing accordingly.

30. For example, a priest now has the opportunity for more shared responsibility with his superior or bishop, in keeping with the renewal of the Church. However, some priests feel that new structures frustrate their ministry. Thus, the exercise of legitimate authority becomes a disproportionate issue in many instances. While the abuse of authority can be a serious issue for many, external tension and conflict and internal dissatisfaction are part of the postconciliar life of the Church.

31. The priest, like other members of the Church, claims his adulthood, which means conscious responsibility for the conduct of his life and ministry. Mature freedom presses toward fuller dialogue with authority and with one's peers; it is an important factor in a priest's continuing formation.

32. The priest discovers demands placed on him which he may or may not be able to manage. Called to servant leadership and effective proclamation of the good news, he is accountable for the mission of the Church—not by himself, but with the community he serves. The People of God expect the priest to exercise responsible ministry, and

---

[11]For a detailed understanding of the importance of the Hispanic presence in our culture and in the Church in the United States, see the United States bishops' recent pastoral letter on Hispanic Ministry, *The Hispanic Presence: Challenge and Commitment* (Washington, D.C.: USCC Office of Publishing and Promotion Services, 1983).

they sometimes will challenge him when that ministry appears less than that.

33. As a spiritual leader, the priest witnesses to the gift of discipleship through a life of holiness. People view him as a person of conversion, as one deepening his life in the Lord, and therefore, as one able to help others deepen their own spiritual lives as well. The priest is more aware than ever of his call to holiness and, at the same time, of his own brokenness.

34. The Church today comprises a variety of organizations, groups, structures, and individuals. It is a community of people with different gifts and ministries designed for the growth of the Body of Christ. The priest needs to work with all these elements and with his peers in a collegial manner. This means he takes seriously the role of the laity and religious, women and men, in the life of the Church.

35. For most priests, ministry unfolds in the local parish community. Faith and prayer are the cornerstone of parish life. Effective preaching and celebration of the sacramental life of the community are the two fundamental avenues by which the priest makes visible and tangible the experience of the death and rising of Christ. Authentic preaching and worship require the priest to enter the ritual moment in such a way that the union between God and humankind is evident.

36. The priest

> stands under the Word he proclaims, the Word which interprets and judges his own life and the life of his people. In other words, he is challenged to the same faith, the same conversion, the same love and thanksgiving to which he calls his people. He immerses himself in the same mystery taking place and involves himself in the action he performs, becoming thereby a transparent witness in his own person to what he expresses in sacred word and symbols.[12]

37. This expression of faith derives from an intimate knowledge of one's community, so that the priest shares word and sacrament with his people in a creative and sensitive way. When he coordinates the ministries of others in his community, and celebrates those ministries in Eucharist, the priest is with his community in an experience of faith.

38. The priest knows how people in many differing situations need compassion and understanding. They look to the priest as friend and counselor in a variety of problems and issues, many of which he has not confronted in previous years of ministry. These situations in ministry call for flexibility and adaptation and sometimes make a priest acutely aware of his own powerlessness.

39. In addition to these demands and possibilities, the priest realizes

---

[12]Ernest E. Larkin, O. Carm., and Gerald T. Broccolo, eds., *Spiritual Renewal of the American Priesthood* (Washington, D.C.: USCC Office of Publishing and Promotion Services, 1972), p. 22.

that justice has a special place in his own life and ministry. Since justice is a constitutive element of the Gospel and mission of the Church, the priest strives to form his own conscience so that he may become more committed to the promotion of justice in the world.

40. Many priests have had the experience of living with minority people, the poor, the oppressed, in this country and in the Third World. The experiences with injustice often galvanize the priest's own option for the poor and challenge him to reflect on his own life style and ministry. In many respects, the priest finds that he is being evangelized by the poor as he ministers among them.

41. Still, it becomes difficult for a priest to confront injustice in society in the name of the Church when he observes that the dictates of justice may not always be observed by those within the Church itself. He thus perceives injustice within a Church that at the same time earnestly calls the priest to stand for justice.

42. Attentiveness to his own journey allows the priest to see these demands more sharply and to see, also, the possibilities for ministry. When he provides for his own nurture as well as for the nurture of the people he serves, the priest lives the Gospel as both gift and call. Were he to regard demands and pressures from the culture and from the Church only in a negative way, the priest would miss the gift of life and growth that is offered him.

43. Besides the present cultural and church context, the priest encounters other more personal factors which affect his life and ministry. Throughout his journey of faith the priest experiences new questions that previous faith responses cannot always satisfy. This fact presents itself both as challenge and as opportunity.

44. The increasing number of nonordained persons involved in ministry pushes the priest to question his own identity and role within the Church. As people ask him to do many things he does not sense he is equipped to manage, the priest may experience a certain amount of uneasiness about himself.

45. Relating to himself and others as a human person and as a priest, the experience of loneliness, the need to relate intimately with others, and the demands of affective growth compel the priest to look continually at his vocation and life and to see the future in new perspectives.[13] The demands of a celibate commitment also place various pressures on the priest. Though these pressures are normal and to be expected, the priest may not have received the necessary support and resources for coping with his affective life.

46. The average age of priests in the United States is steadily increasing. As the priest looks toward his senior years, he wants to approach them with serenity and dignity. However, due to circumstances, a

---

[13]See *A Reflection Guide on Human Sexuality and the Ordained Priesthood* (Washington, D.C.: USCC Office of Publishing and Promotion Services, 1983), pp. 7-12.

priest is often compelled to view these years with a sense of loss. Thus, it is important that the senior priest be treated as a person of wisdom and experience in spite of the aging process which reduces his energy.[14]

47. Priests today are expected to develop a positive attitude toward shared ministry. This means that they be conscious of the identity of the Church as a fellowship of life, charity, and truth; that it was intended by Christ as an instrument of redemption; and that there is present an interrelationship of their own ministerial priesthood and the priesthood of all the faithful.[15]

48. It is evident that the demands on time and energy create a stress unknown in former times. This stress compounds that created by heavy involvement in administrative work, fund raising, and personnel management for which the priest often has had little or no training.[16] Sharing ministry with others, however, stimulates and nourishes the priest in his ministry. This experience itself creates a receptive attitude toward shared ministry which is especially appropriate for one who is a "steward of the mysteries of God."[17]

49. There is, to be sure, much that is disquieting in the life and ministry of the priest. Yet, the possibilities for future growth that the present age offers far outweigh the problems at hand. Therefore, a pressing task before the Church is to design a course of action to promote the continuing formation of the priest. This is not simply a problem to be solved, but more important an opportunity for new life, conversion, and commitment to service as the dialogue-journey continues.

Chapter II
Motivation, Assessment, and Responsible Persons

May the God of our Lord Jesus Christ, the Father of glory, grant you a spirit of wisdom and insight to know him clearly. May he enlighten your innermost vision that you may know the great hope to which he has called you, the wealth of his glorious heritage to be distributed among the members of the church (Eph 1:17-18).

1. Motivation

50. Generating motivation for continued growth and development is always a challenge. Motivation requires both an internal desire to

---

[14]See *Fullness in Christ: A Report on a Study of Clergy Retirement* (Washington, D.C.: USCC Office of Publishing and Promotion Services, 1979).

[15]See *Lumen Gentium*, nos. 9-10.

[16]See *The Priest and Stress.*

[17]*Spiritual Renewal of the American Priesthood*, p. 14.

grow as well as awareness of the expectations of those served by the priest and of the competent authority.

51. Internal motivation presumes a level of self-knowledge acquired through withdrawal from the rhythm of work to examine one's life in a more receptive mode.

52. The rhythm of Sabbath time and ministry time reflects the dual reality of Christian life. This rhythm is deeply embedded in Hebrew culture and in Scripture, which stresses that being is as important as doing.[18] Currently our society is dominated by the contrary belief that one's existence is worthwhile solely in terms of achievement, production, and success. Christian wisdom says that one's being is as worthwhile as one's doing.[19]

53. The inclusion of Sabbath rest in the overall rhythm of life is essential for all people. A deliberately slowed-down pace, a spirit of play and celebration, time given to open receptive meditative prayer, the stretching of the mind and heart through reading and study, exploration of new avenues and disciplines of learning—all these characterize the quality of Sabbath time. Yet most people neglect this side of life; the complexities and demands of modern living tend to fill up all available space.

54. Priests are in a unique position to model the possibilities of Sabbath time for the People of God. Because the concept may be somewhat new to him, the priest will need the encouragement and support of others to move toward fashioning a schedule that respects this other side of ministry.

55. When he takes time apart, the priest is able to realize the challenges that lie before him. He can more properly assess those challenges and determine the best route to help him on his journey. Periodic reflection occasions the possibility of personal goal setting, another important factor in self-motivation.

56. External motivation is also important for continuing growth. Increasing expectations of the ordained minister by the laity and competent authority can foster a sense of mutual sharing in the life of the Church.

57. When such expectations do not have concrete support, affirmation, and appropriate forms of recognition, they can become pressure points for the priest. It is, therefore, important that the priest know that he is valued and appreciated by those who are in leadership and

---

[18]In Genesis, the creation account suggests that the time of rest at the end of creation is a time not only for worship of the Lord, but also a time for people to be re-created. This time is important as a regular part of one's life.

[19]For a more complete study of Sabbath time concept see Tilden Edwards, *Sabbath Time: Understanding and Practice for Contemporary Christians* (New York: Winston Press, 1985); Niels-Erik A. Andreasen, *The Christian Use of Time* (Nashville, Tenn.: Abingdon Press, 1978); Abraham J. Heschel, *The Sabbath: Its Meaning for Modern Man* (New York: Farrar, Straus, and Young, 1951).

authority and by those with whom he ministers. Each diocese and religious community can establish appropriate means of recognition of a priest's ministry, and each can develop and articulate expectations for each priest's ministry.

2. Assessment

58. Another important factor in motivation is assessment that is both an individual and communal effort. When a priest is drawn into a self-assessment process, his personal motivation is strengthened. When this process includes others in ministry, motivation for continuing formation is supported and affirmed.

59. For many, the term *assessment* raises questions and fears, especially when concerned with one's life, ministry, and competence. However, when placed within the context of servant leadership, assessment takes on a more positive tone.

60. First of all, the process of periodic assessment can be affirming. The primary objective of assessment is to provide the priest with the opportunity to view his ministry from a new perspective. Periodic assessment invites the priest to examine the different elements of his life in an open and positive manner and to critique his dispositions, attitudes, and work in light of the vision for ministry that he and the local Church have articulated and chosen.

61. Valuable insights for growth and development can be derived from one's peers, superior, and those with whom one is working. The purpose of their comments is to affirm what the priest is doing to meet his potential for ministry and to suggest what skills or learning are needed to make his ministry more effective. Obviously, this is a delicate process, but one that can promote trust and conversion.

62. The ordained minister—whether bishop, religious superior, priest, or deacon—should be subject to periodic assessment. Proper assessment implies designation of specific areas for future development in the life of each priest. The priest and those assisting him with periodic assessment need to remember that he is not omniscient, that there will always be areas of weakness, and that development and growth are lifelong endeavors. It is also important that the instruments used for periodic assessment need to be tested and regularly evaluated.

3. Responsible Persons

63. Motivation for continuing formation often comes from the people with whom the priest regularly interacts. These men and women have a responsibility to the priest, and he is likewise responsible to them for his own continued growth.

a. The Priest Himself

64. The priest himself has a responsibility to the Church and the people he serves; these expect that he continue his personal, spiritual development in a manner appropriate to his ministry. This means, among other things, that he will give first priority in his life to a deepening personal relationship with Christ through prayer and His special presence to priests in Word, sacrament, and in the people they serve. In addition, he will live an authentic and fruitful ecclesial life by keeping himself adequately informed of changes in church legislation and pastoral practice. It also means that he must remain alert to his own need for future emotional and attitudinal education and development. This is especially true in terms of colleague relationships with brother priests, deacons, women and men religious, and laity who minister with him side by side. In short, the priest has the obligation to care for whatever personal needs he discovers in his spiritual, intellectual, emotional, or relational life.

b. The Bishop or Religious Superior

65. The religious superior or bishop can encourage the priest to engage in continuing formation by his own participation in programs of personal growth and development. The bishop in collaboration with the presbyteral council ought to establish policies concerning minimal expectations, sabbaticals, adequate financial support, and the care of parishes when a priest is away for continuing formation events.

66. Furthermore, the bishop or superior can demonstrate his own commitment to continuing formation by the appointment of a competent director of continuing formation to whom is given appropriate authority and adequate funding. By so doing, the competent authority clearly states that the primary ministry of the director is the continuing formation of priests; active collaboration with the director underscores the importance of this ministry.

67. The bishop's or the superior's own enthusiasm for ongoing education and renewal is a sign to others of its genuine value. In addition, the priest expects his bishop's participation at continuing formation events designed to meet his own personal needs and to assist him in fulfilling his responsibilities as bishop. The priest should support his bishop when he chooses specific programs to do this.

68. Finally, the bishop must also communicate with and understand the needs of the religious priests serving in his diocese. Even though religious are involved in programs within their own communities, it is important for the bishop to encourage their participation in local and diocesan programs as well.

c. Staff Members

69. Those who work in close relationship with a priest, particularly staff and team members, have the opportunity to motivate and encourage him, especially if they have come to recognize the value of continuing formation in their own lives. When a priest and staff or priest and team experience continuing formation programs together a special bond and shared vision often result. This, too, provides new incentive and motivation for further growth and renewal.

d. The Community in Which the Priest Ministers

70. In addition to staff and team members, the people served also bear some responsibility toward the priest. They exercise this responsibility when they encourage the priest to acquire the appropriate skills and learning to care for their own pastoral needs. Parish council members are in a special position to encourage and motivate the priest for continuing formation.

e. The Presbyteral Council

71. The presbyteral council assists the bishop in his ministry and is thus accountable for promoting and encouraging the continuing formation of each priest. When the council by its advice and recommendations aids the bishop in establishing effective policies, programs, and procedures which support the growth of the priest, it acts in accord with its mandate to assist the bishop in promoting the pastoral welfare of all. Members of the presbyteral council exemplify this commitment to continuing formation by their own participation in the process of growth and renewal.[20]

f. The Diocesan Pastoral Council

72. According to the revised *Code of Canon Law*, the diocesan pastoral council assists the bishop in studying issues of pastoral concerns, and it suggests practical means for dealing with them. The council has the responsibility to make itself aware of the needs of priests and to assist them and the bishop in articulating how best to enrich presbyteral ministry.[21]

---

[20]See canon 495, *Code of Canon Law*, Latin-English Edition, Translation prepared under the auspices of the Canon Law Society of America, Washington, D.C., 1983.
[21]See canon 511, *Code of Canon Law*.

g. The Director of Continuing Education

73. The director of continuing formation of priests is one who has some education and formation in the field of growth and development. Among the director's primary responsibilities are to establish an on-going needs assessment of each priest, done both formally and informally, and to inform the priest of local, regional, and national events that can help him.

74. Personal contact with the director encourages and motivates priests both to pursue new programs of personal growth, education, and renewal and to strengthen their relationships with one another.

75. It is the director's responsibility to provide programs for the spiritual growth of the priest. Such programs include retreats, the designation and formation of spiritual directors, days of prayer and recollection, and the development of support groups which focus on spirituality. The director continually monitors these and other programs and events for their effectiveness. He also encourages priests to have their own personal spiritual director.

76. The director's own ministry and work is open to an evaluation, and the ministry programs and policies that are promoted need to undergo continual assessment. The director models the importance of continuing formation through active participation in continuing formation experiences. The director shares in the responsibility of the bishop and presbyteral council in formulating policies and directions for continuing formation. Finally, it is appropriate that each priest inform the director of his participation in various programs and events. This enables the director to keep accurate records of the personal and professional growth of the priests. The purpose of this record keeping is to inform the diocese or community of the knowledge and skills that a priest may offer because of the training and formation he has acquired.

77. In the future, dioceses and religious communities will need to give serious consideration to the urgency and importance of continuing formation by naming a director who will be able to give sufficient attention, time, and energy to the continuing formation of priests. For larger dioceses and religious communities, this means a full-time person. In other instances, it means giving the director the necessary time, funding, and support to fulfill this primary responsibility.

Chapter III
Programs and Resources

Ever since we heard this we have been praying for you unceasingly and asking that you may attain full knowledge of his will through perfect wisdom and spiritual insight. Then you will lead a life worthy of the Lord and pleasing to him in every way. You will multiply good works of every sort and grow in the knowledge of God (Col 1:9-10).

1. Introductory Remarks

78. Continuing formation events and programs provide for a diversity of needs among all priests in a particular diocese or community. Programs with proper balance of theological information, critical reflection, dialogue, and discussion will help a priest achieve a more integrated growth in his intellectual, emotional, and spiritual life.

79. Continuing formation events for the priest can be greatly enhanced on occasion by the presence and participation of religious and of lay women and men, especially those with whom he works. Also, it is sometimes appropriate to invite continuing formation personnel from other religious traditions to participate in programs for priests.

80. At times the competent authority will require the participation of every priest at a specific program or event. This may be necessary because certain issues need the attention of the entire presbyterate.

81. If at times priests are not mandated to attend all conferences, programs, and events in a given diocese or community, it is important that dioceses and religious communities establish minimal requirements for all priests. The expectations of canon 279, § 2 would seem to warrant such an arrangement.[22] This could be done by requiring a certain number of documented hours each year in continuing formation programs.[23]

---

[22]Canon 279, §2, *Code of Canon Law,* is pertinent in this context: "In accord with the prescriptions of particular law, priests are to attend pastoral lectures which are to be held after priestly ordination; at times determined by the same particular law they are also to attend lectures and theological meetings or conferences which afford them opportunities to acquire a fuller knowledge of the sacred sciences and of pastoral methods."

[23]As an example of this requirement, several dioceses have established policies that require every priest to log between thirty and fifty hours each year in some form of formal continuing formation program.

2. *Programs*

a. Sabbaticals

82. Sabbaticals offer priests the opportunity to be renewed through a rest, a change of pace, and freedom from the stress of ministry and other concerns. When a priest acquires additional theological understanding, pastoral skills, and personal growth during a sabbatical, there are obvious benefits for the people he serves.

83. Superiors exercise responsible leadership when they not only develop and promote sabbatical policies, but also engage in sabbatical time on a regular basis themselves. Periodic sabbaticals are of such importance to the personal development and growth of all clergy that diocesan bishops must educate and interpret to the faithful the need on their part to forego at times some priestly service.

84. Sabbaticals may include a formal program in an established institution of learning, several short-term programs, or an extended period of learning designed by the priest himself. Sabbaticals should concentrate primarily on theological, pastoral, or ministerial areas of concern. However, since human growth in every facet of life contributes to the quality of ministry, a priest might use some sabbatical time for studying in other disciplines (e.g., the arts, music, languages, etc.).

85. When a diocese or religious community establishes a sabbatical policy that includes every priest, it recognizes the importance of periodic renewal and encourages the priest to consider taking time away from his regular ministry. Established sabbatical policies include guidelines for appropriate selection of programs, financial support, and a review process to assess the sabbatical's effectiveness.

b. Spiritual Development Programs

86. *The Program of Continuing Education of Priests* stresses that the most important aspect of continuing formation is that it foster the spiritual growth and renewal of the priest. Spirituality is not separate from ministry. In fact, the spiritual journey finds one of its primary sources of life in ministry. As he interacts with people in ministry, the priest discovers God's presence, and he knows that those he serves look to him to mediate the presence of God and help them unite the human and the divine.

87. Those who prepare programs of spiritual formation for the priest recognize that while the journey of each priest is unique, there are certain common experiences, such as the Liturgy of the Hours and the Eucharist, which are part of every priest's life.[24] Therefore, programs which assist the priest in understanding the liturgy as central in the dynamic of his spiritual journey can do much to help the priest integrate life and ministry.

88. When the priest opens himself to the experience of different forms of prayer and worship, both private and communal, he is better able to assist others in their spiritual lives. Retreat experiences and prayer programs are a vital part of the continuing formation process. With the increasing demand for spiritual direction, it is particularly urgent that dioceses and religious communities provide resources for priests to become more competent as spiritual directors. This implies, of course, that the priest himself has his own spiritual director.

89. Decisions made in a context of prayer and openness to the Spirit of God require some understanding of the nature of discernment and the spiritual dynamics of decision making. Programs concerned with the process of discernment provide an additional service to the priest.

c. Local Workshops and Institutes

90. Local workshops and institutes are especially useful for the priest because they provide him with a common experience shared by his peers in ministry. Not only do these local programs focus on unique needs and issues, but they are also less expensive and eliminate the inconvenience of long travel.

91. Furthermore, programs which enlist the cooperation and support of the presbyterate can affirm the talent and ministry of others who serve in the local Church by inviting them to lead programs and lend their expertise.

---

[24]In this context it is good to recall the traditional wisdom of the Church reflected in canon 276, *Code of Canon Law:*

§1. In leading their lives clerics are especially bound to pursue holiness because they are consecrated to God by a new title in the reception of orders as dispensers of God's mysteries in the service of His people.

§2. In order for them to pursue this perfection:

1° first of all they are faithfully and untiringly to fulfill the duties of pastoral ministry;

2° they are to nourish their spiritual life from the two-fold table of Sacred Scripture and the Eucharist; priests are therefore earnestly invited to offer the sacrifice of the Eucharist daily and deacons are earnestly invited to participate daily in offering it;

3° priests as well as deacons aspiring to the priesthood are obliged to fulfill the liturgy of the hours daily in accordance with the proper and approved liturgical books; permanent deacons, however, are to do the same to the extent it is determined by the conference of bishops;

4° they are also bound to make a retreat according to the prescriptions of particular law;

5° they are to be conscientious in devoting time regularly to mental prayer, in approaching the sacrament of penance frequently, in cultivating special devotion to the Virgin Mother of God, and in using other common and particular means for their sanctification.

92. Cooperative programs between diocesan and religious communities on a regional level are another source of growth and development for the priest.

d. Ministry to Other than Parish Communities

93. In addition to parish service there are many priestly ministries in the Church today.[25] The Church reflects its commitment to provide competent and qualified ministers for these other ministries by the appropriate screening of candidates and by adequate training for priests undertaking these ministries. Policies that require screening and training for such ministries support a commitment to excellence.

e. Newly Ordained

94. The first years of a priest's life are crucial to a healthy life and ministry in the future.[26] The newly ordained clergy have particular concerns which need attention at the local level. An internship program for the new priest is a very effective means to continue his theological reflection begun during the seminary years.

95. An internship program should be made mandatory in every diocese and religious community to achieve the best results. Such a program would include a structured support group in which the new priest experiences the ministry of an experienced priest and would provide an opportunity to establish new friendships. Too, it could help the new priest develop good working habits for ministry and for his continuing formation. Internship programs could also diffuse many potentially volatile situations and help the priest adjust to a new social situation which involves the active ministry of others.

96. In addition to assisting the new priest, an internship program provides continuing formation for parish teams and pastors who will receive him into the parish. In many cases, these latter need as much formation as the new priest if the ministry of all is to benefit. Finally, an internship program can bring the new priest into a healthy rela-

---

[25]These ministries might include chaplains in prisons and hospitals, spiritual directors in seminaries and retreat houses, educators, youth ministers, priests who work in diocesan offices, priests who assume ministry among minority groups, priests who work with separated and divorced Catholics, etc.

[26]The Bishops' Committee on Priestly Life and Ministry has completed a study, *The Health of American Catholic Priests: A Report and a Study* (Washington, D.C.: USCC Office of Publishing and Promotion Services, 1985). It indicates that the first five years of a priest's ministry determine to a large extent how the priest will deal with his life and ministry situations, either in a healthy or unhealthy manner. This data supports the need for good internship programs for the younger priest. See also David O'Rourke, *The First Year of Priesthood* (Huntington, Ind.: Our Sunday Visitor Press, 1978).

tionship with his peers and develop a sense of brotherhood in the presbyterate.

f. New Pastors

97. A priest who is called to be a pastor for the first time faces new challenges and opportunities. He realizes that different skills are required as he looks at parish renewal, staff relationships, administrative questions, and the new context in which he is called to serve. Well-designed programs for new pastors provide some assurance that the priest will enter his first pastorate with confidence and the necessary skills for effective ministry.

98. If a diocese is unable to develop a new pastors' program on its own, this can be accomplished very well on a regional basis in cooperation with other dioceses and religious communities and with the assistance of available national resources.[27]

g. Postordination Degrees

99. Many institutions of higher learning have heeded the recommendation to provide extended and in-depth programs leading to professional and academic degrees for those in ministry. Seminaries, colleges, and universities assist the priest in his continuing formation by developing advanced degree programs in ministry available to those seeking further academic training. These and other degree programs give priests an opportunity to grow in the competent practice of pastoral ministry. Participation in these programs often sparks a desire for lifelong learning.

h. Skills Development

100. Leadership, management, listening, and conflict-resolution skills are but a few of the areas that require special attention in the priest's formation. Dioceses and religious communities can assist priests toward attaining the necessary competencies for pastoral ministry when they provide programs in these areas.

101. Since the Eucharist is the community's focal point, liturgical and preaching skills deserve particular attention. Institutes and workshops designed to improve homily preparation and presentation as well as liturgical celebration assist the priest to be a more effective leader and presider in the eucharistic community. The develoment of these skills,

---

[27]The National Organization for Continuing Education of Roman Catholic Clergy, Inc. (NOCERCC) has a listing of new pastors programs that have been used throughout the country. This organization is also available to assist with the development of diocesan and regional programs for new pastors.

however, requires an openness on the part of the priest to review periodically his own style of celebrating liturgy and his preaching.

i. Preretirement/Retirement

102. The concept of retirement has a unique interpretation for priests. While it may relieve priests of certain administrative burdens or regular pastoral responsibilities, it is not intended to deprive the senior priest of opportunities for priestly ministry.

103. It is true that retirement can provide one of the more difficult moments in the priest's life. It tends to be a time of deep, emotional questioning. A priest may have a sense of anxiety about changing forms of ministry; he may experience loneliness in ways he never had before; he may suffer some lack of self-esteem; he may feel unneeded or even discarded.

104. On the other hand, retirement can be a time of deep fulfillment, a time of bringing one's life and ministry into sharper focus. It is a time when one can move to elderhood in the community of believers.

105. Programs for the senior priest can help make this time in his life fulfilling. Programs that begin several years prior to retirement offer the priest adequate time to prepare for this new phase of ministry. Such programs should enable and encourage those areas of priestly ministry permitted by the health and energies of the retired. It is extremely important that the senior priest feel welcomed and invited to participate in continuing formation programs with other priests and to have programs specifically designed for him.[28]

j. Physical and Emotional Well-Being

106. Ministry requires the health of the whole person. A religious community or diocese provides for the physical, emotional, and psychological development of its priests by actively promoting programs along these lines.

107. It is advantageous to develop a habit of regular exercise and periodic physical examinations so that the ministry and spirituality of one's entire priesthood be pursued in a healthy and holistic context. Of similar importance are issues related to the psychosexual maturity of priests which need to be faced in the course of renewal. Honestly facing issues of loneliness, sexuality, relationships, intimacy, feelings of inadequacy, and psychological immaturity can be positive and healing when discussed with competent professionals. Emotional development is a vital factor in the continuing formation of priests.[29]

---

[28]See *Fullness in Christ*, pp. 14-18.

[29]*A Reflection Guide on Human Sexuality and the Ordained Priesthood* presents an excellent means for priests to reflect together on their call to love and serve all those people whose lives touch theirs.

k. Priest-to-Priest Ministry

108. In several dioceses and religious communities the priest is encouraged to minister to his peers on a one-to-one basis and in small groups. In this way, the priest critically reflects on his own life situation and examines his ministry in light of the mission of the Church. Through such a process he is enabled to make concrete decisions concerning his life and future ministry with the support, challenge, and prayer of fellow priests with whom he shares his journey.

109. When a religious community or diocese establishes such ministry in a formal way, it provides a place for the priest to be at home with his peers, for it gives permission to speak of the hopes and fears that lie deep within the heart and spirit.

l. Self-Education

110. Sometimes new ideas and insights come in the quiet of one's personal reading, prayer, and reflection. Thus, it is important that priests be familiar with at least one good theological journal or periodical and read it on a regular basis to remain abreast of new developments in theology and in pastoral ministry. Current books in theology and pastoral ministry can provide a stimulus for learning and growth. Media materials (e.g., video and audio tapes) are also useful for self-education. In all cases, it is the responsibility of the continuing formation director to advise priests where these current materials can be found.

3. *Resources*

111. Resources within a diocese or religious community may be very rich, but not always obvious. One of the first tasks facing continuing formation is the discovery and promotion of these resources. Some of the resources available for continuing formation are found in the local church community itself, while others are available on a broader level. It is the continuing formation director's responsibility to make these resources known to the priests of the diocese or religious community. During the last decade programs have been developed *nationally* to assist the local Church and religious communities in the spiritual renewal of priests. These national resources continue to give vision and thrust to local renewal efforts.

a. Church Resources

112. Many dioceses and religious communities have seminaries at their disposal. This is a valuable resource for priestly growth. The seminary's primary objective is the preparation and formation of the candidate for ordination, but it can serve other areas as well. By instilling in the seminarian an attitude of lifelong learning, the seminary helps him realize his potential for ministry.[30]

113. The seminary may also provide priests with various academic and degree programs and can open its regular course curriculum and spiritual formation resources to assist priests in their ongoing growth and formation. There are other resources the seminary can provide. The facilities of the seminary may be offered to priests for private study or for group meetings or workshops. The seminary library is a valuable resource for continuing one's reading and reflection on matters of current interest. A priest might also wish to experience the liturgy in a different setting. The seminary affords this opportunity.

114. The faculty and staff of the seminary can be of valuable assistance in the planning and preparation of programs for a diocese or community. Furthermore, students can benefit from interaction with area clergy when these priests are present at the seminary.

115. Since the seminary is usually involved in ecumenism, programs involving other religious traditions can provide a wealth of opportunities for the continuing formation of the priest. Finally, utilization of the seminary's recreational facilities can assist the priest in the maintenance of good health.

116. Catholic colleges and universities also offer a rich arena for learning. While being faithful to their own mission, these institutions can place their resources, personnel, and facilities at the disposal of the local Church for continuing formation activities. The priest might choose courses at these institutions for audit or credit. While his primary concerns should relate to theological disciplines or pastoral skills, his study may include other fields helpful to his personal development.

117. Most dioceses have some type of spiritual or retreat center available to the Catholic community. Priests are encouraged to become familiar with these centers and discover how their resources might provide a valuable means of continuing information for them.

---

[30]See *The Program of Priestly Formation*, Third Edition (Washington, D.C.: USCC Office of Publishing and Promotion Services, 1982), pp 67-68, nos. 243-245. These paragraphs suggest that study leaves and sabbaticals are in order for seminary personnel and they should model this concern for personal and professional growth for seminarians. It should be noted as well that individual or programmed calls upon the seminary for assistance with continuing formation must always recognize that the primary purpose of the seminary is the preparation of candidates for the priesthood. Neither the seminary itself nor its personnel and resources should be diverted from that primary purpose by other needs, however great (cf. *The Program of Priestly Formation*, p. 8, no. 19).

It is also well to emphasize here the recommendations of *The Program of Priestly Formation*, p. 16, no. 44 and pp. 61-62, nos. 224-25, which indicate the importance of the theological proficiency that should be developed throughout a priest's life, as well as the position of the seminary in relation to such development, taking into consideration the caution mentioned above.

118. Communication is essential to learning. One form of ongoing communication is a newsletter which informs priests of programs, institutes, and workshops. A newsletter is an opportunity for priests to share some experiences and reflections in articles and columns, which they themselves may write. The director of continuing formation is responsible for the development of such a newsletter.

b. Ecumenical and Interreligious Resources

119. The ecumenical dimension of continuing formation places the priest in dialogue with Christians of other traditions. These traditions also provide their own ministers with new opportunities for learning, and they may be open to Catholic clergy. The fullest kind of interreligious dialogue initiates contact with the Jewish community and other religious groups, such as Moslems, Hindus, and Buddhists. When a priest learns with members of these traditions, he learns to appreciate and value their spiritual and intellectual disciplines.

c. Community Resources

120. Every civic-social community, no matter how small, has some resources available for the priest's own continuing formation. Secular institutions of higher learning (whether large universities or small community colleges) offer a wide range of programs, events, and activities that are available for the priest's growth.
121. By spending time at local libraries, museums, and concert halls, the priest can grow in his appreciation of the arts, music, poetry, and the sciences. While these subjects are sometimes presumed to be unrelated to ministry, they can bring the priest into contact with a more inclusive life view and thus assist his ongoing formation.
122. Other community resources are courses, seminars, and workshops in almost every field of learning. It would serve the priest well to look for and receive information on a regular basis about these opportunities.

4. Life-sharing Groups

123. Small, intentional, and well-focused faith- and life-sharing groups attend to the growth of the priest at the spirtual, intellectual, emotional, professional, and relational levels. Because priests live in a complex web of relationships and responsibilities, they can benefit from a variety of life-sharing groups. While it is not necessary that priests participate in several, consideration should be given to joining at least one.
124. For some, a group composed only of priests is extremely valuable for a sense of belonging and fraternity with those who share the same

vocation. A healthy group of this kind will not reenforce a status-quo mentality or promote clericalism. Rather, it will challenge every member to grow.

125. The priest can grow in his faith through life-sharing in a group with others who also minister in the Church: lay people and religious, women and men. The dynamics of this kind of group can enable one to appreciate the diversity of gifts residing in the Church. Ordained and lay ministers who share their faith and life struggles together are more likely to grow in trust of one another.

126. Other possibilities for life- and faith-sharing groups are ecumenical gatherings representing several Christian traditions or groups made up of a priest together with laity, whose major responsibility is the *world*. Regular gatherings in these and other groups can strengthen the possibility of sharing in prayer. They can explore relationships of priest and people and can discuss mutual reponsibilities for growth and renewal. All of these, in turn, can provide enrichment when the priest prepares his homilies.

Chapter IV
The Future

127. These reflections on the continuing formation of the priest stem from the experience and developments of the past decade. Much has been accomplished toward renewing the whole Church; yet, the Church and the priest are pilgrims in this world, always encountering new situations and needs. This pilgrimage, however, often tends to leave the Church and the priest with a sense of incompleteness.

128. Our faith is in a living God who calls the priest to continuing growth and renewal through conversion. As the priest approaches the third millennium, he looks to the future with hope. He does not see the responsibility of conversion as a task or burden, but as a wonderful opportunity for his personal life and for his ministry. The priest knows that conversion involves his whole being. Consequently, he looks for ways in the future to develop the spiritual, emotional, intellectual, relational, social, moral, and ecclesial aspects of his life.

129. Genuine growth is possible only when there is openness to change. Looking to the future, the priest may experience ambiguity about appropriate directions for his continued growth and development. In spite of this he can find some indicators which will help him understand his own and the Church's needs for the future. Some of these indicators and factors which point to a society yet to be born include those following.

130. Spirituality remains at the center of growth for priests. Contemporary spirituality emphasizes the growth of the person as holistic. It recognizes the interaction between the spiritual and material and sees the correlation between the personal and communal dimensions of spiritual life.

131. The interrelationship between spiritual and wider human growth calls for understanding and appreciation of the balance between the rational and intuitive. The world of symbols has once again taken its rightful place alongside the rational and discursive. The *rediscovery* of these intuitive elements allows the mystical dimension to play a key role in constructing the Church and society of the future. When a priest explores the spiritual, he can find in the mystical dimension of his life new energy, ideas, and vision to help him in the practical working out of his life and ministry. In so doing, the priest moves away from a vision of ministry seen in purely functional terms and goes beyond management by objectives.

132. As the Church evolves, more new ministries will develop which undoubtedly will challenge the priest to develop new skills and talents. The priest who is open to growth and development will help unfold new gifts and talents in ministry. He will become more knowledgeable of how various sytems work as well as discover better ways of resolving conflict. The priest then will be able to change what no longer serves the needs of the Church or the human family. In the future, social analysis will be an important tool to help the priest reflect and discern with others the signs of the times.

133. Our culture and society will continue to evolve. As they do, and as technology grows, continuing formation programs will need to take note of how these technological developments help or hinder the growth of the priest. Continuing formation oportunities will most likely include interdisciplinary learning which integrates the theological and pastoral dimensions with the technological.

134. As ecumenical developments take place, and as Christians come to greater clarity about our common vision and purpose, the priest will need to be a person who can lead people to new levels of communion.

135. The demands of justice in the world today call for the growth of communities in which personal character is developed and manifested. As leaders of this type of community, priests will need to look for ways to develop their own commitment to values that at times may be countercultural.

136. The priest of the future will need to be open and receptive to qualities and values found in the cultures of racial and ethnic groups as these express their legitimate desire to take their place in the Church in the United States.

137. The experience of the suffering faces of Christ in his sisters and brothers can only open the priest to discover anew the Christian meaning of human suffering, to realize again that conversion and renewal, change and growth are often difficult communally as well as personally. As the priest becomes more acutely aware of threats to humanity in the second half of our century—such as the horrible threat of nuclear war—he will want to find ways to speak to such issues that burden the hearts of men, women, and children.[31]

138. The priest of the future will be one who is himself evangelized by those with whom he works. He will learn what missioners have discovered about *reverse-mission*, that is, that the priest will receive healing and service, will be ministered unto, as he serves his sisters and brothers.

139. All of this requires of the priest a continued willingness to be stretched by the Word of God, as Mary was open to move and respond to the call of God's providence in her life. She, whose receptivity to God's urgings moved her beyond the scope of normal human limits, offers a model for the priest in his journey of continuing formation. This journey, the dynamic of conversion, the call to commitment go on into the future until the Lord shall come to glory.

---

[31] Continuing formation also includes a knowledge and understanding of recent pastoral letters by the United States Catholic bishops, e.g., the pastoral letter *The Challenge of Peace: God's Promise and Our Response* (Washington, D.C.: USCC Office of Publishing and Promotion Services, 1983). This and other recent pastoral letters present an excellent model for the kind of dialogue and collaboration that should occur in the Church and that will bring about future growth and development for all.

Rejection of the MX Missile

*A Letter Written to Each Member of the
U.S. Congress by the President of the
United States Catholic Conference*

March 15, 1985

Dear Members of Congress:

1. I write as president of the U.S. Catholic Conference to urge you to vote against funding for the MX missile. The USCC's opposition is based on two considerations: the potentially destabilizing impact of this weapons system on the nuclear arms race and its cost, viewed in light of pressing human needs here and elsewhere in the world.

2. I am aware of the president's position that the MX is part of the U.S. defense posture and negotiating strategy at the Geneva talks. The USCC strongly supports the resumption of the U.S.-Soviet negotiations; as bishops, we pray for their successful outcome. We do not enter the MX debate to provide new strategic or technical advice. Rather, as our opposition to the MX arises from a prudential but soundly based moral judgment, so our intervention at this time reflects the conviction that key moral values are implicated in the legislative decision that faces you. It is these that I wish to discuss in more detail.

3. In their pastoral letter of 1983, *The Challenge of Peace: God's Promise and Our Response*, the U.S. bishops opposed the deployment of weapons which are themselves "likely to be vulnerable to attack" yet also possess a capability of rendering the other side's retaliatory forces vulnerable. Such weapons, the pastoral observed, "may seem to be useful primarily in a first strike." We specifically noted that the MX raises such fears.

4. Testifying on behalf of USCC before the House Foreign Affairs Committee a year after the pastoral letter's publication, Cardinal Joseph L. Bernardin of Chicago and Archbishop John J. O'Connor of New York took up the question of what the bishops meant by their "strictly conditioned acceptance" of the strategy of deterrence. They made the point that such acceptance requires ongoing scrutiny of weapons proposed for addition to the deterrent force. They then proposed two criteria for assessing any new system: its impact on the dynamic of the arms race and its cost. "If a particular system is found to be of dubious value (i.e., not absolutely necessary to preserve our deterrence posture) and yet is certain to cost large sums of money, then these two criteria lead us to recommend against the system in question."

5.   Our concerns about the MX have intensified since the pastoral letter was written. Significant numbers of expert analysts raise the same objections that we cited in 1983. Simply from the point of view of its relationship to our deterrent posture, we believe the MX should be classified as "a system of dubious value."

6.   Perhaps even more important for us as bishops and pastors is the second criterion. Plainly the United States faces a period of severe budgetary constraints over the next several years. The federal deficit imposes an obligation, at once fiscal and moral, to scrutinize expenditures with great care. Testifying for the USCC March 7 of this year, Archbishop O'Connor addressed the pressing human needs seen every day in New York and throughout the nation. These needs touch matters of basic human dignity: the fact of hunger in our midst, the homeless who walk our streets, the lack of access to adequate health care even for middle-class households. Beyond our borders, the needs are still more desperate. Starvation in Ethiopia and grinding poverty in Central America have complex causes, but it is clear that the drama of life and death being played out daily in these and other parts of the world requires sustained humanitarian and economic assistance from the United States.

7.   Faced with these fundamental challenges to human life and human dignity at home and abroad, I am compelled as president of the USCC to urge you to vote against funding the MX missile. It is our considered judgment—not as strategists certainly, but as religious leaders—that sufficient evidence has been brought forward concerning the potentially destabilizing impact which this weapons system may have on the arms race to support the conclusion that these funds ought instead to be used to meet the human needs enumerated in this letter.

> James W. Malone
> Bishop of Youngstown
> President
> United States Catholic Conference

On the Treasury Department's Tax Proposals

*A Letter Written to the President of the
United States by the President of the
National Conference of Catholic Bishops*

April 19, 1985

Dear Mr. President:

1. I am writing on behalf of the U.S. Catholic Conference to call to your attention the very considerable threat to private charity contained in the Department of Treasury's November 1984 proposals on tax reform. I do so in the spirit of assisting your current review and revision of the Treasury proposals prior to submission of your recommendations to the Congress. I recognize that the Treasury proposals do not represent the settled policy of your administration and that you have welcomed comment and advice from all segments of our society. I also recognize that the Treasury proposals respecting the tax treatment of charitable gifts are only a part of a much broader program of reform which has among its objectives many desirable changes intended to improve the fairness and justice of our federal income tax system.

2. One of the major themes of the Treasury proposals is to remove individuals and families below the poverty level from the income tax rolls. This reform is long overdue, and you can be assured that it has the support of the Catholic bishops and the religious, educational, and charitable agencies and institutions of the Catholic Church in the United States. Tax relief for the poor under the Treasury proposals would be secured primarily by a small increase in the zero-bracket amount and by a substantial increase in the personal exemption for taxpayers and their dependents. I hope that you will retain these reforms as the centerpiece of the tax legislation that you have promised to submit to the Congress.

3. The Catholic Church and its institutions are particularly sensitive to the need for tax relief for the poor and their families because they are the very people in our society and throughout the world whom the Church seeks to serve through its charitable endeavors.

4. Before discussing the extremely adverse effect that the Treasury proposals would have on the ability of private charity to serve the needs of the nation, I want to call your attention to the very considerable commitment that the Catholic people of the United States have made to the work of private charity. The Church in the United States maintains 237 colleges and universities, more than 1,500 secondary schools, and 8,000 elementary schools. There are 710 Catholic hospitals, which treat 37 million patients each year. The Church operates 121 nursing schools, 560 homes for invalids, and 190 orphanages and infant asylums. Most of our 181 dioceses and archdioceses maintain Catholic Charities which, as a group, represents the largest collection of private social service and charitable agencies in the nation. In addition, Catholic Relief Services, the overseas and development agency of the U.S. Catholic bishops, is the largest distributor of food to the starving and hungry of the world. USCC's Migration and Refugee Services annually resettle nearly half of all refugees who come to this nation in search of shelter and a new life.

5.   This great service of the Church is made possible primarily by the voluntary free-will gifts of time and money made by concerned and dedicated citizens of all faiths. A steady and consistent commitment to charitable giving is truly one of the distinguishing marks of our American society, with its tradition of voluntary private initatives in service of the common good of mankind.

6.   Since the beginning of this country, our people have been encouraged by their government in countless ways to support private charity and share their national wealth with the less fortunate among us. One of the greatest of all incentives since the inception of the federal income tax system has been the consistent policy to exempt from taxation that portion of an individual's income which he or she freely gives over to private charity, religion, and education. The Treasury tax proposals contain as one of their principal features a series of changes in the tax treatment of charitable donations which, if approved by you and enacted by Congress, can have the result of reducing the support of private charity and impairing the ability of donors to continue their generosity.

7.   Specifically, I refer to the three major Treasury proposals with respect to charitable gifts:

a) Charitable contributions could only be deducted to the extent they exceed 2 percent of a taxpayer's adjusted gross income.

b) The charitable deduction for nonitemizing taxpayers would be repealed.

c) Deductions for gifts of appreciated property would be reduced to adjusted cost basis or fair market value, whichever is less, thus imposing a burden on this form of charitable donations.

8.   The Treasury estimates that these proposals would result in an annual increase in tax payments by charitable donors in excess of $8.5 billion.

9.   I am convinced that these tax collections would be made at the expense of private charity. Many taxpayers would be forced to reduce their gifts in order to pay their taxes. Indeed, an econometric study commissioned by the Independent Sector identifies a multiplier effect

and estimates a total contribution decline of about $13 billion, a reduction of some 20 percent in the annual contribution income of private charity.

10. Mr. President, I believe these Treasury proposals are inconsistent with the stated policy of your administration. You have stressed the need to encourage voluntary private action. In *Building Partnerships*, the report of your Task Force on Private Sector Initiatives, the prevention of new government impediments to the private sector is a central feature of the report. The report thus states the criteria that should be used in evaluating tax reform proposals: "While recognizing that broad changes in the tax structure must be judged by many other standards, what would be the *impact on charitable contributions* and could these methods of taxation be adjusted so they would not decrease such contributions?" (emphasis added).

11. I am in agreement with the criteria of your task force. I call upon you to apply these standards to the Treasury proposals and trust that you will conclude, as I have, that they represent an unwarranted assault upon our historical national commitment to encourage charitable giving. The reductions already made in funds available for public charity and welfare programs sponsored by the government have placed a growing burden on the private sector. Additional cuts in public spending for the poor and disadvantaged are now pending before the Congress in the current budget proposals. This is no time, Mr. President, for the federal government to take money away from private charity. I call upon you to reject these parts of the Treasury tax proposals.

James W. Malone
Bishop of Youngstown
President
National Conference of Catholic Bishops

Tax Reform and the Poor

*A Statement Submitted to the
House Ways and Means Committee
by the General Secretary of the
United States Catholic Conference*

August 15, 1985

1. I am pleased to submit for the record a statement on tax reform on behalf of the U.S. Catholic Conference. The USCC is the public policy agency of the Catholic bishops of the United States. Reforming the federal tax system in a fair and equitable manner is an issue of great importance for American society. As the tax-reform debate continues, the Catholic Church and its institutions are particularly sensitive to the need for tax relief for the poor because they are the very people in our society whom the Church seeks to serve through many of its charitable and institutional endeavors. This statement addresses the impact of tax reform on the poor, provisions for charitable deductions and the issue of tuition tax credits.

2. The federal tax code is one of the most important documents in our nation. It embodies many of the values and priorities of our nation's social and economic policies. The tax code is, to be sure, a complex, technical document. But it is also a moral document, for it has direct and far-reaching effects on the well-being of millions of American families and individuals. It plays a large part in shaping the quality of life in our country. In a very real way the tax code embodies our nation's answers to some fundamental questions of equity. Who will be helped? Who will bear the burden? What is a fair distribution of income and wealth, and how should we achieve it?

3. Because the tax code has such an important role to play in our overall search for social and economic justice, it is both appropriate and necessary to examine the major tax-reform issues from an explicitly moral and ethical perspective. With that in mind, the conference speaks not on behalf of technical experts in the intricacies of tax policy, but rather as a religious organization that has a long and well-developed tradition of social teaching. Using the ethical norms of this tradition as a starting point, this statement offers some brief reflections on this important debate over tax reform.

Ethical Principles

4.   Among the ethical principles that are relevant to this debate, it is important to call attention to three guidelines that are of particular significance in the effort to achieve a just tax system.

1. Concern for the Poor

5.   From the perspective of Catholic social teaching, one of the most important questions to ask in judging economic policies is this: *What will this policy do to the poor and powerless members of the human community?* Our tradition holds that all human beings have a right to the basic necessities required for human dignity. Among these rights is the right to an income sufficient to support oneself and one's family. The tax system clearly has the capacity to enhance or to threaten this basic right.

6.   It is no secret that in the halls of Congress and in the larger arena of public debate the voice of the poor is not always well represented. They have no special interest organization, no sophisticated team of lobbyists, no financial power with which to bargain. Therefore, without a special effort to protect the interests of the poor they will be all too readily overlooked. It is part of the task of all of us, including public officials, to make sure that does not happen.

2. Distributive Justice

7.   One of the most basic principles of Catholic social teaching is "distributive justice." This principle poses the question: *How are the benefits and burdens of the society distributed among its members?* It is a principle that leads us not only to a concern about the overall equity of economic policies, but more precisely to a strong presumption against extreme inequities in the distribution of income and wealth. As long as there are people in our midst who lack the basic necessities of life, severe inequality in the distribution of economic resources cannot be morally justified.

3. The Principle of "Ability to Pay"

8.   When applied to the subject of taxation, the principle of distributive justice yields a more specific norm—namely, that taxes ought to be assessed according to the ability to pay. This principle has been articulated both in Catholic social encyclicals and in the U.S. bishops' policy statements on the economy (cf. *Mater et Magistra*, no. 132; and *The Economy: Human Dimensions*, 1975). In the language of tax policy, this means that "progressivity" ought to be a major principle reflected in the tax code. As a general rule, those with greater wealth and income ought to pay taxes at a higher rate than those with fewer resources.

9.   With these ethical norms as background, I would like to address several aspects of the tax-reform debate in a more specific way. My purpose here is not to endorse any individual tax-reform package, but to suggest several guidelines that I believe should govern congressional debate of all the proposals.

Taxes and the Poor

10. I am pleased to note that the effects of the tax system on the poor have been the subject of increased public attention in recent months. Numerous other witnesses have pointed out to this committee that the federal tax burden on the poor has increased dramatically in recent years. For example, since 1978 the combined federal income and payroll taxes for a family of four at the poverty line have increased from 4 percent of their income to over 10 percent of their income.[1] For a family of four headed by a single parent with earnings at the poverty line, the tax burden has risen from $343 in 1978 to $1,285 today.[2] This family's taxes jumped by more than 125 percent after adjusting for inflation. Overall, the number of poverty-level families paying federal taxes has more than doubled since 1980.[3] This trend stands in sharp contrast to the large tax cuts in 1981 that were enjoyed by other Americans, especially those in the high-income categories.

11. Even families with gross incomes below the poverty line have been affected. Many families and individuals at or below the poverty line are paying a steadily increasing share of their small incomes in taxes. As a result, they are being pushed deeper into poverty. The tax system is actually making the poor poorer. This increasing burden of the tax system on the poor is even more troubling when viewed in the context of recent trends in the overall economic status of the poor. The last five years have witnessed severe cuts in funding for basic needs programs for the poor and the near poor. They have borne a disproportionate share of the burden of federal budget cuts at the very same time that their tax burden was increasing.

12. Partly as a result of these factors, as well as the persistent high levels of unemployment, the status of the poor in our nation has declined dramatically in recent years. The number of poor in America

---

[1]Joint Committee on Taxation. *Federal Tax Treatment of Individuals Below the Poverty Level*, June 5, 1985, p. 12.

[2]Ibid., p. 14.

[3]*Characteristics of the Population Below the Poverty Level: 1983*, U.S. Department of Commerce, Bureau of the Census, Series P-60, No. 147, p. 5, Table 1.

has grown by 6 million since 1980. Over 35 million people—more than one in every seven Americans—now live in poverty.[4] This is a scar on the face of our nation, a scar that can and must be removed.

13. These data on poverty represent far more than mechanical calculations and abstract descriptions of inequality. They represent human hardship and suffering for the poor—three-fourths of whom are women and children.[5] These are families who by definition lack the minimum level of resources required for a decent life. Requiring them to pay part of their meager income in taxes, therefore, must be judged as unfair and an unacceptable burden.

14. From 1975 to 1980, families and individuals in poverty generally were not required to pay income tax.[6] Three major provisions—the personal exemption, the zero-bracket amount, and the earned-income tax credit—worked together to protect those people and families in poverty from paying taxes. In recent years, however, these policies have not been adequately adjusted to keep up with inflation and the needs of the poor. Inflation has driven up the wages of the poor with the result that a larger share of their earnings is now being taxed. In 1978, the poverty line was $858 below the income-tax threshold—the income level at which families and individuals begin to pay taxes. Currently the poverty line is $1,567 *above* the tax threshold. Thus a family of four with income more than $1,500 below the poverty line must still pay income tax.[7] Clearly the protection of the poor from paying taxes has been severely eroded.

15. We believe that it is essential that Congress take the necessary steps to repair the damage that has been done to the poor in recent years. A major step in that direction can be achieved by once again exempting the poor from federal income taxes and offsetting for them a substantial portion of the highly regressive Social Security tax.

16. I am pleased to see that the administration's plan and the other tax-reform proposals would significantly reduce or eliminate income taxes on the poor. There appears to be a growing consensus that significant tax relief for the poor must be an element of federal tax reform. On behalf of the USCC, I want to urge you to make this growing consensus an ironclad commitment. Eliminating the tax burden on families and individuals who are poor must, in our view, be a top priority. Exempting those at or near the poverty line from federal income taxation should be a condition of any tax-reform plan which Congress ultimately adopts.

17. Among the specific mechanisms that could be used to eliminate taxes for the poor and the near poor are: (1) expansion of the earned-

---

[4]Ibid., p. 25, Table 7.
[5]Ibid., p. 5, Table 1.
[6]*Federal Tax Treatment*, pp. 2, 3.
[7]Ibid., p. 10.

income tax credit; (2) raising the zero-bracket amount; and (3) modifying the personal exemption. In the end, some combination of these provisions must be adopted to ensure that all families and individuals at or near the poverty line are exempt and continue to be exempt from federal income taxes.

Earned-Income Tax Credit

18. In choosing the appropriate combination of these provisions, emphasis should be given to those provisions which are most efficient in providing relief to low-income families and individuals. In several respects the earned-income tax credit is the most effective in this regard. The earned-income tax credit was enacted in 1975 in order to provide tax relief to working, low-income taxpayers with children, to provide relief from payroll taxes and to improve work incentives. An especially important aspect of the earned-income tax credit is that it is a refundable credit.

19. I urge this committee to expand the earned-income tax credit so that it not only eliminates income taxes below the poverty line, but also helps to offset the growing burden of payroll taxes on low-income families. Such an expansion should include an increase in the rate of the earned-income tax credit above the current 11 percent and a substantial increase in the earnings level at which the credit is phased out. In order to prevent future erosion of the value of the earned-income tax credit, it should also be indexed for inflation.

20. One proposal under consideration calls for increasing the credit to 16 percent of the first $5,000 of earned income or $500. The credit would be phased out at a rate of 16 percent for incomes between $11,000 and $16,000. Such a plan would build on and improve the administration's helpful initiative since it would help families slightly above the poverty line. In addition to exempting all families in poverty from federal income taxes, it would also provide some offset against payroll taxes for those slightly above the poverty line, and it would increase the work incentive for poor families. I urge the committee to give serious consideration to this type of proposal. In doing so, please note that these proposed increases in the earned-income tax credit would essentially compensate for the earned-income tax credit's erosion by inflation since 1979. They would not constitute a significant new benefit.

21. I wish to urge your consideration of one additional improvement that could be made in the earned-income tax credit. Currently, the earned-income tax credit is unrelated to family size. A family of five or six receives the same credit as a family of three. Would it not be more fair and more supportive of family values to structure the earned-income tax credit to that the size of the credit would be correlated with family size? This could be done by simply increasing the earned-income tax credit with an allowance for each dependent child. Providing an additional allowance for every child under the age of six would be further improvement that would help poor families with young children and child-care costs. Adding this kind of children's allowance to the earned-income tax credit would, in our view, be an effective and efficient way to target benefits to America's needy children.

Single-Parent Families

22. Both current law and several of the proposed tax-reform packages treat single-parent families differently than married couples with children. As a result, single-parent families bear a heavier federal tax burden than married two-parent families of the same size with the exact same income.

23. We can see no legitimate reason for this discrepancy and therefore urge that the zero-bracket amount for single heads of households be raised to the same level as that for married couples filing jointly.

Dependent-Care Tax Credit

24. Current law provides a credit for child and dependent-care expenses necessary for gainful employment. Since 1982 the credit has been targeted so that it provides the greater benefit to low-income taxpayers. Affordable child care is essential to enable parents, especially single parents, to work and remain self-sufficient. In the face of the great unmet need for child care in our nation, it is important to maintain the assistance provided by the dependent-care tax credit. This credit is the largest source of federal financial support for child care.

25. All of the major tax-reform proposals would make significant changes in the dependent-care credit—either by changing it to a deduction or by eliminating it altogether. Such changes would greatly reduce the value of the credit, especially for low-income families. They would effectively eliminate the targeting of the current credit to low- and moderate-income taxpayers and would provide a disproportionate benefit to upper-income families. Therefore, on behalf of the USCC, I urge you to reject the proposed changes.

26. In addition, several important steps could be taken to improve the dependent-care tax credit. Currently, in spite of its targeted structure, two-thirds of the benefits of the credit go to families above the median income.[8] This is due to the fact that most poor families cannot afford to incur the initial costs of child care in order to receive tax

---

[8] *The President's Tax Proposals*, p. 21.

relief at a later date. Only those families who can afford the initial expenses can effectively benefit from the credit. In addition, poor families with incomes below the income-tax threshold receive no benefits because the credit is not refundable.

27. Therefore, in order to make the dependent-care tax credit effectively serve low-income families, some modifications are necessary. We agree with those who have proposed that the credit be made refundable and be indexed to avoid erosion from inflation.

Personal Exemption

28. Although the proposed increases in the personal exemption would provide some relief for low-income people and would help large families, it is a very expensive way to do so. Since it is a deduction to the taxpayer, the value of the personal exemption rises as the tax bracket increases. I would urge you to examine carefully the pros and cons of changing the personal exemption to a nonrefundable credit. This might make it as valuable to low-income families as to those with higher incomes.

29. The above suggestions for changes in the earned-income tax credit, the zero-bracket amount, the personal exemption and the dependent-care tax credit could be used to eliminate effectively the payment of federal taxes by the poor. We recognize that it may be unrealistic and impractical to implement all of these changes at the same time. However, we urge that some combination of these provisions be enacted to ensure that families and individuals at or near the poverty line are exempt and continue to be exempt from paying federal income tax.

Health Insurance Benefits

30. Another item of concern that would affect working low-income families is the proposal to tax employer-provided health insurance. In particular, the proposal to tax the first $10 of an individual monthly premium and the first $25 of a family premium would, in our view, be unwise and unfair. The $10 and $25 amounts would be charged to employees at all income levels, regardless of their different earnings. This would have a clearly regressive effect — placing a proportionately greater burden on low-income workers.

Progressivity in the Tax System

31. As indicated earlier in my remarks, Catholic teaching on social justice supports the principle of progressivity in the tax system. In

our view, it is essential that this principle be incorporated as a major characteristic of any revision in the federal tax code.

32. The gap between the rich and the poor in our nation is widening — a trend that is especially alarming in view of the growing and widespread evidence of hunger, homelessness, and poverty in our nation. There can be no legitimate excuse for this scandal of poverty in a nation as wealthy as ours. We simply must take the necessary measures to eradicate the severe human suffering that confronts us every day on the streets and sidewalks of our national community.

33. Economic growth is an important means of reducing poverty. We must do all in our power to promote a growing, productive and efficient economy. But this is clearly not enough. We must also face head-on the issues of distributive justice. For, as Pope John XXIII said in his famous encyclical *Mater et Magistra*, "Economic prosperity is to be assessed not so much from the sum total of goods and wealth possessed as from the distribution of goods according to the norms of justice" (*Mater et Magistra*, 73).

34. This concern about distributive justice is particularly relevant to discussions about tax reform because the tax system is one of the most important vehicles that we have to affect the distribution of income and wealth. The current tax code already redistributes income and wealth in ways that reflect social goals and values. Upon undertaking major tax reform, therefore, Congress ought to take a careful look at the overall distributional effects of the changes under consideration.

35. Traditionally, our federal income-tax system has been progressive. It has served, in effect, to offset the regressivity of payroll taxes and most state and local taxes. As a result, the nation's overall tax structure is roughly neutral. People in different income classes pay about the same proportion of their income in taxes.

36. As I indicated earlier, Catholic social teaching suggests that progressivity be a central feature of any tax system. Our strong emphasis on distributive justice would lead us to oppose flat-rate income-tax proposals and to suggest that tax reform should move in the direction of significantly more progressivity.

37. Some of the current tax-reform proposals, because they would radically reduce the number of brackets and lower the upper rates, would have the effect of producing a disproportionate benefit for the wealthy. Upper-income taxpayers have already received large tax reductions as a result of the 1981 tax bill. The maximum tax rate was cut from 70 percent to 50 percent. It would be reduced to 35 percent or lower by the major reform proposals now under consideration. This would mean very large tax cuts for the wealthy and relatively small amounts of tax relief for middle-income and working-class Americans. Must we not question the equity of such a result? Should we allow a large windfall for the rich at a time when the gap between

rich and poor is widening, at a time when millions lack even the most basic necessities required for human dignity?

38. I urge the committee to consider appropriate measures to increase the progressivity of the proposals under consideration. I agree with those who have urged you to examine the possibility of adding one or more brackets at the upper end of the tax structure. This could significantly improve the proposed reforms and could be done without adding greatly to the complexity of the proposals.

Raising Adequate Revenues

39. One of the most basic and obvious goals of the tax system is to raise the necessary revenues to pay for the common needs of our society. At a time when deficits in the federal budget are at unprecedented levels and when many social needs continue to go unmet, the question of adequate federal revenues cannot be ignored.

40. I urge this committee to examine carefully all of the tax-reform proposals to ensure that they would raise the necessary revenues to meet our social goals and obligations. If in the long run these proposals were to produce a revenue shortfall, we fear that the added pressure on the federal budget would result in further and unacceptable cuts in human-needs programs.

41. In view of the need to share equitably the burden of funding our common needs in society, I urge you to ensure that the corporate sector pay its fair share of federal taxes. The significant decline in the corporate income tax in recent years—and the resulting shift in the tax burden onto average wage earners—is cause for concern, especially in view of the magnitude of the federal deficit. The average effective corporate tax rate has been cut in half since 1980. In the 1950s and 1960s, corporate income taxes paid for about a quarter of the cost of federal spending, apart from the self-financed Social Security system. By 1984, the share paid for by corporate income tax had shrunk to less than 9 percent.[9]

42. If we are to have a fair and effective tax structure—one that raises sufficient revenues to meet our nation's social needs—then wealthy individuals and corporations must pay their fair share. It is simply not acceptable to force middle-income and working-class Americans to bear a greater and greater share of the federal tax burden.

43. In arguing on behalf of the proposals which I have suggested to benefit the poor and the near poor, I do not mean to suggest that the added costs be borne by moderate-income Americans. They too need tax relief and have sometimes been overlooked in the broad debate

---

[9]Joint Economic Committee, U.S. Congress, *Tax Reform*, November 29, 1984, p. 44.

about reform. It is possible and desirable to both protect the poor and provide tax relief to moderate-income Americans. By significantly increasing the progressivity of the system, by closing loopholes, and by restoring the corporate income tax to more appropriate levels, the necessary revenue can be raised in a fair and efficient manner.

Charitable Deductions

44. The work of the Catholic Church and its various agencies committed to serving the less fortunate of our society has been made possible primarily through the voluntary, free-will gifts of time and money made by concerned and dedicated citizens of all faiths. Through this giving, the Catholic people of the United States make a valuable contribution to the nation in the areas of education, health and human services.[10]

45. These activities constitute one part of the total charitable activities engaged in by thousands of organizations, representing a wide variety of religious and philanthropic groups, among them the Salvation Army and the United Way.

46. A steady and consistent commitment to charitable giving is truly one of the distinguishing marks of our American society with its tradition of voluntary, private initiatives in service of the common good of mankind.

47. Since the beginning of this country, our people have been encouraged by their government in countless ways to support private charity and share their national wealth with the less fortunate among us. One of the greatest of all incentives since the inception of the federal income-tax system has been the consistent policy to exempt from taxation that portion of an individual's income which he or she freely gives over to private charity, religion, and education.

48. Although the president's proposal has modified the changes in charitable deductions contained in the Department of the Treasury's plan, the above-the-line deduction for nonitemizers is still slated for elimination at the end of taxable year 1985. If this deduction were in effect in 1985, it is estimated that charitable giving by nonitemizers

---

[10]The Catholic Church in the United States maintains 237 colleges and universities, more than 1,500 secondary schools, and 8,000 elementary schools. There are 710 Catholic hospitals which treat 37 million patients each year. The Church operates 121 nursing schools, 560 homes for invalids, and 190 orphanages and infant asylums. Most of our 181 dioceses and archdioceses maintain Catholic Charities, which as a group represent the largest collection of private social services and charitable agencies in the nation. In addition, Catholic Relief Services, the overseas-development agency of the U.S. Catholic bishops, is the largest distributor of food to the starving and hungry of the world. USCC's Migration and Refugee Services annually resettle nearly half of all refugees who come to this nation in search of shelter and new life.

would increase more than $4 billion. It would go up by $6.7 billion in 1986.[11] It is in view of this effect on charitable giving that the Catholic conference supports the continuation of the above-the-line charitable deduction.

Tuition Tax Credits

49. Recognizing that none of the proposed tax-reform measures address the issue of tuition tax credits, we want to state our strong conviction that these proposals would be incomplete without adequate provisions for tuition tax credits for those low- and middle-income families who exercise their natural right as parents by sending their children to private and parochial schools. The president has long been an ardent advocate of tuition tax credits to help relieve the financial hardships of such parents by changing the tax system to provide more equitable and just treatment for them. Now is an appropriate time to enact tuition tax credits by integrating them into the comprehensive tax-reform legislation. Failure to consider tuition tax credits germane to the overall issue of tax reform would be unjust to millions of American families who have long shouldered the dual burden for making a conscientious decision in favor of their children. We urge the Ways and Means Committee to give serious consideration to tuition tax credits.

50. On behalf of the USCC, I appreciate the opportunity to present to you our views on the issue of tax reform. We are most interested in the continuing debate on tax reform before the Congress.

---

[11] *The Effect of the Treasury Plan on Charitable Giving,* by Professor Larry B. Lindsey, assistant professor of economics, Harvard University, February 12, 1985.

Statement on South Africa

A Statement Issued by the
Administrative Board of the
United States Catholic Conference

September 11, 1985

1. The relationship between the United States and South Africa has entered a new period of tension and trouble. The determined resistance of the black population of South Africa to the whole political, legal, economic, and social system of apartheid presents a moral and political challenge to the rest of the world.

2. The attention of the international community is now focused on South Africa because of recent instances of violent resistance to apartheid. In South Africa violence has spawned violence. The system of apartheid inflicts its own kind of violence on the human person every day.

3. The Catholic bishops of South Africa characterized apartheid in 1957 as "something intrinsically evil." Their judgment found resounding affirmation in the address of Pope John Paul II at The Hague in May 1985:

> For Christians and for all who believe in a covenant, that is, an unbreakable bond between God and man and between all human beings, no form of discrimination — in law or in fact — on the basis of race, origins, color, culture, sex or religion can ever be acceptable. Hence no system of apartheid or separate development will ever be acceptable as a model for the relations between people or races.

4. On August 3, 1985, after a state of emergency was declared by the South African government, the Catholic bishops of that country declared:

> Hearing of the tragic events in our country, Pope John Paul II last week spoke of this apartheid policy in these words: "To those who suffer the violence of such an inhuman situation I express sentiments of profound participation and support." And we say now, as long as the system of apartheid prevails, the resentment and the unrest will never die down.
>
> In our report on police conduct during township protests, in December 1984, and our statement of March 22 on the Langa tragedy, we deplored the unnecessary force and violence used by the police. We deplore the violence that has continued: the violence of the system. The violence of the police — acknowledging proper fulfillment of duty where this has occurred — and the violence of those who, angered and frustrated beyond measure, have pursued in reprisal and political antagonism the path of destruction, injury, intimidation and even killing.

This is the way of anarchy and chaos. The system bears the gravest
responsibility for it. And unless the system is changed, the violence
is not likely to abate.

5.   The religious and moral significance of the South African problem
is evident in these statements. The central question posed by apartheid
is a direct attack on the dignity of the human person. At the foundation
of the biblical vision that the Christian tradition is the conviction that
every person is created in the image of God. Every person reflects
the presence of God among us; apartheid tries to define the ultimate
value of the person on the basis of race and color. Christian teaching
demands that the unique dignity of every person should find expression in the protection and promotion of the human rights of the
person; apartheid is a systematic assault on the basic rights of black
and coloured races in South Africa. Christian teaching holds that the
state has a positive moral responsibility toward the welfare of every
person; the apartheid system places the resources of the state decisively in the service of the minority of the South African population.
On item after item apartheid stands as a contradiction to the basic
Christian teaching on human dignity and the human person.

6.   It is clear on human, moral, and political grounds that change
must come in South Africa. It is also clear that the primary agents of
change are within South Africa. But nations and institutions which
have a relationship with South Africa are part of the political and
moral drama being played out in that nation.

7.   External forces can be catalysts for positive change or they can be
obstacles to change. Insofar as this is true, external actors are not
passive spectators of the South African problem, but participants in
it. Moreover, they are not "interfering" in an internal issue when
they evaluate their policies or exert pressure on South Africa; they
are simply exercising moral responsibility for their actions as nations
or other social institutions. The policy choices of nations which have
diplomatic relations with South Africa and the practices of institutions
which affect South African society from the outside are filled with
moral content. Determining how a given policy choice will influence
the apartheid system is not a simple matter. But this is no excuse for
avoiding choices or ignoring the moral responsibility external actors
have in South Africa.

8.   Different parts of U.S. society—our government, churches, corporations, foundations—have a direct influence on South Africa; they
affect how the people and government of South Africa see the United
States.

9.   We speak as bishops and pastors of a Church whose religious
and moral teaching is daily contradicted by apartheid, and whose
brother bishops are actively opposing apartheid. We also speak as
citizens of a nation which exercises a significant influence in South

African society. We use this statement to express our episcopal solidarity with the Southern African Catholic Bishops' Conference and to express our deep respect for the exemplary ecumenical witness for justice being made by the churches of South Africa. The words and actions of church leaders in South Africa challenge us to address the moral choices our own society faces concerning South Africa.

I. The Church

10. As members of the Administrative Board of the United States Catholic Conference, we recommend the following actions:

First, that the members of the Catholic Church in the United States be informed about the basic facts of life in South Africa, including the nature of apartheid, its concomitant denial of basic human rights, and its disastrous effects upon individuals and families in the political, legal, economic, and social spheres.

Second, that the members of the Catholic Church in the United States be urged to pray for the people and churches of South Africa and Namibia, as requested by the churches of those countries.

Third, that the U.S. Catholic Conference continue to strengthen its fraternal relationship with the Southern African Catholic Bishops' Conference through visits, communications, and collaboration.

Fourth, that the U.S. Catholic Conference, in consultation with the Southern African Catholic Bishops' Conference, support appropriate legislation in the U.S. Congress and communicate its views on matters of policy to members of the executive branch of the U.S. government.

Fifth, that the U.S. Catholic Conference, in consultation with the Southern African Catholic Bishops' Conference, consider ways in which assistance may be given to those South Africans who conscientiously object to service in the military forces of South Africa.

Sixth, that the USCC Committee on Social Development and World Peace continue its study of the question of divestment of church funds from business enterprises and banks doing business in South Africa and report on this subject to the Administrative Board.

II. The U.S. Government

11. The United States is a major force in the diplomatic life of South Africa, and this offers the possibility of effective action by the United States government to bring about fundamental change in South Africa before that country is engulfed in a full-scale civil war. As Bishop Desmond Tutu said on August 15, 1985, "Our last hope is the intervention of the international community." Aware of this responsibility, we recommend the following policies or actions to the U.S. government:

First, an unambigious U.S. policy of commitment to human rights in South Africa. It should be clear to all interested parties that the urgency of the human rights problem there has made it the principal concern of the United States in U.S.-South African relations.

Second, the voice and vote of the United States in multinational institutions, including the United Nations General Assembly and Security Council, should be used to help make the international community's opposition to the policy of apartheid ever more vigorous and effective.

Third, the U.S. government should engage in the aggressive diplomatic pursuit of every reasonable action in support of the dismantling of the system of apartheid as called for by the Southern African Catholic Bishops' Conference.

Fourth, the approval of the Anti-Apartheid Action Act of 1985, now pending before the Congress, which includes the following measures:

- prohibits the importation of South African krugerrands or other gold coins from South Africa;
- prohibits the exportation of computers, software, and technology to the South African police, military, and other government entities that enforce restrictions on blacks' freedom of movement;
- prohibits loans to the South African government (except for loans for any educational, housing, or health facility which is available to all persons on a nondiscriminatory basis);
- prohibits the export of goods or technology to be used in any South African nuclear production or utilization facility;
- imposes mandatory fair employment practices (the Sullivan principles) for U.S. nationals controlling companies in South Africa;
- establishes a policy calling for the imposition of economic sanctions against South Africa if significant progress has not been made within twelve months toward ending apartheid;
- provides monies for scholarships for black South Africans to attend South African universities, colleges, and secondary schools;
- provides monies for a human rights fund for the legal defense of victims of apartheid.

The Executive Order of September 9, 1985, addresses some of these measures and we welcome it as a development in U.S. policy. Nevertheless, the Anti-Apartheid Action Act of 1985 offers a stronger and broader approach, which we still believe is necessary.

Fifth, in addition to U.S. action directed toward the internal problems of South Africa, there should be a renewed U.S. commitment to achieve the implementation of UN Resolution 435 in Namibia, guaranteeing the withdrawal of South Africa from Namibia, a cease-fire, and the holding of elections under UN auspices.

III. The Private Sector

12. Nongovernmental institutions based in the United States with operations in South Africa can play a very significant role in promoting a consistent policy vision toward South Africa; the private sector, particularly the business and banking communities, has unique opportunities in the South Africa situation. We recommend consideration of the following:

- Investment policies are particularly sensitive and crucial issues; the intense debate surrounding the disinvestment question highlights its importance; similar debate should be encouraged concerning the question of *no further investment* in South Africa and *no further bank loans* without corresponding specific steps on political, social, and legal issues at stake in South Africa. It should be made clear that investments and bank loans to South Africa carry grave moral burdens and have critical impact on issues of human rights.
- Labor practices and working conditions constitute another visible forum for action by U.S.-based businesses; adherence to the Sullivan principles, support for black trade unions in South Africa, and creative steps to improve the general working conditions and access to positions of responsibility for blacks are all steps we find worthy of support.

13. No list of specifics will capture the range of choices facing individuals and institutions in the United States concerning South Africa. We use these principles and examples to press forward the widespread public debate now engaging the U.S. government, the Congress, the business and financial communities, the media, and the U.S. public.
14. Change in South Africa cannot come too quickly for those bearing the indignity and the injustice of apartheid. The United States as a nation and a society should be and should be seen by others to be unambiguously in support of profound, rapid, and thorough change in the political, legal, social, and economic sectors of South African society.

Background Paper on South Africa

USCC Department of Social Development and World Peace

15. Because many Americans are likely to think of the system of apartheid as simply a more extreme version of the system of racial discrimination that existed in the United States before the mid-1960s, an attempt has been made in this paper to describe in some detail the purposes and functioning of that system. In the background paper on southern African issues approved by the Administrative Board on March 23, 1983, it was stated that "at the beginning of 1983, 'constructive engagement' appears to be seriously deficient. South Africa's response has been to delay the Namibian settlement, to attack neighboring nations, and to intensify, rather than mitigate, restrictions on its own black majority population."

16. There is no reason to modify that assessment. In recent months "South African commandos have launched forays, first into Angola's northern enclave of Cabinda, then into Gaberone, capital of Botswana" (Alan Cowell, *New York Times*, June 30, 1985). The insurgency originally backed by South Africa in Mozambique, but repudiated in 1984, has not diminished; on the contrary, "rarely a day goes by without reports of a guerrilla attack on a truck or bus just a few miles outside Maputo (the capital city). Many highways are unsafe. Some rail routes have been closed for months" (ibid). In Namibia, instead of complying with UN Security Council Resolution 435, South Africa installed in 1985 a new "conditional" government, despite urgent and repeated appeals from the Namibian Council of Churches (which includes the Catholic Church) for South Africa's immediate withdrawal, a cease-fire, and genuine, independent elections.

17. "Constructive engagement" was envisioned also as providing an impetus to internal change in the Republic of South Africa; it presupposed a government interested in continuing and significant progress in moving away from apartheid. Some changes have, indeed, taken place, but without seriously affecting "grand apartheid," i.e., the plan that preserves white dominance indefinitely. A new constitution has been installed granting voting rights and parliamentary representation to the "coloured" and Indian segments of the population. Since it excludes the black majority, the Southern African Catholic Bishops' Conference (SACBC) has stated that in reality it entrenches apartheid. Even the groups affected showed minimal support in referendums and elections for the new Indian and "coloured" members of Parliament. Some of the restrictve "petty apartheid" laws have been repealed (interracial marriage and sex relations; business establishments by blacks in "white" downtown areas), but such changes are regarded by church authorities and a majority of blacks as merely cosmetic, without promise of dismantling the fundamental inequality imposed by the apartheid system.

18. The reaction of the black population has been an upsurge of sabotage or violence against the police and security forces as well as against blacks who were, or seemed to be, collaborators with the government. Nonviolent protest has been effectively rendered almost impossible by prohibitions against all gatherings of blacks for political purposes, and the jailing of black political leaders. The churches, Catholic, Protestant, and Anglican, remain almost the only legitimate voices of the black majority.

19. Late in 1984, the SACBC, "shocked by the violent attacks on so many people during the last three months of turmoil," compiled and published a *Report on Police Conduct during Township Protests, August-November 1984*. In the introduction, the bishops state:

> We see no hope of reaching a reasonable settlement embracing everyone in South Africa and an end to the continually smouldering unrest, unless all its causes and aggravations are honestly faced. For instance, one of the reasons for organizing the two-day stayaway (November 5/6) was the masssive presence of the police in the townships. . . . In a number of cases the presence, and especially the attitude of the police, has itself provoked public violence. We regret to say that, instead of being accepted as protectors of the people, the police are now regarded by many people in the black townships as disturbers of the peace and perpetrators of violent crime. . . .
>
> The estimated number of people killed in the townships as a result of the disturbances (August-November 1984) is 150. Our statements indicated that the police used their firearms without provocation on occasion and frequently indiscriminately. Many of the victims of this indiscriminate shooting will bear the injuries for life.

20. The Church has also risen to the defense of white South Africans, particularly conscientious objectors to compulsory military service. In the summer of 1985, the End Conscription Campaign drew the support of Archbishop Denis Hurley, OMI, of Durban, president of the SACBC. Under the present law, which the Church has opposed for many years:

- young men are conscripted to maintain the illegal occupation of Namibia and to wage unjust war against foreign countries;
- they are conscripted to assist in the implementation and defense of apartheid policies;
- those who refuse to serve are faced with the choice of a life of exile or a possible six years in prison.

21. The SACBC in June 1985 invited Cardinal Arns of São Paulo, Brazil, to address a rally for peace and the end of conscription. On the eve of his departure from Brazil, the cardinal was confronted by a demand from the South African government that he promise not to so participate. As he refused to make such a commitment, his visa was withdrawn and the visit was cancelled.

22. In the United States, reactions to the above developments have weakened the arguments for "constructive engagement" to the point where the U.S. ambassador to South Africa was recalled for consultation (traditionally a sign of grave diplomatic disapproval). Both houses of the Congress were moving toward legislation asserting economic sanctions against South Africa when the Executive Order of September 9, 1985, forestalled, at least temporarily, the completion of congressional action.

Part I: The South African System of Apartheid

23. The gravity of the internal situation in South Africa is inadequately understood by many Americans. While the word *apartheid* conveys the notion of racial segregation, it does not reveal the abysmal conditions under which the great majority of blacks, so-called coloureds, and Asians live in South Africa. In any written description of the system of apartheid in South Africa, it is impossible to describe the inhumane conditions under which millions of people in that country are forced to live—the humiliation resulting from the pass laws; the rampant poverty and malnutrition; the intentionally watered-down education made available to black children; the breakup of families; the acute stress caused by the forced relocations; the psychological effect of living in what must be considered by the blacks, coloureds, and Indians to be a police state. An attempt will be made in this paper to give some idea of the apartheid system itself, of the legal apparatus that supports it, and of the ideologies that are used to justify it. The system of apartheid is one of the most reprehensible and all-pervasive systems of repression in the world today.

24. In reflecting upon the development and implementation of apartheid (sometimes referred to as "separate development") in South Africa, one must begin with population and land distribution in that country. The population, divided along racial lines, is approximately as follows:

Blacks	20,862,000	73%
Whites	4,500,000	15%
Coloureds	2,600,000	9%
Indians	821,000	3%

25. But while blacks constitute 73 percent of the population of South Africa, under the laws of that country, only 13 percent of the land is allocated to blacks. It must be emphasized that this allocation of land is controlled by South African laws and is not simply a matter of market forces.

26. The system of apartheid in South Africa is based upon a series of interlocking laws enacted by a parliament in which, between 1936 and 1984, blacks, coloureds, and Indians had no direct representation or participation. Even after the institution of a tricameral legislature in 1984 (whites, coloureds, Indians), blacks are still excluded from participation. Reference will be made below to some of these laws that are key to the maintenance of apartheid.

27. Influx control has been one of the central pillars of segregation pursued by successive governments in South Africa. The black population, excluded from participation in the political process, has had no say in the development of those policies, and black persons have been prevented by the government from mobilizing themselves to have the policies changed.

28. Influx control has always borne a close relationship to land policy. The Native Lands Act of 1913 set aside certain land for ownership and occupation by black persons. Black persons were not permitted to acquire ownership of land outside these areas, which then accounted for about 7 percent of the total area of the country and has since been increased to approximately 13 percent. The right of black persons to be in other parts of the country has been regulated and controlled by the influx control laws. In time this led to the concentration of black persons in particular rural areas which have, as a result, become overpopulated while restrictions on the mobility of black persons imposed by the influx control laws curtailed migration to the towns and inhibited the acquisition by them of skills necessary for full participation in a modern technological society. Towns have been seen by the white population as being their preserve, and their government has used the influx control laws to maintain this position and to restrict the presence of black persons in the towns to what is needed to meet the labor requirements of the white economy.

29. While black ownership of land was thus severely restricted, the Group Areas Act of 1950 imposed control countrywide over all inter-racial changes in ownership and empowered the government to decide where members of the different racial groups should live and trade.

30. The Native Laws Amendment Act of 1952 provided that only those blacks had a right to live permanently in urban areas (i.e., in a black township adjacent to a white area) who had been born there or who had lived their continuously for fifteen years or who had worked continuously for the same employer for ten years (so-called Section 10 rights, which every black, literate or illiterate, seems to know by heart).

31. Influx control laws regulate the movement of black people in South Africa. Every black, beginning at the age of sixteen years, must carry a passbook that will indicate whether he or she is authorized to be in a white area or even in a black township. (One study indicates that in 1983 alone, over 142,000 blacks were arrested for pass law offenses.)

32. If a black person is not authorized to live in an urban area (either in a black township adjacent to a center of white population or in accommodations provided by the employer at the place of employment, as is often the case for domestic servants) and is not a laborer on a white-owned farm, then that black person is required to live in one of the ten homelands established by the South African government for the various language groups: Zulus, Xhosas, Sotho, etc.

33. The purpose of these homelands can be easily seen by a review of the major provisions of the Bantu Homeland Citizenship Act of 1970. This Act says that every black South African is a citizen of one of the homelands. Citizenship is determined by the language spoken, not by place of residence. When homelands are declared to be "independent states" (as has happened in the case of four out of ten homelands), citizens of those so-called independent homelands lose their South African citizenship and thus become foreigners in South Africa. Between 1976 and 1981, 8 million blacks lost their South African citizenship. Once a person loses citizenship in South Africa, he or she cannot claim a share of political power or in the land and wealth of South Africa. He or she has no right to a South African passport and can be deported as an alien from South Africa. A bill enacted in 1984 restricts the employment in South Africa of aliens from the "independent" homelands. The homelands, independent and nonindependent, are underdeveloped and overpopulated areas in which the majority of black South Africans are supposed to live.

34. As a result of these laws concerning the homelands, unemployment is exported from white South Africa to the black homelands. Workers are easily replaceable and this weakens labor's bargaining power. Social welfare responsibilities are transferred to homeland governments which have scant resources. The 13 percent of land allocated to the black homelands includes much land that has either little or no potential for agricultural production.

35. Since the establishment of the black homelands, a program of removals or relocations has resulted in removal of approximately 3,500,000 people from areas designated for white residency and control. While the vast majority of relocated persons are black, about 600,000 persons of other racial groups have been forced to move. An estimated 2,000,000 more people are scheduled for relocation. As a report published in 1984 by the South African Council of Churches (SACC) and the Southern African Catholic Bishops' Conference (SACBC) states: "The process of forced removals and relocations, which has accelerated since the early 1960s, has brought the Apartheid dream of ten independent black nations-states close to realization, although in the eyes of the state the map is still very 'untidy,' since there are over seventy blocks of land distributed among the ten Bantustans (homelands)" (*Relocations*, 1984, p. 14).

36. Some of the consequences of this program of forced removals are summed up in the following statement taken from the churches' report on relocations:

> Inadequate or polluted water supplies, a shortage of productive land, an inhospitable climate and the lack of suitable housing are frequent and well-known features of resettlement camps. People's basic survival is threatened, and this leads to great strain in the family. It weighs heavily on parents if they are unable to provide for their children. Even if a family does not face actual starvation, it is still unlikely to enjoy full health, since resettlement camps are designed for mere survival with only a toilet, a tin hut or tent, and commuter transport being provided. To avoid destitution some family members become migrant workers, but that splits the family and causes further stress. Usually conditions in relocation areas are so meagre that a family cannot enjoy a sufficient standard of living to maintain itself in good health. Any family or community that was formerly living somewhat above the minimum level for suvival is likely to experience relocation as a debilitating loss (ibid., p. 31).

37. The system of apartheid is built upon control over employment and control over residence. Persons living in the homelands are prevented from being in the cities by the controls exercised over their right to reside or take up employment there. As noted above, these controls are brought together by the passbook that every black over the age of sixteen years is required to possess and the passbook that every citizen of an "independent" homeland who does not have a South African passbook is required to carry. No contract of employment may be entered into with anybody who does not possess a passbook nor may any such person become a tenant of a house in an urban black township. The right to be in a prescribed area and the right to take up employment are recorded in the passbook, which must be produced upon demand to an authorized officer. (Passbooks or passports from the "independent" homelands may be demanded in the streets; and if these are not in order, the persons concerned are arrested; and where they do not qualify to be in the city, they may be fined or imprisoned.)

38. As a result of the implementation of the laws designed to further the system of apartheid, South Africa can be said to be today both a "First World country" and a "Third World country." White South Africa's standard and mode of living is comparable to that of western European countries, Canada, and the United States. Black South Africa's standard and mode of living is comparable to that of some of the poorer countries of Africa, Asia, and Latin America. And it is the black South African community that makes possible the high standard of living of the white South African community.

39. In the 1984 report on forced relocations published by the SACC and the SACBC, it is stated that "certain prevalent ideologies held by white South Africans encourage and justify the removal and relocation of other South Africans." The first such ideology is racism which, using spurious biological and anthropological theories, together with a falsified view of history, regards domination by the whites as normal. Another ideology is unrestricted capitalism which views all forms of modernization, wealth accumulation, and economic growth as good, no matter what effect they have on other people. The function of workers is to sell their labor to employers; apart from that the workers are unimportant. Unemployment is not considered a problem, except when it threatens security for the employed.

40. "Afrikaner nationalism" is another ideology used to justify apartheid. Since its victory in 1948, the National Party has used its power to ensure the survival of the Afrikaner nation at all cost. It has sought to maintain the racial "purity" of the white people and the preservation of the chief symbols of the Afrikans' language and heritage. Since this type of nationalism has increasingly come under attack, in reaction it has committed itself to developing a national security state. The ideology of national security regards the preservation of the state as the highest ideal, and any and every means may be used to defend the state and the existing social order. Some acute observers of the South African scene believe that the present parliamentary government may be replaced in the future by authoritarian rule by the state president and state Security Council. This is the view expressed by the Catholic Institute of International Relations in London: "The military, who have for the past two years been involved in road blocks and garrison duties outside townships, have been used since September [1984] on a more regular footing in [black] township control. For the first time, observers in South Africa with a knowledge of the [black] townships have begun using the words 'civil war.'"

41. The South African government has enacted a series of laws to discourage activities and organizations critical to apartheid. The Suppression of Communism Act and the Terrorism Act allow the police to arrest and hold anyone in detention for three months without charging the person with a crime. Detainees cannot contact family members or a lawyer. There is no legal recourse against such detention.

42. Torture is believed to be frequently used on political prisoners. They are sometimes deprived of sleep, beaten, and forced to stand for days without food, water, or toilet facilities and may be kept in solitary confinement. Electric shocks are sometimes applied, and deaths in detention are not uncommon.

43. Less violent is *banning*, a measure that may be taken against an individual or an organization. An organization, when banned, must cease operations. For individuals, banning is a form of house arrest by which the person is compelled to reside in a place designated by the goverment. Such a place may be far distant from the person's normal residence. Banned persons cannot be published or quoted, and their movements are restricted. They may receive only one visitor at a time and may not enter the premises of a school, labor union, newspaper, or other publisher. The banning penalty may last as long as five years and may be renewed. Again, there is no legal recourse against the banning order.

44. There is, of course, the normal legal process of charging an individual with a crime and bringing that person to trial. A notable example of this is the current "treason trial" involving sixteen persons, some of whom comprise the leadership of the United Democratic Front (UDF), a significant broadly based organization that has led nonviolent protests against the new constitution and forced removals. Even if the trial results in not-guilty verdicts, the government will have effectively crippled the UDF during the many months of the legal process.

45. Apartheid is a system of control and repression which is much hated within the black community that constitutes over 70 percent of the population of South Africa. Its byproducts are broken families, poor living conditions, poverty and malnutrition, a sense of insecurity, a loss of respect for the law, and a loathing of officialdom. The Catholic bishops of southern Africa in 1957 stated that apartheid is "something intrinsically evil" (SACBC *Statement on Apartheid*, 1957). That the Church's view has not changed in the intervening years is illustrated by the words of Pope John Paul II spoken on May 13, 1985, at The Hague:

> For Christians and for all who believe in a covenant, that is, an unbreakable bond between God and man and between all human beings, no form of discrimination—in law or in fact—on the basis of race, origins, color, culture, sex or religion can ever be acceptable. Hence no system of apartheid or separate development will ever be acceptable as a model for the relations between people or races.

Part II: U.S. Policy and South Africa

46. The significance of South Africa in the U.S. foreign policy debate has increased dramatically in 1985. The new visibility is the result of efforts of groups in the United States (e.g., on college campuses and at the South African embassy or consulates) as well as a dramatic upsurge of protest from the black community in South Africa. The declaration of a state of emergency on July 20, 1985, by the South African government was both a sign of the seriousness of the internal situation and a cause of sharp diplomatic protest by other governments, including the United States.

47. The basic situation of apartheid sketched above has not changed dramatically; it has been solidly in place for decades. The change has been in the attention the outside world is giving to South Africa.

48. The policy debate in the United States focuses on three topics: the *perspective* by which the South Africa case is viewed; the basic *posture* that the U.S. government and U.S.-based institutions should take toward South Africa; and the specific *means* the United States should use to respond to the policy of apartheid.

49. The debate about perspective affects many issues of U.S. foreign policy. In essence it is whether the South Africa problem should be seen principally as an aspect of the geopolitical struggle of East and West or whether the South Africa policy should be conceived in terms of the intrinsic issues in South Africa and the role of U.S. policy in Africa as a continent. The distinction between these two perspectives is not absolute, but accepting one or the other as a starting point does have direct implications for the specific choices in U.S. policy. For example, the question of how "security interests" (e.g., the sea lanes around South Africa or access to key minerals) are balanced against human rights objectives in U.S. policy is substantially influenced by which perspective one holds on the place of South Africa in U.S. foreign policy.

50. The perspective issue is related to the question of the basic posture that American institutions take toward South Africa. It is the debate about posture that divides the supporters and critics of "constructive engagement." The premises of constructive engagement are that the U.S. government is in a unique position to influence South Africa, but this leverage will be effective only if South Africa sees the United States as an ally, not an adversary. Within the context of a positive atmosphere, the architects of constructive engagement seek to move South Africa toward positive steps on Namibia and internal political questions in South Africa.

51. The critics of constructive engagement argue that such a posture has a high moral price (symbolic and substantive identification of U.S. policy with an apartheid regime) and has had little political payoff. The critics propose a clear posture of U.S. distance from the South African government without breaking diplomatic relations; they push for a limited adversarial relationship between the United States and South Africa. They argue that this makes a clear distinction between the goals of U.S. policy and the South African regime, but the importance of the United States to South Africa will mean that we still will have some leverage on South African policy.

52. The advocates and critics of constructive engagement agree that the United States is too important to South Africa to be ignored by it. They disagree on how best to express a political-moral critique of apartheid and its consequences.

53. The debate about posture moves finally to a question of effective means of policy. The issues debated include major policy measures like invoking economic sanctions against South Africa, depriving it of government or private bank loans, calling for corporations to disinvest, and reducing the U.S. diplomatic presence in South Africa; they also include measures like restricting visas for South Africans in response to South Africa's visa policy and depriving South African Airways of landing rights in the United States. The means debate is both political and moral; it involves questions of tactical effectiveness, timing, and prudence.

Part III: The USCC and South Africa

54. The U.S. bishops have two direct ties to South Africa. First, bonds of episcopal solidarity make the Catholic Church one of a handful of institutions that can act in a coordinated way in both countries. Second, the members of the Church in the United States are citizens of a country with a significant impact on South Africa.

55. USCC links to the SACBC are a significant reality. Few institutions—if any—rival the role of the churches in South Africa as channels of black protest against the existing regime. Bishop Tutu holds a unique position, but the Catholic bishops' conference and its president, Archbishop Denis Hurley of Durban, are playing a major role in the South African crisis. The SACBC positions against the policies of South Africa in Namibia and at home in South Africa have increased in frequency and force in the last decade. There is little doubt that the Catholic bishops are seen as severe critics of their own government and the system of apartheid.

56. The USCC and the SACBC have worked closely in the 1980s on Namibia, culminating in the 1983 USCC Administrative Board *Statement on Namibia*. The general principles the USCC uses on human rights questions apply with particular urgency to South Africa. These include the affirmation that human rights issues are never purely internal questions in a country; that outside actors—particularly governments—have moral responsibility for their policy choices as these affect human rights; and that the USCC statements seek to encourage a public and policy response in the United States that will foster respect for human rights in those situations we can influence. Such USCC statements are based on moral principles but involve the same testing of concrete choices, weighing of consequences, and assessment of effective action that runs through the wider U.S. policy debate.

57. The USCC Administrative Board *Statement on South Africa* seeks to define some of the key moral values at stake in the South Africa case and to make some recommendations for different parts of U.S. society in responding to South Africa.

In the Sight of All, Communications A Vision All Can Share

*Statement Issued by the
Administrative Board of the
United States Catholic Conference*

September 1985

Part I: Introduction

1. "Your light must shine in the sight of all, so that, seeing your good works, they may give the praise to your Father in heaven."[1]
2. As the Administrative Board of the United States Catholic Conference, we address our brother bishops and all communicators serving the Catholic Church in the United States. We write to stress the importance of communication work as a ministry today and to encourage bishops to implement fully in their local churches the communication dimension of their pastoral task. We wish to affirm the efforts begun by communicators who seek a vision of communication and Church that all can share.[2] In this reflection, we recognize the link between the Church and communication, and we propose that all church communication efforts work to establish a public dialogue of faith.
3. As bishops, we rejoice in the unparalleled pastoral opportunity we have to share the light of the Gospel with all people, inviting them into this public dialogue of faith. The communication dimension of our pastoral task is clear: to build up one community of faith that gives witness to Christ in the sight of all,[3] to proclaim the Gospel to all people, believers and unbelievers alike,[4] and to promote dialogue among all people, especially on religious values and issues.[5] This task begins with the community of believers and includes all available communication media,[6] so that we might "communicate the truth,

---

[1]Mt 5:16.

[2]A Vision All Can Share Conference, "Mission Statement," in William J. Thorn, ed., *A Vision All Can Share: Report on the Conference at Marquette University: June 11-13, 1984* (Washington, D.C.: United States Catholic Conference, 1985), p. 8.

[3]*Christus Dominus* in Vatican Council II, *The Conciliar and Post Conciliar Documents,* Austin Flannery, ed. (Collegeville, Minn.: Liturgical Press, 1975), p. 569.

[4]Ibid., no. 12.

[5]Ibid., no. 13.

[6]Ibid.

nourish charity, defend justice, spread joy, and foster and confirm among all people that peace which Christ the Lord brings.'"[7]

4. Recent popes and the Council have given a clear mandate for this.[8] We now reaffirm the Second Vatican Council's approbation of communication media as an integral part of the pastoral role of bishops.[9] We embrace also the challenge of Pope Paul VI in *Evangelii Nuntiandi:* "The Church would feel guilty before the Lord if she did not utilize these powerful means that human skill is daily rendering more perfect. It is through them that she proclaims 'from the housetops' the message of which she is the depository."[10] Further, we urge implementation of the 1983 *Code of Canon Law*, which requires that the means of social communication become an integral part of Catholic evangelization.[11]

A Church That Communicates

5. The communication dimension of our pastoral task is not new. Our predecessors made important commitments to communication. From the publication of the first American Catholic journal in 1822 and the spread of Catholic schools in the nineteenth century, Catholics have attempted to enlarge the role that communication holds in the life of our society. In our day, our conference of bishops has invested $6 million in the development of the Catholic Telecommunications Network of America (CTNA); individual dioceses have doubled this amount in local involvement in CTNA affiliation; and we have authorized a national collection (the Catholic Communication Campaign) that has raised over $30 million since 1979 for church communication activities on the national and local levels.

6. While many aspects of the Church involve communication in the broadest sense, and while the traditional means of communication are well established in the Church, the newer means of communication pose new questions and alternatives today. On the one hand, existing channels of church communication do not reach everyone:

- Forty-seven percent of adult Americans attend church less than

---

[7]"Ordo Benedictionis Aedium ad Communicationes Sociales Promovendas," no. 630 in *Rituale Romanum: De Benedictionibus* (Vatican City: Typis Polyglottis Vaticanis, 1984), p. 247.

[8]*Inter Mirifica.*

[9]*Christus Dominus*, no. 13.

[10]Paul VI, *Evangelii Nuntiandi*, no. 45.

[11]Canons 761, 799, 822, in *Codex Iuris Canonici* (Vatican City: Typis Polyglottis Vaticanis, 1983).

twice a year; among Catholics, 30 percent have not attended Mass in the last month.[12]

- Although the level of education among Catholics has risen dramatically in the last generation, young Catholics do not read religious newspapers or magazines.[13]
- Religious issues are not discussed in depth. The major media often treat religious issues only as one news story among others or treat them only in a weekly religion section.[14]
- People don't know the Catholic Church in the United States as a communion of churches[15] with a heritage drawn from every part of the earth. In this country, we represent one religious ideal among many.

On the other hand, through these newer means of communication, the Church in the United States today has the opportunity to touch the life of every citizen:

- The press coverage of our pastoral letter *The Challenge of Peace: God's Promise and Our Response* made its themes known to virtually every American home.
- Millions of Americans—Catholics and non-Catholics alike—entered into the dialogue process of *The Challenge of Peace* through televised debates, teleconferences, and group study.
- Young Catholic parents use hundreds of video titles in sacramental preparation for their children. Catalogues of religious books and films list thousands of other available titles.
- In 1985 one television drama with a religious theme reached 21 percent of the television audience, or approximately 40 million people.[16]

Thus, as bishops in the United States, we face a challenge and an opportunity different from that of most of the world in communicating Christ's presence and in establishing a dialogue of faith.

---

[12]The Gallup Organization, *The Catholic Press Today: What We Know and How You Can Find Out More* (Princeton, N.J.: The Gallup Organization, 1982), pp. 39-43.

[13]Gallup, pp. 34-35.

[14]George Gerbner, Larry Gross, et al., *Religion and Television* (Philadelphia: The Annenberg School of Communications, 1984), p. 1.

[15]Cf. John Paul II, "Address to the College of Cardinals," December 21, 1984, no. 3, *Origins* 14 (January 10, 1985): 499.

[16]"The Fourth Wise Man," produced by Rev. Ellwood Kieser, CSP. Cf. Neilson Rating, *Broadcasting*, 108 (April 8, 1985): 150.

Part II: A Public Dialogue of Faith as the General Principle of Church Communication

7.   The Church is communicative by nature. We recognize that our faith comes by hearing[17] and by seeing.[18] We also recognize that as we have heard and seen, so must we speak and tell. Our Christian community built up by the proclamation of God's Word must be a sign and an instrument of union among all people.[19]

This community joins people in parishes as part of the universal Church, joins parish communities to local churches, and joins local churches into global union, particularly through the ease of communication "which no longer allows any one part of society to live in isolation."[20] Communication not only fosters the communion of the Church, but also Christ's presence to the world, as that presence is mediated by the community of believers: through sacrament and word, in prayer and works of charity, in the struggle for justice and peace.[21] Part of our ministry, then, is to represent Christ through the various media available to the Catholic Church in the United States today. While doing so, we look to the Scriptures and creeds as touchstones for any message that can be termed Christian. Because of this, teaching forms another part of our communication ministry: we who believe, believe the same Gospel and acknowledge one faith, one baptism, and one Lord.[22]

8.   The Catholic Church in the United States is affected by communication in other ways, too. First, the Church is an object of other people's communication. The witness of Christian living leads people to proclaim God's goodness.[23] Journalists write about the Church; television networks cover papal travels; films, plays, novels, and television drama find in the Church fascinating subject matter. Whether in news or entertainment, the Church in its institutions, officials, and individuals is part of the information society of the United States.

Second, church members form an audience that is a religious audience, hearing, reading, and sharing the message of the Lord. At the same time, however, we form an audience for other messages — messages about power, about consumption, about many values we do not hold.

---

[17]Rom 10:17.
[18]Mt 11:7.
[19]*Lumen Gentium*, no. 4.
[20]*Apostolicam Actuositatem*, no. 10.
[21]*Sacrosanctum Concilium*, no. 7.
[22]Eph 4:5-6.
[23]*Lumen Gentium*, no. 38.

Why Our Faith Dialogue Is Public

9. Thus, the Catholic Church in the United States is in public dialogue with American society. From the perspective of communication, the Church represents a public dialogue of faith.

First, the Church is *public*. We proclaim the Gospel and build up our community openly — "in the sight of all." Because no one can be excluded, the Church publicly manifests Christ's presence in the world. Communication implies this public quality: to communicate is to share, to overcome isolation and individuality, and to become community.

Second, the nature of our community and its place within American society lead to *dialogue*. For true communication, people must listen as well as speak; in this way, communication leads to communion. The Second Vatican Council committed the Church in the contemporary world to dialogue that leads to "a feeling of deep solidarity with the human race and its history."[24] As American bishops, we aim to enter into such dialogue with our nation and our culture. We also recognize that genuine communication must allow all men and women a voice in that dialogue.

Third, the Church is a community of *faith* whose communication always engages that faith. Our dialogue is rooted in faith; its subject ultimately is the Lord. Through our prayer and our teaching, as pastors of the Catholic Church in the United States, we gather the community of disciples. This faith reaches its fullness not in doctrine alone, but in acts of charity, justice, and peace.[25] Communication, too, reaches its fullness in mutual love.[26] Thus we share a common vision of communication in Jesus Christ, the living Word, the perfect communicator, the Teacher and Listener who unites us in his Body and in the Kingdom of God.[27]

10. Within this general sense of communication, a distinct ministry of communication has a place, involving communication professionals and specialists. We have not yet adequately addressed what this expertise requires of us as bishops; but we recognize factors that make this ministry complex: regional diversity, variety of media, need for creative responses, and costs. We therefore see a pastoral duty to guide the ministry of communication in the Catholic Church in the United States by applying the threefold criteria of the public dialogue of faith to five key issues.

---

[24]*Gaudium et Spes,* no. 1; see also no. 3. "And so, the Council, as witness and guide to the faith of the whole people of God, gathered together by Christ, can find no more eloquent expression of its solidarity and respectful affection for the whole human family, to which it belongs, than to enter into dialogue with it."

[25]Jas 2:14-26.

[26]1 Jn 4.

[27]A Vision All Can Share, "Mission Statement," p. 8.

Part III: Communication Issues
for the Church in the
United States

11. Five key issues demand our active involvement: (a) the *style* of church communication; (b) communication as *ministry*; (c) Church use of communication *resources*: (d) responses to communication *content*; and (e) questions of *public policy*.

With regard to each area, we must keep three questions in mind. First, is our witness public? Are we as a Church a sign of the presence of Jesus?[28] Second, do we as bishops foster the dialogue of faith by our teaching and our listening?[29] Third, do we proclaim the discipleship of a common vision of faith in Jesus the Lord?[30]

a. The Style of Church Communication

12. As a community of believers the Church must foster a true dialogue. The dominant mass communication industries promote one-way communication; we must change that attitude. The Church cannot accept only one-way communication systems as models for its own communication. Communicators must listen as well as speak: human dignity demands respect for people's right to communicate. Following the lead of *Communio et Progressio*, we accept the role of dialogue, critical inquiry, access to information, legitimate privacy and confidentiality, and two-way communication in the Church.[31] We also encourage active collaboration among communicators in the Church to foster the dialogue of faith and build up the Body of Christ. This dialogue both strengthens the *sensus fidelium* and helps the Church to discern the signs of the times so that Christ's mandate to preach the good news to all people may be fulfilled.

13. Thus, the right to communicate and the necessity for dialogue are rooted not only in an ecclesiological vision of the People of God but also in the dignity with which we are created. The international community has recognized this fact[32] as has the United States in its basic communication law.[33] These principles also reflect a clear understanding that the human race as a whole is the steward of the gifts of

---

[28] *Evangelii Nuntiandi*, no. 15.

[29] *Gaudium et Spes*, no. 3.

[30] A Vision All Can Share, "Mission Statement," p. 8.

[31] *Communio et Progressio*, nos. 115, 117, 120, 121, 122. See also John Paul II, "Address to UNESCO," *The Month at UNESCO*, 97 (April-June 1980): 1, no. 16.

[32] United Nations, *Universal Declaration of Human Rights*, 1948, art. 19.

[33] U.S. Congress, *The Radio Act of 1912* and *The Communications Act of 1934* in setting forth the charter of the Federal Communications Commission, states that communication should serve "the public interest, convenience, and necessity."

communication and fully exercises its right to communicate only in a dialogue from which none are excluded.

At the same time, men and women, as well as institutions, have rights generally recognized by all to determine what to communicate and when.[34] Therefore, privacy and confidentiality must be respected. In addition, we must continue our past efforts to make society, governments, industry, and other institutions more receptive to public service, local access, and other communication practices that lead to a fuller and more balanced dialogue.[35]

14. This same right and need of all people for true dialogue lies at the heart of communication policy as well. Effective communication demands a knowledge and love that come only from dialogue. Because the Church desires to enter into communication with church members and nonmembers alike, the style of our communication must reflect the loving, communicative nature of the Church. We must learn the needs, concerns, symbols, and language of the people, as well as the media in which they are literate. To this end, we endorse communication research on behalf of the Church and urge that our bishops, in their dioceses and through the USCC Department of Communication, foster national cooperation for communication research, planning, and strategy.[36]

b. Communication as Ministry

15. Communication work within the Catholic Church is a shared pastoral ministry which is never isolated. Just as the Church itself has a communicative dimension,[37] so has each ministry. The ministry of professional communicators serves every ministry of the Church but stands also on its own, giving concrete expression on the Church's fundamental mission to communicate. For this reason, the whole range of communication activities should be submitted to theological scrutiny in order to be integrated more closely with the mission of the Church.

The many different theological points of origin for reflection on communication (pastoral, evangelical, prophetic, Christological, ecclesiological, and so on[38]) prompt us to call theologians and church

---

[34]*Communio et Progressio*, no. 121. Address of Pope John Paul II to the International Catholic Press Union's XII World Congress, September 1981, no. 5.

[35]USCC, letter to senators regarding S.2172, 1982.

[36]A Vision All Can Share, "Recommendations," II. A. 2, p. 11. In addition, we commend the Catholic Press Association for commissioning the Annenberg/Gallup study of the Catholic press, and the Catholic Communication Campaign for commissioning the Annenberg study of Religion and Television.

[37]*Presbyterium Ordinis*, nos. 2, 4.. *Christus Dominus*, nos. 12, 13.

[38]"World Council of Churches Agreed Statement on the Media," *Media Development*, 31:1 (January 1984): 7; *Communio et Progressio*, no. 11.

communicators to collaborate in developing a theological understanding of the role of communication within and on behalf of the Catholic Church in the United States.[39]

16. Because of the communicative dimensions inherent in every form of pastoral ministry, all pastoral workers should receive some education in communications as an integral part of their pastoral education. In our information society, the Church owes pastoral workers this education so that they can understand and minister to the information-rich and the information-poor, with a clear grasp of the impact of new information technologies on individuals and social structures.[40] Pastoral ministers need to be educated particularly in ways of inviting others into dialogue and avoiding communication that involves domination, manipulation, or personal gain.

A Shared Ministry

17. Because the ministry of the Church is one in which all have a part in the public dialogue of faith, the Church looks to professionals in the communication and information industries for their technical, artistic, and creative help. These members of the Church most directly make Christ present in their workplace. Many seek guidance from the Church in integrating the values of their faith with their creative lives. And so we ask each bishop to provide whatever pastoral care communication professionals may seek and to support their efforts to shape the media for the service of community and human progress.[41] We also appeal to those working in these industries to bear witness to their faith and values, never hesitating to ask the church community for whatever assistance they need.

---

[39] A Vision All Can Share, "Recommendations" II.A.1, p. 11.

[40] Cf. Puebla, Third General Conference of Latin American Bishops, *Puebla: Evangelization at Present and in the Future of Latin America*, nos. 1083, 1085. (Washington, D.C.: National Conference of Catholic Bishops, 1979), pp. 171-172. "It is urgently necessary that the hierarchy and pastoral agents in general, all of us, become acquainted with the phenomenon of social communication, understand it, and gain a deeper experiential contact with it. In this way we can adapt our pastoral responses to this new reality and integrate communication into our overall, coordinated pastoral effort. . . . The task of providing training in the field of social communication is a priority one. Hence we must train all the agents of evangelization in this field."

[41] *Communio et Progressio*, no. 1. Agreed Statement of the Swiss Churches on Communication, *Media Development*, 31:1 (January 1984), no. 2, cf. The bishops and religious leaders of Switzerland: "The Church must share the concerns of communicators and support them in their duties: to develop human knowledge and judgment; to provide entertainment and other services; to maintain a concern for truth, freedom and solidarity; to educate the young; to inform public opinion; and to express a concern for human society."

c. Church Use of Communication Resources

18. The Catholic Church in the United States makes some use of almost all means of communication. Catholics experience church communication regularly, from the Sunday homily to broadcast television. Catholic institutions in the United States maintain the National Catholic News Service and publish 156 diocesan newspapers, 5 national newspapers, and 335 magazines. Religious educators and parishes use the so-called group media—films and filmstrips, audio and videocassettes, puppets, and so on that lend themselves to a person-to-person evangelization.[42] Religious educators in larger dioceses have also pioneered the use of Instructional Television Fixed Service (ITFS), a microwave transmission facility for parishes and schools. The Church also uses church-related production houses and church-sponsored radio and television programming. Even the newer technologies of cable television and computers find a place in communication ministry. The Catholic Telecommunications Network of America, a satellite mediated information system designed to provide program distribution, teleconferencing, and electronic mail, is the newest church use of communication technology.

Talking among Ourselves . . .

19. In our use of these means of communication, the Church communicates with two different groups. Pastorally, communication is directed to the members of the Catholic Church—to teach, to support, to admonish, to encourage one another;[43] to give the Church in the United States a sense of identity and unity; and to reflect on our faith, to retell the story of the crucified and risen Lord in our contemporary language.[44] Many media carry this word directly to the various communities of the Church, in homes or through Catholic schools and religious education programs, parishes, and diocesan organizations. Administratively, the Church uses communications media to link parishes with each other and the local bishop; bishops in regional and national conferences; religious communities and provinces; Catholic colleges and universities; hospitals and associations, and so on. Institutional networking on these levels provides strong support and cooperation in an efficient and cost-effective manner. Effective networking

---

[42]Cf. Puebla documents, no. 1090, p. 172: "Besides being less costly and easier to handle, they (group media) offer the possibility of dialogue and they are more suited to a person-to-person type of evangelization that will evoke truly personal adhesion and commitment."

[43]Col 3:16.

[44]*Christus Dominus*, no. 13.

shares resources, utilizes talent, and lowers the cost of both the communication media and the goods and services involved.

... And with Others

20. Our communication is also directed outside the Catholic Church. Whether under the name of "pre-evangelization," "evangelization," or "pastoral outreach," the Church has the duty to preach the Gospel to all. In our own country, where millions have left the Christian churches and millions more have little religious background, the Church must go outside itself. And it is here that the Church uses communications media to provide a way to begin its outreach. The dialogue of faith is public; without it, no one will be drawn to that faith;[45] through public communication, the Church also challenges society according to the Gospel and introduces a moral voice into the discussion of vital issues.[46]

What We Can Do

21. Within the context of communication, there still remains much to be done, because of the impact of the information society and also because our efforts do not reach everyone.

We urge each diocese, therefore, to develop a strategy for using the means of communication, fitted into an overall diocesan pastoral plan.[47]

We support particularly the Catholic press. People should have access to Catholic publications that present national and international news of the Church and that form and inform the local church. We urge all dioceses, either locally or through regional cooperation, to provide Catholic newspapers.[48] We encourage a high priority on the discussion of serious contemporary issues and on a serious effort to reach Catholic young adults.

We renew our commitment to the CTNA as a means of promoting communication within the Church and providing quality religious programming for redistribution to radio, television, and cable outlets.[49] We urge dioceses to affiliate with CTNA as soon as possible, either individually or through a local consortium so that this telecommunications network may reach the potential of service to the Catholic

---

[45]Rom 10:14-17.

[46]Cf. National Conference of Catholic Bishops, *The Challenge of Peace: God's Promise and Our Response* (Washington, D.C.: United States Catholic Conference, 1983), nos. 139-140.

[47]A Vision All Can Share, "Recommendations," II.B.2, p. 12.

[48]Ibid., I.3, p. 9.

[49]Ibid., I.2, p. 8.

Church in the United States that motivated our initial funding for the network.

Where local churches, religious communities, and individuals within the Church have already invested in establishing media libraries and structures (publishing houses, journals, film production facilities, radio and television studios and stations, and even satellite links), we urge the whole Church to utilize these resources fully through cooperative and equitable ventures.[50]

Consonant with this, we also urge Catholic communicators to cooperate in ecumenical communication projects to make the gospel message better known.[51]

We commend and encourage the efforts of the various associations of Catholic communicators—the Catholic Press Association, UNDA (National Catholic Association for Communicators), the International Catholic Press Union, the International Catholic Film Organization—in establishing interpersonal networks among communicators.

Finally, we direct the USCC Department of Communication to serve as our agent in identifying and providing for any needs of church communicators that are not met by an existing organization.

22. In addition, we call upon everyone in the Church to exercise responsibility and creativity in fostering a public dialogue of faith. Many resources remain insufficiently utilized: public service announcements, advertising, public relations, news coverage, and cable access channels. We ask all bishops and church communicators to encourage secular news media and public affairs agencies to cover major issues of religious and ethical import and to provide those agencies with whatever information and expertise they can. In using these structures, church communicators should indicate clearly the capacity in which they speak. The press and mass media must be able to recognize the differences between an individual speaking personally, speaking for a local church, and speaking for the Church in the United States.[52]

Overcoming Limitations of the Media

23. We recognize that the various media of communication have their own limitations and inherent weaknesses. The North American patterns of communication already invest these media with values. The American broadcast industry—producers, networks, broadcasters, sponsors, and so forth—have formed radio and television primarily

---

[50]Ibid., II.A.3, p. 11; I.4, p. 9.
[51]Ibid., II.A.3, p. 11.
[52]Ibid., II.B.3, p. 12.

into entertainment and sales media.[53] Our brother bishops in Latin America have recognized and pointed out at their Puebla meeting the dangers of consumerism and reduction to a lowest common denominator audience that mass media and their advertising tend to promote.[54] Other communications media have their drawbacks as well. Cable television does not necessarily extend the religious viewing audience. Rather than making new converts, its religious programming attracts an audience of believers.[55] Diocesan newspapers reach less than half of the Catholic population.[56] Despite their benefits, cable television and some small media (videocassette recorders, film projectors, and increasingly the telephone) are too expensive for the poor and the elderly. Some people are unable to subscribe; others lack the technical training to make use of what is available. Not everyone possesses the skills essential to critical use of print and broadcast communication.

24. But no communication medium is, in and of itself, foreign to religious use. The broadcast media can obviously be used for purposes other than entertainment and sales: educational, public affairs, cultural events, and religious programming also exist. Despite any disadvantages and the added limitations that the recent industry and Federal Communications Commission deregulatory initiatives have placed on access and financing, we must use these media as part of our educational, catechetical, ethical, and evangelical outreach. In doing this, we issue an important challenge to the very definition of the broadcast media in the United States. We must also explore new and effective uses of cable and other media to reach the unchurched. Recognizing the dangers of the smaller media does not mean we should not use them: we must plan carefully so that the Church is truly present to all people without violating their rights or cutting them off from the dialogue of faith. Decisions about communication planning and policy cannot be purely technical or economic, but must take into account both the limiting aspects and the positive values of human dignity, church identity, and church mission.

---

[53]This fact has been canonized by the Federal Communications Commission in the recent deregulation of radio (USCC comments before FCC re: BC Docket No. 79-219, RM-3099, RM-3273) and has been challenged by community and church leaders in the debate over a "family viewing hour." Cf. Administrative Board, United States Catholic Conference, *Statement on the Family Viewing Policy of the Television Networks* (Washington, D.C.: United States Catholic Conference, 1975).

[54]Puebla documents, nos. 1069, 1073, pp. 170-171; Address of Pope John Paul II to the International Catholic Press Union XII World Congress, September 1981, no. 4.

[55]Gerbner et al., pp. 64-65.

[56]Gallup, p. 5.

The Catholic Communication Campaign

25. The Catholic Communication Campaign should support a variety of communication efforts, following its mission and priorities. Its overall mission is to aid the Church's evangelization efforts through the proclamation of the Gospel and the advancement and integral development of all men and women.

Within this framework, the priorities are to create the Church's messages, to deliver those messages especially through the development of CTNA, to educate audiences and train religious communicators, to share resources, to protect the Church's media access, to strengthen the Church's relations with the communication establishment in this country, and to serve the universal Church.[57] The CCC's sole source of financial support is an annual appeal to parishioners throughout the United States. We urge each diocese to support the CCC in these efforts; we are concerned that the CCC collection is not supported to the extent needed to finance the kinds and number of projects our conference endorsed in voting for this annual national fund-raising effort. It is important to remember that half the money raised annually stays in the local dioceses, where it is used for a variety of communication-related activities matching the national mission and priorities.

26. The decision to communicate has already been made. The task now is to support that decision and to evaluate it according to these criteria: the public manifestation of the presence of Christ, openness to the dialogue of faith in society, and the witness to the shared vision of American Catholic communication. These goals have a substantial cost in trained personnel and in financial resources; but on a per capita basis of people reached, however, it is considerably less than the cost of traditional channels of church information, such as personal contact, preaching, or education.[58] We cannot allow the impression of cost to discourage us from our pastoral duty. We urge all bishops to see through on the local level the decisions they have made on the national level.

---

[57] Catholic Communication Campaign, "Communication Committee Adopts New CCC Funding Priorities," *Proclaim* (August/September 1985): 1.

[58] In 1984, *Merton*, the one-hour film biography of the social activist and spiritual writer Thomas Merton was carried by over 85 percent of the stations of the Public Broadcasting Service in the United States. The CCC provided matching funds of $175,000 for this major film documentary which cost $340,000. According to the standard survey procedures of the broadcast industry, this 85 percent PBS coverage factor translates conservatively into a minimum of 70 million viewers. Thus it cost U.S. Catholics less than .003 cents per viewer to air a quality religious program seen nationally and rebroadcast in major markets several times over in 1984–1985.

d. Responses to Communication Content

27. In our information society, people often feel deluged by messages that promote values contrary to their own and contrary to the Gospel. Many people find television and radio programming, dramatic productions, some popular music, rock music videos, many films, and some written materials offensive, insulting, or degrading. The United States Catholic Conference has consistently and emphatically opposed any communication content that is destructive of human and religious values.[59] At the same time, recognizing the legitimate rights and duties of artistic expression,[60] we oppose censorship;[61] our policy instead is to urge artists, producers, and communicators to seek sincerely the truth and to be motivated by a love for humanity, rather than by financial gain or base instinct.

Therefore, we support industry self-regulation, and we strongly remind communicators that some communication content—pornography, for example—is not protected by the First Amendment. As religious leaders, we oppose pornography, not only on legal grounds, but especially on moral grounds since pornography demeans the human person and denies any possibility of dialogue, discipleship, or communication. Those citizen efforts to take legal action against pornography deserve our support.

What We Can Do

23. On our part, we too bear a responsibility to provide guidance and education regarding media content.[62] Just as literary and dramatic criticism has had a place in Catholic education, so too should the evaluation of popular culture in all its forms. Media education and the formation of the individual conscience are absolute necessities. This responsibility, though, cannot be solely the task of educators. It forms a part of the shared pastoral ministry of communication in the Church.

Newspapers, journals, books, radio, and television materials should aid media education so that all can experience this liberating pedagogy. Media education is an essential response to the invasion of unwanted programming into the home, to the degradation of human sexuality and women in particular by the pornography industry, and to the violence unthinkingly portrayed as the sole solution to any human conflict. In addition, media literacy courses educate children

---

[59]USCC, comments before the FCC, GEN Docket 83-989.
[60]*Communio et Progressio,* no. 57.
[61]USCC, Administrative Board, *Statement on the Family Viewing Policy,* 1975, p. 7.
[62]*Inter Mirifica,* no. 21.

and adults in the use of the media, preparing them to participate more fully in a communication society and helping them to know the value of the dialogue we esteem.[63]

29. Since the discussion of religious and moral issues is paramount to the development of responsible, adult Christians, church communication activities must promote this discussion through both printed materials and electronic programming. Catholic media should also provide information on the whole scope of Christian living — the teaching of the Magisterium; instruction in church doctrine; news coverage of the community, both local and global; discussion of issues of justice and peace; spiritual and reflective material. This listing does not exhaust the possibilities of religious communication: Catholic communicators should exercise imagination and creativity, drawing on the whole tradition of the Church in this important educative role.[64]

e. Questions of Public Communication Policy

30. As a Church committed to a public dialogue of faith, our interest in communication goes beyond the boundaries of our own faith community. Representing the religious beliefs of one quarter of the citizens of the United States, the Church has a right to be heard by government and a duty to speak out on the moral and ethical dimension of national and international communication issues. This dimension is too often submerged by questions of financial gain.

In these issues, we apply the same criteria of the public dialogue of faith that we have already noted: the right of all men and women to communicate, the duties of the human race as stewards of the gifts of creation (including the broadcast spectrum), and the defense against exploitation and dehumanizing communication. In *Communio et Progressio*, an instruction noted for its defense of the right to communicate,[65] the Church has spoken already of the freedom to assess and compare differing views, the right to information, the freedom of access to the sources and channels of information, the freedom of communication, and the free flow of information and opinion.[66]

Other issues are interrelated with communication: issues of control and manipulation; exploitation of passions, feelings, violence, and sex for commercial purposes; attacks on the family; misrepresen-

---

[63]A Vision All Can Share, "Recommendations," I.8, p. 10.

[64]Ibid., I.8, p. 10; cf. also Pope John Paul II's comment to Catholic journalists, "One of the Catholic journalist's responsibilities is the conscientious exercise of an educative role, so that his readers may perceive, desire and seek the best and most just and truthful attitude, the most beneficial one for them and for society." Address to the XII World Congress of the International Catholic Press Union, September 1981, no. 3.

[65]UNESCO, *Many Voices, One World* (Paris: UNESCO, 1980), p. 137, note 1.

[66]*Communio et Progressio*, nos. 26, 33, 34, 46.

tation of religion; domination of the means of communication for political purposes.[67] As representatives of the Catholic Church in a country which is a leader in world communication, we call for justice in communication and encourage the application of gospel values and teaching to communication in our country, even where this means taking controversial positions. These issues are complex; briefly, we stand for a just resolution of the conflicting rights of international access and individual governments; of those who have invested in communication facilities and local or national communities; of individuals and groups.[68]

A Place for Discussion

31. The mass communication media often supply the most appropriate forum for church discussion of a variety of moral issues: national defense policies, respect for human life, citizens' rights, conduct of foreign policy (particularly where the Church's perspective goes beyond a national self-interest), rights of the weak, and so forth. In entering into a national dialogue through mass communication, we not only fulfill our teaching role, but also seek to persuade all people according to the Gospel. To do this, we must bring a credibility to our public communication by being aware of our own intentions, consistent with the moral teaching of the Church, and clear in our witness to the Gospel.[69] Moreover, all church communicators should be well prepared, both in content and in communication skills, and be readily available to make the Church's position and reasoning known to all.

Part IV: Summary

32. In the many communication-related concerns and challenges today facing the Catholic Church in the United States, it is our commitment to a public dialogue of faith that leads us. No single solution or communication plan can answer all questions or needs. In this reflection, therefore, we have outlined only an approach to communication and offered general recommendations. Local dioceses must implement

---

[67]Puebla documents, nos. 1068, 1069, p. 170.

[68]Some of these areas of conflicting communication rights appear in the debates of the World Administrative Radio Conferences, the Federal Communication Commission regulatory policies, cable television legislation, and local franchising agreements regarding cable.

[69]Cf. The World Council of Churches at its 1983 Vancouver Assembly (Declaration, *Media Development*, 31:1 [January 1984]: 7). "Credibility involves more than simply telling the truth. It must take the following into account: (a) Intention . . . (b) Content . . . (c) Style . . . (d) Dialogue . . . (e) Appropriateness . . . (f) Mystery . . . (g) Value reversal.

these recommendations. In this effort, we encourage the "Vision All Can Share" process already begun by church communication personnel.

We call all to a change of attitude so that we may communicate *with* rather than *to* people. As a Church we wish to foster a dialogue of faith rooted in the proclamation of the Gospel (no. 12). To this end, we ask:

- that every diocesan pastoral plan incorporate communications as an integral component (no. 21);
- that all pastoral workers receive education in communication (no. 16);
- that scholars and teachers undertake communication research on behalf of the Church (no. 14);
- that theologians and communication specialists collaborate in a theological reflection on communication (no. 15); and
- that bishops exercise special pastoral care for those men and women who work in the communication and information industries (no. 17).

We call church leaders, especially our brother bishops, to fulfill the mandate of the universal Church and of our own conference in actively supporting communication efforts already undertaken (no. 3). In particular, we call for:

- renewed support of the Catholic press and for a particular outreach to young Catholic adults (no. 21);
- renewed commitment to the Catholic Communication Campaign in order to provide adequate funding for common projects (no. 25);
- effective local implementation of the Catholic Telecommunications Network of America (no. 21);
- greater cooperation among Catholic media houses in making resources available (no. 21);
- greater efforts in media education (no. 28);
- diocesan support for the public communication policy decisions agreed upon by the conference (no. 30).

"All the members of the Church should make a concerted effort to ensure that the means of communication are put at the service of the multiple forms of the apostolate without delay and as energetically as possible, where and when they are needed."[70] We need them today.

---

[70] *Inter Mirifica*, no. 13.

Statement on the Ukraine

A Statement Issued by the
National Conference of Catholic Bishops

November 14, 1985

Be it resolved that the National Conference of Catholic Bishops at their annual meeting in Washington, D.C. is aware and concerned about the ongoing persecution of the Catholic Church in the Ukraine and requests the President of the United States at the summit meetings in Geneva to include this denial of freedom and worship and human rights as a paramount issue in his discussion with the Soviet authorities and that the members of this conference gratefully acknowledge the sacrifices of our modern Ukrainian Catholic martyrs and come to the assistance of our brothers and sisters in the Ukrainian Catholic Underground Church.

Pastoral Plan for Pro-Life Activities
A Reaffirmation

A Statement Issued by the
National Conference of Catholic Bishops

November 14, 1985

Introduction

All human beings ought to value every person for his or her uniqueness as a creature of God, called to be a brother or sister of Christ
by reason of the incarnation and the universal redemption. For us,.
the sacredness of human life is based on these premises. And it is
on these same premises that there is based our celebration of life—
all human life. This explains our efforts to defend human life against
every influence or action that threatens or weakens it, as well as our
endeavors to make every life more human in all its aspects.

And so, we will stand up every time that human life is threatened
(Pope John Paul II, Homily on the Capitol Mall, Washington, D.C.,
October 7, 1979).

1. Respect for human life was declining in our society when the
Pastoral Plan for Pro-Life Activities was first issued in 1975. In part this
reflected a secularizing trend, a rejection of moral imperatives based
on belief in God and his plan for creation. It also reflected social trends
encouraging individuals to give precedence to their own well-being
to the detriment of others. These and other trends had helped bring
about laws and judicial decisions which denied or ignored basic human
rights and our moral responsibility to protect and promote the common good. Conspicuous in this category were the 1973 decisions of
the United States Supreme Court removing any effective legal protection from unborn children and the efforts to justify euthanasia,
which were stimulated by those decisions.

2. A decade later these destructive trends continue to exert their
effect, though resistance to them is stronger than it was ten years
ago. In several later rulings, the Supreme Court has reaffirmed and
broadened its 1973 abortion decisions, spurring the growth of an
abortion industry which now destroys the lives of over one and a half
million unborn children in the United States every year. This situation
in turn has encouraged a trend toward lethal neglect of newborn
children with disabilities, a practice sometimes rationalized by appeal
to the same "right of privacy" used in the attempt to establish a right
to abortion. Increasingly, public debate over "death with dignity" has
become a debate regarding the legitimacy of "rational suicide" and
the active hastening of death for elderly patients. In other areas of
public concern—including nuclear deterrence, capital punishment,

immigration policy, and social spending for the poor—respect for the intrinsic dignity of human life does not play the central role it deserves.

3.   For these reasons, it is highly appropriate not only to revise the original *Pastoral Plan* in light of the contemporary situation, but also to reaffirm its central message regarding the dignity of human life while urging intensified efforts to implement this plan.

4.   In fulfillment of our pastoral responsibilities, we the members of the National Conference of Catholic Bishops reaffirm that human life is a precious gift from God; that each person who receives this gift has responsibilities toward God, toward self, and toward others; and that society, through its laws and social institutions, must protect and sustain human life at every stage of its existence. These convictions grow out of our Church's constant witness that "life must be protected with the utmost care from the moment of conception" (*Gaudium et Spes*, 51). In stating this principle, and in condemning abortion and infanticide as "abominable crimes," the Second Vatican Council restated a teaching which has been a constant part of the Christian message since the Apostolic Age.

5.   This principle of the absolute inviolability of innocent human life has emerged intact from centuries of discussion, during which some have argued for a compromise of principle in certain cases to serve various aspects of human well-being. The Church has always known that the fear and desperation of some who take human life in circumstances of severe hardship can so cloud their conscience as to reduce their moral guilt. Thus, it recognizes a need to remove or alleviate those circumstances which may lead otherwise responsible people to choose such actions. But it does not and cannot conclude that any circumstance gives a person the right directly to destroy an innocent human life.

6.   Ultimately, the duty of individuals and society to respect human life is grounded in the dignity of the human person, made in the image of God. Recognition of this duty is thoroughly consistent with the legal traditions of our own nation, whose Declaration of Independence names the right to life as first among the unalienable rights conferred by our Creator.

7.   Basic human rights are violated in many ways: by abortion and euthanasia, by injustice and the denial of equality to individuals or various groups of persons, by some forms of human experimentation, by neglect of the underprivileged and disadvantaged who deserve society's concern and support. But society's responsibility to ensure and protect human rights demands recognition and protection of the right to life as antecedent to all other rights and the necessary condition for their realization. It is unlikely that efforts to protect other rights will ultimately be successful if life itself is continually diminished in value.

8.   Moreover, among the many important issues involving the dignity

of human life with which the Church is concerned, abortion necessarily plays a central role. Abortion's direct attack on innocent human life is precisely the kind of violent act that can never be justified. Because victims of abortion are the most vulnerable and defenseless members of the human family, it is imperative that we, as Christians called to serve the least among us, give urgent attention and priority to this issue of justice. Our concern is intensified by the realization that a policy and practice allowing over one and a half million abortions annually cannot but diminish respect for life in other areas. As we said in our pastoral letter *The Challenge of Peace*: "Abortion in particular blunts a sense of the sacredness of human life. In a society where the innocent unborn are killed wantonly, how can we expect people to feel righteous revulsion at the act or threat of killing noncombatants in war?" (no. 285). In a society where abortion is claimed as "a woman's right," the most fundamental right—the right to life—is denied, and the basis for defending the rights of all women and men is, thereby eroded. In this *Pastoral Plan* we, therefore, focus attention especially on the pervasive threat to human life arising from the present situation of abortion virtually on demand.

9.   This focus and the Church's firm commitment to a consistent ethic of life complement each other. A consistent ethic, far from diminishing concern for abortion or equating all issues touching on the dignity of human life, recognizes the distinctive character of each issue while giving each its proper role within a coherent moral vision. Within this vision, different issues are linked at the level of moral principle because they involve the intrinsic dignity of human life and our obligation to protect and nurture this great gift. At the same time, each issue requires its own moral analysis and practical response. In addressing a specific issue—whether it be abortion, nuclear war, capital punishment, degrading poverty, or racism, sexism, and other forms of discrimination—the Church highlights a particular aspect of the Christian message, without forgetting its place within a larger moral framework. Taken together, the Church's diverse pastoral statements and practical programs constitute no mere assortment of unrelated initiatives but a consistent strategy in support of human life in its various stages and circumstances.

10. Thus, we are fully committed to taking up the many issues touching on the dignity of human life and examining their interdependence. This is already clear from the diversity of concerns we have addressed and continue to address as an episcopal conference through pastoral letters and other statements, and from the range of matters discussed every year in our educational effort known as the Respect Life Program. But, in this *Pastoral Plan*, we are guided by a key insight regarding the linkage between abortion and these other important issues: Precisely *because* all issues involving human life are interdependent, a society which destroys human life by abortion under the mantle of law unavoidably undermines respect for life in all other contexts. Likewise, protection in law and practice of unborn human life will benefit all life, not only the lives of the unborn.

11. In focusing attention on the sanctity of human life, we hope to generate a greater respect for the life of all persons. We are confident that greater respect for human life will result from continuing the public discussion of abortion and from efforts to shape our laws so as to protect the life of all, including the unborn.

12. This *Pastoral Plan* calls into action the resources of the Church in three major areas:

    a) a public information and education effort to deepen understanding of the humanity of the unborn, the sanctity of human life, the moral evil of abortion, and the consistent efforts of the Church to witness on behalf of all human life;

    b) a pastoral effort addressed to the special needs of women with problems related to pregnancy, of men and women struggling to accept responsibility for their power to generate human life, and of all persons who have had or have taken part in an abortion; and

    c) a public policy effort directed to ensuring effective legal protection for the right to life of the unborn.

13. This *Pastoral Plan* is addressed to and calls upon all church-sponsored or identifiably Catholic national, diocesan, and parish organizations and agencies to pursue this threefold effort with renewed determination. This plan envisages dialogue and cooperation between the NCCB/USCC and clergy, religious, and lay persons, individually and collectively. We seek the collaboration of all national Catholic organizations in this effort.

14. At the same time, we urge Catholics in the professions to discuss these issues with their colleagues and carry the dialogue into their own professional organizations. We recognize the important role of Catholic health care professionals, who are called to act as models of responsible stewardship for human life. We also urge those in the legal profession and in research, education, and academic life to make an effective presentation of the Church's commitment to respect for life at every stage and in every condition.

15. Dialogue among churches and religious groups is essential and has already proven fruitful. We are grateful that many other religious groups have voiced their strong opposition to abortion in recent years and have actively joined in the effort to restore legal protection for the unborn. We encourage continued national efforts at interreligious consultation and dialogue with other Christian bodies and with Judaism, as well as with other religious traditions and with those who have no specific denominational allegiance. Dialogue among ethicists is an important part of this effort.

16. The most effective structures for pastoral action are in the diocese and the parish. While recognizing the roles of national, regional, and statewide groups, this plan places primary emphasis and responsibility on the clergy, religious, and laity who serve the Church through diocesan and parish structures. While the work of informed and committed lay people at the parish level is clearly indispensable to the success of any large-scale pastoral effort, they must be able to rely on the support of religious and ordained ministers. The success of this *Pastoral Plan* depends in a special way on the support and encouragement given it by parish priests.

I. Public Information and Education Program

17. To deepen respect for human life and heighten public opposition to abortion, there is need for a twofold educational effort presenting the case for the sanctity of life from conception on.

18. The first aspect is a public information effort directed to the general public. This effort creates awareness of the threats to human dignity inherent in evils such as abortion, infanticide and euthanasia, and of the need to correct the present situation by establishing legal safeguards for the right to life. It gives pro-life issues continued visibility, while sensitizing those who have general perceptions of these issues but little firm conviction of commitment. This public information effort is necessary to inform public discussion and demonstrate the Church's commitment to a long-range pro-life effort. It will take a variety of forms: accurately reporting newsworthy events, issuing public statements, sponsoring conferences on pro-life issues, preparing and distributing information materials, etc.

19. The second aspect is an intensive, long-range educational effort leading people to a clearer understanding of the issues, to firm conviction, and to commitment. The Church has a duty to carry forward such an effort, directed primarily to the Catholic community. Those engaged in this effort should use the best legal, sociological, and medical information available, emphasizing advances in medical technology which call attention to the continuity of human development from conception on. Ultimately, however, moral and theological arguments present the central issue of respect for human life in its most intellectually compelling terms.

20. This intensive educational effort should present scientific information on the humanity of the unborn child and the continuity of human growth and development before birth; the biblical and theological foundations which sustain our commitment to human life and the dignity of the human person; society's responsibility to safeguard the life of the child at every stage of its existence; and humane and morally acceptable solutions to problems that may exist for a woman during and after pregnancy.

21. This effort should be carried on by all who participate in the Church's educational ministry, notably:

- clergy and religious, exercising their teaching responsibility in the pulpit, in other teaching roles, through parish programs, and through their public support for pro-life projects;
- all church-sponsored or identifiably Catholic organizations — national, regional, diocesan, and parochial — conducting adult education efforts;
- schools, catechetical programs, and other church-sponsored educational agencies providing moral teaching and motivation, bolstered by medical, legal, and sociological data;
- seminaries and houses of religious formation conducting academic and pastoral ministry programs;
- Catholic social service and health care agencies conducting educational efforts through seminars and other appropriate programs, including special efforts to publicize programs and services offering alternatives to abortion; and
- lay people instructing each other through discussion of critical public issues and forming the values of the next generation by their example and parental guidance.

22. The primary purpose of this intensive educational program is the development of pro-life attitudes and the determined avoidance of abortion. There is need for accurate information regarding the nature of abortion, a compelling explanation of how it violates God's plan for his children, and efforts to motivate people to act responsibly toward human life even though they may encounter hardships in doing so. Success will depend in part on promoting a moral and emotional climate in which human persons, human sexuality, and the power to generate human life are treated with the respect and sensitivity they deserve. At the same time, ethical consistency requires extending the program to related issues involving respect for human life.

23. The Respect Life Program, through its program manual and other materials, helps parishes call attention to specific problems and provides appropriate program formats and resources. It highlights the relationships among many of the Church's concerns and serves as a model for education on Christian responsibility. It sets abortion in the context of other issues involving threats to human life, such as certain problems facing the family, youth, the unemployed, the elderly, and persons with disabilities. It addresses specific issues such as poverty, housing, war, capital punishment, population control, infanticide, and euthanasia. While each of these issues demands its own moral analysis and response, the Repect Life Program calls attention to the way in which each touches on the dignity of human life.

II. Pastoral Care Program

24. Pastoral care includes the range of services which the Church offers people in dealing with their problems. Both spiritual assistance, extended with compassion and dignity, and essential material assistance, including supplementary services beyond those available in the community, express the Church's love for all human beings.
25. Three facets of the Church's program of pastoral care deserve particular attention.

1. Prayer and Worship

26. Responsibility for the least among us transcends all social theories and finds its root in the teaching of Jesus Christ. Appreciation for this responsibility is deepened by prayer and fasting. Participation in the sacramental life of the worshiping Catholic community sustains us in our ministry of service.
27. In the Eucharist, which renews and celebrates the saving mystery of Christ's death and resurrection and his gift of life to the Church, we are continually called to reconciliation and new life. Those entrusted with the ministry of preaching the homily should preach the truth about the dignity of all human life, born and unborn, and about the moral evil of abortion and other attacks on life. They should call forth compassion for individuals and families who find themselves in stressful situations and should motivate the Catholic community to offer practical assistance to help them make life-affirming decisions. The readings of the Church's liturgy give ample opportunity to proclaim respect for the dignity of human life throughout the liturgical year.
28. The Liturgy of the Hours and paraliturgical services also offer opportunities for the celebration of life and instruction in the moral teaching of the Church.

2. Service and Care

29. Respect for human life leads individuals and groups to reach out to those with special needs. With the support of the Catholic community, Catholic organizations and agencies will continue to provide services and care to pregnant women, especially to those who would otherwise find it difficult or impossible to obtain high-quality care. Ideally, these programs should include:

- material assistance, including nutritional, prenatal, childbirth, and postnatal care for the mother and nutritional and pediatric care for the child throughout the first year of life;
- continued research into and development of prenatal and neonatal medicine;
- extension of agency-sponsored adoption and foster care services to all who need them and concerted educational efforts to present adoption in a positive light;
- spiritual assistance and counseling services to provide support for women and men who face difficulties related to pregnancy and parenting;
- opportunities for teenage parents to continue their education before and after childbirth, including school policies which make it possible for them to complete their high school education;
- special understanding, encouragement, and support for victims of rape and other forms of abuse and violence;
- efforts to promote the virtue of chastity and to enable young men and women to take responsibility for their power to generate human life; and
- education in fertility awareness for young men and women and expansion of natural family planning services for married couples.

30. Many of these services, involving the dedicated efforts of professionals and volunteers, have been and will continue to be provided by church-sponsored health care and social service agencies. Collaboration with other private and public agencies, with volunteer groups, and with local communities, as well as efforts to obtain government assistance, are necessary extensions of the long-range effort.

3. Reconciliation

31. Christ's redeeming act, the paschal mystery of his death and resurrection, is the cause of human reconciliation in its twofold aspect: liberation from sin and communion with God. The whole Church has the mission of proclaiming this reconciliation.

32. Priests have a privileged opportunity to serve others by offering the unconditional and efficacious love of Christ in the sacrament of penance and fostering conversion and healing in women and men who have been involved in the destruction of innocent human life. Clergy education should reflect this reality, especially by training seminarians and priests to understand the painful experience of women who have had abortions. Many lay people, by God's grace, also serve directly or indirectly in this process of restoration to spiritual, mental, and emotional health.

33. Effective pastoral programs of reconciliation will draw upon these God-given resources to rebuild the penitent's bond with God, with the child, with the family, and with the community.

III. Public Policy Program

34. Protecting and promoting the inviolable rights of persons are essential duties of civil authority. As Americans, and as religious leaders, we are committed to governance by a system of law that protects the rights of individuals and maintains the common good. Consistent with our nation's legal tradition, we hold that all human law must be measured against the natural law engraved in our hearts by the Creator. A human law or policy contrary to this higher law, especially one which ignores or violates fundamental human rights, surrenders its claim to the respect and obedience of citizens while in no way lessening their obligation to uphold the moral law.

35. This relationship between morality and law is highlighted in the case of abortion. The abortion decisions of the United States Supreme Court violate the moral order and have disrupted the legal process which previously attempted to safeguard the rights of unborn children.

36. All in our society who are pledged to protect human rights through law have a moral responsibility to address this injustice by seeking the restoration of legal protection to the unborn. While at any given time human law may not fully articulate this moral imperative, our legal system can and must be continually reformed so that it increasingly fulfills its proper task of protecting the weak and preserving the right to life.

37. A comprehensive public policy program on behalf of the unborn must include the following long- and short-term goals:

a) a constitutional amendment providing protection for the unborn child to the maximum degree possible;

b) federal and state laws and administrative policies to eliminate government support of abortion and restrict the practice of abortion as much as possible;

c) continual refinement, precise interpretation, and ultimate reversal of decisions by the Supreme Court and other courts denying the right to life; and

d) support for legislation that provides morally acceptable alternatives to abortion, including efforts to expand education, health, nutrition, and other services for disadvantaged parents and their children.

38. Implementing this aspect of the *Pastoral Plan* will undoubtedly require well-planned and coordinated advocacy by citizens at the national, state, and local levels. This activity is not solely the responsibility of Catholics, nor should it be limited to Catholic groups or agencies. It calls for widespread cooperation and collaboration. As citizens of this democracy, and as leaders of a religious institution in this society, we see a moral imperative for public policy efforts to ensure the protection of human life. As participants in the American democratic process, we appeal to our fellow citizens to recognize the justice of this cause. Since our goal is to eliminate violence against the unborn, we oppose any use of violence to achieve this objective.

IV. Implementing the Program

39. Restoring respect for human life in our society is an essential task of the Church that extends through all its institutions, agencies, and organizations and embraces diverse tasks and goals. The following schema suggests a model for organizing and allocating the Church's resources of people, institutions, and finances at various levels to help restore protection of the right to life for the unborn and to foster respect for all human life. We recommend that the Committee for Pro-Life Activities periodically inform the NCCB on the status of the implementation of the plan.

1. State Coordinating Committee

40. The state Catholic conference or its equivalent should provide overall coordination in each state. Where a state Catholic conference is in process of formation or does not exist, bishops' representatives from each diocese should be appointed as the core members of the state coordinating committee.

41. The state coordinating committee may be comprised of the director of the state Catholic conference and the diocesan pro-life directors. At this level, it is valuable to have one or more persons who are knowledgeable about and experienced in legislative activity. The primary purposes of the state coordinating committee are

    a) to monitor social and political trends in the state and their implications for the pro-life effort;

    b) to coordinate the efforts of the various dioceses and to evaluate progress in the dioceses and congressional districts;

    c) to analyze relationships within the various political parties and coalitions at the state level as they affect local implementation efforts; and

d) to encourage unity and cooperation among pro-life groups in the state.

2. The Diocesan Pro-Life Committee

42. The general purpose of the committee is to coordinate activities within the diocese to implement this *Pastoral Plan*. In its coordinating role, the committee will receive information and guidance from the Bishops' Office for Pro-Life Activities and may also seek advice and assistance from the National Committee for a Human Life Amendment. The committee should be directed by the diocesan pro-life director, who is appointed by and responsible to the diocesan bishop. Its membership may include the diocesan pro-life director; the respect life coordinator; representatives of diocesan agencies (Family Life, Education, Youth Ministry, Catholic Charities, Health Affairs, etc.); representatives of lay organizations (Knights of Columbus, Diocesan Council of Catholic Women, etc.); medical, legal, and public affairs advisors; representatives of pro-life groups (Right to Life, Emergency Pregnancy Services, Congressional District Action Committee); and representatives of parish pro-life committees. The committee's objectives are

a) to provide direction and coordination of diocesan and parish information and educational efforts;
b) to support ongoing programs provided by Catholic Charities and other groups which counsel and assist women who have problems related to pregnancy and promote development of new programs where needed;
c) to maintain working relationships with local pro-life groups and encourage the development of local lobbying networks;
d) to maintain communications with the Bishops' Office for Pro-Life Activities and, as appropriate, with the National Committee for a Human Life Amendment regarding federal activity;
e) to maintain a local public information effort directed to print and broadcast media (this includes monitoring the public media's treatment of pro-life issues, seeking response time under the Fairness Doctrine, etc.); and
f) to develop responsible and effective communication with each elected representative.

3. The Parish Pro-Life Committee

43. The general purpose of the parish pro-life committee is to make parishioners more aware of pro-life issues and needs and to recruit volunteers to help meet those needs. Whether it is a distinct committee or a part of the parish council or other parish organization, it should include representatives of both adult and youth parish groups, as well as those responsible for educational and pastoral care.

44. The parish committee relies on the diocesan pro-life director for information and guidance. The committee should play a vital role in parish life and enjoy the strong support of clergy and other key personnel. Its objectives are

- a) to coordinate parish implementation of the Respect Life Program by promoting it to all groups within the parish, especially schools and religious education programs;
- b) to promote and assist pregnancy counseling and comprehensive maternity support services, as well as postabortion counseling and reconciliation programs; and
- c) to foster public awareness of the need for a constitutional amendment and other laws and policies to restore legal protection to the unborn.

4. The Pro-Life Effort in the Congressional District

45. Passage of a constitutional amendment and other pro-life legislation requires the support of members of Congress. Efforts to persuade them to vote for such measures are part of the democratic process and are most effective when carried on in the congressional districts or states which legislators represent. Ongoing public information activities and careful, detailed organization are required. Thus, it is necessary to encourage the development of identifiable, tightly knit and well-organized pro-life units at the local level. Such a unit can be described as a congressional district action committee or a citizens' lobby; but no matter what it is called, its task is to organize people to persuade their elected representatives to support a constitutional amendment and other pro-life legislation.

46. As such, the congressional district action committee differs from the diocesan, regional, and parish pro-life coordinators and committees, whose task includes educational and motivational as well as legislative aspects, and whose range of action extends to a variety of efforts calculated to enhance respect for human life. Moreover, it is an organization of Catholic and non-Catholic citizens, operated, controlled, and financed by these same citizens. It is not an agency of the Church, nor is it operated, controlled, or financed by the Church. The congressional district action committee should be nonpartisan, nonsectarian, and dedicated to influencing public policy. It is complementary to groups primarily involved in educational and pastoral care efforts.

47. The objectives of a congressional district action committee may include:

a) educating fellow citizens on the destructiveness of abortion to society and the need for a constitutional amendment and other pro-life legislation;

b) helping pro-life citizens to organize more effectively, so that their views will be heard and taken into account by party officials and elected representatives; and

c) lobbying elected officials and candidates for public office to support effective legal protection of human life from conception on.

48. These goals can be effectively pursued by a small, dedicated, and politically alert group. It merits financial support from other pro-life groups and individuals. Its greatest need, however, is for encouragement from those who recognize its potential and are prepared to work with it to achieve such goals.

Conclusion

49. As a result of the judicial and legislative endorsement of abortion, American society today faces enormous challenges. So do the Church and individual Catholics. But this is nothing new, for every age confronts the Church with challenges. In our time and nation, restoring respect for human life and reestablishing a system of justice which protects the most basic of human rights constitute not just a challenge, but an oportunity for the Church to proclaim anew its commitment to Christ's teaching concerning human dignity. This emphasis on restoring protection to the lives of the unborn is part of our commitment to a consistent ethic of life. The special urgency of addressing and ending the evil of abortion is evident in our nation today; our determination to pursue this goal until it is achieved also reinforces our determination to speak and act on behalf of the sanctity of life whenever and wherever it is threatened. Demanding and prolonged as it will be, this work, as it applies to abortion and to the other life-related issues of our times, fully merits our unstinting courage, patience, and determination.

50. In the ten years since the *Pastoral Plan for Pro-Life Activities* was first issued, much progress has been made. This is due in large part to the dedication and hard work of many women and men of faith who, operating with limited resources, have devoted themselves to its implementation at the parish and diocesan levels. We commend these tireless workers and urge them to recommit themselves to this effort. At the same time, we renew our appeal to the entire Catholic community to join them in fostering respect for human life in our society. For our part, we reaffirm our commitment as expressed in this *Pastoral Plan*, and we pledge all possible support to its continued implementation and ultimate success.

51. Prayer and sacrifice are essential to every aspect of this program. Without God's merciful assistance, we labor in vain. We, therefore, invoke that assistance today by entrusting this plan to the intercession of the Virgin Mary, Mother of Jesus Christ, and of all who have life through him, and we ask all the faithful to pray the Hail Mary daily for the success of this effort.

I came that you might have life and have it to the full (Jn 10:10).

Resolution on Immigration Reform

A Resolution Passed by the
National Conference of Catholic Bishops

November 14, 1985

1. For many reasons, the Catholic Church has a strong interest in immigration and immigration-related legislation. We now express our specific concern for legislative proposals pertaining to undocumented immigration and foreign agricultural workers.

2. Although the Catholic bishops share the concerns of many other persons on these matters, we believe that the approaches now being most actively pursued are neither workable nor morally acceptable. In particular, we hold that any viable program of immigration reform must be based on legalization as its foundation, rather than as an ancillary and conditional component. An acceptable program must, therefore, include the following elements:

- legalization opportunities for the maximum number of undocumented aliens;
- an extensive, aggressive outreach effort to eligible aliens;
- application deadlines and requirements for qualification that are both generous in respect to the number of aliens included and realistic in terms of the time-frame for application;
- no administrative arbitrariness in determining who shall be excluded;
- the provision of adequate appellate recourse for those disqualified by the Immigration and Naturalization Service (INS);
- active participation in planning by representative ethnic groups and by responsible community and denominational migration agencies;
- screening of applications by responsible agencies before submission to the INS in order to ensure eligibility; and
- provision to the newly legalized of the same protections and benefits available to all resident aliens.

3. Only when legalization is treated as the centerpiece of immigration reform is it conceivable that the bishops will judge employer sanctions tolerable. Until that time, we shall oppose employer sanctions. This means that we shall consider accepting sanctions only if they

- are part of a generous and fair legalization program that will benefit most undocumented persons now in the country;

- are accompanied by stringent antidiscrimination legislation;
- call for the development of a secure and uniform national employment identification system (e.g., a tamper-proof social security card) required of all applicants for employment; and
- offer substantive reassurances that enforcement will not fall disproportionately on employers employing Hispanics and Orientals and on employers in areas with high concentrations of foreign-born and other minority persons.

4.   As for foreign temporary agricultural worker programs, the Catholic bishops cannot accept any large-scale new program, nor can we accept "reforms" of existing programs whose net effect would be the erosion of protections offered U.S. farm workers and the deterioration of wages, as well as living and working conditions, for all farm workers.

5.   In conclusion, we submit that this might be a useful time for Congress and the nation to pause and reevaluate the model on which current proposals for immigration reform are based and separate the legalization/sanctions reforms from the issue of temporary agricultural workers. The Catholic bishops in the United States are committed to help fashion legislation that will truly reflect the American commitment to social and economic justice for all.

Statement on Lithuania

A Statement Issued by the
National Conference of Catholic Bishops

November 15, 1985

1. The National Conference of Catholic Bishops has for many years been aware of and concerned about the systematic repression of religious freedom in Lithuania, particularly the drastic restrictions on adequate facilities for worship.

2. This situation has been aggravated by a specific section of the Soviet government which illegally seized the Church of Mary Queen of Peace in Klaipeda in 1961 and has never returned it.

3. We protest the continuing injustice of this action, and we take this occasion to call upon the Soviet authorities to adhere to the Helsinki Final Accords of 1975 which guarantee the right of the Lithuanian people to practice their faith freely.

4. In accord with the obligations of the Helsinki Accords, we call upon the Lithuanian authorities to return the Klaipeda church before 1987, the observance of the 600th anniversary of the conversion of the Lithuanian nation to Christianity.

Empowered by the Spirit
Campus Ministry Faces the Future

A Pastoral Letter on Campus Ministry
Issued by the
National Conference of Catholic Bishops

November 15, 1985

Introduction

1. "I pray that he will bestow on you gifts in keeping with the riches of his glory. May he strengthen you inwardly through the working of his Spirit. May Christ dwell in your hearts through faith and may charity be the root and foundation of your life" (Eph 3:16-17). For over a century, Catholic campus ministry in our country, empowered by the Spirit, has been forming communities of faith which witness to the presence of the risen Christ. Now we are at the beginning of a new era filled with opportunities to build up the faith community on campuses and to promote the well-being of higher education and society as a whole. In this pastoral letter addressed to the Catholic Church in the United States and especially to the Church on campus, we offer our prayerful support, encouragement, and guidance to the men and women who are committed to bringing the message of Christ to the academic world. In preparing this letter, we have consulted with many of them and have come to a deeper appreciation of their dedication and achievements, as well as their concerns and frustrations. This new era, which is filled with promise, challenges campus ministry to respond creatively to the promptings of the Spirit for the well-being of the Church and higher education.

2. Our 1981 statement on Catholic higher education concluded by noting "the excellent intellectual and pastoral leadership of many Catholics engaged as teachers, administrators, and campus ministers in the colleges and universities which are not Catholic."[1] We said at that time that "we hope for a future opportunity to speak of their invaluable contribution to the intellectual life of our country."[2] In this

---

[1] "Catholic Higher Education and the Pastoral Mission of the Church," in *Pastoral Letters of the United States Catholic Bishops*, 4 vols., Hugh J. Nolan, ed. (Washington, D.C.: USCC Office of Publishing and Promotion Services, 1983-1984), vol. IV, 1975-1983, no. 64, footnote 32. (Hereafter all pastoral letters will be cited from the Nolan text.)

[2] Ibid.

pastoral letter, we fulfill that hope and turn our attention primarily to the ministry of the Church on these public and private campuses, where each year millions of Catholics are being prepared as future leaders of society and Church.[3] We are mindful of our previous comments on the crucial importance of Catholic higher education, especially the distinctive task of campus ministry on Catholic campuses to call the total institution to spread the Gospel and to preserve and enrich its religious traditions.[4] In addition, the suggestions for this document made by those who serve at Catholic institutions affirmed that all who minister in the world of higher education have certain common concerns and similar desires for cooperation. Collaboration among all colleges and universities within a diocese enhances the Church's ministry to higher education. Mutual support, joint sponsorship of programs, and sharing of resources improve the total efforts of campus ministry. Many of the perspectives, suggestions, and directions in this pastoral letter should be helpful to those who serve so well in our Catholic institutions of higher education.

3.   Campus ministry is best understood in its historical, sociological, and theological context. Thus, the first section discusses our hopes for the Church on campus in the light of its previous history. The next section locates campus ministry within the relationship between the Church and the world of higher education, highlighting the need for renewed dialogue. Campus ministry derives its life from the persons who bring the Gospel of Christ to the academic world. Therefore, the third section focuses on the members of the Church on campus, emphasizing the call of all the baptized to collaborate in the work of the Church, as well as the special responsibility of professional campus ministers to empower others for this task. The fourth section examines six aspects of campus ministry that flow from the nature of the Church and the situation on campus. Here we state principles and suggest strategies for carrying out this ministry. The epilogue notes our own responsibilities as bishops to serve the Church on campus and calls the Church to an exciting new phase in the history of campus ministry in our country.

---

[3]There are over 3,300 institutions of higher learning in the United States. The 1985 fall enrollment was 12,247,000 of which approximately 9.6 million attend public colleges and universities and 2.7 million attend private institutions. In the total student population, 43% are 25 or older and 45% attend part time. In recent times Catholics have constituted around 39% of the freshmen class. For these statistics, see *Chronicle of Higher Education*, September 4, 1985.

[4]"Catholic Higher Education," nos. 45-46.

I. History and Current Opportunities

A. *History and Contemporary Developments*

4.   The Church's response to current opportunities on campus will benefit from an awareness of the history of the Newman Movement in the United States.[5] This ministry began in 1883 at the University of Wisconsin with the founding, through lay initiative, of the Melvin Club which was designed to keep Catholics on campus in touch with their religious heritage. A decade later the first Newman Club was established at the University of Pennsylvania, with much the same purpose. It was named after John Henry Cardinal Newman, who was the English leader in the nineteenth-century intellectual renewal in the Church and later was chosen the great patron of campus ministers in our country. During this initial stage, farsighted leaders recognized that the growing number of Catholic collegians attending public institutions needed support and instruction in their religious heritage. They responded by establishing clubs for Catholic students, with their own chaplains and residence halls.

5.   In 1908, the second stage began with the establishment of the first association of Catholic clubs in state universities. What would become the National Newman Club Federation replaced this first effort about the time of World War I. This phase, which lasted until 1969, was often characterized by a defensive and even hostile attitude on the part of Catholic students and their chaplains toward the academic world, which was perceived as dominated by a secularist philosophy. During this period, many students and chaplains in the Newman Movement felt estranged from the rest of the Church and decried the lack of support from the hierarchy.

6.   The third stage, begun in 1969 in response to the Second Vatican Council and continuing until the present, has produced some healthy new developments. First, the Church as a whole has grown in appreciation and support of campus ministry. It is true there are still problems: some colleges and universities lack officially appointed campus ministers and many others are understaffed and suffer from financial problems. At times, there are misunderstandings between the Church on campus and local parishes and diocesan offices. However, progress has clearly been made in integrating campus ministry into the life of the Church. Today, there are over two thousand Catholics ministering on campuses throughout the country—a significant increase over a couple of decades ago. There is an increased commitment to providing

---

[5]See John Whitney Evans, *The Newman Movement* (Notre Dame: University of Notre Dame Press, 1980).

well-trained campus ministers who appreciate the need for continued professional and theological development. Student groups at all levels collaborate with official representatives of the Church. Diocesan directors of campus ministry help keep campus concerns before the whole Church. More Catholics appreciate the importance of campus ministry and support diocesan funding of this work. Through this pastoral letter, we affirm these positive developments and pledge to work with others to build on them. We bring to the attention of the whole Church the importance of campus ministry for the future well-being of the Church and society. Our goal is to foster a closer relationship and a greater spirit of cooperation between campus ministry and the rest of the local Church. Campus ministry is an integral part of the Church's mission to the world and must be seen in that light.

7.   Second, we endorse the improving relationship between the Church on campus and the academic community. While problems remain, Catholics have developed a greater understanding of the positive values and legitimate concerns of higher education. Many campus ministers have established good working relationships with administrators, faculty, and staff. There is greater appreciation of the way the Church benefits from the teaching, research, and service carried on by colleges and universities. Similarly, many administrators view campus ministry as an ally in the common effort to provide an integrated learning experience for the students. Faculty members frequently value the presence of campus ministers who demonstrate an appreciation of the spiritual life and can articulate their Catholic heritage. In our consultations, we found that many leaders in the academic community welcome a word from the Church on matters of mutual concern.[6] Our hope in this letter is to build on this fund of good will and to heal any wounds which linger from past mistakes and misunderstandings. With respect for the freedom and autonomy of the academic community, we believe it is time to foster a renewed dialogue between the Church and higher education, to the benefit of society as a whole.

8.   Third, we affirm the development of ecumenical and interfaith relationships. There are, of course, problems in resolving longstanding differences, and at some colleges and universities dialogue and cooperation have been difficult to establish and maintain. However, on many campuses, the Catholic community and other religious groups who share a common vision of ministry and who are interested in ecumenical and interfaith cooperation have developed strong working relationships. This occurs especially with other Christian Churches,

---

[6]Among the many consultations with administrators, faculty, students, selected experts, and others, we found especially helpful the close to 300 responses received from presidents and elected faculty leaders representing institutions of higher education from all 50 states who informed us of their hopes and concerns.

with whom we share a common commitment to Jesus Christ, and with the Jewish community, with whom we hold a common heritage and shared Scriptures. In some situations, Catholic campus ministers share an interfaith center and collaborate in some ministerial tasks. In other places, the Catholic community cooperates with other religious groups through regular meetings, joint study, and shared prayer. Mutual trust has grown as members of various religious traditions work together on common programs, such as projects to promote social justice. We commend this ecumenical and interfaith progress and give full support to greater and more creative efforts in this direction. Catholics who are deeply rooted in their tradition and who maintain a strong sense of identity with their religious heritage will be better prepared to carry out this mission. We appreciate the contributions and cooperative attitudes of most of the various religious communities on campus. The Catholic community on campus might also seek to engage those who are concerned with human ethical values of our society but do not directly relate their concerns to a faith tradition. To those who demonstrate less tolerant attitudes, we extend an invitation to join in the dialogue. In this pastoral message, we address the Catholic campus community and discuss its particular challenges and opportunities. While we will not treat directly the ecumenical and interfaith dimensions of campus ministry today, we hope that the Catholic communities on individual campuses will be prompted by this letter to renewed dialogue and collaboration in serving the common good.

9.   Finally, this third stage in the history of the Newman Movement has produced a remarkable diversity of legitimate styles and approaches to campus ministry, designed to match available resources with the unique situations at particular colleges and universities. These creative responses range from well-organized teams serving the needs of a large university parish to an individual ministering part time in a small community college. The styles include ministries that are primarily sacramental and those that rely mainly on the ministry of presence. Some campus ministers work on Catholic campuses where they can influence policy decisions, while others serve in public institutions where they have little or no access to the centers of power. In some situations priests are working full time, while in others the ministry is carried out almost entirely by members of religious orders and lay people. Ministers on residential campuses can offer many set programs for students, while those who serve on commuter campuses must be attentive to the creative possibilities demanded by such a fluid situation. Most serve on one campus, although some are responsible for several colleges and universities. While we cannot discuss in detail all styles of ministry, we will offer principles and strategies designed to encourage all those concerned with the Church on campus to make vigorous and creative applications to their own situations.

B. Current Challenges and Opportunities

10. We believe this is the opportune time to address a challenging word to the Church on campus. Catholics are attending colleges and universities in numbers that far exceed their percentage of the general population.[7] It is crucial that these emerging leaders of Church and society be exposed to the best of our Catholic tradition and encounter dedicated leaders who will share their journey of faith with them. Thus, the time is right to encourage campus ministers to renew their own spiritual lives and to facilitate the faith development of the Catholics on campus.

11. Today, there is a growing interest among many Catholics in various ministries. On campus, there is a great reservoir of energy and talent that could be utilized in the service of the Church and the world. Therefore, the time is right to challenge faculty members, administrators, support staff, and students to contribute their time and gifts to the common effort to help the academic community achieve its goals and to build up the Church on campus.

12. The academic world is in the midst of an important debate on how to improve the quality of higher education in our country.[8] Fundamental questions about the purpose, methods, and direction of higher education must be addressed, as colleges and universities continue to define their mission and to improve their performance. Therefore, the time is right to encourage Catholics on campus to participate in these local debates and, thus, to contribute their insights and values to this crucial national discussion.

II. Campus Ministry and the Relationship between the Church and Higher Education

A. History

13. Campus ministry is an expression of the Church's special desire to be present to all who are involved in higher education. Throughout

---

[7] In both 1983 and 1984, 39.3% of college freshmen were Roman Catholic. See Alexander W. Astin, *The American Freshman National Norms for Fall 1983* (and *1984*), published by the American Council on Education and the University of California at Los Angeles. Catholics constitute about 25% of the general population in the United States.

[8] Cf. "Involvement in Learning: Realizing the Potential of American Education" (National Institute of Education, 1984); William J. Bennett, "To Reclaim a Legacy" (National Endowment for the Humanities, 1984); "Integrity in the College Curriculum: A Report to the Academic Community" (Association of American Colleges, 1985); and "Higher Education and the American Resurgence" (Carnegie Foundation for the Advancement of Teaching, 1985).

its history, the Church has been instrumental in cultivating the intellectual life. During the period of the Fathers, great centers of learning at Antioch and Alexandria instructed the faithful and promoted the integration of faith and culture. The Church contributed her resources to the task of forming medieval universities and founded many of them, including the great schools of Bologna, Paris, Oxford, and Cambridge. In the modern world, government increasingly has taken over the responsibility for higher education, with a resulting split between the Church and the university. This has occurred in our own country with the establishment of a massive system of public higher education that has its own autonomy. Shortly after 1900, it was evident that enrollments in this system were growing faster than those in the Catholic and Protestant colleges, which for so long had constituted higher education in the United States. From the perspective of faith, Christians often detected in public institutions a growing secularism that celebrated the autonomy of reason and left little room for consideration of religious questions or moral values. This situation intensified after World War I, and the Church responded not only by increasing her traditional commitment to higher education, but also by trying to protect Catholic students from the antireligious elements perceived on public campuses. During this period, the Church and higher education experienced a good deal of mutual misunderstanding. Some people in the academic world feared that the Church would try to reassert, in more subtle ways, its control over higher education. On the other side, members of the Church, at times, regarded secular higher education as a threat to the Christian way of life. The time has come to move beyond these misunderstandings and to forge a new relationship between the Church and higher education that respects the unique character of each. We remain convinced that "cooperation between these two great institutions, Church and university, is indispensable to the health of society."[9]

B. *The Contribution of Higher Education*

14. We respect the autonomy of the academic community and appreciate its great contributions to the common good. Higher education benefits the human family through its research, which expands our common pool of knowledge. By teaching people to think critically and to search for the truth, colleges and universities help to humanize our world. The collegiate experience provides individuals with attitudes and skills that can be used in productive work, harmonious living, and responsible citizenship. Since higher education in the United States has taken on public service as one of its tasks, society has

---

[9]"To Teach as Jesus Did: A Pastoral Message on Catholic Education," in *Pastoral Letters*, vol. III, 1962-1974, no. 63.

received significant assistance in solving human and technical problems. The Second Vatican Council placed this contribution in a personal context when it said that people who apply themselves to philosophy, history, science, and the arts help "to elevate the human family to a more sublime understanding of truth, goodness, and beauty and to the formation of judgments which embody universal values."[10]

15. The Church, as well as society as a whole, benefits from the contributions of higher education. The members of the Church hold a common faith in Jesus Christ, a faith that seeks understanding. When the academic world produces new knowledge and encourages critical thinking, it assists Christians in the process of deepening and articulating their faith. When higher education fosters fidelity toward truth in scientific research and collaborative efforts to improve the quality of life in our world, it helps to prepare for the acceptance of the gospel message."[11]

16. There is no doubt that the world of higher education has its own problems that must be addressed and dehumanizing practices that must be challenged. Fidelity to the Gospel demands critical judgment, as well as affirmation. It is, however, vital that campus ministry maintains a fundamental appreciation of the contributions made by higher education to society and the Church.

C. The Contribution of the Church

17. The Church brings to the dialogue with higher education its general mission to preach the Gospel of Christ and to help the human family achieve its full destiny.[12] Thus, the Church seeks to help higher education attain its lofty goal of developing a culture in which human beings can realize their full potential.[13] In providing this assistance, the Church joins its voice with others in promoting the ideal of educating the whole person. From our perspective, this means keeping the dignity and worth of human beings in the center of our reflections on the purpose of higher education. Education is the process by which persons are "assisted in the harmonious development of their physical, moral, and intellectual endowments."[14] It aims at the formation of individuals who have a sense of ultimate purpose and are moving toward greater freedom, maturity, and integration. At the same time,

---

[10]"Pastoral Constitution on the Church in the Modern World," in *The Documents of Vatican II*, Walter M. Abbott, SJ, ed. (New York: America Press, 1966), no. 57. (Hereafter all documents from Vatican II will be cited from the Abbott text.)

[11]Ibid.

[12]Ibid., no. 92.

[13]"The Church of the University," *The Pope Speaks*, vol. 27, no. 3 (Fall 1982): 252.

[14]"Declaration on Christian Education," in *Documents of Vatican II*, no. 1.

genuine education nurtures a sense of responsibility for the common good and provides skills for active involvement in community life.

18. We think that it is important to keep the problems of higher education in a larger societal and educational context. Thus, family life must be seen as central to the process of educating the whole person, since "the family is the first and fundamental school of social living."[15] Moreover, improvement in the quality of higher education is dependent on primary and secondary schools doing a better job of cultivating the intellect, passing on the cultural heritage, and fostering constructive values. If students are better prepared by a healthy family life and solid primary and secondary education, institutions of higher learning can attend to their primary purpose, "the passionate and disinterested search for the truth," which makes human beings free and helps them achieve their full humanity in accord with their dignity and worth.[16] The search for truth should also include the ability to handle ethical issues and to achieve a harmonious integration of intellect and will.

19. The Church also brings to the dialogue its traditional understanding of wisdom. We believe that the faith community and the institution of higher learning are involved in a common pursuit of the life of wisdom.[17] There are various interpretations of wisdom, but we agree with those who hold that its pursuit includes discovering the highest principles that integrate all knowledge; uncovering the deepest secrets that constitute human nature; and achieving a personal synthesis in which knowledge and love are ultimately united. For us, the mystery of human existence is fully revealed in Jesus Christ. He reminds us of our profound dignity and our immense potential. He provides us with perspective and teaches by example how love illumines knowledge. The wisdom that we learn from Christ includes the cross, which confounds the wisdom of the world (1 Cor 1:18-24). From the perspective of the cross, we are called to challenge the limitations and contradictions of the world (1 Cor 3:18-23). At the same time, our wisdom tradition includes an understanding of God's mysterious plan to bring all things in the heavens and on earth into unity under the headship of Christ (Eph 1:9-10). The risen Lord has poured out his Spirit on all creation and so we are moved to celebrate truth, goodness, and beauty wherever they are to be found. Since no single community can monopolize the gift of wisdom, the Church joins with the university and others in the search for wisdom. But, when the quest for wisdom is forgotten or diminished, then the Church must keep the ideal alive for the good of society. When the so-called wisdom of the

---

[15]John Paul II, *On the Family* (Washington, D.C.: USCC Office of Publishing and Promotion Services, 1982), no. 37.
[16]"The Church of the University," p. 250.
[17]Ibid., p. 252.

world is employed in support of injustice, the Church must proclaim the wisdom of the cross, which challenges all oppressive structures. In the Church, the practical wisdom enunciated by the Hebrew sages is celebrated; the traditional philosophical wisdom is remembered; and the integrating wisdom of faith is proclaimed. For Christians, this whole quest for wisdom finds its summation and final fulfillment in Jesus Christ, who is the wisdom of God (1 Cor 1:24). We are convinced that the Christian wisdom synthesis, merely sketched out here, is a valuable resource in the continuing dialogue between the Church and higher education.

20. In a new relationship, the Church can work with higher education in improving the human community and establishing a culture that enables all human beings to reach their full potential. While admitting our failures in the past, we are concentrating on the future and a new era of cooperation. In the dialogue, we expect to learn and benefit from the work of higher education and will contribute our support, experience, and insights.

D. Campus Ministry Described and Defined

21. Campus ministry is one of the important ways the Church exercises her mission in higher education. Its goals include promoting theological study and reflection on the religious nature of human beings "so that intellectual, moral, and spiritual growth can proceed together; sustaining a Christian community on campus, with the pastoral care and liturgical worship it requires; integration of its apostolic ministry with other ministries of the local community and the diocese; and helping the Christian community on campus to serve its members and others, including the many nonstudents who gravitate toward the university."[18] Campus ministry gathers the Catholics on campus for prayer, worship, and learning in order that they might bring the light of the Gospel to illumine the concerns and hopes of the academic community. All the members of the Church on campus are called, according to their own gifts, to share in this ministry, guided by the professional campus ministers. "The work of campus ministry requires continual evaluation of traditional methods of ministry and also new approaches which are licitly and responsibly employed. These latter can be highly appropriate in the campus setting, where there exists an audience receptive to the kind of sound innovation which may in the future prove beneficial to the larger Catholic community."[19] Such creativity has produced great diversity in organization, style, and approach, as campus ministers strive to form a searching, believing,

---

[18]"To Teach as Jesus Did," no. 67.
[19]Ibid., no. 49.

loving, worshiping Catholic presence on campus. With this diversity in mind, campus ministry can be defined as the public presence and service through which properly prepared baptized persons are empowered by the Spirit to use their talents and gifts on behalf of the Church in order to be sign and instrument of the kingdom in the academic worlds. The eye of faith discerns campus ministry where commitment to Christ and care for the academic world meet in purposeful activity to serve and realize the kingdom of God.

III. Persons Who Serve on Campus

A. The Baptized

22. The Church carries out its pastoral mission to the academic world both through its communal life and through the Christian witness of its individual members. "The baptized by the regeneration and the anointing of the Holy Spirit are consecrated as a spiritual house and a holy priesthood" (cf. 1 Pt 2:4-5), in order that through all their works they may "proclaim the power of Him who has called them out of darkness into His marvelous light."[20] All the faithful on campus, by virtue of their baptism, share in the task of bringing the humanizing light of the Gospel to bear on the life of the academic community. They are called to live out Christian values while engaging in the teaching, learning, research, public service, and campus life that constitute the academic world. They are united with other believers in this work but make their own unique contributions, according to their personal talents and specific circumstances. "As generous distributors of God's manifold grace, put your gifts at the service of one another" (1 Pt 4:10). The Second Vatican Council further specified this scriptural teaching: "From the reception of these charisms or gifts, including those which are less dramatic, there arise for each believer the right and duty to use them in the Church and in the world for the good of [humankind] and for the upbuilding of the Church."[21] Thus, all the baptized members of the academic community have the opportunity and the obligation, according to their unique talents and situations, to join with others to help higher education reach its full potential.

23. The faithful are called not only to bring Christian witness to the academic world, but also to exercise their baptismal prerogatives by helping to build up the Church on campus. While many persons today generously contribute their time, talent, and experience to the faith

---

[20] "Dogmatic Constitution on the Church," in *Documents of Vatican II*, no. 10.
[21] "Decree on the Apostolate of the Laity," in *Documents of Vatican II*, no. 3.

community, Catholic faculty, staff, and administration have a unique opportunity and calling to lead and direct campus ministry programs, according to their gifts. These individuals are particularly needed on the many campuses throughout the country where no campus ministry programs presently exist. This contribution is enhanced when individuals take time to prepare themselves through prayer and study for this work. In section four of this letter, perspectives and strategies will be enunciated to build the various aspects of campus ministry. We hope that students, including the large number of older students,[22] administrators, faculty members, and all who are concerned with higher education will be able to make creative applications to their own situations based on the conviction that the Spirit moves among all the People of God, promoting them, according to their own talents, to discern anew the signs of the times and to interpret them boldly in the light of the faith.[23]

B. Professional Campus Ministers

24. Some members of the Church on campus are called to lead the faith community. Ideally, these men and women are professionally trained and exercise the kind of leadership that serves and empowers others. As officially appointed campus ministers, they are sent to form the faith community so that it can be a genuine sign and instrument of the kingdom. Their task is to identify, call forth, and coordinate the diverse gifts of the Spirit possessed by all the members of the faith community. Their challenge is to educate all the baptized to appreciate their own calls to service and to create a climate where initiative is encouraged and contributions are appreciated. One of the most important functions of campus ministers is to provide a vision and a sense of overall direction that will encourage and guide the other members to contribute to the well-being of the academic community and the Church on campus. If they understand their own family relationships in a faith perspective, they will be able to help others who are trying to improve the quality of their family lives. Setting up programs that embody this vision is a concrete way of encouraging others and of demonstrating what can be done with cooperative efforts. The goal of this style of leadership is to multiply the centers of activity and to unleash the creative power of the Spirit so that the community of faith can be an authentic sign and instrument of the kingdom.

25. Some professional campus ministers exercise the universal priest-

---

[22]Over two-fifths of the current student population are 25 years of age or older. See footnote 3.

[23]"Called and Gifted: The American Catholic Laity," in *Pastoral Letters*, vol. IV, 1975-1983, no. 19.

hood based on baptism, and others are ordained priests or deacons through the sacrament of holy orders. It is a sign of hope that a growing number of lay people serve as leaders in the faith community on campus. We commend members of religious orders who continue to make important contributions by gathering and encouraging the faithful. It is of historical significance that women "who in the past have not always been allowed to take their proper role in the Church's ministry"[24] find greater opportunities on campus to exercise their leadership abilities. Deacons often possess special talents and important life experiences that enhance their leadership skills. We encourage the priests who help form the faith community in a great variety of ways. Their prayerful celebration of the Eucharist, which invites active participation and manifests the unity of the congregation, as well as their compassionate celebration of the sacrament of reconciliation are especially important. All those officially appointed to lead the Church on campus have a great responsibility to form vibrant communities of faith and an exciting challenge to bring forth the gifts of individual believers.

26. In order to meet these challenges, campus ministers often form teams which provide a broader base of leadership to the faith community. Individual members bring their unique personalities and gifts to the team and work cooperatively to set direction and carry out some programs. The team members are co-responsible for the well-being of the faith community and accountable in their own areas of activity and competency. At the same time, they have the support of their colleagues when needed. Praying together helps the men and women on the team to keep in mind the true source and goal of their mission and to experience a sense of solidarity. We encourage the formation of such team ministries, which serve as models of ministry and community for the rest of the Church.

27. There are certain general challenges faced by all campus ministers. To be effective, ministers must attend to their own spiritual development. Campus ministers who are serious about their prayer life and can speak openly about their relationship to God will be able to direct others. Ministers who have wrestled with the great questions of meaning, purpose, and identity can offer helpful guidance to other genuine searchers. Those who have appropriated the faith and mined the riches of the Catholic heritage will be in a better position to invite others to join the faith community. If they genuinely care about the weak and oppressed, they will inspire others to work for social justice. Finally, campus ministers who have achieved an integration of faith and culture will naturally serve as role models for students and faculty members who are trying to achieve a similar synthesis. In summation,

---

[24]Ibid., no. 27.

the leaders of the faith community must be perceived as persons who know the struggles of life and who are working to develop themselves spiritually.

28. Campus ministers are also called to empower the faith community and its individual members in the task of helping their colleges or universities to reach their full potential. Ministers who have a genuine respect for academic life and for institutions of higher education will see clearly the importance of this work and find creative ways to respond. A healthy self-confidence will enable them to relate openly with faculty members and administrators and to empathize with students who are struggling with their personal growth. By gaining the respect and confidence of the various members of the academic community, they will find many ways to get involved on campus and promote human values in the institution. Campus ministers with solid training and good credentials will have more opportunities to enter into the mainstream of academic life on campus. Today, it is clear that campus ministers must not remain on the margins of the academic community but must accept the call to bring the light of the Gospel to the very center of that world.

29. To prepare for meeting all these challenges, we encourage campus ministers to take responsibility for their own personal and professional development. Clear contractual arrangements that include carefully defined expectations and procedures for accountability and evaluation help to set a proper framework for their personal enrichment. Membership in appropriate professional organizations, participation in activities on diocesan, regional, and national levels, involvement in support groups with other campus ministers, and regular interaction with a spiritual director can provide motivation and direction for improving their performance. If campus ministers are to remain flexible in response to the rapidly changing needs of the campus community, they need to study contemporary developments in Scripture and theology while deepening their knowledge of the Christian tradition. Attaining an advanced degree or achieving competency in a particular area not only contributes to professional development, but helps gain respect in the academic world. Today, skills in counseling and spiritual direction, as well as knowledge of family systems and life cycles, group dynamics, and adult education are especially valuable for leaders of the faith community. An understanding of the nature and dynamics of the academic world enables campus ministers to apply Christian teachings and values more effectively.

30. In addition to these common challenges, campus ministers find that the unique situations of their particular campuses create their own concerns and opportunities. For example, campus ministers at community colleges must respond to the needs of students who live at home and have jobs. They often need assistance in defining their roles and responsibilities in the home. Many students are married

and are present on campus only for their classes. Some ministers have been able, in these situations, to form small faith communities around shared prayer or social action projects. At these two-year colleges, the ministry of presence is especially important, as is securing the support and active involvement of interested faculty members. These institutions are often open to the addition of religion courses into the curriculum. Skills in marriage and career counseling are especially valuable. It is important for these campus ministers to maintain close relationships with neighboring parishes because that is where many students will find their primary faith community.

31. It is possible also to identify other particular challenges. Campus ministers on private denominational campuses must be especially attentive to the ecumenical dimension. Those who work primarily with minority students, including recently arrived immigrants, refugees, and international students, must be in touch with their cultural background and family experiences, as well as the unique challenges they face in the academic world. Large state schools produce logistical problems for campus ministers in handling so many students. On commuter campuses, making contact with students is difficult in itself. All of these particular challenges represent opportunities for creative ministry.

32. Professional campus ministers are crucial to the work of the Church on campus. They bear the heavy responsibility of guiding the faith community and empowering others to assist in the task of helping higher education reach its full potential. The extent and intensity of these demands remind them that they must gather others to assist them. They should expect support and guidance from the diocesan director of campus ministry, who is the usual liaison with the bishop and the local diocese. The director can help facilitate their personal growth, call for a proper accountability, and possible diocesan-wide programming. As the diocesan bishop's representative, the director encourages the interaction among campus ministers in the diocese who serve on public, Catholic, and other private campuses. We recognize our responsibility as bishops to offer all campus ministers moral support, to provide financial assistance to the degree this is needed and possible, and to help them achieve the competency they need to be effective witnesses of the Gospel.

IV. Aspects of Campus Ministry

33. After situating campus ministry in the relationship between the Church and higher education and discussing the persons who perform this service, we now turn our attention to six aspects of campus ministry. These ministerial functions reflect the general mission of the Church on campus and the distinctive situation of higher education

today. In her ministry, the faith community on campus must be faithful to the essential teachings of the Church and, at the same time, read the signs of the times and accordingly adapt the message of the Gospel to meet the needs of the academic community.[25]

A. Forming the Faith Community

1. Community and Alienation on Campus

34. Campus ministry attempts to form faith communities in an academic environment that knows both a healthy sense of solidarity and a good deal of alienation. Ideally, colleges and universities gather teachers and students together into a community of shared values and common dedication to the pursuit of truth. In fact, on campuses there is a good deal of collaborative effort. Organizations abound, close friendships are formed, interest groups gather the like-minded. Many administrators, faculty members, and students move easily in this world and find that it satisfies their needs for companionship and involvement. Many Christians freely gather into communities of faith in which they share their strengths and gifts with others.

35. On the other hand, lonely voices on campus cry out for intimacy, and mildly estranged individuals express a desire for more personal inteaction. Students who leave home and come to large universities often feel lost in the vast impersonal world. The world of research and scholarship can seem cold and demeaning to graduate students. Commuter students who are on campus only briefly for classes do not have the opportunity to form close bonds with others. Some sense of alienation seems inevitable for international students who must cope with a new culture. Recently arrived immigrant and refugee students experience the isolation and loneliness of being separated from family and homeland. Older students worry about fitting in and being accepted and, at times, have the added complication of marital and family pressures. Even students in small private colleges can experience a lack of depth in their relationships and a consequent sense of estrangement. Complaints are also heard from faculty members about the supeficiality of their relationships with close colleagues and the lack of opportunities for interaction with those in other departments. Some feel cut off from the centers of power, as important academic decisions are made without their input. The difficulty of gathering students for anything except social events and concerts is a continuing problem for student affairs leaders. Administrators speak openly about the fragmentation of campus life and search for ways to overcome it. The voices of estrangement are many and varied.

---

[25]"The Church in the Modern World," no. 44.

Campus ministers who listen well know that there is a genuine hunger for community in the academic world, as well as a strong sense of solidarity.

2. The Importance of Christian Community

36. The call to form communities of faith flows both from the very nature of the Gospel itself and from the pastoral situation on campus. Christianity is ecclesial by its very nature. The communal character of salvation is already clear in the Hebrew Scriptures: "It has pleased God, however, to make [human beings] holy and save them not merely as individuals without any mutual bonds, but by making them into a single people, a people which acknowledges Him in truth and serves Him in holiness."[26] This truth was exemplified in the life of Jesus Christ who, led by the Spirit, gathered together a community of followers. The Twelve served as official witnesses of his saving mission and symbolic representation of the new People of God. Through his striking parables and miraculous signs he proclaimed the kingdom in which all human beings, animated by the Spirit, were to live in peace and harmony. The death and resurrection of Jesus brought a new outpouring of the Spirit which "makes the Church grow, perpetually renews Her and leads Her to perfect union with Her Spouse."[27] Under the influence of the Spirit, the Church remembers the prayer of Jesus that "all may be one, Father, as you are in me and I am in you, so that the world may believe" (Jn 17:21). All the baptized, empowered by the Spirit, share responsibility for forming the Church into a genuine community of worship and service. Guided by the Holy Spirit, the Church is called, with all of its limitations and sinfulness, to wend its way through history as the visible sign of the unity of the whole human family and as an instrument of reconciliation for all.[28]

37. Today, the Church on campus is challenged to be a credible sign of unity and a living reminder of the essential interdependence and solidarity of all people. Thus, the faith community seeks to gather those who wish to serve others and to bring healing to those in the academic world who are restricted by artificial bariers and wounded by alienating practices. The Church gains credibility when the dream of community produces genuine commitment and intelligent effort. In the ideal community of faith, the Mystery that rules over our lives is named and worshiped. Dedication to Christ is fostered, and openness to all truth, goodness, and beauty is maintained. The life of the

---

[26]"Dogmatic Constitution on the Church," no. 9.
[27]Ibid., no. 4.
[28]Ibid., no. 48.

Spirit is nourished and discussed. Positive images of God, Christ, Mary, and the afterlife warm the heart and structure the imagination. The common good is emphasized and personal development encouraged. Individuals experience true freedom and at the same time accept responsibility for the well-being of the group. Traditional wisdom is available and the best contemporary insights are valued. Prayerful liturgies enable us to praise God with full hearts and create a sense of belonging, as well as nourish people for a life of service. Members are known by name and newcomers are welcomed. Unity of faith is celebrated while legitimate pluralism is recognized. Individuals find both support and challenge and can share their joys and sorrows. The members hunger for justice and have the courage to fight the dehumanizing tendencies in the culture. The community knows the sorrows of life but remains a people of hope. In this ideal community of faith, the members are of one heart and mind (Acts 4:32) and receive the spirit of wisdom which brings them to full knowledge of Jesus Christ who is the head of the Church (Eph 1:17-23).

38. By working toward the dream of genuine community, campus ministry unleashes human potential and contributes to the common struggle against the forces of alienation. A Church serious about building community reminds others of the beauty and nobility of a life lived in harmony and peace. The baptized who experience acceptance, healing, and empowerment in the faith community are better prepared to bring an understanding ear, a reconciling touch, and an encouraging voice to alienated persons on campus.

3. The Challenge of Forming the Faith Community

39. When the dream of a genuine faith community is alive, then the search for effective strategies is intensified. Attitudes are crucial. Campus ministers whose personal outreach is warm and welcoming are likely to gain the active participation of others in the community. The ministry of presence in which leaders of the faith community make themselves available by being on campus regularly and getting involved in activities and events is a valuable way of making initial contact with potenial members of the faith community and of enhancing existing relationships. Administrators, faculty members, and students who sense that they are valued as persons and that their talents and initiatives are appreciated, will find involvement more attractive.

40. On many campuses, Mass and communion services have proven to be powerful means of building community. Ministers who put a great deal of effort into preparing liturgies that are in accord with the Church's liturgical directives and are prayerful, coherent, and aesthetically pleasing, generally find an enthusiastic response. If they keep in mind the sensibilities of the academic community and strive for wide participation, the broad use of legitimate liturgical options, and a flexible style, the inherent community-building power of the Eucharist is enhanced. There is a greater recognition today that stimulating homilies that apply the Gospel realistically and convey positive religious images are especially important in fostering genuine religious conversion and a sense of closeness to the worshiping community and the Church as a whole.[29] It is a sign of hope for the future that so many collegians are gaining a deeper appreciation of the power of the Eucharist to rise the mind and heart to God and to serve as "a sacrament of love, a sign of unity, a bond of charity."[30]

41. In many sacramentally oriented campus ministries, the adult catechumenate process has become an especially valuable means of incorporating new members into the Catholic Church and strengthening the faith of those who are already members. As a result, the Catholic faith community becomes stronger, more attractive, and inviting. The presence of adults who have freely chosen to join the Church moves some members to think more deeply about their own relationships to the Church. Those who serve as sponsors often gain a new appreciation of their faith and a renewed sense of the Church as a community of committed believers. A community will attract newcomers as more and more of its members demonstrate enthusiasm for the faith and an attractive style of Christian living.

42. On other campuses, different forms of community building predominate. For example, campus ministers at some commuter colleges form community through bible study programs. Through personal contact, they gather together faculty members and students for shared reading and discussion of the Scriptures. This leads into group prayer and joint projects to serve others. Such programs reveal the power of the Scriptures to call individuals out of their isolation and to give them a sense of solidarity as they struggle to live out the Christian life in the academic world.

43. The experience of Christian community on campus is important to the life of the whole Church. Students who have such a positive experience and are taught their responsibilities to the larger Church will continue to be a very valuable resource for family, parish, and diocesan life when they leave school. Campus ministers can prepare for this by maintaining good ties with local parishes and giving students the opportunity to be of service there.

44. Building up the community of faith on campus is the responsibility of all baptized persons. The desire to serve and the hunger for community must be tapped. Individuals who are personally invited to join in this task and given freedom and encouragement to use their gifts and talents for the benefit of the community are more likely to

---

[29]Fee et al., *Young Catholics* (New York: William H. Sadlier, Inc., 1980), pp. 154-155.
[30]"Constitution on the Sacred Liturgy," in *Documents of Vatican II*, no. 47.

respond. It is the duty of leaders to provide vision and encourage others to accept their responsibilities. The task of forming Christian communities on campus encounters great difficulties but also brings deep satisfaction. This crucial aspect of campus ministry is worthy of vigorous and creative efforts so that the Catholic community can be an authentic sign and instrument of the kingdom on campus.

B. *Appropriating the Faith*

1. The Challenges to Faith on Campus

45. Campus ministry has the task of enabling Catholics to achieve a more adult appropriation of their faith so that they can live in greater communion with God and the Church, give more effective witness to the Gospel, and face the challenges to belief that exist in the academic world. In the classroom, students learn to question traditional assumptions and to tolerate diverse opinions on important questions that cause some to doubt their religious beliefs. Most students eventually encounter the modern critics of religion who charge that belief is either infantile or dehumanizing. In some classes, the scientific method that has advanced human learning so effectively is presented as a total world view, which supplants religion and renders obsolete other approaches to truth. Some professors give the impression that maturation involves rejection of religious beliefs. In these and other ways, the academic world challenges the traditional belief systems of many students.

46. Campus life tends to reinforce these intellectual challenges. Catholic students, at times, find their faith shaken by encountering peers who profess widely divergent world views and life styles. Today, a significant number of Catholics are attracted away from their religious heritage by fundamentalist groups that employ aggressive proselytizing tactics and promise clear answers and instant security in the midst of a frightening and complex world. When students learn more about the harsh realities of life and monstrous evils that have been part of human history, they are, at times, forced to question their belief in a God who seems callous in allowing such human suffering. Finally, the whirl of campus life, with its exhilarating freedom and the pressure of making good grades, can so dominate the attention of students that they drift away from their faith without much real thought.

47. Many Catholics on campus, including faculty members, are unprepared to deal with intellectual challenges to the faith. They are unable to explain their belief to interested friends or to defend it against attacks by hostile critics. Their understanding of the faith has not kept pace with their knowledge in other areas. The legitimate pluralism of theology and spirituality in the Church confuses them. They have not achieved an adult appropriation of their religion that would enable them to speak about it not only with conviction but also with intelligence. At times, this produces frustration and anger over the inadequacy of their religious training.

48. These problems are intensified by the general religious illiteracy in our culture. Public education is not committed to passing on the religious heritage. Many good people do not recognize the importance of religious knowledge for a well-rounded education. Most colleges and universities still do not have departments or programs of religious studies, nor do they provide adequate opportunities to explore the religious dimension of various disciplines in the curriculum. In the academic world, there are still those who think that teaching about religion necessarily involves proselytizing and that it cannot be done in an academically sound way. This attitude compounds the problems of campus ministers who seek to promote a more mature appropriation of the faith among Catholics.

49. On the positive side, the challenges on campus prompt some Catholics to explore and deepen their belief. Doubts, which are frequently a part of faith development, at times lead to further study and renewed convictions. The academic world provides intellectual stimulation and helpful resources for those who want to explore their religious tradition. There is a growing interest in religious studies and an increase in programs and courses around the country. Some public institutions have excellent departments or programs in religious studies that demonstrate that this can be done legally and according to proper academic standards. Today, within the academic community a few voices are heard insisting that a well-educated person should have a knowledge of religion. At some institutions, campus ministry has produced excellent programs in theological studies that supplement the offerings in the curriculum through a wide variety of credit and noncredit courses, seminars, and lectures. The faculty members and students who have achieved a more mature appropriation of their faith provide important witness on campus and are a sign of hope in the struggle against religious illiteracy.

2. Principles for Appropriating the Faith

50. By its very nature, Christianity calls us to an ever-deeper understanding and appreciation of our faith. Baptism initiates us into a lifelong process in which we are gradually formed anew in the image of our Creator and thus grow in knowledge (Col 3:10). The Scriptures remind us that this process means moving beyond childish ways to more mature approaches: "Let us, then, be children no longer, tossed here and there, carried about by every wind of doctrine that originates in human trickery and skill in proposing error. Rather, let us profess

the truth in love and grow to the full maturity of Christ the head"
(Eph 4:14-16). The Scriptures also call us to move beyond illusion to
a deeper way of thinking and relating to God: "You must lay aside
your former way of life and the old self which deteriorates through
illusion and desire, and acquire a fresh, spiritual way of thinking"
(Eph 4:22-23). Members of the faith community who achieve a more
mature grasp of their Christian faith are in a better position to understand themselves and their world. Those who continue their theological education are better able to reflect on their experiences in the
light of the Gospel. By assimilating the meanings and values in the
Christian tradition, believers are better equipped to affirm the positive
meanings and values in the culture and to resist those who are opposed
to the Gospel. Individuals who are well grounded in their own Catholic heritage are better prepared to enter into ecumenical and interfaith
dialogue and cooperation. The Second Vatican Council reminded us
that Christians have the task of achieving "a public, persistent, and
universal presence in the whole enterprise of advancing higher culture."[31] The Council called upon Christians to "shoulder society's
heavier burdens and to witness the faith to the world."[32] Those best
qualified for this great work are the believers who have understood
the implications of their faith and are able to articulate their deepest
beliefs. The Scriptures offer us this advice: "Should anyone ask you
the reason for this hope of yours, be ever ready to reply, but speak
gently and respectfully" (1 Pt 3:15-16). To respond credibly, intelligently, and sensitively to honest inquiry requires careful and systematic preparation. All the members of the community of faith have a
right to the kind of theological education that prepares them to meet
this responsibility.[33] When we consider the demands of the academic
world, it is clear that the Church on campus has a special responsibility
to enable all of its members to appropriate the faith more deeply in
order to give effective witness to the academic community.

51. The importance of achieving an intelligent appropriation of the
faith can also be established by examining the nature and purpose of
education. As we have noted elsewhere, "a truly liberating and ele-
vating education is incomplete without the study of theology or religion."[34] We must continue to encourage the study of religion in our
society as a whole because, as Cardinal Newman insisted, religious
truth has an inherent value and is "not only a portion but a condition

---

[31]"Declaration on Christian Education," no. 10.

[32]Ibid.

[33]Ibid., no. 2.

[34]"Catholic Higher Education," no. 22. In this regard, it is important to distinguish
theology, which involves a faith perspective and commitment, from religious studies,
which can proceed in a more neutral fashion.

of general knowledge."[35] Educated persons should know something of the history, teachings, and practices of the various world religions and be especially versed in the Judeo-Christian tradition, which shaped Western civilization in general and our own culture in particular. Furthermore, they should be aware of the religious aspects of other disciplines, such as literature, history, and art, as well as the religious dimension of our contemporary culture.[36]

52. Traditionally, theology has been known to the Church as the "Queen of the Sciences." Today, we must emphasize its continuing power to keep alive the great questions of meaning, purpose, and identity and to provide a coherent vision of life, which serves as a framework and unifying principle for all learning. Theological study helps to produce the kind of intellect described by Cardinal Newman "which cannot be partial, cannot be exclusive, cannot be impetuous, cannot be at a loss, cannot but be patient, collected, and majestically calm, because it discerns the end in every delay; because it ever knows where it stands, and how its path lies from one point to another."[37] The study of theology not only helps us gain this kind of perspective, but also helps us to understand in greater depth Jesus Christ who reveals to us the secrets of the Father. In a well-rounded Christian education, the teachings of the Church are presented with fidelity to the magisterium and with the contemporary situation in mind. This kind of solid theological training enables the members of the faith community to achieve a genuine synthesis of their rich religious heritage and the best in the contemporary culture.

53. A Christian faith that fails to seek a more mature understanding is not faithful to its own inner dynamism. A culture that is unaware of its religious roots and substance is impoverished and weakened. Educated Christians who have not grown beyond an adolescent level of faith development are limited in their ability to achieve personal integration and to make a contribution to society. These dangers remind campus ministry to maintain its dedication to forming the best possible learning community. The goal is that all of the members of the community achieve a deep understanding of their faith so that they are better prepared to witness to the kingdom of truth in the world.

3. Strategies for Appropriating the Faith

54. In order to move toward these goals, it is vital that campus ministry creates a climate in which theological learning is respected. Campus ministers help to produce this climate by reminding all the members

---

[35]John Henry Cardinal Newman, *The Idea of a University* (Garden City, N.Y.: Image Books, 1959), p. 103.

[36]"Catholic Higher Education," no. 22.

[37]Newman, *The Idea of a University*, p. 159.

that they need an adult appropriation of the faith that matches their learning in other areas, in order to function as effective Christians in the world. This message is strengthened if the campus ministers are perceived as being serious about continuing their own theological education. The presence of faculty members and students who are already finding enlightenment and satisfaction in theological studies is a powerful motivation for others. A tradition of pursuing theological learning must be established in which all the members sense their responsibility to achieve a more mature understanding of their faith.

55. If the faith community shares this broad appreciation of the importance of religious studies, then individual programs are more likely to be successful. Program planners should be aware of the courses on campus that deal with religious matters, as well as the current needs and interests of faculty and students. For example, the existence on campus of an increasing number of fundamentalist groups has intensified the need for scripture courses that combine the historical-critical method with opportunities for personal application and shared prayer. Such courses tap the current interest in relating the Scriptures to everyday life and prepare members of the faith community to deal with the aggressive recruiting methods employed by some fundamentalist groups. In general, campus ministry should supplement the religious offerings in the curriculum and provide a wide variety of opportunities for Catholics to study and appropriate their religious heritage and to reflect critically on their experiences in the light of the Gospel.

56. Effective strategies must deal realistically with the situations of the targeted audiences. Theological studies can be made more attractive for students by arranging credit for courses offered by the campus ministry program. For example, through a theologian-in-residence program, students on a state university campus could gain academic credit from a nearby Catholic college for theology courses taught at the campus ministry center on the state campus. Programs for faculty members and administrators must respect their vast experience while, at the same time, taking into account their general lack of systematic theological training.

57. Campus ministry has the responsibility not only to provide theological education for Catholics, but also to work with others to improve the response of higher education to the problem of religious illiteracy in our culture. The key to making progress in this idea is to overcome the unfortunate assumption that the study of religion cannot be a genuine academic discipline. The academic community must be shown that religion is worthy of careful and systematic study because it is central to human existence and is an important well-spring of our culture. Professors who deal with religious questions in their courses can help to overcome this bias by teaching this material according to rigorous academic standards of objectivity and with obvious respect

for opposing opinions. If the bias against religion as an academic subject can be overcome, then a variety of positive steps might be possible, such as establishing a religious studies program, organizing a lectureship devoted to religious questions, and founding an endowed chair for Catholic thought. If the climate on campus were more open, then campus ministers with advanced degrees might find opportunities to teach part time in appropriate departments or programs. Even if some of these larger initiatives are not possible, campus ministers still can provide a valuable service for students by identifying the courses on campus in which the religious aspect is treated well and fairly.

58. In the faith community, it is understood that religious literacy is for the well-being of society and that theological learning is for the sake of a deepened faith. The goal is an adult appropriation of the faith that fosters personal commitment to Christ and encourages intelligent witness in the world on behalf of the Gospel.

C. Forming the Christian Conscience

1. Moral Relativism on Campus

59. The Church on campus must facilitate the formation of a Christian conscience in its members so that they can make decisions based on gospel values and, thereby, resist moral relativism. Many questions of personal values and ethics inevitably arise for individuals in the academic community. Students are concerned with the moral dimension of such matters as relating to family members, abortion, sexual conduct, drinking and drugs, forming friendships, honesty in their studies, and pursuing a career. At times, faculty members experience a conflict of values as they try to balance their research and teaching and attempt to remain objective in the classroom while expressing their personal opinions. Their integrity can be tested as they fight against grade inflation and struggle to maintain academic freedom while accepting external funding for research. Individual courses often produce particular ethical and value questions. This occurs in obvious ways in philosophy, literature, and the life sciences and in more subtle ways in the physical sciences and technology courses. For example, a computer course may be based on assumptions about human nature that need to be discussed. Ethical questions also arise in relation to institutional policies and practices, such as whether a particular college or university is demonstrating a proper respect and care for the athletes it recruits and utilizes.

60. As members of the academic community deal with these questions, they unavoidably come under the influence of the moral climate that dominates their particular college or university. The eyes of faith discern, in the academic world as a whole, the predictable mixture of grace and sin that characterizes all institutions. On the one hand, the climate is shaped by high idealism, dedicated service, a long tradition of civil discourse, great tolerance for opposing views, sensitive care for individuals, hard work, and a deep love for freedom. Examples of personal virtue are evident in students who resist intense peer pressure and maintain their high moral standards; in faculty members who make financial sacrifices to stay in the academic world and who carry on their teaching and research with responsibility and integrity; in administrators who consistently speak the truth and treat all members of the academic community humanely. Organizations and groups often help raise the moral tone of the campus by being involved in charitable activities and espousing high ideals. In some fields, such as business, medicine, law, and the life sciences, more courses are being offered that deal with ethical questions. Periodically, a wave of idealism sweeps our campuses which reminds us of the great potential for goodness in the academic community.

61. On the other hand, Christians recognize in the academic world a strong strain of moral relativism that tends to reduce genuine freedom to license and an open-minded tolerance to mindlessness. Rational discourse about ethical questions degenerates into nothing more than sharing personal feelings. Sin is reduced to neurosis or blamed on societal pressures. The project of forming a healthy conscience is neglected in favor of a selfish individualism. In this climate, some persons assume that it is impossible or useless to make judgments about whether particular actions are right or wrong, whether some values are better than others, and whether certain patterns of behavior are constructive or destructive.

62. If this philosophy predominates on campus, Catholics are hard-pressed to maintain their values and principles. They find it harder to mount an effective critique of institutional practices that violate the high ideals of higher education and fail to respect the dignity of human beings. Young adults who are moving through various stages of moral development are often confused by mixed messages and conflicting philosophies. Students must contend with peer pressures to enter into the drug scene, to cheat on exams, to engage in promiscuous sexual activity, to have abortions, and, in general, to adopt a hedonistic life style. Some other students find that their commitments to spouses and families are called into question. Faculty members and administrators, at times, experience subtle pressures to go along with morally questionable institutional policies and practices.

2. Conscience in a Catholic Perspective

63. In this situation, campus ministry has the crucial task of assisting in the formation of Catholic consciences so that individuals who will continue to face very complex ethical issues throughout their lives are prepared to make good moral judgments according to gospel values. The Scriptures remind us: "Do not conform yourself to this age but be transformed by the renewal of your mind so that you may judge what is God's will, what is good, pleasing and perfect" (Rom 12:2). Conscience formation involves just such a transforming renewal of mind in accord with the will of God.[38] For, conscience is that "most secret core and sanctuary of a person where one is close with God."[39] There we hear the voice of God echoing in the depths of our being and calling us to heed the law written on our hearts. As Cardinal Newman wrote in the last century: "Conscience does not repose on itself, but vaguely reaches forward to something beyond itself and dimly discerns a sanction higher than self for its decisions, as is evidenced in that keen sense of obligation and responsibility which informs them."[40] "Conscience, then, though it is inviolable, is not a law unto itself."[41] It is rather through our conscience that we detect a call from God, summoning us to love the good and avoid evil. It is in response to this call, heard in the secret recesses of our hearts, that we make the judgments of conscience required by the concrete circumstances of our daily lives. This requires an informed conscience, one nourished in prayer, enlightened by study, structured by the Gospel, and guided by the teachings of the Church. Self-deception is all too easy; blindness and illusion can easily mislead us. "Beloved, do not trust every spirit, but put the spirits to a test to see if they belong to God" (1 Jn 4:1). Thus, we need the community of faith to challenge our illusions and to call us to greater self-honesty.

64. In emphasizing the objective call from God, mediated through the Church, we do not want to lose sight of the fact that the divine summons must be answered freely and intelligently. "Morality, then, is not simply something imposed on us from without, but is ingrained in our being; it is the way we accept our humanity as restored to us in Christ."[42] Thus, all human beings are bound to follow their conscience faithfully in order that they may set the course of their lives directly toward God.[43] We are freely responsible for ourselves and cannot shift that burden to anyone else. We come to the full measure of freedom by putting on the mind of Christ. When Christ freed us, he meant us to remain free (Gal 5:1). By preaching Christ and his message of freedom, the community of faith seeks to inform the consciences of all of its members. The Christian who possesses a

---

[38]"The Church in the Modern World," no. 16.

[39]Ibid.

[40]Cited in "The Church in Our Day," in *Pastoral Letters*, vol. III, 1962-1974, no. 205.

[41]Ibid., no. 206.

[42]"To Live in Christ Jesus," in *Pastoral Letters*, vol. IV, 1975-1983, no. 22.

[43]"Declaration on Religious Freedom," in *Documents of Vatican II*, no. 3.

conscience structured by the Gospel of Christ and who is guided by the continuing presence of Christ's spirit in the Church is better prepared to deal with the rapidly changing complexities of the world today. When genuine virtue is acquired, then good actions flow more spontaneously and new strength is found to live according to one's ideals. Individuals whose conscience has been tutored by the Gospel understand that their task is not only to resist evil but to help transform the world.

65. This portrayal of the informed Christian conscience stands in stark contrast to moral relativism. If morality is based on the call of God, then it cannot be totally arbitrary. Moral relativism betrays the essential structure of human persons who are ultimately dependent on a God who calls all of us to account. A conscience that remembers its source and is nourished and supported by the community of faith is the best resource for dealing with the complex questions of personal values and ethics.

3. Methods of Conscience Formation

66. Campus ministry is called to bring the Gospel of Christ to bear on the moral problems faced by members of the academic community. This can be done by personal encounters such as spiritual direction and counseling, as well as through homilies, classes, and seminars. When campus ministers address these questions, it is vital that they are perceived as being in touch with the texture and complexities of the moral problems generated by campus life. They also must have a working knowledge of the wisdom found in the Catholic tradition on particular moral questions. A good way for campus ministers to multiply their effectiveness is by facilitating peer ministry programs in which individuals who have successfully dealt with particular moral problems can help others in similar situations. For example, a senior athlete who managed to keep a healthy perspective on sports and maintain good grades could be prepared to speak with other athletes struggling to keep their values intact in highly pressurized situations. Students who have freed themselves from the drug scene could help others interested in breaking their drug habits. For older students struggling to keep their marriages together, conversations with faculty members who kept their commitments in similar circumstances could be mutually beneficial in enriching their married lives. In all such peer ministry approaches, it is important that those serving others are well prepared through a proper grounding in gospel ideals and church teachings on these moral questions. Engaging members of the faith community in such peer ministry programs is a valuable way of extending the effort to form Christian consciences.

67. Courses or seminars provide a more structured approach to the formation of conscience. For example, undergraduate students can be gathered for a seminar on the question of premarital sex, contraception, and abortion. An open atmosphere is needed so that the students can speak freely about the prevailing attitudes and peer pressures on campus, as well as about their own outlooks and modes of decision making. A skillful leader can use the discussion as a basis for bringing out the Christian teaching that insists that sexuality is best understood in terms of personal relationships and that intercourse is a sign of the total commitment associated with marriage. In dealing with this and all areas of personal morality, the Catholic tradition must be presented as containing a wisdom that illuminates the mystery of human existence and encourages behavior that is in the best interest of the individual and society.

68. A good deal of conscience formation must be done on an individual basis. Counseling, spiritual direction, and the celebration of the sacrament of reconciliation provide excellent opportunities to apply Christian teachings to an individual's precise situation and current stage of moral development. Through these means, persons can gradually discover the illusions and destructive patterns that impede the development of a conscience fully attuned to the Gospel. Such settings also provide the occasion to proclaim the great mercy of our God, who deals patiently with our weaknesses and guides us gradually to full growth in Christ.

69. If campus ministry hopes to deal effectively with questions of personal values and ethics, it must be concerned with the general moral climate on campus. When individuals maintain high moral standards despite pressures, they make an important personal contribution to the moral tone of the academic community. Since colleges and universities have the task of fostering critical thinking and transmitting our cultural heritage, they should include questions of values and ethics in this general mission. Members of the faith community who understand the importance of the moral dimension of life are called to join with others in promoting a more extensive and informed discussion of ethical issues on campus. This can be done in a great variety of ways, such as facilitating an appreciation of the need for courses on ethics in each department and program, encouraging professors to treat the questions of ethics and values that arise in their courses, and sponsoring lectures and seminars on particular moral questions. It is especially helpful to get the whole academic community involved in concentrated discussions. For example, campus ministers could join with other interested groups in sponsoring a "Values and Ethics Week" on campus, designed to deal directly with moral issues. During this week, all professors are encouraged to spend class time discussing the ethical implications of their courses. Informal discussions and structured seminars are arranged throughout the week. In order to give the whole program momentum and status, major speakers are brought in to address current ethical concerns. The important element in these strategies is to move the academic community to carry on its proper task of promoting critical thinking in the area of values and ethics.

D. Educating for Justice

1. The Search for Justice on Campus

70. Campus ministry is called to make the struggle for social justice an integral part of its mission. The academic world generates questions not only of personal morality but also of social justice, which includes issues of peace and war, as well as reverence for life in all phases of its development. Some questions arise as colleges and universities determine their internal policies and practices. How, for instance, should they balance their concern for quality education with a policy of open access that gives disadvantaged students the opportunity for higher education?[44] Issues also emerge as higher education interacts with other institutions. A prime example is whether universities can maintain their integrity, freedom, and a balanced research program while accepting massive funding from the Department of Defense for research on weapons systems. Periodically, a social justice issue captures the imagination of a significant number of students on campus, producing demonstrations and an appeal for direct action. A more sustained commitment to particular justice issues is demonstrated by some individuals, such as those who remain active in the peace movement over a long period of time and those who maintain the effort to gain legal protection for unborn human life. Such persons of conscience often encounter apathy, misunderstanding, and rejection and therefore deserve the special support and encouragement of the Church.
71. The academic community could generate intense debate over all these issues. In general terms, some want the university to remain detached from social issues, while others look for more active involvement to achieve a more just society. Most agree that higher education makes a valuable contribution by providing a forum for discussing the great questions of the day in a civil and reasoned fashion so that constructive solutions can be worked out.
72. Finally, it must be admitted that there is a great deal of apathy in evidence on campus today. Many are caught up in their own concerns and have little if any interest in social matters. Others who have been actively involved are now weary of the battles and have retreated into less demanding activities. Most students do not even think in terms of altering unjust structures through political action or

---

[44]See the report by the Southern Regional Education Board's Commission for Educational Quality, "Access to Quality Undergraduate Education," *Chronicle of Higher Education*, July 3, 1985, p. 9 ff.

social involvement. In general, alongside striking examples of personal commitment to justice, we sense a strong current of individualism that undercuts concern for the common good and eclipses the urgency of social concerns.

2. Principles of Catholic Social Teaching

73. Campus ministry is called to be a consistent and vigorous advocate for justice, peace, and the reverence for all life. All the baptized should understand that "action on behalf of justice is a significant criterion of the Church's fidelity to its missions. It is not optional, nor is it the work of only a few in the Church. It is something to which all Christians are called according to their vocations, talents, and situations in life."[45] With this in mind, campus ministers have the responsibility of keeping alive the vision of the Church on campus as a genuine servant community that is dedicated to the works of justice, peace, and reverence for life, in all stages of its development.

74. As we noted in our pastoral letter on peace, "at the center of all Catholic social teaching are the transcendence of God and the dignity of the human person. The human person is the clearest reflection of God's presence in the world; all of the Church's work in pursuit of both justice and peace is designed to protect and promote the dignity of every person. For each person not only reflects God but is the expression of God's creative work and the meaning of Christ's redemptive ministry."[46] In our day, the sanctity of the life of the unborn calls everyone to protect vigorously the life of the most defenseless among us. When we reflect further upon Christ's redemptive ministry, we see that he demonstrated a special care for the poor and the outcasts of his society. He came "to bring glad tidings to the poor, to proclaim liberty to the captives" (Lk 4:18). In identifying himself with suffering persons, he provided us with the strongest motivation to work for justice for all (Mt 25:31-46). In word and deed, Jesus taught us the essential unity between love of God and love of neighbor. His followers understood that if you claim to love God and hate your neighbor, you are a liar (1 Jn 4:20). The Gospel he proclaimed and the Spirit he sent were to transform and renew all of human existence, the social and institutional dimensions, as well as the personal.[47] This analysis suggests a rationale for the commitment to justice, a rationale that should be known and understood by all members of the Church.

---

[45] United States Catholic Conference, *Sharing the Light of Faith: National Catechetical Directory for Catholics of the United States* (Washington, D.C.: USCC Office of Publishing and Promotion Services, 1979), no. 160.

[46] "The Challenge of Peace: God's Promise and Our Response," in *Pastoral Letters*, vol. IV, 1975-1983, no. 15.

[47] "The Church in the Modern World," No. 26.

75. In the struggle for justice, we need Christians who understand that "knowledge of economics and politics will not in itself bring about justice, unless it is activated by human and religious ideals. However, religious ideals without the necessary secular expertise will not provide the kind of leadership needed to influence our complex society."[48] The faith community on campus, which includes individuals with significant academic achievements, is especially well equipped to achieve the integration of an informed faith with knowledge and skill in the social arena. To accomplish this, there must be great emphasis on "teaching and learning the tradition of Catholic social thought, the creation of an environment for learning that reflects a commitment to justice, and an openness on the part of all Catholics to change personal attitudes and behavior."[49] We call special attention to the coherent body of Catholic social thought developed during the past century in papal encyclicals and reflected in our pastoral letters.[50] It is especially important for Catholics on campus to assimilate these teachings and to use them in their work for justice.

76. As the faith community carries on this educational task, it must remember that the goal is not learning alone, but constructive action to eradicate injustice and to transform society. Christians must learn how to empower individuals and groups to take charge of their own lives and to shape their own destinies. The sin that infects the social order must be not merely analyzed, but attacked. Unjust structures and institutions must be changed, as must policies and laws that fail to respect human life. To be a credible partner in this task, the Church on campus should remember that "any group which ventures to speak to others about justice should itself be just, and should be seen as such. It must therefore submit its own politics, programs, and manner of life to continuing review."[51]

3. Working for Justice

77. Considering the apathy on campus, the faith community has the vital task of raising consciousness on social issues and providing motivation for study and action. Leaders in the faith community who are

---

[48]"Catholic Higher Education," no. 39.

[49]To Do the Work of Justice," in *Pastoral Letters*, vol. IV, 1975-1983, no. 8.

[50]For important papal documents, see David J. O'Brien and Thomas A. Shannon, eds., *Renewing the Earth: Catholic Documents of Peace, Justice, and Liberation* (Garden City, N.Y.: Doubleday, 1977). Among our more recent pastoral letters and statements on social justice and peace we call attention to: "The Challenge of Peace: God's Promise and Our Response"; "Brothers and Sisters to Us"; "To Do the Work of Justice"; and our forthcoming pastoral letter on the economy. Finally, we note the valuable insights in the pastoral letter *What We Have Seen and Heard: A Pastoral Letter on Evangelization from the Black Bishops of the United States* (Cincinnati: St. Anthony Messenger Press, 1984).

[51]*Sharing the Light of Faith*, no. 160.

already actively committed to the struggle for justice are a valuable resource in this effort. Drawing on their own experience, they can try to recruit others to work on specific justice issues. The very presence in the faith community of a core group dedicated to justice serves as an example and invitation to others to contribute their own talents and gifts to create a more humane society. Since apathy and excessive individualism are such pervasive problems, it is important for all those who are concerned about social justice to sustain their efforts even in the midst of limited successes.

78. Education for justice can be carried out in a variety of ways, ranging from scripture studies and liturgies with a justice orientation to seminars and guided readings on a particular justice issue. Education for justice is enhanced by including an action component. For example, a seminar on hunger that raises consciousness on the issue should include suggested actions, such as joining an appropriate organization, writing congresspersons, or helping out in a local food distribution center. Given the gravity of the nuclear threat, it is especially important to study the issue of peace and war. Such studies should include a discussion of ways to implement the summons to peacemaking contained in our pastoral letter *The Challenge of Peace: God's Promise and Our Response.*

79. Since the struggle for social justice demands involvement and not simply objective analysis, the Church on campus should provide ample opportunities for all of its members to work directly in programs and projects designed to create a more just social order in which peace and reverence for life are possible. Students who are involved in service projects, such as visiting nursing homes, tutoring disadvantaged children, or helping out during vacations in impoverished areas of the country, often grow in appreciation of the people they serve, as well as discover more about the complexity of institutional problems. Systematic reflection on such experiences in the light of the Gospel and the social teachings of the Church enhances their learning and prepares them to be lifelong seekers after justice.

80. Campus ministry has the responsibility to work with others to enable higher education to live up to its commitments and ideals in the area of social justice. Individuals have many opportunities to speak on behalf of those who are powerless. For instance, administrators and faculty members who are helping to set admissions policies or who are involved in hiring decisions can raise up the concerns of the disadvantaged and underrepresented. Students in various organizations can be vigilant so that the rights and sensibilities of international and minority students are respected. Individuals and groups who are attuned to the social dimension of the Gospel can raise ethical questions about institutional policies.

81. Periodically, issues arise that call for a more public response by the Church on campus. Campus ministers, for instance, may be asked to be advocates for a group of students who are seeking redress of legitimate grievances or to provide leadership on a particular issue, such as combating the problems of racism and sexism. These are important opportunities, and campus ministers should respond by drawing on the social teaching of the Church and giving public witness to the Church's concern for justice and peace.

82. Finally, the faith community can touch the conscience of the academic world by sponsoring programs on campus designed to raise consciousness and to promote justice and peace. For example, the Church could organize a day of fasting on campus, with the meal money saved going to help feed hungry people. This is a means of alerting individuals to the magnitude of the problem, of offering concrete help to the hungry, and of witnessing to the social dimension of the Gospel.

E. Facilitating Personal Development

1. Self-fulfillment in the Academic World

83. Campus ministry has the task of promoting the full personal development of the members of the academic community in a setting that is filled with rich, if often neglected, resources for self-fulfillment. Colleges and universities provide marvelous opportunities for healthy personal growth. Classes, lectures, and seminars provide intellectual stimulation. Cultural and social events broaden horizons and facilitate emotional growth. The greatest catalyst for development comes from interaction with the concerned people who make up the academic community. There are campus ministers who can provide guidance for the spiritual quest; administrators who possess broad visions and sensitive hearts; faculty members who are generous in sharing the results of their scholarship; international students who bring the richness of different cultures; and peers who are willing to share friendship and the common struggle for greater maturity. With all of these resources, many individuals find the academic world to be an ideal setting for establishing their identities, forming relationships, developing their talents, preparing for leadership, discerning their vocations, and charting the direction of their lives.

84. On the other hand, this vast potential for growth is often ignored or impeded. Some students think of college only in terms of opening the door to a good job and a secure future. They attend classes, gain credits, and manage to graduate. Learning to think critically and achieving a well-rounded personality through involvement on campus are not part of their program. For these students, the call to self-fulfillment either falls on deaf ears or is interpreted exclusively in terms of a lucrative career and material success. The great potential of higher education to promote personal development can also lie

dormant because of the policies and practices of colleges and universities themselves. The traditional task of producing well-rounded individuals who are prepared to serve the common good can recede into the background, as policy decisions are made on the basis of declining enrollments and financial pressures. Recently, voices from within the academic community have been raised, claiming that higher education has not remained faithful to its traditional goals and is not living up to its potential. Some say this is because students are not involved enough in the whole learning process.[52] One report claims that administrators and faculty have lost their nerve in the face of cultural trends and student pressures. It charges that leaders, by failing to insist on the systematic study of the humanities, have effectively deprived students of the cultural heritage that is needed for a well-rounded education.[53] Others decry the lack of a coherent curriculum and call for diverse learning experiences that foster critical thinking and help produce integrated persons who can live responsibly and joyfully as individuals and democratic citizens.[54] Among the critics, there is general agreement that reform is needed so that colleges and universities can achieve their proper goal of facilitating the full personal development of students.

2. Christian Perspectives on Self-fulfillment

85. The Church has the task of distinguishing and evaluating the many voices of our age.[55] Campus ministry must be attuned to the voices of reform in the academic community and be prepared to function as the friend of genuine personal development and as an ally in the quest for healthy self-fulfillment. Our Scriptures remind us that the Spirit calls us to put aside childish ways and to live with greater maturity (1 Cor 14:20). For us Christians, Jesus Christ is the perfectly fulfilled human being.[56] In him, we see the depth of our potential and sublime character of our call. "He blazed a trail, and if we follow it, life and death are made holy and take on a new meaning."[57] By following this path of truth and love, we can grow to full maturity in Christ (Eph 4:15). The Spirit of Jesus, poured out through his death and resurrection, energizes us for the task of developing our potential. The same Spirit enables us to recognize and overcome the selfishness in our hearts and the contradictions in the culture that distort the quest for healthy self-fulfillment. When individuals pursue personal

---

[52]See "Involvement in Learning."

[53]See Bennett, "To Reclaim a Legacy."

[54]See "Integrity in the College Curriculum."

[55]"The Church in the Modern World," no. 44.

[56]Ibid., no. 22.

[57]Ibid.

development within the community of faith, they are constantly challenged to use their talents in the service of others and to stay open to the Spirit, who accomplishes surprising things in us (Jn 3:8).

86. The Second Vatican Council has given contemporary expression to these biblical insights.[58] Human dignity demands that persons act according to intelligent decisions that are motivated from within. We should pursue our goals in a free choice of what is good and find apt means to achieve these laudable goals. The Christian vision of human existence safeguards the ideal of full human development by rooting it in the sacredness of the person. All persons are worthy of respect and dignity and are called to perfection because they are "a living image of God"[59] and possess a "godlike seed" that has been sown in them.[60] This intrinsic relationship with God, far from limiting the drive for personal development, frees human beings to pursue their fulfillment and happiness with confidence.[61] Furthermore, life in community teaches us that personal freedom acquires new strength when it consents to the requirements of social life, takes on the demands of human partnership, and commits itself to the service of the human family.[62]

87. These principles remind us that Christians must proclaim an ideal of self-fulfillment that is solidly rooted in the sacredness of persons, is placed in the service of the common good, and stays open to the God who is the source of all growth.

88. When campus ministry brings the light of the Gospel to the educational process, the search for personal development leads to a Christian humanism that fuses the positive values and meanings in the culture with the light of faith.[63] Genuine Christian humanists know that the heart is restless until it rests in God and that all persons are unsolved puzzles to themselves, always awaiting the full revelation of God.[64] Thus, for them, personal development is perceived as a lifelong adventure, completed only in the final fulfilling union with the Lord. Christian humanists know that history and all cultures are a mysterious mix of grace and sin[65] and that where sin exists, there grace more abounds (Rom 5:20). Thus, while rejecting the sinful ele-

---

[58]Ibid., no. 17.

[59]"Pastoral Letter on Marxist Communism," in *Pastoral Letters*, vol. IV, 1975-1983, no. 14.

[60]"The Church in the Modern World," no. 3.

[61]Ibid., no. 21.

[62]Ibid., no. 31.

[63]This term, *Christian humanism*, has been used in the Church to suggest the ideal of integrating positive cultural values and meanings in a faith perspective. For a recent usage of this term, see "Catholic Higher Education," no. 19.

[64]"The Church in the Modern World," no. 21.

[65]Ibid.

ments in the culture, they are able to assimilate the grace-inspired meanings and values in the world into a comprehensive and organic framework, built on faith in Jesus Christ. As individuals pursue their personal development, the ideal of Christian humanism lights the path and sets the direction.

3. Achieving Personal Development in a Christian Context

89. Campus ministry can facilitate personal development through vibrant sacramental life, courses, seminars, and retreats that enable Catholics on campus to integrate their collegiate experience with their Christian faith. Through pastoral counseling and spiritual direction, campus ministers can encourage individuals to make use of the resources on campus and guide them on the path toward a Christian humanism. This important work is enhanced when the ministers are perceived as persons of prayer who are serious about their own personal growth.
90. It is helpful to multiply these efforts by bringing together, in a personal encounter, those who share the journey toward Christian maturity. A program that enables an individual faculty member to meet on a regular basis outside the classroom with a particular student for friendly conversation and serious discussion provides great opportunities for the kind of exchange that is mutually enriching. Faculty members who are inspired by gospel ideals and undergo training for this kind of program are in an excellent position to be role models for students and, perhaps, spiritual mentors. Students, in turn, bring to the relationship their distinctive experience and challenging questions, which can be a catalyst for mutual growth. A great variety of such programs is possible. The key is to increase the opportunities for more personal contact between members of the faith community so that they can assist one another in the quest for a genuine Christian humanism.
91. Since there is a temptation to reduce self-fulfillment to a selfish individualism, campus ministry provides a valuable service by keeping alive the ideal of Christian humanism, which recognizes that personal growth must be open to the transcendent and in service to the common good. Through prayer groups and liturgical celebrations that link life and worship, in lectures and seminars that relate current questions and the Christian tradition, by service projects and actions for justice that put personal gifts at the service of others, the community of faith publicly manifests the Christian ideal of self-fulfillment. The sacrament of reconciliation is a powerful means for personal development since it enables individuals to confront the sins and destructive patterns that inhibit their progress and to hear again the compassionate summons to grow into greater maturity in Christ. Communal penance services that encourage an examination of the dis-

tinctive challenges and opportunities for personal development presented by campus life are especially effective in making the ideal of Christian humanism more concrete.

92. Inspired by this ideal, individual members of the faith community have the responsibility to assist their colleges or universities in the task of educating whole persons for lifelong growth and responsible citizenship. This is done in obvious ways by students who study hard and take advantage of cultural opportunities on campus and by faculty members who teach well and take a personal interest in students. In addition, there is the challenge of establishing institutional policies and practices that better facilitate these goals. Today, there is a general consensus that undergraduate education must be improved by various means, such as setting higher standards for classroom work, establishing a more coherent curriculum, and improving teacher performance through better preparation and proper incentives.[66] As the precise shape of the reforms is debated on particular campuses, it is vital that the voices of Christian humanists be joined with others of good will, on behalf of reform, which makes possible the education of the whole person. Trustees, administrators, and deans, as well as faculty members and students who serve on appropriate committees can promote policies that clearly place the well-being of students in the center of the academic enterprise. The opportunities are many and varied for members of the faith community to work with others in an effort to improve the quality of higher education so that a healthy personal development is facilitated. What is needed is the conviction that this is an essential aspect of bringing Christian witness to the campus.

F. Developing Leaders for the Future

1. Potential Leaders on Campus

93. Campus ministry has the great opportunity to tap the immense pool of talent in our colleges and universities and to help form future leaders for society and the Church. Large numbers of intelligent and ambitious young people are on campuses, gaining the knowledge and skills needed to launch them into eventual positions of leadership in the world. Many of the older students at our colleges and universities are acquiring new knowledge and skills that will enhance their opportunities to influence their world for the good. The intense course of studies pursued by graduate students equips them with specialized knowledge that can be used for the common good. When international students, trained on our campuses, return to their own countries,

---

[66]We recall the four reports cited in footnote 8.

they carry with them knowledge and skills that can be extremely valuable in promoting progress in their own societies. While not all of the students on campuses today will assume prominent leadership positions, everyone will have opportunities to provide some leadership in their various communities.

94. The large numbers of Catholics attending colleges and universities are potential leaders not only of society, but of the Church as well. Parishes require women and men who, in actively proclaiming the Gospel, combine commitment and good will with knowledge and skills. The Catholic community is in great need of more priests who will dedicate themselves to serving the needs of others. The religious orders are looking for new members who will live a life of dedicated service. In searching for this kind of church leadership for the future, we naturally turn to our colleges and universities, where so many of our talented young people are being educated.

95. The search for church leaders on campus should also extend to Catholic administrators and faculty. The local Church should make every effort to train individuals to carry out campus ministry on campuses where there are no professional campus ministry personnel. These men and women who are blessed with extensive education perform an important Christian service in the academic world and constitute an immense resource for church leadership. Not all of these individuals have the time or calling to assume leadership positions within the faith community. However, as a whole, they constitute a valuable pool of leadership talent that could be better utilized for the benefit of the Church.

2. Leadership in the Christian Perspective

96. From the perspective of faith, the Scriptures present a distinctive understanding of leadership. Jesus told his followers, "You are the light of the world . . . your light must shine before all so that they may see goodness in your acts and give praise to your heavenly Father" (Mt 5:14-19). This suggests that all the disciples of Jesus carry the responsibility of offering personal witness in order to make a difference in the world and using their influence to bring others to a greater appreciation of the goodness of God. This kind of leadership is to be carried out according to one's own unique talents. As the Apostle Paul indicated: "Just as each of us has one body with many members, and not all the members have the same function, so too we, though many, are one body in Christ and individually members one of another. We have gifts that differ according to the favor bestowed on each of us" (Rom 12:4-6). Paul also reminds us of the deep purpose involved in such gifts when he says, "To each person the manifestation of the Spirit is given for the common good" (1 Cor 12:7). In the Christian community, genuine leadership is based not on coercive power or high status, but on loving service that leads to the empowerment of others (Mk 10:42-45). Thus, the clear teaching of Scripture is that gifts and talents are not given simply for personal advantage; they are to be used generously for the benefit of others and for the good of society and the Church.

97. The Second Vatican Council recognized the great opportunities for this kind of Christian leadership and called on all adult Christians to prepare themselves for this task. "Indeed, everyone should painstakingly ready himself [or herself] personally for the apostolate, especially as an adult. For the advance of age brings with it better self-knowledge, thus enabling each person to evaluate more accurately the talents with which God has enriched [each] soul and to exercise more effectively those charismatic gifts which the Holy Spirit has bestowed on [all] for the good of [others]."[67] Thus, from the perspective of faith, it is clear that effective leadership in the contemporary world is connected both with a sense of loving service and with a more mature development in self-knowledge.

98. The nature of Christian leadership can also be understood from the viewpoint of the vocation we all receive from God. Through baptism, "all the faithful of Christ of whatever rank or status are called to the fullness of the Christian life and to the perfection of charity. By this holiness a more human way of life is promoted even in this earthly society."[68] This baptismal vocation gives to every Christian the special task "to illumine and organize" temporal affairs of every sort "in such a way that they may start out, develop, and persist according to Christ's mind."[69] Individuals may choose to live out this general vocation as single persons, as members of the clergy or religious orders, or as married couples. In all of these states of life, there are opportunities large and small for exercising a leadership that is based on service and helps to humanize our world.

3. Strategies for Forming Christian Leaders

99. Campus ministers can facilitate the development of Christian leaders by encouraging members of the faith community to identify their gifts and to use them for the common good. Individuals must be helped to overcome their fears and to gain confidence in their abilities. They need proper training and opportunities to improve their leadership skills. For example, retreats for liturgical ministers can help them sense the importance of their roles at Mass and enable them to perform these roles prayerfully and competently. A leadership train-

---

[67]"Decree on the Laity," no. 30.
[68]"Dogmatic Constitution on the Church," no. 40.
[69]Ibid., no. 9.

ing session for officers in Catholic student organizations, at the beginning of the academic year, can give them added confidence and practical skills. Campus ministers who work with student organizers of a social justice project can provide them with Christian principles and practical advice that will enhance their effectiveness as current and future leaders.

100. In addition to developing leaders within the faith community, campus ministers should also encourage students to exercise their influence in other groups and activities. It helps to remind them that involvement in the life of their college or university is a significant factor in getting more out of the collegiate experience and that all Catholics on campus have the responsibility to work for the betterment of the academic community.

101. The development of leaders involves helping students to discern their vocations in life and to prepare for them. Most young people on campus today need guidance in preparing for marriage and family life. The preparation should include programs that encompass the following elements: the sacrament of marriage as an interpersonal relationship; the identity and mission of the family; the role of human sexuality and intimacy; conjugal love as union and as sharing in the creative power of God; responsible parenthood; and the couple's responsibilities to the larger community.[70] A significant number of collegians seriously consider vocations to the priesthood or religious life.[71] Campus ministers are in an excellent position to promote these vocations. A program in which campus ministers gather interested students together regularly for discussions and prayer is a valuable way of helping them discern the promptings of the Spirit. Students moving in the direction of the single life often need personal assistance in order to deal with societal pressures and cultural stereotypes.

102. In order to get more faculty members and administrators to exercise leadership in the faith community, campus ministers need to establish personal contact with them, offer them opportunities that fit their particular expertise, and provide them with training, if necessary. For example, counselors on campus could run marriage preparation and enrichment programs for the faith community, after studying the Church's teachings on marriage. It would also be helpful to gather the Catholic faculty and administrators together, on occasion, to give them a sense of group identity and to encourage their active participation in the Church on campus. This could be done through a retreat in which they explore ways of integrating their faith with their professional concerns. The more this integration takes place, the better role models they will be for students, who are the emerging leaders of society and the Church.

---

[70]John Paul II, *On the Family*, no. 66.
[71]Fee et al., *Young Catholics*, pp. 154-155.

Epilogue

103. In this pastoral letter, we have placed campus ministry in its historical and cultural context and have examined it from the viewpoint of the persons who carry it out, as well as the tasks they perform. We are convinced that this ministry is vitally important for the future of Church and society. As bishops, we recognize our responsibility to "see to it that at colleges and universities which are not Catholic there are Catholic residences and centers where priests, religious, and [lay persons] who have been judiciously chosen and trained can serve as on-campus sources of spiritual and intellectual assistance to young college people."[72]

104. The revised *Code of Canon Law* has reinforced this responsibility by reminding us that the diocesan bishop is to be zealous in his pastoral care of students, even by the creation of a special parish or, at least, by appointing priests with a stable assignment to this care.[73] We know it is important to find dedicated persons for this ministry who have a solid faith, a love for the academic world, and the ability to relate well to both inquiring students and an educated faculty. They need proper training, which includes personal development, practical experience, and theological study. Advanced degrees are helpful in order to gain credibility in the academic world. We are committed to providing the best professional campus ministers possible and intend to hold them accountable for dedicated and creative service to the academic community. Our responsibilities extend to ensuring that within each diocese adequate funding is available for campus ministry and that there is an overall plan for allocating resources.

105. Our hope is that this pastoral letter will mark the beginning of a new phase in the history of Catholic campus ministry in the United States. In our vision of the new era, campus ministry will succeed more than ever before in forming the faithful into vibrant communities of faith and in empowering them to bring the light of the Gospel to the academic world. Campus ministry will be better understood and supported by the Church as a whole and will therefore be strengthened to make its voice heard in the center of campus life. The spiritual life of the Church on campus will be renewed so that it can be a more potent force, enabling the academic community to live up to its own ideals. The faith community will be more in touch with its Catholic roots so that it can confidently enter into deeper dialogue and more productive relationships with other religious groups on campus. A contemporary Christian humanism will flourish, which will demonstrate to all the value of an adult faith that has integrated the best

---

[72]"Declaration on Christian Education," no. 10.
[73]*Code of Canon Law* (Washington, D.C.: Canon Law Society of America, 1983), cc. 813, 814.

insights of the culture. The Church on campus will be seen more clearly as a genuine servant community, dedicated to social justice, and therefore will be a more effective sign and instrument of the kingdom of peace and justice in the world. In the new era, the Church and higher education will find more productive ways of working together for the well-being of the whole human family. In our vision, campus ministry, empowered by the Spirit, faces a future bright with promise.

Statement on Food and Agriculture

*A Message to President Ronald Reagan and
Members of Congress Issued by the
National Conference of Catholic Bishops*

November 15, 1985

1. We, the bishops of the National Conference of Catholic Bishops, at our annual November meeting in Washington, D.C., wish to express our concern about the present trend in the development of the 1985 Farm Bill as it relates to food and agriculture, including the present "farm crisis."

2. Unless there is sufficient government support forthcoming in the short term and effective methods of managing food supply in the long term, this trend will destroy a large number of our competent and dedicated owners and operators of moderate-sized farms.

3. We ask that any legislation have the following goals:

  a) a just return for farmers and a just wage for farmworkers;
  b) incentives for long-term conservation of the soil—a regenerative agriculture; and
  c) enabling more owner-operator farms rather than fewer.

4. We recognize that while many of our people are suffering from economic problems at this time, such as small business, millions unemployed, millions of others working but poor, the further concentration of land and food production will only add to their suffering. Our reason for issuing this message is not only that we are concerned for farmers and ranchers experiencing economic disaster, but even more so because of the vital place that the production, distribution, and consumption of food hold in the lives of all. We believe that the further concentration of our agricultural land in the hands of a few could ultimately produce oppression, hunger, and powerlessness of the general population.

5. We fear that unless we recognize and address the gravity of this situation today, the economic and social disasters that now threaten our farming communities will only foreshadow social and economic disruption in our cities and metropolitan areas in the future. The food and agriculture crisis facing us is an issue far wider than just a rural question. The success or failure of our efforts to address this problem will have serious effects on every consumer and thus every citizen of the land.

6.   As pastors, we pledge ourselves to provide continued liturgical, spiritual, and moral support for farmers and farmworkers presently suffering because of the farm crisis.

7.   In the development of our pastoral letter *Catholic Social Teaching and the U.S. Economy,* we are devoting an entire section to questions regarding food and agriculture.

8.   Our concern for these matters has been expressed as early as 1972, when we issued the statement *Where Shall the People Live?* and again in 1979, in the statement *The Family Farm.* Our concerns and our positions remain the same.

Resolution on the Supreme Court's Aguilar Decision

A Resolution Passed by the
National Conference of Catholic Bishops

November 15, 1985

1. We, the Catholic bishops of the United States, deplore the harm and the hurt that so many children are suffering from the unjust, discriminatory, and narrow decision of the U.S. Supreme Court in the *Aguilar* vs. *Felton* case. We find the decision deeply disturbing in that it deprives some of the nation's poorest and most disadvantaged children of equitable participation in the compensatory education program which Congress authorized in Title 1 of the Elementary and Secondary Education Act of 1965.

2. Ironically, this adverse decision was handed down on the twentieth anniversary of that act, truly a landmark piece of legislation, which provided desperately needed remedial services for educationally deprived children, regardless of the school they attend. The court made its decision despite a twenty-year record of implementation which, in the words of the court of appeals, "had done so much good and little, if any, detectable harm."

3. As Chief Justice Warren Burger said in his dissenting opinion, "It borders on paranoia. The notion that denying these services to students in religious schools is a neutral act to protect us from an established church has no support in logic, experience, or history. Rather than showing the neutrality the court boasts of, it exhibits nothing less than hostility toward religion and the children who attend church-sponsored schools."

4. While we are outraged by the deprivation and harm caused by this decision, we remind our fellow citizens that our national policy, enshrined in the law of the land, continues to call for equitable participation of the nation's children in this federal program. This tragic decision only strengthens our resolve to achieve justice for all children whose parents exercise their God-given rights to choose a religious education. We will never abandon the struggle for fair treatment for the poorest and neediest of all children. We join all parents and concerned citizens in working for that day when justice and compassion will prevail in education.

A Vision of Evangelization

A Statement Issued by the
National Conference of Catholic Bishops

November 15, 1985

1. Our hope and earnest prayer as Catholic bishops is that all people of the United States, and indeed the whole world, will receive the fullness of Christ's word and the fullness of divine assistance to live according to that word. Jesus insisted, "I must proclaim the good news of the kingdom of God" (Lk 4:43). We accept evangelization as our priority, too, aware that our activity and witness must be "made explicit by a clear and unequivocal proclamation of the Lord Jesus" (*Evangelii Nuntiandi,* 23). "To evangelize is first of all to bear witness, in a simple and direct way, to God revealed by Jesus Christ in the Holy Spirit" (ibid., 26). Thus, the essence of evangelization is the proclamation of salvation in Jesus Christ and the person's response in faith (ibid., 27, 28), both of which can be achieved solely through the power of the Father and the action of the Holy Spirit (ibid., 75).

2. With Pope Paul VI, we affirm the profound link between Christ, the Church, and evangelization. "The presentation of the gospel message is not an optional contribution for the Church. It is the duty incumbent on her by the command of the Lord Jesus, so that people can believe and be saved" (ibid., 5; cf. 16).

3. The Holy Father also presents the content of evangelization. "As the kernel and center for his good news, Christ proclaims salvation, this great gift of God which is liberation from everything that oppresses man but which is above all liberation from sin and the Evil One." This salvation is "begun during the life of Christ and definitively accomplished by his death and resurrection. But it must be carried on during the course of history, in order to be realized fully on the day of the final coming of Christ" (ibid., 9; cf. Mt 24:36; Acts 1:7; 1 Thes 5:1-2).

4. Jesus said: "The reign of God is at hand! Reform your lives and believe in the Gospel" (Mk 1:15). The gospel transformation we seek includes first of all a conversion experience—a deeper knowledge of and commitment to the Lord Jesus Christ—among Catholics themselves, as well as the reconciliation of alienated Catholics. All members of the Catholic community are called and sent to evangelize one another. "The Church is an evangelizer, but she begins by being evangelized herself" (*Evangelii Nuntiandi,* 15).

5. Second, this transformation, this call to open our hearts to the life and joy of the risen Christ as poured out by the Holy Spirit, leads us to receive individuals into full communion with the Catholic Church.

6. This transformation also challenges all Catholics to work for the unity for which Jesus prayed and for the restoration of full communion with other church bodies. For "the division among Christians is a serious reality which impedes the very work of Christ . . . and damages the most holy cause of preaching the Gospel to all" (ibid., 77).

7. Third, this transformation includes reaching out to those who are not Christians or who have no religious affiliation (ibid., 53). In all these efforts, however, we are called to act as Jesus did, sensitive to others as persons blessed with freedom by showing "respect for their religious and spiritual situation . . ., their tempo and pace . . ., their conscience and conviction" (ibid., 79, 80).

8. Finally, authentic evangelization must include a response in justice to the needs of suffering human beings. The fullness of the Christian message must be extended to our nation's familial, economic, educational, political, and recreational systems. Christ's message must be embedded not only in the hearts of people, but in social systems and cultures as well (ibid., 20; cf. 31).

9. In conclusion, we repeat these words of Paul VI, which so well capture our vision for the evangelization of America: "For the Church, evangelizing means bringing the good news into all the strata of humanity, and through its influence transforming humanity from within and making it new. . . . The purpose of evangelization is therefore precisely this interior change, and . . . the Church evangelizes when she seeks to convert, solely through the divine power of the message she proclaims, both the personal and collective consciences of people, the activities in which they engage, and the lives and concrete milieus which are theirs" (ibid., 18).

II. Pathways to the Next Centennial
1986-1988

Introduction

The United States Catholic Conference, in a March 17, 1986 letter signed by Monsignor Daniel Hoye, general secretary, urged members of the House of Representatives to reject a proposal by the Reagan administration that would provide military aid to rebels, known as "contras," seeking to overthrow Nicaragua's Sandinista government. While admitting "intensified" restrictions on the Church in Nicaragua, the letter maintained that "military assistance by outside powers to either side in Nicaragua" is not a useful solution of the problem. Instead, the USCC suggested a "full-scale, high-level commitment by the United States to support and facilitate the renewed Contadora peace process, which has now been given new impetus by the Carabelleda Message of January 12, 1986."

The following week, in a *Statement on the Federal Budget, the Deficit, and Taxes*, issued March 24, 1986, at their semiannual meeting, the Administrative Board of the United States Catholic Conference used three criteria in addressing the problem of the federal budget: (1) that the poor, "the most vulnerable people in our society, should be protected from the effects of these cuts"; (2) that necessary cuts "should be allocated fairly between defense and nondefense spending"; and (3) that in cutting the defense budget "attention should be given to arms control criteria as well as fiscal criteria." Regarding tax policy, the statement quotes recent USCC testimony before Congress: "At a time when deficits in the federal budget are at unprecedented levels, and when many social needs continue to go unmet, the question of adequate federal revenues cannot be ignored." The bishops' statement was intended to address generally their concerns about budget, deficit, and tax matters. They indicated that they would take specific stands as the Congress and administration made changes in current proposals.

That fall, at their September 1986 meeting, the Administrative Board of the USCC issued a policy statement on *Divestment, Disinvestment, and South Africa*. While admitting that the primary agents for improvement of the situation were in South Africa, the bishops stated that nations and institutions having a relationship with South Africa bear some moral responsibility for that devastating political situation.

The prelates set May 15, 1987, as a deadline for the South African government to take some positive steps to correct apartheid, which the Catholic bishops of South Africa denounced as "something intrinsically evil." If that government failed to meet this deadline, then Catholic organizations were to begin prudent divestment from business enterprises involved in South Africa and to promote, where possible with other shareholders, a program of divestment from that troubled country.

When the May 15 deadline passed without significant progress toward dismantling the government's apartheid policy, the USCC divested itself of $18 million worth of South African ties by June 8, 1987, and most dioceses and Catholic institutions followed suit.[1] In addition, according to a national newspaper, "the Board's Policy Statement was received warmly by the media, thus, many secular and non-Catholic organizations were also prompted to adopt the program of divestment."[2]

Back in March 1985, the NCCB Committee on Migration began the process of preparing a statement on the complicated problems of immigration. After wide consultation, the committee submitted the final draft to the Administrative Committee of the National Conference of Catholic Bishops prior to the November 1986 bishops' meeting. *Together a New People: Pastoral Statement on Migrants and Refugees* was approved on November 8, 1986, and issued as a statement of the Administrative Committee.

In several ways, this pastoral statement is a development of the *Resolution on the Pastoral Concern of the Church for People on the Move* passed in 1976 by the National Conference of Catholic Bishops. The dominant note of this statement is that from its beginning the Church in the United States has followed as its guiding light the words of our Lord: "I was a stranger and you welcomed me."

Responding to the avid opponents of immigration, the bishops reminded them that now our annual immigration amounts to only 0.3 percent as compared to 1.5 percent at the turn of the century: "The 1980 Census shows that the foreign born population of the United States is 7 percent, while it is 11 percent for France, 16 percent for Canada, and 20 percent for Australia."

Consistent with its teaching on the dignity of the human person, the statement insists that the Church must continue its mission of acceptance and support of all human beings regardless of culture. Developing this point, the bishops quote Pope John Paul II: "More fully than other social groups, Catholic communities should experience this dynamic fraternal unity and respect differences. Thanks to the Holy Spirit, they should work ceaselessly to build up a people of God speaking the language of love, to be a ferment in a construction of human love."[3]

After developing "Evangelization and Service" to these "New People of God," the prelates conclude their pastoral statement with excellent "Pastoral Suggestions and Resources," beginning on the parish level.

---

[1] *Crux of the News*, June 8, 1987.

[2] The *New York Times*, September 14, 1986.

[3] John Paul II, *Addresses to the World Congress on the Pastoral Care of Immigrants*, October 17, 1985.

The 1986 general meeting of the NCCB, November 10-13, was unique. On the first day, papal pronuncio Archbishop Pio Laghi's address consisted principally of reading Pope John Paul II's letter to the bishops. In his letter, the Holy Father stated his role is "to promote the universality of the Church, to protect her legitimate variety, to guarantee her Catholic unity, to confirm the bishops in their apostolic faith and ministry, to preside in love."He cited the Vatican-commissioned study of the U.S. seminaries and the decision to establish a commission on religious life as "specific ways I have tried to be of service" to the Church in the United States. His Holiness mentioned the purpose of his 1987 trip to the United States would be to "celebrate with you one unity in Jesus Christ and his Church." This papal letter to a general meeting of the U.S. bishops was a first and set a tone for the meeting—a tone of unity with our Holy Father.

On the opening day of the meeting, in his presidential address, Bishop James W. Malone (Youngstown) stated that during our days together we will consider a major pastoral letter on Catholic Social Teaching and the U.S. Economy. "We do so as those committed to moral analysis, as teachers. We do so with an unwavering sense of duty to both society and the Church." He also cited that for the first time, the Church has taught not simply through a finished product, but through the *process* that led to the finished product. "We have found a method in which our collegial teaching engages and gathers into community all sectors of the Church and many of those outside the Church, men and women of good will who are as concerned as we are about nuclear war and economic justice."

But first there had to be the election of his successor. On Tuesday morning, November 11, the outgoing president, Bishop Malone, announced that Archbishop John L. May (St. Louis) was elected president of the conference on the second ballot, and Archbishop Daniel E. Pilarczyk (Cincinnati) was elected vice president. Both were considered to be moderates. The assembled bishops also elected four delegates to the 1987 World Synod of Bishops on the Laity. As expected, the newly elected president, Archbishop May, was named as one of the delegates. The others were Cardinal Joseph L. Bernardin (Chicago), Archbishop Rembert G. Weakland, OSB (Milwaukee), and Bishop Stanley J. Ott (Baton Rouge), who was also chairman of the Bishops' Committee on the Laity. Bishop Raymond A. Lucher (New Ulm) and Bishop Ricardo Ramirez (Las Cruces) were elected as alternates.

On November 12, prompted by the realization that the policy of the United States could be decisive for Lebanon, the National Conference of Catholic Bishops passed unanimously a *Resolution on Lebanon* to enlist international aid to protect the rights of Christians in Lebanon and to promote peaceful coexistence among all Lebanese. In their conclusion to the resolution, the bishops called for a U.S.

policy that would "assist all the Lebanese to guarantee the freedom, territorial integrity, and sovereignty of their nation."

On the same day, the bishops noted the 600th anniversary of the conversion of the Lithuanian nation in their *Resolution on Lithuania.* The U.S. bishops asked all their ordinaries to proclaim, in unison with the Holy Father, June 28, 1987, as a day of prayer for the persecuted Church of Lithuania and to observe the anniversary year in a fitting manner. In few nations has the Church suffered more under crushing Soviet repression than in Lithuania. In their resolution, the American prelates pleaded with the Soviet authorities "to honor the human rights of all Lithuanians." Specifically, the bishops sought permission to publish a new Lithuanian translation of the Scriptures and requested the return of three prominent churches to religious use.

The State Department Country Reports on Human Rights Practices 1986 stated, however, "Soviet authorities have apparently mounted a large-scale assault on all religious activists not controlled and sponsored by the State, with special emphasis on the Catholic Church."[4] The report noted that although the Lithuanian Church was preparing for the 1987 celebrations marking the 600th anniversary of Christianity in Lithuania, "there was a fear that the Soviet authorities might restrict or totally forbid large gatherings."[5] Unfortunately, that fear was realized. The anticipated action materialized, for "in a mean-spirited effort to minimize the jubilee, the government banned all travel to Lithuania during June."[6]

On June 28, in Rome, Pope John Paul II did commemorate the sixth centennial with a solemn papal Mass and beatified George Matulaitis (1871-1927) a Lithuanian archbishop, observing that to their credit, over 75 percent of the Lithuanians persevere in their faith although its practice, even in so-called *glasnost,* is both difficult and dangerous.

A third piece of business that took place on November 12, 1986, was the approval by the body of bishops of a pastoral statement on world mission entitled *To the Ends of the Earth.*

In 1984, at the request of the Committee on the Missions, the NCCB voted to publish a pastoral on the Church's missionary activity. Limiting the pastoral's scope to only foreign missions, the conference wished to commemorate two anniversaries: the twentieth of Vatican II's decree *Ad Gentes* and the tenth of Pope Paul VI's apostolic exhortation *Evangelii Nuntiandi.*

Bishop James W. Malone, then president of the conference, asked the Committee on the Missions to prepare the pastoral. Bishop Joseph

---

[4]The *Florida Catholic,* March 6, 1987.
[5]Ibid.
[6]"The Lithuanian Cross," *America,* June 13, 1987.

A. Fiorenza was chairman of the committee, which included Archbishop Edward O'Meara and Bishops Terry Steib, Richard Ham, Thomas O'Brien, Thaddeus Shubsda, and William Connare.

In his presentation of the final draft at the November 1986 meeting, Bishop Fiorenza explained that three hearings were held to which theologians, scripture scholars, men and women missionaries, and representatives of mission-sending societies were invited to present their response to an outline on mission theology and practice. Based on their responses, the first draft was sent to active missionaries for their input; over 900 replied from every continent. Subsequent drafts had input from diocesan mission directors, presbyteral councils, and other interested persons. Members of the NCCB Administrative Committee and other members of the NCCB then offered several helpful suggestions, which were incorporated into the fourth and final draft.

After the presentation of this final draft to the general body of the bishops, a few further amendments were added to the document. On November 12, 1986, the mission pastoral was passed unanimously by voice vote.

To the Ends of the Earth was meant to be an appropriate companion to the peace pastoral and to the economic pastoral. Before the Church can promote peace and economic justice, it must proclaim salvation in Christ. So the world mission pastoral can be read as the final work in a trilogy of pastorals that teach mankind's salvation, peace, and justice.

This statement offered a sound theological basis "for the role of the Church in the missions and specifically the role of the United States."[7] The pastoral also affirmed missionaries in their efforts to proclaim the Gospel. By its very nature, the Church is missionary and all are faithful to the Church "to the degree we love and sincerely promote her missionary activity."[8]

A thoroughly honest statement, lamenting colonial and political evils that often plague mission endeavors, it noted "the shifting of the Church's center of gravity from the West, from Europe and North America toward the East and South. . . . In Latin America, Africa, and Asia the Church is experiencing either profound revitalization or enormous growth." Reminding Catholics that every local church is "both mission-sending and mission-receiving," the prelates proclaimed, "To say 'Church' is to say 'mission.' Any local church," the bishops taught, "has no choice but to reach out to others with the Gospel of Christ's love for all people." Specifically, the bishops warned: "When missionaries come from a country like the United States, which

---

[7]The *Catholic Standard and Times*, November 20, 1986.

[8]*To the Ends of the Earth* (Washington, D.C.: USCC Office of Publishing and Promotion Services, 1986).

has great political and economic interests throughout the world, their participation in the life of the local church can place them in conflict with the policies of their own government or, indeed, of their host government. Nevertheless, they must be in union with the diocesan bishops and the local church which they have been sent to serve."

These teachers emphasized that true inculturation occurs only when the Gospel penetrates the heart of the cultural experience and shows how Christ gives new meaning to authentic human values. "In this work of dialogue and evangelization, the Church must be a leaven for all cultures, at home in each culture."

To the Ends of the Earth presented liberation theology at its best, stressing a "special option for the poor," and declaring: "central to the Church's missionary task is a mission spirituality." Citing several contemporary American martyred missionaries, this comprehensive document concluded: "We challenge the young to consider following Christ as missionaries."

Unfortunately, at its publication, this carefully researched, well-organized, lucidly written, and timely pastoral did not get the attention or acclaim it so richly deserved, principally because of the Archbishop Raymond Hunthausen case, which was discussed in executive session at the November 1986 meeting. Fortunately, from all appearances, this pastoral seems to be gaining momentum: Father William Young, SSS, wrote an excellent reflection on part III, "A Mission Spirituality," of *To the Ends of the Earth* entitled "Send to Receive From."[9] Father William M. Boteler, superior general of the Maryknoll Fathers, observed that missioners who stand up for oppressed Third World peoples sometimes find themselves under fire back home, criticized for becoming too socially or politically involved, but the bishops' pastoral statement "strongly endorses the work our missioners are doing around the world."[10] Bishop William J. McCormack, national director for the Society for the Propogation of the Faith, in a brief but excellent analysis of the pastoral noted: "The bishops of the United States ask each Catholic to take a personal sense of responsibility for mission, for bringing the good news of God's love to the world by word and example."[11]

Time may prove *To the Ends of the Earth* to be one of the better and more important pastorals produced by the U.S. hierarchy.

The most noted document to come out of the November 1986 general meeting was the bishops' economic pastoral. Since both the "Pastoral Message" and their letter on *Economic Justice for All* are published here in their entirety, there will be no attempt to summarize the pastoral in this introduction. Only some of the key teachings and

---

[9]*Emmanuel* (April 1987): 14ff.

[10]*Maryknoll* (April 1987): 40.

[11]Ibid. (October 1987): 58.

the more significant historical facts in the development and refinement of the document will be noted here.

Contrary to what some people think and to what some journalists write, the idea of such a pastoral letter did not originate from the thought of correcting recent economic difficulties here and elsewhere in the world. After the letter on Marxism was issued by the National Conference of Catholic Bishops in 1980, the Most Rev. Peter Rosazza, auxiliary bishop of Hartford, suggested that the NCCB issue one on capitalism.

The then president of the NCCB, Archbishop John R. Roach (St. Paul and Minneapolis), named the Most Rev. Rembert G. Weakland, OSB, archbishop of Milwaukee, chairman of the ad hoc Committee on Christianity and Capitalism, later limited for practical reasons to Catholic Social Teaching and the U.S. Economy. One of the most intelligent members of the American Hierarchy, an able linguist, a cultured man, graduate of Julliard Conservatory, whose father died when Rembert was a small boy (so his family had to live on welfare until the promising young man was nearly through high school), Archbishop Weakland was an excellent choice for chairman.

The other members of the ad hoc committee were well qualified for their posts: Bishop Peter A. Rosazza studied in Paris and then worked for ten years with the Hispanic immigrants in Hartford, experiencing their poverty firsthand. Archbishop Thomas A. Donnellan of Atlanta was seasoned in law, holding an earned doctorate in canon law. His many years of service in the New York Archdiocesan Tribunal had shown him how broken marriages can produce poverty. Bishop William K. Weigand of Salt Lake City, formerly a priest of the Diocese of Boise, worked for nine and a half years with the poor in Peru, South America. The final member, Bishop George H. Speltz of St. Cloud, Minnesota, earned a doctorate in economics and is an expert in rural life, having been born into it and having served all his priesthood in rural areas.

Even before the first draft of the pastoral appeared, there were shouts of "unpatriotic," "un-American" and even "socialistic." Incidentally, there is hardly a major reform that now constitutes an accepted part of the American way of life that was not at one time tarred as "socialistic"—from free schooling for everyone to child-labor laws; from the eight-hour working day to Social Security; from women's suffrage to the right to organize labor unions and engage in collective bargaining. In daring to examine and, where necessary, criticize our economic system, the bishops were not betraying the American part; they were being faithful to it.[12]

---

[12]Cf. Most Rev. Roger Mahony, "There Your Heart Will Be: A Pastoral Reflection on the American Economy," *Catholicism in Crisis*, July 1984.

Referring to the first drafting of the pastoral, representatives of principal Jewish organizations emphasized that in their Talmudic tradition, individuals and governments have a duty to care for the needs of the poor. "Jewish law resorts to coercive measures when personal charity does not meet the needs of the public good," noted Rabbi Walter Wurzburger, chairman of Interreligious Affairs of the Synagogue Council of America. "The free-marketing system cannot be relied upon exclusively to ensure the well-being of all human beings."[13]

In his 1984 Labor Day Statement, then Archbishop O'Connor of New York rejected the view that the bishops were intruding in political affairs. "Rather," he said, "[the Church] is seeking to make clear the human and moral consequences of the technical choices we make as a nation. Catholic social teaching is neither widely known nor understood," O'Connor stated, claiming this pastoral letter "will provide the opportunity to raise up this *buried treasure* and dust off its many valuable contents."[14]

The pastoral is based on six moral principles drawn from Scripture and the social teachings of the Church. These constitute part I of the letter:

1. Human rights are the minimum conditions for life in community. In Catholic teaching, human rights include not only civil and political rights (freedom of speech, worship, etc.), but also economic rights. As Pope John XXIII declared, all people have a right to life, food, clothing, shelter, rest, medical care, education, and employment.
2. Human dignity can be realized and protected only in community. Although the obligation to "love our neighbor" has an individual dimension, it also requires a broader social commitment to the common good.
3. All people have a right to participate in the economic life of society. No person or group should be unfairly excluded or unable to participate in or contribute to the economy.
4. Every economic decision and institution must be judged in the light of whether it protects or undermines the dignity of the human person. The economy should serve people, not the other way around.
5. Society as a whole, acting through public and private institutions, has the moral responsibility to enhance human dignity and protect human rights. In addition to the clear responsibility of private institutions, government also has an essential responsibility.

---

[13]The *National Catholic Reporter,* August 17, 1984.
[14]*Origins* (September 6, 1984): 181-184.

6. All members of society have a special obligation to the poor and vulnerable. As followers of Christ, we are challenged to make a "fundamental option for the poor"—to speak for the voiceless, to defend the defenseless.

Part II of the letter was originally going to deal with five policy issues: (1) unemployment; (2) poverty; (3) planning; and (4) trade with developing nations, which soon broadened to include "aid" to those nations. The fifth issue, "natural resources," because of its vastness, much to the regret of the chairman, who felt the letter did not do justice to the whole ecological question, had to be reduced to "food and agriculture," then a most urgent area.

In 1984 and 1985, there arose a moderate-sized family farm crisis. The committee, convinced that food and its production occupy a special place in the economy, and that the erosion of family farming brings with it a serious erosion of both moral and economic values connected with stewardship of the land, decided to devote a separate chapter to food production and land use.

Regarding the process used for the pastoral "from beginning to completion," one of the chief consultants, Monsignor George Higgins, declared that it would be fair to say that no other ecclesiastical body, including the Vatican, has ever engaged in a consultative process as extensive, as open-ended, as that of the American bishops in the drafting of their two pastorals *The Challenge of Peace* and *Economic Justice for All*. "I agree with those who say that this process may well prove to have more lasting influence that the two documents themselves."[15]

Although the same expert agreed that liberation is absolutely essential to evangelization, he conceded, "the Church cannot find a future simply in secular concerns, however pressing and urgent these may be, for the Church is meant to be a community of the transcendent."[16]

Archbishop Roger Mahony reflected that this composing procedure, like the process that led up to the pastoral letter, *The Challenge of Peace: God's Promise and Our Response*, represents something new and very important in the Church in our country, something based on a deepening understanding of the Church, which we owe to the profound renewal of Catholicism inaugurated by the Second Vatican Council. "The model adopted by the United States Bishops' Conference believes," in Archbishop Weakland's words, "that the Holy Spirit resides in all members of the Church and that the hierarchy must listen to what the Spirit is saying to the whole Church. . . . Discern-

---

[15]Higgins, "The Social Mission of the Church after Vatican II," *America*, July 26, 1986.
[16]Ibid.

ment," as Archbishop Weakland points out, "becomes part of the teaching process."[17]

On November 11, 1984, the committee released the first draft of the pastoral. Presiding Bishop Malone advised: "The most important thing for all of us to do is to respond in writing after this meeting and after we have had a chance to study and reflect on this document."[18] At that meeting, Archbishop Weakland made a report, answered several general questions, and requested further written comments. No detailed discussion was held.

Despite its length—112 pages of text—the proposed pastoral was a limited document, written in language the average person could understand. It did not pretend to offer a panoramic view of all economics.

On Wednesday morning, November 14, Archbishop Weakland in his presentation to the general assembly of bishops, pointed out: "We [the committee] approached our work not as economists. We approached our work as concerned teachers."

Among the thirteen bishops who commented on the first draft of the pastoral, Archbishop Philip Hannan of New Orleans asked for an inclusion of low-cost housing. Cardinal Joseph Bernardin warned against a "laundry list of economic issues," and Archbishop John O'Connor of New York told of how eager a Wall Street group of financiers was to hear the pastoral and how he was personally going to conduct weekly classes for them. Archbishop Francis Hurley of Anchorage advised his brother bishops to "get to know poor people firsthand. Set an example of personal contact with poor people. Jesus was seen personally and visibly with the poor."

The Reagan administration, according to White House spokesperson Larry Speakes, shared the bishops' concern for the poor expressed in the first draft of the pastoral letter on the economy (November 13, 1984). Although Speakes noted that President Reagan welcomed the draft of the pastoral letter, he observed it would be inappropriate to comment on it, since it would not be in final form for at least another year.[19]

The first draft of the pastoral had a difficult entry. Michael Novak of the self-described Lay Commission on Catholic Social Teaching and the U.S. Economy published a completely distorted review of the pastoral in the *Washington Post*. "It was so inaccurate one wondered whether he actually read the draft of the pastoral."[20]

---

[17]*Catholicism in Crisis,* July 1984.

[18]"Minutes of the General Meeting of the National Conference of Catholic Bishops," November 12, 1984.

[19]The *Catholic Standard and Times,* November 22, 1984.

[20]Thomas J. Reese, SJ, *America,* December 8, 1984.

Critics concentrated on three arguments:

1. The bishops are incompetent in economics (yet every ordinary has numerous business dealings in his lifetime).
2. The bishops are politically naive and out of step with the American people (but the bishops can afford to oppose public opinion, for they do not seek election; they work to FORM public opinion rather than CONFORM to it).
3. The most serious argument: these proposals have been tried before and they failed. Archbishop Weakland agreed that many of the programs had been tried in the past, but just because those poorly designed programs did not work was no reason to give up entirely on attempts to help the poor. "If the bishops' proposals do not work, it is up to the critics to come up with better ones that will take care of the unemployed, hungry, and homeless both in the United States and around the world."[21]

The first draft had been held up because of the national presidential election. It was given to the bishops only a few days before the November 1984 meeting in Washington. So the following June meeting in Collegeville was the first opportunity the assembled prelates had for a full discussion of the first draft. Meanwhile 10,000 pages of suggestions from home and abroad were received by the drafting committee.

Repeatedly, the drafting committee and commentators explained that part I of the pastoral, dealing with ethical principles, was more important than part II, which offered only prudential judgments about application of these principles to concrete problems.[22]

Generally, the negative critics faulted the second part of the letter, with its concrete recommendations for solving specific economic problems: unemployment, poverty, and so forth. Critics contended that the proposals were expensive, warmed-over programs that had not worked in the past. For instance, Leonard Silk, noted writer on economic affairs, commenting on section VII, "The United States and the World Economy," stated: "Perhaps the most controversial element in the bishops' letter may be its harsh criticism of the United States policy towards Third World countries."[23]

In contrast, Gordon Welty wrote sympathetically in his "Reflections on the Bishops' Pastoral Letter," noting that, given our present definition of national security and such an agency as the modern corporation, international policy suffers the most dehumanizing dis-

---

[21]Ibid.
[22]Cf. Thomas J. Reese, SJ, "The Economic Pastoral: Part I," *America*, April 19, 1985.
[23]The *New York Times*, November 19, 1984.

tortions. The greater portion of foreign aid goes to a few nations in the Middle East (cf. also para. 291), seemingly to exacerbate the perennial conflict there. Armament sales clog international trade (para. 314; cf. also para. 12)."[24]

By the June 1985 meeting in Collegeville, Minnesota, the bishops were able to focus on five areas of concern elicited mostly from diocesan consultation on the first draft of the economy pastoral: (1) the specificity of the draft; (2) the place for preferential option for the poor; (3) the plan for the summary of the pastoral; (4) the implementation of the pastoral; and (5) the connection between this pastoral and the earlier peace pastoral.

Archbishop Weakland summarized the bishops' input for these five major areas. On specificity, he stated the writing committee would take a closer look at the whole matter and clarify the issues. Regarding the preferential option for the poor, he noted the majority of the bishops favored retaining the term, but the committee would devise an American context so as not to polarize the middle class. Archbishop Weakland hoped the dual purpose of the pastoral (namely, formation of conscience and preparation for participation in the public debate) would give substance and impetus to the implementation. Further, the committee saw an opportunity for making the linkage with the peace pastoral in the discussion of the world economy or in the militarization of the economy.[25]

There was unanimous support for a briefer pastoral message issued in conjunction with the larger document (a summary to be sent to the bishops well in advance of the November 1985 meeting.)

At the conclusion of Archbishop Weakland's remarks, the bishops were once again invited to meet in small groups to respond to the Milwaukee prelate's summary of their concerns and to address any additional substantive concerns not easily included in the five discussion questions presented the previous day. Nineteen tables and seventeen individuals requested time to speak to the assembly. Nearly every table representative and most of the individual speakers expressed confidence in and gratitude to the writing committee for the work on and the general content of the pastoral letter.

Again Archbishop Weakland responded to the lengthy discussion, addressing the following points:

1. The idea of inviting people to consider solutions and of avoiding apodictic statements where possible is a good one (the writing committee had heard this from its European colleagues as well).

---

[24] *Social Justice Review*, May-June 1985.

[25] "Minutes of the Thirty-Second General Meeting of the National Conference of Catholic Bishops," p. 14.

2. The writing committee will have to discuss whether the brief pastoral message could be produced by November without delaying the process of producing a second draft of the pastoral letter itself.

3. The distinction between levels of authority, necessary in all conference documents, is treated in part II. Perhaps this treatment should be highlighted at the beginning of part I.

4. The discussion on food and agriculture is very helpful, but it is difficult to keep long-range and short-range solutions in proper focus when the immediate situation is so urgent. This is the most specific section and one which most clearly calls for government intervention because of its urgency.

5. Others have criticized us for not dealing with population. We could attempt a treatment of this, drawing from *Mater et Magistra* and the Vatican statement at the U.N. Population Conference in Mexico City, as well as other church documents.[26]

6. The idea of specific responses to the critics is a good one, but the problem is deciding which economists to draw on. The writing committee will look into this.

7. The committee considered drawing up a systematic critique of capitalism, but decided that it would be very difficult since capitalism has not one single spokesman—as does Marxism, for example. The current document is capitalistic; although it proposes modifications of capitalism to serve the common good more adequately. Some may interpret these modifications as socialistic, but socialism does not address the perennial problem of the tension between efficiency and equity. Capitalism is the best system for producing wealth, but needs communitarian values drawn from the outside. The writing committee could attempt to incorporate some of this theme into the next text.

8. The writing committee is not opposed to citing achievements of capitalism, but will also have to deal with the costs. The Industrial Revolution, for example, only developed safeguards for equity because of the outside force exerted by the labor movement. The committee is concerned that the incorporation of too much of this kind of discussion would make the document lose its pastoral character and take on a theoretical cast.

Archbishop Weakland concluded by expressing the appreciation of the entire writing committee for all the comments the bishops'

---

[26]In a later talk on the economic pastoral, principally to New York City's business community, Archbishop Weakland explained regarding population control that the lack of discussion of that question is a *"lacuna* in the total economy picture . . ."* He did not expand upon the issue, but admitted it would require a separate paper in the future. The *National Catholic Reporter,* June 21, 1985.

discussions had engendered and said that they would try to take them all into account. Bishop Malone, in the name of the assembly, commended the committee for its work in introducing the first draft.

The initial reaction to the pastoral throughout the country was generally negative. *America* devoted its entire January 5, 1985, issue to a wide-ranging discussion of the first draft of the pastoral and to the comments already made on it; with two exceptions, the January issue reflected that negative attitude. During the next month, however, other voices were heard praising the strengths of the bishops' proposals and the urgency of their call. The May 1985 issue of *America*, more ecumenical in scope, included the opinions of a Protestant, a Jew, and a secular humanist. That issue reflected well the change to a more promising positive attitude.

The second draft of the pastoral letter on economy, released on October 5, 1985, affirmed once again that the fundamental criterion for all economic decisions and institutions is that they serve all people, especially the poor. At that time, Archbishop Weakland asserted: "In the second draft, we do not back away from our strong conviction that more can and must be done to fight poverty and unemployment."[27]

"Every perspective of economic life that is human, moral, and Christian," says the draft, "must be shaped by three questions—What does the economy do for the people? What does it do to the people? And how do people participate in it?"[28] Using both biblical concepts and ethical norms, the draft set forth moral criteria for assessing economic life and called for a "new American experiment" to enhance human dignity through the determined pursuit of greater economic justice.

The Archbishop emphasized the importance of the open process used in drafting and discussing the pastoral letter: "We have sought to stimulate a public discussion that gives explicit attention to the moral values inherent in economic decisions. . . . We have been very pleased by the richness and the extent of the response thus far."[29]

One frequent response to the first draft had been that the emphasis on the preferential option for the poor pitted the middle class against the poor. The second draft maintained the strong emphasis on concern for the poor, but presented this theme in the context of the common good: "The deprivation and powerlessness of the poor wounds the whole of society."[30]

---

[27] The *Catholic Standard and Times,* October 17, 1985.

[28] *Origins* 15 (October 10, 1985).

[29] *USCC News,* October 7, 1985.

[30] The second draft of "Catholic Social Teachings and the U.S. Economy," *Origins* 15 (October 15, 1985).

One new element in the second draft was a briefer discussion of the American economic system as such:

> The Church is not bound to any particular economic, political, or social system or ideology. It has existed and will continue to exist in many different environments with different forms of economic and social organization. We must evaluate all these economic systems in terms of our moral and ethical principles. Our primary criterion in judging any economy is not its adherence to a particular ideology but the impact it has on human beings. Does it promote or impede the realization of human dignity?[31]

This pastoral letter was being written both to provide guidance for Catholics and to contribute to the public discussion about U.S. economic policies. "As pastors and teachers," said Archbishop Weakland, "we have the challenge of applying 100 years of Catholic social teaching to the most powerful economy on earth. What we're trying to do is to take that teaching and explore its meaning in this complex diverse economy. We're exploring what an authentic 'option for the poor' means for the Church in the United States, and how we measure our economic life by gospel values."

The document proposed three priority points that should shape economic policies and institutions both domestically and internationally:

1. fulfilling the basic needs of the poor;[32]
2. increasing participation in economic life by those who are presently excluded or vulnerable; and
3. targeting the investment of wealth, talent, and human energy to benefit those who are poor or economically insecure.

Chapter III of the second draft discussed several specific economic issues. The drafting committee selected four issues that exemplify the interaction of moral values and economic policy: (1) employment; (2) poverty; (3) food and agriculture; and (4) international economic concerns. Archbishop Weakland cautioned that these were not intended to be a comprehensive list of issues: "We have selected only four issues, with the full realization that these four do not encompass all economic topics. We hope and expect that others will apply Catholic moral principles to the full range of economic issues that confront the nation."[33]

In April 1986, the drafting committee met in private sessions with some bishops from Latin America to discuss international issues con-

---

[31] Ibid.
[32] *USCC News*, October 7, 1985.
[33] Ibid.

tained in the letter. The entire committee also fanned out to address various groups in the United States, seeking further input for the final draft after the second draft was discussed at the bishops' meeting.

As the third draft was being prepared, some critics—Catholic and non-Catholic—complained that the Church had no right to speak on public issues. At the University of Notre Dame, NCCB President Bishop James W. Malone countered that when religion speaks to the issues of the day we rightfully insist that its voice be heard.

> The moral norms authoritatively proposed by the Church are essentially negative—they say what may not be done (though of course such prohibitions defend positive values). As for what should be done after proposing certain broad goals—life, liberty, and the pursuit of happiness, say—the Church's authoritative teaching leaves it to the moral creativity of the individuals and groups to determine how best to pursue and realize them.[34]

At the release of the third draft on June 2, 1986, Archbishop Weakland emphasized that the final vote on the pastoral letter would not be the end of the process. The "Pastoral Message" (the abbreviated version) itself stated that "the completion of a letter such as this is but the beginning of a long process of education, discussion, and action [to reshape the economy] so that human dignity prospers and the human person is served. This is the unfinished work and the challenge of our faith."

Governor Mario Cuomo of New York commented on the third draft:

> There's a renewed belief that we have it in our own power to help people to improve the condition of their lives, to break the cycle of dependency, to realize the promise that is supposed to be the birthright of all Americans. The bishops deserve our thanks for helping to lead us to all these realizations.[35]

Recalling the ridicule that greeted the first draft, Cuomo responded:

> I admire [the bishops'] dedication and persistence in improving each draft. But what's more important is that as a nation we seem no longer content to avoid the issue. Motivated by both compassion and common sense, by both clarity and self-interest, we're determined now, I think, to do something. . . . We are ready again to bear true faith and allegiance to the traditions that have always America at its best.[36]

The *Wall Street Journal*, in contrast, concluded a critical article with

---

[34]The *Catholic Standard and Times*, March 6, 1986.
[35]*Our Sunday Visitor*, August 10, 1986.
[36]Ibid.

a lamenting tone that the third draft would not be changed substantially: "Archbishop Weakland said that while there will be some further amendments to the draft, he felt the Church's U.S. hierarchy was nearing a consensus on the document."[37]

This draft called for the sweeping reforms or replacement of the World Bank, the International Monetary Fund, and the General Agreement on Tariffs and Trade. These institutions were neither "representative nor capable of dealing adequately with current problems."[38]

The criticism of institutions like the World Bank, IMF, and GAT followed consultations the previous December with Third World economists and in April with representatives of Latin American bishops' conferences. Writing in the *National Catholic Reporter*, Archbishop Weakland said that the much longer section on the urgency of the Third World debt crisis reflected the fact that "so often . . . we ignore the effects that it is having on the lives of people already disadvantaged."[39] These pastoral concerns had been pointed out to the drafting committee "in vivid terms" during their discussions with bishops from Central and South America. "Most Americans are not conscious of the grave consequences that could follow if this question is not solved at once," he added [40]

The third draft also gave more attention to the family. It did not suggest that the family be the basic economic unit of society, as research had shown 40 percent of wage earners to be single, but recommended that a criterion for economic policies and decisions should be "their impact of strength and stability of family life." The draft pointed out that destructive trends that militated against the stability of the family were more evident among the poor, with more damaging economic consequences; but such trends had to be counteracted in the whole of society by reviving a sense of personal responsibility and commitment. Education, too, was stressed as an aid to help overcome powerlessness and marginalization.

The draft challenged Americans about their life style. On this, Archbishop Weakland said, "Serious questions must be asked and prophetic stances be taken," adding that this section of the pastoral would "surely remain one of the most challenging for all who take the Gospel seriously."[41] The draft further included a few paragraphs about leisure, intended to balance a possible overemphasis on work in recent Catholic social teaching, which might make it seem the total means of self-definition and self-fulfillment.

---

[37] June 3, 1986.
[38] Cf. *The Tablet* (England), October 12, 1986.
[39] June 6, 1986.
[40] Ibid.
[41] Ibid.

Never neglecting the role of the spiritual, the third draft of the pastoral stressed: "The transformation of social structures begins with and is always accompanied by a conversion of the heart."

Archbishop Weakland, in his presentation at the November 1986 meeting, stated that all the bishops were aware of the impact that the three drafts of the letter had not only on the Catholic population of the country but on the world. He maintained that the Christian moral vision of *Economic Justice for All* was the document's central contribution, citing the very first sentence of the letter: "Every perspective on economic life that is human, moral, and Christian must be shaped by three questions: What does the economy do *for* the people? What does it do *to* the people? And how do the people *participate* in it?"

The Archbishop then traced the long tedious journey from the concept of the pastoral to the third draft, observing that the decision to limit detailed analysis to five themes was crucial to the development of the document. The five areas finally selected were (1) employment, (2) poverty, (3) food and agricultural issues, (4) international questions, and (5) collaboration in economic life (which evolved as a special chapter called "A New American Experiment: Partnership for the Public Good"). The pastoral's final title became *Economic Justice for All: Pastoral Letter on Catholic Social Teaching and the U.S. Economy.*

The troubling question of length and style was, according to the Archbishop, at least partially solved through the decision to write a "Pastoral Message" to accompany the entire document. The message, which had been sent to the bishops a few weeks earlier would also be the object of amendments and debate.

Archbishop Philip Hannan requested that a new principle be inserted in the pastoral: "Workers must be willing to use and/or seek opportunities to work." And Cardinal Bernardin refuted at length those critics of the third draft who alleged that an underlying theme behind the final draft appears to be a vision not of justice based on liberty, but of equality based on income and wealth.

Reporting on that same draft, the *Wall Street Journal* observed: "The final amendments include a plea for efforts to overcome the effects of sexism, which the report calls immoral."[42]

The bishops also added an acknowledgment that the new tax law did much to achieve the goal of letting poor families avoid taxes. In addition, the bishops agreed to sharpen language asserting that allegations of welfare fraud are overstated and attacking the belief that individuals are poor by choice or laziness.

The bishops did not intend to limit the letter to Catholics alone. Although they proposed to write first of all to provide guidance for Catholics seeking to form their conscience about economic matters,

---

[42]Ibid.

they asserted, "No one may claim the name Christian and be comfortable in the face of hunger, homelessness, insecurity, and injustice . . . that there are so many poor people in a nation as rich as ours is a social and moral scandal that we cannot ignore."

The bishops wanted to join the public debate about the directions in which the U.S. economy should be moving, seeking also the cooperation and support of those not of the Catholic faith and tradition. The third draft was critical of what it sees as misguided and insufficient U.S. efforts to spur development and reduce poverty in the Third World.

Despite the enormous problems involved nationally and internationally, a constant strong optimism characterizes the pastoral: "We believe that with your prayers, reflection, service, and action, our economy can be shaped so that human dignity prospers and the human person is served. This is the unfinished work of our nation. This is the challenge of our faith."

Archbishop Weakland processed a long series of amendments to the third draft into Thursday morning, November 13, when Bishop Robert J. Banks (auxiliary, Boston) moved that the floor be closed to amendments, thus eliminating any further discussion of the pastoral or the briefer message. The motion was approved, much to the chagrin of some bishops. According to the unpublished minutes of the general meeting, Bishop Malone called for the question and the tally was 210 to 40 in support of the motion, far more than the necessary two-thirds majority.

Passage of the pastoral required 195 votes (two-thirds of the *de jure* members attending). On November 13, it was adopted by a vote of 225 to 9. There was a loud round of applause for the committee and for the successful accomplishment of such a work.

The letter received solid notices both on national and international levels. On December 22, 1986, the pastoral was debated before the Joint Economic Committee of the U.S. Congress by a panel that included Archbishop Weakland, the USCC expert Father Bryan Hehir, and Father David Hollenback of Weston School of Theology, as well as several social scientists and economists. This was most unusual for any congressional committee to gather solely to discuss a policy statement by a religious organization.

Lamenting the high rate of unemployment in the United States, Archbishop Weakland saw that probably the most important issue is participation in the economy through jobs. He reminded the committee that more than 33 million Americans are poor and paraphrased the pastoral: "the fact that so many are poor in a nation as wealthy as ours is a social and moral scandal."

The archbishop reminded the committee that between the "collectivist" type of economics and the school that teaches "the free market automatically produces justice," there is a positive, constructive role for government in the economy of the nation.

Father Hollenback stressed that the minimum wage has now fallen 15 to 20 percent below poverty level.

Father Hehir emphasized the pressing need to revamp global economy which keeps 800 million people in dire poverty and 500 million in daily hunger despite an abundance of food stuffs. The Boston diocesan priest declared that the difference of the Western and Eastern outlook distorts our allotment of international aid.

Their presentation made a significant impact. Representative David Obey (D-Wis.), chairman of the committee, added that as a former chairman of the Foreign Operations Subcommittee, he could attest to the fact that "well over two-thirds of the U.S. foreign aid is provided not on the basis of need but for military purposes." Obey also mentioned his grave concern over the current U.S. economic policy and offered support for many of the bishops' suggestions.

Then chairman of the Joint Economic Committee Paul Sarbanes (D-Md.) was quite familiar with the pastoral and was reported to be "vitally concerned with the issue it has raised."

On November 14, 1986, the White House in its *Report of the Working Group on the Family* agreed with the bishops' letter on a major point: "The economy must help, not hinder, American families."[43]

Father Thomas Gannon, SJ, in a lengthy and scholarly critique of the pastoral concluded that the real difference that the bishops' letter makes does not lie in its diagnosis of the American economy or in its recommendations about how economic life should be organized.

> The difference lies, rather, in the possibility it offers that ordinary Catholic and non-Catholic citizens could be more sensitized, more concerned, more compassionate, and more committed to the cause of those who, having no cause to promote, have no one to promote their own. This is a significant step for the Catholic community, which both illuminates the complexity and breadth of the Catholic social agenda and manifests the Church's effectiveness when confronting important and troubling issues of our time. In the end, the real success of the pastoral will lie not in its public response, but in the renewal of each person who hears its message.[44]

In a January 1987 speech to social justice officials Owen Bieber, president of the United Auto Workers, endorsed the pastoral on economic justice as a guide for economic reform. He also declared that the U.S. bishops "confront the American dream" (currently perverted by greed) with "the American reality" that demands economic justice.[45]

---

[43]The *Washington Post*, November 15, 1986.

[44]*Month* (December 1986): 350.

[45]The *National Catholic Register*, February 8, 1987.

There was also an encouraging international acceptance of the pastoral. Auxiliary Bishop Genaro Alamilla of Mexico City said Mexico's bishops fundamentally agreed with the American bishops' letter on the economy, especially with regard to the world economic order and the Third World debt problems—a serious question facing Mexico and other developing nations. Mexico is second only to Brazil among debtor nations.[46]

One set of critics, however, accused the bishops of a "preferential option for the state" and averred the prelates put too much faith in government intervention as a means of helping the poor.[47]

In contrast, the *National Catholic Reporter* queried, "So you want to know why the bishops write pastorals? Barely days after the U.S. Catholic bishops overwhelmingly approved their economic justice letter . . . the greed-fed ambitions of the insider traders and corporate raiders treat as incidental the lives and livelihood of millions of ordinary people."[48]

A Maryknoll missionary sagely remarked that the bishops would be criticized, but they could take consolation in being denounced: "Missionaries have long known the cost of defending the oppressed against the powerful. Unfortunately, it is sometimes impossible to confront the afflicted without in turn afflicting the comfortable."[49]

Commonweal applauded the bishops for, quite properly, delivering the Good News. "But the Good News is always difficult to hear. For one thing, it is too good to believe. For another, it's too good to live up to."[50]

The same article asked: "Are the bishops serious about the statement they've so publicly and painstakingly put together? One indication that they are, is implicitly economic. They have allocated more than a half-million dollars for spreading and implementing the pastoral's message during the next three years. That is the commitment of the U.S. Catholic Conference."

Dioceses, parishes, religious orders, universities, and Catholic organizations have marshalled their own individual efforts. The pastoral is being ever more widely studied and discussed here and abroad. In the spring of 1987, Georgetown University Press published *The Deeper Meaning of Economic Life: Critical Essays on the U.S. Bishops' Pastoral Letter on the Economy*, edited by R. Bruce Douglass. This interdisciplinary study takes up the fundamental challenge to rethink our economic philosophy. Archbishop Weakland called this study "most

---

[46]*The Tablet* (English), December 8, 1986.
[47]Cf. *Florida Catholic*, January 2, 1987.
[48]December 5, 1986.
[49]Rev. John Geitner, MM, *Florida Catholic*, November 26, 1986.
[50]December 5, 1986.

helpful in outlining certain of the more philosophical questions involved and for discussing them at a level and in the depth they deserve."[51]

Certainly, from the second draft on, many bishops were concerned about the lasting effect of the economic pastoral. Accordingly, early in 1986 Bishop James Malone, then president of the conference, appointed an ad hoc committee to further the implementation of the letter. Bishop Anthony Pilla (Cleveland) was named chairman of the committee, which included Bishops Matthew H. Clark (Rochester), Francis A. Quinn (Sacramento), and John H. Ricard, SSJ (Baltimore).

They drafted a widely researched, diocesan-centered, follow-up plan that included a digest of the letter called a *Pastoral Message*. In a later explanatory article, Bishop Pilla remarked that all in the Church must be convinced that everyday economic choices cannot be separated from religious and moral convictions. "What we do in the marketplace Monday through Friday must not be divorced from what we do around the altar." The pastoral's moral principles bind all.[52]

The committee insisted that especially the laity, whose lives are touched in very direct ways by the country's economy, have a most important role in the implementation of the pastoral. "They must take the lead in articulating the values of our faith in the complex marketplace of the U.S. economy."[53]

Because the topic was complex and difficult for many to grasp, in his presentation Bishop Pilla suggested a systematic three-pronged effort to promote the teaching and application of the pastoral's message: (1) education and public information; (2) pastoral life; and (3) institutional response. He favored the formation of a new three-year ad hoc committee, consisting of three bishops and experts from the USCC, to implement and explore further the issues treated in the pastoral as well as other related topics not treated.

Bishop Pilla insisted that the implementation of the letter must include a strong advocacy for economic justice in the legislative arena. "Our goal is to be a competent and effective advocate in the legislative process . . . seeking to speak clearly on behalf of economic justice for all."[54] Efforts, principally through the USCC, are already being made in this legislative direction.

In addition, at the end of his presentation, Bishop Pilla promised the following: a national conference on implementing the letter; a resource manual for diocesan leaders; and a half-hour videotape giv-

---

[51]*Commonweal*, June 19, 1987.

[52]Most Rev. Anthony M. Pilla, "How to Implement Economic Justice for All," *America*, January 31, 1987.

[53]Ibid.

[54]"Minutes of the General Meeting of the National Conference of Catholic Bishops," November 13, 1986.

ing an overview of the pastoral. He also promised a more detailed report to be mailed to all the bishops within three weeks.[55]

Bishop Malone then asked if there were any comments. Archbishop Szoka cautioned that the implementation of the pastoral could cost $525,000 over three years, and the bishops were voting to authorize this. He did not necessarily object, but he wanted this point understood. Bishop Malone observed that according to Bishop McGann's report on the 1987 budget, the amount to be spent in 1987 for this was already budgeted. He asked Bishop McGann what percentage of this figure would be spent in the first year. Bishop McGann said the 1987 figure would be $300,000 and this has been approved by the Finance and Administrative Committees, adding that expenditures for the future would be voted on when the time came.

There being no further comment, Bishop Pilla thanked his implementation committee members and staff for their work. Then, Bishop Malone called for the question. The implementation plan and its message were adopted unanimously.

Fulfillment of the plan began immediately after that November meeting so that the economic pastoral has enjoyed the most complete implementation of any pastoral ever published by the American bishops.

The following year, on February 2, 1987, written *Testimony on Welfare Reform* was submitted to the Senate Finance Committee's Subcommittee on Social Security and Family Policy by Father J. Bryan Hehir, secretary for Social Development and World Peace, on behalf of the United States Catholic Conference. "The Aid to Families with Dependent Children Program is of deep concern to the bishops," stated Father Hehir, who explained that the bishops' views are founded on the principle that human dignity is the fundamental criterion for judging public policy, and on the conviction "that in a society as rich as ours there is no excuse for the extremes of deprivation and poverty that leave millions without even the bare necessities of life."

Father Hehir questioned the AFDC program, asking whether states should be permitted "to deny aid to otherwise eligible needy children solely because they live with both their parents"; What should be done "about unmarried teenage mothers who do not live with their own families?" How can welfare dependency be prevented? He cited that welfare benefits are "woefully inadequate," and proposed "a national minimum-standard benefit" to cover basic human needs. "We urge the committee to begin an examination of a family allowance or children's allowance system that would supplement other income to ensure a floor of support for all children."

Then, on March 4, 1987, Archbishop Rembert Weakland, OSB,

---

[55] Ibid.

representing the United States Catholic Conference, testified before the House Subcommittee on Foreign Operations regarding the *International Debt*. "As we hear from American missionaries overseas and from the Latin American bishops, the international debt problem calls for more than a technical solution," said Archbishop Weakland. He urged that any solution to the debt problem "be shared in an equitable fashion by both creditor and debtor countries." He prayed that the "primary objective of any approach" be to improve life for the poorest people and that any structured adjustment or debt-solution package "preserve the basic human rights of the citizens of the debtor country and the integrity of its government."

The Archbishop hoped that one effect of the recent economic pastoral would be to identify the Roman Catholic community with the cause of economic justice—"especially for the poor, both in the United States and in the Third World." He then presented seven sets of principles "which we and many other religious groups believe should underlie a normative approach to a solution to the problem of Third World debt."

The seeds for *A Pastoral Statement for Catholics on Biblical Fundamentalism* were actually sown at the November 1984 meeting, when several bishops expressed their concern about the proselytizing activities of fundamentalist Christian churches among Catholics, especially Hispanics. President Malone named the following committee to study the question: Archbishop John F. Whealon (Hartford) chairman; Archbishops Theodore E. McCarrick (Newark) and J. Francis Stafford (Denver); and Auxiliary Bishops Alvaro Corrado (Washington), Richard J. Sklba (Milwaukee), and Donald W. Trautman (Buffalo). They were assisted in their task not only by consultants but also by some Catholic converts from fundamentalism.

To underline the seriousness of the problem, Archbishop Whealon recalled giving a talk in a small city (Waterbury, Connecticut) in his archdiocese. After the talk, a local fundamentalist pastor told the Archbishop that 90 percent of his congregation was composed of former Catholics.[56]

On March 26, 1987, the Administrative Committee of the NCCB authorized publication of the pastoral statement, as drafted by the ad hoc Committee on Biblical Fundamentalism.[57] Biblical fundamentalism's basic characteristic is to eliminate "from Christianity the Church as the Lord Jesus founded it. That Church is a community of faith, worldwide, with pastoral and teaching authority."[58]

According to the pastoral, unfortunately, a minority of fundamentalist churches not only put down the Catholic Church as a "man-

---

[56] *Our Sunday Visitor*, November 8, 1987.
[57] United States Catholic Conference, March 31, 1987.
[58] Ibid., p. 2.

made organization" with "man-made" rules but "indulge in crude anti-Catholic bigotry." Biblical fundamentalism is especially attractive to young Catholics who do not understand properly the Church's teaching on the Scriptures. "It is important for every Catholic to realize that the Church produced the New Testament and not vice versa." Adding to the attractiveness for Catholic youth is the great warmth in the fundamentalist congregation in comparison to the larger, colder, Catholic congregation, whose members seldom greet the stranger. "We Catholics need to redouble our efforts to make parish Masses an expression of worship in which all . . . feel the warmth and know that here the Bible is clearly reverenced and preached. The current trend toward smaller faith-sharing and Bible-studying groups within a parish family is strongly to be encouraged."[59]

The committee closed with a request for further research on this entire question.

Because of a revival of racism in some areas of the United States, on March 27, 1987, the Administrative Board of the United States Catholic Conference released a *Statement on the Ku Klux Klan*. This statement reminds all Catholics that membership in such racist organizations is in violation of Church teaching. "Every person and every institution that bears the name Catholic should proclaim to all that the sin of racism defiles the image of God and degrades the sacred dignity of mankind. . . . To struggle against it demands an equally radical transformation, in our own minds and hearts as well as in the structure of our society."

This statement was received favorably in the secular press.

On April 9, 1987, Bishop James Malone, representing the United States Catholic Conference, gave *Testimony on the Fair Housing Amendments Act of 1987* before the Subcommittee on the Constitution of the U.S. Senate Committee on the Judiciary. Affirming the bishops' strong support for the legislation, which would provide an effective enforcement mechanism against unjust discrimination in housing, Bishop Malone commended the subcommittee's work and pledged the assistance of the United States Catholic Conference in working to see that the legislation is approved.

"While the most blatant forms of housing discrimination, such as restrictive covenants, have been largely eliminated, other forms of exclusion and segregation are still commonplace practice in our society," testified Bishop Malone. "Racial steering, redlining, discriminatory mortgage and lease restrictions, and providing false information to minority buyers or renters are among the techniques that are still often used against blacks, Hispanics, and other minorities in communities across the nation," he continued.

---

[59] Ibid., p. 8.

Further explaining the bishops' particular interest in this legislative process, Bishop Malone stated: "In the Catholic tradition our moral vision begins with the dignity of the human person. All persons are deserving of a special reverence because they are made in the image and likeness of God. To offend that human dignity is, therefore, in a very real way, to offend against God. . . . Unjust discrimination on the basis of race is clearly a violation of the dignity of the human person and the basic rights which protect this dignity."

In concluding his remarks on behalf of the United States Catholic Conference, the bishop said: "The passage of these Fair Housing Amendments will contribute in a very real way to the good of individuals and to the common good as well. It will be a necessary and appropriate reflection of our nation's constitutional heritage that recognizes the equality, dignity, and inalienable rights of all its citizens."

In the summer of 1987, after concerns were raised by a number of Jewish leaders regarding plans for Austrian President Kurt Waldheim to meet at the Vatican with Pope John Paul II on June 25, 1987— and in light of the bearing of those concerns on the pope's planned meeting in Miami with Jewish leaders the following September— Archbishop John May (St. Louis), president of the National Conference of Catholic Bishops, issued a *Statement on Waldheim* on June 22, 1987.

"As the Holy See has stated publicly, the Holy Father did not initiate the meeting with President Waldheim. Moreover, such a meeting is in keeping with the standard practice of the Holy See to receive duly elected political leaders. It can also be noted that to be received by the pope does not mean that the Holy See is making a statement on the personal character of the one being received," Archbishop May explained.

In concluding his statement, the president of the NCCB said: "I pray that the good relations the conference of bishops has with our Jewish brothers and sisters in this country will be strong enough to overcome any specific difficulty of the moment."

More than a decade ago, in 1975, the United States Catholic Conference began making representative statements on political responsibility prior to each national election. At their September 1987 meeting, the Administrative Board of the United States Catholic Conference approved *Political Responsibility: Choices for the Future*, a document that updated the 1984 statement on political responsibility. The 1987 statement was intended to clarify the position of the Church with regard to politics—a position misunderstood at a time when the Church's tax-exempt privilege was being challenged in a lawsuit.[60]

Tracing the question from the inaugural address of George Wash-

---

[60]*Origins*, November 5, 1987.

ington to the opinion polls of the 1980s, the bishops proved "the role of religion in public life is neither new nor surprising." They explained that the disestablishment principle governing state-church relations has as its purpose "to distinguish key elements in our heritage not to silence or suppress religious witness or influence. . . . The role of religion in our public life has been visible and constant."

The Administrative Board stressed that the role of the Church includes "education regarding the teachings of the Church and the responsibilities of the faithful; analysis of issues for their social and moral dimensions; measuring public policy against gospel values; participating in debate over public policy; and speaking out with courage, skill, and concern on public issues involving human rights, social justice, and the life of the Church in society."

The bishops explained that the Church's participation in public affairs is not a threat to the political process, nor to genuine pluralism, but an affirmation of their importance. "The Church recognizes the legitimate autonomy of government and the right of all, including the Church itself, to be heard in the formulation of public policy." And, according to the Vatican II document *Gaudium et Spes:* "She [the Church] also has the right to pass moral judgments, even on matters touching the political order, whenever basic personal rights or the salvation of souls makes such judgments necessary."The prelates endeavored to promote a greater understanding of the important link between faith and politics and to express their belief "that our nation is enriched when its citizens and social groups approach public affairs from positions grounded in moral conviction and religious belief."

Becoming specific, the bishops then listed as pertinent issues: abortion; arms control and disarmament; capital punishment; civil rights; the economy; education; family life; food and agricultural policy; health; housing; human rights; immigration and human rights policy; mass media; and regional conflict in the world. "We hope these reflections will contribute to a renewed vitality in our land, both in terms of citizen participation . . . and in accountability of those who seek and hold public office."Urging all citizens to use their franchise, the bishops prayed that Americans would be blessed with a spirit of responsible political involvement and, following the example of Jesus, give special concern to the poor, ever guided by a deep love of God and neighbor.

Also in September 1987, concerned principally with the contraceptive information offered in some public school systems—allegedly to prevent the spread of the AIDS epidemic—the Administrative Board of the United States Catholic Conference issued a statement entitled *Value and Virtue: Moral Education in the Public School.* The bishops affirmed that, as American citizens concerned for children and young people, they would like to add their voice to the public debate on the issue of moral education in the public schools of this nation. "We do not wish to impose a religious viewpoint on our fellow citizens, but we do wish to provide our reasoned reflection on what we perceive to be a national concern." Earlier, the prelates proclaimed that our children and young people are the future of our country, our civilization, and our world.

In a very practical approach, the bishops offered several valuable points for national discussion, for example, "that a renewed shared moral vision within the public schools is possible . . . that the values, virtues, moral ideals, and truth of our heritage should be infused into the curriculum . . . that peer pressure among students need not be solely for ill, but can be a great support in the pursuit of moral excellence." The statement insisted that school communities must see themselves as moral communities involving students, parents, teachers, administrators, and support staff. All must be involved. The American Catholic hierarchy pledged its support and concluded by thanking those educators and parents who are already working conscientiously to provide children and young people with a solid grounding in moral values.

In the history of the United States Catholic Conference, *The Many Faces of AIDS: A Gospel Response* caused more division among the American bishops than any other statement. Some might say it even caused "a visible split in the U.S. hierarchy."[61] On November 14, 1987, the Administrative Board of the USCC approved this statement in its own name.

In the introduction of their gospel response, the board recognizes "the ominous presence of the disease known as AIDS" and see this disease as "a significant pastoral issue." To meet this challenge, these fifty prelates issued this statement with its six major reflections.

The following passage is the one that prompted the greatest reaction—even from Rome:

> Because we live in a pluralistic society, we acknowledge that some will not agree with our understanding of human sexuality. We recognize that public educational programs addressed to a wide audience will reflect the fact that some people will not act as they can and should; that they will not refrain from the type of sexual or drug-abuse behavior that can transmit AIDS. In such situations, educational efforts, grounded in the broader moral vision outlined above, could include accurate information about prophylactic devices or other practices proposed by some medical experts as potential means of preventing AIDS. We are not promoting the use of prophylactics, but merely providing information that is part of the factual picture.

Cardinal Law (Boston) expressed possibly the harshest episcopal criticism of the AIDS statement, insisting that the Administrative Board

---

[61]David M. Hollenbach, SJ, "AIDS Education: Moral Substance," *America*, December 26, 1987.

make it clear "that this document has no official standing" and hoping that "something could be done now to withdraw the statement."

Archbishop Roger Mahoney (Los Angeles) published his own emendations of the Administrative Board's text, including a warning that "recommendations in educational material concerning the use of prophylactic devices are not to be endorsed by educators under Catholic auspices."

Archbishop May, NCCB president, noted: "Since the publication of the Catholic bishops' Administrative Board statement on AIDS, I have become aware of a misunderstanding in media reports. I encourage a full reading of the document, not just headlines and excerpts, perhaps out of context." Few of the media surpassed the distortion of the *New York Times* which, without qualification, dashed off this front-page headline: "U.S. Bishops Back Condom Education as a Move on AIDS."[62] On the supportive side for the statement was Bishop William Hughes (Covington), head of the task force that drafted the statement:

> The Catholic Church exists in a pluralistic society, and many people do not follow the teachings of the Church. AIDS is a fatal disease, a fact that puts it into a category very different from other sexually transmitted communicable diseases. Because of these two factors, they believe they could not object to education programs that presented all important facts that could help in decreasing the spread of this fatal disease.

Equally supportive, Archbishop Daniel Pilarczyk (Cincinnati), vice president of the NCCB, explained:

> Not to address such aspects of the AIDS phenomenon frankly and critically would leave people to learn of them from factually misleading campaigns designed to sell certain products or to advocate 'safe sex' without reference to a moral perspective. Telling people what public health officials say and pointing out to them that their recommendations are unacceptable hardly constitutes advocacy or dissemination of contraceptive information.

Much stronger in his support of the statement was Bishop Timothy J. Harrington (Worcester): "A response to the confusion by those who have questioned the excellent statement of the National Conference of Catholic Bishops on a gospel response to *The Many Faces of AIDS* would take more than a seminar."

Archbishop J. Francis Stafford (Denver) wrote to Archbishop May, expressing his "serious doubts" that the AIDS statement "is correct in either its analysis of the situation or its utilization of the canonical principles and procedures" by which the statement was released. He suggested that the Administrative Board had overreached its author-

---

[62]December 11, 1987.

ity in issuing the statement. In addition, Archbishop Stafford issued a 2,300 word theological and canonical critique of the statement, as well as a letter he released in his archdiocese saying he could not implement the AIDS statement until he has received an acceptable response from Archbishop May. The Denver prelate based his theological objection upon the statement's alleged misinterpretation of the theological principal of the "toleration of the lesser evil."[63]

The Pennsylvania bishops issued a release in which they said: "In view of the widespread confusion about the moral teaching on contraceptive devices unfortunately generated by the statement and its coverage in the media, we would presume that this matter will be brought to the attention of the National Conference of Catholic Bishops at its next plenary session."

As a result of many bishops rejecting the Administrative Board's November 1987 statement on AIDS, a discussion of Acquired Immunodeficiency Syndrome was slated for the June 24-27, 1988 meeting of the U.S. bishops at St. John's University in Collegeville, Minnesota, to focus on pastoral, theological, and moral concerns raised by the disease. Shortly before the bishops' meeting, Vatican concerns about *The Many Faces of AIDS* were expressed in a letter from Cardinal Joseph Ratzinger, prefect of the Congregation for the Doctrine of the Faith. Ratzinger sent his letter to Archbishop Pio Laghi, apostolic pronuncio in the United States. The letter was then forwarded to Archbishop John L. May (St. Louis), president of the National Conference of Catholic Bishops and United States Catholic Conference and, subsequently, to each U.S. bishop. The text of the letter was released by the bishops' conference during the Collegeville meeting.

While expressing approval of certain aspects of *The Many Faces of AIDS*, including its call for solidarity with those suffering from the disease, Cardinal Ratzinger's letter suggested that there are some cases when the bishops should consult the Vatican prior to publication of such a document. He expressed concern about the lack of unity among the bishops in this; he also observed that the principle tolerance of the lesser evil "hardly seems pertinent" with regard to public education programs providing instruction on prophylactics and AIDS prevention.

"In fact," the letter continued, "even when the issue has to do with educational programs promoted by the civil government, one would not be dealing with a form of passive toleration but rather with a kind of behavior which would result in at least the facilitation of evil.

"The Church's responsibility is to give that kind of witness which is proper to her, namely, an unequivocal witness of effective and

---

[63]*Origins*, January 7, 1988.

unreserved solidarity with those who are suffering and, at the same time, a witness of defense of the dignity of human sexuality which can be realized only within the context of moral law."

At the November 1987 meeting of the National Conference of Catholic Bishops Archbishop Robert Sanchez (Santa Fe) explained that ten years previously the late bishop James Rausch, then general secretary of the NCCB/USCC, had asked him to serve as chairman of an ad hoc Committee on Hispanic Ministry. He began with two major objectives: (1) to raise conference awareness of the needs of Hispanic Catholics in the United States and (2) to start a training program for permanent deacons and lay ministers to complement the insufficient number of Spanish-speaking priests in the country.[64]

Thanking the bishops for their cooperation since 1977, Archbishop Sanchez said both goals are now largely achieved, and 130 dioceses have an office for Hispanic ministries. He also noted that the United States now has six pastoral centers for training in the Hispanic ministry, each with a mobile unit to reach out to other parts of the country.

In 1983, his committee produced the pastoral letter *The Hispanic Presence: Challenge and Commitment*. Further, the ad hoc committee's proposal that this be followed by a *National Pastoral Plan for Hispanic Ministry* was approved by the NCCB. The drafting committee of the plan consisted of Bishop Ricardo Ramirez (Las Cruces); Bishop Peter Rosazza (Hartford); and Archbishop Roger Mahony (Los Angeles).

At the November 1987 meeting, Bishop Ramirez presented the proposed national plan and divided the suggested amendments into group 1 (those *accepted* by the committee) and group 2 (those *not* accepted by the committee).

Group 1 amendments included the addition of a table of contents; a new section on marriage and family life ministry; a rewriting of a passage about a National Encuentro to be conducted by regional representation; an emphasis on vocations (requested by the Texas bishops); a definition of *Mestizaje*, placing ("historical" before "cultural"); a new definition of *proselytism* from Archbishop McCarrick (Newark); and the modification suggested by Cardinal Bernard Law (Boston): "We encourage dioceses and parishes to incorporate this with due regard for local adaptation."The group 1 amendments, without objection, were declared adopted.

When Bishop Ramirez presented the group 2 amendments (those not accepted by the committee), Bishop Lessard asked two questions related to the Trinity. Bishop Ramirez answered that the first passage had been caused by a printing error, and the second concern was

---

[64]Unless otherwise noted, all the data of this introduction to the *National Pastoral Plan for Hispanic Ministry* has been drawn from the Minutes of the November 1987 Meeting of the NCCB.

corrected by the elimination of a line from the document. The remainder of the group 2 amendments were declared rejected.

Archbishop May asked if there were any further comments on the plan itself. Cardinal Law wished to express only what he was sure would be the sentiments of many bishops: support for and thanks to the committee for its fine work, affirming that this ministry is at the heart of the Church's work in the United States.

Cardinal Bernardin (Chicago) also favored the pastoral plan, adding, "This is a critical moment in the life of the Church—what is done or not done in the next few years will determine whether the Hispanic community in the United States will retain and strengthen its Catholic faith and enrich the whole Church." He observed that although the plan looks overwhelming, and the temptation is to throw up one's hands and do nothing, many of these things are actually already being done in several dioceses; the pastoral plan will provide both motivation and framework to improve these efforts. He noted his own experiences in Chicago (800,000 to 1 million Hispanics and a large percentage of undocumented aliens): ninety parishes are now largely or entirely Hispanic, and a diocesan task force has been established to promote the kinds of programs for which this new pastoral plan calls. He, too, thanked the committee for work well done.

Archbishop Patrick F. Flores (San Antonio) also began by expressing his admiration for the American hierarchy, particularly for their response to the needs of European immigrants at the turn of the century, including enormous sacrifices to provide them with churches, schools, and so forth, in order to help them retain their Catholic faith. The archbishop declared we are in a similar crisis now, for the Catholic commitment of Hispanics in the United States is weakening. He observed that he has visited almost all dioceses in the United States and often sees a single Catholic church serving Hispanics, surrounded by nineteen or twenty non-Catholic churches. He admitted the pastoral plan's challenge is tremendous but necessary, observing that Hispanics leave the Catholic Church because they feel it does not provide nourishment and support; they see the Catholic Church as a huge and impersonal structure (thus, *communidades de base* has become so popular). He begged for heroic efforts to keep Hispanic immigrants in the Catholic Church.

Archbishop Rembert Weakland (Milwaukee) added his support to the pastoral plan and said he would indeed vote for it, but expressed one hesitation: the plan did not clearly indicate where this great effort should begin. He thought appreciation of a wider context necessary: "After Vatican II there was a scriptural renewal, but not enough focus on promoting a Catholic approach to Scripture to protect Hispanic Catholics and others from fundamentalism." He feared Hispanics face the danger of becoming a people of the Word only; this must be prevented by an emphasis on the Church's sacramental traditions.

At present, this focus is so weak that when Hispanics lose the sacraments by moving to a fundamentalist church, they do not realize the magnitude of their loss. Archbishop Weakland urged the bishops to make a concerted effort to meet this threat.

The vote was called and the *National Pastoral Plan for Hispanic Ministry* was unanimously approved. [The text, as published in this volume, contains some minor revisions that were approved for inclusion in 1989.] This plan calls for small parish-based communities, youth ministries, family life support, and leadership formation adapted to the Hispanic culture. Because most Hispanic people feel distant or marginated from the Catholic Church, the Church in Hispanic ministry must recognize the role that small neighborhood ecclesial communities play in promoting faith and conversion in addition to concern for the individual. Hispanic Catholics often experience a lack of unity and community in the Church's pastoral ministry. On all levels of church life, greater collaboration and coordination of ministry for Hispanics must come to be.

The pastoral explains further: "Proselytism embraces whatever violates the rights of the human person, Christian or non-Christian, to be free from external coercion in religious matters or whatever in the proclamation of the Gospel does not conform to the ways God draws free men to himself in response to his call to serve in spirit and truth."

Regarding proselytism conducted by other religious groups in the Hispanic community, the plan requests *integration* of Hispanic Catholics into the United States Catholic Church rather than *assimilation*. "Hispanic people are to be welcomed by our church institutions at all levels. They are to be served in their language when possible, and their religious traditions are to be respected." Accordingly, the pastoral plan requires an explicit affirmation of the concept of cultural pluralism in our Church within a fundamental unity of doctrines. The plan also moves from the spiritual realm to urge the promotion of social justice for these often impoverished peoples.

In a press conference, Bishop Ramirez noted that small communities offer *one* of the answers, not the total answer to proselytism.[65]

Archbishop Sanchez commented that the hope is that the pastoral plan will assist our Catholic Hispanics in their efforts to achieve integration and participation in the life of our Church and in the building of the kingdom of God.[66]

The seriousness of this problem is evident in "Defection among the Hispanics," an article by Andrew M. Greeley: "In the past fifteen years, nearly one million Hispanic men and women in the United States have left the Catholic Church." In the same article, Father

---

[65]National Catholic News Service, November 18, 1987.
[66]Ibid.

Greeley added "that the *National Pastoral Plan for Hispanic Ministry* . . . seems to be an impressive document."[67]

On November 18, 1987, at the thirty-fifth general meeting of the NCCB, President Archbishop May called on Bishop Joseph Sullivan (auxiliary, Brooklyn) to present, in the name of the bishops, a *Resolution on Korea*. In their resolution, the U.S. bishops urged their government to recognize the Korean desire for representative democracy and "the importance of the Korean people to be the sole architects of their own political, economic, and social resolutions." The prelates stressed the longstanding cooperation between the Korean Catholic community and that of the United States, as well as the important role of the Church in Korea. The resolution was approved unanimously.

At the same meeting, Bishop Joseph Sullivan was asked to present a second resolution in the name of the bishops, also on November 18. The *Resolution on Lebanon* began: "After eleven years of war, the people of Lebanon are tired of death and destruction. They yearn for peace." The resolution protested outside interference in Lebanon's affairs and called "again on the U.S. government to shape a policy that will assist all the Lebanese to guarantee the freedom, territorial integrity, and sovereignty of their nation. The resolution was passed unanimously.

Another significant action that took place on November 18, was the approval by the NCCB's general membership of the bishops' statement entitled *Norms for Priests and Their Third Age*. In line with the 1983 *Code of Canon Law*, these guidelines gave more attention to the retirement years of priests and to their "suitable support and housing" than did the earlier *Code*.[68]

Diocesan policy generally determines the age and circumstances for the retirement of its priests from a certain diocesan appointment, while not implying an end to his priestly ministry. The norms of canon law speak, instead, of an entry into "a third age where the Spirit is calling us to reflect upon, to integrate, and to complete the ministry to which we are called." Ordinaries should offer programs to assist priests to prepare for their third age. These clerics should be allowed to indicate the kinds of ministry they wish to continue, and provisions should be made for their physical, emotional, and spiritual health. Normally, the retiring priest shall be given a choice in regard to his retirement housing and be guaranteed adequate support both financially and spiritually.

One of the more important subjects discussed at the November

---

[67] *America*, July 30, 1988.
[68] Cf. c. 538:3.

1987 general meeting was school-based clinics, a topic being discussed nationwide. A prime promoter of this project with such a deadly potential is Planned Parenthood, so richly financed by American tax dollars.

The previous November the Bishops' Committee for Pro-Life Activities had planned a pastoral statement on this subject. The committee had already addressed this issue briefly in 1986, when the U.S. Senate was considering reauthorization of the federal government's Title X family planning program. Then the prelates asked the Senate to "bar Title X grants to school-based family planning clinics in order *to prevent further undermining of parental authority.*"

The bishops noted that the already difficult problems of teenage sexuality and pregnancy can only be aggravated by placing school authority figures in the position of seeming to condone teenage sexual activity so long as contraception is used. Legislative advisors told the bishops that this issue was likely to receive increased attention in Congress in future months and that a longer and more authoritative pastoral statement would be helpful to them in their study of this serious matter. This, in great part, explains the present *Statement on School-based Clinics,* which discussed the problem fully and offered a sound solution. Many experts in several kindred fields were consulted during the production of this statement.

Briefly, what do the bishops say about school-based clinics? First, they state that their interest in this issue stems from their concern for the physical, emotional, and spiritual well-being of young people. Problems facing the youth of our country must be addressed in ways that will give them ideals for the future and challenge them to live up to those ideals. Most significant:

> In this context, we address the seemingly intractable problem of teenage pregnancy as one that will not admit of an amoral or purely technological solution. *To the extent* that school-based clinics offer a program for more efficient promotion of contraceptives and abortion-related services to minors, they are part of the problem rather than a key to a solution.

The *Washington Times* editorialized:

> Birth control and reproductive counseling programs fail in part because they avoid discussing the tried-and-true traditional values—abstinence, self-respect, respect for the rights and feelings of others—that in the past have provided youngsters with the maturity and responsibility to defer their gratifications. The sterile rhetoric of health care professionaldom ignores the fact that sex is necessarily a moral activity, and that one cannot sensibly discuss sexual activity without making a strong case for the traditional values mentioned above.

"The bishops' *Statement on School-based Clinics,*" editorialized *Our*

Sunday Visitor, "presents strong and cogent arguments against a growing anti-life propaganda campaign in the United States."[69]

On November 19, Bishop Joseph Sullivan (Brooklyn), chairman of the USCC Committee on Social Development and World Peace, made the preliminary presentation of the *Statement on Central America* to the bishops. By way of background, His Excellency told his audience: "As mentioned at the September 1987 meeting of the Administrative Board, we are well aware of the sensitivity of this moment in the peace process and will insert an introductory explanation that takes note of the situation and the development of this statement." The bishop noted that prospects for peace look brighter now and mentioned that his committee had rejected most of the proposed modifications in an effort to preserve the statement's careful balance. He assured the bishops that the document is consistent with previous conference statements on Central America and examines the present reality in that region. Bishop Sullivan invited the bishops to ask questions or to submit further written amendments to the committee.

Cardinal Bernard Law (Boston) suggested that since several bishops held different views on the problem, and since current peace negotiations in the region are at a delicate stage, perhaps the U.S. bishops should say nothing at this time. Bishop Sullivan responded that the Central American bishops want the U.S. hierarchy to reaffirm its past statements opposing military intervention there. The Brooklyn prelate warned that withdrawing the expected statement now would deeply disappoint the Central American hierarchy. Later at a press conference, he explained that the statement did not favor any political side; principally, it repeated the pleas for a peaceful resolution to the destructive violence.

After several questions from the assembled bishops, most of whom were seeking further clarifications, the statement was adopted.

In their statement, the bishops urge that U.S. policy toward all of Latin America should give highest priority to economic rather than military aid. They lament that, thus far in the 1980s, poverty and suffering have increased tremendously in Latin America. Twenty million children in Central America live on the streets, always hungry and in physical and moral peril.

The bishops continue: "We have joined with our Central American brothers in the episcopate in urging the adoption of sincere parties. . . . With them we have insisted, as we continue to insist, that true peace can come about only when the fundamental causes of the conflict are sincerely faced."

In regard to U.S. responsibility, much of Central America is owned by U.S. companies that send produce and profits to the United States while peasants working the land are reduced to murderous poverty.

---

[69]December 6, 1987.

But the U.S. policy long antedates the iniquitous assaults against the poor in Central America. The driving force is a ruthless determination to keep these countries in servitude as cheap supply sources of fruit, vegetables, timber, and minerals for North America, with all their attendant profits.[70]

In conclusion, the bishops urge that peace in Central America can and must be built up through dialogue and political, rather than military, activities and that it must be sustained by the solidarity of the other nations, including the needed economic assistance that the wealthier countries can provide.

While the statement was well received in this country, it even had an international impact. England's *Tablet* carried an editorial denouncing "all who think that church people critical of the policy of the United States in Central America are simply Communist dupes. . . . Those who lend an ear to the siren voices of bogus patriotism, bogus national security, and bogus anti-Communism are the real simpletons and the real enemies of America."[71]

On February 24, 1988, Bishop John Ricard (auxiliary, Baltimore), representing the United States Catholic Conference, submitted *Testimony on Emergency Hunger Policy* before the Subcommittee on Domestic Marketing, Consumer Relations and Nutrition of the U.S. House Committee on Agriculture. Calling hunger "a fundamentally moral issue," the bishop went on to say: "In traditional Catholic social teaching, the right to a sufficient amount of food to sustain life is a human right, one linked to the right to life itself. . . . We cannot permit the human dignity of so many of our fellow citizens to be undermined because they are too poor to feed themselves and their families."

Taking exception to the government's position that the voluntary sector— churches in particular—ought to be able to take up the slack caused by the cutback in federal food assistance programs, the bishops stated: "Our experience teaches us that it is not possible for the private voluntary sector to replace government programs. [This] was recently confirmed in testimony before the House Select Committee on Hunger, where so many witnesses testified to the inability of the private agencies to fill the gap. Certainly, the churches have and will continue to increase their efforts and resources to assist the hungry and the poor. However, the churches cannot and should not substitute for the essential responsibility that just public policy and government programs must play in meeting basic human needs. We can be effective partners; we cannot go it alone."

The bishops urged legislative support for nine measures that they felt would strenghten existing federal food assistance programs, emphasizing four additional changes to current child nutrition pro-

---

[70]*The Tablet* (England), November 28, 1987.
[71]Ibid.

grams. In addition, they urged the extension of the authorization of the Temporary Emergency Food Assistance Program (TEFAP) at its current $50 million level and the increase of administrative funds that must go to emergency feeding organizations.

The following month, on March 22, 1988, the U.S. Congress voted to override President Reagan's veto of the Civil Rights Restoration Act. Almost angrily, Monsignor Daniel Hoye, then general secretary of the United States Catholic Conference, declared that the president had vetoed one of the most important pieces of civil rights legislation to come along in many years. Once the veto was overridden, Monsignor Hoye issued a *Statement on Civil Rights,* in which he noted that this new law ensures that no institution will be required to provide abortion services as a condition for receiving federal funds; and that this bill safeguards religious liberty. He also expressed the hope that Congress will build on its significant civil rights victory by strengthening federal fair-housing laws to combat more effectively housing discrimination in our land. The statement received mostly a politically partisan reaction.

The next day, on March 23, the Administrative Committee of the National Conference of Catholic Bishops voted to approve *The Statement to Youth on School-based Clinics.* In this companion document to their 1987 *Statement on School-based Clinics,* the bishops address the youth of the nation: "Human sexuality is a gift from God and an important part of your total personality. Integrating your sexuality with all the facets of your life is a lifelong process that can be most difficult in the teen years when you face so many changes and challenges."

In this statement, the bishops respond to five claims made by supporters of school-based clinics and offer their support and encouragement to Catholic youth as they face "the pressures . . . to become involved in sexual activity."

In conclusion, the bishops reaffirm: "We the Catholic bishops of the United States pledge our energies in working with you, your families, and your schools to help build a society in which the positive values of human sexuality will be lived and appreciated."

For the last decade the problem of homelessness has steadily worsened, especially in large American cities. The Church had done much to solve this problem, but it does lack the means to meet the ever-increasing demands of homeless families.

To alert the public and governments to their responsibility to heal this social evil, the Administrative Board of the United States Catholic Conference released the statement *Homelessness and Housing: A Human Tragedy, A Moral Challenge* on March 24, 1988. The bishops stated that the "national disgrace of widespread homelessness" must prompt a renewed commitment to preserving and constructing affordable housing for all people. "As Americans and believers, we are haunted by the tragic reality of so many without decent housing in our land, a sign of serious social neglect and moral failure."

Federal, state, and municipal governments have now become conscious of the problem and are trying to alleviate it. Many volunteer groups from the various Catholic parishes and institutions are also offering their help every night.

On May 10, 1988, Mr. Frank J. Monahan, director of the USCC Government Liaison Office, presented *Testimony to the Democratic and Republican National Convention Platform Committees* on behalf of the U.S. Catholic Conference. According to this testimony, the bishops joined in the public debate not to impose some sectarian doctrine but to speak for themselves as citizens, to share their experience in serving the poor and vulnerable, and to voice their hope that our nation might be an effective force for true justice and genuine peace. This document presents the bishops' position on abortion, arms control, economic policy on the domestic and international levels, education, employment, food, health care, housing, human rights, immigration, mass media, and regional conflicts in the world.

In their testimony, the bishops cited that American Catholics have a dual heritage: "As believers, we are heirs of a tradition that calls us to measure our society by how it touches the least. . . . As citizens, we are part of a remarkable tradition that sets before us the pledge of 'liberty and justice for all.' " The bishops asked both parties to fashion a platform that respects the life, enhances the dignity, and protects the rights of all, "especially the poor and the most vulnerable."

Following the November 1985 general meeting of the National Conference of Catholic Bishops, an ad hoc committee of bishops was appointed to assess whether the stated conditions for the moral acceptability of deterrence, which were set forth in the 1983 pastoral letter *The Challenge of Peace: God's Promise and Our Response*, were being met. In April 1988, the ad hoc committee submitted to the bishops the first draft of a pastoral reflection along with the committee's report. Approval of the pastoral reflection and the committee report was given during the plenary assembly in Collegeville, Minnesota on June 25, 1988. Accordingly, publication of this pastoral reflection, *Building Peace: A Pastoral Reflection on the Response to "The Challenge of Peace"* and *A Report on "The Challenge of Peace" and Policy Developments 1983-1988*, was authorized by the general secretary on July 7, 1988.

The report sought to assess that facts of the nuclear problem in 1988 in light of the principles of that pastoral letter. The committee called for a renewed commitment to pray, educate, and work for peace at every level of the Church's life: "Now is a time to build on the activities of the past five years, to renew our efforts to educate and advocate for peace, to help make our Church a truly peacemaking community, and to work with all the people of good-will to help shape a world of peace and justice." The bishops hoped that believers will become more effective witnesses and workers for peace, helping our world to say "no" to the violence of war, "no" to nuclear destruction, "no" to an arms race that robs the poor and endangers all.

"We are skeptical about escaping the strategic and moral dilemmas of the nuclear age through technology," wrote the bishops. They favored a complementary strategy, pressing a creative and sustained effort to reshape the political dimension of U.S.-Soviet relations. Admitting that this is an enormously complex process—tried often before with few positive results—the prelates pleaded that it is worth another effort, not only to lessen the danger of a superpower confrontation but also to limit the ways in which present East-West competition is injected into the conflicts of others: "This is a call to fundamental change in international politics."

Begging the superpowers to go beyond "the logic of the blocs" in keeping the nuclear peace and building peace through just relations with the poor of the world, the bishops warned that nothing less than this kind of vision— joining the East-West issues and the North-South issues in a coherent plan—is equal to the world in which we live. The committee ends their report on a positive encouraging note: "But changes do occur. . . . the twentieth century—after two major wars—has a record of sustained peace among the democracies."

That summer, on July 15, 1988, Monsignor Daniel Hoye, general secretary of the National Conference of Catholic Bishops and the United States Catholic Conference, issued a *Statement on Federal Funding of "in vitro" Fertilization Experiments.* The statement protested the recent U.S. Department of Health and Human Services' decision to appoint an Ethics Advisory Board, which could lead to the approval of *in vitro* fertilization experiments in humans. The statement denounced the abortifacient aspects of the procedure and the unethical practice of laboratory-generated embryos solely for experimentation. The general secretary voiced grave concern that this procedure was to render more efficient the elimination of prenatal lives considered genetically imperfect. In conclusion, he urged Health and Human Services Secretary Bowen "to reconsider his decision to pursue this kind of research, which does not conform to the administration's [Reagan's] stated policy of respect for human life from the moment of conception."

On September 13, 1988, the Administrative Board of the United States Catholic Conference unanimously approved the *Statement on Principles for Legal Immigration Policy.* While recognizing the need to reshape the immigration system, the bishops strongly encouraged Congress "to engage in extensive, thoughtful, and public debate before any new immigration law is enacted." In their statement, the bishops offer five principles "to guide the development of any legal immigration policy."

At the bishops' thirty-seventh general meeting, held November

14-17, 1988, in Washington D.C., a singular happening took place. A document entitled *Doctrinal Responsibilities*, in which the bishops endeavored to establish the rightful roles of the bishops and of theologians, was withdrawn from the meeting. Bishop Raymond Lessard, chairman of the Committee on Doctrine explained that he had received from Archbishop Bovone of the Congregation for the Doctrine of the Faith, by way of a November 10, 1988, letter from Apostolic Pro-Nuncio Pio Laghi, observations concerning the document and the information that "the Congregation will send a letter on this subject, but I am not certain that it will arrive before the opening of your meeting."[72] The letter did not arrive on time so action on this document was deferred to the spring 1989 meeting. Cardinal O'Connor explained the congregation's delayed action by saying "the congregation is badly understaffed."

Archbishop John Roach, chairman of the ad hoc task force, presented the *Report of the Ad Hoc Task Force on Food, Agriculture, and Rural Concerns*, in answer to a new mandate on rural issues. The archbishop called the 85,000 foreclosure warnings being sent to American farmers a "tragedy not only for those families but for the nation. This is a sign of the crisis our task force was formed to deal with." The USCC expresses deep concern and solidarity with the many farmers who face the loss of their farms unless they can convince the federal government within the next forty-five days that they should be given another chance to continue farming.

The burdens of possible foreclosure will fall most heavily on small farmers, especially minority farmers. Representatives of black farmers estimate that nearly all of the 40 percent of black farmers served by the Farmers' Home Administration will receive foreclosure notices. "As pastors we have seen firsthand the human agony, the tragedy that farm failures and foreclosures inflict on individuals," lamented the archbishop. "The family loses everything, even a place to live. The conference hopes that the Farmers' Home Administration will delay actual foreclosures until farmers have an ample opportunity to present their case. Archbishop Roach mentioned that the USCC is sending important information on potential foreclosures to over 200 diocesan offices to prompt farmers to act swiftly in filling out the forms necessary to protect their livelihood and way of life, if possible. "This is just a symbol of the problems our country faces in bringing both justice and compassion to the issues of food and agriculture in our land."

Archbishop James Francis Stafford of Denver asked if the report included ranching, which is now in its worst condition since the Depression of the 1930s. Archbishop Roach replied that the task force made a conscious effort to address such industries as ranching, fish-

---

[72]Archbishop Pio Laghi to NCCB President Archbishop John May.

ing, and lumbering. Admitting that the report was an excellent follow-up on the pastoral *Economic Justice for All*, Milwaukee Archbishop Rembert Weakland wondered if more could be said regarding the international situation. Archbishop Roach replied that his task force was asked to investigate only how the bishops could respond to the situation in the United States.

When the report came up for debate and vote, Cardinal O'Connor encouraged Archbishop Roach in his efforts on behalf of the rural people. However, His Eminence cautioned against a tendency to overemphasize agriculture to the exclusion of food issues such as burning crops, leaving fields fallow, and failing to feed the urban poor in a truly dignified way. He urged the task force to approach its work from a spiritual perspective. The bishop must feed people both spiritually and physically. Archbishop Roach assured all that the task force would be very sensitive to the agricultural food issue because the National Rural Life Conference has long been weakened by its identification as a midwestern farm organization. It is important to be more expansive since the four largest food-producing states are California, Texas, Florida, and New York.

Archbishop Roach moved for the approval of the *Report of the Ad Hoc Task Force on Food, Agriculture, and Rural Concerns*, and the motion passed unanimously.

Archbishop Eugene Marino (Atlanta) made the presentation of the compassionate *Resolution on the Tenth Anniversary of the NCCB Pastoral Statement on Handicapped People*. The archbishop mentioned that it was drafted by the board of directors of the National Catholic Office for Persons with Disabilities, composed of bishops and pastoral ministers working with disabled people. The assembled bishops then saw an excellent videotape presentation on ministry with handicapped people. The videotape stressed making the handicapped feel most welcome in the Church and encouraged the use of their various talents for the benefit of the Church. The resolution was approved unanimously.

On November 16, the bishops issued a *Policy Statement on Employer Sanctions*, briefly summarizing the history of this particular aspect of the Immigration Reform and Control Act of 1986 and highlighting the bishops' extreme skepticism as well as their opposition to the concept of having employers take an active role in immigration control. The prelates recognized, with profound concern, the very large number of undocumented persons living desperate lives in the shadows of our society.

In place of Archbishop Theodore McCarrick (Newark), who was unable to attend the meeting, Archbishop Anthony Bevilacqua (Philadelphia) made the presentation. Archbishop Bevilacqua explained that the policy statement expresses concern for the worsening plight of the undocumented aliens in the United States, many of them Catholics, whose situation has deteriorated as a result of the employers sanctions provision of the Immigration Reform and Control Act of 1986.

While the recent legalization program did enable many undocumented persons to begin the process of becoming legal citizens—a process in which the Church took an important leadership role nationwide—"still vast numbers remain outside the protection of our nation's laws and basic guarantees of human rights," noted Archbishop Mahony (Los Angeles). His Excellency warned that the employer sanctions provision continues to place enormous burdens upon this remnant population, found in so many cities and dioceses. Unprecedented hardships are now being borne by parents struggling to feed and clothe their children.

Under this Act, it is unlawful knowingly to hire or recruit any worker who is not legally authorized to work in the United States. A system of fines and criminal penalties is imposed on employers who violate the law. The committee felt that these *sanctions* (hence the name) are causing severe hardships for some of the most vulnerable members of society. Carefully avoiding any counseling of civil disobedience, the statement opposes the employer sanctions and offers some social actions that could help the Catholic community's efforts to assist the undocumented and change or modify this harsh law.

For decades, the bishops have been crusading to change the nation's immigration laws. They called for mitigating provisions of the Immigration Reform and Control Act of 1986 that penalize employers of undocumented workers. Also, in this statement, they pledged their efforts to stop employer discrimination against undocumented workers. (In a report released earlier in the week of the bishops' meeting, the government's General Accounting Office cited the need for educating employers on the provisions of the Act. The report also observed that, under the new immigration law, one employer in six may have committed discriminatory acts.) The bishops, through the United States Catholic Conference, have begun compiling records of cases of discrimination against migrants in order to provide documentation for future attempts to change the law, affirming: "If enough cases of discrimination can be reported through the GAO, Congress must revisit the law."

The bishops also will seek to inform employers about the law: "Many employers do not realize that employees hired before November 6, 1986, are 'grandfathered' by the law," the bishops' statement said. "These employees should not be dismissed or asked to show documents demonstrating their immigration status, and employers cannot be sanctioned for failing to do so."

The Committee on Migration urged their brother bishops to confirm the mandate to implement the recommended six action steps: "We recommend that you accept this policy statement for your own guidance at the diocesan level, and that your local staff continue to collaborate with our conference office of migration to reverse the discrimination and suffering being felt so deeply across the land."The policy statement was accepted unanimously.

On the last day of the meeting, November 17, the bishops voted their approval of *A Word of Solidarity, A Call for Justice: A Statement on Religious Freedom in Eastern Europe and the Soviet Union.* In his final presentation of this marvelous document, Archbishop Mahony feared that a statement that enjoys such broad and enthusiastic support could get lost in the crowded agenda of the meeting. This statement may lack the drama and controversy of some others, but it is a major contribution to the conference's effort to share Catholic social teaching and a word of genuine solidarity with sisters and brothers of faith in the Soviet Union and Eastern Europe. It challenges the leaders of those countries to match their recent talk of reform with concrete action demonstrating respect for the principles of religious liberty. It challenges American Catholics and our nation's leaders to support the courageous struggle of believers to practice their faith.

His Excellency stated that the Committee on Social Development and World Peace had consulted widely to further refine what we believe is a strong and sophisticated treatment of these complex issues. Asking their help in sharing it widely, he assured the assembled bishops: "We will be seeking an early opportunity to share our concerns with leaders of our nation and the countries addressed in the statement. We want our support and solidarity to be felt by our sisters and brothers in Eastern Europe and the Soviet Union and by those who rule those lands."

Most Reverend Paul Baltakis, bishop for the spiritual assistance of Lithuanians outside Lithuania, made a lengthy and significant intervention in which he noted that, after having met with all the bishops of Lithuania and many of its priests and faithful during the past year, he finds this document "extremely well prepared, balanced, and up to date." This statement "will enable *perestroika's* limits to be tested and even expanded."After mentioning that under Mr. Gorbachev the experience of the people in the Baltic States has improved and citing several specific improvements, he quoted Lithuanian Cardinal Sladkevicius' assessment of the Lithuanian Church's present situation: "hope mixed with great caution." Bishop Baltakis urged the assembly to vote for this statement.

Cardinal Hickey (Washington) mentioned that this statement was in accord with the conference's recent peace pastoral and that it is most timely. Bishop William Keeler (Harrisburg), an expert in ecumenism, remarked how warmly this statement will be received by the Jews and the Greek Orthodox, who are so restricted by the Soviets in the practice of their religion. Several bishops commented that this statement will offer a blueprint to the Soviets on how to implement *glasnost* and *perestroika*.

A Word of Solidarity, A Call for Justice was approved by a unanimous vote.

Opposition of Military Aid to Contras

*A Letter Written to Members of the
House of Representatives by the
General Secretary of the
United States Catholic Conference*

March 17, 1986

1.   I write about the upcoming vote on March 20, 1986, on U.S. policy toward Nicaragua.

2.   The position of the U.S. Catholic Conference on Nicaragua has three elements: (1) to protest and oppose human rights violations in Nicaragua, particularly those which restrict the ministry of the Church; (2) to oppose military aid to any party in Nicaragua, including U.S. military aid to the *contras*; and (3) to urge a more creative and intensive effort by the United States and other key governments toward a diplomatic-political solution for Nicaragua and the Central American region. These three positions have been spelled out in previous congressional testimony; here we simply comment on each.

3.   In the past year, the human rights problem in general and the specific issues surrounding the full and free exercise of the Catholic Church's ministry have reached very critical proportions. In previous congressional testimony, the USCC has addressed human rights restrictions in Nicaragua regarding freedom of the press, freedom of assembly, the rights of free trade unions, and the exercise of the Church's ministry, particularly as it pertains to the work of the Catholic bishops of Nicaragua. In recent months, the restrictions on crucial aspects of the Church's work have intensified. In his presentation to the secretary general of the United Nations, Cardinal Obando has enumerated some of the most serious issues: the harassment of church institutions, the closing of the publication *Iglesia* and of Radio Catolica, the summoning of priests by state security forces for questioning, and a general pattern of restricting the freedom of the Church to preach the Gospel. The USCC believes that the human rights issues in Nicaragua are a necessary concern of U.S. foreign policy and of other states in the international community.

4.   The USCC does not believe, however, that the provision of military assistance by outside powers to either side in Nicaragua is a useful contribution to a peaceful solution of the problem. Hence, the USCC opposes the measure before the House of Representatives to provide military aid to forces in conflict with the Nicaraguan government. Such aid, in our view, simply intensifies the conflict, has contributed to several thousand deaths, and does not serve a useful political or humanitarian purpose. We urge the Congress to reject the provision of the military-assistance package.

5.   In contrast to this proposal, we believe a productive road is open to U.S. action. It involves a full-scale, high-level commitment by the United States to support and facilitate the renewed Contadora peace process, which has now been given new impetus by the Carabelleda Message of January 12, 1986. This new effort, supported by the original Contadora group and the foreign ministers of Argentina, Brazil, Peru, and Uruguay and affirmed by all five Central American states on January 14, 1986, is a very useful Latin American initiative. But it cannot succeed without the active support of the United States. It is this road which we hope the Congress will support for U.S. policy.

6.   Thank you for your consideration of our views.

Statement on the Federal Budget, the Deficit, and Taxes

A Statement Issued by the
Administrative Board of the
United States Catholic Conference

March 24, 1986

1. In 1986, the United States will face particularly stark choices about national priorities and the principles that determine them. The choices arise now because the deficit must be reduced and because the targets in the Gramm-Rudman-Hollings law set the framework for the debate about budget, deficits, and taxes.

2. Decisions about these matters are not purely technical. Embedded in the technical debate are moral decisions about justice and fairness and moral judgments about how best to provide for the common defense and promote the general welfare. At the heart of the budget-deficit-taxes debate are questions that directly touch human dignity, human rights, and human needs in the United States and beyond our borders. It is these human questions — which are always moral questions — that move us to address these issues.

3. Clearly, there is a consensus that the deficit must be systematically reduced. The key policy differences lie in the means of achieving this objective. One set of choices is the relationship of budget cuts and tax policy. A second set of choices concerns allocation of the cuts between defense and nondefense spending. A third set of choices involves what kinds of decisions on defense policy contribute to both arms control objectives and deficit reduction.

4. Addressing the problem of the federal budget, we use three criteria. First, distributive and social justice require that when the federal budget is cut, the most vulnerable people in our society should be protected from the effects of these cuts. This principle calls for a conscious policy choice to protect the poor. The reasons supporting this choice are not only the vulnerability of the poor, but also the deep cuts that have been made in recent years in programs affecting them.

5. Second, the necessary reductions in the federal budget should be allocated fairly between defense and nondefense spending. To insulate defense spending from budget reductions would greatly increase the possibility that the most vulnerable people in our society would bear a disproportionate share of budget cuts.

6. Third, when deciding upon reductions in the defense budget, attention should be given to arms control criteria as well as fiscal criteria. Specifically, we urge consideration of the guidelines found in our 1983 pastoral letter *The Challenge of Peace*. Based on that letter, the USCC has proposed that major weapons systems which are of questionable effectiveness, but which are certain to cost large sums of money, should not be pursued in this time of severe budget stringency.

7.   Budgetary decisions require consideration not only of cuts but also of federal revenues. In recent USCC testimony on tax policy, we said:

> One of the most basic and obvious goals of the tax system is to raise the necessary revenues to pay for the common needs of our society. At a time when deficits in the federal budget are at unprecedented levels and when many social needs continue to go unmet, the question of adequate federal revenues cannot be ignored.

8.   We urge a careful review of tax proposals to ensure that any measure adopted will meet our social goals and obligations. The debate and decisions we face as a nation in the months ahead will be complex and will require the best resources of vision, wisdom, and compassion we can muster as a society. We should address the issues of budget, deficits, and taxes in a manner that binds us together as a nation, supporting each other and shaping our common future in a spirit of faith, hope, and trust.

Divestment, Disinvestment, and South Africa

A Policy Statement Issued by the
Administrative Board of the
United States Catholic Conference

September 10, 1986

1. The Catholic bishops of South Africa have characterized apartheid as "something intrinsically evil." The United States Catholic Conference has frequently condemned the system of apartheid and protested specific actions of the South African government. The repressive measures recently imposed by that government under the guise of a State of Emergency are an additional intolerable affront to the dignity of all South African people and to the common opinion of humankind.

2. It is clear on human, moral, and political grounds that change must come in South Africa. It is also clear that the primary agents of change are within South Africa. But nations and institutions that have a relationship with South Africa are part of the political and moral drama being played out in that nation.

3. We speak as bishops and pastors of a Church whose religious and moral teaching is daily contradicted by apartheid, and whose brother bishops are actively opposing apartheid. We also speak as citizens of a nation that exercises a significant influence in South African society.

4. The Administrative Board of the United States Catholic Conference, therefore, recommends that dioceses and church-related institutions give consideration to the adoption of the following policy statement:

5. If, by May 15, 1987, the government of South Africa has failed to undertake significant progress toward the dismantling of the system of apartheid and has not sincerely attempted to enter into serious and substantial negotiations with legitimate black leaders, then those agents managing the investment portfolio will be instructed to:

    a) institute a program for the prudent and fiscally responsible divestment from business enterprises doing business in South Africa, or

    b) file, encourage, and join with others in filing shareholder resolutions with portfolio corporations doing business in South Africa, requiring them to implement a disinvestment program by withdrawal from South Africa.

6. These alternatives are not mutually exclusive and may be combined even in dealing with the same company. Divestment may be

adopted with regard to some companies, stockholder resolutions with regard to others; or while generally divesting from a company, a small block of stock may be retained in order to allow the introduction or support of stockholders' resolutions.

Explanatory Notes

Note A:

What constitutes "significant progress toward the dismantling of the system of apartheid"? A convenient listing of steps in this direction is provided in the text of the Anti-Apartheid Act of 1985, which was endorsed by the Administrative Board in September 1985:

1) The government of South Africa has eliminated the system which makes it impossible for black employees and their families to be housed in family accommodations near the place of employment.

2) The government of South Africa has eliminated all policies that restrict the rights of black people to seek employment in South Africa and to live wherever they find employment in South Africa.

3) The government of South Africa has eliminated all policies that make distinctions between the South African nationality of blacks and whites.

4) The government of South Africa has eliminated removals of black populations from certain geographic areas on account of race or ethnic origin.

5) The government of South Africa has eliminated all residence restriction based on race or ethnic origin.

6) The government of South Africa has entered into meaningful negotiations with truly representative leaders of the black population for a new political system providing for the full national participation of all the people of South Africa in the social, political, and economic life in that country and an end to discrimination based on race or ethnic origin.

7) An internationally recognized settlement for Namibia has been achieved.

8) The government of South Africa has freed all political prisoners.

Note B:

Judgment about "significant progress" or the lack of it in the light of these criteria would be made by the diocesan bishop for those funds subject to his care and by the chief executive officers of other Catholic institutions. Numerous sources are available to assist them in arriving at their conclusion. One such source is the USCC Office of International Justice and Peace, which is in continuing contact with the Southern African Catholic Bishops' Conference.

Divestment, Disinvestment, and South Africa
A Background Paper

USCC Department of
Social Development and World Peace

I. *Introduction*

1. At the June 1985 meeting of the Committee on Social Development and World Peace, staff presented to the members of the committee a memorandum pertaining to South Africa. That memorandum, dated June 6, 1985, consisted of two major parts.

2. Part I contained a discussion of the South African system of apartheid. Following upon the approval of the committee, this material was prepared for the consideration of the Administrative Board in September 1985. The Administrative Board unanimously approved the proposed *Policy Statement on South Africa* and also called for the publication of the *Background Paper on South Africa,* which had been prepared by the staff.

3. Part II of the memorandum pertained to the divestment of church funds. Following upon an extended discussion, the Committee on Social Development and World Peace, at its June meeting, asked the staff to continue its study and analysis of the issues involved. Special mention was made of the need to examine the economic impact of divestment. At its September 1985 meeting, the Administrative Board recommended that "the USCC Committee on Social Development and World Peace continue its study of the question of divestment of church funds from business enterprises doing business in South Africa and report on this subject to the Administrative Board."

4. During its meeting of December 10-11, 1985, the Administrative Board received, discussed, and approved a draft of this present paper, with the proviso that the views of the Southern African Catholic Bishops' Conference be solicited and taken into account.

II. *Divestment: Arguments Pro and Con*

5. At the outset, it should be noted that while the terms *divestment* and *disinvestment* are often used interchangeably, it is preferable to define these terms as follows:

> *divestment:* investors selling their stock in companies that do business in South Africa and depositors withdrawing their funds from banks that lend monies to the South African government and its agencies.

> *disinvestment:* the withdrawal of foreign corporation investment and business from South Africa.

6. It should be clear that the purpose of a divestment campaign aimed at companies and banks doing business in South Africa is to bring about disinvestment, that is, the withdrawal of investments and business by those companies and banks from South Africa, in order to impose strong pressure on the white business and political leaders so that meaningful negotiations might result.

7. Those who argue in favor of divestment often advance two major reasons in support of their position: (1) that the withdrawal of foreign investments from South Africa (the purpose of the divestment campaign) will weaken the South African economy and, therefore, the South African government, and that this will assist those South Africans who are working to dismantle the system of apartheid; and (2) that such foreign investments are questionable from an ethical standpoint in that they support and perpetuate the white minority government at the expense of the well-being and human rights of the black majority.

8. Those who oppose divestment and advocate the continuation of foreign investment in South Africa argue that investment in South Africa's economy actually breaks down apartheid by providing opportunities for blacks, coloureds, and Asians to improve their lot economically and thus acquire political power as labor union members, entrepreneurs, and consumers.

9. While some opponents of divestment contend that it is the black population in South Africa that will suffer the most from any impairment of the South African economy, those in favor of divestment can quote statements such as that of Nobel Peace Laureate Albert Luthuli, who said as long ago as 1959:

> The economic boycott of South Africa will entail undoubted hardship for Africans. We do not doubt that. But if it is a method which shortens the day of bloodshed, the suffering to us will be a price we are willing to pay.

10. Another set of arguments concern the effect of economic growth upon apartheid. Opponents of divestment assert that it is South Africa's economic growth that is weakening apartheid and, as evidence for this, they will cite the dismantling of some of the racial discrimination laws (known as *petty apartheid*). But, the proponents of economic disengagement firmly believe that the interests of the majority in South Africa will not be served by the mere reform of apartheid. Rather, they hold that apartheid cannot be reformed but must be ended in its entirety. They also argue that because of the tight rein the South African government keeps on all elements of the society, and the intertwining of political and economic power, any capital infusions that bolster the South African economy necessarily serve to strengthen the forces that maintain apartheid.

11. It is hoped that the above paragraphs will provide at least some understanding of the lines of argumentation followed by both the proponents and opponents of divestment from banks and enterprises doing business in South Africa.

III. *Economic Sanctions against South Africa United States Law*

12. On August 1, 1985, a conference committee reported on the Anti-Apartheid Action Act of 1985, a compromise between bills previously adopted by the House and the Senate, respectively. This compromise legislation was approved overwhelmingly by the House of Representatives and secured a majority of votes in the Senate, although it failed to achieve the sixty votes required under the procedural rules of the Senate then in force.

13. The USCC Administrative Board, on September 11, 1985, in its *Policy Statement on South Africa*, recommended the approval of the Anti-Apartheid Action Act of 1985, which included the following measures:

- prohibit the importation of South African Krugerrands or other gold coins from South Africa;
- prohibit the exportation of computers, software, and technology to the South African police, military, and other government entities that enforce restrictions on blacks' freedom of movement;
- prohibit loans to the South African government (except for loans for any educational, housing, or health facility that is available to all persons on a nondiscriminatory basis);
- prohibit the export of goods or technology to be used in any South African nuclear production or utilization facility;
- impose mandatory fair employment practices (the Sullivan Principles) for U.S. business enterprises employing more than twenty-five persons;
- provide monies for scholarships for black South Africans to attend South African universities, colleges, and secondary schools;
- provide monies for a human rights fund for the legal defense of victims of apartheid;
- establish a policy calling for the imposition of economic sanctions against South Africa if significant progress has not been made within twelve months toward ending apartheid.

14. One of the principal reasons why this anti-apartheid legislation failed adoption in the Senate (although it did receive a majority of votes in that chamber) is that on September 9, 1985, two days before the scheduled Senate vote, President Reagan issued an Executive

Order prohibiting trade and certain other transactions involving South Africa.

15. The provisions of the Anti-Apartheid Action Act of 1985 and of the President's Executive Order of September 9 are parallel in many respects, although the proposed legislation was more extensive in its reach than the Executive Order. However, the principal difference between the proposed congressional legislation and the presidential Executive Order is that the former would have established a policy calling for the imposition of economic sanctions against South Africa if significant progress had not been made within twelve months toward ending apartheid. No such provision is contained in the Executive Order which, on September 4, 1986, was renewed for a period of one year.

16. Cognizant of the differences between the congressional proposal and the Executive Order, the USCC Administrative Board, in its policy statement of September 11, 1985, said:

> The Executive Order of September 9, 1985, addresses some of these measures and we welcome it as a development in U.S. policy. Nevertheless, the Anti-Apartheid Action Act of 1985 offers a stronger and broader approach, which we still believe is necessary.

17. Finally, it should be noted that among the economic sanctions envisioned by the Anti-Apartheid Action Act of 1985—if significant progress was not made within twelve months toward dismantling the system of apartheid—were the following:

- a ban on new commercial investment in South Africa;
- a denial of most-favored-nation status to South Africa;
- a ban on the importation of coal, uranium ore, and uranium oxide from South Africa and Namibia.

IV. Economic Impact of Divestment

18. A recent issue of an influential investment letter describes the opposing arguments over divestment in the following terms:

> Just how U.S. companies operating in South Africa figure into the present and future of apartheid has become a very hot issue. On one side, opposition to our commercial involvement in that country has risen in federal and local governments, universities, and church groups, many of whose investment portfolios have begun to be realigned accordingly. Proponents of disinvestment, or corporate withdrawal, argue that companies who invest in South Africa are "financiers of apartheid," whose capital, skills, technology, and products help keep the present system running smoothly. Disinvestment, they argue, therefore would pressure the government to change its policies.
> On the other side, proponents of "responsible involvement" feel

that U.S. companies can exert a greater influence by staying, particularly if they adhere to the Sullivan Principles, a code of conduct that promotes equality both in and outside of the workplace. By actively pushing for social reform, say Sullivan advocates, U.S. companies can set an example that is a stimulus for other companies to follow and is in the best interest of South African blacks" (*TAMCO Investment Letter*, July 3, 1985).

19. In the opinion of many students of the South African scene, the inner dynamics of apartheid are economic in nature, and apartheid has been described as racial capitalism. (Cf. *Relocations: The Churches' Report on Forced Removals in South Africa*, published by the South African Council of Churches and the Southern African Catholic Bishops' Conference in 1984.)

20. While it has been argued that investment and trade with South Africa would induce changes in the system of apartheid, this would seem to ignore the fact that foreign investors and business enterprises trading with South Africa have been among the principal beneficiaries of the system of apartheid. Investors do not invest in South Africa as acts of charity or to end apartheid, but rather to make profits. The controlled supply of cheap labor provided by apartheid assured that this objective would be achieved.

21. Since September 1977, when the European Economic Community's code of conduct went into operation, and since July 1978, when the United States equivalent, the so-called Sullivan Principles, began to be effective, companies doing business in South Africa have been under some pressure to improve working conditions for the black labor force. These codes have had significant effects in that they have defined a base-line below which the treatment of black labor might be deemed improper and immoral. A limited number of black workers have enjoyed improved wages, working conditions, and opportunities for advancement. Some employers have actively promoted beneficial developments outside the workplace, such as improved education and housing.

22. Critics of these codes, however, see them as encouraging trade and investment without altering the system of apartheid in any fundamental way. The political economy of apartheid remains untouched. While some of the oppressive laws controlling the lives of black South Africans have been repealed, others have replaced them and no progress has been made toward full political participation by the black majority. One cannot see in the application of the codes, even if strictly enforced and universally observed (which they are not), an instrument of more than superficial change in South Africa.

23. Bishop Desmond Tutu wrote in 1981:

Many who are concerned to see fundamental change happen in our country peacefully believe that economic prosperity will of itself erode apartheid. . . . I wish this were true. Unfortunately, contemporary South African history proves the opposite. We have experienced several boom periods during the 30 years of Nationalist apartheid rule. There has been no real liberalization of apartheid. Some of the most vicious legislation has come at times not of a recession but of a boom.

24. United States economic involvement in South Africa more than tripled in the period between 1970 and 1981, yet apartheid was in no way weakened. On the contrary, the repressive power of the white minority increased during those years.

25. In the June 6, 1985, memorandum from staff to the Committee on Social Development and World Peace, consideration was given to proposals for withdrawing funds from banks making loans to the South African government and its state agencies and to proposals for divestment from business enterprises operating in South Africa. Since the presidential Executive Order of September 9, 1985, prohibits "the making or approval of any loans by financial institutions in the United States to the Government of South Africa or to entities owned or controlled by that Government," this paper will concentrate on an examination of proposals for divestment from business enterprises operating in South Africa.

26. First of all, what is the current extent of United States corporate investment and activity in South Africa?

27. While there are varying reports on this subject, it is estimated that during the fifteen-year period (1966-1981), total United States corporate fixed investment (defined as plant, equipment, and inventories) in South Africa rose at a 12 percent annual rate from $490 million to $2.6 billion. Since 1981, however, this total has declined to roughly $2.3 billion at present. The most tangible reason for this downward trend is general weakening of the South African economy. Also, the strong dollar has reduced the value of U.S. direct investments in South Africa.

28. About 280 U.S. companies have direct investments in South Africa. Roughly 5,700 others sell products in the country without a local office. Most of the direct investors are major corporations and respectively constitute a very large percentage of several key industry sectors in the country, including oil, office equipment, automobiles, drugs, and chemicals.

29. From a United States point of view, South African exposure is relatively small, accounting for about 1 percent of total U.S. foreign direct investment. Also, for the majority of the U.S. companies in question, South African investments represent less than 1 percent of total corporate assets. From a South African point of view, while the United States is said to be South Africa's second largest investor, as of 1983, U.S. companies operated only 3 percent of South Africa's industrial plants.

30. According to the 1984 report on the signatory companies to the Sullivan Principles, U.S. companies employ approximately 65,000 South

African workers, of whom about two-thirds, or 43,500 are black. Other estimates of black workers employed by U.S. firms range as high as 58,000, but it should be kept in mind that South Africa has a black population in excess of 20 million persons.

31. Arguments and counterarguments concerning divestment can be summed up as follows:

a) Divestment will hurt most the very people we are trying to help, that is, the black South Africans. Bishop Tutu comments on this point as follows:

> The argument that Blacks would be the first to suffer may be true, yet there are at least two rejoinders: a cynical one is, when did Whites become so altruistic? After all, they have benefited from black misery engendered by low wages, migratory labor, etc., for so long. The less cynical is that Blacks would probably be ready to accept suffering that has a goal and a purpose and would therefore end, rather than continue to suffer endlessly.

Bishop Tutu's view was substantially supported in a recent poll (by a Gallup-affiliated organization) in which 73 percent of urban black South Africans were shown to be in favor of some form of disinvestment.

b) If U.S. business enterprises leave South Africa, then other investors, less sensitive to human rights, will move in quickly and fill the void, and the United States will lose its leverage. But, as the statistics given above would seem to indicate, the impact of U.S. business enterprises and the resulting leverage from their presence in South Africa have not produced significant change for the vast majority of black workers. It may also be pointed out that the current violence and instability in South Africa would be discouraging to prudent investors of whatever country or origin.

c) Disinvestment would lead to increased violence and instability in South Africa. This argument seems to assume that the presence of U.S. firms in South Africa has been a stabilizing factor, but, although United States investment has tripled since 1970, this has occurred at a time when the South African government became even more repressive. The purpose of sanctions, including disinvestment, is to impose strong pressure on the white business and political leaders so that meaningful negotiations might result, leading to the elimination of the causes of the present violence and instability.

d) Disinvestment will cause the United States to lose its influence in South Africa. The U.S. business enterprises investing and operating in South Africa have not had any significant effect on the structure of grand apartheid. At best, they have merely affected some changes in petty apartheid such as desegregation of dining rooms, toilet facilities, and so forth. This concerns only the working conditions of a very small percentage of the black work force. Disinvestment would not be the end of United States influence. Other economic sanctions and political actions would remain available to U.S. policy-makers.

e) Disinvestment would seriously injure the economies of countries that border on South Africa, such as Botswana, Lesotho, Swaziland, and Mozambique. When the South African economy is healthy, it absorbs thousands of migrant workers from these countries, and the external trade of these countries centers upon South Africa. The imposition of economic sanctions on South Africa may well require emergency assistance to its neighboring countries that are dependent, in large measure, upon the South African economy. In a memorandum submitted to the Organization of African Unity at its July 1985 meeting, the Southern African Development Coordination Conference stated:

> Those opposed to sanctions argue that they will hurt neighboring states. Undoubtedly, this is true. But if it accelerated the ending of apartheid, it would be well worth the additional cost. And those who are concerned about the negative effects of sanctions on the neighboring states should provide assistance to those states to minimize it. . . . South Africa destabilizes its neighbors to keep them dependent so that they will be harmed by sanctions. South Africa's capacity to maintain its destabilization is buttressed by support from the same western states who point to the harm that sanctions would do.

32. In the preceding paragraphs, an attempt has been made to summarize some of the arguments surrounding the economic and political impact of disinvestment.

33. It may not be out of place to note that there are also strictly *economic* arguments for disinvestment these days. As stated in the September 30, 1985, issue of *Fortune* Magazine:

> South Africa has been in deep recession for three years, battered by a prolonged drought, falling gold prices, and double-digit inflation. Interest rates of 20% and more have dried up consumer spending. The average after-tax return on investments of the fewer than 300 American companies that have direct investments in South Africa shrank from 31% in 1980 to only 7% in 1983, the latest year available. The rand, South Africa's unit of currency, has lost 50% of its value since January. International banks, led by Chase Manhattan, have refused to roll over about half of South Africa's $12 billion short-term debt. In late August, the government declared a moratorium on repaying the debt and, to head off an outflow of capital, reimposed foreign-exchange controls that it had lifted in 1983.
> Thirteen U.S. companies, mostly those with small South African holdings, have left the country this year. . . . The 13 include General Foods, Pan American World Airways, and PepsiCo. A number of companies with bigger stakes in the country, including Ford Motor, Coca-Cola, and Union Carbide, have quietly reduced their holdings or are trying to.

V. The Church in South Africa and Divestment

34. The Southern African Catholic Bishops' Conference met in extraordinary session in May 1986, and on May 2 issued a statement entitled *Economic Pressure on the South African Government*, which states in part:

> Anyone who does not appreciate the untold daily sufferings of the people, the pain, the insecurity of starvation, the horrors of widespread unemployment that are associated with the present system, will also not appreciate the need for drastic and extraordinary measures to put an end to all of this misery as quickly as possible. The system of apartheid has caused so much suffering and so much harm in human relations in our country for so long and is now being defended, despite some reforms, with so much repressive violence, that the people have had to resort to the strongest possible forms of pressure to change the system. It seems that the most effective of nonviolent forms of pressure left is economic pressure.
>
> We are deeply concerned about the additional suffering that some forms of economic pressure might cause, and we remain very sensitive to the possibility of further unemployment and escalating violence. But against this, we have to balance the enormity of the present suffering and rate of unemployment and the prospect for the future if the system of apartheid is not dismantled soon. The aim and purpose of economic pressure is to change our society so that the present sufferings may be removed together with the obstacles to employment deriving from the apartheid system. . . .
>
> We ourselves believe that economic pressure has been justifiably imposed to end apartheid. Moreover, we believe that such pressure should continue and, if necessary, be intensified should . . . developments . . . show little hope of fundamental change. However, we do not need to point out that, in our view, intensified pressure can only be justified if applied in such a way as not to destroy the country's economy and to reduce as far as possible any additional suffering to the oppressed through job loss. At the moment, we can see no justification for the sort of pressure that would leave a liberated South Africa in an economically nonviable situation.

(The full text of the bishops' statement is given in the appendix to this document.)

VI. The Church in the United States, South Africa, and Divestment: A Proposal

35. In view of the above statements from the bishops, what prudent and responsible actions might be recommended to Catholic dioceses and church-related institutions in the United States?

36. *First,* the presidential Executive Order of September 9, 1985, renewed on September 4, 1986, prohibits new bank loans to the South African government and its agencies; makes mandatory the application of the Sullivan Principles to U.S. enterprises employing more than twenty-five employees in South Africa; and prohibits the importation of Krugerrands.

37. It is *assumed* that dioceses and church-related institutions will deposit their money only in those banks and invest their money only in those enterprises that strictly observe these and related provisions of this Executive Order.

38. *Second,* it is recommended that dioceses and church-related institutions invest their monies only in those enterprises that are in *full* compliance with the Sullivan Principles *regardless of the number of persons they presently employ.* While, for purposes of ease in monitoring compliance with the law, the United States government has adopted twenty-five employees as a cut off point, there is no ethical reason for saying that an employer with only twenty-four employees may treat its employees any differently than an employer with twenty-six employees.

39. *Third,* it is recommended that dioceses and church-related institutions give serious consideration to the adoption of the USCC Administrative Board Policy Statement, which this Background Paper accompanies.

40. The two strategies suggested should be seen as complementary since both are aimed at pressuring U.S. and international companies to disinvest in South Africa unless and until apartheid is dismantled. It is believed that their adoption will be of assistance to those in the U.S. and South African business communities who are attempting to convince the South African government of the urgent need to dismantle the system of apartheid. It would enable these business leaders to tell the South African government that if significant progress toward this end is not made within a specified period of time, then their investors will begin withdrawing their monies, to the detriment of the South African economy. The rentention of some shares would allow the investor to voice demands for withdrawal at stockholders' meetings, to compel the consideration of motions for divestment, and to impress upon management and other stockholders the moral dimension of doing business in South Africa. Such action by Catholic institutions and dioceses can, in some cases, be coordinated with similar moves by other like-minded stockholders. In short, in this approach investments in companies doing business in South Africa are seen as a means of leverage, and this strategy is designed to increase that leverage.

41. It will be recalled that the USCC Administrative Board, at its September 1985 meeting, called for the enactment of the Anti-Apartheid Action Act of 1985. That act provided for economic sanctions against South Africa if significant progress had not been made within twelve months toward ending the system of apartheid. Thus, the Administrative Board is on record as favoring some type of economic sanction if progress toward ending apartheid is not achieved within a stated period of time.

42. This idea of asserting a period of time within which significant progress toward dismantling the system of apartheid must be made if economic sanctions are to be avoided also appears in the statements of Bishop Tutu (two years from early winter 1984) and Rev. Leon Sullivan (May 1987). Some legislation currently before the Congress provides a "grace period" of six months.

43. What constitutes "significant progress toward the dismantling of the system of apartheid?" A convenient listing of steps in this direction is provided in the text of the Anti-Apartheid Act of 1985, which was endorsed by the Administrative Board in September 1985:

a) The government of South Africa has eliminated the system that makes it impossible for black employees and their families to be housed in family accommodations near the place of employment.

b) The government of South Africa has eliminated all policies that restrict the rights of black people to seek employment in South Africa and to live wherever they find employment in South Africa.

c) The government of South Africa has eliminated all policies that make distinctions between the South African nationality of blacks and whites.

d) The government of South Africa has eliminated removals of black populations from certain geographic areas on account of race or ethnic origin.

e) The government of South Africa has eliminated all residence restriction based on race or ethnic origin.

f) The government of South Africa has entered into meaningful negotiations with truly representative leaders of the black population for a new political system providing for the full national participation of all the people of South Africa in the social, political, and economic life in that country and an end to discrimination based on race or ethnic origin.

g) An internationally recognized settlement for Namibia has been achieved.

h) The government of South Africa has freed all political prisoners.

44. Judgment about "significant progress" or the lack of it in the light of these criteria would be made by the diocesan bishop for those funds subject to his care and by the chief executive officers of other Catholic institutions. Numerous sources are available to assist them in arriving at their conclusion. One such source is the USCC Office of International Justice and Peace, which is in continuing contact with the Southern African Catholic Bishops' Conference.

45. As the USCC Administrative Board concluded in its 1985 *Policy Statement on South Africa*:

> Change in South Africa cannot come too quickly for those bearing the indignity and the injustice of apartheid. The United States as a nation and a society should be and should be seen by others to be unambiguously in support of profound, rapid, and thorough change in the political, legal, social, and economic sectors of South African society.

. . . the primary agents of change are within South Africa. But nations and institutions that have a relationship with South Africa are part of the political and moral drama being played out in that nation.

46. It is suggested that this recommendation, if adopted, will encourage Catholic dioceses and church-related institutions in the United States to act further in support of the goal of bringing to an end the system of apartheid in South Africa.

Economic Pressure on the South Africa Government

Statement of the Southern African Catholic Bishops' Conference

May 2, 1986

1. Our fundamental role as bishops is pastoral care. That is to say, we are called at all times and in all circumstances to give pastoral guidance to those who are in our care. We do this by preaching the Gospel, by interpreting it for our times, and by bringing to bear upon a situation its hope and courage.

2. In times of serious conflict, there is usually a great deal of conflict and confusion about issues so central to people's well-being that clear vision of the issues and of what God demands from people committed to his Gospel is difficult. In such times, all Christians are called upon to open themselves to that gift of the Spirit known as discernment. As for ourselves, it is our pastoral duty to give a lead in exercising that gift. This prophetic task of ours—as it is called—demands of us that we reflect on the issues in the light of the Gospel (cf. Mt 5), to see them through eyes opened by Jesus' teaching and to decide on what the Lord is demanding of us here and now. This decision is a decision of conscience, a decision or option that might open up new perspectives for others and, thus, give them a lead and provide them with a definite direction. It is a decision that inevitably involves taking a bold stand on controversial issues in the sphere of politics and economics, since it is these very areas that are at the root of the conflict.

3. In such circumstance, our prophetic witness might provide a challenge to people far beyond our dioceses, our country, and our Christian field. It might also provide encouragement and bring some measure of hope to millions of people who are beyond our usual pastoral care.

4. It is this prophetic calling that requires us, at certain times, to make a direct intervention in the affairs of our country. We realize that our stand represents a point of view that not all Catholics will agree with. While we realize that in such matters our decision of conscience about how to pressurize the present government to change does not oblige all Catholics to agree with us, it does give a lead that must be taken seriously. For, what we have done, we have not done lightly. It was only after much reflection, discussion, listening, consulting, and prayer that we have decided upon this stand that we are now taking on the issue of putting economic pressure on the apartheid government. As Saint Paul once said about another matter, another issue, "I have no directions from the Lord but give my own opinion . . . and I think that I too have the Spirit of God" (1 Cor 7:5,25,40).

5.   We must emphasize from the start, it is the unprecedented seriousness of our present crisis, the enormity of the present suffering of the oppressed people of South Africa, the horrifying spectre of escalating violence that have led us to take this stand. Anyone who does not appreciate the untold daily sufferings of the people, the pain, the insecurity of starvation, the horrors of widespread unemployment that are associated with the present system, will also not appreciate the need for drastic and extraordinary measures to put an end to all this misery as quickly as possible. The system of apartheid has caused so much suffering and so much harm in human relations in our country for so long and is now being defended—despite some reforms—with so much repressive violence that people have had to resort to the strongest possible forms of pressure to change the system. It seems that the most effective of nonviolent forms of pressure left is economic pressure.

6.   We are deeply concerned about the additional suffering that some forms of economic pressure might cause, and we remain very sensitive to the possibility of further unemployment and escalating violence. But, against this, we have to balance the enormity of the present suffering and rate of unemployment and the prospect for the future if the system of apartheid is not dismantled soon. The purpose of economic pressure is to change our society so that the present sufferings may be removed, together with the obstacles to employment deriving from the apartheid system.

7.   In considering economic pressure, we recognize that it can be a morally justifiable means of bringing about the elimination of injustices. In deciding in a particular case whether such pressure is justified or not, one needs to balance the degree of injustice and the pressing need to eliminate it against the hardship such pressure may cause.

8.   Many have already judged that the situation in our country is one in which economic pressure is justified. We not only respect their decision but express our admiration for their dedicated service in working for justice here. We assure them that their efforts have not

been in vain, but have helped bring about some of the changes that have occurred thus far.

9. We are aware that certain developments are imminent, such as the initiative of the Commonwealth Eminent Persons group and the forthcoming federal congress of the National Party. These may demand a reassessment of the issue of economic pressure. Should the government announce real basic changes, there may be a mitigation of economic pressure or at least its maintenance at the present level until the genuineness of such changes is clear. On the other hand, there may be an increase in economic pressure should the government prove intransigent.

10. We, ourselves, believe that economic pressure has been justifiably imposed to end apartheid. Moreover, we believe that such pressure should continue and, if necessary, be intensified should the developments just referred to show little hope of fundamental change. However, we do not need to point out that, in our view, intensified pressure can only be justified if applied in such a way as not to destroy the country's economy and to reduce, as far as possible, any additional suffering to the oppressed through job loss. At the moment, we can see no justification for the sort of pressure that would leave a liberated South Africa in an economically nonviable situation. However, we also recognize that the most important factor in deciding on how much suffering should be allowed to flow from economic pressure is the opinion of the oppressed of our land. It is imperative, therefore, that their views be canvassed as fully as possible. Such consultation is especially important in local consumer boycotts, where in order to achieve conformity, not infrequently forms of intimidation are used that range from the regrettable to the most inhuman imaginable. The latter cannot be condemned strongly enough.

11. We realize that we cannot give specific advice on exactly how economic pressure can or should be applied. The feasibility, effectiveness, and consequences of each method vary from one case to another and change with circumstances. Only those with the necessary expertise can make those judgments, and in doing so, they need to keep in mind always the conditions justifying such pressures.

12. Recognizing that the final word is far from being said, we will set up a commission to advise on various aspects of the overall issues that will arise.

13. We acknowledge yet again that in taking steps such as scrapping of the influx control, the government has initiated certain potentially genuine changes. However, if these are not linked to the issue of negotiation with accepted leaders of the people, the current civil war situation will continue and with it an escalating spiral of violence. Such negotiations are possible only if all political prisoners are released and their organizations unbanned. The release of such leaders is therefore a vital element in considering the degree to which change is genuine and economic pressure needs to be applied.

14. We have taken a decision of conscience over which we have agonized. It has been a Gethsemane experience, torn as we have been between the need to provide positive nonviolent actions against apartheid and the fear of adding to the misery and violence. We now call on you, the People of God, to reflect on what we have said. To some, it may be inadequate; to others, deeply disturbing. We beg you not to make hasty judgments about it but to reflect in the light of the Gospel on the crisis through which we are passing. In such a time, we must all examine our consciences in order to make sure that what we seek is God's will and not our own. Together, we must pray long and hard, and we must fast or do other acts of penance. As your bishops, we call for an intensification of the campaign of prayer for justice and peace and for the observance of a special day of prayer and fasting on the first Friday of each month. In this, we shall be cooperating with other believers who are embarking on similar observances. May the Spirit who has transformed God's people so often in the past do so again in our midst here in South Africa.

Together, A New People
Pastoral Statement on
Migrants and Refugees

*A Pastoral Statement Approved by the
Administrative Committee of the
National Conference of Catholic Bishops*

November 8, 1986

A Pastoral Statement on
Migrants and Refugees

1. Introduction

1. The loving concern of the Church for immigrants and refugees is a thread that ties together more than three centuries of its history in the United States. The growth and crises, the achievements and occasional failures of the Church are linked to its struggle to include in one community of faith, peoples from a hundred diverse cultures and then lead this new People of God toward a creative service in a pluralistic society. In fact, as a land of liberty and opportunity, the United States has drawn immigrants from every race, creed, and ethnic background, more than 52 million of them since 1820. Through policies and through family and ethnic group history, our national identity is rooted in the immigrant experience and in the enrichment provided by the sweat and skills, intelligence and dynamism of the immigrants.
2. The observance of the 100th anniversary of the Statue of Liberty gave witness to this awareness in a festive national celebration and reaffirmed the vision of a country that remains today a land of promise and a refuge for the oppressed, for "the huddled masses, yearning to breathe free."

2. A Tradition of Welcome

3. From its earliest days, in council debates and pastoral directives, the Church of the United States recalled as a guiding light the words of the Lord: "I was a stranger and you welcomed me" (Mt 25:35). It rejoiced in the growth of the Catholic family; it provided priests for the different language groups; it deplored the loss of members who could not worship according to their customs; it thanked the churches of origin of the immigrants for assisting in preserving their faith; it defended persecuted immigrants.[1] The Church extended its pastoral care to every new arriving group and devised innovative responses in the context of the times: educating immigrant children, caring for the orphans, establishing parishes of various languages, teaching seminarians the language of newcomers, forming immigrant associations, offering Christian sympathy, and instilling understanding of the duties of citizenship. The pastoral letters of the United States Catholic bishops and the pastoral practices of dioceses and parishes document a tradition of welcome into the social church where there are no more distinctions between Jew and Greek, slave and free, male and female, but all are one in Christ Jesus (Gal 3:28). A Church of many nations, the Catholic community was called to develop an attitude of welcome, mindful of the Lord's words: "He who welcomes you welcomes me" (Mt 10:40). It was challenged to reach out to the poor and the marginal and open ways to full participation, because when a stranger sojourns with you in your land, you shall not do him wrong . . . he shall be to you as the native among you, and you shall love him as yourself (Lv 19:33-34). At the same time, the presence of the immigrants made evident a living communion of churches throughout the world; the immigrants became a natural link with their countries of origin, advocates for their needs, and bearers of new cultural expressions in the American mosaic.

4.　The Second Vatican Council enunciated clearly the principles for a comprehensive pastoral response to the situation of people obliged to live outside their country and ethnic community.[2] Conciliar and papal teaching on human solidarity, the right to emigrate, cultural pluralism, equality of treatment, the rights and dignity of the human person, access to pastoral care, the evil of racism, and the demands of justice have been frequently highlighted for reflection and action. In the context of this rich and authoritative teaching explicitly formulated as a foundation for the pastoral care of immigrants, we bishops formally raised our voice on behalf of refugees and displaced persons, asylum seekers, boat people.

---

[1]Cf. *Pastoral Letters of the United States Catholic Bishops, 1792-1983*. Washington, D.C.: USCC Office of Publishing and Promotion Services, 1984. Volumes 1-IV.

[2]Vatican II. *Decree on the Pastoral Office of Bishops in the Church* (*Christus Dominus*), no. 18. "Special concern should be shown for those among the faithful who, on account of their condition or way of life, cannot sufficiently make use of the common and ordinary pastoral services of the parish priests or are quite cut off from them. Among this group are quite many migrants, exiles and refugees, seamen, airplane personnel, gypsies, and others of this kind. Suitable pastoral methods should also be developed to sustain the spiritual life of those who journey to other lands for a time for the sake of recreation. Episcopal conferences, especially national ones, should pay energetic attention to the more pressing problems confronting the aforementioned groups. Through common agreement and united efforts, such conferences should look to and promote the spiritual care of these people by means of suitable methods and institutions." (Cf. in the same document, no. 23, and *Pastoral Constitution on the Church in the Modern World* [*Gaudium et Spes*], no. 66.)

5.   The concern of the Church for people forced out of their country by political upheavals and economic conditions has been articulated in advocacy for fair immigration laws and a generous sharing in assistance and relief, together with the international community. In particular, ten years ago we issued a *Resolution on the Pastoral Concern of the Church for People on the Move* (1976), calling for amnesty for undocumented immigrants and other immigration reforms. In more recent statements, respect for racial and ethnic groups, celebration to aid small-boat refugees in Southeast Asia and the Caribbean and displaced persons from Central America were indicated as appropriate Christian responses in a world of increasing mobility and sudden tragedies. Conscious that the gospel message must take root and grow within each culture, the relationship between pastoral care and the many language and ethnic groups within the Catholic community was discussed in the statement *Cultural Pluralism in the United States* (1980) and in the pastoral letter *The Hispanic Presence: Challenge and Commitment* (1983). Now the sustained influx of new arrivals from all over the world and new preoccupations expressed in the current public debate on the impact of immigration in parishes, dioceses, and the whole society challenge anew the pastoral creativity of the Church.

3. Today's Immigration Reality

6.   From distant lands and neighboring countries, people enter our national community attracted by the labor demand of the economy and the hope of personal success. They are also pushed out of their native environment by the disruption or destruction of family, social, and religious life on the part of economic and political systems where human dignity is disregarded or violated. They follow in the footsteps of the Holy Family of Nazareth, who had to flee into exile for the safety of Jesus and seek refuge in an unfamiliar country (Mt 2:13). All seek freedom, security, and better living conditions for themselves and their families.

7.   The newest immigrants to the United States continue a familiar process of enrichment and diversification that reshapes the face of America. The numbers of people and their countries of origin have changed from past decades. The average annual legal immigration rate is over half a million. An additional annual residue of the inflow of undocumented immigrants remains as a permanent part of our society. In the past, the greatest number of immigrants were Europeans. Today, the largest percentage of legal arrivals is from Asia and from Latin America. In 1985, the top fifteen countries of birth for immigrants who became legal permanent residents were: Mexico, the Philippines, Korea, Vietnam, India, China, the Dominican Republic, Cuba, Jamaica, Iran, Taiwan, Cambodia, United Kingdom, Colombia, and Canada. Of the total immigration (570,009), 268,745 came from

Asia-Oceania (47 percent); 126,437 came from Mexico and Central and South America (22 percent); 83,281 came from the Caribbean (14 percent); and the balance from other regions of the world.

8. The continuity of immigration and its changed sources are understandable not only as an integral aspect of America always in the making, but also as a consequence of the increasing shift of direction of United States interests toward the countries of the Pacific rim.

9. The turmoil and violence still disrupting some Central American and Caribbean countries and the desperate poverty and repression in some have forced large numbers of their people on a perilous journey by land or in flimsy boats toward the haven of the United States. Thus, for the first time in its history, the United States has had to face the experience of becoming a country of first asylum.

10. This more complex and more diverse population has affected cities with a long immigration tradition as well as others which had developed a more homogeneous ethnic identity. On the other hand, immigration remains a comparative trickle when taken as a percentage of national population. Annual immigration, in fact, amounts to 0.3 percent of our population, as against 1.5 percent at the historic peak of immigration at the turn of the century and 0.6 percent average over two centuries.

11. Welcoming refugees and immigrants, as other countries are doing, expresses our solidarity with the international community of people. The 1980 Census shows that the foreign-born population of the United States is 7 percent, while it is 11 percent for France, 16 percent for Canada, and 20 percent for Australia.

4. *The Voice of the Church in the Current Debate*

12. Today, as often in our history, immigration is viewed with both optimism and apprehension. A national debate is underway on how welcoming the country is; how much diversity it can accept and at what pace; how it can diffuse fear and occasional conflict and discrimination in housing, health services, and employment; how best it can resolve the critical issues of undocumented workers and their families; of detention of asylum seekers and interception at sea of boat people seeking to reach the shores of the United States. The Church has contributed to answering these old and new questions with concrete proposals and insights from its long experience in social services and pastoral care. Through congressional testimony and policy statements and resolutions, it has publicly articulated its position, insisting that the application of basic principles of human rights takes precedence over legal rights.

13. Building on its past tradition and consistent with its teaching on the dignity of the human person and our common relationship whom we address as "our" Father (Mt 6:9), the Church renews its mission of acceptance of and support for all brothers and sisters from any different culture. "In all this," says the Holy Father John Paul II,

> the Church has a leading educative role to play amongst the people, the leaders and the structures of society, in order to enlighten public opinion and stimulate consciences. But she herself must bear witness to the quality of integration that she practices in her own bosom. Is she not the "sacrament of unity," welcoming diversity in unity, giving testimony to the reconciliation that Christ obtained through his cross. More fully than other social groups, Catholic communities should experience this dynamic of fraternal unity and respect for differences. Thanks to the Holy Spirit, they should work ceaselessly to build up a people of brothers, speaking the language of love, to be a ferment in the construction of human unity, of a civilization of love.[3]

5. Evangelization and Service

14. The mission of the Church, then, as the trusted and familiar home for most of the nation's newest arrivals, is a ministry of evangelization and service. The task of welcoming immigrants, refugees, and displaced persons into full participation in the Church and society with equal rights and duties continues the biblical understanding of the justice of God reaching out to all peoples and rectifying the situation of the poor, the orphans, the widows, the disadvantaged, and especially in the Old Testament, the alien and the stranger. It reflects the biblical version of universality expressed in the words of the Lord through Isaiah: "I come to gather nations of every language; they shall come and see my glory. . . . They shall bring all your brethren from all the nations as an offering to the Lord" (Is 66:18-20).

A. Together, a New People of God

15. In the community of faith, an attitude of welcome is a prerequisite for any possibility of journeying together "to build up the Body of Christ" (Eph 4:11-12). In the various local churches, different strategies have been utilized, from multicultural parishes to parallel language communities in the same physical structure to personal transitional language parishes, missions, or chaplaincies. In all circumstances, the pastoral solicitude of the Church is at work as its own directives require.[4]

16. In the parish, first of all, the encounter of newcomers and established members offers the opportunity to live the new commandment

---

[3]John Paul II. *Address to the World Congress on the Pastoral Care of Immigrants,* October 17, 1985.

[4]Cf. *Code of Canon Law,* cc. 518, 529; Paul VI. *New Norms for the Care of Migrants (Pastoralis Migratorium);* Sacred Congregation for Bishops. *Instruction on the Pastoral Care of People Who Migrate.* Washington, D.C.: USCC Office of Publishing and Promotion Services, 1969, ch. IV.

of the Lord: ". . . Such as my love has been for you, so must your love be for each other" (Jn 13:34). Pastors and parish teams can play a key role. If aware and sensitive to the presence of newcomers, they can lead the whole community to welcome them: there are no aliens in the Church. In fact, pastoral awareness is the practical recognition of the spiritual and social needs of migrants and refugees. In order to know what these needs are and to respond accordingly, it is first necessary to meet the newcomer with openness. The biblical injunction to extend hospitality to the stranger overcomes the tendency to see newcomers as a threat to our comfort, institutions, culture, and life styles. It allows newcomers to adapt in such a way that they will not lose their identity in the process of incorporation. It helps the imagination to devise and adopt initiatives and structures which empower immigrants to be themselves and which make it possible for their presence to enrich all with a pluralism of gifts in celebration of diversity.

17. The proclamation of the good news, in fact, needs to take into account this diversity. Christ's message must be embedded not only in the hearts of people, but in social systems and cultures as well.[5] The inculturation of the faith in the cultural communities in the United States remains an ongoing commitment of the Church's mission.

18. For many newcomers, however, there are not sufficient clergy and religious with appropriate language and culture training to provide pastoral care. In the absence of ordinary pastoral ministry, the newcomers are at risk of developing an attitude of passivity which leads to cultural and social alienation, religious indifference, and the search for the warmth of friendship and belonging in other religious movements and groups. Many priests, sisters, deacons, and church workers have learned to speak new languages and immersed themselves in new cultures for the sake of the Gospel. In several seminaries, the requirement of a second language is mandatory, and courses or workshops on the cultures and pastoral care of new immigrants are offered. Parishes avail themselves of the specialized assistance of itinerant missionaries and of catechists and leaders from the refugee and immigrant communities. Dioceses reorganize their pastoral coordination of immigrant apostolates and ask new questions on the meaning for evangelization of the increasing numbers of non-Christians among the most recent newcomers. All these initiatives point out a real partnership in faith and the maternal concern of the Church that responds to uprooted and needy people with special attention, in order to help them overcome the isolation of cultural and linguistic barriers and rebuild a normal existence. Thus, through ministry to the newest brothers and sisters, parishes and dioceses "place them-

---

[5]Paul VI. *On Evangelization in the Modern World* (*Evangelii Nuntiandi*), no. 20. Washington, D.C.: USCC Office of Publishing and Promotion Services, 1975.

selves, in a certain sense, at the service of the world" and thus they discover their catholicity in an experiential way.[6]

19. On the part of newcomers, faith requires commitment to active membership in the life of their parishes and worship communities. It asks them to appreciate their new country and its people, traditions, and culture. It invites them to contribute their intelligence and skills for the common good.

20. Together, then, as we grow strong in the familiarity of God's love, we build a more perfect and more inclusive community. We seek those who are not yet full and equal members; we reach out to immigrants and refugees whose faith needs community in order to flourish. In fact, the principal aspect of pastoral care is to create a true community where the Eucharist, sacrament of unity, is celebrated. The right of participation in the Eucharist enhances all forms of participation in the life of the community and society. Equality before God is the model of equality which requires that all persons have access to the resources and services of the local church so that all may experience and celebrate true community. In the dynamic process of creating community with all, the Church favors the most needy, and among these are migrants, refugees, and culturally different groups. In this way, welcoming new individuals and groups into the life of the parish and of the diocese becomes an exercise of incorporation that in this new historical moment calls for creativity and flexibility. The preservation and protection of the identity of the individual and the group, and the expression of this identity in community life, will be safeguarded. In the specific context of the local church, new forms of more effective ministry can be contributed by recent migrants and refugees themselves. In a mutuality of services, the local church becomes an anticipation of a more perfect and final communion, a reflection of the whole world in the diversity and gifts of its peoples and in the celebration of Christ's love for all in the message of salvation. This message, like the Eucharist to which it leads, remains a source of renewal. It prompts the Church to extend welcome, create community, defend human rights, announce the Gospel, and evangelize all different peoples and groups and make of them the new People of God.

B. In Ministry of Service

21. The promise of America to newcomers is equality and respect both as individuals and as ethnic and cultural groups. For the individual immigrant and refugee, this promise is met in equal opportunities in education, employment, housing, and health care. For the

---

[6]Pontifical Commission for the Pastoral Care of Migrants and Itinerant Peoples. *The Church and People on the Move*, no. 27. Washington, D.C.: USCC Office of Publishing and Promotion Services, 1978.

ethnic or cultural groups, this promise recognizes the desire to preserve and maintain the precious heritage which identifies the group as a group and the past experience which indicates that successful integration takes place from a position of strength. The promise of America, on the other hand, requires the newcomers to exercise the rights and duties of citizens to build community and nation.

22. This task should become a concern also of the many immigrants who dream of returning to their countries of origin but, in fact, are daily becoming more deeply rooted in their new environment, especially when their children are educated here. The longing to return, as the historical experience of many groups shows, can distract from an immediate, active participation in the life of society and Church. At the same time, those immigrant workers who regularly come to perform services for a time should be extended every protection and, in turn, they should abide by the laws of this country.

23. In this reciprocal relationship, an orderly society can prosper. The transition from homeland to a new life in America is for many refugees a period of tremendous instability. In the absence of strong community, women, children, and the elderly, who depend on community for support and care, are particularly at risk. The plight of the undocumented assumes a particular urgency. It is against the common good and unacceptable to have a double society, one visible with rights and one invisible without rights—a voiceless underground of undocumented persons. For political and economic reasons, these persons have settled into the country and are now part of its life. While the government has a right to safeguard the common good by controlling immigration, an effort should be pursued to regularize as many undocumented immigrants as possible. Other displaced persons avail themselves of the recognized right to seek asylum and end up in detention, a policy in need of revision.

24. In compassion and fairness, the Church reaches out to these multiple needs with its ministry of service and advocacy. A leaven in society, it promotes the rights of immigrants, migrants, and refugees and protects them before local, state, and federal institutions. As the Church calls us to action in the process of incorporation so that it becomes a home for every person and culture, so it places itself at the service of all newcomers without distinctions and conditions. Dioceses in particular are encouraged to provide the proper social services for new immigrants, refugees, and all uprooted people. As the bishops of Texas have observed:

> The response of the Church must be to offer these people safety, encouragement, food, clothing, health care, and the opportunity to practice their Faith. Our concern is not to support any particular effort that assists immigrants or refugees, but to help people in need in the tradition of the Church's ministry. As Church, we accept these people regardless of the economic or political causes that generated their journey. We ourselves shall not sit in judgment on the conflict

and tensions that may have initiated the process. We minister to their physical and spiritual needs without regard to their country of origin or their political beliefs. We do know that we, ourselves, will be judged on the basis of our response to the stranger, to the hungry, to these our brothers and sisters who find themselves in a foreign land.[7]

25. At the same time, our vision of the future includes a broader understanding of the root causes of migrations in contemporary society and a clearer acceptance of international responsibility. In the interrelated and interdependent community of nations, our policy decisions concerning foreign relations, trade, and economic and social development bear directly on the movements of peoples. These decisions should be directed in such a way as to facilitate the right of people to remain in their homelands where they may find a decent standard of living and where their basic needs are met.

26. The advocacy, however, of the right to stay in one's country should not be used as an excuse to deny the right to migrate. Nor should it impede our tradition of generosity in welcoming people, especially those escaping religious, political, and cultural or racial oppression. Current legislation must, therefore, reflect our best traditions which the Statue of Liberty continues to symbolize: the ongoing American democratic experiment, our past achievements, and our current welcome to newcomers.

6. Invitation to Commitment

27. We invite all people of good will to open their hearts to welcome and love the migrant and refugee. "For the Lord, your God . . . executes justice for the orphan and the widow, and befrieds the alien, feeding and clothing him. So, you, too, must befriend the alien, for you were once aliens yourselves . . ." (Dt 10:17-19).

28. We have before us the example of many men and women in this special ministry, beginning with St. John Neumann and St. Frances Cabrini, who walked together with the newcomers as fellow pilgrims on the journey to the Father. The Lord himself gave us the best motivation and example by identifying with the immigrant and the refugee when he said, "I was a stranger and you welcomed me" (Mt 25:35).

29. The commitment to welcome is a call to dispel attitudes, stereotypes, and prejudices which are harmful to others and which make us inhospitable. It asks us to show the universality of God's love by imitating him: "Accept one another, then, as Christ accepted you, for the glory of God" (Rom 15:7). Hospitality educates, forms, and enlightens us in the mission of the pilgrim Church of God on earth and on

---

[7] A statement from the Catholic bishops of Texas. *The Pastoral Care of Hispanic Immigrants in Texas*, October 1985.

our journey, "the sublime migration towards the total Communion of the Kingdom of God, where everyone and everything is restored in Christ."[8]

Pastoral Suggestions and Resources

30. To help welcome immigrants and refugees, we offer suggestions to encourage the development and growth of this commitment through creative and flexible initiatives according to the reality of the local church.

1. The Parish

31. Newcomers experience the Church first in their neighborhoods and parishes. Pastors and parish teams, therefore, should acquire an evangelical openness and strive to learn the language and cultural background of their new people, when different from their own, and the rich teaching of the Church on the pastoral care of immigrants and refugees. Communication will be enhanced and the process of building community can start. The many facets and moments of this process require an active pastoral outreach. Some suggestions are offered around which parish programs can be planned, discussion groups formed, and new steps taken on the part of newcomers and the receiving community.

A. Works of Evangelization

1. Catechesis for adults, youth, and children in an approach which is multicultural in its content and context of teaching.

2. Bible study groups where the meaning of migration and exile in the history of salvation is highlighted for the understanding of today's migrations.

3. Mobile leadership teams to visit, seek, and catechize all members of the faith community who are alienated or isolated from the Church by reason of language, culture, or mobility.

4. Emphasize family unity as the foundation of Christian community and have parishioners sponsor refugees and help immigrants to have their families with them, as it is their natural right.

5. Encourage the immigrant and refugee in Catholicism with knowledge of his or her cultural background.

---

[8]*Pastoral Constitution on the Church in the Modern World (Gaudium et Spes)*, no. 22.

B. Worship

1. Seek understanding of the immigrants' faith practices, their devotions, and popular piety.

2. Integrate the languages of the parishioners into prayers and hymns for special liturgies.

3. Provide bilingual liturgical and catechetical materials for the different language and culture groups.

4. Assist in the development of the newcomers' liturgical and devotional life, with special sensitivity to new Catholics from non-European cultures.

C. Education

1. Organize programs for immigrant parents as primary educators in the faith.

2. Provide family orientation programs for newcomers and special counselors in the parochial schools when needed.

3. Host a forum to discuss the Church's concern for people on the move and have the parish team familiarize itself with the main teaching documents of the Church in this area of pastoral concern.

4. Promote the development of cultural identity through special programs on the background of newcomers in the parochial school.

5. Orient the immigrants to the expectations of the Church.

6. Provide scholarships for poor immigrant children.

D. Youth

1. Offer programs for youth that take into account their special needs, caught as they often are between the traditions and culture of their immigrant parents and their American peer group.

2. Encourage youth participation in parochial pastoral councils and parochial associations.

3. Organize programs for youth to share in the social, recreational, educational, cultural, and religious reality of the parish.

4. Ask the youth to be a bridge between cultures for their parents and the faith community.

5. Invite parents to share their concerns for their children and provide assistance to resolve these concerns.

E. Lay Leadership

1. Appoint an immigrant or refugee representative to the parish council.

2. Encourage the development and training of lay leadership in the newcomer communities.

3. Involve the English-speaking laity in ministry to newcomers.

F. Building Community

1. Seek a vision of community and Church that all can share and have all cultural communities in the parish and in the diocese participate in shaping this vision.

2. Make parish facilities available for events of the immigrant communities at a time suitable for them.

3. Invite the newcomer to dramatize in song, dance, or narrative the moral and ethical teachings of his or her culture to make it known in the local church.

2. *The Diocese*

32. "The pastoral care of immigrants . . . is the task of the whole local church." These words of John Paul II sum up the challenge confronting every diocese when refugees, immigrants, and different cultural groups become part of its life. It is particularly in the local diocese that the unity and diversity of the Church are witnessed in the variety of people and institutions that make it "sign and instrument of communion with God and unity among men" (Vatican II, *Dogmatic Constitution on the Church* [*Lumen Gentium*], no. 1). The areas of concern that follow suggest opportunities for diocesan action.

A. Pastoral Plan for Newcomers

1. Be aware of the presence of various ethnic and cultural groups within the diocese.

2. Appoint specific individuals to care for the specific needs of these groups.

3. Sensitize the entire diocese to the richness of the cultural values present in the diocese.

4. Provide funds to support special projects to meet the needs of the various ethnic groups: refugee resettlement, family reunification services for refugees and immigrants, legal services for those in need of assistance with immigration laws, assistance on naturalization.

B. Pastoral Offices and Services for Newcomers

1. Provide diocesan coordination of pastoral services for ethnic and cultural groups through one rather than many offices as pastoral concerns indicate (e.g., a secretariat, office, or episcopal vicar).

2. Publicize Catholic pastoral and social services in the immigrant communities.

3. Develop diocesan, interdocesan, and regional pastoral centers for leadership formation to form, evangelize, and develop faith and culture.

4. Once a year, diocesan offices and agencies can review their outreach to newcomers in the context of the total pastoral action of the diocese.

C. Training for Priests, Brothers, Seminarians, Religious Women, Lay Catechists, and Permanent Deacons

1. Develop programs to sensitize and conscientize diocesan personnel which reflect the concern of the Church for newcomers.

2. Integrate into ongoing programs curriculum materials, church documents, and factual information relating to language and culture groups, especially in seminaries.

3. Welcome and integrate into the local presbytery the priests from other local churches serving their cultural group.

D. Communications

1. Develop a plan for the utilization of media on behalf of the newcomers and support the various language programs.

2. Enable the newcomers to have access to the diocesan media and articulate their aspirations and contributions.

3. Ask all who serve as communicators to use their skills to share the message of the Gospel with different language and culture groups to help overcome their isolation and become community.

3. National Migration Week

33. Since 1980, the NCCB Committee on Migration and Tourism has coordinated National Migration Week (NMW). The observance occurs immediately following the Feast of the Epiphany, with the general scriptural theme, "I was a stranger and you welcomed me" (Mt 25:35). Each year a more specific focus is given to NMW by drawing upon the annual statement the Holy Father issues on various aspects of pastoral care of immigrants and refugees. National Migration Week provides a teaching instrument to create awareness of the rich mosaic of peoples that is the Church in the United States, to counter prejudice and discrimination, and to encourage practical services. It is a week of prayer, reflection, and action reflecting the social teachings of the Church. The endorsement of the local ordinary is indispensable to the success of NMW on the diocesan and parish levels. So, too, is the wholehearted support of pastors, parish councils, school administrators, CCD directors, and all parishioners.

4. *Resources*

34. The historical concern of the Church for all immigrants and refugees is documented in the variety and depth of its teaching statements on this area of pastoral care. There are dozens of decrees, apostolic letters, statements, instructions, constitutions, and papal pronouncements from the Holy See dealing with the many facets of human mobility. The bishops of the United States have responded with individual and collective directives and statements to the pastoral expectations of many refugee and immigrant groups. Some basic documents are listed here.

A. Documents of the Holy See on Immigration

Pius XII. Apostolic Constitution *Exsul Familia*. A.A.S. XXXXIV (1952) English text: "The Church's Magna Charta for Migrants." Staten Island: Center of Migration Studies, 1962.

Paul VI. *New Norms for the Care of Migrants (Pastoralis Migratorum)* Apostolic Letter Motu Proprio (August 15, 1969). *Instruction on the Pastoral Care of People Who Migrate*. Congregation for Bishops, Vatican City, August 22, 1969. Washington, D.C.: USCC Office of Publishing and Promotion Services. No. 881.

Pontifical Commission for the Pastoral Care of Migrants and Itinerant Peoples. *The Church and People on the Move*. Letter to Episcopal Conferences (May 4, 1978). Washington, D.C.: USCC Office of Publishing and Promotion Services, 1978.

_____. *General Directory for the Pastoral Ministry in the Field of Tourism*. Vatican City, 1982.

_____. *Migrations*. Interdisciplinary Studies. Vatican City, 1985.

_____. *Chiesa e Mobilita Umana* ("Church and Human Mobility," Documents of the Holy See from 1883 to 1983). Rome, 1985, p. 1043.

B. Documents of the National Conference of Catholic Bishops on Immigration

National Conference of Catholic Bishops/United States Catholic Conference. *Pastoral Letters of the United States Catholic Bishops, 1792-1983*. Vol. I-IV. Washington, D.C.: USCC Office of Publishing and Promotion Services, 1984.

_____. *Pastoral Letters*, "World Refugee Year and Migration" (November 19, 1959), Vol. II, pp. 226-231.

_____. *Pastoral Letters*, "Resolution on the Pastoral Concern of the Church for People on the Move" (November 11, 1976), Vol. IV, pp. 167-169.

_____. *Pastoral Letters*, "Resolution on Haitian Refugees" (May 2, 1977, Vol. IV, pp. 198-199.

_____. *Pastoral Letters*, "Statement on Small-Boat Refugees in Southeast Asia" (February 16, 1978), Vol. IV, pp. 241-242.

_____. *Pastoral Letters*, "Cultural Pluralism in the United States" (April 14, 1980), Vol. IV, pp. 364-376.

_____. *Pastoral Letters*, "Resolution on Cuban and Haitian Refugees" (May 1980), Vol. IV, p. 378.

_____. *The Hispanic Presence: Challenge and Commitment* (December 12, 1983). Washington, D.C.: USCC Office of Publishing and Promotion Services, 1984. No. 891.

_____. *Resolution on Immigration Reform* (November 14, 1985). Washington, D.C.: USCC Office of Publishing and Promotion Services, 1986. No. 984.

Resolution on Lebanon

A Resolution Passed by the
National Conference of Catholic Bishops

November 12, 1986

1. After eleven years of war, the people of Lebanon are tired of death and destruction. They yearn for peace. The persistence of the conflict and its complexity have combined to produce in the wider international community a sense of frustration and a pattern of neglect. It is to resist this trend that we speak again about Lebanon.

2. The Lebanese are the first to acknowledge that they must be the architects of their destiny: they must find the solution to their conflict. But they cannot do it alone. Without the interest and assistance of the international community—moral, humanitarian, and diplomatic interest—the Lebanese cannot move beyond the present tragic impasse.

3. As Catholic bishops in the United States, we have a double interest in and relationship to the Lebanese question. First, we share bonds of faith with the Christian communities in Lebanon; these create specific responsibilities and obligations for us. Second, we are concerned for the welfare of Lebanon as a whole—all of its people and its future status as a free sovereign state in the community of nations. We know the policy of the United States can be decisive for Lebanon; this fact also creates obligations for us as bishops in this country.

4. To respond to both of these responsibilities, we speak again about Lebanon and our concern for it. The fate and future of Lebanon is at stake. In a particular way, the survival and welfare of the Christian community in Lebanon is at stake. The Christians of Lebanon hold a special significance for all the Christians of the Middle East. As bishops, we must stand in their defense and speak for their legitimate interests.

5. We intend by this resolution to call the attention of the international community to the fragile status of Lebanon and its need for help. We intend to speak to the Christians of Lebanon; we will be advocates of your rights to remain a free Christian community independent of Islamic law; the rights of freedom of worship, freedom to educate, and full participation of Christians in the life of Lebanese society must be protected.

6. We encourage the continuing dialogue and the peaceful coexistence of all Lebanese, and we reject violence against innocent people. We look for the day that people of all religious persuasions will again be able to live in harmony and freedom in accord with the great religious heritage of Lebanon.

7. Finally, we call again on the U.S. government to shape a policy which will assist all the Lebanese to guarantee the freedom, territorial integrity, and sovereignty of their nation.

Resolution on Lithuania

A Resolution Passed by the
National Conference of Catholic Bishops

November 12, 1986

1. In anticipation of the 600th anniversary of the conversion of the Lithuanian nation, to be marked in 1987, the National Conference of Catholic Bishops in the United States wishes to express solidarity with our brothers, the Lithuanian bishops, and the Lithuanian people.

2. We respectfully request all ordinaries to proclaim June 28, the day on which the anniversary will be celebrated with a papal Mass in Rome, a day of prayer for the persecuted Church of Lithuania, with an appropriate intention inserted in the Prayer of the Faithful that day.

3. We call upon Soviet authorities, in keeping with the Universal Declaration on Human Rights, the Helsinki Final Accords of 1975, and other international agreements, to honor the human rights of all Lithuanians. We call upon the Soviet authorities to honor the request of the bishops of Lithuania for restoration to religious use of the Cathedral of Vilnius and of the Church of St. Casimir in Vilnius, together with the Church of the Queen of Peace in Klaipeda.

4. We also call upon the Soviet government to honor the request of the bishops of Lithuania to allow publication of a new Lithuanian translation of the Scriptures.

To the Ends of the Earth
A Pastoral Statement on World Mission

A Pastoral Statement Issued by the
National Conference of Catholic Bishops

November 12, 1986

Introduction

1. *Jesus the Missionary*—Jesus was a missionary. As the Word of God, he is the light of all nations.[1] As the Word made flesh, he brought God's own life into our midst.[2] Before returning to the Father, he sent the Church to continue the mission given him by the Father and empowered her with his Spirit: "As the Father has sent me, so I send you" (Jn 20:21).[3]

2. *A Missionary Church*—The Church, therefore, is missionary by her very nature. She continues the mission of the Son and the mission of the Holy Spirit by proclaiming to the ends of the earth the salvation Christ offers those who believe in him.[4] We are faithful to the nature of the Church to the degree that we love and sincerely promote her missionary activity. As teachers and pastors, we are responsible for keeping alive a vibrant Catholic missionary spirit in the United States.

3. *Purpose of Statement*—Our purpose in writing this pastoral letter is twofold:

First, to provide a theological and pastoral instrument for mission animation in order to stimulate interest in and a personal sense of responsibility for the Church's mission to other peoples. Jesus' great commission to the first disciples is now addressed to us. Like them, we must go and make disciples of all the nations, baptize them in the name of the Father, and the Son, and the Holy Spirit, and teach them everything that Jesus has commanded.[5] This mission to the peoples of all nations must involve all of us personally in our parishes and at the diocesan and universal levels of the Church.

Second, to affirm missionaries in their efforts to proclaim the gospel and promote the reign of God. Jesus Christ, the Lord of all,

---

[1]Second Vatican Council. *Lumen Gentium* (*Dogmatic Constitution on the Church*), November 21, 1964, no. 1.

[2]See John 1:1-5, 10-12, 16.

[3]See also John 17:18.

[4]Vatican II, *Ad Gentes* (*Decree on the Church's Missionary Activity*), December 7, 1965, nos. 2-3; Mark 16:15-16.

[5]See Matthew 28:16-20.

is with them as they go forth in his name.[6] So must the entire Church in the United States be with them as they carry out our common mission under difficult and often dangerous circumstances. Our focus in this pastoral is the proclamation of the gospel to peoples outside the United States. While we are acutely conscious of our continuing need to evangelize in our own country, that challenge, as great as it is, must never cause us to forget our responsibility to share the good news of Jesus with the rest of the world.

4. *Documents on Mission*—Over the centuries, the Church has frequently reflected on her founding by Christ as a missionary community with a vision of God's reign that stretches beyond the horizon of history. Our own time has seen the promulgation of the Second Vatican Council's *Decree on the Church's Missionary Activity* (*Ad Gentes*) and Pope Paul VI's Apostolic Exhortation *On Evangelization in the Modern World* (*Evangelii Nuntiandi*). These important documents stress the essential missionary nature of the Church and outline a contemporary charter for her mission through sensitive adaptation to new conditions.

5. *World Mission*—We commemorate *Ad Gentes* and *Evangelii Nuntiandi* with this pastoral letter on the mission of the Church in the United States to other lands. We do so as members of the college of bishops, all of whom "are consecrated not just for one diocese alone, but for the salvation of the whole world."[7] Our concern must be for the whole Church, but especially for "those parts of the world where the Word of God has not yet been proclaimed."[8]

6. *Mission and "The Challenge of Peace"*—Concern for world mission springs from the same principles we set forth in our pastoral letters *The Challenge of Peace* and *Economic Justice for All: Catholic Social Teaching and the U.S. Economy*. These letters offer substantial help for understanding our Church's mission to other peoples and nations. As we said in *The Challenge of Peace*:

> The theological principle of unity has always affirmed a human interdependence; but today this bond is complemented by the growing political and economic interdependence of the world, manifested in a whole range of international issues.[9]

When the Church brings Christ's message to the ends of the earth, she helps foster this unity. As we stated:

---

[6]See Matthew 28:20.

[7]*Ad Gentes*, no. 38; see also *Lumen Gentium*, no. 23, and Vatican II, *Christus Dominus* (*Decree on the Pastoral Office of Bishops in the Church*), October 28, 1965, no. 6.

[8]*Christus Dominus*, no. 6.

[9]NCCB, *The Challenge of Peace: God's Promise and Our Response* (Washington, D.C.: USCC Office of Publishing and Promotion Services), no. 240.

The risen Lord's gift of peace is inextricably bound to the call to follow Jesus and to continue the proclamation of God's reign. Matthew's Gospel (Mt 28:16-20; cf. Lk 24:44-53) tells us that Jesus' last words to his disciples were a sending forth and a promise: "And know that I am with you always, until the end of the world!" In the continuing presence of Jesus, disciples of all ages find the courage to follow him. To follow Jesus Christ implies continual conversion in one's own life as one seeks to act in ways which are consonant with the justice, forgiveness and love of God's reign. Discipleship reaches out to the ends of the earth and calls for reconciliation among all peoples so that God's purpose, "to be carried out in the fullness of time: namely, to bring all things in the heavens and on earth into one under Christ's headship," (Eph 1:10) will be fulfilled.[10]

7. *Mission and "Economic Justice for All"* —Our pastoral *Economic Justice for All: Catholic Social Teaching and the U.S. Economy* shows how the Church's mission in an interdependent world has important implications for economic policy. Here we follow the traditional principles of Catholic teaching on interdependence as expressed in the writings of recent popes. These principles affirm the dignity of the human person, the unity of the human family, the right of all to share in the goods of the earth, the need to pursue the international common good, and the imperative of distributive justice in a world ever more sharply divided between rich and poor.[11]

8. *Unity and the Universal Church*—This pastoral letter presents the challenge to the Church in the United States with regard to world mission. We write conscious of our unity with John Paul II, our pope, and with the Church throughout the world.

I. The New Missionary Context

9. *New Context*—In their publications and personal communications, missionaries emphasize how greatly the missionary context has changed since the Second World War, and even since the promulgation of *Ad Gentes* and *Evangelii Nuntiandi*.[12] It is important that we understand this change.

---

[10]Ibid., no. 54.

[11]See Pope John XXIII, *Mater et Magistra* (*On Christianity and Social Progress*), May 15, 1961 and *Pacem in Terris* (*On Establishing Universal Peace in Truth, Justice, Charity and Liberty*), April 11, 1963; Pope Paul VI, *Populorum Progressio* (*On the Development of Peoples*), March 26, 1967 and *Octogesima Adveniens* (*On the Occasion of the Eightieth Anniversary of the Encyclical Rerum Novarum*), May 14, 1971; and Pope John Paul II, *Laborem Exercens* (*On Human Work*), September 14, 1981.

[12]See *Mission in Dialogue, the Sedos Research Seminar on the Future of Mission*, March 8-19, 1981, Rome, Italy. Edited by Mary Motte, FMM, and Joseph R. Lang, MM (Maryknoll, N.Y.: Orbis Books, 1982).

Historical Background

10. *Missionary Roots of U.S. Church*—From the earliest days, European missionaries served immigrants to the New World and the native people they found on these shores. Many journeyed from Spain, France, England, and other countries to give heroic witness to the gospel in colonial America. Missionaries such as Isaac Jogues and Junipero Serra made major contributions to shaping our identity as Catholics with a mission.

11. *Missionaries and Immigrants*—Missionaries accompanied the millions of poor and destitute people who vitalized our growing nation in the 19th and early 20th centuries. At this time, too, heroic witness was not uncommon. Two of these missionaries, Mother Frances Xavier Cabrini and Bishop John Neumann, are celebrated as saints.

12. *Missionaries in Our Turn*—In God's providence, our own people have accepted the challenge of sharing the gift of faith we have received. Especially in this century, but even in the last, missionaries were sent to announce the gospel to other nations and peoples. Religious congregations and missionary societies, some of them founded in our own country, played a prominent part in this work. The bishops of the United States underscored their commitment to world mission when they established Maryknoll as The Catholic Foreign Mission Society of America in 1911. Dioceses also sent priests, religious, and laity to mission lands. This proud tradition continues at the present time.

13. *Pontifical Mission Aid Societies*—People young and old encouraged these missionaries with prayers and sacrifices, assisted them financially, and welcomed them on visits home. The Society for the Propagation of the Faith and The Association of the Holy Childhood—the Pontifical Mission Aid Societies—have been principally responsible for fostering this popular support, performing the central role in universal missionary cooperation that the Second Vatican Council has affirmed:

> It is right that these works [i.e., the Pontifical Mission Aid Societies] be given first place, because they are a means by which Catholics are imbued from infancy with a truly universal and missionary outlook and also as a means for instigating an effective collecting of funds for all the missions, each according to its needs.[13]

The Church has commissioned these organizations to awaken and deepen the missionary conscience of the People of God; to inform them about the needs of universal mission; and to encourage local

---

[13] *Ad Gentes*, no. 38. See Canon 791, *Code of Canon Law* (Washington, D.C.: Canon Law Society of America, 1983).

churches to pray for and support one another with personnel and material aid.

Contemporary Developments

14. *A New Vitality*—A significant contemporary development in world mission is the shifting of the Church's center of gravity from the West, from Europe and North America, toward the East and South. In Latin America, Africa, and Asia the Church is experiencing either profound revitalization or enormous growth. Indeed, the Christian energy of these local churches has begun to overflow into missionary service of the gospel.[14]

15. *Mission-Sending, Mission-Receiving*—The lands to which missionaries went used to be called "the missions." These countries were seen as mission-receiving. Other countries were thought of as mission-sending; they did not see themselves in need of receiving missionaries. A deeper understanding of the theology of mission leads us to recognize that these distinctions no longer apply. Every local church is both mission-sending and mission-receiving.

A New Self-Understanding

16. *Church Is Mission*—These changes have brought about a new self-understanding, both for the former "mission countries" which have taken the missionary mandate of the Church as their own, and for those which have long ceased to think of themselves as "mission countries." Together we are coming to see that any local church has no choice but to reach out to others with the gospel of Christ's love for all peoples. To say "Church" is to say "mission."

17. *Basic Task of Mission*—Missionaries have always seen their principal tasks as preaching the gospel to those who have not heard it, baptizing them with the waters of salvation, caring for their physical well-being, and forming Christian communities. These missionaries were also sent to lend pastoral assistance to other established churches in need. The magnificent work of these men and women has been an invaluable service to the Church, and today's missionaries build on their achievements.

18. *Influence of Colonial Attitudes*—At times in the past, missionaries brought not only the strengths but also some of the weaknesses of Western civilization. It often happened that they labored in lands where their own country had political and economic interests. In areas where their home country was the colonial power, those to whom

---

[14]See Omer Degrijse, CICM, *Going Forth: Missionary Consciousness in Third World Catholic Churches* (Maryknoll, N.Y.: Orbis Books, 1984).

they were sent sometimes found it difficult to distinguish the Church's missionary effort from the colonizing effort, which proved critical when the colonial empires were dismantled after World War II.

19. *Solidarity with Local Church*—Today missionaries work primarily in established local churches, to whose life and vitality they want to contribute. The need to cooperate with diocesan bishops and authorized pastoral workers requires adaptation to local institutions and culture. When missionaries come from a country like the United States, which has great political and economic interests throughout the world, their participation in the life of the local church can place them in conflict with the policies of their own government or, indeed, of their host government. Nevertheless, they must be in union with the diocesan bishop and the local church which they have been sent to serve.[15]

20. *Overcoming Colonial Attitudes*—In the postcolonial era, missionaries inevitably confront the effects of long Western domination in the Third World. As they work with others to promote the reign of God, they face the challenge of clearly distinguishing their Christian mission from colonial and neocolonial practices. Missionaries sometimes work in countries where freedom of conscience, freedom of religion, and other basic human rights are either overtly or subtly restricted. These, especially, need to know that we are one with them and understand the very difficult situations in which they labor.

21. *Heroic Witness*—Mission work still calls for heroic witness to the faith. We are proud of Jean Donovan, a lay woman; Ita Ford and Maura Clarke, Maryknoll sisters; Dorothy Kazel, an Ursuline sister; James Miller, a De La Salle Christian Brother; William Woods, a Maryknoll priest; Stanley Rother, an Oklahoma diocesan priest; and many others who have died violent deaths serving their brothers and sisters in Christ. Nor can we forget missionaries like Bishops Francis X. Ford and James E. Walsh, who have suffered imprisonment or exile because of their Christian witness. May their courageous response to the gospel inspire us to expand our missionary commitment to all peoples.

II. Today's Missionary Task

22. *Mission and the Trinity*—The missionary task of the Church is rooted theologically in the Blessed Trinity. The very origin of the Church is from the missions of the Son and the Holy Spirit as decreed by the Father, "the fountain of love," who desires the salvation of the whole

---

[15]See Pope Paul VI, *Evangelii Nuntiandi (On Evangelization in the Modern World)*, December 8, 1975, no 60. "If each individual evangelizes in the name of the Church, who herself does so by virtue of a mandate from the Lord, no evangelizer is the absolute master of his evangelizing action, with a discretionary power to carry it out in accordance with the individualistic criteria and perspectives; he acts in communion with the Church and her pastors."

human race.[16] To continue his mission in time, Christ gave the missionary mandate to his followers to "make disciples of all the nations" (Mt 28:19), and he sent the Holy Spirit, the promised one of the Father,[17] who impels the Church to share the gospel with the world. Like all good news, the gospel of salvation is irrepressible. The spontaneous need to communicate it comes from the quickening presence of the Holy Spirit in every aspect of church life. The Holy Spirit is the spirit of universal mission[18] and reconciliation.[19] The same Spirit who accompanies and quickens the missionary activity of the Church likewise precedes that activity, offering those beyond the Church's visible limits a participation in the paschal mystery of Christ.[20]

23. *Urgency of Mission*—We must pray for and earnestly desire a sense of urgency regarding our missionary task. This sense of urgency flows from the demands of being faithful disciples of Jesus, from our responsibility to share his gospel and from a concern that all our brothers and sisters participate as fully as possible in his life and saving mystery. We see this urgency in the life of Jesus, God's beloved Son, who was sent to proclaim the good news of the kingdom: "This is the time of fulfillment. The reign of God is at hand! Reform your lives and believe in the gospel!" (Mk 1:15).

24. *Coming of the Kingdom*—When the people of Capernaum tried to restrict Jesus' mission to themselves, he answered, "To other towns I must announce the good news of the reign of God, because that is why I was sent" (Lk 4:43). In his very person, in all that he said and did, and especially in his death and resurrection, that kingdom was already breaking into the world. It will be perfectly established, however, only in the fullness of time.

25. *Foundation of the Church*—Jesus called a small number of men and women to be his disciples, to share intimately in his life and his vision of God's reign, and to spread his word to other times and places.[21] He selected twelve of them to be his apostles,[22] promised them the Holy Spirit as an abiding presence, and commissioned them to be his "witnesses in Jerusalem, throughout Judea and Samaria, yes, even to the ends of the earth" (Acts 1:8). These apostles were established as the foundation of the Church,[23] which was divinely constituted as

---

[16]See *Evangelii Nuntiandi*, nos. 13-15; *Ad Gentes*, nos. 2-3.

[17]See Luke 24:49; John 14:26.

[18]See Acts 2:1-11.

[19]See John 20:19-23.

[20]*Ad Gentes*, no. 4; *Lumen Gentium*, no. 16; Vatican II, *Gaudium et Spes* (*Pastoral Constitution on the Church in the Modern World*), December 7, 1965, no. 22.

[21]See Mark 1:16-20.

[22]See Luke 6:12-16.

[23]See Ephesians 2:20.

the effective sign, the herald, the seed, and the promoter of the kingdom, indeed its initial budding forth on earth.[24]

26. *Church Continues Jesus' Mission*—Nearly twenty centuries of Christian history have elapsed, and Jesus' prayer: "Your kingdom come!" (Mt 6:9-13; Lk 11:2-4) is still our prayer. The mission he gave his apostles and disciples continues to be the Church's mission. As we read in the preface to the decree *Ad Gentes*: "Having been divinely sent to the nations that she might be 'the universal sacrament of salvation' (*Lumen Gentium*) the Church, in obedience to the command of her Founder (Mk 16:15), strives to preach the Gospel to all men."[25]

Like the men and women who first responded to Jesus' invitation, those who respond in our time develop a personal relationship with Christ that sustains them in their mission.

27. *Holiest Duty of the Church*—St. Paul expressed the urgency of mission when he wrote to the Corinthians: "Preaching the gospel is not the subject of a boast; I am under compulsion and have no choice. I am ruined if I do not preach it!" (1 Cor 9:16). And preach the gospel he did, not only in neighboring towns and cities, but to every nation he was able to reach. Like St. Paul, we are called to share the gospel by the witness of our lives and the explicit proclamation of salvation in Jesus Christ.[26] The Council calls this "the greatest and holiest duty of the Church."[27]

28. *Needs of Others*—The human and spiritual needs of peoples beyond our borders call us to the urgency of mission. Mission always expresses a concern for the life of others. Moved by the Spirit, we ardently desire that our brothers and sisters have life, and in abundance,[28] and that they be saved by faith in Christ through the grace of God. This is our prayer in the name of Jesus Christ our Lord.

29. *Ecumenical Cooperation*—We rejoice that Christians of other churches share and participate in the mission of our Lord. John Paul II has urged that those who share Christ's mission "must show forth his unifying love in action."[29] Today the dangers from proselytizing are real. Nevertheless, where there can be mutual respect among the different religious traditions, there are increasing opportunities in mission work for collaboration in prayer, good works, the use of media, community service, and social action. Such collaboration is itself a witness to the reconciling spirit of God.

---

[24]*Lumen Gentium*, no. 5; See *Instruction on Christian Freedom and Liberation*, Congregation for the Doctrine of the Faith, March 22, 1986 (USCC: Washington, D.C.), no. 58.

[25]*Ad Gentes*, no. 1.

[26]*Evangelii Nuntiandi*, nos. 40-48.

[27]*Ad Gentes*, no. 29.

[28]See John 10:10

[29]John Paul II, Homily, Ecumenical Service, Synod of Bishops, December 1985; *Origins*, vol. 15, no. 27, p. 454.

Hungry for the Word

30. *Spiritual and Material Poverty*—Often those who have not heard the gospel are doubly poor, doubly hungry, doubly oppressed. They are materially poor, lacking possessions; they are spiritually poor, lacking that hope which springs from the knowledge and love of Christ. Their hunger is not only for bread and rice, but also for the Word that gives meaning to their existence. They are oppressed not only by social injustice but also by the sin at its root.

31. *Mission to the Whole Person*—By the same token, people are saved not only as individuals but also as members of sociocultural groups. They must experience the redemption not only of their souls but also of their whole bodily existence, not only in a world to come but also beginning here on earth. They must participate in the mystery of Christ not passively or minimally but rather as fully as possible, with intelligence, freedom, and a lively sense of responsibility. Those who rejoice in the life poured into their hearts by the Spirit of Christ must be not only receivers of the Word but also missionaries to others.

32. *Planting in Holy Ground*—Mission is characterized not by power and the need to dominate, but by a deep concern for the salvation of others and a profound respect for the ways they have already searched for and experienced God. The ground in which we are called to plant the gospel is holy ground, for before our arrival God has already visited the people he knows and loves.[30] In this ground, sown with the seeds of God's word, a local church is born, a church that expresses its vitality in the language of its own culture, a church also called to be missionary beyond its own borders.

Mutuality in Mission

33. *United with Human Family*—As soon as a local church is established, Christ calls it to share the gospel it has received. Such sharing is essential for the Church's vitality, since those who give life to others find it for themselves. So it was with Jesus throughout his life, and especially in his death and resurrection. Sharing is essential to every level of church life; it applies to dioceses and parishes as well as families and individuals. The local church cannot live in isolation, unconcerned for other peoples. As human beings created by the Father of all, as disciples of the risen Jesus who is Lord of all, and as Christians who have received the Holy Spirit, we are united with the entire human family. This union shapes our attitudes and moves us to respect other peoples and their cultures, to make their concerns our

---

[30]See Acts 7:33; 10:1-11:18.

own, and to share with them the gospel riches we have received.[31]

34. *Missionary Institutes in Other Lands*—The Church has now been planted on all the continents and in most nations. It has grown and matured in countries once thought of as mission territories. Local churches in these countries recognize the importance of sharing the unique insights which accompanied the gospel's flowering in their cultures. Several, like Nigeria, South Korea, Mexico, Colombia, and the Philippines, have established their own foreign mission societies. Moreover, missionary institutes, orders, and congregations are drawing members from former mission countries and sending them to other peoples.

35. *Sharing the Gospel*—Each new incarnation of the gospel must be shared, even if the growth of the local church is as yet modest. As we have seen, mission is mutual, not one-directional. Christian peoples and local churches will share the gospel with one another in various ways, from each according to its special gifts and abilities, to each according to its needs.[32]

36. *Openness to Others*—Even as we go out to other nations to announce the good news, we must remain open to the voice of the gospel speaking to us in a myriad of cultural and social expressions. We must be willing to welcome new immigrants into our parishes, to respect the cultural treasures of these newcomers and allow ourselves to be enriched and strengthened by their witness to the faith. In this, we come to see more clearly how the local church expresses the life of the universal Church. As Pope John Paul II said in a message to the curial cardinals, "The Church is a communion of churches, and indirectly a communion of nations, languages, and cultures. Each of these brings its gifts to the whole."[33] Mission involves mutual ministry and dialogue among the local churches of the world.

37. *Sensitivity in Mission*—Each local church must carry out its mission to other nations and cultures with great sensitivity. Peoples inevitably communicate out of their historical experience. Nevertheless, we must constantly strive to transcend culturally based limitations in our manifestation of the Church's life. If we fail to link Christian values with what is already good in a culture, we merely export an expression of faith foreign to that culture, one the people cannot fully accept. It expresses someone else's faith experience, not their own.[34] Mission must therefore humbly imitate the example of Jesus, who did not cling to his divine privileges but became like us in all things save sin.[35]

---

[31] *Evangelii Nuntiandi,* nos. 19, 30-31.

[32] *Ad Gentes,* no. 38; Acts 2:42-47; 4:32-35.

[33] Pope John Paul II, "Message to the Curial Cardinals," Christmas 1984.

[34] See Pope John Paul II, "Address to the Amerindians of Canada at the Shrine of St. Anne de Beaupre," September 10, 1984.

[35] See Philippians 2:6-11; Hebrews 4:14-15.

38. *Common Elements*—There are, it is true, expressions of faith and morals in the Scriptures that are meaningful in every cultural milieu. The Lord's Prayer, the beatitudes, the commandments, the story of Jesus, and the sacraments all tend to bond human beings together in one faith and one Church.[36] Cultural differences remain significantly important, however.

39. *Mission Is Not Coercive*—Jesus' call to discipleship was a free invitation. In the same way, the Church does not coerce others to accept the gospel and join her ranks. Mission presupposes love for those being evangelized and, as Paul VI said, "the first sign of this love is respect for the religious and spiritual situation of those being evangelized."[37] The Church extends an invitation, realizing that others may not respond. If we extend our invitation well, witnessing in the love of God and the image of Christ, and with the fire of the Holy Spirit, we have fulfilled Christ's mandate.[38] Acceptance of the gospel and conversion to Christ is the working of God's grace, a mystery beyond comprehension which we accept in faith.[39]

Mission and Dialogue

40. *Role of Dialogue*—The way we extend Christ's free invitation to others differs according to local circumstances.[40] The context of mission in Japan or India, for example, is vastly different from that in Bolivia or the Philippines. The recent document on dialogue and mission of the Vatican Secretariat for Non-Christians emphasizes the role of dialogue with adherents of other great religions.[41] While dialogue takes many forms,

> before all else, dialogue is a manner of acting, an attitude and a spirit which guides one's conduct. It implies concern, respect, and hospitality toward the other. It leaves room for the other person's identity, his modes of expression, and his values. Dialogue is thus the norm and necessary manner of every form of Christian mission, as well as of every aspect of it, whether one speaks of simple presence and witness, service, or direct proclamation. Any sense of mission not permeated by such a dialogical spirit would go against the demands of true humanity and against the teachings of the gospel.[42]

---

[36] *Evangelii Nuntiandi*, nos. 20, 65.

[37] Ibid., no. 79.

[38] See Matthew 28:16-20.

[39] See Matthew 10:16-42; 12:16-24; John 6:61-70.

[40] *Ad Gentes*, no. 6.

[41] Secretariat for Non-Christians. "The Attitude of the Church towards the Followers of Other Religions, Reflections and Orientations on Dialogue and Mission," Pentecost, 1984. See also Paul VI, *Ecclesiam Suam* (*Paths of the Church*), August 6, 1964.

[42] Ibid., n. 29.

41. *Other Great Religions*—Dialogue goes beyond collaboration and discussion with members of other great religions. It includes the sharing of faith, religious experiences, prayer, contemplation. In such sharing, all parties are mutually enriched. "The sometimes profound differences beween the faiths do not prevent this dialogue. Those differences, rather, must be referred back in humility and confidence to God who 'is greater than our hearts' (1 Jn 3:20)."[43]

42. *Conversion the Goal of Mission*—Though dialogue is a vital characteristic of mission, it is not the goal of missionary proclamation. The Secretariat for Non-Christians goes on to say: "According to the Second Vatican Council, missionary proclamation has conversion as its goal: 'that non-Christians be freely converted to the Lord under the action of the Holy Spirit who opens their hearts so that they may adhere to him' (AG 13)."[44]

43. *Church Offers the Fullness of Revealed Truth*—Pope John Paul II emphasized this same point in his homily in Calcutta:

> While esteeming the value of these (non-Christian) religions, and seeing in them at times the action of the Holy Spirit who is like the wind which "blows where it will" (Jn 3:8), the Church remains convinced of the need for her to fulfill her task of offering to the world the fullness of revealed truth, the truth of the redemption in Jesus Christ.[45]

The fact that the Holy Father spoke these important words in India, a predominantly non-Christian country, makes them especially significant.

44. *True Inculturation*—In this work of dialogue and evangelization, the Church must be a leaven for all cultures, at home in each culture. True inculturation occurs when the gospel penetrates the heart of cultural experience and shows how Christ gives new meaning to authentic human values. However, the Church must never allow herself to be absorbed by any culture,[46] since not all cultural expressions are in conformity with the gospel. The Church retains the indispensable duty of testing and evaluating cultural expressions in the light of her understanding of revealed truth. Cultures, like individual human beings and societies, need to be purified by the blood of Christ.

---

[43]Ibid., n. 35.

[44]Ibid., n. 37.

[45]Pope John Paul II, "Homily," February 5, 1986.

[46]See *Final Report*, the Extraordinary Synod of 1985, II, D.4.; John Paul II, *Catechesi Tradendae* (*On Catechesis in Our Time*), October 16, 1979, no. 53 and *Familiaris Consortio* (*On the Family*), December 15, 1981, nos. 10-16.

A Holistic Approach

45. *Response to Suffering*—Solidarity with others and faithfulness to the gospel demand that we respond to people's genuine needs and hungers, even those of which they may be unaware. As noted above, human hunger takes two forms. While spiritual hungers reflect our highest aspirations, physical hungers can be so great as to blunt or even block them. Some social hungers may indicate the presence of oppression, preventing people from developing in an atmosphere of peace and justice. In a human being, in a society, in the world, when one member suffers all suffer.

46. *Mission of Jesus Was Liberation*—A holistic approach to mission recognizes that humanity's hungers are so interwoven that the spirit cannot be satisfied without attending to the body.[47] As we read in a recent instruction from the Holy See:

> Liberation is first and foremost from the radical slavery of sin. Its end and its goal is the freedom of the children of God, which is the gift of grace. As a logical consequence, it calls for freedom from many different kinds of slavery in the cultural, economic, social, and political spheres, all of which derive ultimately from sin and so often prevent people from living in a manner befitting their dignity.[48]

The Church's seriousness about responding to all genuine human needs is further stressed in a subsequent document:

> The Church is firmly determined to respond to the anxiety of contemporary man as he endures oppression and yearns for freedom. The political and economic running of society is not a direct part of her mission. But the Lord Jesus has entrusted to her the word of truth which is capable of enlightening consciences. Divine love, which is her life, impels her to a true solidarity with everyone who suffers.[49]

47. *Jesus' Mission Is Now Ours*—Clearly, then, neither the Church as a whole nor the Church in the United States can remain indifferent to the suffering, inequities, and oppression that afflict so much of the world's population. These evils openly contradict Christ's gospel. Jesus came to bring good news to the poor, proclaim liberty to captives,

---

[47] *Evangelii Nuntiandi*, no. 33.

[48] *Instruction on Certain Aspects of the "Theology of Liberation,"* Sacred Congregation for the Doctrine of the Faith, 1984. (Washington, D.C.: USCC Office of Publishing and Promotion Services), Introduction.

[49] *Instruction on Christian Freedom and Liberation*, Congregation for the Doctrine of the Faith, March 22, 1986 (Washington, D.C.: USCC Office of Publishing and Promotion Services), no. 61.

give sight to the blind, and release prisoners.[50] His mission became that of the Church, and it is now ours.[51]

48. *Liberation Requires Action*—Had Jesus merely said that his mission was to set people free from sin and all forms of oppression,[52] his words would have fallen on deaf ears. He had to work at this task of liberation. He not only talked about freeing the poor and oppressed but, undeterred by criticism, actually welcomed the poor and sinners to share at his table. Like Jesus, we must be able to accompany others in their suffering and be willing to suffer with them.

49. *Special Option for the Poor*—In its openness to all, the Church's mission makes a special option for the poor and powerless. "The special option for the poor, far from being a sign of particularism or sectarianism, manifests the universality of the Church's being and mission."[53] This special option is deeply rooted in the mission of Jesus, who rejected no one but was especially sensitive to those who needed him most. The poor, destitute, and powerless of the world help us see and evaluate the evils of our society and the evils that one society or nation inflicts on another. Accompanying the poor assures us of the relevance of our message of salvation.

50. *Evangelizing the Powerful*—The option for the poor also implies the need to evangelize the powerful and influential. If the gospel call to conversion can reach their hearts, they will help construct a new society. In our option for the poor, we join our aspirations and commitment to those of our brother bishops of Latin America, Africa, Asia, and Oceania as expressed in their pastoral statements.[54]

III. A Mission Spirituality

51. *Spirituality Is Central*—Central to the Church's missionary task is a mission spirituality. This is true for those personally engaged in bringing the gospel to other nations as well as those at home who pray, work, and sacrifice for the world mission of the Church. Mission spirituality begins with the gospel, a commitment to following Christ, and openness to the Holy Spirit. We need to hear the gospel and be

---

[50]See Luke 4:18.

[51]"The evil inequities and oppression of every kind which afflict millions of men and women today openly contradict Christ's gospel and cannot leave the conscience of any Christian indifferent." *Instruction on Christian Freedom and Liberation*, no. 57.

[52]See Luke 4:16-19.

[53]*Instruction on Christian Freedom and Liberation*, no. 68.

[54]See, for example, Second General Conference of Latin American Bishops, "The Church in the Present-Day Transformation of Latin America in the Light of the Council" (Medellin, 1968); Third General Conference of Latin American Bishops, "Evangelization at Present and in the Future of Latin America" (Puebla, 1979); First Plenary Assembly of the Federation of Asian Bishops' Conferences, "Evangelization in Modern Day Asia," (Taipei, April 1974).

continually formed by it. When we listen to the Word, we experience Christ present to us, calling us to a new life and giving us the Spirit who transforms us into missionaries. In order to share the gospel with others, we must love it deeply and have a profound appreciation of its values. Equally important is a loving relationship with the person of Christ and his Church. Faithfulness to Christ in communion with the Church is the cornerstone of the entire missionary edifice.

52. *Baptism and Confirmation*—In baptism and confirmation, where human commitment and divine grace become one, we respond to Christ's invitation and are empowered to join in his mission. Through these sacraments, the Church, a missionary community, welcomes us and pledges her support. We need this support to take the risks required for our mission to the whole human family. Baptism expresses in word and symbol our readiness to die and be buried with Christ in the hope one day of rising with him.[55] Confirmation, in which all share in the spirit of Pentecost, expresses our eagerness to take part in the Church's mission to all nations.

53. *Multiplication of Loaves*—The connection between Christian discipleship and Christian mission is well expressed in the ancient tradition of the multiplication and sharing of loaves.[56] Although each Gospel presents the tradition in its own way, all of them emphasize the missionary implications of the passage. The disciples are overwhelmed by the demands of the mission and ask Jesus to send the people away to provide for their own needs. Jesus replies that the disciples themselves should give the crowd something to eat. He then takes bread, blesses, breaks, and gives it to the disciples to distribute. When they share the little they have, everyone is wonderfully nourished. Through these accounts, some of the most beautiful and moving in Scripture, the New Testament relates mission to the Christian experience of hospitality and Eucharist. Like the disciples in Mark's Gospel who gathered in small communities of fifty and a hundred, we must be willing to share Christ's nourishment with other parishes and dioceses.[57] We must also be willing to bring this nourishment to other lands and gather all nations, all peoples, at the table of the Lord.[58]

54. *Act of Sharing*—Hospitality and food sharing are important symbolic events in all cultures. Like the disciples, we must be prepared to share what we have and to accept what others offer us. In the simple act of sharing, we join others in their joys and suffering and accompany them on their life's journey.[59]

---

[55] See Romans 6:3-5.

[56] Mark 6:34-44; 8:1-10; Matthew 14:13-21; 15:32-39; Luke 9:10-17; John 6:1-15.

[57] See Mark 6:34-44.

[58] See Mark 8:1-9.

[59] *Gaudium et Spes*, no. 1.

55. *Mission and the Eucharist*—The Eucharist sustains and nourishes each Christian's commitment to the Church's mission. In the Eucharist, where Christ shares his very person with us, we learn to share the gospel, prayer, our resources, our very selves. We thus imitate the ideal of Christian sharing which Acts 2:42-47 attributes to the early Christian community in Jerusalem.[60] Maturity in that sharing fosters the impulse to reach out to the whole world with the good news of salvation.

56. *Cost of Discipleship*—The universal sharing inspired by the Eucharist is very demanding. This is why the New Testament authors emphasized it in their accounts of Jesus' Last Supper. Before the multiplication of loaves, the disciples protested that sharing with all would be costly. They thought in material terms. Financial sacrifice, however, is nothing compared with the real cost of discipleship with Jesus, which requires the gift of our lives. Sometimes this gift means the shedding of blood. For most people, however, it means daily giving, a sharing which requires the dying with Christ that we pledge in baptism.

57. *United with Christ and One Another*—To share in Christ's glory, each person must be willing to be baptized in Christ's passion and drink his cup of suffering.[61] That is Jesus' message to his disciples.[62] By this willingness to suffer with Christ and with one another in him, we commit ourselves to the new covenant, to new relationships which transcend every consideration of race, sex, family, nationality, economic or social standing.

58. *Eucharist Nourishes Mission Spirituality*—The Eucharist is the primary proclamation of the love Christ showed by his death and resurrection. It is the heart of the gospel. Like those who first ate and drank at the table of the Lord, we who gather today at that table have no choice but to proclaim his gospel to all.[63] The Eucharist nourishes our mission spirituality and strengthens our commitment to give of ourselves and our resources to the development of the diocesan and universal Church as a people aware of our responsibility for, and interdependence with, all peoples of the earth. Vatican Council II

---

[60]"They devoted themselves to the apostles' instruction and the communal life, to the breaking of bread, and the prayers. A reverent fear overtook them all, for many wonders and signs were performed by the apostles. Those who believed shared all things in common; they would sell their property and goods, dividing everything on the basis of each other's need. They went to the temple area together every day, while in their homes they broke bread. With exultant and sincere hearts they took their meals in common, praising God and winning the approval of all the people. Day by day the Lord added to their number those who were being saved" (Acts 2:42-47).

[61]See Romans 8:17.

[62]"Can you drink the cup I shall drink or be baptized in the same bath of pain as I?" (Mk 10:38).

[63]See Acts 10:34-43.

clearly equates the renewal of local churches with the degree of their gracious sharing and loving concern for those beyond their borders. This sharing and concern should not be limited to prayers and financial assistance, but should include sharing personnel as well.[64]

59. *Self-denial*—Spirituality is lived in a specific culture. The environment in which American Catholics are called to witness their faith is strongly marked by individualism, consumerism, and materialism. Thus our mission spirituality must embrace a developed asceticism, the virtue of self-denial that fosters life and authentic freedom. If we lack the spirit of mortification and sacrifice, we cannot hear Jesus' call to follow the narrow path. Our natural inclination toward avarice and greed will dominate and hold us in bondage. Jesus' call is clear: we are not only to pray and give alms, we are also to fast.[65]

60. *Prayer and Mission Spirituality*—Prayer is likewise a key element in mission spirituality. In the garden of Gethsemane, Jesus prayed that the Father take away the cup of suffering, but only if it were according to the Father's will. He also asked the disciples to pray that they might be spared the test. Without prayer, our commitments risk remaining mere words. In prayer, we join Mary in her Magnificat and show ourselves to be a people of hope, confident that God's promises will be fulfilled. With Mary and the apostles and disciples,[66] we pray to be empowered by the Holy Spirit as we pursue the Church's mission to all nations.

Conclusion

61. *Missionary Vocations*—In concluding this letter, we challenge young people to consider following Christ as missionaries. There is no doubt that Jesus is calling many of you to serve the Church as priests and religious in foreign lands. We pray that you will have the courage to respond to that call with the complete gift of yourselves. Your brothers and sisters in mission lands are counting on you to share the riches of the gospel with them. The Church is counting on you, too.

62. *Need for Missionaries*—While some of you are called to dedicate your whole life to Christ in another culture, others are called to devote a few important years. It is true that secular agencies accomplish much good, but the Church's mission extends beyond earthly realities and requires heroic sacrifice for the sake of the kingdom.[67]

---

[64]"The grace of renewal cannot grow in communities unless each of them expands the range of its charity to the ends of the earth, and has the same concern for those who are far away as it has for its members" (*Ad Gentes*, no. 37).

[65]See Matthew 6:1-18.

[66]See Acts 1:14.

[67]*Evangelii Nuntiandi*, no. 33.

63. *Lay Missionaries*—We are inspired by the increase of committed lay missionaries who answer the call to serve the gospel in other lands. You bring important expertise and enthusiasm into missionary activities. Your growing number is a sign of great hope for the future of world mission. We recognize the special difficulties lay persons face in missionary work and your enormous trust that God will provide for you and your families.

64. *Generosity of U.S. Catholics*—We are grateful to the Catholics of the United States for your continued concern for the missionary activity of the Church, for missionaries themselves, and for the young churches of the developing world. You have responded generously to missionaries who visit your parishes through the Missionary Cooperation Plan to explain their work and needs. Many of you also belong to parish mission societies, and others participate in special programs of daily prayer and regular sacrifice for world mission. Your tradition of prayer and generous giving is a strong witness to the missionary vitality of the Church.

65. *Parents and Families of Missionaries*—We are grateful to families of missionaries, especially to parents who have encouraged their sons and daughters to serve the Church. The need has not diminished. We pray that young families will continue to follow this example of generosity.

66. *Support of Pontifical Mission Aid Societies*—We renew our prayer that all will continue to support missionary activity in every way, especially through the Pontifical Societies, namely, The Society for the Propagation of the Faith and The Association of the Holy Childhood. We commend the work of the directors of these societies for their continued efforts to educate the faithful to the mission challenge. The Secretariat for Latin America, established by the bishops of the United States to assist the Church in Central and South America, also merits continued support. Like Paul, we rejoice "at the way you have continually helped promote the gospel from the very first day" and pray that "he who has begun the good work in you will carry it through to completion, right up to the day of Christ Jesus" (Phil 1:3-6).

67. *U.S. Church Leaders*—We also express our gratitude to you in the service of the Church in the United States. Whether as lay leaders, religious, educators, deacons or priests, you share the service of leadership with us. In this time of transition from one missionary context to another, you have worked hard to preserve unity in our missionary efforts even when our faith was tested and many were confused. We ask that you join us in praying for an increase in missionary vocations, in supporting those involved in mission education, and in helping to make others more aware of the needs of the universal Church and their role in meeting these needs.

68. *Missionary Congregations*—We extend special thanks to religious congregations and societies of men and women who educate, form, and give so many of their members to the missionary work of the Church. Much of your work goes unrecognized. We commend you especially for the sensitive care you give those missionaries who return home because of illness or age, or who have been exiled from their missions by political oppression.

69. *Diocesan Mission Projects*—We are encouraged by the large number of dioceses that send priests, religious, and laity to staff special mission projects. We hope their example will inspire other dioceses to undertake similar programs.

70. *Education for Mission*—We appeal to all educators to help give Catholics a better understanding of the task and demands of mission today. Theological studies should include a strong missionary emphasis, so necessary for the formation of future priests and leaders.[68] Further, authors of catechetical texts should highlight the missionary responsibility of every Christian so that young people may be educated from an early age in this essential aspect of the Church's life.

71. *World Mission Sunday*—We urge the fullest celebration of World Mission Sunday in every parish. The Church has designated this day for Catholics worldwide to recommit themselves to the missionary task and to support the Church financially in its outreach. World Mission Sunday, under the aegis of the Propagation of the Faith, uniquely celebrates the unity and universality of the Church. It gives us, in the words of Pope John Paul II, "an excellent occasion for an examination of conscience with regard to our missionary obligation, and for reminding all the faithful . . . that each one is involved in this duty."[69]

72. *Gratitude to Missionaries*—Our gratitude to you, the missionaries, is especially profound. You have left home and family, even risking your lives for the sake of the gospel to the nations. Moreover, this time of transition has imposed an additional burden: the challenge of adapting your missionary efforts to a new context.

73. *Support for Missionaries*—As missionaries you are sent to place yourselves at the service of the local church in union with its bishop.[70] Your role is a humble and difficult one. We affirm our solidarity with you and pledge you our support. You make visible the universal commitment of the Church in the United States, sometimes at the cost of misunderstanding or indifference from those who lack your experience.

---

[68]"University and seminary professors will instruct the young as to the true condition of the world and the Church, so that the need for a more intense evangelization of non-Christians will be clear to them and feed their zeal. In teaching dogmatic, biblical, moral, and historical subjects, they should focus attention on their missionary aspects, so that in this way a missionary awareness will be formed in future priests" (*Ad Gentes*, no. 39).

[69]Pope John Paul II, *Message for World Mission Sunday*, 1981. See Canon 791.

[70]*Evangelii Nuntiandi*, no. 60; see the Eucharistic Prayers of the Mass.

74. *Learning from Missionaries*—We ask that you share with us your experience as well as the faith experience of the people you serve. On your visits home, you are a missionary from another local church to ours. Our faith is deepened and broadened as we learn from you. You enrich us in our understanding of the problems and challenges of the universal Church.

75. *Jesus the Missionary*—Jesus is "the missionary of the Father";[71] each Christian is his witness. Let his voice proclaim the gospel through us as we bring the good news of salvation to the ends of the earth.

---

[71]Pope John Paul II, *Talk to Chapter Delegates of the Vincentian Fathers*, June 30, 1986.

Economic Justice for All
Pastoral Letter on Catholic Social Teaching and the U.S. Economy

A Pastoral Letter Issued by the
National Conference of Catholic Bishops

November 13, 1986

A Pastoral Message

Brothers and Sisters in Christ:

1.   We are believers called to follow Our Lord Jesus Christ and proclaim his Gospel in the midst of a complex and powerful economy. This reality poses both opportunities and responsibilities for Catholics in the United States. Our faith calls us to measure this economy, not only by what it produces, but also by how it touches human life and whether it protects or undermines the dignity of the human person. Economic decisions have human consequences and moral content; they help or hurt people, strengthen or weaken family life, advance or diminish the quality of justice in our land.

2.   This is why we have written *Economic Justice for All: Pastoral Letter on Catholic Social Teaching and the U.S. Economy.* This letter is a personal invitation to Catholics to use the resources of our faith, the strength of our economy, and the opportunities of our democracy to shape a society that better protects the dignity and basic rights of our sisters and brothers, both in this land and around the world.

3.   The pastoral letter has been a work of careful inquiry, wide consultation, and prayerful discernment. The letter has been greatly enriched by this process of listening and refinement. We offer this introductory pastoral message to Catholics in the United States seeking to live their faith in the marketplace—in homes, offices, factories, and schools; on farms and ranches; in boardrooms and union halls; in service agencies and legislative chambers. We seek to explain why we wrote the pastoral letter, to introduce its major themes, and to share our hopes for the dialogue and action it might generate.

Why We Write

4.   We write to share our teaching, to raise questions, to challenge one another to live our faith in the world. We write as heirs of the biblical prophets who summon us "to do the right, and to love goodness, and to walk humbly with your God" (Mi 6:8). We write as followers of Jesus who told us in the Sermon on the Mount: "Blessed are the poor in spirit. . . . Blessed are the meek. . . . Blessed are they who hunger and thirst for righteousness. . . . You are the salt of the earth. . . . You are the light of the world" (Mt 5:1-6,13-14). These words challenge us not only as believers but also as consumers, citizens, workers, and owners. In the parable of the Last Judgment, Jesus said, "For I was hungry and you gave me food, I was thirsty and you gave me drink. . . . As often as you did it for one of my least brothers, you did it for me" (Mt 25:35-40). The challenge for us is to discover in our own place and time what it means to be "poor in spirit" and "the salt of the earth" and what it means to serve "the least among us" and to "hunger and thirst for righteousness."

5.   Followers of Christ must avoid a tragic separation between faith and everyday life. They can neither shirk their earthly duties nor, as the Second Vatican Council declared, "immerse [them]selves in earthly activities as if these latter were utterly foreign to religion, and religion were nothing more than the fulfillment of acts of worship and the observance of a few moral obligations" (*Pastoral Constitution on the Church in the Modern World*, no. 43).

6.   Economic life raises important social and moral questions for each of us and for society as a whole. Like family life, economic life is one of the chief areas where we live out our faith, love our neighbor, confront temptation, fulfill God's creative design, and achieve our holiness. Our economic activity in factory, field, office, or shop feeds our families—or feeds our anxieties. It exercises our talents—or wastes them. It raises our hopes—or crushes them. It brings us into cooperation with others—or sets us at odds. The Second Vatican Council instructs us "to preach the message of Christ in such a way that the light of the Gospel will shine on all activities of the faithful" (*Pastoral Constitution*, no. 43). In this case, we are trying to look at economic life through the eyes of faith, applying traditional church teaching to the U.S. economy.

7.   In our letter, we write as pastors, not public officials. We speak as moral teachers, not economic technicians. We seek not to make some political or ideological point but to lift up the human and ethical dimensions of economic life, aspects too often neglected in public discussion. We bring to this task a dual heritage of Catholic social teaching and traditional American values.

8.   As *Catholics* we are heirs of a long tradition of thought and action on the moral dimensions of economic activity. The life and words of Jesus and the teaching of his Church call us to serve those in need and to work actively for social and economic justice. As a community of believers, we know that our faith is tested by the quality of justice among us, that we can best measure our life together by how the poor and the vulnerable are treated. This is not a new concern for us.

It is as old as the Hebrew prophets, as compelling as the Sermon on the Mount, and as current as the powerful voice of Pope John Paul II defending the dignity of the human person.

9.   As *Americans*, we are grateful for the gift of freedom and committed to the dream of "liberty and justice for all." This nation, blessed with extraordinary resources, has provided an unprecedented standard of living for millions of people. We are proud of the strength, productivity, and creativity of our economy, but we also remember those who have been left behind in our progress. We believe that we honor our history best by working for the day when all our sisters and brothers share adequately in the American dream.

10. As bishops, in proclaiming the Gospel for these times we also manage institutions, balance budgets, meet payrolls. In this we see the human face of our economy. We feel the hurts and hopes of our people. We feel the pain of our sisters and brothers who are poor, unemployed, homeless, living on the edge. The poor and vulnerable are on our doorsteps, in our parishes, in our service agencies, and in our shelters. We see too much hunger and injustice, too much suffering and despair, both in our own country and around the world.

11. As pastors, we also see the decency, generosity, and vulnerability of our people. We see the struggles of ordinary families to make ends meet and to provide a better future for their children. We know the desire of managers, professionals, and business people to shape what they do by what they believe. It is the faith, good will, and generosity of our people that gives us hope as we write this letter.

Principal Themes of the Pastoral Letter

12. The pastoral letter is not a blueprint for the American economy. It does not embrace any particular theory of how the economy works, nor does it attempt to resolve the disputes between different schools of economic thought. Instead, our letter turns to Scripture and to the social teachings of the Church. There, we discover what our economic life must serve, what standards it must meet. Let us examine some of these basic moral principles.

13. *Every economic decision and institution must be judged in light of whether it protects or undermines the dignity of the human person.* The pastoral letter begins with the human person. We believe the person is sacred — the clearest reflection of God among us. Human dignity comes from God, not from nationality, race, sex, economic status, or any human accomplishment. We judge any economic system by what it does *for* and *to* people and by how it permits all to *participate* in it. The economy should serve people, not the other way around.

14. *Human dignity can be realized and protected only in community.* In our teaching, the human person is not only sacred but also social. How we organize our society — in economics and politics, in law and policy—directly affects human dignity and the capacity of individuals to grow in community. The obligation of "love our neighbor" has an individual dimension, but it also requires a broader social commitment to the common good. We have many partial ways to measure and debate the health of our economy: gross national product, per capita income, stock market prices, and so forth. The Christian vision of economic life looks beyond them all and asks, Does economic life enhance or threaten our life together as a community?

15. *All people have a right to participate in the economic life of society.* Basic justice demands that people be assured a minimum level of participation in the economy. It is wrong for a person or group to be excluded unfairly or to be unable to participate or contribute to the economy. For example, people who are both able and willing, but cannot get a job are deprived of the participation that is so vital to human development. For, it is through employment that most individuals and families meet their material needs, exercise their talents, and have an opportunity to contribute to the larger community. Such participation has a special significance in our tradition because we believe that it is a means by which we join in carrying forward God's creative activity.

16. *All members of society have a special obligation to the poor and vulnerable.* From the Scriptures and church teaching, we learn that the justice of society is tested by the treatment of the poor. The justice that was the sign of God's covenant with Israel was measured by how the poor and unprotected—the widow, the orphan, and the stranger—were treated. The kingdom that Jesus proclaimed in his word and ministry excludes no one. Throughout Israel's history and in early Christianity, the poor are agents of God's transforming power. "The Spirit of the Lord is upon me, therefore he has anointed me. He has sent me to bring glad tidings to the poor" (Lk 4:18). This was Jesus' first public utterance. Jesus takes the side of those most in need. In the Last Judgment, so dramatically described in St. Matthew's Gospel, we are told that we will be judged according to how we respond to the hungry, the thirsty, the naked, the stranger. As followers of Christ, we are challenged to make a fundamental "option for the poor"—to speak for the voiceless, to defend the defenseless, to assess life styles, policies, and social institutions in terms of their impact on the poor. This "option for the poor" does not mean pitting one group against another, but rather, strengthening the whole community by assisting those who are most vulnerable. As Christians, we are called to respond to the needs of *all* our brothers and sisters, but those with the greatest needs require the greatest response.

17. *Human rights are the minimum conditions for life in community.* In Catholic teaching, human rights include not only civil and political rights but also economic rights. As Pope John XXIII declared, "all people have a right to life, food, clothing, shelter, rest, medical care, education, and employment." This means that when people are without a chance to earn a living, and must go hungry and homeless, they are being denied basic rights. Society must ensure that these rights are protected. In this way, we will ensure that the minimum conditions of economic justice are met for all our sisters and brothers.

18. *Society as a whole, acting through public and private institutions, has the moral responsibility to enhance human dignity and protect human rights.* In addition to the clear responsibility of private institutions, government has an essential responsibility in this area. This does not mean that government has the primary or exclusive role, but it does have a positive moral responsibility in safeguarding human rights and ensuring that the minimum conditions of human dignity are met for all. In a democracy, government is a means by which we can act together to protect what is important to us and to promote our common values.

19. These six moral principles are not the only ones presented in the pastoral letter, but they give an overview of the moral vision that we are trying to share. This vision of economic life cannot exist in a vacuum; it must be translated into concrete measures. Our pastoral letter spells out some specific applications of Catholic moral principles. We call for a new national commitment to full employment. We say it is a social and moral scandal that one of every seven Americans is poor, and we call for concerted efforts to eradicate poverty. The fulfillment of the basic needs of the poor is of the highest priority. We urge that all economic policies be evaluated in light of their impact on the life and stability of the family. We support measures to halt the loss of family farms and to resist the growing concentration in the ownership of agricultural resources. We specify ways in which the United States can do far more to relieve the plight of poor nations and assist in their development. We also reaffirm church teaching on the rights of workers, collective bargaining, private property, subsidiarity, and equal opportunity.

20. We believe that the recommendations in our letter are reasonable and balanced. In analyzing the economy, we reject ideological extremes and start from the fact that ours is a "mixed" economy, the product of a long history of reform and adjustment. We know that some of our specific recommendations are controversial. As bishops, we do not claim to make these prudential judgments with the same kind of authority that marks our declarations of principle. But, we feel obliged to teach by example how Christians can undertake concrete analysis and make specific judgments on economic issues. The Church's teachings cannot be left at the level of appealing generalities.

21. In the pastoral letter, we suggest that the time has come for a "New American Experiment" — to implement economic rights, to broaden the sharing of economic power, and to make economic decisions more accountable to the common good. This experiment can create new structures of economic partnership and participation within

firms at the regional level, for the whole nation, and across borders.
22. Of course, there are many aspects of the economy the letter does
not touch, and there are basic questions it leaves to further exploration.
There are also many specific points on which men and women of
good will may disagree. We look for a fruitful exchange among differing viewpoints. We pray only that all will take to heart the urgency
of our concerns; that together we will test our views by the Gospel
and the Church's teaching; and that we will listen to other voices in
a spirit of mutual respect and open dialogue.

A Call to Conversion and Action

23. We should not be surprised if we find Catholic social teaching to
be demanding. The Gospel is demanding. We are always in need of
conversion, of a change of heart. We are richly blessed, and as St.
Paul assures us, we are destined for glory. Yet, it is also true that we
are sinners; that we are not always wise or loving or just; that, for all
our amazing possibilities, we are incompletely born, wary of life, and
hemmed in by fears and empty routines. We are unable to entrust
ourselves fully to the living God, and so we seek substitute forms of
security in material things, in power, in indifference, in popularity,
in pleasure. The Scriptures warn us that these things can become
forms of idolatry. We know that, at times, in order to remain truly a
community of Jesus' disciples, we will have to say "no" to certain
aspects in our culture, to certain trends and ways of acting that are
opposed to a life of faith, love, and justice. Changes in our hearts
lead naturally to a desire to change how we act. With what care,
human kindness, and justice do I conduct myself at work? How will
my economic decisions to buy, sell, invest, divest, hire, or fire serve
human dignity and the common good? In what career can I best
exercise my talents so as to fill the world with the Spirit of Christ?
How do my economic choices contribute to the strength of my family
and community, to the values of my children, to a sensitivity to those
in need? In this consumer society, how can I develop a healthy detach-
ment from things and avoid the temptation to assess who I am by
what I have? How do I strike a balance between labor and leisure that
enlarges my capacity for friendships, for family life, for community?
What government policies should I support to attain the well-being
of all, especially the poor and vulnerable?
24. The answers to such questions are not always clear—or easy to
live out. But, conversion is a lifelong process. And, it is not undertaken
alone. It occurs with the support of the whole believing community,
through baptism, common prayer, and our daily efforts, large and
small, on behalf of justice. As a Church, we must be people after
God's own heart, bonded by the Spirit, sustaining one another in
love, setting our hearts on God's kingdom, committing ourselves to

solidarity with those who suffer, working for peace and justice, acting as a sign of Christ's love and justice in the world. The Church cannot redeem the world from the deadening effects of sin and injustice unless it is working to remove sin and injustice in its own life and institutions. All of us must help the Church to practice in its own life what it preaches to others about economic justice and cooperation.

25. The challenge of this pastoral letter is not merely to think differently, but also to act differently. A renewal of economic life depends on the conscious choices and commitments of individual believers who practice their faith in the world. The road to holiness for most of us lies in our secular vocations. We need a spirituality that calls forth and supports lay initiative and witness not just in our churches but also in business, in the labor movement, in the professions, in education, and in public life. Our faith is not just a weekend obligation, a mystery to be celebrated around the altar on Sunday. It is a pervasive reality to be practiced every day in homes, offices, factories, schools, and businesses across our land. We cannot separate what we believe from how we act in the marketplace and the broader community, for this is where we make our primary contribution to the pursuit of economic justice.

26. We ask each of you to read the pastoral letter, to study it, to pray about it, and match it with your own experience. We ask you to join with us in service to those in need. Let us reach out personally to the hungry and the homeless, to the poor and the powerless, and to the troubled and the vulnerable. In serving them, we serve Christ. Our service efforts cannot substitute for just and compassionate public policies, but they can help us practice what we preach about human life and human dignity.

27. The pursuit of economic justice takes believers into the public arena, testing the policies of government by the principles of our teaching. We ask you to become more informed and active citizens, using your voices and votes to speak for the voiceless, to defend the poor and the vulnerable, and to advance the common good. We are called to shape a constituency of conscience, measuring every policy by how it touches the least, the lost, and the left-out among us. This letter calls us to conversion and common action, to new forms of stewardship, service, and citizenship.

28. The completion of a letter such as this is but the beginning of a long process of education, discussion, and action. By faith and baptism, we are fashioned into new creatures, filled with the Holy Spirit and with a love that compels us to seek out a new profound relationship with God, with the human family, and with all created things. Jesus has entered our history as God's anointed son who announces the coming of God's kingdom, a kingdom of justice and peace and freedom. And, what Jesus proclaims, he embodies in his actions. His ministry reveals that the reign of God is something more powerful

than evil, injustice, and the hardness of hearts. Through his crucifixion and resurrection, he reveals that God's love is ultimately victorious over all suffering, all horror, all meaninglessness, and even over the mystery of death. Thus, we proclaim words of hope and assurance to all who suffer and are in need.

29. We believe that the Christian view of life, including economic life, can transform the lives of individuals, families, schools, and our whole culture. We believe that with your prayers, reflection, service, and action, our economy can be shaped so that human dignity prospers and the human person is served. This is the unfinished work of our nation. This is the challenge of our faith.

I. The Church and the Future of the U.S. Economy

1. Every perspective on economic life that is human, moral, and Christian must be shaped by three questions: What does the economy do *for* people? What does it do *to* people? And how do people *participate* in it? The economy is a human reality: men and women working together to develop and care for the whole of God's creation. All this work must serve the material and spiritual well-being of people. It influences what people hope for themselves and their loved ones. It affects the way they act together in society. It influences their very faith in God.[1]

2. The Second Vatican Council declared that "the joys and hopes, the griefs and anxieties of the people of this age, especially those who are poor or in any way afflicted, these too are the joys and hopes, the griefs and anxieties of the followers of Christ."[2] There are many signs of hope in U.S. economic life today:

- Many fathers and mothers skillfully balance the arduous responsibilities of work and family life. There are parents who pursue a purposeful and modest way of life and by their example encourage their children to follow a similar path. A large number of women and men, drawing on their religious tradition, recognize the challenging vocation of family life and childrearing in a culture that emphasizes material display and self-gratification.

---

[1]Vatican Council II, *The Pastoral Constitution on the Church in the Modern World,* 33. [Note: This pastoral letter frequently refers to documents of the Second Vatican Council, papal encyclicals, and other official teachings of the Roman Catholic Church. Most of these texts have been published by the United States Catholic Conference Office of Publishing and Promotion Services; many are available in collections, though no single collection is comprehensive. See selected bibliography.]

[2]*Pastoral Constitution,* 1.

- Conscientious business people seek new and more equitable ways to organize resources and the workplace. They face hard choices over expanding or retrenching, shifting investments, hiring or firing.
- Young people choosing their life's work ask whether success and security are compatible with service to others.
- Workers whose labor may be toilsome or repetitive try daily to ennoble their work with a spirit of solidarity and friendship.
- New immigrants brave dislocations while hoping for the opportunities realized by the millions who came before them.

3.   These signs of hope are not the whole story. There have been failures—some of them massive and ugly:

- Poor and homeless people sleep in community shelters and in our church basements; the hungry line up in soup lines.
- Unemployment gnaws at the self-respect of both middle-aged persons who have lost jobs and the young who cannot find them.
- Hardworking men and women wonder if the system of enterprise that helped them yesterday might destroy their jobs and their communities tomorrow.
- Families confront major new challenges: dwindling social supports for family stability; economic pressures that force both parents of young children to work outside the home; a driven pace of life among the successful that can sap love and commitment; lack of hope among those who have less or nothing at all. Very different kinds of families bear different burdens of our economic system.
- Farmers face the loss of their land and way of life; young people find it difficult to choose farming as a vocation; farming communities are threatened; migrant farmworkers break their backs in serf-like conditions for disgracefully low wages.

4.   *And beyond our own shores, the reality of 800 million people living in absolute poverty and 450 million malnourished or facing starvation casts an ominous shadow over all these hopes and problems at home.*
5.   Anyone who sees all this will understand our concern as pastors and bishops. People shape the economy and in turn are shaped by it. Economic arrangements can be sources of fulfillment, of hope, of community—or of frustration, isolation, and even despair. They teach virtues—or vices—and day by day help mold our characters. They affect the quality of people's lives; at the extreme even determining whether people live or die. Serious economic choices go beyond purely technical issues to fundamental questions of value and human pur-

pose.[3] We believe that in facing these questions the Christian religious and moral tradition can make an important contribution.

A. The U.S. Economy Today: Memory and Hope

6.   The United States is among the most economically powerful nations on earth. In its short history the U.S. economy has grown to provide an unprecedented standard of living for most of its people. The nation has created productive work for millions of immigrants and enabled them to broaden their freedoms, improve their families' quality of life, and contribute to the building of a great nation. Those who came to this country from other lands often understood their new lives in the light of biblical faith. They thought of themselves as entering a promised land of political freedom and economic opportunity. The United States *is* a land of vast natural resources and fertile soil. It *has* encouraged citizens to undertake bold ventures. Through hard work, self-sacrifice, and cooperation, families have flourished; towns, cities, and a powerful nation have been created.

7.   But we should recall this history with sober humility. The American experiment in social, political, and economic life has involved serious conflict and suffering. Our nation was born in the face of injustice to Native Americans, and its independence was paid for with the blood of revolution. Slavery stained the commercial life of the land through its first two hundred and fifty years and was ended only by a violent civil war. The establishment of women's suffrage, the protection of industrial workers, the elimination of child labor, the response to the Great Depression of the 1930s, and the civil rights movement of the 1960s all involved a sustained struggle to transform the political and economic institutions of the nation.

8.   The U.S. value system emphasizes economic freedom. It also recognizes that the market is limited by fundamental human rights. Some things are never to be bought or sold.[4] This conviction has prompted positive steps to modify the operation of the market when it harms vulnerable members of society. Labor unions help workers resist exploitation. Through their government, the people of the United States have provided support for education, access to food, unemployment compensation, security in old age, and protection of the

---

[3]See ibid., 10, 42, 43; Congregation for the Doctrine of the Faith, *Instruction on Christian Freedom and Liberation*, (Washington, D.C.: USCC Office of Publishing and Promotion Services, 1986), 34-36.

[4]See Pope John Paul II, *On Human Work* (1981), 14; and Pope Paul VI, *Octogesima Adveniens* (1971), 35. See also Arthur Okun, *Equality and Efficiency: The Big Tradeoff* (Washington, D.C.: The Brookings Institution, 1975), ch. 1; Michael Walzer, *Spheres of Justice: A Defense of Pluralism and Equality* (New York: Basic Books, 1983), ch. 4; Jon P. Gunnemann, "Capitalism and Commutative Justice," paper presented at the 1985 meeting of the Society of Christian Ethics.

environment. The market system contributes to the success of the U.S. economy, but so do many efforts to forge economic institutions and public policies that enable *all* to share in the riches of the nation. The country's economy has been built through a creative struggle; entrepreneurs, business people, workers, unions, consumers, and government have all played essential roles.

9.   The task of the United States today is as demanding as that faced by our forebears. Abraham Lincoln's words at Gettysburg are a reminder that complacency today would be a betrayal of our nation's history: "It is for us, the living, rather to be dedicated here to the unfinished work . . . they have thus far nobly advanced."[5] There is unfinished business in the American experiment in freedom and justice for all.

B. Urgent Problems of Today

10.   The preeminent role of the United States in an increasingly interdependent global economy is a central sign of our times.[6] The United States is still the world's economic giant. Decisions made here have immediate effects in other countries; decisions made abroad have immediate consequences for steelworkers in Pittsburgh, oil company employees in Houston, and farmers in Iowa. U.S. economic growth is vitally dependent on resources from other countries and on their purchases of our goods and services. Many jobs in U.S. industry and agriculture depend on our ability to export manufactured goods and food.

11.   In some industries the mobility of capital and technology makes wages the main variable in the cost of production. Overseas competitors with the same technology but with wage rates as low as one-tenth of ours put enormous pressure on U.S. firms to cut wages, relocate abroad, or close. U.S. workers and their communities should not be expected to bear these burdens alone.

12.   All people on this globe share a common ecological environment that is under increasing pressure. Depletion of soil, water, and other natural resources endangers the future. Pollution of air and water threatens the delicate balance of the biosphere on which future generations will depend.[7] The resources of the earth have been created by God for the benefit of all, and we who are alive today hold them in trust. This is a challenge to develop a new ecological ethic that will help shape a future that is both just and sustainable.

13.   In short, nations separated by geography, culture, and ideology

---

[5] Abraham Lincoln, Address at Dedication of National Cemetery at Gettysburg, November 19, 1863.

[6] Pope John XXIII, *Peace on Earth* (1963), 130-131.

[7] Synod of Bishops, *Justice in the World* (1971), 8; Pope John Paul II, *Redeemer of Man* (1979), 15.

are linked in a complex commercial, financial, technological, and environmental network. These links have two direct consequences. First, they create hope for a new form of community among all peoples, one built on dignity, solidarity, and justice. Second, this rising global awareness calls for greater attention to the stark inequities across countries in the standards of living and control of resources. We must not look at the welfare of U.S. citizens as the only good to be sought. Nor may we overlook the disparities of power in the relationships between this nation and the developing countries. The United States is the major supplier of food to other countries, a major source of arms sales to developing nations, and a powerful influence in multilateral institutions such as the International Monetary Fund, the World Bank, and the United Nations. What Americans see as a growing interdependence is regarded by many in the less developed countries as a pattern of domination and dependence.

14. Within this larger international setting, there are also a number of challenges to the domestic economy that call for creativity and courage. The promise of the "American dream"—freedom for all persons to develop their God-given talents to the full—remains unfulfilled for millions in the United States today.

15. Several areas of U.S. economic life demand special attention. Unemployment is the most basic. Despite the large number of new jobs the U.S. economy has generated in the past decade, approximately 8 million people seeking work in this country are unable to find it, and many more are so discouraged they have stopped looking.[8] Over the past two decades the nation has come to tolerate an increasing level of unemployment. The 6 to 7 percent rate deemed acceptable today would have been intolerable twenty years ago. Among the unemployed are a disproportionate number of blacks, Hispanics, young people, or women who are the sole support of their families.[9] Some cities and states have many more unemployed persons than others as a result of economic forces that have little to do with people's desire to work. Unemployment is a tragedy no matter whom it strikes, but the tragedy is compounded by the unequal and unfair way it is distributed in our society.

16. Harsh poverty plagues our country despite its great wealth. More than 33 million Americans are poor; by any reasonable standard another 20 to 30 million are needy. Poverty is increasing in the United States, not decreasing.[10] For a people who believe in "progress," this should

---

[8]U.S. Department of Labor, Bureau of Labor Statistics, *The Employment Situation: August 1985* (September 1985), Table A-1.

[9]Ibid.

[10]U.S. Bureau of the Census, Current Population Reports, Series P-60, 145, *Money Income and Poverty Status of Families and Persons in the United States: 1983* (Washington, D.C.: U.S. Government Printing Office, 1984), 20.

be cause for alarm. These burdens fall most heavily on blacks, Hispanics, and Native Americans. Even more disturbing is the large increase in the number of women and children living in poverty. Today children are the largest single group among the poor. This tragic fact seriously threatens the nation's future. That so many people are poor in a nation as rich as ours is a social and moral scandal that we cannot ignore.

17. Many working people and middle-class Americans live dangerously close to poverty. A rising number of families must rely on the wages of two or even three members just to get by. From 1968 to 1978 nearly a quarter of the U.S. population was in poverty part of the time and received welfare benefits in at least one year.[11] The loss of a job, illness, or the breakup of a marriage may be all it takes to push people into poverty.

18. The lack of a mutually supportive relation between family life and economic life is one of the most serious problems facing the United States today.[12] The economic and cultural strength of the nation is directly linked to the stability and health of its families.[13] When families thrive, spouses contribute to the common good through their work at home, in the community, and in their jobs; and children develop a sense of their own worth and of their responsiblity to serve others. When families are weak or break down entirely, the dignity of parents and children is threatened. High cultural and economic costs are inflicted on society at large.

19. The precarious economic situation of so many people and so many families calls for examination of U.S. economic arrangements. Christian conviction and the American promise of liberty and justice for all give the poor and the vulnerable a special claim on the nation's concern. They also challenge all members of the Church to help build a more just society.

20. The investment of human creativity and material resources in the production of the weapons of war makes these economic problems even more difficult to solve. Defense Department expenditures in the United States are almost $300 billion per year. The rivalry and mutual fear between superpowers divert into projects that threaten death, minds and money that could better human life. Developing countries engage in arms races they can ill afford, often with the encouragement of the superpowers. Some of the poorest countries of the world use scarce resources to buy planes, guns, and other weapons when they lack the food, education, and health care their people need. Defense

---

[11]Greg H. Duncan, *Years of Poverty, Years of Plenty: The Changing Economic Fortunes of American Workers and Their Families* (Ann Arbor, Mich.: Institute for Social Research, University of Michigan, 1984).

[12]See Pope John Paul II, *Familiaris Consortio* (1981), 46.

[13]*Pastoral Constitution*, 47.

policies must be evaluated and assessed in light of their real contribution to freedom, justice, and peace for the citizens of our own and
other nations. We have developed a perspective on these multiple
moral concerns in our 1983 pastoral letter, *The Challenge of Peace: God's
Promise and Our Response.*[14] When weapons or strategies make questionable contributions to security, peace, and justice and will also be
very expensive, spending priorities should be redirected to more
pressing social needs.[15]

21. Many other social and economic challenges require careful analysis: the movement of many industries from the Snowbelt to the
Sunbelt, the federal deficit and interest rates, corporate mergers and
takeovers, the effects of new technologies such as robotics and information systems in U.S. industry, immigration policy, growing international traffic in drugs, and the trade imbalance. All of these issues
do not provide a complete portrait of the economy. Rather they are
symptoms of more fundamental currents shaping U.S. economic life
today: the struggle to find meaning and value in human work, efforts
to support individual freedom in the context of renewed social cooperation, the urgent need to create equitable forms of global interdependence in a world now marked by extreme inequality. These deeper
currents are cultural and moral in content. They show that the long-
range challenges facing the nation call for sustained reflection on the
values that guide economic choices and are embodied in economic
institutions. Such explicit reflection on the ethical content of economic
choices and policies must become an integral part of the way Christians
relate religious belief to the realities of everyday life. In this way, the
"split between the faith which many profess and their daily lives,"[16]
which Vatican II counted among the more serious errors of the modern
age, will begin to be bridged.

C. The Need for Moral Vision

22. Sustaining a common culture and a common commitment to moral
values is not easy in our world. Modern economic life is based on a
division of labor into specialized jobs and professions. Since the industrial revolution, people have had to define themselves and their work
ever more narrowly to find a niche in the economy. The benefits of
this are evident in the satisfaction many people derive from contributing their specialized skills to society. But the costs are social frag-

---

[14]National Conference of Catholic Bishops, *The Challenge of Peace: God's Promise and Our
Response* (Washington, D.C.: USCC Office of Publishing and Promotion Services, 1983).
[15]Cardinal Joseph L. Bernardin and Cardinal John J. O'Connor, Testimony before the
House Foreign Relations Committee, June 26, 1984, *Origins* 14:10 (August 10, 1984):
157.
[16]*Pastoral Constitution*, 43.

mentation, a decline in seeing how one's work serves the whole community, and an increased emphasis on personal goals and private interests.[17] This is vividly clear in discussions of economic justice. Here it is often difficult to find a common ground among people with different backgrounds and concerns. One of our chief hopes in writing this letter is to encourage and contribute to the development of this common ground.[18]

23. Strengthening common moral vision is essential if the economy is to serve all people more fairly. Many middle-class Americans feel themselves in the grip of economic demands and cultural pressures that go far beyond the individual family's capacity to cope. Without constructive guidance in making decisions with serious moral implications, men and women who hold positions of responsibility in corporations or government find their duties exacting a heavy price. We want these reflections to help them contribute to a more just economy.

24. The quality of the national discussion about our economic future will affect the poor most of all, in this country and throughout the world. The life and dignity of millions of men, women, and children hang in the balance. Decisions must be judged in light of what they do *for* the poor, what they do *to* the poor, and what they enable the poor to do *for themselves.* The fundamental moral criterion for all economic decisions, policies, and institutions is this: They must be at the service of *all people, especially the poor.*

25. This letter is based on a long tradition of Catholic social thought, rooted in the Bible and developed over the past century by the popes and the Second Vatican Council in response to modern economic conditions. This tradition insists that human dignity, realized in community with others and with the whole of God's creation, is the norm against which every social institution must be measured.[19]

26. This teaching has a rich history. It is also dynamic and growing.[20] Pope Paul VI insisted that all Christian communities have the responsibility "to analyze with objectivity the situation which is proper to their own country, to shed on it the light of the Gospel's unalterable words and to draw principles of reflection, norms of judgment, and

---

[17]See, for example, Peter Berger, Brigitte Berger, and Hansfried Kellner, *The Homeless Mind: Modernization and Consciousness* (New York: Vintage, 1974).

[18]For a recent study of the importance and difficulty of achieving such a common language and vision see Robert N. Bellah, Richard Madsen, William M. Sullivan, Ann Swidler, and Stephen M. Tipton, *Habits of the Heart: Individualism and Commitment in American Life* (Berkeley, Calif.: University of California Press, 1985). See also Martin E. Marty, *The Public Church* (New York: Crossroads, 1981).

[19]Pope John XXIII, *Mater et Magistra* (1961), 219; *Pastoral Constitution,* 40.

[20]Congregation for the Doctrine of the Faith, *Instruction on Certain Aspects of the Theology of Liberation* (Washington, D.C.: USCC Office of Publishing and Promotion Services, 1984); Pope Paul VI, *Octogesima Adveniens* (1971), 42.

directives for action from the social teaching of the Church."[21] Therefore, we build on the past work of our own bishops' conference,
including the 1919 Program of Social Reconstruction and other pastoral
letters.[22] In addition many people from the Catholic, Protestant, and
Jewish communities, in academic, business, or political life, and from
many different economic backgrounds have also provided guidance.
We want to make the legacy of Christian social thought a living,
growing resource that can inspire hope and help shape the future.
27. We write, then, first of all to provide guidance for members of
our own Church as they seek to form their consciences about economic
matters. No one may claim the name Christian and be comfortable
in the face of the hunger, homelessness, insecurity, and injustice
found in this country and the world. At the same time, we want to
add our voice to the public debate about the directions in which the
U.S. economy should be moving. We seek the cooperation and support of those who do not share our faith or tradition. The common
bond of humanity that links all persons is the source of our belief that
the country can attain a renewed public moral vision. The questions
are basic and the answers are often elusive; they challenge us to serious
and sustained attention to economic justice.

II. The Christian Vision of Economic Life

28. The basis for all that the Church believes about the moral dimensions of economic life is its vision of the transcendent worth—the
sacredness—of human beings. *The dignity of the human person, realized
in community with others, is the criterion against which all aspects of economic
life must be measured.*[1] All human beings, therefore, are ends to be
served by the institutions that make up the economy, not means to
be exploited for more narrowly defined goals. Human personhood
must be respected with a reverence that is religious. When we deal
with each other, we should do so with the sense of awe that arises
in the presence of something holy and sacred. For that is what human
beings are: we are created in the image of God (Gn 1:27). Similarly,
all economic institutions must support the bonds of community and

---

[21] *Octogesima Adveniens*, 4.

[22] Administrative Committee of the National Catholic War Council, *Program of Social
Reconstruction*, February 12, 1919. Other notable statements on the economy by our
predecessors are *The Present Crisis*, April 25, 1933; *Statement on Church and Social Order*
February 4, 1940; *The Economy: Human Dimensions*, November 20, 1975. These and
numerous other statements of the U.S. Catholic episcopate can be found in Hugh J.
Nolan, ed., *Pastoral Letters of the United States Catholic Bishops*, 4 vols. (Washington,
D.C.: USCC Office of Publishing and Promotion Services, 1984).

[1] *Mater et Magistra*, 219-220. See *Pastoral Constitution*, 63.

solidarity that are essential to the dignity of persons. Wherever our economic arrangements fail to conform to the demands of human dignity lived in community, they must be questioned and transformed. These convictions have a biblical basis. They are also supported by a long tradition of theological and philosophical reflection and through the reasoned analysis of human experience by contemporary men and women.

29. In presenting the Christian moral vision, we turn first to the Scriptures for guidance. Though our comments are necessarily selective, we hope that pastors and other church members will become personally engaged with the biblical texts. The Scriptures contain many passages that speak directly of economic life. We must also attend to the Bible's deeper vision of God, of the purpose of creation, and of the dignity of human life in society. Along with other churches and ecclesial communities who are "strengthened by the grace of Baptism and the hearing of God's Word," we strive to become faithful hearers and doers of the word.[2] We also claim the Hebrew Scriptures as common heritage with our Jewish brothers and sisters, and we join with them in the quest for an economic life worthy of the divine revelation we share.

A. Biblical Perspectives

30. The fundamental conviction of our faith is that human life is fulfilled in the knowledge and love of the living God in communion with others. The Sacred Scriptures offer guidance so that men and women may enter into full communion with God and with each other, and witness to God's saving acts. We discover there a God who is creator of heaven and earth, and of the human family. Though our first parents reject the God who created them, God does not abandon them, but from Abraham and Sarah forms a people of promise. When this people is enslaved in an alien land, God delivers them and makes a covenant with them in which they are summoned to be faithful to the *torah* or sacred teaching. The focal points of Israel's faith—creation, covenant, and community—provide a foundation for reflection on issues of economic and social justice.

1. Created in God's Image

31. After the exile, when Israel combined its traditions into a written *torah*, it prefaced its history as a people with the story of the creation of all peoples and of the whole world by the same God who created them as a nation (Gn 1-11). God is the creator of heaven and earth

---

[2]Vatican Council II, *Decree on Ecumenism,* 22-23.

(Gn 14:19-22; Is 40:28; 45:18); creation proclaims God's glory (Ps 89:6-12) and is "very good" (Gn 1:31). Fruitful harvests, bountiful flocks, a loving family are God's blessings on those who heed God's word. Such is the joyful refrain that echoes throughout the Bible. One legacy of this theology of creation is the conviction that no dimension of human life lies beyond God's care and concern. God is present to creation, and creative engagement with God's handiwork is itself reverence for God.

32. At the summit of creation stands the creation of man and woman, made in God's image (Gn 1:26-27). *As such every human being possesses an inalienable dignity that stamps human existence prior to any division into races or nations and prior to human labor and human achievement (Gn 2:4-11).* Men and women are also to share in the creative activity of God. They are to be fruitful, to care for the earth (Gn 2:15), and to have "dominion" over it (Gn 1:28), which means they are "to govern the world in holiness and justice and to render judgment in integrity of heart" (Wis 9:3). Creation is a gift; women and men are to be faithful stewards in caring for the earth. They can justly consider that by their labor they are unfolding the Creator's work.[3]

33. The narratives of Genesis 1-11 also portray the origin of the strife and suffering that mar the world. Though created to enjoy intimacy with God and the fruits of the earth, Adam and Eve disrupted God's design by trying to live independently of God through a denial of their status as creatures. They turned away from God and gave to God's creation the obedience due to God alone. For this reason the prime sin in so much of the biblical tradition is idolatry: service of the creature rather than of the creator (Rom 1:25), and the attempt to overturn creation by making God in human likeness. The Bible castigates not only the worship of idols, but also manifestations of idolatry, such as the quest for unrestrained power and the desire for great wealth (Is 40:12-20; 44:1-20; Wis 13:1-14:31; Col 3:5, "the greed that is idolatry"). The sin of our first parents had other consequences as well. Alienation from God pits brother against brother (Gn 4:8-16), in a cycle of war and vengeance (Gn 4:22-23). Sin and evil abound, and the primeval history culminates with another assault on the heavens, this time ending in a babble of tongues scattered over the face of the earth (Gn 11:1-9). Sin simultaneously alienates human beings from God and shatters the solidarity of the human community. Yet this reign of sin is not the final word. The primeval history is followed by the call of Abraham, a man of faith, who was to be the bearer of the promise to many nations (Gn 12:1-4). Throughout the Bible we find

---

[3]C. Westermann, *Creation* (Philadelphia: Fortress Press, 1974); and B. Vawter, *On Genesis: A New Reading* (Garden City, N.Y.: Doubleday, 1977). See also *Pastoral Constitution*, 34.

this struggle between sin and repentance. God's judgment on evil is followed by God's seeking out a sinful people.

34. The biblical vision of creation has provided one of the most enduring legacies of church teaching. To stand before God as the creator is to respect God's creation, both the world of nature and of human history. *From the patristic period to the present, the Church has affirmed that misuse of the world's resources or appropriation of them by a minority of the world's population betrays the gift of creation since "whatever belongs to God belongs to all."*[4]

2. A People of the Covenant

35. When the people of Israel, our forerunners in faith, gathered in thanksgiving to renew their covenant (Jos 24:1-15), they recalled the gracious deeds of God (Dt 6:20-25; 26:5-11). When they lived as aliens in a strange land and experienced oppression and slavery, they cried out. The Lord, the God of their ancestors, heard their cries, knew their afflictions, and came to deliver them (Ex 3:7-8). By leading them out of Egypt, God created a people that was to be the Lord's very own (Jer 24:7; Hos 2:25). They were to imitate God by treating the alien and the slave in their midst as God had treated them (Ex 22:20-22, Jer 34:8-14).

36. In the midst of this saving history stands the covenant at Sinai (Ex 19-24). It begins with an account of what God has done for the people (Ex 19:1-6; cf. Jos 24:1-13) and includes from God's side a promise of steadfast love (*hesed*) and faithfulness (*'emeth*, Ex 34:5-7). The people are summoned to ratify this covenant by faithfully worshiping God alone and by directing their lives according to God's will, which was made explicit in Israel's great legal codes such as the Decalogue (Ex 20:1-17) and the Book of the Covenant (Ex 20:22-23:33). Far from being an arbitrary restriction on the life of the people, these codes made life in community possible.[5] The specific laws of the covenant protect human life and property, demand respect for parents and the spouses and children of one's neighbor, and manifest a special concern for the vulnerable members of the community: widows, orphans, the poor, and strangers in the land. Laws such as that for the Sabbath year when the land was left fallow (Ex 23:11; Lv 25:1-7) and for the year of release of debts (Dt 15:1-11) summoned people to

---

[4]St. Cyprian, *On Works and Almsgiving*, 25, trans. R. J. Deferrari, *St. Cyprian: Treatises*, 36 (New York: Fathers of the Church, 1958), 251. Original text in Migne, *Patrologia Latina*, vol. 4, 620. On the Patristic teaching, see C. Avila, *Ownership: Early Christian Teaching* (Maryknoll, N.Y.: Orbis Books, 1983). Collection of original texts and translations.

[5]T. Ogletree, *The Use of the Bible in Christian Ethics* (Philadelphia: Fortress Press, 1983), 47-85.

respect the land as God's gift and reminded Israel that as a people freed by God from bondage they were to be concerned for the poor and oppressed in their midst. Every fiftieth year a jubilee was to be proclaimed as a year of "liberty throughout the land" and property was to be restored to its original owners (Lv 25:8-17, cf. Is 61:1-2; Lk 4:18-19).[6] The codes of Israel reflect the norms of the covenant; reciprocal responsibility, mercy, and truthfulness. They embody a life in freedom from oppression: worship of the One God, rejection of idolatry, mutual respect among people, care and protection for every member of the social body. Being free and being a co-responsible community are God's intentions for us.

37. When the people turn away from the living God to serve idols and no longer heed the commands of the covenant, God sends prophets to recall his saving deeds and to summon them to return to the one who betrothed them "in right and in justice, in love and in mercy" (Hos 2:21). The substance of prophetic faith is proclaimed by Micah: "to do justice and to love kindness, and to walk humbly with your God" (Mi 6:8, RSV). Biblical faith in general, and prophetic faith especially, insist that fidelity to the covenant joins obedience to God with reverence and concern for the neighbor. The biblical terms which best summarize this double dimension of Israel's faith are *sedaqah*, justice (also translated as righteousness), and *mishpat* (right judgment or justice embodied in a concrete act or deed). The biblical understanding of justice gives a fundamental perspective to our reflections on social and economic justice.[7]

38. God is described as a "God of justice" (Is 30:18) who loves justice (Is 61:8, cf. Pss 11:7; 33:5; 37:28; 99:4) and delights in it (Jer 9:23). God demands justice from the whole people (Dt 16:20) and executes justice for the needy (Ps 140:13). Central to the biblical presentation of justice is that the justice of a community is measured by its treatment of the powerless in society, most often described as the widow, the orphan, the poor, and the stranger (non-Israelite) in the land. The Law, the Prophets, and the Wisdom literature of the Old Testament all show deep concern for the proper treatment of such people.[8] What these groups of people have in common is their vulnerability and lack of power. They are often alone and have no protector or advocate. There-

---

[6]Though scholars debate whether the Jubilee was a historical institution or an ideal, its images were continually evoked to stress God's sovereignty over the land and God's concern for the poor and the oppressed (e.g., Is 61:1-2; Lk 4:16-19). See R. North, *Sociology of the Biblical Jubilee* (Rome: Biblical Institute, 1954); S. Ringe, *Jesus, Liberation and the Biblical Jubilee: Images for Ethics and Christology* (Philadelphia: Fortress Press, 1985).

[7]On justice, see J. R. Donahue, "Biblical Perspectives on Justice," in Haughey, ed., *The Faith That Does Justice* (New York: Paulist Press, 1977), 68-112; and S. C. Mott, *Biblical Ethics and Social Change* (New York: Oxford University Press, 1982).

[8]See Ex 22:20-26; Dt 15:1-11; Jb 29:12-17; Pss 69:34, 72:2, 4, 12-24; 82;3-4; Prv 14:21, 31; Is 3:14-15; 10:2; Jer 22:16; Zec 7:9-10.

fore, it is God who hears their cries (Pss 109:21; 113:7), and the king who is God's anointed is commanded to have special concern for them.

39. Justice has many nuances.[9] Fundamentally, it suggests a sense of what is right or of what should happen. For example, paths are just when they bring you to your destination (Gn 24:48; Ps 23:3), and laws are just when they create harmony within the community, as Isaiah says: "Justice will bring about peace; right will produce calm and security" (Is 32:17). God is "just" by acting as God should, coming to the people's aid and summoning them to conversion when they stray. People are summoned to be "just," that is, to be in a proper relation to God, by observing God's laws which form them into a faithful community. Biblical justice is more comprehensive than subsequent philosophical definitions. It is not concerned with a strict definition of rights and duties, but with the rightness of the human condition before God and within society. Nor is justice opposed to love; rather, it is both a manifestation of love and a condition for love to grow.[10] Because God loves Israel, he rescues them from oppression and summons them to be a people that "does justice" and loves kindness. The quest for justice arises from loving gratitude for the saving acts of God and manifests itself in wholehearted love of God and neighbor.

40. These perspectives provide the foundation for a biblical vision of economic justice. Every human person is created as an image of God, and the denial of dignity to a person is a blot on this image. Creation is a gift to all men and women, not to be appropriated for the benefit of a few; its beauty is an object of joy and reverence. The same God who came to the aid of an oppressed people and formed them into a covenant community continues to hear the cries of the oppressed and to create communities which are responsive to God's word. God's love and life are present when people can live in a community of faith and hope. These cardinal points of the faith of Israel also furnish the religious context for understanding the saving action of God in the life and teaching of Jesus.

3. The Reign of God and Justice

41. Jesus enters human history as God's anointed Son who announces the nearness of the reign of God (Mk 1:9-14). This proclamation summons us to acknowledge God as creator and covenant partner and

[9] J. Pedersen, *Israel: Its Life and Culture*, vol. I-II (London: Oxford University Press, 1926), 337-340.

[10] J. Alfaro, *Theology of Justice in the World* (Rome: Pontifical Commission on Justice and Peace, 1973), 40-41; E. McDonagh, *The Making of Disciples* (Wilmington, Del.: Michael Glazier, 1982), 119.

challenges us to seek ways in which God's revelation of the dignity and destiny of all creation might become incarnate in history. It is not simply the promise of the future victory of God over sin and evil, but that this victory has already begun—in the life and teaching of Jesus.

42. What Jesus proclaims by word, he enacts in his ministry. He resists temptations of power and prestige, follows his Father's will, and teaches us to pray that it be accomplished on earth. He warns against attempts to "lay up treasures on earth" (Mt 6:19) and exhorts his followers not to be anxious about material goods but rather to seek first God's reign and God's justice (Mt 6:25-33). His mighty works symbolize that the reign of God is more powerful than evil, sickness, and the hardness of the human heart. He offers God's loving mercy to sinners (Mk 2:17), takes up the cause of those who suffered religious and social discrimination (Lk 7:36-50; 15:1-2), and attacks the use of religion to avoid the demands of charity and justice (Mk 7:9-13; Mt 23:23).

43. When asked what was the greatest commandment, Jesus quoted the age-old Jewish affirmation of faith that God alone is One and to be loved with the whole heart, mind, and soul (Dt 6:4-5) and immediately adds: "You shall love your neighbor as yourself" (Lv 19:18; Mk 12:28-34). This dual command of love that is the basis of all Christian morality is illustrated in the Gospel of Luke by the parable of a Samaritan who interrupts his journey to come to the aid of a dying man (Lk 10:29-37). Unlike the other wayfarers who look on the man and pass by, the Samaritan "was moved with compassion at the sight"; he stops, tends the wounded man, and takes him to a place of safety. In this parable compassion is the bridge between mere seeing and action; love is made real through effective action.[11]

44. Near the end of his life, Jesus offers a vivid picture of the last judgment (Mt 25:31-46). All the nations of the world will be assembled and will be divided into those blessed who are welcomed into God's kingdom or those cursed who are sent to eternal punishment. The blessed are those who fed the hungry, gave drink to the thirsty, welcomed the stranger, clothed the naked, and visited the sick and imprisoned; the cursed are those who neglected these works of mercy and love. Neither the blessed nor the cursed are astounded that they are judged by the Son of Man, nor that judgment is rendered according to works of charity. The shock comes when they find that in neglecting the poor, the outcast, and the oppressed, they were rejecting Jesus himself. Jesus who came as "Emmanuel" ("God with us," Mt 1:23) and who promises to be with his people until the end of the age (Mt 28:20) is hidden in those most in need; to reject them is to reject God made manifest in history.

---

[11]Pope John Paul II has drawn on this parable to exhort us to have a "compassionate heart" to those in need in his Apostolic Letter *On the Christian Meaning of Human Suffering* (*Salvifici Doloris*) (Washington, D.C.: USCC Office of Publishing and Promotion Services, 1984), 34-39.

4. Called to Be Disciples in Community

45. Jesus summoned his first followers to a change of heart and to take on the yoke of God's reign (Mk 1:14-15; Mt 11:29). They are to be the nucleus of that community which will continue the work of proclaiming and building God's kingdom through the centuries. As Jesus called the first disciples in the midst of their everyday occupations of fishing and tax collecting, so he again calls people in every age in the home, in the workplace, and in the marketplace.

46. The Church is, as Pope John Paul II reminded us, "a community of disciples" in which "we must see first and foremost Christ saying to each member of the community: follow me."[12] To be a Christian is to join with others in responding to this personal call and in learning the meaning of Christ's life. It is to be sustained by that loving intimacy with the Father that Jesus experienced in his work, in his prayer, and in his suffering.

47. Discipleship involves imitating the pattern of Jesus' life by openness to God's will in the service of others (Mk 10:42-45). Disciples are also called to follow him in the way of the cross and to heed his call that those who lose their lives for the sake of the Gospel will save them (Mk 8:34-35). Jesus' death is an example of that greater love which lays down one's life for others (cf. Jn 15:12-18). It is a model for those who suffer persecution for the sake of justice (Mt 5:10). The death of Jesus was not the end of his power and presence, for he was raised up by the power of God. Nor did it mark the end of the disciples' union with him. After Jesus had appeared to them and when they received the gift of the Spirit (Acts 2:1-12), they became apostles of the good news to the ends of the earth. In the face of poverty and persecution they transformed human lives and formed communities which became signs of the power and presence of God. Sharing in this same resurrection faith, contemporary followers of Christ can face the struggles and challenges that await those who bring the gospel vision to bear on our complex economic and social world.

5. Poverty, Riches, and the Challenge of Discipleship

48. The pattern of Christian life as presented in the Gospel of Luke has special relevance today. In her *Magnificat*, Mary rejoices in a God who scatters the proud, brings down the mighty, and raises up the poor and lowly (Lk 1:51-53). The first public utterance of Jesus is "The Spirit of the Lord is upon me, because he has anointed me to preach the good news to the poor" (Lk 4:18; cf. Is 61:1-2). Jesus adds to the blessing on the poor a warning, "Woe to you who are rich, for you

---

[12] *Redeemer of Man*, 21.

have received your consolation" (Lk 6:24). He warns his followers against greed and reliance on abundant possessions and underscores this by the parable of the man whose life is snatched away at the very moment he tries to secure his wealth (Lk 12:13-21). In Luke alone, Jesus tells the parable of the rich man who does not see the poor and suffering Lazarus at his gate (Lk 16:19-31). When the rich man finally "sees" Lazarus, it is from the place of torment and the opportunity for conversion has passed. Pope John Paul II has often recalled this parable to warn the prosperous not to be blind to the great poverty that exists beside great wealth.[13]

49. Jesus, especially in Luke, lives as a poor man, like the prophets takes the side of the poor, and warns of the dangers of wealth.[14] The terms used for poor, while primarily describing lack of material goods, also suggest dependence and powerlessness. The poor are also an exiled and oppressed people whom God will rescue (Is 51:21-23) as well as a faithful remnant who take refuge in God (Zep 3:12-13). Throughout the Bible, material poverty is a misfortune and a cause of sadness. A constant biblical refrain is that the poor must be cared for and protected and that when they are exploited, God hears their cries (Prv 22:22-23). Conversely, even though the goods of the earth are to be enjoyed and people are to thank God for material blessings, wealth is a constant danger. The rich are wise in their own eyes (Prv 28:11) and are prone to apostasy and idolatry (Am 5:4-13; Is 2:6-8), as well as to violence and oppression (Jas 2:6-7).[15] Since they are neither blinded by wealth nor make it into an idol, the poor can be open to God's presence; throughout Israel's history and in early Christianity the poor are agents of God's transforming power.

50. The poor are often related to the lowly (Mt 5:3,5) to whom God reveals what was hidden from the wise (Mt 11:25-30). When Jesus calls the poor "blessed," he is not praising their condition of poverty, but their openness to God. When he states that the reign of God is theirs, he voices God's special concern for them and promises that they are to be the beneficiaries of God's mercy and justice. When he summons disciples to leave all and follow him, he is calling them to share his own radical trust in the Father and his freedom from care and anxiety (cf. Mt. 6:25-34). The practice of evangelical poverty in

---

[13] Address to Workers at São Paulo, 8, *Origins,* 10:9 (July 31, 1980): 139; and Address at Yankee Stadium, *Origins* 9:19 (October 25, 1979): 311-312.

[14] J. Dupont and A. George, eds. *La pauvrete evangelique* (Paris: Cerf, 1971); M. Hengel, *Property and Riches in the Early Church* (Philadelphia: Fortress Press, 1974); L. Johnson, *Sharing Possessions: Mandate and Symbol of Faith* (Philadelphia: Fortress Press, 1981); D. L. Mealand, *Poverty and Expectation in the Gospels* (London: SPCK, 1980); W. Pilgrim, *Good News to the Poor: Wealth and Poverty in Luke-Acts* (Minneapolis: Augsburg, 1981); and W. Stegemann, *The Gospel and the Poor* (Philadelphia: Fortress Press, 1984).

[15] See Am 4:1-3; Jb 20:19; Sir 13:4-7; Jas 2:6; 5:1-6, Rv 18:11-19.

the Church has always been a living witness to the power of that trust and to the joy that comes with that freedom.

51. Early Christianity saw the poor as an object of God's special love, but it neither canonized material poverty nor accepted deprivation as an inevitable fact of life. Though few early Christians possessed wealth or power (1 Cor 1:26-28; Jas 2:5), their communities had well-off members (Acts 16:14; 18:8). Jesus' concern for the poor was continued in different forms in the early Church. The early community at Jerusalem distributed its possessions so that "there was no needy person among them," and held "all things in common"—a phrase that suggests not only shared material possessions, but more fundamentally, friendship and mutual concern among all its members (Acts 4:32-34; 2:44). While recognizing the dangers of wealth, the early Church proposed the proper use of possessions to alleviate need and suffering, rather than universal dispossession. Beginning in the first century and throughout history, Christian communities have developed varied structures to support and sustain the weak and powerless in societies that were often brutally unconcerned about human suffering.

52. Such perspectives provide a basis today for what is called the "preferential option for the poor."[16] Though in the Gospels and in the New Testament as a whole the offer of salvation is extended to all peoples, Jesus takes the side of those most in need, physically and spiritually. The example of Jesus poses a number of challenges to the contemporary Church. It imposes a prophetic mandate to speak for those who have no one to speak for them, to be a defender of the defenseless, who in biblical terms are the poor. It also demands a compassionate vision that enables the Church to see things from the side of the poor and powerless and to assess lifestyle, policies, and social institutions in terms of their impact on the poor. It summons the Church also to be an instrument in assisting people to experience the liberating power of God in their own lives so that they may respond to the Gospel in freedom and in dignity. Finally, and most radically, it calls for an emptying of self, both individually and corporately, that allows the Church to experience the power of God in the midst of poverty and powerlessness.

6. A Community of Hope

53. The biblical vision of creation, covenant, and community, as well as the summons to discipleship, unfolds under the tension between promise and fulfillment. The whole Bible is spanned by the narratives of the first creation (Gn 1-3) and the vision of a restored creation at the end of history (Rv 21:1-4). Just as creation tells us that God's desire was one of wholeness and unity between God and the human family

---

[16]See paras. 85-91.

and within this family itself, the images of a new creation give hope that enmity and hatred will cease and justice and peace will reign (Is 11:4-6; 25:1-8). Human life unfolds "between the times," the time of the first creation and that of a restored creation (Rom 8:18-25). Although the ultimate realization of God's plan lies in the future, Christians in union with all people of good will are summoned to shape history in the image of God's creative design, and in response to the reign of God proclaimed and embodied by Jesus.

54. A Christian is a member of a new community, "God's own people" (1 Pt 2:9-10), who, like the people of Exodus, owes its existence to the gracious gift of God and is summoned to respond to God's will made manifest in the life and teaching of Jesus. A Christian walks in the newness of life (Rom 6:4), and is "a new creation; the old has passed away, the new has come" (2 Cor 5:17). This new creation in Christ proclaims that God's creative love is constantly at work, offers sinners forgiveness, and reconciles a broken world. Our action on behalf of justice in our world proceeds from the conviction that, despite the power of injustice and violence, life has been fundamentally changed by the entry of the Word made flesh into human history.

55. Christian communities that commit themselves to solidarity with those suffering and to confrontation with those attitudes and ways of acting which institutionalize injustice, will themselves experience the power and presence of Christ. They will embody in their lives the values of the new creation while they labor under the old. The quest for economic and social justice will always combine hope and realism, and must be renewed by every generation. It involves diagnosing those situations that continue to alienate the world from God's creative love as well as presenting hopeful alternatives that arise from living in a renewed creation. This quest arises from faith and is sustained by hope as it seeks to speak to a broken world of God's justice and loving kindness.

7. A Living Tradition

56. Our reflection on U.S. economic life today must be rooted in this biblical vision of the kingdom and discipleship, but it must also be shaped by the rich and complex tradition of Catholic life and thought. Throughout its history, the Christian community has listened to the words of Scripture and sought to enact them in the midst of daily life in very different historical and cultural contexts.

57. In the first centuries, when Christians were a minority in a hostile society, they cared for one another through generous almsgiving. In the patristic era, the church fathers repeatedly stressed that the goods of the earth were created by God for the benefit of every person without exception, and that all have special duties toward those in need. The monasteries of the Middle Ages were centers of prayer, learning, and education. They contributed greatly to the cultural and economic life of the towns and cities that sprang up around them. In the twelfth century, the new mendicant orders dedicated themselves to following Christ in poverty and to the proclamation of the good news to the poor.

58. These same religious communities also nurtured some of the greatest theologians of the Church's tradition, thinkers who synthesized the call of Christ with the philosophical learning of Greek, Roman, Jewish, and Arab worlds. Thomas Aquinas and the other scholastics devoted rigorous intellectual energy to clarifying the meaning of both personal virtue and justice in society. In more recent centuries Christians began to build a large network of hospitals, orphanages, and schools, to serve the poor and society at large. And beginning with Leo XIII's *Rerum Novarum*, down to the writings and speeches of John Paul II, the popes have more systematically addressed the rapid change of modern society in a series of social encyclicals. These teachings of modern popes and of the Second Vatican Council are especially significant for efforts to respond to the problems facing society today.[17]

59. We also have much to learn from the strong emphasis on Protestant traditions on the vocation of lay people in the world and from ecumenical efforts to develop an economic ethic that addresses newly emergent problems. And in a special way our fellow Catholics in developing countries have much to teach us about Christian response to an ever more interdependent world.

60. Christians today are called by God to carry on this tradition through active love of neighbor, a love that responds to the special challenges of this moment in human history. The world is wounded by sin and injustice, in need of conversion and of the transformation that comes when persons enter more deeply into the mystery of the death and Resurrection of Christ. The concerns of this pastoral letter are not at all peripheral to the central mystery at the heart of the Church.[18] They are integral to the proclamation of the Gospel and part of the vocation of every Christian today.[19]

B. Ethical Norms for Economic Life

61. These biblical and theological themes shape the overall Christian perspective on economic ethics. This perspective is also subscribed to by many who do not share Christian religious convictions. Human understanding and religious belief are complementary, not contra-

---

[17]See Selected Bibliography.

[18]Extraordinary Synod of Bishops (1985) *The Final Report*, II, A (Washington, D.C.: USCC Office of Publishing and Promotion Services, 1986).

[19]Pope Paul VI, *On Evangelization in the Modern World*, 31.

dictory. For human beings are created in God's image, and their dignity is manifest in the ability to reason and understand, in their freedom to shape their own lives and the life of their communities, and in the capacity for love and friendship. In proposing ethical norms, therefore, we appeal both to Christians and to all in our pluralist society to show that respect and reverence owed to the dignity of every person. Intelligent reflection on the social and economic realities of today is also indispensable in the effort to respond to economic circumstances never envisioned in biblical times. Therefore, we now want to propose an ethical framework that can guide economic life today in ways that are both faithful to the Gospel and shaped by human experience and reason.

62. First we outline the *duties* all people have to each other and to the whole community: love of neighbor, the basic requirements of justice, and the special obligation to those who are poor or vulnerable. Corresponding to these duties are the *human rights* of every person; the obligation to protect the dignity of all demands respect for these rights. Finally these duties and rights entail several *priorities* that should guide the economic choices of individuals, communities, and the nation as a whole.

1. The Responsibilities of Social Living

63. Human life is life in community. Catholic social teaching proposes several complementary perspectives that show how moral responsibilities and duties in the economic sphere are rooted in this call to community.

a. Love and Solidarity

64. *The commandments to love God with all one's heart and to love one's neighbor as oneself are the heart and soul of Christian morality.* Jesus offers himself as the model of this all-inclusive love: ". . . love one another as I have loved you" (Jn 15:12). These commands point out the path toward true human fulfillment and happiness. They are not arbitrary restrictions on human freedom. Only active love of God and neighbor makes the fullness of community happen. Christians look forward in hope to a true communion among all persons with each other and with God. The Spirit of Christ labors in history to build up the bonds of solidarity among all persons until the day on which their union is brought to perfection in the kingdom of God.[20] Indeed Christian theological reflection on the very reality of God as a trinitarian unity of

---

[20]Ibid., 24.

persons—Father, Son, and Holy Spirit—shows that being a person means being united to other persons in mutual love.[21]

65. What the Bible and Christian tradition teach, human wisdom confirms. Centuries before Christ, the Greeks and Romans spoke of the human person as a "social animal" made for friendship, community, and public life. These insights show that human beings achieve self-realization not in isolation, but in interaction with others.[22]

66. The virtues of citizenship are an expression of Christian love more crucial in today's interdependent world than ever before. These virtues grow out of a lively sense of one's dependence on the commonweal and obligations to it. This civic commitment must also guide the economic institutions of society. In the absence of a vital sense of citizenship among the businesses, corporations, labor unions, and other groups that shape economic life, society as a whole is endangered. Solidarity is another name for this social friendship and civic commitment that make human, moral, and economic life possible.

67. The Christian tradition recognizes, of course, that the fullness of love and community will be achieved only when God's work in Christ comes to completion in the kingdom of God. This kingdom has been inaugurated among us, but God's redeeming and transforming work is not yet complete. Within history, knowledge of how to achieve the goal of social unity is limited. Human sin continues to wound the lives of both individuals and larger social bodies and places obstacles in the path toward greater social solidarity. If efforts to protect human dignity are to be effective, they must take these limits on knowledge and love into account. Nevertheless, sober realism should not be confused with resigned or cynical pessimism. It is a challenge to develop a courageous hope that can sustain efforts that will sometimes be arduous and protracted.

b. Justice and Participation

68. Biblical justice is the goal we strive for. This rich biblical understanding portrays a just society as one marked by the fullness of love, compassion, holiness, and peace. On their path through history, however, sinful human beings need more specific guidance on how to move toward the realization of this great vision of God's kingdom. This guidance is contained in the norms of basic or minimal justice. These norms state the *minimum* levels of mutual care and respect that all persons owe to each other in an imperfect world.[23] Catholic social teaching, like much philosophical reflection, distinguishes three

---

[21]*Pastoral Constitution*, 32.

[22]Ibid., 25.

[23]See para. 39.

dimensions of basic justice: commutative justice, distributive justice, and social justice.[24]

69. *Commutative justice calls for fundamental fairness in all agreements and exchanges between individuals or private social groups.* It demands respect for the equal human dignity of all persons in economic transactions, contracts, or promises. For example, workers owe their employers diligent work in exchange for their wages. Employers are obligated to treat their employees as persons, paying them fair wages in exchange for the work done and establishing conditions and patterns of work that are truly human.[25]

70. *Distributive justice requires that the allocation of income, wealth, and power in society be evaluated in light of its effects on persons whose basic material needs are unmet.* The Second Vatican Council stated: "The right to have a share of earthly goods sufficient for one's self and one's family belongs to everyone. The fathers and doctors of the Church held this view, teaching that we are obliged to come to the relief of the poor and to do so not merely out of our superfluous goods."[26] Minimum material resources are an absolute necessity for human life. If persons are to be recognized as members of the human community, then the community has an obligation to help fulfill these basic needs unless an absolute scarcity of resources makes this strictly impossible. No such scarcity exists in the United States today.

71. Justice also has implications for the way the larger social, economic, and political institutions of society are organized. *Social justice implies that persons have an obligation to be active and productive participants in the life of society and that society has a duty to enable them to participate in this way.* This form of justice can also be called "contributive," for it stresses the duty of all who are able to help create the goods, services, and other nonmaterial or spiritual values necessary for the welfare of the whole community. In the words of Pius XI, "It is of the very essence of social justice to demand from each individual all that is necessary for the common good."[27] Productivity is essential if the community is to have the resources to serve the well-being of all. Productivity, however, cannot be measured solely by its output in

---

[24]Josef Pieper, *The Four Cardinal Virtues* (Notre Dame, Ind.: University of Notre Dame Press, 1966), 43-116; David Hollenbach, "Modern Catholic Teachings concerning Justice," in John C. Haughey ed., *The Faith That Does Justice* (New York: Paulist Press, 1977), 207-231.

[25]Jon P. Gunnemann, "Capitalism and Commutative Justice," presented at the 1985 meeting of the Society of Christian Ethics, forthcoming in *The Annual of the Society of Christian Ethics.*

[26]*Pastoral Constitution*, 69.

[27]Pope Pius XI, *Divini Redemptoris*, 51. See John A. Ryan, *Distributive Justice*, third edition (New York: Macmillan, 1942), 188. The term "social justice" has been used in several different but related ways in the Catholic ethical tradition. See William Ferree, "The Act of Social Justice," *Philosophical Studies*, vol. 72 (Washington, D.C.: The Catholic University of America Press, 1943).

goods and services. Patterns of production must also be measured in light of their impact on the fulfillment of basic needs, employment levels, patterns of discrimination, environmental quality, and sense of community.

72. The meaning of social justice also includes a duty to organize economic and social institutions so that people can contribute to society in ways that respect their freedom and the dignity of their labor. Work should enable the working person to become "more a human being," more capable of acting intelligently, freely, and in ways that lead to self-realization.[28]

73. Economic conditions that leave large numbers of able people unemployed, underemployed, or employed in dehumanizing conditions fail to meet the converging demands of these three forms of basic justice. Work with adequate pay for all who seek it is the primary means for achieving basic justice in our society. Discrimination in job opportunities or income levels on the basis of race, sex, or other arbitrary standards can never be justified.[29] It is a scandal that such discrimination continues in the United States today. Where the effects of past discrimination persist, society has the obligation to take positive steps to overcome the legacy of injustice. Judiciously administered affirmative action programs in education and employment can be important expressions of the drive for solidarity and participation that is at the heart of true justice. Social harm calls for social relief.

74. Basic justice also calls for the establishment of a floor of material well-being on which all can stand. This is a duty of the whole of society and it creates particular obligations for those with greater resources. This duty calls into question extreme inequalities of income and consumption when so many lack basic necessities. Catholic social teaching does not maintain that a flat, arithmetical equality of income and wealth is a demand of justice, but it does challenge economic arrangements that leave large numbers of people impoverished. Further, it sees extreme inequality as a threat to the solidarity of the human community, for great disparities lead to deep social divisions and conflict.[30]

75. This means that all of us must examine our way of living in light of the needs of the poor. Christian faith and the norms of justice impose distinct limits on what we consume and how we view material goods. The great wealth of the United States can easily blind us to the poverty that exists in this nation and the destitution of hundreds of millions of people in other parts of the world. Americans are challenged today as never before to develop the inner freedom to resist

---

[28] *On Human Work,* 6, 9.
[29] *Pastoral Constitution,* 29.
[30] Ibid. See below, paras. 180-182.

the temptation constantly to seek more. Only in this way will the nation avoid what Paul VI called "the most evident form of moral underdevelopment," namely greed.[31]

76. These duties call not only for individual charitable giving but also for a more systematic approach by businesses, labor unions, and the many other groups that shape economic life—as well as government. The concentration of privilege that exists today results far more from institutional relationships that distribute power and wealth inequitably than from differences in talent or lack of desire to work. These institutional patterns must be examined and revised if we are to meet the demands of basic justice. For example, a system of taxation based on assessment according to ability to pay[32] is a prime necessity for the fulfillment of these social obligations.

c. Overcoming Marginalization and Powerlessness

77. These fundamental duties can be summarized this way: *Basic justice demands the establishment of minimum levels of participation in the life of the human community for all persons.* The ultimate injustice is for a person or group to be treated actively or abandoned passively as if they were nonmembers of the human race. To treat people this way is effectively to say that they simply do not count as human beings. This can take many forms, all of which can be described as varieties of marginalization, or exclusion from social life.[33] This exclusion can occur in the political sphere: restriction of free speech, concentration of power in the hands of a few, or outright repression by the state. It can also take economic forms that are equally harmful. Within the United States, individuals, families, and local communities fall victim to a downward cycle of poverty generated by economic forces they are powerless to influence. The poor, the disabled, and the unemployed too often are simply left behind. This pattern is even more severe beyond our borders in the least-developed countries. Whole nations are prevented from fully participating in the international economic order because they lack the power to change their disadvantaged position. Many people within the less developed countries are excluded from sharing in the meager resources available in their homelands by unjust elites and unjust governments. These patterns of exclusion are created by free human beings. In this sense they can be called forms of social sin.[34] Acquiescence in them or failure to correct

---

[31] Pope Paul VI, *On the Development of Peoples* (1967), 19.

[32] *Mater et Magistra*, 132.

[33] *Justice in the World*, 10, 16; and *Octogesima Adveniens*, 15.

[34] *Pastoral Constitution*, 25; *Justice in the World*, 51; Pope John Paul II, *The Gift of the Redemption*, Apostolic Exhortation on Reconciliation and Penance (Washington, D.C.: USCC Office of Publishing and Promotion Services, 1984), 16; Congregation for the Doctrine of the Faith, *Instruction on Christian Freedom and Liberation*, 42, 74.

them when it is possible to do so is a sinful dereliction of Christian duty.

78. Recent Catholic social thought regards the task of overcoming these patterns of exclusion and powerlessness as a most basic demand of justice. Stated positively, justice demands that social institutions be ordered in a way that guarantees all persons the ability to participate actively in the economic, political, and cultural life of society.[35] The level of participation may legitimately be greater for some persons than for others, but there is a basic level of access that must be made available for all. Such participation is an essential expression of the social nature of human beings and of their communitarian vocation.

2. Human Rights: The Minimum Conditions for Life in Community

79. Catholic social teaching spells out the basic demands of justice in greater detail in the human rights of every person. These fundamental rights are prerequisites for a dignified life in community. The Bible vigorously affirms the sacredness of every person as a creature formed in the image and likeness of God. The biblical emphasis on covenant and community also shows that human dignity can only be realized and protected in solidarity with others. In Catholic social thought, therefore, respect for human rights and a strong sense of both personal and community responsibility are linked, not opposed. Vatican II described the common good as "the sum of those conditions of social life which allow social groups and their individual members relatively thorough and ready access to their own fulfillment."[36] These conditions include the rights to fulfillment of material needs, a guarantee of fundamental freedoms, and the protection of relationships that are essential to participation in the life of society.[37] These rights are bestowed on human beings by God and grounded in the nature and dignity of human persons. They are not created by society. Indeed society has a duty to secure and protect them.[38]

80. The full range of human rights has been systematically outlined by John XXIII in his encyclical *Peace on Earth*. His discussion echoes the United Nations Universal Declaration of Human Rights and implies that internationally accepted human rights standards are strongly supported by Catholic teaching. These rights include the civil and

---

[35]In the words of the 1971 Synod of Bishops: "Participation constitutes a right which is to be applied in the economic and in the social and political field," *Justice in the World*, 18.

[36]*Pastoral Constitution*, 26.

[37]Pope John Paul II, Address at the General Assembly of the United Nations (October 2, 1979), 13, 14.

[38]See Pope Pius XII, 1941 Pentecost Address, in V. Yzermans, *The Major Addresses of Pope Pius XII*, vol. I (St. Paul: North Central, 1961), 32-33.

political rights to freedom of speech, worship, and assembly. A number of human rights also concern human welfare and are of a specifically economic nature. First among these are the rights to life, food, clothing, shelter, rest, medical care, and basic education. These are indispensable to the protection of human dignity. In order to ensure these necessities, all persons have a right to earn a living, which for most people in our economy is through remunerative employment. All persons also have a right to security in the event of sickness, unemployment, and old age. Participation in the life of the community calls for the protection of this same right to employment, as well as the right to healthful working conditions, to wages, and other benefits sufficient to provide individuals and their families with a standard of living in keeping with human dignity, and to the possibility of property ownership.[39] These fundamental personal rights—civil and political as well as social and economic—state the minimum conditions for social institutions that respect human dignity, social solidarity, and justice. They are all essential to human dignity and to the integral development of both individuals and society, and are thus moral issues.[40] Any denial of these rights harms persons and wounds the human community. Their serious and sustained denial violates individuals and destroys solidarity among persons.

81. Social and economic rights call for a mode of implementation different from that required to secure civil and political rights. Freedom of worship and of speech imply immunity from interference on the part of both other persons and the government. The rights to education, employment, and social security, for example, are empowerments that call for positive action by individuals and society at large.

82. However, both kinds of rights call for positive action to create social and political institutions that enable all persons to become active members of society. Civil and political rights allow persons to participate freely in the public life of the community, for example, through free speech, assembly, and the vote. In democratic countries these rights have been secured through a long and vigorous history of creating the institutions of constitutional government. In seeking to secure the full range of social and economic rights today, a similar effort to shape new economic arrangements will be necessary.

83. The first step in such an effort is the development of a new cultural

---

[39] *Peace on Earth*, 8-27. See *On Human Work*, 18-19. *Peace on Earth* and other modern papal statements refer explicitly to the "right to work" as one of the fundamental economic rights. Because of the ambiguous meaning of the phrase in the United States, and also because the ordinary way people earn their living in our society is through paid employment, the NCCB has affirmed previously that the protection of human dignity demands that the right to useful employment be secured for all who are able and willing to work. See NCCB, *The Economy: Human Dimensions* (November 20, 1975), 5, in NCCB, *Justice in the Marketplace*, 470. See also Congregation for the Doctrine of the Faith, *Instruction on Christian Freedom and Liberation*, 85.

[40] *The Development of Peoples*, 14.

consensus that the basic economic conditions of human welfare are essential to human dignity and are due persons by right. Second, the securing of these rights will make demands on *all* members of society, on all private sector institutions, and on government. A concerted effort on all levels in our society is needed to meet these basic demands of justice and solidarity. Indeed political democracy and a commitment to secure economic rights are mutually reinforcing.

84. Securing economic rights for all will be an arduous task. There are a number of precedents in U.S. history, however, which show that the work has already begun.[41] The country needs a serious dialogue about the appropriate levels of private and public sector involvement that are needed to move forward. There is certainly room for diversity of opinion in the Church and in U.S. society on *how* to protect the human dignity and economic rights of all our brothers and sisters.[42] In our view, however, there can be no legitimate disagreement on the basic moral objectives.

3. Moral Priorities for the Nation

85. *The common good demands justice for all, the protection of the human rights for all.*[43] Making cultural and economic institutions more supportive of the freedom, power, and security of individuals and families must be a central, long-range objective for the nation. Every person has a duty to contribute to building up the commonweal. All have a responsibility to develop their talents through education. Adults must contribute to society through their individual vocations and talents. Parents are called to guide their children to the maturity of Christian adulthood and responsible citizenship. Everyone has special duties toward the poor and the marginalized. Living up to these responsibilities, however, is often made difficult by the social and economic patterns of society. Schools and educational policies both public and private often serve the privileged exceedingly well, while the children of the poor are effectively abandoned as second-class citizens. Great stresses are created in family life by the way work is organized and scheduled, and by the social and cultural values communicated on TV. Many in the lower middle class are barely getting by and fear becoming victims of economic forces over which they have no control.

86. *The obligation to provide justice for all means that the poor have the single most urgent economic claim on the conscience of the nation.* Poverty can take many forms, spiritual as well as material. All people face struggles of the spirit as they ask deep questions about their purpose

---

[41]Martha H. Good, "Freedom from Want: The Failure of United States Courts to Protect Subsistence Rights," *Human Rights Quarterly*, 6 (1984): 335-365.

[42]*Pastoral Constitution*, 43.

[43]*Mater et Magistra*, 65.

in life. Many have serious problems in marriage and family life at some time in their lives, and all of us face the certain reality of sickness and death. The Gospel of Christ proclaims that God's love is stronger than all these forms of diminishment. Material deprivation, however, seriously compounds such sufferings of the spirit and heart. To see a loved one sick is bad enough, but to have no possibility of obtaining health care is worse. To face family problems, such as the death of a spouse or a divorce, can be devastating, but to have these lead to the loss of one's home and end with living on the streets is something no one should have to endure in a country as rich as ours. In developing countries these human problems are even more greatly intensified by extreme material deprivation. This form of human suffering can be reduced if our own country, so rich in resources, chooses to increase its assistance.

87. As individuals and as a nation, therefore, we are called to make a fundamental "option for the poor."[44] The obligation to evaluate social and economic activity from the viewpoint of the poor and the powerless arises from the radical command to love one's neighbor as one's self. Those who are marginalized and whose rights are denied have privileged claims if society is to provide justice for *all*. This obligation is deeply rooted in Christian belief. As Paul VI stated:

> In teaching us charity, the Gospel instructs us in the preferential respect due to the poor and the special situation they have in society: the more fortunate should renounce some of their rights so as to place their goods more generously at the service of others.[45]

John Paul II has described this special obligation to the poor as "a call to have a special openness with the small and the weak, those that suffer and weep, those that are humiliated and left on the margin of society, so as to help them win their dignity as human persons and children of God."[46]

88. The prime purpose of this special commitment to the poor is to enable them to become active participants in the life of society. It is to enable *all* persons to share in and contribute to the common good.[47]

---

[44]On the recent use of this term see: Congregation for the Doctrine of the Faith, *Instruction on Christian Freedom and Liberation*, 46-50, 66-68; *Evangelization in Latin America's Present and Future*, Final Document of the Third General Conference of the Latin American Episcopate (Puebla, Mexico; January 27-February 13, 1979), esp. part VI, ch. 1, "A Preferential Option for the Poor," in J. Eagleson and P. Scharper, eds., *Puebla and Beyond* (Maryknoll: Orbis Books, 1979), 264-267; Donal Dorr, *Option for the Poor: A Hundred Years of Vatican Social Teaching* (Dublin: Gill and Macmillan/Maryknoll, N.Y.: Orbis Books, 1983).

[45]*Octogesima Adveniens*, 23.

[46]Address to Bishops of Brazil, 6, 9, *Origins* 10:9 (July 31, 1980): 135.

[47]Pope John Paul II, Address to Workers at São Paulo, 4, *Origins* 10:9 (July 31, 1980): 138; Congregation for the Doctrine of the Faith, *Instruction on Christian Freedom and Liberation*, 66-68.

The "option for the poor," therefore, is not an adversarial slogan that pits one group or class against another. Rather it states that the deprivation and powerlessness of the poor wounds the whole community. The extent of their suffering is a measure of how far we are from being a true community of persons. These wounds will be healed only by greater solidarity with the poor and among the poor themselves.

89. In summary, the norms of love, basic justice, and human rights imply that personal decisions, social policies, and economic institutions should be governed by several key priorities. These priorities do not specify everything that must be considered in economic decision making. They do indicate the most fundamental and urgent objectives.

90. a. *The fulfillment of the basic needs of the poor is of the highest priority.* Personal decisions, policies of private and public bodies, and power relationships must all be evaluated by their effects on those who lack the minimum necessities of nutrition, housing, education, and health care. In particular, this principle recognizes that meeting fundamental human needs must come before the fulfillment of desires for luxury consumer goods, for profits not conducive to the common good, and for unnecessary military hardware.

91. b. *Increasing active participation in economic life by those who are presently excluded or vulnerable is a high social priority.* The human dignity of all is realized when people gain the power to work together to improve their lives, strengthen their families, and contribute to society. Basic justice calls for more than providing help to the poor and other vulnerable members of society. It recognizes the priority of policies and programs that support family life and enhance economic participation through employment and widespread ownership of property. It challenges privileged economic power in favor of the well-being of all. It points to the need to improve the present situation of those unjustly discriminated against in the past. And it has very important implications for both the domestic and the international distribution of power.

92. c. *The investment of wealth, talent, and human energy should be specially directed to benefit those who are poor or economically insecure.* Achieving a more just economy in the United States and the world depends in part on increasing economic resources and productivity. In addition, the ways these resources are invested and managed must be scrutinized in light of their effects on nonmonetary values. Investment and management decisions have crucial moral dimensions: they create jobs or eliminate them; they can push vulnerable families over the edge into poverty or give them new hope for the future; they help or hinder the building of a more equitable society. Indeed they can have either positive or negative influence on the fairness of the global economy. Therefore, this priority presents a strong moral challenge to policies that put large amounts of talent and capital into the production of luxury consumer goods and military technology while failing to invest sufficiently in education, health, the basic infrastructure of our society, and economic sectors that produce urgently needed jobs, goods, and services.

93. d. *Economic and social policies as well as the organization of the work world should be continually evaluated in light of their impact on the strength and stability of family life.* The long-range future of this nation is intimately linked with the well-being of families, for the family is the most basic form of human community.[48] Efficiency and competition in the marketplace must be moderated by greater concern for the way work schedules and compensation support or threaten the bonds between spouses and between parents and children. Health, education, and social service programs should be scrutinized in light of how well they ensure both individual dignity and family integrity.

94. These priorities are not policies. They are norms that should guide the economic choices of all and shape economic institutions. They can help the United States move forward to fulfill the duties of justice and protect economic rights. They were strongly affirmed as implications of Catholic social teaching by Pope John Paul II during his visit to Canada in 1984: "The needs of the poor take priority over the desires of the rich; the rights of workers over the maximization of profits; the preservation of the environment over uncontrolled industrial expansion; production to meet social needs over production for military purposes."[49] There will undoubtedly be disputes about the concrete applications of these priorities in our complex world. We do not seek to foreclose discussion about them. However, we believe that an effort to move in the direction they indicate is urgently needed.

95. The economic challenge of today has many parallels with the political challenge that confronted the founders of our nation. In order to create a new form of political democracy they were compelled to develop ways of thinking and political institutions that had never existed before. Their efforts were arduous and their goals imperfectly realized, but they launched an experiment in the protection of civil and political rights that has prospered through the efforts of those who came after them. *We believe the time has come for a similar experiment in securing economic rights: the creation of an order that guarantees the minimum conditions of human dignity in the economic sphere for every person.* By drawing on the resources of the Catholic moral-religious tradition, we hope to make a contribution through this letter to such a new "American Experiment": a new venture to secure economic justice for all.

---

[48] *Pastoral Constitution*, 47.

[49] Address on Christian Unity in a Technological Age (Toronto, September 14, 1984) in *Origins* 14:16 (October 4, 1984): 248.

C. Working for Greater Justice: Persons and Institutions

96. The economy of this nation has been built by the labor of human hands and minds. Its future will be forged by the ways persons direct all this work toward greater justice. The economy is not a machine that operates according to its own inexorable laws, and persons are not mere objects tossed about by economic forces. Pope John Paul II has stated that "human work is a key, probably the essential key, to the whole social question."[50] The pope's understanding of work includes virtually all forms of productive human activity: agriculture, entrepreneurship, industry, the care of children, the sustaining of family life, politics, medical care, and scientific research. Leisure, prayer, celebration, and the arts are also central to the realization of human dignity and to the development of a rich cultural life. It is in their daily work, however, that persons become the subjects and creators of the economic life of the nation.[51] Thus, it is primarily through their daily labor that people make their most important contributions to economic justice.

97. All work has a threefold moral significance. First, it is a principal way that people exercise the distinctive human capacity for self-expression and self-realization. Second, it is the ordinary way for human beings to fulfill their material needs. Finally, work enables people to contribute to the well-being of the larger community. Work is not only for one's self. It is for one's family, for the nation, and indeed for the benefit of the entire human family.[52]

98. These three moral concerns should be visible in the work of all, no matter what their role in the economy: blue-collar workers, managers, homemakers, politicians, and others. They should also govern the activities of the many different, overlapping communities and institutions that make up society: families, neighborhoods, small businesses, giant corporations, trade unions, the various levels of government, international organizations, and a host of other human associations including communities of faith.

99. Catholic social teaching calls for respect for the full richness of social life. The need for vital contributions from different human associations—ranging in size from the family to government—has been classically expressed in Catholic social teaching in the "principle of subsidiarity":

> Just as it is gravely wrong to take from individuals what they can accomplish by their own initiative and industry and give it to the community, so also it is an injustice and at the same time a grave

---

[50]*On Human Work,* 3.
[51]Ibid., 5, 6.
[52]Ibid., 6, 10.

evil and disturbance of right order to assign to a greater and higher association what lesser and subordinate organizations can do. For every social activity ought of its very nature to furnish help (*subsidium*) to the members of the body social, and never destroy and absorb them."[53]

100. This principle guarantees institutional pluralism. It provides space for freedom, initiative, and creativity on the part of many social agents. At the same time, it insists that *all* these agents should work in ways that help build up the social body. Therefore, in all their activities these groups should be working in ways that express their distinctive capacities for action, that help meet human needs, and that make true contributions to the common good of the human community. The task of creating a more just U.S. economy is the vocation of all and depends on strengthening the virtues of public service and responsible citizenship in personal life and on all levels of institutional life.[54]

101. Without attempting to describe the tasks of all the different groups that make up society, we want to point to the specific rights and duties of some of the persons and institutions whose work for justice will be particularly important to the future of the United States economy. These rights and duties are among the concrete implications of the principle of subsidiarity. Further implications will be discussed in chapter IV of this letter.

1. Working People and Labor Unions

102. Though John Paul II's understanding of work is a very inclusive one, it fully applies to those customarily called "workers" or "labor" in the United States. Labor has great dignity, so great that all who are able to work are obligated to do so. The duty to work derives both from God's command and from a responsibility to one's own humanity and to the common good.[55] The virtue of industriousness is also an

---

[53]*Quadragesimo Anno*, 79. The meaning of this principle is not always accurately understood. For studies of its interpretation in Catholic teaching see: Calvez and Perrin in John F. Cronin, *Catholic Social Principles* (Milwaukee: Bruce, 1950), 328-342; Johannes Messner, "Freedom as a Principle of Social Order: An Essay in the Substance of Subsidiary Function," *Modern Schoolman* 28 (1951): 97-110; Richard E. Mulcahy, "Subsidiarity," *New Catholic Encyclopedia* vol. 13 (New York: McGraw-Hill, 1966), 762; Franz H. Mueller, "The Principle of Subsidiarity in Christian Tradition," *American Catholic Sociological Review* 4 (October 1943): 144-157; Oswald von Nell-Breuning, "Zur Sozialreform, Erwagungen zum Subsidiaritätsprinzip," *Stimmen der Zeit* 157, Bd. 81 (1955-1956): 1-11; id., "Subsidiarity," *Sacramentum Mundi*, vol. 6 (New York: Herder and Herder, 1970), 6, 114-116; Arthur Fridolin Utz, *Formen und Grenzen des Subsidiaritätsprinzips* (Heidelberg: F. H. Kerle Verlag, 1956); id., "The Principle of Subsidiarity and Contemporary Natural Law," *Natural Law Forum* 3 (1958): 170-183; id., *Grundsätze der Sozialpolitik: Solidarität und Subsidiarität in der Alterversicherung* (Stuttgart: Sewald Verlag, 1969).

[54]*Pastoral Constitution*, 31.

[55]*On Human Work*, 16.

expression of a person's dignity and solidarity with others. All working people are called to contribute to the common good by seeking excellence in production and service.

103. Because work is this important, people have a right to employment. In return for their labor, workers have a right to wages and other benefits sufficient to sustain life in dignity. As Pope Leo XIII stated, every working person has "the right of securing things to sustain life."[56] The way power is distributed in a free market economy frequently gives employers greater bargaining power than employees in the negotiation of labor contracts. Such unequal power may press workers into a choice between an inadequate wage and no wage at all. But justice, not charity, demands certain minimum guarantees. The provision of wages and other benefits sufficient to support a family in dignity is a basic necessity to prevent this exploitation of workers. The dignity of workers also requires adequate health care, security for old age or disability, unemployment compensation, healthful working conditions, weekly rest, periodic holidays for recreation and leisure, and reasonable security against arbitrary dismissal.[57] These provisions are all essential if workers are to be treated as persons rather than simply as a "factor of production."

104. The Church fully supports the right of workers to form unions or other associations to secure their rights to fair wages and working conditions. This is a specific application of the more general right to associate. In the words of Pope John Paul II, "The experience of history teaches that organizations of this type are an indispensable element of social life, especially in modern industrialized societies."[58] Unions may also legitimately resort to strikes where this is the only available means to the justice owed to workers.[59] No one may deny the right to organize without attacking human dignity itself. Therefore, we firmly oppose organized efforts, such as those regrettably now seen in this country, to break existing unions and prevent workers from organizing. Migrant agricultural workers today are particularly in need of the protection, including the right to organize and bargain collectively. U.S. labor law reform is needed to meet these problems as well as to provide more timely and effective remedies for unfair labor practices.

105. Denial of the right to organize has been pursued ruthlessly in many countries beyond our borders. We vehemently oppose violations of the freedom to associate, wherever they occur, for they are an intolerable attack on social solidarity.

---

[56]*Rerum Novarum*, 62; see also 9.

[57]*On Human Work*, 19.

[58]Ibid., 20.

[59]Ibid.

106. Along with the rights of workers and unions go a number of important responsibilities. Individual workers have obligations to their employers, and trade unions also have duties to society as a whole. Union management in particular carries a strong responsibility for the good name of the entire union movement. Workers must use their collective power to contribute to the well-being of the whole community and should avoid pressing demands whose fulfillment would damage the common good and the rights of more vulnerable members of society.[60] It should be noted, however, that wages paid to workers are but one of the factors affecting the competitiveness of industries. Thus, it is unfair to expect unions to make concessions if managers and shareholders do not make at least equal sacrifices.

107. Many U.S. unions have exercised leadership in the struggle for justice for minorities and women. Racial and sexual discrimination, however, have blotted the record of some unions. Organized labor has a responsibility to work positively toward eliminating the injustice this discrimination has caused.

108. Perhaps the greatest challenge facing United States workers and unions today is that of developing a new vision of their role in the United States economy of the future. The labor movement in the United States stands at a crucial moment. The dynamism of the unions that led to their rapid growth in the middle decades of this century has been replaced by a decrease in the percentage of U.S. workers who are organized. American workers are under heavy pressures today that threaten their jobs. The restrictions on the right to organize in many countries abroad make labor costs lower there, threaten American workers and their jobs, and lead to the exploitation of workers in these countries. In these difficult circumstances, guaranteeing the rights of U.S. workers calls for imaginative vision and creative new steps, not reactive or simply defensive strategies. For example, organized labor can play a very important role in helping to provide the education and training needed to help keep workers employable. Unions can also help both their own members and workers in developing countries by increasing their international efforts. A vital labor movement will be one that looks to the future with a deepened sense of global interdependence.

109. There are many signs that these challenges are being discussed by creative labor leaders today. Deeper and broader discussions of this sort are needed. This does not mean that only organized labor faces these new problems. All other sectors and institutions in the U.S. economy need similar vision and imagination. Indeed new forms of cooperation among labor, management, government, and other social groups are essential and will be discussed in chapter IV of this letter.

---

[60] Ibid.

2. Owners and Managers

110. The economy's success in fulfilling the demands of justice will depend on how its vast resources and wealth are managed. Property owners, managers, and investors of financial capital must all contribute to creating a more just society. Securing economic justice depends heavily on the leadership of men and women in business and on wise investment by private enterprises. Pope John Paul II has pointed out, "The degree of well-being which society today enjoys would be unthinkable without the dynamic figure of the business person, whose function consists of organizing human labor and the means of production so as to give rise to the goods and services necessary for the prosperity and progress of the community."[61] The freedom of entrepreneurship, business, and finance should be protected, but the accountability of this freedom to the common good and the norms of justice must be assured.

111. Persons in management face many hard choices each day, choices on which the well-being of many others depends. Commitment to the public good and not simply the private good of their firms is at the heart of what it means to call their work a vocation and not simply a career or a job. We believe that the norms and priorities discussed in this letter can be of help as they pursue their important tasks. The duties of individuals in the business world, however, do not exhaust the ethical dimensions of business and finance. The size of a firm or bank is in many cases an indicator of relative power. Large corporations and large financial institutions have considerable power to help shape economic institutions within the United States and throughout the world. With this power goes responsibility and the need for those who manage it to be held to moral and institutional accountability.

112. Business and finance have the duty to be faithful trustees of the resources at their disposal. No one can ever own capital resources absolutely or control their use without regard for others and society as a whole.[62] This applies first of all to land and natural resources. Short-term profits reaped at the cost of depletion of natural resources or the pollution of the environment violate this trust.

113. Resources created by human industry are also held in trust. Owners and managers have not created this capital on their own. They have benefited from the work of many others and from the local

---

[61] Pope John Paul II, Address to Businessmen and Economic Managers (Milan, May 22, 1983) in *L'Osservatore Romano*, weekly edition in English (June 20, 1983): 9:1.

[62] Thomas Aquinas, *Summa Theologiae*, IIa, IIae, q. 66.

communities that support their endeavors.[63] They are accountable to these workers and communities when making decisions. For example, reinvestment in technological innovation is often crucial for the long-term viability of a firm. The use of financial resources solely in pursuit of short-term profits can stunt the production of needed goods and services; a broader vision of managerial responsibility is needed.

114. The Catholic tradition has long defended the right to private ownership of productive property.[64] This right is an important element in a just economic policy. It enlarges our capacity for creativity and initiative.[65] Small and medium-sized farms, businesses, and entrepreneurial enterprises are among the most creative and efficient sectors of our economy. They should be highly valued by the people of the United States, as are land ownership and home ownership. Widespread distribution of property can help avoid excessive concentration of economic and political power. For these reasons ownership should be made possible for a broad sector of our population.[66]

115. The common good may sometimes demand that the right to own be limited by public involvement in the planning or ownership of certain sectors of the economy. Support of private ownership does not mean that anyone has the right to unlimited accumulation of wealth. "Private property does not constitute for anyone an absolute or unconditioned right. No one is justified in keeping for his exclusive use what he does not need, when others lack necessities."[67] Pope John Paul II has referred to limits placed on ownership by the duty to serve the common good as a "social mortgage" on private property.[68] For example, these limits are the basis of society's exercise of eminent domain over privately owned land needed for roads or other essential public goods. The Church's teaching opposes collectivist and statist economic approaches. But it also rejects the notion that a free market automatically produces justice. Therefore, as Pope John Paul II has argued, "One cannot exclude the socialization, in suitable conditions, of certain means of production."[69] The determination of when such conditions exist must be made on a case-by-case basis in light of the demands of the common good.

116. United States business and financial enterprises can also help

---

[63] As Pope John Paul II has stated: "This gigantic and powerful instrument—the whole collection of the means of production that in a sense are considered synonymous with 'capital'—is the result of work and bears the signs of human labor" (*On Human Work*, 12).

[64] *Rerum Novarum*, 10, 15, 36.

[65] *Mater et Magistra*, 109.

[66] *Rerum Novarum*, 65, 66; *Mater et Magistra*, 115.

[67] *On the Development of Peoples*, 23.

[68] Pope John Paul II, Opening Address at the Puebla Conference (Puebla, Mexico; January 28, 1979) in John Eagleson and Philip Scharper, eds., *Puebla and Beyond*, 67.

[69] *On Human Work*, 14.

determine the justice or injustice of the world economy. They are not all-powerful, but their real power is unquestionable. Transnational corporations and financial institutions can make positive contributions to development and global solidarity. Pope John Paul II has pointed out, however, that the desire to maximize profits and reduce the cost of natural resources and labor has often tempted these transnational enterprises to behavior that increases inequality and decreases the stability of the international order.[70] By collaborating with those national governments that serve their citizens justly and with intergovernmental agencies, these corporations can contribute to overcoming the desperate plight of many persons throughout the world.

117. Business people, managers, investors, and financiers follow a vital Christian vocation when they act responsibly and seek the common good. We encourage and support a renewed sense of vocation in the business community. We also recognize that the way business people serve society is governed and limited by the incentives which flow from tax policies, the availability of credit, and other public policies.

118. Businesses have a right to an institutional framework that does not penalize enterprises that act responsibly. Governments must provide regulations and a system of taxation which encourage firms to preserve the environment, employ disadvantaged workers, and create jobs in depressed areas. Managers and stockholders should not be torn between their responsibilities to their organizations and their responsibilities toward society as a whole.

3. Citizens and Government

119. In addition to rights and duties related to specific roles in the economy, everyone has obligations based simply on membership in the social community. By fulfilling these duties, we create a true commonwealth. Volunteering time, talent, and money to work for greater justice is a fundamental expression of Christian love and social solidarity. All who have more than they need must come to the aid of the poor. People with professional or technical skills needed to enhance the lives of others have a duty to share them. And the poor have similar obligations: to work together as individuals and families to build up their communities by acts of social solidarity and justice. These voluntary efforts to overcome injustice are part of the Christian vocation.

120. Every citizen also has the responsibility to work to secure justice and human rights through an organized social response. In the words of Pius XI, "Charity will never be true charity unless it takes justice

---

[70]Ibid., 17.

into account. . . . Let no one attempt with small gifts of charity to exempt himself from the great duties imposed by justice."[71] The guaranteeing of basic justice for all is not an optional expression of largesse but an inescapable duty for the whole of society.

121. The traditional distinction between society and the state in Catholic social teaching provides the basic framework for such organized public efforts. The Church opposes all statist and totalitarian approaches to socioeconomic questions. Social life is richer than governmental power can encompass. All groups that compose society have responsibilities to respond to the demands of justice. We have just outlined some of the duties of labor unions and business and financial enterprises. These must be supplemented by initiatives by local community groups, professional associations, educational institutions, churches, and synagogues. All the groups that give life to this society have important roles to play in the pursuit of economic justice.

122. For this reason, it is all the more significant that the teachings of the Church insist that *government has a moral function: protecting human rights and securing basic justice for all members of the commonwealth.*[72] Society as a whole and in all its diversity is responsible for building up the common good. But it is government's role to guarantee the minimum conditions that make this rich social activity possible, namely, human rights and justice.[73] This obligation also falls on individual citizens as they choose their representatives and participate in shaping public opinion.

123. More specifically, it is the responsibility of all citizens, acting through their government, to assist and empower the poor, the disadvantaged, the handicapped, and the unemployed. Government should assume a positive role in generating employment and establishing fair labor practices, in guaranteeing the provision and maintenance of the economy's infrastructure, such as roads, bridges, harbors, public means of communication, and transport. It should regulate trade and commerce in the interest of fairness.[74] Government may levy the taxes necessary to meet these responsibilities, and citizens have a moral obligation to pay those taxes. The way society responds

---

[71] *Divini Redemptoris*, 49.

[72] *Peace on Earth*, 60-62.

[73] Vatican Council II, *Declaration on Religious Freedom* (*Dignitatis Humanae*), 6. See John Courtney Murray, *The Problem of Religious Freedom*, Woodstock Papers, no. 7 (Westminster, Md.: Newman Press, 1965).

[74] *Peace on Earth*, 63-64. *Quadragesimo Anno*, 80. In *Rerum Novarum* Pope Leo XIII set down the basic norm that determines when government intervention is called for: "If, therefore, any injury has been done to or threatens either the common good or the interests of individual groups, which injury cannot in any other way be repaired or prevented, it is necessary for public authority to intervene" *Rerum Novarum*, 52. Pope John XXIII synthesized the Church's understanding of the function of governmental intervention this way: "The State, whose purpose is the realization of the common

to the needs of the poor through its public policies is the litmus test of its justice or injustice. The political debate about these policies is the indispensable forum for dealing with the conflicts and tradeoffs that will always be present in the pursuit of a more just economy.

124. The primary norm for determining the scope and limits of governmental intervention is the "principle of subsidiarity" cited above. This principle states that, in order to protect basic justice, government should undertake only those initiatives which exceed the capacity of individuals or private groups acting independently. Government should not replace or destroy smaller communities and individual initiative. Rather it should help them to contribute more effectively to social well-being and supplement their activity when the demands of justice exceed their capacities. This does not mean, however, that the government that governs least governs best. Rather it defines good government intervention as that which truly "helps" other social groups contribute to the common good by directing, urging, restraining, and regulating economic activity as "the occasion requires and necessity demands."[75] This calls for cooperation and consensus-building among the diverse agents in our economic life, including government. The precise form of government involvement in this process cannot be determined in the abstract. It will depend on an assessment of specific needs and the most effective ways to address them.

D. Christian Hope and the Courage to Act

125. The Christian vision is based on the conviction that God has destined the human race and all creation for "a kingdom of truth and life, of holiness and grace, of justice, love, and peace."[76] This conviction gives Christians strong hope as they face the economic struggles of the world today. This hope is not a naive optimism that imagines that simple formulas for creating a fully just society are ready at hand. The Church's experience through history and in nations throughout the world today has made it wary of all ideologies that claim to have the final answer to humanity's problems.[77] Christian hope has a much stronger foundation than such ideologies, for it rests

---

good in the temporal order, can by no means disregard the economic activity of its citizens. Indeed it should be present to promote in suitable manner the production of a sufficient supply of material goods, . . . contribute actively to the betterment of the living conditions of workers, . . . see to it that labor agreements are entered into according to the norms of justice and equity, and that in the environment of work the dignity of the human being is not violated either in body or spirit" (*Mater et Magistra*, 20-21).

[75]*Quadragesimo Anno*, 79.

[76]Preface for the Feast of Christ the King, *The Sacramentary of the Roman Missal*.

[77]*Octogesima Adveniens*, 26-35.

on the knowledge that God is at work in the world, "preparing a new dwelling place and a new earth where justice will abide."[78]

126. This hope stimulates and strengthens Christian efforts to create a more just economic order in spite of difficulties and setbacks.[79] Christian hope is strong and resilient, for it is rooted in a faith that knows that the fullness of life comes to those who follow Christ in the way of the cross. In pursuit of concrete solutions, all members of the Christian community are called to an ever finer discernment of the hurts and opportunities in the world around them, in order to respond to the most pressing needs and thus build up a more just society.[80] This is a communal task calling for dialogue, experimentation, and imagination. It also calls for deep faith and courageous love.

III. Selected Economic Policy Issues

127. We have outlined this moral vision as a guide to all who seek to be faithful to the Gospel in their daily economic decisions and as a challenge to transform the economic arrangements that shape our lives and our world. These arrangements embody and communicate social values and therefore have moral significance both in themselves and in their effects. Christians, like all people, must be concerned about how the concrete outcomes of their economic activity serve human dignity; they must assess the extent to which the structures and practices of the economy support or undermine their moral vision.

128. Such an assessment of economic practices, structures, and outcomes leads to a variety of conclusions. Some people argue that an unfettered free-market economy, where owners, workers, and consumers pursue their enlightened self-interest, provides the greatest possible liberty, material welfare, and equity. The policy implication of this view is to intervene in the economy as little as possible because it is such a delicate mechanism that any attempt to improve it is likely to have the opposite effect. Others argue that the capitalist system is inherently inequitable and therefore contradictory to the demands of Christian morality, for it is based on acquisitiveness, competition, and self-centered individualism. They assert that capitalism is fatally flawed and must be replaced by a radically different system that abolishes private property, the profit motive, and the free market.

129. Catholic social teaching has traditionally rejected these ideological extremes because they are likely to produce results contrary to human dignity and economic justice.[1] Starting with the assumption

---

[78] *Pastoral Constitution,* 39.

[79] Ibid.

[80] *Octogesima Adveniens,* 42.

[1] *Octogesima Adveniens,* 26-41; and *On Human Work,* 7, 13.

that the economy has been created by human beings and can be changed by them, the Church works for improvement in a variety of economic and political contexts; but it is not the Church's role to create or promote a specific new economic system. Rather, the Church must encourage all reforms that hold out hope for transforming our economic arrangements into a fuller systemic realization of the Christian moral vision. The Church must also stand ready to challenge practices and institutions that impede or carry us farther away from realizing this vision.

130. In short, the Church is not bound to any particular economic, political, or social system; it has lived with many forms of economic and social organization and will continue to do so, evaluating each according to moral and ethical principles: What is the impact of the system on people? Does it support or threaten human dignity?

131. In this document we offer reflections on the particular reality that is the U.S. economy. In doing so we are aware of the need to address not only individual issues within the economy but also the larger question of the economic system itself. Our approach in analyzing the U.S. economy is pragmatic and evolutionary in nature. We live in a "mixed" economic system which is the product of a long history of reform and adjustment. It is in the spirit of this American pragmatic tradition of reform that we seek to continue the search for a more just economy. Our nation has many assets to employ in this quest—vast economic, technological, and human resources and a system of representative government through which we can all help shape economic decisions.

132. Although we have chosen in this chapter to focus primarily on some aspects of the economy where we think reforms are realistically possible, we also emphasize that Catholic social teaching bears directly on larger questions concerning the economic system itself and the values it expresses—questions that cannot be ignored in the Catholic vision of economic justice.[2] For example, does our economic system place more emphasis on maximizing profits than on meeting human needs and fostering human dignity? Does our economy distribute its benefits equitably or does it concentrate power and resources in the hands of a few? Does it promote excessive materialism and individualism? Does it adequately protect the environment and the nation's natural resources? Does it direct too many scarce resources to military purposes? These and other basic questions about the economy need to be scrutinized in light of the ethical norms we have outlined. We urge continuing exploration of these systematic questions in a more comprehensive way than this document permits.

133. We have selected the following subjects to address here:

---

[2]*Program of Social Reconstruction*, 33-40.

(1) employment, (2) poverty, (3) food and agriculture, and (4) the U.S. role in the global economy. These topics were chosen because of their relevance to both the economic "signs of the times" and the ethical norms of our tradition. Each exemplifies U.S. policies that are basic to the establishment of economic justice in the nation and the world, and each illustrates key moral principles and norms for action from Catholic social teaching. Our treatment of these issues does not constitute a comprehensive analysis of the U.S. economy. We emphasize that these are illustrative topics intended to exemplify the interaction of moral values and economic issues in our day, not to encompass all such values and issues. This document is not a technical blueprint for economic reform. Rather, it is an attempt to foster a serious moral analysis leading to a more just economy.

134. In focusing on some of the central economic issues and choices in American life in the light of moral principles, we are aware that the movement from principle to policy is complex and difficult and that although moral values are essential in determining public policies, they do not dictate specific solutions. They must interact with empirical data, with historical, social, and political realities, and with competing demands on limited resources. The soundness of our prudential judgments depends not only on the moral force of our principles, but also on the accuracy of our information and the validity of our assumptions.

135. Our judgments and recommendations on specific economic issues, therefore, do not carry the same moral authority as our statements of universal moral principles and formal church teaching; the former are related to circumstances which can change or which can be interpreted differently by people of good will. We expect and welcome debate on our specific policy recommendations. Nevertheless, we want our statements on these matters to be given serious consideration by Catholics as they determine whether their own moral judgments are consistent with the Gospel and with Catholic social teaching. We believe that differences on complex economic questions should be expressed in a spirit of mutual respect and open dialogue.[3]

A. Employment

136. Full employment is the foundation of a just economy. The most urgent priority for domestic economic policy is the creation of new jobs with adequate pay and decent working conditions. We must make it possible as a nation for everyone who is seeking a job to find employment within a reasonable amount of time. Our emphasis on

---

[3]See *The Challenge of Peace: God's Promise and Our Response,* 9-10.

this goal is based on the conviction that human work has a special dignity and is a key to achieving justice in society.[4]

137. Employment is a basic right, a right which protects the freedom of all to participate in the economic life of society. It is a right which flows from the principles of justice which we have outlined above. Corresponding to this right is the duty on the part of society to ensure that the right is protected. The importance of this right is evident in the fact that for most people employment is crucial to self-realization and essential to the fulfillment of material needs. Since so few in our economy own productive property, employment also forms the first line of defense against poverty. Jobs benefit society as well as workers, for they enable more people to contribute to the common good and to the productivity required for a healthy economy.

1. The Scope and Effects of Unemployment

138. Joblessness is becoming a more widespread and deep-seated problem in our nation. There are about 8 million people in the United States looking for a job who cannot find one. They represent about 7 percent of the labor force.[5] The official rate of unemployment does not include those who have given up looking for work or those who are working part time, but want to work full time. When these categories are added, it becomes clear that about one-eighth of the workforce is directly affected by unemployment.[6] The severity of the unemployment problem is compounded by the fact that almost three-fourths of those who are unemployed receive no unemployment insurance benefits.[7]

139. In recent years there has been a steady trend toward higher and higher levels of unemployment, even in good times. Between 1950 and 1980 the annual unemployment rate exceeded current levels only during the recession years of 1975 and 1976. Periods of economic recovery during these three decades brought unemployment rates down to 3 and 4 percent. Since 1979, however, the rate has generally been above 7 percent.

140. Who are the unemployed? Blacks, Hispanics, Native Americans, young adults, female heads of households, and those who are inad-

---

[4]*On Human Work*, 3.

[5]U.S. Department of Labor, Bureau of Labor Statistics, *The Employment Situation: April 1986* (May 1986).

[6]Full Employment Action Council, *Employment in America: Illusory Recovery in a Decade of Decline* (Washington, D.C., February 1985), 19. Calculations based on data from the U.S. Department of Labor's Bureau of Labor Statistics.

[7]U.S. Department of Labor, Bureau of Labor Statistics, *The Employment Situation: August 1985;* and U.S. Department of Labor Employment and Training Administration, *Unemployment Insurance Claims*, Reference week of June 22, 1985.

equately educated are represented disproportionately among the ranks of the unemployed. The unemployment rate among minorities is almost twice as high as the rate among whites. For female heads of households the unemployment rate is over 10 percent. Among black teenagers, unemployment reaches the scandalous rate of more than one in three.[8]

141. The severe human costs of high unemployment levels become vividly clear when we examine the impact of joblessness on human lives and human dignity. It is a deep conviction of American culture that work is central to the freedom and well-being of people. The unemployed often come to feel they are worthless and without a productive role in society. Each day they are unemployed our society tells them: We don't need your talent. We don't need your initiative. We don't need *you*. Unemployment takes a terrible toll on the health and stability of both individuals and families. It gives rise to family quarrels, greater consumption of alcohol, child abuse, spouse abuse, divorce, and higher rates of infant mortality.[9] People who are unemployed often feel that society blames them for being unemployed. Very few people survive long periods of unemployment without some psychological damage even if they have sufficient funds to meet their needs.[10] At the extreme, the strains of job loss may drive individuals to suicide.[11]

142. In addition to the terrible waste of individual talent and creativity, unemployment also harms society at large. Jobless people pay little or no taxes, thus lowering the revenues for cities, states, and the federal government. At the same time, rising unemployment requires greater expenditures for unemployment compensation, food stamps, welfare, and other assistance. It is estimated that in 1986, for every one percentage point increase in the rate of unemployment, there will be roughly a $40 billion increase in the federal deficit.[12] The costs to

[8]*The Employment Situation: August 1985.*

[9]Brenner, "Fetal, Infant and Maternal Mortality during Periods of Economic Instability," *International Journal of Health Services* (Summer 1973); P.H. Ellison, "Neurology of Hard Times," *Clinical Pediatrics* (March 1977); S. V. Kasl and S. Cobb, "Some Mental Health Consequences of Plant Closings and Job Loss," in L. Ferman and J. P. Gordus, eds., *Mental Health and the Economy* (Kalamazoo, Mich.: W. E. Upjohn Institute for Employment Research, 1979), 255-300; L. E. Kopolow and F. M. Ochberg, "Spinoff from a Downward Swing," *Mental Health* 59 (Summer 1975); D. Shaw, "Unemployment Hurts More than the Pocketbook," *Today's Health* (March 1978).

[10]Richard M. Cohn, *The Consequences of Unemployment on Evaluation of Self,* Doctoral dissertation, Department of Psychology (University of Michigan, 1977); John A. Garraty, *Unemployment in History: Economic Thought and Public Policy* (New York: Harper and Row, 1978); Harry Maurer, *Not Working: An Oral History of the Unemployed* (New York: Holt, Rinehart, and Winston, 1979).

[11]M. Harvey Brenner, *Estimating the Social Cost of National Economic Policy* (U.S. Congress, Joint Economic Committee, 1976); see Brenner, *Mental Illness and the Economy* (Cambridge, Mass.: Harvard University Press, 1973).

[12]Congressional Budget Office, *Economic and Budget Outlook: FY 1986-FY 1990* (Washington, D.C., February 1985), 75.

society are also evident in the rise of crime associated with joblessness. The Federal Bureau of Prisons reports that increases in unemployment have been followed by increases in the prison population. Other studies have shown links between the rate of joblessness and the frequency of homicides, robberies, larcenies, narcotics arrests, and youth crimes.[13]

143. Our own experiences with the individuals, families, and communities that suffer the burdens of unemployment compel us to the conviction that as a nation we simply cannot afford to have millions of able-bodied men and women unemployed. We cannot afford the economic costs, the social dislocation, and the enormous human tragedies caused by unemployment. In the end, however, what we can least afford is the assualt on human dignity that occurs when millions are left without adequate employment. Therefore, we cannot but conclude that current levels of unemployment are intolerable, and they impose on us a moral obligation to work for policies that will reduce joblessness.

2. Unemployment in a Changing Economy

144. The structure of the U.S. economy is undergoing a transformation that affects both the quantity and the quality of jobs in our nation. The size and makeup of the workforce, for example, have changed markedly in recent years. For a number of reasons, there are now more people in the labor market than ever before in our history. Population growth has pushed up the supply of potential workers. In addition, large numbers of women have entered the labor force not only in order to put their talents and education to greater use, but also out of economic necessity. Many families need two salaries if they are to live in a decently human fashion. Female-headed households often depend heavily on the mother's income to stay off the welfare rolls. Immigrants seeking a better existence in the United States have also added to the size of the labor force. These demographic changes, however, cannot fully explain the higher levels of unemployment.

145. Technological changes are also having dramatic impacts on the employment picture in the United States. Advancing technology brings many benefits, but it can also bring social and economic costs, including the downgrading and displacement of workers. High technology and advanced automation are changing the very face of our nation's industries and occupations. In the 1970s, about 90 percent of all new jobs were in service occupations. By 1990, service industries are expected

---

[13]*Correlation of Unemployment and Federal Prison Population* (Washington, D.C.: U.S. Bureau of Prisons, March 1975); M. Yeager, "Unemployment and Imprisonment," *Journal of Criminal Law and Criminology* 70:4 (1979); Testimony of M. H. Brenner in *Unemployment and Crime* (U.S. Congress, House Hearings, 1977), 25.

to employ 72 percent of the labor force. Much of the job growth in the 1980s is expected to be in traditionally low-paying, high-turnover jobs such as sales, clerical, janitorial, and food service.[14] Too often these jobs do not have career ladders leading to higher skilled, higher paying jobs. Thus, the changing industrial and occupational mix in the U.S. economy could result in a shift toward lower paying and lower skilled jobs.

146. Increased competition in world markets is another factor influencing the rate of joblessness in our nation. Many other exporting nations have acquired and developed up-to-the-minute technology, enabling them to increase productivity dramatically. Combined with very low wages in many nations, this has allowed them to gain a larger share of the U.S. market to cut into U.S. export markets. At the same time, many corporations have closed plants in the United States and moved their capital, technology, and jobs to foreign affiliates.

147. Discrimination in employment is one of the causes for high rates of joblessness and low pay among racial minorities and women. Beyond the normal problems of locating a job, blacks, Hispanics, Native Americans, immigrants, and other minorities bear this added burden of discrimination. Discrimination against women is compounded by the lack of adequate child care services and by the unwillingness of many employers to provide flexible employment or extend fringe benefits to part-time employees.

148. High levels of defense spending also have an effect on the number of jobs in our economy. In our pastoral letter *The Challenge of Peace,* we noted the serious economic distortions caused by the arms race and the disastrous effects that it has on society's ability to care for the poor and the needy. Employment is one area in which this interconnection is very evident. The hundreds of billions of dollars spent by our nation each year on the arms race create a massive drain on the U.S. economy as well as a very serious "brain drain." Such spending on the arms race means a net loss in the number of jobs created in the economy, because defense industries are less labor-intensive than other major sectors of the economy.[15] Moreover, nearly half of the American scientific and engineering force works in defense-related

---

[14]Committee on the Evolution of Work, AFL-CIO, *The Future of Work* (Washington, D.C.: AFL-CIO, 1983), 11.

[15]Congressional Budget Office, *Defense Spending and the Economy* (Washington, D.C.: Government Printing Office, 1983). See also Michael Edelstein, *The Economic Impact of Military Spending* (New York: Council on Economic Priorities, 1977); and Robert De Grasse, Jr., *Military Expansion, Economic Decline* (New York: Council on Economic Priorities, 1983). See also U.S. Department of Labor, Bureau of Labor Statistics Report, "Structure of the U.S. Economy in 1980 and 1985" (Washington, D.C.: Government Printing Office, 1975); and Marion Anderson, *The Empty Pork Barrel* (Lansing, Mich.: Employment Research Associates, 1982).

programs and over 60 percent of the entire federal research and development budget goes to the military.[16] We must ask whether our nation will ever be able to modernize our economy and achieve full employment if we continue to devote so much of our financial and human resources to defense-related activities.

149. These are some of the factors that have driven up the rate of unemployment in recent years. Although our economy has created more than 20 million new jobs since 1970,[17] there continues to be a chronic and growing job shortage. In the face of this challenge, our nation's economic institutions have failed to adapt adequately and rapidly enough. For example, failure to invest sufficiently in certain industries and regions, inadequate education and training for new workers, and insufficient mechanisms to assist workers displaced by new technology have added to the unemployment problem.

150. Generating an adequate number of jobs in our economy is a complex task in view of the changing and diverse nature of the problem. It involves numerous trade-offs and substantial costs. Nevertheless, it is not an impossible task. Achieving the goal of full employment may require major adjustments and creative strategies that go beyond the limits of existing policies and institutions, but it is a task we must undertake.

3. Guidelines for Action

151. We recommend that the nation make a major new commitment to achieve full employment. At present there is nominal endorsement of the full employment ideal, but no firm commitment to bringing it about. If every effort were now being made to create the jobs required, one might argue that the situation today is the best we can do. But such is not the case. The country is doing far less than it might to generate employment.

152. Over the last decade, economists, policy makers, and the general public have shown greater willingness to tolerate unemployment levels of 6 to 7 percent or even more.[18] Although we recognize the

[16]U.S. Office of Management and Budget, *Historical Tables*, Budget of the United States Government Fiscal Year 1986 (Washington, D.C.: U.S. Government Printing Office, 1985). Table 10.2, 10.2(3). See also, National Science Foundation Report, "Characteristics of Experienced Scientists and Engineers" (1978), Detailed Statistical Tables (Washington, D.C.: U.S. Government Printing Office, 1978).

[17]"Statistical Supplement to International Comparison of Unemployment," Bureau of Labor Statistics (May 1984): 7. Unpublished.

[18]Isabel V. Sawhill and Charles F. Stone state the prevailing view among economists this way: "High employment is usually defined as the rate of unemployment consistent with no additional inflation, a rate currently believed by many, but not all, economists to be in the neighborhood of 6 percent." "The Economy: The Key to Success," in John L. Palmer and Isabel V. Sawhill, eds., *The Reagan Record: An Assessment of America's Changing Domestic Priorities* (Cambridge, Mass.: Bollinger, 1984), 72. See also Stanley Fischer and Rudiger Dornbusch, *Economics* (New York: McGraw-Hill, 1983), 731-743.

complexities and trade-offs involved in reducing unemployment, we believe that 6 to 7 percent unemployment is neither inevitable nor acceptable. While a zero unemployment rate is clearly impossible in an economy where people are constantly entering the job market and others are changing jobs, appropriate policies and concerted private and public action can improve the situation considerably, if we have the will to do so. No economy can be considered truly healthy when so many millions of people are denied jobs by forces outside their control. The acceptance of present unemployment rates would have been unthinkable twenty years ago. It should be regarded as intolerable today.

153. We must first establish a consensus that everyone has a right to employment. Then the burden of securing full employment falls on all of us—policy makers, business, labor, and the general public—to create and implement the mechanisms to protect that right. We must work for the formation of a new national consensus and mobilize the necessary political will at all levels to make the goal of full employment a reality.

154. Expanding employment in our nation will require significant steps in both the private and public sectors, as well as a joint action between them. Private initiative and entrepreneurship are essential to this task, for the private sector accounts for about 80 percent of the jobs in the United States, and most new jobs are being created there.[19] Thus, a viable strategy for employment generation must assume that a large part of the solution will be with private firms and small businesses. At the same time, it must be recognized that government has a prominent and indispensable role to play in addressing the problem of unemployment. The market alone will not automatically produce full employment. Therefore, the government must act to ensure that this goal is achieved by coordinating general economic policies, by job creation programs, and by other appropriate policy measures.

155. Effective action against unemployment will require a careful mix of general economic policies and targeted employment programs. Taken together, these policies and programs should have full employment as their number one goal.

a. General Economic Policies

156. The general or macroeconomic policies of the federal government are essential tools for encouraging the steady economic growth that produces more and better jobs in the economy. *We recommend that the fiscal and monetary policies of the nation—such as federal spending, tax, and interest rate policies—should be coordinated so as to achieve the goal of full employment.*

---

[19]W. L. Birch, "Who Creates Jobs?" *The Public Interest* 65 (Fall 1981): 3-14.

157. General economic policies that attempt to expand employment must also deal with the problem of inflation.[20] The risk of inflationary pressures resulting from such expansionary policies is very real. Our response to this risk, however, must not be to abandon the goal of full employment, but to develop effective policies that keep inflation under control.

158. While economic growth is an important and necessary condition for the reduction of unemployment, it is not sufficient in and of itself. In order to work for full employment and restrain inflation, it is also necessary to adopt more specific programs and policies targeted toward particular aspects of the unemployment problem.[21]

b. Targeted Employment Programs

159. (1) *We recommend expansion of job-training and apprenticeship programs in the private sector administered and supported jointly by business, labor unions, and government.* Any comprehensive employment strategy must include systematic means of developing the technical and professional skills needed for a dynamic and productive economy. Investment in a skilled work force is a prerequisite both for sustaining economic growth and achieving greater justice in the United States. The obligation to contribute to this investment falls on both the private and public sectors. Today business, labor, and government need to coordinate their efforts and pool their resources to promote a substantial increase in the number of apprenticeship programs and to expand on-the-job-training programs. We recommend a national commitment to eradicate illiteracy and to provide people with the skills necessary to adapt to the changing demands of employment.

160. With the rapid pace of technological change, continuing education and training are even more important today than in the past. Businesses have a stake in providing it, for skilled workers are essential to increased productivity. Labor unions should support it, for their members are increasingly vulnerable to displacement and job loss unless they continue to develop their skills and their flexibility on the job. Local communities have a stake as well, for their economic well-

---

[20]Martin Neil Baily and Arthur M. Okun, eds., *The Battle Against Unemployment and Inflation*, third edition (New York: Norton, 1982); and Martin Neil Baily, "Labor Market Performance, Competition and Inflation," in Baily, ed., *Workers, Jobs and Inflation* (Washington, D.C.: The Brookings Institution, 1982). See also, Lawrence Klein, "Reducing Unemployment Without Inflation"; and James Tobin, "Unemployment, Poverty, and Economic Policy," testimony before the Subcommittee on Economic Stabilization, U.S. House of Representatives Committee on Banking, Finance and Urban Affairs (March 19, 1985), serial no. 99-5 (Washington, D.C.: U.S. Government Printing Office, 1985), 15-18, 31-33.

[21]Tobin, "Unemployment, Poverty, and Economic Policy"; and Klein, "Reducing Unemployment Without Inflation."

being will suffer serious harm if local industries fail to develop and are forced to shut down.

161. The best medicine for the disease of plant-closings is prevention. Prevention depends not only on sustained capital investment to enhance productivity through advanced technology but also on the training and retraining of workers within the private sector. In circumstances where plants are forced to shut down, management, labor unions, and local communities must see to it that workers are not simply cast aside. Retraining programs will be even more urgently needed in these circumstances.

162. (2) *We recommend increased support for direct job-creation programs targeted on the long-term unemployed and those with special needs.* Such programs can take the form of direct public service employment and also of public subsidies for employment in the private sector. Both approaches would provide jobs for those with low skills less expensively and with less inflation than would general stimulation of the economy.[22] The cost of providing jobs must also be balanced against the savings realized by the government through decreased welfare and unemployment insurance expenditures and increased revenues from the taxes paid by the newly employed.

163. Government funds, if used effectively, can also stimulate private sector jobs for the long-term unemployed and for groups particularly hard to employ. Experiments need to be conducted on the precise ways such subsidies would most successfully attract business participation and ensure the generation of permanent jobs.

164. These job generation efforts should aim specifically at bringing marginalized persons into the labor force. They should produce a net increase in the number of jobs rather than displacing the burden of unemployment from one group of persons to another. They should also be aimed at long-term jobs and should include the necessary supportive services to assist the unemployed in finding and keeping jobs.

165. Jobs that are created should produce goods and services needed and valued by society. It is both good common sense and sound economics to create jobs directly for the purpose of meeting society's unmet needs. Across the nation, in every state and locality, there is ample evidence of social needs that are going unmet. Many of our parks and recreation facilities are in need of maintenance and repair. Many of the nation's bridges and highways are in disrepair. We have a desperate need for more low-income housing. Our educational systems, day-care services, senior citizen services, and other community programs need to be expanded. These and many other elements of our national life are areas of unmet need. At the same time, there are

---

[22]Robert H. Haveman, "Toward Efficiency and Equity through Direct Job Creation," *Social Policy* 11:1 (May/June 1980): 48.

more than 8 million Americans looking for productive and useful work. Surely we have the capacity to match these needs by giving Americans who are anxious to work a chance for productive employment in jobs that are waiting to be done. The overriding moral value of enabling jobless persons to achieve a new sense of dignity and personal worth through employment also strongly recommends these programs.

166. These job-creation efforts will require increased collaboration and fresh alliances between the private and public sectors at all levels. There are already a number of examples of how such efforts can be successful.[23] We believe that the potential of these kinds of partnerships has only begun to be tapped.

c. Examining New Strategies

167. In addition to the actions suggested above, we believe there is also a need for careful examination and experimentation with alternative approaches that might improve both the quantity and quality of jobs. More extensive use of job sharing, flex time, and a reduced work week are among the topics that should continue to be on the agenda of public discussion. Consideration should also be given to the possibility of limiting or abolishing compulsory overtime work. Similarly, methods might be examined to discourage the overuse of part-time workers, who do not receive fringe benefits.[24] New strategies also need to be explored in the area of education and training for the hard-to-employ, displaced workers, the handicapped, and others with special needs. Particular attention is needed to achieve pay equity between men and women, as well as upgrading the pay scale and working conditions of traditionally low-paying jobs. The nation should renew its efforts to develop effective affirmative action policies that assist those who have been excluded by racial or sexual discrimination in the past. New strategies for improving job placement services at the national and local levels are also needed. Improving occupational safety is another important concern that deserves increased attention.

---

[23]William H. McCarthy, *Reducing Urban Unemployment: What Works at the Local Level* (Washington, D.C.: National League of Cities, October 1985); William Schweke, "States that Take the Lead on a New Industrial Policy," in Betty G. Lall, ed., *Economic Dislocation and Job Loss* (New York: Cornell University, New York State School of Industrial and Labor Relations, 1985), 97-106; David Robinson, *Training and Jobs Programs in Action: Case Studies in Private Sector Initiatives for the Hard to Employ* (New York: Committee for Economic Development, 1978). See also ch. IV of this pastoral letter.

[24]Rudy Oswald, "The Economy and Workers' Jobs, The Living Wage and a Voice," in John W. Houch and Oliver F. Williams, eds. *Catholic Social Teaching and the U.S. Economy: Working Papers for a Bishops' Pastoral* (Washington, D.C.: University Press of America, 1984), 77-89. On the subject of shortening the work week, Oswald points out that in the first 40 years of this century, the average work week fell from 60 hours to 40 hours. However, the standard work week has been unchanged now for almost 50 years.

168. Much greater attention also needs to be devoted to the long-term task of converting some of the nation's military production to more peaceful and socially productive purposes. The nation needs to seek more effective ways to retool industries, to retrain workers, and to provide the necessary adjustment assistance for communities affected by this kind of economic conversion.

169. These are among the avenues that need to be explored in the search for just employment policies. A belief in the inherent dignity of human work and in the right to employment should motivate people in all sectors of society to carry on that search in new and creative ways.

B. Poverty

170. More than 33 million Americans—about one in every seven people in our nation—are poor by the government's official definition. The norms of human dignity and the preferential option for the poor compel us to confront this issue with a sense of urgency. Dealing with poverty is not a luxury to which our nation can attend when it finds the time and resources. Rather, it is a moral imperative of the highest priority.

171. Of particular concern is the fact that poverty has increased dramatically during the last decade. Since 1973 the poverty rate has increased by nearly a third. Although the recent recovery has brought a slight decline in the rate, it remains at a level that is higher than at almost any other time during the last two decades.[25]

172. As pastors we have seen firsthand the faces of poverty in our midst. Homeless people roam city streets in tattered clothing and sleep in doorways or on subway grates at night. Many of these are former mental patients released from state hospitals. Thousands stand in line at soup kitchens because they have no other way of feeding themselves. Millions of children are so poorly nourished that their physical and mental development are seriously harmed.[26] We have also seen the growing economic hardship and insecurity experienced by moderate-income Americans when they lose their jobs and their income due to forces beyond their control. These are alarming signs and trends. They pose for our nation an urgent moral and human challenge: to fashion a society where no one goes without the basic material necessities required for human dignity and growth.

---

[25]U.S. Bureau of the Census, Current Population Reports, Series P-60, no. 149, *Money Income and Poverty Status of Families in the United States: 1984* (Washington, D.C.: U.S. Government Printing Office, 1985).

[26]Massachusetts Department of Public Health, *Massachusetts Nutrition Survey* (Boston, Mass.: 1983).

173. Poverty can be described and defined in many different ways. It can include spiritual as well as material poverty. Likewise, its meaning changes depending on the historical, social, and economic setting. Poverty in our time is different from the more severe deprivation experienced in earlier centuries in the U.S. or in Third World nations today. Our discussion of poverty in this chapter is set within the context of present-day American society. By poverty, we are referring here to the lack of sufficient material resources required for a decent life. We use the government's official definition of poverty, although we recognize its limits.[27]

1. Characteristics of Poverty

174. Poverty is not an isolated problem existing solely among a small number of anonymous people in our central cities. Nor is it limited to a dependent underclass or to specific groups in the United States. It is a condition experienced at some time by many people in different walks of life and in different circumstances. Many poor people are working but at wages insufficient to lift them out of poverty.[28] Others are unable to work and are therefore dependent on outside sources of support. Still others are on the edge of poverty; although not officially defined as poor, they are economically insecure and at risk of falling into poverty.

175. While many of the poor manage to escape from beneath the official poverty line, others remain poor for extended periods of time. Long-term poverty is concentrated among racial minorities and fam-

---

[27] There is considerable debate about the most suitable definition of poverty. Some argue that the government's official definition understates the number of the poor, and that a more adequate definition would indicate that as many as 50 million Americans are poor. For example, they note that the poverty line has declined sharply as a percent of median family income—from 48% in 1959 to 35% in 1983. Others argue that the official indicators should be reduced by the amount of in-kind benefits received by the poor, such as food stamps. By some calculations that would reduce the number counted as poor to about 12 million. We conclude that for present purposes the official government definition provides a suitable middle ground. That definition is based on a calculation that multiplies the cost of USDA's lowest cost food plan times three. The definition is adjusted for inflation each year.

Among other reasons for using the official definition is that it allows one to compare poverty figures over time. For additional readings on this topic see: L. Rainwater, *What Money Buys: Inequality and the Social Meanings of Income* (New York: Basic Books, 1975); id., *Persistent and Transitory Poverty: A New Look* (Cambridge, Mass.: Joint Center for Urban Studies, 1980); M. Orshansky, "How Poverty is Measured," *Monthly Labor Review* 92 (1969): 37-41; M. Anderson, *Welfare* (Stanford, Calif.: Hoover Institution Press, 1978); and Michael Harrington, *The New American Poverty* (New York: Holt, Rinehart, and Winston, 1984), 81-82.

[28] Of those in poverty, 3 million work year-round and are still poor. Of the 22.2 million poor who are 15 years or over, more than 9 million work sometime during the year. Since 1979, the largest increases of poverty in absolute terms have been among those who work and are still poor. U.S. Bureau of the Census, *Money, Income and Poverty*.

ilies headed by women. It is also more likely to be found in rural areas and in the South.[29] Of the long-term poor, most are either working at wages too low to bring them above the poverty line or are retired, disabled, or parents of preschool children. Generally they are not in a position to work more hours than they do now.[30]

a. Children in Poverty

176. Poverty strikes some groups more severely than others. Perhaps most distressing is the growing number of children who are poor. Today one in every four American children under the age of six, and one in every two black children under six, are poor. The number of children in poverty rose by 4 million over the decade between 1973 and 1983, with the result that there are now more poor children in the United States than at any time since 1965.[31] The problem is particularly severe among female-headed families, where more than half of all children are poor. Two-thirds of black children and nearly three-quarters of Hispanic children in such families are poor.

177. Very many poor families with children receive no government assistance, have no health insurance, and cannot pay medical bills. Less than half are immunized against preventable diseases such as diphtheria and polio.[32] Poor children are disadvantaged even before birth; their mothers' lack of access to high quality prenatal care leaves them at much greater risk of premature birth, low-birth weight, physical and mental impairment, and death before their first birthday.

---

[29]U.S. Bureau of the Census, Current Population Reports, series P-60, no. 149, 19. Blacks make up about 12% of the entire population but 62% of the long-term poor. Only 19% of the overall population live in families headed by women, but they make up 61% of the long-term poor. Twenty-eight percent of the nation's total population reside in nonmetropolitan areas, but 34% of the nation's poor live in these areas.

[30]G. J. Duncan et al., *Years of Poverty, Years of Plenty: The Changing Economic Fortunes of American Workers and Their Families* (Ann Arbor, Mich.: Institute for Social Research, The University of Michigan, 1984). This book is based on the Panel Study of Income Dynamics, a survey of 5,000 American families conducted annually by the Survey Research Center of the University of Michigan. See G. J. Duncan and J. N. Morgan, *Five Thousand American Families—Patterns of Economic Progress*, vol. III (Ann Arbor: University of Michigan, 1975).

[31]Congressional Research Service and Congressional Budget Office, *Children in Poverty* (Washington, D.C., May 22, 1985), 57. This recent study also indicates that children are now the largest age group in poverty. We are the first industrialized nation in the world in which children are the poorest age group. See Daniel Patrick Moynihan, *Family and Nation* (New York: Harcourt, Brace, Jovanovich, 1986), 112.

[32]Children's Defense Fund, *American Children in Poverty* (Washington, D.C., 1984).

b. Women and Poverty

178. The past twenty years have witnessed a dramatic increase in the number of women in poverty.[33] This includes women raising children alone as well as women with inadequate income following divorce, widowhood, or retirement. More than one-third of all female-headed families are poor. Among minority families headed by women the poverty rate is over 50 percent.[34]

179. Wage discrimination against women is a major factor behind these high rates of poverty. Many women are employed but remain poor because their wages are too low. Women who work outside their homes full time and year round earn only 61 percent of what men earn. Thus, being employed full time is not by itself a remedy for poverty among women. Hundreds of thousands of women hold full-time jobs but are still poor. Sixty percent of all women work in only ten occupations, and most new jobs for women are in areas with low pay and limited chances of advancement. Many women suffer discrimination in wages, salaries, job classifications, promotions, and other areas.[35] As a result, they find themselves in jobs that have low status, little security, weak unionization, and few fringe benefits. Such discrimination is immoral and efforts must be made to overcome the effects of sexism in our society.

180. Women's responsibilities for childrearing are another important factor to be considered. Despite the many changes in marriage and family life in recent decades, women continue to have primary responsibility in this area. When marriages break up, mothers typically take custody of the children and bear the major financial responsibility for supporting them. Women often anticipate that they will leave the labor force to have and raise children, and often make job and career choices accordingly. In other cases, they are not hired or promoted to higher paying jobs because of their childrearing responsibilities. In addition, most divorced or separated mothers do not get child support payments. In 1983, less than half of women raising children alone had been awarded child support, and of those, only half received the full amount to which they were entitled. Even fewer women (14 percent) are awarded alimony, and many older women are left in

---

[33]This trend has been commonly referred to as the "feminization of poverty." This term was coined by Dr. Diana Pierce in the *1980 Report to the President* of the National Advisory Council on Economic Opportunity to describe the dramatic increase in the proportion of the poor living in female-headed households.

[34]U.S. Bureau of the Census, Technical Paper 55, *Estimates of Poverty Including the Value of Non-Cash Benefits: 1984* (Washington, D.C., August 1985), 5, 23.

[35]Barbara Raskin and Heidi Hartmann, *Women's Work, Men's Work, Sex Segregation on the Job*, National Academy of Sciences (Washington, D.C.: National Academy Press, 1986), pp. 10-126.

poverty after a lifetime of homemaking and childrearing.[36] Such women have great difficulty finding jobs and securing health insurance.

c. Racial Minorities and Poverty

181. Most poor people in our nation are white, but the rates of poverty in our nation are highest among those who have borne the brunt of racial prejudice and discrimination. For example, blacks are about three times more likely to be poor than whites. While one out of every nine white Americans is poor, one of every three blacks and Native Americans and more than one of every four Hispanics are poor.[37] While some members of minority communities have successfully moved up the economic ladder, the overall picture indicates that black family income is only 55 percent of white family income, reflecting an income gap that is wider now than at any time in the last fifteen years.[38]

182. Despite the gains which have been made toward racial equality, prejudice and discrimination in our own time as well as the effects of past discrimination continue to exclude many members of racial minorities from the mainstream of American life. Discriminatory practices in labor markets, in educational systems, and in electoral politics create major obstacles for blacks, Hispanics, Native Americans, and other racial minorities in their struggle to improve their economic status.[39] Such discrimination is evidence of the continuing presence of racism in our midst. In our pastoral letter *Brothers and Sisters to Us*, we have described this racism as a sin—"a sin that divides the human family, blots out the image of God among specific members of that family, and violates the fundamental human dignity of those called to be children of the same Father."[40]

2. Economic Inequality

183. Important to our discussion of poverty in America is an understanding of the degree of economic inequality in our nation. Our economy is marked by a very uneven distribution of wealth and income. For example, it is estimated that 28 percent of the total net wealth is held by the richest 2 percent of families in the United States.

---

[36]U.S. Bureau of the Census, series P-23, no. 124, *Special Study Child Support and Alimony: 1981 Current Population Report* (Washington, D.C., 1981).

[37]U.S. House of Representatives Subcommittee on Oversight and Public Assistance and Unemployment Compensation, Committee on Ways and Means, *Background Material on Poverty* (Washington, D.C., October 1983). See also Committee on Ways and Means, U.S. House of Representatives, *Children in Poverty*, 3.

[38]The National Urban League, *The Status of Black America 1984* (New York, January 1984).

[39]Ibid.

[40]NCCB, *Brothers and Sisters to Us: U.S. Bishops' Pastoral Letter on Racism in Our Day* (Washington, D.C.: USCC Office of Publishing and Promotion Services, 1979).

The top 10 percent holds 57 percent of the net wealth.[41] If homes and other real estate are excluded, the concentration of ownership of "financial wealth" is even more glaring. In 1983, 54 percent of the total net financial assets were held by 2 percent of all families, those whose annual income is over $125,000. Eighty-six percent of these assets were held by the top 10 percent of all families.[42]

184. Although disparities in the distribution of income are less extreme, they are still striking. In 1984 the bottom 20 percent of American families recieved only 4.7 percent of the total income in the nation and the bottom 40 percent received only 15.7 percent, the lowest share on record in U.S. history. In contrast, the top one-fifth received 42.9 percent of the total income, the highest share since 1948.[43] These figures are only partial and very imperfect measures of the inequality in our society.[44] However, they do suggest that the degree of inequality is quite large. In comparison with other industrialzed nations, the United States is among the more unequal in terms of income distribution.[45] Moreover, the gap between rich and poor in our nation has increased during the last decade.[46] These inequities are of particular concern because they reflect the uneven distribution of power in our society. They suggest that the level of participation in the political and social spheres is also very uneven.

185. Catholic social teaching does not require absolute equality in the distribution of income and wealth. Some degree of inequality not only is acceptable, but also may be considered desirable for economic and social reasons, such as the need for incentives and the provision of greater rewards for greater risks. However, unequal distribution should be evaluated in terms of several moral principles we have enunciated: the priority of meeting the basic needs of the poor and the importance of increasing the level of participation by all members of society in the economic life of the nation. These norms establish a strong presumption against extreme inequality of income and wealth as long as

---

[41]Federal Reserve Board, "Survey of Consumer Finances, 1983: A Second Report," reprint from the *Federal Reserve Bulletin* (Washington, D.C., December 1984), 857-868. This survey defines net worth as the difference between gross assets and gross liabilities. The survey's estimates include all financial assets, equity in homes and other real property, as well as all financial liabilities such as consumer credit and other debts.

[42]Ibid., 863-864.

[43]U.S. Bureau of the Census, series P-60, no. 149, 11.

[44]Income distribution figures give only a static picture of income shares. They do not reflect the significant movement of families into and out of different income categories over an extended period of time. See *Years of Poverty, Years of Plenty*, 13. It should also be noted that these figures reflect pre-tax incomes. However, since the national tax structure is proportional for a large segment of the population, it does not have a significant impact on the distribution of income. See Joseph Pechman, *Who Paid Taxes, 1966-85?* (Washington, D.C.: The Brookings Institution, 1985), 51.

[45]Lars Osberg, *Economic Inequality in the United States* (New York: M.E. Sharpe, Inc., 1984), 24-28.

[46]U.S. Bureau of the Census, series P-60, no. 149, 11.

there are poor, hungry, and homeless people in our midst. They also suggest that extreme inequalities are detrimental to the development of social solidarity and community. In view of these norms we find the disparities of income and wealth in the United States to be unacceptable. Justice requires that all members of our society work for economic, political, and social reforms that will decrease these inequities.

3. Guidelines for Action

186. Our recommendations for dealing with poverty in the United States build upon several moral principles that were explored in chapter II of this letter. The themes of human dignity and the preferential option for the poor are at the heart of our approach; they compel us to confront the issue of poverty with a real sense of urgency.

187. The principle of social solidarity suggests that alleviating poverty will require fundamental changes in social and economic structures that perpetuate glaring inequalities and cut off millions of citizens from full participation in the economic and social life of the nation. The process of change should be one that draws together all citizens, whatever their economic status, into one community.

188. The principle of participation leads us to the conviction that the most appropriate and fundamental solutions to poverty will be those that enable people to take control of their own lives. For poverty is not merely the lack of adequate financial resources. It entails a more profound kind of deprivation, a denial of full participation in the economic, social, and political life of society and an inability to influence decisions that affect one's life. It means being powerless in a way that assaults not only one's pocketbook but also one's fundamental human dignity. Therefore, we should seek solutions that enable the poor to help themselves through such means as employment. Paternalistic programs which do too much *for* and too little *with* the poor are to be avoided.

189. The responsibility for alleviating the plight of the poor falls upon all members of society. As individuals, all citizens have a duty to assist the poor through acts of charity and personal commitment. But private charity and voluntary action are not sufficient. We also carry out our moral responsibility to assist and empower the poor by working collectively through government to establish just and effective public policies.

190. Although the task of alleviating poverty is complex and demanding, we should be encouraged by examples of our nation's past successes in this area. Our history shows that we can reduce poverty. During the 1960s and early 1970s, the official poverty rate was cut in half, due not only to a healthy economy, but also to public policy decisions that improved the nation's income transfer programs. It is estimated, for example, that in the late 1970s federal benefit programs were lifting out of poverty about 70 percent of those who would have otherwise been poor.[47]

191. During the last twenty-five years, the Social Security Program has dramatically reduced poverty among the elderly.[48] In addition, in 1983 it lifted out of poverty almost 1.5 million children of retired, deceased, and disabled workers.[49] Medicare has enhanced the life expectancy and health status of elderly and disabled people, and Medicaid has reduced infant mortality and greatly improved access to health care for the poor.[50]

192. These and other successful social welfare programs are evidence of our nation's commitment to social justice and a decent life for everyone. They also indicate that we have the capacity to design programs that are effective and provide necessary assistance to the needy in a way that respects their dignity. Yet it is evident that not all social welfare programs have been successful. Some have been ill-designed, ineffective, and wasteful. No one has been more aware of this than the poor themselves, who have suffered the consequences. Where programs have failed, we should discard them, learn from our mistakes, and fashion a better alternative. Where programs have succeeded, we should acknowledge that fact and build on those successes. In every instance, we must summon a new creativity and commitment to eradicate poverty in our midst and to guarantee all Americans their right to share in the blessings of our land.

193. Before discussing directions for reform in public policy, we must speak frankly about misunderstandings and stereotypes of the poor. For example, a common misconception is that most of the poor are racial minorities. In fact, about two-thirds of the poor are white.[51] It is also frequently suggested that people stay on welfare for many years, do not work, could work if they wanted to, and have children

---

[47]"Poverty in the United States: Where Do We Stand Now?" *Focus* (University of Wisconsin: Institute for Research on Poverty, Winter 1984). See also Danzinger and Gottschalk, "The Poverty of Losing Ground," *Challenge* 28:2 (May/June 1985). As these studies indicate, the slowing of the economy after 1969 tended to push more people into poverty, a trend that was offset to a great extent by the broadening of federal benefit programs for the poor in recent years have contributed to the increase in poverty. For other analyses of the causes and cures of poverty see Charles Murray, *Losing Ground: American Social Policy 1950-1980* (New York: Basic Books, Inc., 1984); Ben J. Wattenberg, *The Good News Is the Bad News Is Wrong* (New York: Simon and Shuster, 1984); and Michael Harrington, *The New American Poverty* (New York: Holt, Rinehart, and Winston, 1984).

[48]*Family and Nation*, 111-113.

[49]Committee on Ways and Means, *Children in Poverty*. Calculation based on Tables 6-1 and 6-2, 180-181; and estimates of social insurance transfers on 221-222.

[50]Paul Starr, *The Social Transformation of American Medicine* (New York: Basic Books, Inc., 1982), 373.

[51]U.S. Bureau of the Census, series P-60, no. 149, 11.

who will be on welfare. In fact, reliable data show that these are not accurate descriptions of most people who are poor and on welfare. Over a decade people move on and off welfare, and less than 1 percent obtain these benefits for all ten years.[52] Nor is it true that the rolls of Aid to Families with Dependent Children (AFDC) are filled with able-bodied adults who could but will not work. The majority of AFDC recipients are young children and their mothers who must remain at home.[53] These mothers are also accused of having more children so that they can raise their allowances. The truth is that 70 percent of AFDC families have only one or two children and that there is little financial advantage in having another. In a given year, almost half of all families who receive AFDC include an adult who has worked full or part time.[54] Research has consistently demonstrated that people who are poor have the same strong desire to work that characterizes the rest of the population.[55]

194. We ask everyone to refrain from actions, words, or attitudes that stigmatize the poor, that exaggerate the benefits received by the poor, and that inflate the amount of fraud in welfare payments.[56] These are symptoms of a punitive attitude towards the poor. The belief persists in this country that the poor are poor by choice or through laziness, that anyone can escape poverty by hard work, and that welfare programs make it easier for people to avoid work. Thus, public attitudes toward programs for the poor tend to differ sharply from attitudes about other benefits and programs. Some of the most generous subsidies for individuals and corporations are taken for granted and are not even called benefits but entitlements.[57] In contrast, programs for the poor are called handouts and receive a great deal of critical attention, even though they account for less than 10 percent of the federal budget.[58]

---

[52]*Years of Poverty, Years of Plenty,* 13.

[53]Center on Social Welfare Policy and Law, *Beyond the Myths: The Families Helped by the AFDC Program* (New York, 1985).

[54]Ibid. This booklet cites Census Bureau data showing that in 1980 about 45% of those families who received AFDC also had earned income during that year, and that the average number of weeks worked during the year was 32.1.

[55]Leonard Goodwin, *Causes and Cures of Welfare* (Lexington, Mass.: Lexington Books, 1983), ch. 1. See also Leonard Goodwin, "Can Workfare Work?" *Public Welfare* 39 (Fall 1981): 19-25.

[56]*Beyond the Myths.* With respect to error and fraud rates in AFDC, this booklet notes that erroneous payments in the AFDC program account for less than 10% of the benefits paid. No more than 8.1% of the families on AFDC received overpayments as a result of client error. In less than 4.5% of all AFDC cases nationally are questions of fraud raised. Moreover, in over 40% of these cases, a review of the facts indicated that there was insufficient evidence to support an allegation of fraud.

[57]P. G. Peterson, "No More Free Lunch for the Middle Class," *New York Times Magazine* (January 17, 1982).

[58]Interfaith Action for Economic Justice, *End Results: The Impact of Federal Policies Since 1980 on Low-Income Americans* (Washington, D.C.), 2.

195. We now wish to propose several elements which we believe are necessary for a national strategy to deal with poverty. We offer this not as a comprehensive list but as an invitation for others to join the discussion and take up the task of fighting poverty.

196. a. *The first line of attack against poverty must be to build and sustain a healthy economy that provides employment opportunities at just wages for all adults who are able to work.* Poverty is intimately linked to the issue of employment. Millions are poor because they have lost their jobs or because their wages are too low. The persistent high levels of unemployment during the last decade are a major reason why poverty has increased in recent years.[59] Expanded employment especially in the private sector would promote human dignity, increase social solidarity, and promote self-reliance of the poor. It should also reduce the need for welfare programs and generate the income necessary to support those who remain in need and cannot work: elderly, disabled, and chronically ill people, and single parents of young children. It should also be recognized that the persistence of poverty harms the larger society because the depressed purchasing power of the poor contributes to the periodic cycles of stagnation in the economy.

197. In recent years the minimum wage has not been adjusted to keep pace with inflation. Its real value has declined by 24 percent since 1981. We believe Congress should raise the minimum wage in order to restore some of the purchasing power it has lost due to inflation.

198. While job creation and just wages are major elements of a national strategy against poverty, they are clearly not enough. Other more specific policies are necessary to remedy the institutional causes of poverty and to provide for those who cannot work.

199. b. *Vigorous action should be undertaken to remove barriers to full and equal employment for women and minorities.* Too many women and minorities are locked into jobs with low pay, poor working conditions, and little opportunity for career advancement. So long as we tolerate a situation in which people can work full time and still be below the poverty line—a situation common among those earning the minimum wage—too many will continue to be counted among the "working poor." Concerted efforts must be made through job training, affirmative action, and other means to assist those now prevented from obtaining more lucrative jobs. Action should also be taken to upgrade poorer paying jobs and to correct wage differentials that discriminate unjustly against women.

200. c. *Self-help efforts among the poor should be fostered by programs and policies in both the private and public sectors.* We believe that an effective way to attack poverty is through programs that are small in scale, locally based, and oriented toward empowering the poor to become

---

[59]"The Poverty of Losing Ground," 32-38.

self-sufficient. Corporations, private organizations, and the public sector can provide seed money, training and technical assistance, and organizational support for self-help projects in a wide variety of areas such as low-income housing, credit unions, worker cooperatives, legal assistance, and neighborhood and community organizations. Efforts that enable the poor to participate in the ownership and control of economic resources are especially important.

201. Poor people must be empowered to take charge of their own futures and become responsible for their own economic advancement. Personal motivation and initiative, combined with social reform, are necessary elements to assist individuals in escaping poverty. By taking advantage of opportunities for education, employment, and training, and by working together for change, the poor can help themselves to be full participants in our economic, social, and political life.

202. d. *The tax system should be continually evaluated in terms of its impact on the poor.* This evaluation should be guided by three principles. First, the tax system should raise adequate revenues to pay for the public needs of society, especially to meet the basic needs of the poor. Second, the tax system should be structured according to the principle of progressivity, so that those with relatively greater financial resources pay a higher rate of taxation. The inclusion of such a principle in tax policies is an important means of reducing the severe inequalities of income and wealth in the nation. Action should be taken to reduce or offset the fact that most sales taxes and payroll taxes place a disproportionate burden on those with lower incomes. Third, families below the official poverty line should not be required to pay income taxes. Such families are, by definition, without sufficient resources to purchase the basic necessities of life. They should not be forced to bear the additional burden of paying income taxes.[60]

203. e. *All of society should make a much stronger commitment to education for the poor.* Any long-term solution to poverty in this country must pay serious attention to education, public and private, in school and out of school. Lack of adequate education, especially in the inner-city setting, prevents many poor people from escaping poverty. In addition, illiteracy, a problem that affects tens of millions of Americans, condemns many to joblessness or chronically low wages. Moreover, it excludes them in many ways from sharing in the political and spiritual life of the community.[61] Since poverty is fundamentally a problem of powerlessness and marginalization, the importance of education as a means of overcoming it cannot be overemphasized.

204. Working to improve education in our society is an investment in the future, an investment that should include both the public and

---

[60]The tax reform legislation of 1986 did a great deal to achieve this goal. It removed from the federal income tax rolls virtually all families below the official poverty line.

[61]Jonathan Kozol, *Illiterate America* (New York: Anchor Press/Doubleday, 1985).

private school systems. Our Catholic schools have the well-merited reputation of providing excellent education, especially for the poor. Catholic inner-city schools provide an otherwise unavailable educational alternative for many poor families. They provide one effective vehicle for disadvantaged students to lift themselves out of poverty. We commend the work of all those who make great sacrifices to maintain these inner-city schools. We pledge ourselves to continue the effort to make Catholic schools models of education for the poor.

205. We also wish to affirm our strong support for the public school system in the United States. There can be no substitute for quality education in public schools, for that is where the large majority of all students, including Catholic students, are educated. In Catholic social teaching, basic education is a fundamental human right.[62] In our society a strong public school system is essential if we are to protect that right and allow everyone to develop to their maximum ability. Therefore, we strongly endorse the recent calls for improvements in and support for public education, including improving the quality of teaching and enhancing the rewards for the teaching profession.[63] At all levels of education we need to improve the ability of our institutions to provide the personal and technical skills that are necessary for participation not only in today's labor market but also in contemporary society.

206. f. *Policies and programs at all levels should support the strength and stability of families, especially those adversely affected by the economy.* As a nation, we need to examine all aspects of economic life and assess their effects on families. Employment practices, health insurance policies, income security programs, tax policy, and service programs can either support or undermine the abilities of families to fulfill their roles in nurturing children and caring for infirm and dependent family members.

207. We affirm the principle enunciated by John Paul II that society's institutions and policies should be structured so that mothers of young children are not forced by economic necessity to leave their children

---

[62]*Peace on Earth*, 13.

[63]These reports and studies include: E. Boyer, *High School: A Report on Secondary Education in America* (Princeton: Carnegie Foundation for the Advancement of Teaching, 1983); P. Cusick, *The American High School and the Egalitarian Ideal* (New York: Longman, 1983); J. I. Goodlad, *A Place Called School: Prospects for the Future* (New York: McGraw-Hill, 1983); The National Commission on Excellence in Education, *A Nation at Risk: The Imperative for Educational Reform* (Washington, D.C.: U.S. Department of Education, 1983); D. Ravitch, *The Troubled Crusade: American Education, 1945-1980* (New York: Basic Books, 1983); T. R. Sizer, *Horace's Compromise: The Dilemma of the American High School* (Boston: Houghton Mifflin, 1984); Task Force on Education for Economic Growth, *Action for Excellence: A Comprehensive Plan to Improve our Nation's Schools* (Denver: Education Commission of the States, 1983); and The Twentieth Century Fund Task Force on Federal Elementary and Secondary Education Policy, *Making the Grade* (New York: Twentieth Century Fund, 1983). For a discussion of the issues raised in these reports see *Harvard Educational Review* 54:1 (February 1984): 1-31.

for jobs outside the home.[64] The nation's social welfare and tax policies should support parents' decisions to care for their own children and should recognize the work of parents in the home because of its value for the family and for society.

208. For those children whose parents do work outside the home, there is a serious shortage of affordable, quality day care. Employers, governments, and private agencies need to improve both the availability and the quality of child care services. Likewise, families could be assisted by the establishment of parental leave policies that would assure job security for new parents.

209. The high rate of divorce and the alarming extent of teenage pregnancies in our nation are distressing signs of the breakdown of traditional family values. These destructive trends are present in all sectors of society: rich and poor; white, black, and brown; urban and rural. However, for the poor they tend to be more visible and to have more damaging economic consequences. These destructive trends must be countered by a revived sense of personal responsibility and commitment to family values.

210. g. *A thorough reform of the nation's welfare and income-support programs should be undertaken.* For millions of poor Americans the only economic safety net is the public welfare system. The programs that make up this system should serve the needs of the poor in a manner that respects their dignity and provides adequate support. In our judgment the present welfare system does not adequately meet these criteria.[65] We believe that several improvements can and should be made within the framework of existing welfare programs. However, in the long run, more far-reaching reforms that go beyond the present system will be necessary. Among the immediate improvements that could be made are the following:

211. (1) *Public assistance programs should be designed to assist recipients, wherever possible, to become self-sufficient through gainful employment.* Individuals should not be worse off economically when they get jobs than when they rely only on public assistance. Under current rules, people who give up welfare benefits to work in low-paying jobs soon lose their Medicaid benefits. To help recipients become self-sufficient and reduce dependency on welfare, public assistance programs should work in tandem with job creation programs that include provisions

---

[64]The Vatican, *Charter of the Rights of the Family* (Washington, D.C.: USCC Office of Publishing and Promotion Services, 1983). See also *On Human Work*, 19; *Familiaris Consortio*, 23, 81; and "Christian Solidarity Leads to Action," Address to Austrian Workers (Vienna, September 1983) in *Origins* 13:16 (September 29, 1983): 275.

[65]H. R. Rodgers, Jr., *The Cost of Human Neglect: America's Welfare* (Armonk, N.Y.: W. E. Sharpe, Inc., 1982); C. T. Waxman, *The Stigma of Poverty*, second edition (New York: Pergamon Press, 1983), especially ch. 5; and S. A. Levitan and C. M. Johnson, *Beyond the Safety Net: Reviving the Promise of Opportunity in America* (Cambrdige, Mass.: Ballinger, 1984).

for training, counseling, placement, and child care. Jobs for recipients of public assistance should be fairly compensated so that workers recieve the full benefits and status associated with gainful employment.

212. (2) *Welfare programs should provide recipients with adequate levels of support.* This support should cover basic needs in food, clothing, shelter, health care, and other essentials. At present only 4 percent of poor families with children receive enough cash welfare benefits to lift them out of poverty.[66] The combined benefits of AFDC and food stamps typically come to less than three-fourths of the official poverty level.[67] Those receiving public assistance should not face the prospect of hunger at the end of the month, homelessness, sending children to school in ragged clothing, or inadequate medical care.

213. (3) *National eligibility standards and a national minimum benefit level for public assistance programs should be established.* Currently welfare eligibility and benefits vary greatly among states. In 1985 a family of three with no earnings had a maximum AFDC benefit of $96 a month in Mississippi and $558 a month in Vermont.[68] To remedy these great disparities, which are far larger than the regional differences in the cost of living, and to assure a floor of benefits for all needy people, our nation should establish and fund national minimum benefit levels and eligibility standards in cash assistance programs.[69] The benefits should also be indexed to reflect changes in the cost of living. These changes reflect standards that our nation has already put in place for aged and disabled people and veterans. Is it not possible to do the same for the children and their mothers who receive public assistance?

214. (4) *Welfare programs should be available to two-parent as well as single-parent families.* Most states now limit participation in AFDC to families headed by single parents, usually women.[70] The coverage of this program should be extended to two-parent families so that fathers who are unemployed or poorly paid do not have to leave home in order for their children to receive help. Such a change would be a significant step toward strengthening two-parent families who are poor.

---

[66]*Children in Poverty.*

[67]U.S. House of Representatives Committee on Ways and Means, *Background Materials and Data on Programs Within the Jurisdiction of the Committee on Ways and Means* (Washington, D.C., February 22, 1985), 345-346.

[68]Ibid., 347-348.

[69]In 1982, similar recommendations were made by eight former Secretaries of Health, Education, and Welfare (now Health and Human Services). In a report called "Welfare Policy in the United States," they suggested a number of ways in which national minimal standards might be set and strongly urged the establishment of a floor for all states and territories.

[70]Committee on Ways and Means, *Background Materials and Data on Programs.*

4. Conclusion

215. The search for a more human and effective way to deal with poverty should not be limited to short-term reform measures. The agenda for public debate should also include serious discussion of more fundamental alternatives to the existing welfare system. We urge that proposals for a family allowance or a children's allowance be carefully examined as a possible vehicle for ensuring a floor of income support for all children and their families.[71] Special attention is needed to develop new efforts that are targeted on long-term poverty, which has proven to be least responsive to traditional social welfare programs. The "negative income tax" is another major policy proposal that deserves continued discussion.[72] These and other proposals should be part of a creative and ongoing effort to fashion a system of income support for the poor that protects their basic dignity and provides the necessary assistance in a just and effective manner.

C. Food and Agriculture

216. The fundamental test of an economy is its ability to meet the essential human needs of this generation and future generations in an equitable fashion. Food, water, and energy are essential to life; their abundance in the United States has tended to make us complacent. But these goods—the foundation of God's gift of life—are too crucial to be taken for granted. God reminded the people of Israel that "the land is mine; for you are strangers and guests with me" (Lv 25:23, RSV). Our Christian faith calls us to contemplate God's creative and sustaining action and to measure our own collaboration with the Creator in using the earth's resources to meet human needs. While Catholic social teaching on the care of the environment and the management of natural resources is still in the process of development, a Christian moral perspective clearly gives weight and urgency to their use in meeting human needs.

217. No aspect of this concern is more pressing than the nation's food system. We are concerned that this food system may be in jeopardy as increasing numbers of farm bankruptcies and foreclosures result

---

[71]France adopted a "family" or "children's" allowance in 1932, followed by Italy in 1936, The Netherlands in 1939, the United Kingdom in 1945, and Sweden in 1947. Arnold Heidenheimer, Hugh Heclo, and Carolyn Teich Adams, *Comparative Public Policy: The Politics of Social Choice in Europe and America* (New York: St. Martin's Press, 1975), 189, 199. See Also Robert Kuttner, *The Economic Illusion* (Boston: Houghton Mifflin Co., 1984), 243-246; and Joseph Piccione, *Help for Families on the Front Lines: The Theory and Practice of Family Allowances* (Washington, D.C.: The Free Congress Research and Education Foundation, 1983).

[72]Milton Friedman, *Capitalism and Freedom* (University of Chicago Press, 1962), 190-195.

in increased concentration of land ownership.[73] We are likewise concerned about the increasing damage to natural resources resulting from many modern agricultural practices: the overconsumption of water, the depletion of topsoil, and the pollution of land and water. Finally, we are concerned about the stark reality of world hunger in spite of food surpluses. Our food production system is clearly in need of evaluation and reform.

1. U.S. Agriculture—Past and Present

218. The current crisis has to be assessed in the context of the vast diversity of U.S. crops and climates. For example, subsistence farming in Appalachia, where so much of the land is absentee-owned and where coal mining and timber production are the major economic interests, has little in common with the family farm grain production in the central Midwest or ranching in the Great Plains. Likewise, large-scale irrigated fruit, vegetable, and cotton production in the central valley of California is very different from dairy farming in Wisconsin or tobacco and peanut production in the Southeast.

219. Two aspects of the complex history of U.S. land and food policy are particularly relevant. First, the United States entered this century with the ownership of productive land widely distributed. The Pre-emption Acts of the early nineteenth century and the Homestead Act of 1862 were an important part of that history. Wide distribution of ownership was reflected in the number and decentralization of farms in the United States, a trend that reached its peak in the 1930s. The U.S. farm system included nearly 7 million owner-operators in 1935.[74] By 1983 the number of U.S. farms had declined to 2.4 million, and only about 3 percent of the population were engaged in producing food.[75] Second, U.S. food policy has had a parallel goal of keeping the consumer cost of food low. As a result, Americans today spend less of their disposable income on food than people in any other industrialized country.[76]

220. These outcomes require scrutiny. First of all, the loss of farms and the exodus of farmers from the land have led to the loss of a

---

[73]*The Current Financial Conditon of Farmers and Farm Lenders*, Ag. Info. Bulletin no. 490 (Washington, D.C.: U.S. Department of Agriculture Economic Research Service, March 1985), viii-x.

[74]Data on farms and farm population are drawn from *Agricultural Statistics*, annual reports of the U.S. Department of Agriculture, Washington, D.C.

[75]Irma T. Elo and Calvin L. Beale, *Rural Development, Poverty, and Natural Resources* (Washington, D.C.: National Center for Food and Agricultural Policy, Resources for the Future, 1985).

[76]*National Food Review*, USDA, no. 29 (Winter/Spring 1985). In 1984 Americans were spending 15.1% of their disposable income on food. This is an average figure. Many low-income people spent a good deal more and others much less.

valued way of life, the decline of many rural communities, and the increased concentration of land ownership. Second, while low food prices benefit consumers who are left with additional income to spend on other goods, these pricing policies put pressure on farmers to increase output and hold down costs. This has led them to replace human labor with cheaper energy, expand farm size to employ new technologies favoring larger scale operations, neglect soil and water conservation, underpay farmworkers, and oppose farmworker unionization.[77]

221. Today nearly half of U.S. food production comes from the 4 percent of farms with over $200,000 in gross sales.[78] Many of these largest farms are no longer operated by families, but by managers hired by owners.[79] Nearly three-quarters of all farms, accounting for only 13 percent of total farm sales, are comparatively small. They are often run by part-time farmers who derive most of their income from off-farm employment. The remaining 39 percent of sales comes from the 24 percent of farms grossing between $40,000 and $200,000. It is this group of farmers, located throughout the country and caught up in the long-term trend toward fewer and larger farms, who are the center of the present farm crisis.

222. During the 1970s, new markets for farm exports created additional opportunities for profit and accelerated the industrialization of agriculture, a process already stimulated by new petroleum-based, large-scale technologies that allowed farmers to cultivate many more acres. Federal tax policies and farm programs fostered this tendency by encouraging too much capital investment in agriculture and overemphasizing large-scale technologies.[80] The results were greater production, increases in the value of farmland, and heavy borrowing to finance expansion. In the 1980s, with export markets shrinking and commodity prices and land values declining, many farmers cannot repay their loans.

223. Their situation has been aggravated by certain "external" factors: persistent high interest rates that make it difficult to repay or refinance loans, the heavy debt burden of food-deficient countries, the high value of the dollar, dramatically higher U.S. budget and trade deficits, and generally reduced international trade following the worldwide

---

[77]Luther Tweeten, *Causes and Consequences of Structural Change in the Farming Industry*, (Washington, D.C.: National Planning Association, 1984), 7.

[78]*Economic Indicators of the Farm Sector: Income and Balance Sheet Statistics, 1983*, ECIFS 3-3 (Washington, D.C.: U.S. Department of Agriculture Economic Research Service, September 1984).

[79]Marion Clawson, *Ownership Patterns of Natural Resources in America: Implications for Distribution of Wealth and Income* (Washington, D.C.: Resources for the Future, Summer 1983).

[80]*Causes and Consequences*, 7; and *A Time to Choose: Summary Report on the Structure of Agriculture* (Washington, D.C.: U.S. Department of Agriculture, January 1981).

recession of the early 1980s. The United States is unlikely to recapture its former share of the world food and fiber trade, and it is not necessarily an appropriate goal to attempt to do so. Exports are not the solution to U.S. farm problems. Past emphasis on producing for overseas markets has contributed to the strain on our natural resource base and has also undermined the efforts of many less developed countries in attaining self-reliance in feeding their own people. In attempting to correct these abuses, however, we must not reduce our capability to help meet emergency food needs.

224. Some farmers face financial insolvency because of their own eagerness to take advantage of what appeared to be favorable investment opportunities. This was partly in response to the encouragement of public policy incentives and the advice of economists and financiers. Nevertheless, farmers should share some responsibility for their current plight.

225. Four other aspects of the current situation concern us: first, land ownership is becoming further concentrated as units now facing bankruptcy are added to existing farms and nonfarm corporations. Diversity of ownership and widespread participation are declining in this sector of the economy as they have in others. Since differing scales of operation and the investment of family labor have been important for American farm productivity, this increasing concentration of ownership in almost all sectors of agriculture points to an important change in that system.[81] Of particular concern is the growing phenomenon of "vertical integration" whereby companies gain control of two or three of the links in the food chain: as suppliers of farm inputs, landowners, and food processors. This increased concentration could also adversely affect food prices.

226. Second, diversity and richness in American society are lost as farm people leave the land and rural communities decay. It is not just a question of coping with additional unemployment and a need for retraining and relocation. It is also a matter of maintaining opportunities for employment and human development in a variety of economic sectors and cultural contexts.

227. Third, although the United States has set a world standard for food production, it has not done so without cost to our natural resource base.[82] On nearly one-quarter of our most productive cropland, topsoil

---

[81]The nature of this transformation and its implications have been addressed previously by the USCC Committee on Social Development and World Peace in a February 1979 statement *The Family Farm* and again in May 1980 by the bishops of the Midwest in a joint pastoral letter *Strangers and Guests: Toward Community in the Heartland*.

[82]*Soil Conservation in America: What Do We Have to Lose?* (Washington, D.C.: American Farmland Trust, 1984); E. Philip LeVeen, "Domestic Food Security and Increasing Competition for Water," in Lawrence Busch and William B. Lacy, eds., *Food Security in the United States* (Boulder, Colo.: Westview Press, 1984), 52. See also *America's Soil and Water: Condition and Trends* (Washington, D.C.: U.S. Department of Agriculture Soil Conservation Service, 1981).

erosion currently exceeds the rate at which it can be replaced by natural processes. Similarly, underground water supplies are being depleted in areas where food production depends on irrigation. Furthermore, chemical fertilizers, pesticides, and herbicides, considered now almost essential to today's agriculture, pollute the air, water, and soil, and pose countless health hazards. Finally, where the expansion of residential, industrial, and recreational areas makes it rewarding to do so, vast acreages of prime farmland, 3 million acres per year by some estimates, are converted to nonfarm use. The continuation of these practices, reflecting short-term investment interests or immediate income needs of farmers and other landowners, constitutes a danger to future food production because these practices are not sustainable.

228. Farm owners and farmworkers are the immediate stewards of the natural resources required to produce the food that is necessary to sustain life. These resources must be understood as gifts of a generous God. When they are seen in that light and when the human race is perceived as a single moral community, we gain a sense of the substantial responsibility we bear as a nation for the world food system. Meeting human needs today and in the future demands an increased sense of stewardship and conservation from owners, managers, and regulators of all resources, especially those required for the production of food.

229. Fourth, the situation of racial minorities in the U.S. food system is a matter of special pastoral concern. They are largely excluded from significant participation in the farm economy. Despite the agrarian heritage of so many Hispanics, for example, they operate only a minute fraction of America's farms.[83] Black-owned farms, at one time a signficant resource for black participation in the economy, have been disappearing at a dramatic rate in recent years,[84] a trend that the U.S. Commission on Civil Rights has warned "can only serve to further diminish the stake of blacks in the social order and reinforce their skepticism regarding the concept of equality under the law."[85]

230. It is largely as hired farm laborers rather than farm owners that minorities participate in the farm economy. Along with many white farmworkers, they are, by and large, the poorest paid and least benefited of any laboring group in the country. Moreover, they are not as well protected by law and public policy as other groups of workers, and their efforts to organize and bargain collectively have been systematically and vehemently resisted, usually by farmers themselves. Migratory field workers are particularly susceptible to exploitation.

---

[83] *1982 Census of Agriculture.*

[84] U.S. Commission on Civil Rights, *The Decline of Black Farming in America* (Washington, D.C.: U.S. Commission on Civil Rights, February 1982), esp. 65-69 regarding their property.

[85] Ibid., 8.

This is reflected not only in the characteristically low wages but also in the low standards of housing, health care, and education made available to these workers and their families.[86]

2. Guidelines for Action

231. We are convinced that current trends in the food sector are not in the best interests of the United States or of the global community. The decline in the number of moderate-sized farms, increased concentration of land ownership, and the mounting evidence of poor resource conservation raise serious questions of morality and public policy. As pastors, we cannot remain silent while thousands of farm families caught in the present crisis lose their homes, their land, and their way of life. We approach this situation, however, aware that it reflects longer-term conditions that carry consequences for the food system as a whole and for the resources essential for food production.

232. While much of the change needed must come from the cooperative efforts of farmers themselves, we strongly believe that there is an important role for public policy in the protection of dispersed ownership through family farms, as well as in the preservation of natural resources. We suggest three guidelines for both public policy and private efforts aimed at shaping the future of American agriculture.

233. First, moderate-sized farms operated by families on a full-time basis should be preserved and their economic viability protected. Similarly, small farms and part-time farming, particularly in areas close to cities, should be encouraged. As we have noted elsewhere in this pastoral letter,[87] there is genuine social and economic value in maintaining a wide distribution in the ownership of productive property. The democratization of decision making and control of the land resulting from wide distribution of farm ownership are protections against concentration of power and a consequent possible loss of responsiveness to public need in this crucial sector of the economy.[88] Moreover, when those who work in an enterprise also share in its ownership, their active commitment to the purpose of the endeavor and their participation in it are enhanced. Ownership provides incentives for diligence and is a source of increased sense that the work being done is one's own. This is particularly singificant in a sector as vital to human well-being as agriculture.

234. Furthermore, diversity in farm ownership tends to prevent excessive consumer dependence on business decisions that seek maximum

---

[86]U.S. Department of Labor, *Hearings Concerning Proposed Full Sanitation Standards*, document no. H-308 (Washington, D.C., 1984).

[87]Ch. II, para. 112.

[88]*A Time to Choose*, 148.

return on invested capital, thereby making the food system overly susceptible to fluctuations in the capital markets. This is particularly relevant in the case of nonfarm corporations that enter agriculture in search of high profits. If the return drops substantially, or if it appears that better profits can be obtained by investing elsewhere, the corporation may cut back or even close down operations without regard to the impact on the community or on the food system in general. In similar circumstances full-time farmers, with a heavy personal investment in their farms and strong ties to the community, are likely to persevere in the hope of better times. Family farms also make significant economic and social contributions to the life of rural communities.[89] They support farm suppliers and other local merchants, and their farms support the tax base needed to pay for roads, schools, and other vital services.

235. This rural interdependence has value beyond the rural community itself. Both Catholic social teaching and the traditions of our country have emphasized the importance of maintaining the rich plurality of social institutions that enhances personal freedom and increases the opportunity for participation in community life. Movement toward a smaller number of very large farms employing wage workers would be a movement away from this institutional pluralism. By contributing to the vitality of rural communities, full-time residential farmers enrich the social and political life of the nation as a whole. Cities, too, benefit soundly and economically from a vibrant rural economy based on family farms. Because of out-migration of farm and rural people, too much of this enriching diversity has been lost already.

236. *Second, the opportunity to engage in farming should be protected as a valuable form of work.* At a time when unemployment in the country is already too high, any unnecessary increase in the number of unemployed people, however small, should be avoided. Farm unemployment leads to further rural unemployment as rural businesses lose their customers and close down. The loss of people from the land also entails the loss of expertise in farm and land management and creates a need for retraining and relocating another group of displaced workers.

237. Losing any job is painful, but losing one's farm and having to leave the land can be tragic. It often means the sacrifice of a family heritage and a way of life. Once farmers sell their land and their equipment, their move is practically irreversible. The costs of returning are so great that few who leave ever come back. Even the small current influx of people into agriculture attracted by lower land values will not balance this loss. Society should help those who would and could continue effectively in farming.

---

[89]Luther Tweeten, "The Economics of Small Farms," *Science* vol. 219 (March 4, 1983): 1041.

238. *Third, effective stewardship of our natural resources should be a central consideration in any measures regarding U.S. agriculture.* Such stewardship is a contribution to the common good that is difficult to assess in purely economic terms, because it involves the care of resources entrusted to us by our Creator for the benefit of all. Responsibility for the stewardship of these resources rests on society as a whole. Since farmers make their living from the use of this endowment, however, they bear a particular obligation to be caring stewards of soil and water. They fulfill this obligation by participating in soil and water conservation programs, using farm practices that enhance the quality of the resources, and maintaining prime farmland in food production rather than letting it be converted to nonfarm uses.

3. Policies and Actions

239. The human suffering involved in the present situation and the long-term structural changes occurring in this sector call for responsible action by the whole society. A half-century of federal farm-price supports, subsidized credit, production-oriented research and extension services, and special tax policies for farmers have made the federal government a central factor in almost every aspect of American agriculture.[90] No redirection of current trends can occur without giving close attention to these programs.

240. A prime consideration in all agricultural trade and food assistance policies should be the contribution our nation can make to global food security. This means continuing and increasing food aid without depressing Third World markets or using food as a weapon in international politics. It also means not subsidizing exports in ways that lead to trade wars and instability in international food markets.

241. We offer the following suggestions for governmental action with regard to the farm and food sector of the economy.

242. a. The current crisis calls for special measures to assist otherwise viable family farms that are threatened with bankruptcy or foreclosure. Operators of such farms should have access to emergency credit, reduced rates of interest, and programs of debt restructuring. Rural lending institutions facing problems because of nonpayment or slow payment of large farm loans should also have access to temporary assistance. Farmers, their families, and their communities will gain immediately from these and other short-term measures aimed at keeping these people on the land.

243. b. Established federal farm programs, whose benefits now go

---

[90]U.S. Department of Agriculture, *History of Agricultural Price-Support and Adjustment Programs, 1933-1984*, Ag. Info. Bulletin no. 485 (Washington, D.C.: U.S. Department of Agriculture Economic Research Service, December 1984).

disproportionately to the largest farmers,[91] should be reassessed for their long-term effects on the structure of agriculture. Income-support programs that help farmers according to the amount of food they produce or the number of acres they farm should be subject to limits that ensure a fair income to all farm families and should restrict participation to producers who genuinely need such income assistance. There should also be a strict ceiling on price-support payments which assist farmers in times of falling prices, so that benefits go to farms of moderate or small size. To succeed in redirecting the benefits of these programs while holding down costs to the public, consideration should be given to a broader application of mandatory production control programs.[92]

244. c. We favor reform of tax policies which now encourage the growth of large firms, attract investments into agriculture by non-farmers seeking tax shelters, and inequitably benefit large and well-financed farming operations.[93] Offsetting nonfarm income with farm "losses" has encouraged high-income investors to acquire farm assets with no intention of depending on them for a living as family farmers must. The ability to depreciate capital equipment faster than its actual decline in value has benefitted wealthy investors and farmers. Lower tax rates on capital gains have simulated farm expansion and larger investments in energy-intensive equipment and technologies as substitutes for labor. Changes in estate tax laws have consistently favored the largest estates. All of these results have demonstrated that reassessment of these and similar tax provisions is needed.[94] We continue, moreover, to support a progressive land tax on farm acreage to discourage the accumulation of excesssively large holdings.[95]

245. d. Although it is often assumed that farms must grow in size in order to make the most efficient and productive use of sophisticated and costly technologies, numerous studies have shown that medium-sized commercial farms achieve most of the technical cost efficiencies available in agriculture today. We, therefore, recommend that the research and extension resources of the federal government and the

---

[91] *The Distribution of Benefits from the 1982 Federal Crop Programs* (Washington, D.C.: U.S. Senate Committee on the Budget, November 1984).

[92] "The Great Debate on Mandatory Production Controls" in *Farm Policy Perspectives: Setting the Stage for 1985 Agricultural Legislation* (Washington, D.C.: U.S. Senate Committee on Agriculture, Nutrition, and Forestry, April 1984).

[93] *A Time to Choose*, 91.

[94] Richard Dunford, *The Effects of Federal Income Tax Policy on U.S. Agriculture* (Washington, D.C.: Subcommittee on Agriculture and Transportation of the Joint Economic Committee of the Congress of the United States, December 21, 1984).

[95] This proposal was put forward thirteen years ago in *Where Shall the People Live?* A Special Message of the United States Catholic Bishops (Washington, D.C.: USCC Office of Publishing and Promotion Services, 1972).

nation's land grant colleges and universities be redirected toward improving the productivity of small and medium-sized farms.[96]

246. e. Since soil and water conservation, like other efforts to protect the environment, are contributions to the good of the whole society, it is appropriate for the public to bear a share of the cost of these practices and to set standards for environmental protection. Government should, therefore, encourage farmers to adopt more conserving practices and distribute the costs of this conservation more broadly

247. f. Justice demands that worker guarantees and protections such as minimum wages and benefits and unemployment compensation be extended to hired farmworkers on the same basis as all other workers. There is also an urgent need for additional farmworker housing, health care, and educational assistance.

4. Solidarity in the Farm Community

248. While there is much that government can and should do to change the direction of farm and food policy in this country, that change in direction also depends upon the cooperation and good will of farmers. The incentives in our farm system to take risks, to expand farm size, and to speculate in farmland values are great. Hence, farmers and ranchers must weigh these incentives against the values of family, rural community, care of the soil, and a food system responsive to long-term as well as short-term food needs of the nation and the world. The ever present temptation to individualism and greed must be countered by a determined movement toward solidarity in the farm community. Farmers should approach farming in a cooperative way, working with other farmers in the purchase of supplies and equipment and in the marketing of produce. It is not necessary for every farmer to be in competition against every other farmer. Such cooperation can be extended to the role farmers play through their various general and community organizations in shaping and implementing governmental farm and food policies.[97] Likewise, it is possible to seek out and adopt technologies that reduce costs and enhance productivity without demanding increases in farm size. New technologies are not forced on farmers; they are chosen by farmers themselves.

249. Farmers also must end their opposition to farmworker unionization efforts. Farmworkers have a legitimate right to belong to unions of their choice and to bargain collectively for just wages and working conditions. In pursuing that right they are protecting the value of labor in agriculture, a protection that also applies to farmers who devote their own labor to their farm operations.

---

[96]Thomas E. Miller, et al., *Economies of Size in U.S. Field Crop Farming* (Washington, D.C.: U.S. Department of Agriculture Economic Research Service, July 1981).

[97]See ch. IV.

5. Conclusion

250. The U.S. food system is an integral part of the larger economy of the nation and the world. As such this integral role necessitates the cooperation of rural and urban interests in resolving the challenges and problems facing agriculture. The very nature of agricultural enterprise and the family farm traditions of this country have kept it a highly competitive sector with a widely dispersed ownership of the most fundamental input to production, the land. That competitive, diverse structure, proven to be a dependable source of nutritious and affordable food for this country and millions of people in other parts of the world, is now threatened. The food necessary for life, the land and water resources needed to produce that food, and the way of life of the people who make the land productive are at risk. Catholic social and ethical traditions attribute moral significance to each of these. Our response to the present situation should reflect a sensitivity to that moral significance, a determination that the United States will play its appropriate role in meeting global food needs, and a commitment to bequeath to future generations an enhanced natural environment and the same ready access to the necessities of life that most of us enjoy today. To farmers and farmworkers who are suffering because of the farm crisis, we promise our solidarity, prayers, counseling, and the other spiritual resources of our Catholic faith.

D. *The U.S. Economy and the Developing Nations Complexity, Challenge, and Choices*

1. The Complexity of Economic Relations in an Interdependent World

251. The global economy is made up of national economies of industrialized countries of the North and the developing countries of the South, together with the network of economic relations that link them. It constitutes the framework in which the solidarity we seek on a national level finds its international expression. Traditional Catholic teaching on this global interdependence emphasizes the dignity of the human person, the unity of the human family, the universally beneficial purpose of the goods of the earth, the need to pursue the international common good, as well as the good of each nation, and the imperative of distributive justice. The United States plays a leading role in the international economic system, and we are concerned that U.S. relations with all nations—Canada, Europe, Japan, and our other trading partners, as well as the socialist countries—reflect this teaching and be marked by fairness and mutual respect.
252. Nevertheless, without in the least discounting the importance

of these linkages, our emphasis on the preferential option for the poor moves us to focus our attention mainly on U.S. relations with the Third World. Unless conscious steps are taken toward protecting human dignity and fostering human solidarity in these relationships, we can look forward to increased conflict and inequity, threatening the fragile economies of these relatively poor nations far more than our own relatively strong one. Moreover, equity requires, even as the fact of interdependence becomes more apparent, that the *quality* of interdependence be improved, in order to eliminate "the scandal of the shocking inequality between the rich and the poor"[98] in a world divided ever more sharply between them.

253. Developing countries, moreover, often perceive themselves more as *dependent* on the industrialized countries, especially the United States, because the international system itself, as well as the way the United States acts in it, subordinates them. The prices at which they must sell their commodity exports and purchase their food and manufactured imports, the rates of interest they must pay and the terms they must meet to borrow money, the standards of economic behavior of foreign investors, the amounts and conditions of external aid, etc., are essentially determined by the industrialized world. Moreover, their traditional cultures are increasingly susceptible to the aggressive cultural penetration of Northern (especially U.S.) advertising and media programming. The developing countries are junior partners at best.

254. The basic tenets of church teaching take on a new moral urgency as we deepen our understanding of how disadvantaged large numbers of people and nations are in this interdependent world. Half the world's people, nearly two and a half billion, live in countries where the annual per capita income is $400 or less.[99] At least 800 million people in those countries live in absolute poverty, "beneath any rational definition of human decency."[100] Nearly half a billion are chronically hungry, despite abundant harvests worldwide.[101] Fifteen out of every 100 children born in those countries die before the age of five, and millions of the survivors are physically or mentally stunted. No aggregate of individual examples could portray adequately the appalling inequities within those desperately poor countires and between them and our own. And their misery is not the inevitable result of the march of history or of the intrinsic nature of particular cultures, but of human decisions and human institutions.

---

[98]*Instruction on Certain Aspects of the Theology of Liberation*, I:6. See also *Peace on Earth*, 130-131; and *On Human Work*, 11.

[99]Overseas Development Council, *U.S. Policy and the Third World: Agenda 1985-1986.*

[100]Robert S. McNamara, *Address to the Board of Governors of the World Bank* (Washington, D.C.: World Bank, September 30, 1980).

[101]UN/Food and Agricultural Organization, *Dimensions of Need*, E 9 (Rome 1982). The UN World Food Council uses this figure consistently, most recently at its 11th annual meeting in Paris.

255. On the international economic scene three main sets of actors warrant particular attention: individual nations, which retain great influence; multilateral institutions, which channel money, power, ideas, and influence; and transnational corporations and banks, which have grown dramatically in number, size, scope, and strength since World War II.[102] In less identifiable ways trade unions, popular movements, private relief and development agencies, and regional groupings of nations also affect the global economy. The interplay among all of them sets the context for policy choices that determine whether genuine interdependence is promoted or the dependence of the disadvantaged is deepened.

256. In this arena, where fact and ethical challenges intersect, the moral task is to devise rules for the major actors that will move them toward a just international order. One of the most vexing problems is that of reconciling the transnational corporations' profit orientation with the common good that they, along with governments and their multilateral agencies, are supposed to serve.

257. The notion of interdependence erases the fading line between domestic and foreign policy. Many foreign policy decisions (for example, on trade, investment, and immigration) have direct and substantial impact on domestic constituencies in the United States. Similarly, many decisions thought of as domestic (for example, on farm policy, interest rates, the federal budget, or the deficit) have important consequences for other countries. This increasingly recognized link of domestic and foreign issues poses new empirical and moral questions for national policy.

2. The Challenge of Catholic Social Teaching

258. Catholic teaching on the international economic order recognizes this complexity, but does not provide specific solutions. Rather, we seek to ensure that moral considerations are taken into account. All of the elements of the moral perspective we have outlined above have important implications for international relationships. (1) The demands of *Christian love* and *human solidarity* challenge all economic actors to choose community over chaos. They require a definition of political community that goes beyond national sovereignty to policies that recognize the moral bonds among all people. (2) *Basic justice* implies

---

[102]Joseph Greenwald and Kenneth Flamm, *The Global Factory* (Washington, D.C.: The Brookings Institution, 1985); see also Ronald Muller and Richard Barnet, *Global Reach* (New York: Simon and Schuster, 1974); Raymond Vernon, *The Economic and Political Consequences of Multinational Enterprise* (Cambridge, Mass.: Harvard University Press, 1972); the United Nations Center on Transnational Corporations maintains current data on these institutions.

that all peoples are entitled to participate in the increasingly inter-dependent global economy in a way that ensures their freedom and dignity. When whole communities are effectively left out or excluded from equitable participation in the international order, basic justice is violated. We want a world that works fairly for all. (3) *Respect for human rights*, both political and economic, implies that international decisions, institutions, and policies must be shaped by values that are more than economic. The creation of a global order in which these rights are secure for all must be a prime objective for all relevant actors on the international stage. (4) *The special place of the poor* in this moral perspective means that meeting the basic needs of the millions of deprived and hungry people in the world must be the number one objective of international policy.

259. These perspectives constitute a call for fundamental reform in the international economic order. Whether the problem is preventing war and building peace, or addressing the needs of the poor, Catholic teaching emphasizes not only the individual conscience, but also the political, legal, and economic structures through which policy is deter-mined and issues are adjudicated.[103] We do not seek here to evaluate the various proposals for international economic reform or deal here with economic relations between the United States and other indus-trialized countries. We urge, as a basic and overriding consideration, that both empirical and moral evidence, especially the precarious situation of the developing countries, calls for the renewal of the dialogue between the industrialized countries of the North and the developing countries of the South, with the aim of reorganizing inter-national economic relations to establish greater equity and help meet the basic human needs of the poor majority.[104]

260. *Here, as elsewhere, the preferential option for the poor is the central priority for policy choice.* It offers a unique perspective on foreign policy in whose light U.S. relationships, especially with developing coun-tries, can be reassessed. Standard foreign policy analysis deals with calculations of power and definitions of national interest; but the poor are, by definition, not powerful. If we are to give appropriate weight to their concerns, their needs, and their interests, we have to go beyond economic gain or national security as a starting point for the policy dialogue. We want to stand with the poor everywhere, and we believe that relations between the U.S. and developing nations should be determined in the first place by a concern for basic human needs and respect for cultural traditions.

---

[103] *Peace on Earth,* 56-63.

[104] *On the Development of Peoples,* 44, 58-63; quoted also by Pope John Paul II, *Origins* 14:16 (October 4, 1984): 247.

3. The Role of the United States in the Global Economy Constructive Choices

261. As we noted in *The Challenge of Peace*, recent popes have strongly supported the United Nations as a crucial step forward in the development and organization of the human community; we share their regret that no political entity now exists with the responsibility and power to promote the global common good, and we urge the United States to support UN efforts to move in that direction. Building a just world economic order in the absence of such an authority demands that national governments promote public policies that increase the ability of poor nations and marginalized people to participate in the global economy. Because no other nation's economic power yet matches ours, we believe that this responsibility pertains especially to the United States, but it must be carried out in cooperation with other industrialized countries as in the case of halting the rise of the dollar. This is yet another evidence of the fact of interdependence. Joint action toward these goals not only promotes justice and reduces misery in the Third World, but also is in the interest of the United States and other industrialized nations.

262. Yet in recent years U.S. policy toward development in the Third World has become increasingly one of selective assistance based on East-West assessment of North-South problems, at the expense of basic human needs and economic development. Such a view makes national security the central policy principle.[105] Developing countries have become largely testing grounds in the East-West struggle; they seem to have meaning or value mainly in terms of this larger geopolitical calculus. The result is that issues of human need and economic development take second place to the political-strategic argument. This tendency must be resisted.

263. Moreover, U.S. performance in North-South negotiations often casts us in the role of resisting developing-country proposals without advancing realistic ones of our own.[106] North-South dialogue is bound to be complex, protracted, and filled with symbolic and often unrealistic demands; but the situation has now reached the point where the rest of the world expects the United States to assume a reluctant, adversarial posture in such discussions. The U.S. approach to the developing countries needs urgently to be changed; a country as large, rich, and powerful as ours has a moral obligation to lead in helping to reduce poverty in the Third World.

---

[105]President's Commission on Security and Economic Assistance (Carlucci Commission), *A Report to the Secretary of State* (Washington, D.C., November 1983).

[106]For example: After a dozen years of negotiations, during which nearly all of the issues were resolved to U.S. satisfaction, the United States refused to sign the Law of the Seas treaty; only the United States failed to support the UN infant formula resolution; the United States has not ratified the two UN Covenants on Human Rights, etc.

264. We believe that U.S. policy toward the developing world should reflect our traditional regard for human rights and our concern for social progress. In economic policy, as we noted in our pastoral letter on nuclear war, the major international economic relationships of aid, trade, finance, and investment are interdependent among themselves and illustrate the range of interdependence issues facing U.S. policy. All three of the major economic actors are active in all these relationships. Each relationship offers us the possibility of substantial, positive movement toward increasing social justice in the developing world; in each, regrettably, we fall short. It is urgent that immediate steps be taken to correct these deficiencies.

265. a. *Development Assistance:* The official development assistance that the industrialized and the oil-producing countries provide the Third World in the form of grants; low-interest, long-term loans; commodities; and technical assistance is a significant contribution to their development. Although the annual share of U.S. gross national product (GNP) devoted to foreign aid is now less than one-tenth of that of the Marshall Plan, which helped rebuild devastated but advanced European economies, we remain the largest donor country. We still play a central role in these resource transfers, but we no longer set an example for other donors. We lag proportionately behind most other industrial nations in providing resources and seem to care less than before about development in the Third World. Our bilateral aid has become increasingly militarized and security-related and our contributions to multilateral agencies have been reduced in recent years.[107] Not all of these changes are justifiable. The projects of the International Development Agency, for example, seem worthy of support.

266. This is a grave distortion of the priority that development assistance should command. We are dismayed that the United States, once the pioneer in foreign aid, is almost last among the seventeen industrialized nations in the Organization for Economic Cooperation and Development (OECD) in percentage of GNP devoted to aid. Reduction of the U.S. contribution to multilateral development institutions is particularly regrettable, because these institutions are often better able than the bilateral agencies to focus on the poor and reduce dependency in developing countries.[108] This is also an area in which, in the past, our leadership and example have had great influence. A more affirmative U.S. role in these institutions, which we took the lead in creating,

---

[107]U.S. Agency for International Development, *Congressional Presentation, Fiscal Year 1986, Main Volume* (Washngton, D.C., 1985).

[108]The clients of the International Development Association, the "soft loan window" of the World Bank, are the poorest countries. The United States insisted upon—and obtained—a 25% reduction in IDA's current (seventh) replenishment. Taking inflation into account, this meant a 40% drop in real terms at exactly the moment when developing-country debt levels are punishingly high and the prices of their export commodities are almost at rock bottom.

could improve their performance, send an encouraging signal of U.S. intentions, and help reopen the dialogue on the growing poverty and dependency of the Third World.

267. b. *Trade:* Trade continues to be a central component of international economic relations. It contributed in a major way to the rapid economic growth of many developing countries in the 1960s and 1970s and will probably continue to do so, though at a slower rate. The preferential option for the poor does not, by itself, yield a trade policy, but it does provide a frame of reference. In particular, an equitable trading system that will help the poor should allocate its benefits fairly and ensure that exports from developing countries receive fair prices reached by agreement among all trading partners. Developing nations have a right to receive a fair price for their raw materials that allows for a reasonable degree of profit.

268. Trade policy illustrates the conflicting pressures that interdependence can generate: claims of injustice from developing countries denied market access are countered by claims of injustice in the domestic economies of industrialized countries when jobs are threatened and incomes fall. Agricultural trade and a few industrial sectors present particularly acute examples of this.

269. We believe the ethical norms we have applied to domestic economic questions are equally valid here.[109] As in other economic matters, the basic questions are: Who benefits from the particular policy measure? How can any benefit or adverse impact be equitably shared? We need to examine, for example, the extent to which the success in the U.S. market of certain imports is derived from exploitative labor conditions in the exporting country, conditions that in some cases have attracted the investment in the first place. The United States should do all it can to ensure that the trading system treats the poorest segments of developing countries' societies fairly and does not lead to human rights violations. In particular the United States should seek effective special measures under the General Agreement on Tariffs and Trade (GATT)[110] to benefit the poorest countries.

270. At the same time, U.S. workers and their families hurt by the operation of the trading system must be helped through training and other measures to adjust to changes that advance development and decrease poverty in the Third World. This is a very serious, immediate, and intensifying problem. In our judgment, adjustment assistance programs in the United States have been poorly designed and administered, and inadequately funded. A society and an economy such as

---

[109]See ch. II.

[110]The GATT, third of the Bretton Woods "institutions" (with the World Bank and the IMF) is in fact a treaty, monitored and supported by a secretariat located in Geneva, Switzerland. Periodic "rounds" of negotiations among its several score members, North and South, modify and extend its provisions and regulations.

ours can better adjust to trade dislocations than can poverty-ridden developing countries.

271. c. *Finance:* Aid and trade policies alone, however enlightened, do not constitute a sufficient approach to the developing countries; they must also be looked at in conjunction with international finance and investment. The debtor-creditor relationship well exemplifies both the interdependence of the international economic order and its asymmetrical character, i.e., the *dependence* of the developing countries. The aggregate external debt of the developing countries now approaches $1 trillion,[111] more than one-third of their combined GNP; this total doubled between 1979 and 1984 and continues to rise. On average, the first 20 percent of export earnings goes to service that debt without significantly reducing the principal; in some countries debt service is nearly 100 percent of such earnings, leaving scant resources available for the countries' development programs.

272. The roots of this very complex debt crisis are both historic and systemic. *Historically,* the three major economic actors share the responsibility for the present difficulty because of decisions made and actions taken during the 1970s and 1980s. In 1972 the Soviet Union purchased the entire U.S. grain surplus, and grain prices trebled. Between 1973 and 1979, the Organization of Petroleum Exporting Countries raised the price of oil eightfold and thereafter deposited most of the profits in commercial banks in the North. In order to profit from the interest-rate spread on these deposits, the banks pushed larger and larger loans on eager Third World borrowers needing funds to purchase more and more expensive oil. A second doubling of oil prices in 1979 forced many of these countries to refinance their loans and borrow more money at escalating interest rates. A global recession beginning in 1979 caused the prices of Third World export commodities to fall and thus reduced the ability to meet the increasingly burdensome debt payments out of export earnings.

273. The global *system* of finance, development, and trade established by the Bretton Woods Conference in 1944—the World Bank, the International Monetary Fund (IMF), and the GATT—was created by the North to prevent a recurrence of the economic problems that were perceived to have led to World War II. Forty years later that system seems incapable, without basic changes, of helping the debtor countries—which had no part in its creation—manage their increasingly untenable debt situation effectively and equitably. The World Bank, largest of these institutions, has been engaged primarily in lending for specific projects rather than for general economic health. The IMF was intended to be a short-term lender that would help out with temporary balance of payments, or cash-flow problems; but in the

---

[111]Debt figures have been compiled from data published by the World Bank, the IMF, and the Bank for International Settlements.

current situation it has come to the fore as a monitor of commercial financial transactions and an evaluator of debtors' creditworthiness— and therefore the key institution for resolving these problems. The GATT, which is not an institution, had been largely supplanted, as trade monitor for the developing countries, by UNCTAD[112] in which the latter have more confidence.

274. This crisis, however, goes beyond the system; it affects people. It afflicts and oppresses large numbers of people who are already severely disadvantaged. That is the scandal: it is the poorest people who suffer most from the austerity measures required when a country seeks the IMF "seal of approval" which establishes its creditworthiness for a commerical loan (or perhaps an external aid program). It is these same people who suffer most when commodity prices fall, when food cannot be imported or they cannot buy it, and when natural disasters occur. Our commitment to the preferential option for the poor does not permit us to remain silent in these circumstances. Ways must be found to meet the immediate emergency—moratorium on payments, conversion of some dollar-denominated debt into local-currency debt, creditors' accepting a share of the burden by partially writing down selected loans, capitalizing interest, or perhaps outright cancellation.

275. The poorest countries, especially those in sub-Saharan Africa which are least developed, most afflicted by hunger and malnutrition, and most vulnerable to commodity price declines, are in extremely perilous circumstances.[113] Although their aggregate debt of more than $100 billion (much of it owed to multilateral institutions), is about one-quarter that of Latin America, their collateral (oil, minerals, manufactures, grain, etc.) is much less adequate, their ability to service external debt much weaker, and the possibility of their rescheduling it very small. For low-income countries like these, the most useful immediate remedies are longer payment periods, lower interest rates, and modification of IMF adjustment requirements that exacerbate the already straitened circumstances of the poor.[114] Especially helpful for

---

[112]The United Nations Conference on Trade and Development (UNCTAD) originated in Geneva in 1964 at a meeting convened by the UN to discuss trade, development, and related problems of low-income countries. It established a quadrennial meeting and created permanent machinery in the UN to deal with these problems. A Trade and Development Board (TDB), with standing committees, meets every two years, and there is a small secretariat to staff it. UNCTAD is viewed as representing the developing countries' continuing effort to have a larger voice in international decisions affecting trade and development and to secure more favorable terms of trade.

[113]*U.S. Policy and the Third World*, Table B-5.

[114]When the IMF helps a country adjust to balance-of-payments problems (e.g., by assisting in the rescheduling of its external debt), it negotiates certain conditions with the debtor country in order to improve its immediate financial position. In general, these require the borrowing country to earn and save more. The adjustments, usually referred to as "conditionality," tend to fall most heavily on the poor through reduction of government spending on consumer subsidies and public services, and often of wages.

some African countries would be cancellation of debts owed to governments, a step already taken by some creditor nations.

276. Better off debtor countries also need to be able to adjust their debts without penalizing the poor. Although the final policy decisions about the allocation of adjustment costs belong to the debtor government, internal equity considerations should be taken into account in determining the conditions of debt rescheduling and additional lending; for example, wage reductions should not be mandated, basic public services to the poor should not be cut, and measures should be required to reduce the flight of capital. Since this debt problem, like most others, is systemic, a case-by-case approach is not sufficient: lending policies and exchange-rate considerations are not only economic questions, but are also thoroughly and intensely political.

277. Beyond all this, the growing external debt that has become the overarching economic problem of the Third World also requires systemic change to provide immediate relief and to prevent recurrence. The Bretton Woods institutions do not adequately represent Third World debtors, and their policies are not dealing effectively with problems affecting those nations. These institutions need to be substantially reformed and their policies reviewed at the same time that the immediate problem of Third World debt is being dealt with. The United States should promote, support, and participate fully in such reforms and reviews. Such a role is not only morally right, but is also in the economic interest of the United States; more than a third of this debt is owed to U.S. banks. The viability of the international banking system (and of those U.S. banks) depends in part on the ability of debtor countries to manage those debts. Stubborn insistence on full repayment could force them to default—which would lead to economic losses in the United States. In this connection, we should not overlook the impact of U.S. budget and trade deficits on interest rates. These high interest rates exacerbate the already difficult debt situation. They also attract capital away from investment in economic development in Third World countries.

278. d. *Foreign Private Investment:* Although direct private investment in the developing countries by U.S.-based transnational corporations has declined in recent years, it still amounts to about $60 billion and accounts for sizeable annual transfers. Such investment in developing countries should be increased, consistent with the host country's development goals and with benefits equitably distributed. Particular efforts should be made to encourage investments by medium-sized and small companies, as well as to joint ventures, which may be more appropriate to the developing country's situation. For the foreseeable future, however, private investment will probably not meet the infrastructural needs of the poorest countries—roads, transportation, communications, education, health, etc.—since these do not generally show profits and therefore do not attract private capital. Yet without

this infrastructure, no real economic growth can take place.

279. Direct foreign investment, risky though it may be for both the investing corporation and the developing country, can provide needed capital, technology, and managerial expertise. Care must be taken lest such investment create or perpetuate dependency, harming especially those at the bottom of the economic ladder. Investments that sustain or worsen inequities in a developing country, that help to maintain oppressive elites in power, or that increase food dependency by encouraging cash cropping for export at the expense of local needs, should be discouraged. Foreign investors, attracted by low wage rates in less developed countries, should consider both the potential loss of jobs in the home country and the potential exploitation of workers in the host country.[115] Both the products and the technologies of the investing firms should be appropriate to the developing country, neither catering just to a small number of high-income consumers nor establishing capital-intensive processes that displace labor, especially in the agricultural sector.[116]

280. Such inequitable results, however, are not necessary consequences of transnational corporate activity. Corporations can contribute to development by attracting and training high-caliber managers and other personnel, by helping organize effective marketing systems, by generating additional capital, by introducing or reinforcing financial accountability, and by sharing the knowledge gained from their own research and development activities. Although the ability of the corporations to plan, operate, and communicate across national borders without concern for domestic considerations makes it harder for governments to direct their activities toward the common good, the effort should be made; the Christian ethic is incompatible with a primary or exclusive focus on maximization of profit. We strongly urge U.S. and international support of efforts to develop a code of conduct for foreign corporations that recognizes their quasi-public character and encourages both development and the equitable distribution of their benefits. Transnational corporations should be required to adopt such a code, and to conform their behavior to its provisions.

281. e. *The World Food Problem—A Special Urgency:* These four resource transfer channels—aid, trade, finance, and investment—intersect and overlap in all economic areas, but in none more clearly than in the international food system. The largest single segment of development assistance support goes to the agricultural sector and to food aid for short-term emergencies and vulnerable groups; food constitutes one of the most critical trade sectors; developing countries have borrowed

---

[115]North American Coalition for Human Rights in Korea, *Testimony before the U.S. Trade Representative,* June 24, 1985.

[116]E. F. Schumacher, *Small Is Beautiful: Economics As If People Mattered* (New York: Harper and Row, 1973).

extensively in the international capital markets to finance food imports; and a substantial portion of direct private investment flows into the agricultural sector.

282. The development of U.S. agriculture has moved the United States into a dominant position in the international food system. The best way to meet the responsibilities this dominance entails is to design and implement a U.S. food and agriculture policy that contributes to increased food security—that is, access by everyone to an adequate diet. A world with nearly half a billion hungry people is not one in which food security has been achieved. The problem of hunger has a special significance for those who read the Scriptures and profess the Christian faith. From the Lord's command to feed the hungry, to the Eucharist we celebrate as the Bread of Life, the fabric of our faith demands that we be creatively engaged in sharing the food that sustains life. There is no more basic human need. The gospel imperative takes on new urgency in a world of abundant harvests where hundreds of millions of people face starvation. Relief and prevention of their hunger cannot be left to the arithmetic of the marketplace.[117]

283. The chronic hunger of those who live literally from day to day is one symptom of the underlying problem of poverty; relieving and preventing hunger is part of a larger, coordinated strategy to attack poverty itself. People must be enabled either to grow or to buy the food they need, without depending on an indefinite dole; there is no substitute for long-term agricultural and food-system development in the nations now caught in the grip of hunger and starvation. Most authorities agree that the key to this development is the small farmers, most of whom are prevented from participating in the food system by the lack of a market incentive resulting from the poverty of the bulk of the populations and by the lack of access to productive agricultural inputs, especially land, resulting mainly from their own poverty. In these poor, food-deficit countries, no less than in our own, the small family farm deserves support and protection.

284. But recognizing the long-term problem does not dissolve the short-term obligation of the world's major food-exporting nation to provide food aid sufficient to meet the nutritional needs of poor people, and to provide it not simply to dispose of surpluses but in a way that does not discourage local food production. There can be no successful solution to the problem of hunger in the world without U.S. participation in a cooperative effort that simultaneously increases food aid and launches a long-term program to help develop food self-reliance in food-deficit developing countries.

285. Hunger is often seen as being linked with the problem of population growth, as effect to cause. While this relationship is sometimes presented in oversimplified fashion, we cannot fail to recognize that

---

[117]*On the Development of Peoples*, 44, 58-63.

the earth's resources are finite and that population tends to grow rapidly. Whether the world can provide a truly human life for twice as many people or more as now live in it (many of whose lives are sadly deficient today) is a matter of urgent concern that cannot be ignored.[118]

286. Although we do not believe that people are poor and hungry primarily because they have large families, the Church fully supports the need for all to exercise responsible parenthood. Family size is heavily dependent on levels of economic development, education, respect for women, availability of health care, and the cultural traditions of communities. Therefore, in dealing with population growth we strongly favor efforts to address these social and economic concerns.

287. Population policies must be designed as part of an overall strategy of integral human development. They must respect the freedom of parents and avoid coercion. As Pope Paul VI has said concerning population policies: "It is true that too frequently an accelerated demographic increase adds its own difficulties to the problems of development: the size of the population increases more rapidly than available resources, and things are found to have reached apparently an impasse. From that moment the temptation is great to check the demographic increase by means of radical measures. It is certain that public authorities can intervene, within the limit of their competence, by favoring the availability of appropriate information and by adopting suitable measures, provided that these be in conformity with the moral law and that they respect the rightful freedom of married couples. Where the inalienable right to marriage and procreation is lacking, human dignity has ceased to exist."[119]

4. U.S. Responsibility for Reform in the International Economic System

288. The United States cannot be the sole savior of the developing world, nor are Third World countries entirely innocent with respect to their own failures or totally helpless to achieve their own destinies. Many of these countries will need to initiate positive steps to promote and sustain development and economic growth—streamline bureaucracies, account for funds, plan reasonable programs, and take further steps toward empowering their people. Progress toward development will surely require them to take some tough remedial measures as well: prevent the flight of capital, reduce borrowing, modify price discrimination against rural areas, eliminate corruption in the use of funds and other resources, and curtail spending on inefficient public enterprises. The pervasive U.S. presence in many parts of our inter-

---

[118]Ibid., 37; *Pastoral Constitution,* 87.
[119]*On the Development of Peoples,* 37.

dependent world, however, also creates a responsibility for us to increase the use of U.S. economic power—not just aid—in the service of human dignity and human rights, both political and economic.

289. In particular, as we noted in our earlier letter *The Challenge of Peace*, the contrast between expenditures on armaments and on development reflects a shift in priorities from meeting human needs to promoting "national security" and represents a massive distortion of resouorce allocations. In 1982, for example, the military expenditures of the industrialized countries were seventeen times larger than their foreign assistance; in 1985 the United States alone budgeted more than twenty times as much for defense as for foreign assistance, and nearly two-thirds of the latter took the form of military assistance (including subsidized arms sales) or went to countries because of their perceived strategic value to the United States.[120] *Rather than promoting U.S. arms sales, especially to countries that cannot afford them, we should be campaigning for an international agreement to reduce this lethal trade.*

290. In short, the international economic order, like many aspects of our own economy, is in crisis; the gap between rich and poor countries and between rich and poor people within countries is widening. The United States represents the most powerful single factor in the international economic equation. But even as we speak of crisis, we see an opportunity for the United States to launch a worldwide campaign for justice and economic rights to match the still incomplete, but encouraging, political democracy we have achieved in the United States with so much pain and sacrifice.

291. To restructure the international order along lines of greater equity and participation and apply the preferential option for the poor to international economic activity will require sacrifices of at least the scope of those we have made over the years in building our own nation. We need to call again upon the qualities of leadership and vision that have marked our history when crucial choices were demanded. As Pope John Paul II said during his 1979 visit to the United States, "America, which in the past decades has demonstrated goodness and generosity in providing food for the hungry of the world, will, I am sure, be able to match this generosity with an equally convincing contribution to the establishing of a world order that will create the necessary economic and trade conditions for a more just relationship between all the nations of the world."[121]

292. We share his conviction that most of the policy issues generally called economic are, at root, moral and therefore require the application of moral principles derived from the Scriptures and from the

---

[120]Ruth Leger Sivard, *World Military and Social Expenditures, 1983* (Washington, D.C.: World Priorities, 1983), 23.

[121]Pontifical Commission Justitia et Pax, *The Social Teaching of John Paul II*, 6 (October 6, 1979).

evolving social teaching of the Church and other traditions.[122] We also recognize that we are dealing here with sensitive international issues that cross national boundaries. Nevertheless, in order to pursue justice and peace on a global scale, *we call for a U.S. international economic policy designed to empower people everywhere and enable them to continue to develop a sense of their own worth, improve the quality of their lives, and ensure that the benefits of economic growth are shared equitably.*

E. Conclusion

293. None of the issues we have addressed in this chapter can be dealt with in isolation. They are interconnected, and their resolution requires difficult trade-offs among competing interests and values. The changing international economy, for example, greatly influences efforts to achieve full employment in the United States and to maintain a healthy farm sector. Similarly, as we have noted, policies and programs to reduce unemployment and poverty must not ignore a potential inflationary impact. These complexities and trade-offs are real and must be confronted, but they are not an excuse for inaction. They should not paralyze us in our search for a more just economy.

294. Many of the reforms we have suggested in this chapter would be expensive. At a time when the United States has large annual deficits some might consider these costs too high. But this discussion must be set in the context of how our resources are allocated and the immense human and social costs of failure to act on these pressing problems. We believe that the question of providing adequate revenues to meet the needs of our nation must be faced squarely and realistically. Reforms in the tax code which close loopholes and generate new revenues, for example, are among the steps that need to be examined in order to develop a federal budget that is both fiscally sound and socially responsible. The cost of meeting our social needs must also be weighed against the $300 billion a year allocated for military purposes. Although some of these expenditures are necessary for the defense of the nation, some elements of the military budget are both wasteful and dangerous for world peace.[123] Careful reductions should be made in these areas in order to free up funds for social and economic reforms. In the end, the question is not whether the United States can provide the necessary funds to meet our social needs, but whether we have the political will to do so.

---

[122]*On the Development of Peoples,* 44, 58-63.

[123]See "Testimony on U.S. Arms Control Policy," *Origins* 14:10 (August 9, 1984): 154ff.

IV. A New American Experiment
Partnership for the Public Good

295. For over two hundred years the United States has been engaged in a bold experiment in democracy. The founders of the nation set out to establish justice, promote the general welfare, and secure the blessings of liberty for themselves and their posterity. Those who live in this land today are the beneficiaries of this great venture. Our review of some of the most pressing problems in economic life today shows, however, that this undertaking is not yet complete. Justice for all remains an aspiration; a fair share in the general welfare is denied to many. In addition to the particular policy recommendations made above, a long-term and more fundamental response is needed. This will call for an imaginative vision of the future that can help shape economic arrangements in creative new ways. We now want to propose some elements of such a vision and several innovations in economic structures that can contribute to making this vision a reality.

296. Completing the unfinished business of the American experiment will call for new forms of cooperation and partnership among those whose daily work is the source of the prosperity and justice of the nation. The United States prides itself on both its competitive sense of initiative and its spirit of teamwork. Today a greater spirit of partnership and teamwork is needed; competition alone will not do the job. It has too many negative consequences for family life, the economically vulnerable, and the environment. Only a renewed commitment by all to the common good can deal creatively with the realities of international interdependence and economic dislocations in the domestic economy. The virtues of good citizenship require a lively sense of participation in the commonwealth and of having obligations as well as rights within it.[1] The nation's economic health depends on strengthening these virtues among all its people, and on the development of institutional arrangements supportive of these virtues.[2]

---

[1] *Octogesima Adveniens*, 24.

[2] For different analyses along these lines with quite different starting points see Martin Carnoy, Derek Shearer, and Russell Rumberger, *A New Social Contract* (New York: Harper and Row, 1983); Amatai Etzioni, *An Immodest Agenda: Reconstructing America before the Twenty-First Century* (New York: McGraw-Hill, 1983); Charles E. Lindblom, *Politics and Markets* (New York: Basic Books, 1977), esp. 346-348; George C. Lodge, *The New American Ideology* (New York: Alfred A. Knopf, 1975); Douglas Sturm, "Corporations, Constitutions, and Covenants," *Journal of the American Academy of Religion*, 41 (1973); 331-355; Lester Thurow, *The Zero-Sum Society* (New York: Basic Books, 1980), esp. ch. 1; Roberto Mangabeira Unger, *Knowledge and Politics* (New York: Free Press, 1975); George F. Will, *Statecraft as Soulcraft: What Government Does* (New York: Simon and Schuster, 1982), esp. ch. 6.

297. The nation's founders took daring steps to create structures of participation, mutual accountability, and widely distributed power to ensure the political rights and freedoms of all. We believe that similar steps are needed today to expand economic participation, broaden the sharing of economic power, and make economic decisions more accountable to the common good. As noted above, the principle of subsidiarity states that the pursuit of economic justice must occur on all levels of society. It makes demands on communities as small as the family, as large as the global society, and on all levels in between. There are a number of ways to enhance the cooperative participation of these many groups in the task of creating this future. Since there is no single innovation that will solve all problems, we recommend careful experimentation with several possibilities that hold considerable hope for increasing partnership and strengthening mutual responsibility for economic justice.

A. Cooperation within Firms and Industries

298. A new experiment in bringing democratic ideals to economic life calls for serious exploration of ways to develop new patterns of partnership among those working in individual firms and industries.[3] Every business, from the smallest to the largest, including farms and ranches, depends on many different persons and groups for its success: workers, managers, owners or shareholders, suppliers, customers, creditors, the local community, and the wider society. Each makes a contribution to the enterprise, and each has a stake in its growth or decline. Present structures of accountability, however, do not acknowledge all these contributions or protect these stakes. A major challenge in today's economy is the development of new institutional mechanisms for accountability that also preserve the flexibility needed to respond quickly to a rapidly changing business environment.[4]

299. New forms of partnership between workers and managers are one means for developing greater participation and accountability within firms.[5] Recent experience has shown that both labor and management suffer when the adversarial relationship between them becomes extreme. As Pope Leo XIII stated, "Each needs the other completely:

---

[3] *Pastoral Constitution,* 68. See *Mater et Magistra,* 75-77.

[4] Charles W. Powers provided a helpful discussion of these matters in a paper presented at a conference on the first draft of this pastoral letter sponsored by the Harvard University Divinity School and the Institute for Policy Studies, Cambridge, Massachusetts, March 29-31, 1985.

[5] See John Paul II, "The Role of Business in a Changing Workplace," 3, *Origins* 15 (February 6, 1985): 567.

capital cannot do without labor, nor labor without capital."[6] The organization of firms should reflect and enhance this mutual partnership. In particular, the development of work patterns for men and women that are more supportive of family life will benefit both employees and the enterprises for which they work.

300. Workers in firms and on farms are especially in need of stronger institutional protection, for their jobs and livelihood are particularly vulnerable to the decisions of others in today's highly competitive labor market. Several arrangements are gaining increasing support in the United States: profit sharing by the workers in a firm; enabling employees to become company stockholders, granting employees greater participation in determining the conditions of work; cooperative ownership of the firm by all who work within it; and programs for enabling a much larger number of Americans, regardless of their employment status, to become shareholders in successful corporations. Initiatives of this sort can enhance productivity, increase the profitability of firms, provide greater job security and work satisfaction for employees, and reduce adversarial relations.[7] In our 1919 Program of Social Reconstruction, we observed "the full possibilities of increased production will not be realized so long as the majority of workers remain mere wage earners. The majority must somehow become owners, at least in part, of the instruments of production."[8] We believe this judgment remains generally valid today.

301. None of these approaches provides a panacea, and all have certain drawbacks. Nevertheless we believe that continued research

---

[6]*Rerum Novarum*, 28. For an analysis of the relevant papal teachings on institutions of collaboration and partnership, see John Cronin, *Catholic Social Principles: The Social Teaching of the Catholic Church Applied to American Economic Life* (Milwaukee: Bruce, 1950), ch. VII; Oswald von Nell-Breuning, *Reorganization of Social Economy: The Social Encyclical Developed and Explained*, trans. Bernard W. Dempsey (Milwaukee: Bruce, 1936), chs. X-XII; Jean-Yves Calvez and Jacques Perrin, *The Church and Social Justice*, trans. J. R. Kirwan (Chicago: Regnery, 1961), ch. XIX.

[7]Michael Conte, Arnold S. Tannenbaum, and Donna McCulloch, *Employee Ownership*, Research Report Series, Institute for Social Research (Ann Arbor, Mich.: University of Michigan, 1981); Robert A. Dahl, *A Preface to Economic Democracy* (Berkeley: University of California Press, 1985); Harvard Business School, "The Mondragon Cooperative Movement," case study prepared by David P. Ellerman (Cambridge, Mass.: Harvard Business School, n.d.); Robert Jackall and Henry M. Levin, eds., *Worker Cooperatives in America* (Berkeley: University of California Press, 1984); Derek Jones and Jan Svejnar, eds. *Participatory and Self-Managed Firms: Evaluating Economic Performance* (Lexington, Mass.: D. C. Heath, 1982); Irving H. Siegel and Edgar Weinberg, *Labor-Management Cooperation: The American Experience* (Kalamazoo, Mich.: W. E. Upjohn Institute for Employment Research, 1982); Stuart M. Speiser, "Broadened Capital Ownership—The Solution to Major Domestic and International Problems," *Journal of Post Keynesian Economics* VIII (1985); 426-434; Jaroslav Vanek, ed., *Self-Management: Economic Liberation of Man* (London: Penguin, 1975); Martin L. Weitzman, *The Share Economy* (Cambridge, Mass.: Harvard University Press, 1984).

[8]*Program of Social Reconstruction* in *Justice in the Marketplace*, 381.

[9]*Mater et Magistra*, 32, 77, 85-103; *On Human Work*, 14.

and experimentation with these approaches will be of benefit. Catholic social teaching has endorsed on many occasions innovative methods for increasing worker participation within firms.[9] The appropriateness of these methods will depend on the circumstances of the company or industry in question and on their effectiveness in actually increasing a genuinely cooperative approach to shaping decisions. The most highly publicized examples of such efforts have been in large firms facing serious financial crises. If increased participation and collaboration can help a firm avoid collapse, why should it not give added strength to healthy businesses? Cooperative ownership is particularly worthy of consideration in new entrepreneurial enterprises.[10]

302. Partnerships between labor and management are possible only when both groups possess real freedom and power to influence decisions. This means that unions ought to continue to play an important role in moving toward greater economic participation within firms and industries. Workers rightly reject calls for less adversarial relations when they are a smokescreen for demands that labor make all the concessions. For partnership to be genuine it must be a two-way street, with creative initiative and a willingness to cooperate on all sides.

303. When companies are considering plant closures or the movement of capital, it is patently unjust to deny workers any role in shaping the outcome of these difficult choices.[11] In the heavy manufacturing sector today, technological change and international competition can be the occasion of painful decisions leading to the loss of jobs or wage reductions. While such decisions may sometimes be necessary, a collaborative and mutually accountable model of industrial organization would mean that workers not be expected to carry all the burdens of an economy in transition. Management and investors must also accept their share of sacrifices, especially when management is thinking of closing a plant or transferring capital to a seemingly more lucrative or competitive activity. The capital at the disposal of management is in part the product of the labor of those who have toiled in the company over the years, including currently employed workers.[12] As a minimum, workers have a right to be informed in advance when such decisions are under consideration, a right to negotiate with management about possible alternatives, and a right to fair compensation and assistance with retraining and relocation expenses should these be necessary. Since even these minimal rights are jeopardized without

---

[10]For examples of worker-owned and operated enterprises supported by the Campaign for Human Development's revolving loan fund see CHD's *Annual Report* (Washington, D.C.: USCC).

[11]*Quadragesimo Anno* states the basic norm on which this conclusion is based: "It is wholly false to ascribe to property alone or to labor alone whatever has been obtained through the combined effort of both, and it is wholly unjust for either, denying the efficacy of the other, to arrogate to itself whatever has been produced" (53).

[12]*On Human Work*, 12.

collective negotiation, industrial cooperation requires a strong role for labor unions in our changing economy.

304. Labor unions themselves are challenged by the present economic environment to seek new ways of doing business. The purpose of unions is not simply to defend the existing wages and prerogatives of the fraction of workers who belong to them, but also to enable workers to make positive and creative contributions to the firm, the community, and the larger society in an organized and cooperative way.[13] Such contributions call for experiments with new directions in the U.S. labor movement.

305. The parts played by managers and shareholders in the U.S. corporations also need careful examination. In U.S. law, the primary responsibility of managers is to exercise prudent business judgment in the interest of a profitable return to investors. But morally this legal responsibility may be exercised only within the bounds of justice to employees, customers, suppliers, and the local community. Corporate mergers and hostile takeovers may bring greater benefits to shareholders, but they often lead to decreased concern for the well-being of local communities and make towns and cities more vulnerable to decisions made from afar.

306. Most shareholders today exercise relatively little power in corporate governance.[14] Although shareholders can and should vote on the selection of corporate directors and on investment questions and other policy matters, it appears that return on investment is the governing criterion in the relation between them and management. We do not believe this is an adequate rationale for shareholder decisions. The question of how to relate the rights and responsibilties of shareholders to those of the other people and communities affected by corporate decisions is complex and insufficiently understood. We, therefore, urge serious, long-term research and experimentation in this area. More effective ways of dealing with these questions are essential to enable firms to serve the common good.

---

[13]Ibid., 20. This point was well made by John Cronin twenty-five years ago: "Even if most injustice and exploitation were removed, unions would still have a legitimate place. They are the normal voice of labor, necessary to organize social life for the common good. There is a positive need for such organization today, quite independently of any social evils which may prevail. Order and harmony do not happen; they are the fruit of conscious and organized effort. While we may hope that the abuses which occasioned the rise of unions may disappear, it does not thereby follow that unions will have lost their function. On the contrary, they will be freed from unpleasant, even though temporarily necessary, tasks and able to devote all their time and efforts to a better organization of social life" *Catholic Social Principles*, 418. See also AFL-CIO Committee on the Evolution of Work, *The Future of Work* (Washington, D.C.: AFL-CIO, 1983).

[14]For a classic discussion of the relative power of managers and shareholders see A. A. Berle and Gardiner C. Means, *The Modern Corporation and Private Property* (New York, Macmillan, 1932).

B. Local and Regional Cooperation

307. The context within which U.S. firms do business has direct influence on their ability to contribute to the common good. Companies and indeed whole industries are not sole masters of their own fate. Increased cooperative efforts are needed to make local, regional, national, and international conditions more supportive of the pursuit of economic justice.

308. In the principle of subsidiarity, Catholic social teaching has long stressed the importance of small- and intermediate-sized communities or institutions in exercising moral responsibility. These mediating structures link the individual to society as a whole in a way that gives people greater freedom and power to act.[15] Such groups include families, neighborhoods, church congregations, community organizations, civic and business associations, public interest and advocacy groups, community development corporations, and many other bodies. All these groups can play a crucial role in generating creative partnerships for the pursuit of the public good on the local and regional level.

309. The value of partnership is illustrated by considering how new jobs are created. The development of new businesses to serve the local community is key to revitalizing areas hit hard by unemployment.[16] The cities and regions in greatest need of these new jobs face serious obstacles in attracting enterprises that can provide them. Lack of financial resources, limited entrepreneurial skill, blighted and unsafe environments, and a deteriorating infrastructure create a vicious cycle that makes new investment in these areas more risky and therefore less likely.

310. Breaking out of this cycle will require a cooperative approach that draws on all the resources of the community.[17] Community development corporations can keep efforts focused on assisting those most in need. Existing business, labor, financial, and academic institutions can provide expertise in partnership with innovative entrepreneurs. New cooperative structures of local ownership will give the com-

---

[15]Peter L. Berger and Richard John Neuhaus, *To Empower People: The Role of Mediating Structures in Public Policy* (Washington, D.C.: American Enterprise Institute, 1977).

[16]United States Small Business Administration, *1978 Annual Report* (Washington, D.C.: Government Printing Office, 1979).

[17]For recent discussion from a variety of perspectives see: Robert Friedman and William Schweke, eds., *Expanding the Opportunity to Produce: Revitalizing the American Economy through New Enterprise Development: A Policy Reader* (Washington, D.C.: Corporation for New Enterprise Development, 1981); Jack A. Meyer, ed., *Meeting Human Needs: Toward a New Public Philosophy* (Washington, D.C.: American Enterprise Institute, 1982); Committee for Economic Development, *Jobs for the Hard-to-Employ: New Directions for a Public-Private Partnership* (New York: Committee for Economic Development, 1978); Gar Alperovitz and Jeff Faux, *Rebuilding America: A Blueprint for the New Economy* (New York: Pantheon Books, 1984).

munity or region an added stake in businesses and even more importantly give these businesses a greater stake in the community.[18] Government on the local, state, and national levels must play a significant role, especially through tax structures that encourage investment in hard hit areas and through funding aimed at conservation and basic infrastructure needs. Initiatives like these can contribute to a multilevel response to the needs of the community.

311. The Church itself can work as an effective partner on the local and regional level. Firsthand knowledge of community needs and commitment to the protection of the dignity of all should put church leaders in the forefront of efforts to encourage a community-wide cooperative strategy. Because churches include members from many different parts of the community, they can often serve as mediator between groups who might otherwise regard each other with suspicion. We urge local church groups to work creatively and in partnership with other private and public groups in responding to local and regional problems.

C. Partnership in the Development of National Policies

312. The causes of our national economic problems and their possible solutions are the subject of vigorous debate today. The discussion often turns on the role the national government has played in creating these problems and could play in remedying them. We want to point to several considerations that could help build new forms of effective citizenship and cooperation in shaping the economic life of our country.

313. First, while economic freedom and personal initiative are deservedly esteemed in our society, we have increasingly come to recognize the inescapably social and political nature of the economy. The market is always embedded in a specific social and political context. The tax system affects consumption, saving, and investment. National monetary policy, domestic and defense programs, protection of the environment and worker safety, and regulation of international trade all shape the economy as a whole. These policies influence domestic investment, unemployment rates, foreign exchange, and the health of the entire world economy.

314. The principle of subsidiarity calls for government intervention when small or intermediate groups in society are unable or unwilling to take the steps needed to promote basic justice. Pope John XXIII observed that the growth of more complex relations of interdependence among citizens has led to an increased role for government in

---

[18]Christopher Mackin, *Strategies for Local Ownership and Control: A Policy Analysis* (Somerville, Mass.: Industrial Cooperative Association, 1983).

modern societies.[19] This role is to work *in partnership with* the many other groups in society, helping them fulfill their tasks and responsibilities more effectively, not replacing or destroying them. The challenge of today is to move beyond abstract disputes about whether more or less government intervention is needed, to consideration of creative ways of enabling government and private groups to work together effectively.

315. It is in this light that we understand Pope John Paul II's recommendation that "society make provision for overall planning" in the economic domain.[20] Planning must occur on various levels, with the government ensuring that basic justice is protected and also protecting the rights and freedoms of all other agents. In the pope's words:

> In the final analysis this overall concern weighs on the shoulders of the state, but it cannot mean one-sided centralization by the public authorities. Instead what is in question is a just and rational coordination within the framework of which the initiative of individuals, free groups, and local work centers and complexes must be safeguarded.[21]

316. We are well aware that the mere mention of economic planning is likely to produce a strong negative reaction in U.S. society. It conjures up images of centralized planning boards, command economies, inefficient bureaucracies, and mountains of government paperwork. It is also clear that the meaning of "planning" is open to a wide variety of interpretations and takes very different forms in various nations.[22] The pope's words should not be construed as an endorsement of a highly centralized form of economic planning, much less a totalitarian one. His call for a "just and rational coordination" of the endeavors of the many economic actors is a call to seek creative new partnership and forms of participation in shaping national policies.

317. There are already many forms of economic planning going on within the U.S. economy today. Individuals and families plan for their economic future. Management and labor unions regularly develop both long- and short-term plans. Towns, cities, and regions frequently have planning agencies concerned with their social and economic future. When state legislatures and the U.S. Congress vote on budgets

---

[19]*Mater et Magistra,* 59, 62.

[20]*On Human Work,* 18.

[21]Ibid.

[22]For examples and analyses of different meanings of economic planning see Naomi Caiden and Aaron Wildavsky, *Planning and Budgeting in Poor Countries* (New York: Wiley, 1974); Robert Dahl and Charles E. Lindblom, *Politics, Economics and Welfare: Planning and Politico-Economic Systems Resolved into Basic Social Processes* (Chicago: Unviersity of Chicago Press, 1976); Stephen S. Cohen, *Modern Capitalist Planning: The French Model* (Berkeley: University of California Press, 1977); Albert Waterston, *Development Planning: Lessons of Experience* (Baltimore: Johns Hopkins Press, 1965); *Rebuilding America,* chs. 14, 15.

or on almost any other bill that comes before them, they are engaged in a form of public planning. Catholic social teaching does not propose a single model for political and economic life by which these levels are to be institutionally related to each other. It does insist that reasonable coordination among the different parts of the body politic is an essential condition for achieving justice. This is a moral precondition of good citizenship that applies to both individual and institutional actors. In its absence no political structure can guarantee justice in society or the economy. Effective decisions in these matters will demand greater cooperation among all citizens. To encourage our fellow citizens to consider more carefully the appropriate balance of private and local initiative with national economic policy, we make several recommendations.

318. First, in an advanced industrial economy like ours, all parts of society, including government, must cooperate in forming national economic policies. Taxation, monetary policy, high levels of government spending, and many other forms of governmental regulation are here to stay. A modern economy without governmental interventions of the sort we have alluded to is inconceivable. These interventions, however, should help, not replace, the contributions of other economic actors and institutions and should direct them to the common good. The development of effective new forms of partnership between private and public agencies will be difficult in a situation as immensely complex as that of the United States in which various aspects of national policy seem to contradict one another.[23] On the theoretical level, achieving greater coordination will make demands on those with the technical competence to analyze the relationship among different parts of the economy. More practically, it will require the various subgroups within our society to sharpen their concern for the common good and moderate their efforts to protect their own short-term interests.

319. Second, the impact of national economic policies on the poor and the vulnerable is the primary criterion for judging their moral value. Throughout this letter we have stressed the special place of the poor and the vulnerable in any ethical analysis of the U.S. economy. National economic policies that contribute to building a true commonwealth should reflect this by standing firmly for the rights of those who fall through the cracks of our economy: the poor, the unemployed, the homeless, the displaced. Being a citizen of this land means sharing in the responsibility for shaping and implementing such policies.

320. Third, the serious distortion of national economic priorities produced

---

[23]For example, many students of recent policy point out that monetary policy on the one hand and fiscal policies governing taxation and government expenditures on the other have been at odds with each other, with larger public deficits and high interest rates as the outcome. See Alice M. Rivlin, ed., *Economic Choices 1984* (Washington, D.C.: The Brookings Institution, 1984), esp. ch. 2.

by massive national spending on defense must be remedied. Clear-sighted consideration of the role of government shows that government and the economy are already closely intertwined through military research and defense contracts. Defense-related industries make up a major part of the U.S. economy and have intimate links with both the military and civilian government; they often depart from the competitive model of free-market capitalism. Moreover, the dedication of so much of the national budget to military purposes has been disastrous for the poor and vulnerable members of our own and other nations. The nation's spending priorities need to be revised in the interests of both justice and peace.[24]

321. We recognize that these proposals do not provide a detailed agenda. We are also aware that there is a tension between setting the goals for coherent policies and actually arriving at them by democratic means. But if we can increase the level of commitment to the common good and the virtues of citizenship in our nation, the ability to achieve these goals will greatly increase. It is these fundamental moral concerns that lead us as bishops to join the debate on national priorities.

D. *Cooperation at the International Level*

322. If our country is to guide its international economic relationships by policies that serve human dignity and justice, we must expand our understanding of the moral responsibility of citizens to serve the common good of the entire planet. Cooperation is not limited to the local, regional, or national level. Economic policy can no longer be governed by national goals alone. The fact that the "social question has become worldwide"[25] challenges us to broaden our horizons and enhance our collaboration and sense of solidarity on the global level. The cause of democracy is closely tied to the cause of economic justice. The unfinished business of the American experiment includes the formation of new international partnerships, especially with the developing countries, based on mutual respect, cooperation, and a dedication to fundamental justice.

323. The principle of subsidiarity calls for government to intervene in the economy when basic justice requires greater social coordination and regulation of economic actors and institutions. In global economic relations, however, no international institution provides this sort of coordination and regulation. The UN system, including the World Bank, the International Monetary Fund, and the General Agreement on Tariffs and Trade, does not possess the requisite authority. Pope John XXIII called this institutional weakness a "structural defect" in the organization of the human community. The structures of world

---

[24]*The Challenge of Peace*, 270-271.
[25]*On the Development of Peoples*, 3.

order, including economic ones, "no longer correspond to the objective requirements of the universal common good."[26]

324. Locked together in a world of limited material resources and a growing array of common problems, we help or hurt one another by the economic policies we choose. All the economic agents in our society, therefore, must consciously and deliberately attend to the good of the whole human family. We must all work to increase the effectiveness of international agencies in addressing global problems that cannot be handled through the actions of individual countries. In particular we repeat our plea made in *The Challenge of Peace* urging "that the United States adopt a stronger supportive leadership role with respect to the United Nations."[27] In the years following World War II, the United States took the lead in establishing multilateral bodies to deal with postwar economic problems. Unfortunately, in recent years this country has taken steps that have weakened rather than strengthened multilateral approaches. This is a shortsighted policy and should be reversed if the long-term interests of an interdependent globe are to be served.[28] In devising more effective arrangements for pursuing international economic justice, the overriding problem is how to get from where we are to where we ought to be. Progress toward that goal demands positive and often difficult action by corporations, banks, labor unions, governments, and other major actors on the international stage. But whatever the difficulty, the need to give priority to alleviating poverty in developing countries is undeniable; and the cost of continued inaction can be counted in human lives lost or stunted, talents wasted, opportunities foregone, misery and suffering prolonged, and injustice condoned.

325. Self-restraint and self-criticism by all parties are necessary first steps toward strengthening the international structures to protect the common good. Otherwise, growing interdependence will lead to conflict and increased economic threats to human dignity. This is an important long-term challenge to the economic future of this country and its place in the emerging world economic community.

V. A Commitment to the Future

326. Because Jesus' command to love our neighbor is universal, we hold that the life of each person on this globe is sacred. This commits us to bringing about a just economic order where all, without exception, will be treated with dignity and to working in collaboration with

---

[26] *Peace on Earth*, 134-135.

[27] *The Challenge of Peace*, 268.

[28] See Robert O. Keohane and Joseph S. Nye, Jr., "Two Cheers for Multilateralism," *Foreign Policy* 60 (Fall 1985): 148-167.

those who share this vision. The world is complex and this may often tempt us to seek simple and self-centered solutions, but as a community of disciples we are called to a new hope and to a new vision that we must live without fear and without oversimplification. Not only must we learn more about our moral responsibility for the larger economic issues that touch the daily life of each and every person on this planet, but we also want to help shape the Church as a model of social and economic justice. Thus, this chapter deals with the Christian vocation in the world today, the special challenges to the Church at this moment of history, ways in which the themes of this letter should be followed up, and a call to the kind of commitment that will be needed to reshape the future.

A. The Christian Vocation in the World Today

327. This letter has addressed many matters commonly regarded as secular, for example, employment rates, income levels, and international economic relationships. Yet, the affairs of the world, including economic ones, cannot be separated from the spiritual hunger of the human heart. We have presented the biblical version of humanity and the Church's moral and religious tradition as a framework for asking the deeper questions about the meaning of economic life and for actively responding to them. But words alone are not enough. The Christian perspective on the meaning of economic life must transform the lives of individuals, families, in fact, our whole culture. The Gospel confers on each Christian the vocation to love God and neighbor in ways that bear fruit in the life of society. That vocation consists above all in a change of heart: a conversion expressed in praise of God and in concrete deeds of justice and service.

1. Conversion

328. The transformation of social structures begins with and is always accompanied by a conversion of the heart.[1] As disciples of Christ each of us is called to a deep personal conversion and to "action on behalf of justice and participation in the transformation of the world."[2] By faith and baptism we are fashioned into a "new creature"; we are filled with the Holy Spirit and a new love that compels us to seek out a new profound relationship with God, with the human family, and with all created things.[3] Renouncing self-centered desires, bearing one's daily cross, and imitating Christ's compassion, all involve a personal struggle to control greed and selfishness, a personal com-

---

[1] *Reconciliation and Penance*, 13.

[2] *Justice in the World*, 6.

[3] Medellin Documents: *Justice* (1968), 4.

mitment to reverence one's own human dignity and the dignity of others by avoiding self-indulgence and those attachments that make us insensitive to the conditions of others and that erode social solidarity. Christ warned us against attachments to material things, against total self-reliance, against the idolatry of accumulating material goods and seeking safety in them. We must take these teachings seriously and in their light examine how each of us lives and acts towards others. But personal conversion is not gained once and for all. It is a process that goes on through our entire life. Conversion, moreover, takes place in the context of a larger faith community: through baptism into the Church, through common prayer, and through our activity with others on behalf of justice.

2. Worship and Prayer

329. Challenging U.S. economic life with the Christian vision calls for a deeper awareness of the integral connection between worship and the world of work. Worship and common prayer are the wellsprings that give life to any reflection on economic problems and that continually call the participants to greater fidelity to discipleship. To worship and pray to the God of the universe is to acknowledge that the healing love of God extends to all persons and to every part of existence, including work, leisure, money, economic and political power and their use, and to all those practical policies that either lead to justice or impede it. Therefore, when Christians come together in prayer, they make a commitment to carry God's love into all these areas of life.

330. The unity of work and worship finds expression in a unique way in the Eucharist. As people of a new covenant, the faithful hear God's challenging word proclaimed to them—a message of hope to the poor and oppressed—and they call upon the Holy Spirit to unite all into one Body of Christ. For the Eucharist to be a living promise of the fullness of God's kingdom, the faithful must commit themselves to living as redeemed people with the same care and love for all people that Jesus showed. The Body of Christ which worshipers receive in Communion is also a reminder of the reconciling power of his death on the cross. It empowers them to work to heal the brokenness of society and human relationships and to grow in a spirit of self-giving for others.

331. The liturgy teaches us to have grateful hearts: to thank God for the gift of life, the gift of this earth, and the gift of all people. It turns our hearts from self-seeking to a spirituality that sees the signs of true discipleship in our sharing of goods and working for justice. By uniting us in prayer with all the People of God, with the rich and the poor, with those near and dear, and with those in distant lands, liturgy challenges our way of living and refines our values. Together in the community of worship, we are encouraged to use the goods of this earth for the benefit of all. In worship and in deeds for justice, the Church becomes a "sacrament," a visible sign of that unity in justice and peace that God wills for the whole of humanity.[4]

3. Call to Holiness in the World

332. Holiness is not limited to the sanctuary or to moments of private prayer; it is a call to direct our whole heart and life toward God and according to God's plan for this world. For the laity holiness is achieved in the midst of the world, in family, in community, in friendships, in work, in leisure, in citizenship. Through their competency and by their activity, lay men and women have the vocation to bring the light of the Gospel to economic affairs, "so that the world may be filled with the Spirit of Christ and may more effectively attain its destiny in justice, in love, and in peace."[5]

333. But as disciples of Christ we must constantly ask ourselves how deeply the biblical and ethical vision of justice and love permeates our thinking. How thoroughly does it influence our way of life? We may hide behind the complexity of the issues or dismiss the significance of our personal contribution; in fact, each one has a role to play, because every day each one makes economic decisions. Some, by reason of their work or their position in society, have a vocation to be involved in a more decisive way in those decisions that affect the economic well-being of others. They must be encouraged and sustained by all in their search for greater justice.

334. At times we will be called upon to say no to the cultural manifestations that emphasize values and aims that are selfish, wasteful, and opposed to the Scriptures. Together we must reflect on our personal and family decisions and curb unnecessary wants in order to meet the needs of others. There are many questions we must keep asking ourselves: Are we becoming ever more wasteful in a "throwaway" society? Are we able to distinguish between our true needs and those thrust on us by advertising and a society that values consumption more than saving? All of us could well ask ourselves whether as a Christian prophetic witness we are not called to adopt a simpler lifestyle, in the face of the excessive accumulation of material goods that characterizes an affluent society.

335. Husbands and wives, in particular, should weigh their needs carefully and establish a proper priority of values as they discuss the

---

[4]*Dogmatic Constitution on the Church*, 1; *Pastoral Constitution*, 42, 45; *Constitution on the Liturgy*, 26; *Decree on the Church's Missionary Activity*, 5; *Liturgy and Social Justice*, Mark Searle, ed. (Collegeville, Minn.: Liturgical Press, 1980); National Conference of Catholic Bishops, *The Church at Prayer* (Washington, D.C.: USCC Office of Publishing and Promotion Services, 1983).

[5]*Dogmatic Constitution on the Church*, 36.

questions of both parents working outside the home and the responsibilities of raising children with proper care and attention. At times we will be called as individuals, as families, as parishes, as Church, to identify more closely with the poor in their struggle for participation and to close the gap of understanding between them and the affluent. By sharing the perspectives of those who are suffering, we can come to understand economic and social problems in a deeper way, thus leading us to seek more durable solutions.

336. In the workplace the laity are often called to make tough decisions with little information about the consequences that such decisions have on the economic lives of others. Such times call for collaborative dialogue together with prayerful reflection on Scripture and ethical norms. The same can be said of the need to elaborate policies that will reflect sound ethical principles and that can become a part of our political and social system. Since this is a part of the lay vocation and its call to holiness, the laity must seek to instill a moral and ethical dimension into the public debate on these issues and help enunciate the ethical questions that must be faced. To weigh political options according to criteria that go beyond efficiency and expediency requires prayer, reflection, and dialogue on all the ethical norms involved. Holiness for the laity will involve all the sacrifices needed to lead such a life of prayer and reflection within a worshiping and supporting faith community. In this way the laity will bridge the gap that so easily arises between the moral principles that guide the personal life of the Christian and the considerations that govern decisions in society in the political forum and in the marketplace.

4. Leisure

337. Some of the difficulty in bringing Christian faith to economic life in the United States today results from the obstacles to establishing a balance of labor and leisure in daily life. Tedious and boring work leads some to look for fulfillment only during time off the job. Others have become "workaholics," people who work compulsively and without reflection on the deeper meaning of life and their actions. The quality and pace of work should be more human in scale enabling people to experience the dignity and value of their work and giving them time for other duties and obligations. This balance is vitally important for sustaining the social, political, educational, and cultural structures of society. The family, in particular, requires such balance. Without leisure there is too little time for nurturing marriages, for developing parent-child relationships, and for fulfilling commitments to other important groups: the extended family, the community of friends, the parish, the neighborhood, schools, and political organizations. Why is it one hears so little today about shortening the work week, especially if both parents are working? Such a change would give them more time for each other, for their children, and for their other social and political responsibilities.

338. Leisure is connected to the whole of one's value system and influenced by the general culture one lives in. It can be trivialized into boredom and laziness, or end in nothing but a desire for greater consumption and waste. For disciples of Christ, the use of leisure may demand being countercultural. The Christian tradition sees in leisure, time to build family and social relationships and an opportunity for communal prayer and worship, for relaxed contemplation and enjoyment of God's creation, and for the cultivation of the arts which help fill the human longing for wholeness. Most of all, we must be convinced that economic decisions affect our use of leisure and that such decisions are also to be based on moral and ethical considerations. In this area of leisure we must be on our guard against being swept along by a lack of cultural values and by the changing fads of an affluent society. In the creation narrative God worked six days to create the world and rested on the seventh (Gn 2:1-4). We must take that image seriously and learn how to harmonize action and rest, work and leisure, so that both contribute to building up the person as well as the family and community.

B. Challenges to the Church

339. The Church is all the People of God, gathered in smaller faith communities, guided and served by a pope and a hierarchy of bishops, ministered to by priests, deacons, religious, and laity, through visible institutions and agencies. Church is, thus, primarily a communion of people bonded by the Spirit with Christ as their Head, sustaining one another in love, and acting as a sign or sacrament in the world. By its nature it is people called to a transcendent end, but, it is also a visible social institution functioning in this world. According to their calling, members participate in the mission and work of the Church and share, to varying degrees, the responsibility for its institutions and agencies.[6]

At this moment in history, it is particularly important to emphasize the responsibilities of the whole Church for education and family life.

1. Education

340. We have already emphasized the commitment to quality education that is necessary if the poor are to take their rightful place in the economic structures of our society. We have called the Church to remember its own obligation in this regard and we have endorsed support for improvements in public education.

---

[6]*Justice in the World,* 41.

341. The educational mission of the Church is not only to the poor but to all its members. We reiterate our 1972 statement: "Through education, the Church seeks to prepare its members to proclaim the Good News and to translate this proclamation into action. Since the Christian vocation is a call to transform oneself and society with God's help, the educational efforts of the Church must encompass the twin purposes of personal sanctification and social reform in the light of Christian values."[7] Through her educational mission the Church seeks: to integrate knowledge about this world with revelation about God; to understand God's relationship to the human race and its ultimate destiny in the kingdom of God; to build up human communities of justice and peace; and to teach the value of all creation. By inculcating these values the educational system of the Church contributes to society and to social justice. Economic questions are, thus, seen as a part of a larger vision of the human person and the human family, the value of this created earth, and the duties and responsibilities that all have toward each other and toward this universe.

342. For these reasons, the Church must incorporate into all levels of her educational system the teaching of social justice and the biblical and ethical principles that support it. We call on our universities, in particular, to make Catholic social teaching and the social encyclicals of the popes a part of their curriculum, especially for those whose vocation will call them to an active role in U.S. economic and political decision making. Faith and technological progress are not opposed one to another, but this progress must not be channeled and directed by greed, self-indulgence, or novelty for its own sake, but by values that respect human dignity and foster social solidarity.

343. The Church has always held that the first task and responsibility for education lies in the hands of parents: they have the right to choose freely the schools or other means necessary to educate their children in the faith.[8] The Church also has consistently held that public authorities must ensure that public subsidies for the education of children are allocated so that parents can freely choose to exercise this right without incurring unjust burdens. This parental right should not be taken from them. We call again for equitable sharing in public benefits for those parents who choose private and religious schools for their children. Such help should be available especially for low-income parents. Though many of these parents sacrifice a great deal for their children's education, others are effectively deprived of the possibility of exercising this right.

---

[7]National Conference of Catholic Bishops, *To Teach as Jesus Did*, A Pastoral Message on Education (Washington, D.C.: USCC Office of Publishing and Promotion Services, 1972), 7.

[8]Cf. Vatican Council II, *Declaration on Christian Education* 3, 6. See also, *Charter of the Rights of the Family*, 5b; *Instruction on Christian Freedom and Liberation*, 94.

2. Supporting the Family

344. Economic life has a profound effect on all social structures and particularly on the family. A breakdown of family life often brings with it hardship and poverty. Divorce, failure to provide support to mothers and children, abandonment of children, pregnancies out of wedlock, all contribute to the amount of poverty among us. Though these breakdowns of marriage and the family are more visible among the poor, they do not affect only that one segment of our society. In fact, one could argue that many of these breakdowns come from the false values found among the more affluent—values which ultimately pervade the whole of society.

345. More studies are needed to probe the possible connections between affluence and family and marital breakdowns. The constant seeking for self-gratification and the exaggerated individualism of our age, spurred on by false values often seen in advertising and on television, contribute to the lack of firm commitment in marriage and to destructive notions of responsibility and personal growth.[9]

346. With good reason, the Church has traditionally held that the family is the basic building block of any society. In fighting against economic arrangements that weaken the family, the Church contributes to the well-being of society. The same must be said of the Church's teaching on responsible human sexuality and its relationship to marriage and family. Economic arrangements must support the family and provide its solidarity.

3. The Church as Economic Actor

347. Although all members of the Church are economic actors every day in their individual lives, they also play an economic role united together as Church. On the parish and diocesan levels, through its agencies and institutions, the Church employs many people; it has investments; it has extensive properties for worship and mission. *All the moral principles that govern the just operation of any economic endeavor apply to the Church and its agencies and institutions; indeed the Church should be exemplary.* The Synod of Bishops in 1971 worded this challenge most aptly: "While the Church is bound to give witness to justice, she recognizes that anyone who ventures to speak to people about justice must first be just in their eyes. Hence, we must undertake

---

[9]Pope John Paul II, *On the Family* (Washington, D.C.: USCC Office of Publishing and Promotion Services, 1981), 6. See also Robert N. Bellah, Richard Madsen, William M. Sullivan, Ann Swidler, Steven M. Tipton, *Habits of the Heart: Individualism and Commitment in American Life* (Berkeley: University of California Press, 1985); *The Family Today and Tomorrow: The Church Addresses Her Future* (Boston, Mass.: The Pope John Center, 1985).

an examination of the modes of acting and of the possessions and lifestyle found within the Church herself."[10]

348. Catholics in the United States can be justly proud of their accomplishments in building and maintaining churches and chapels, and an extensive system of schools, hospitals, and charitable institutions. Through sacrifices and personal labor our immigrant ancestors built these institutions. For many decades religious orders of women and men taught in our schools and worked in our hospitals with very little remuneration. Right now, we see the same spirit of generosity among the religious and lay people even as we seek to pay more adequate salaries.

349. We would be insincere were we to deny a need for renewal in the economic life of the Church itself and for renewed zeal on the part of the Church in examining its role in the larger context of reinforcing in U.S. society and culture those values that support economic justice.[11]

350. We select here five areas for special reflection: (1) wages and salaries, (2) rights of employees, (3) investments and property, (4) works of charity, and (5) working for economic justice.

351. We bishops commit ourselves to the principle that those who serve the Church—laity, clergy, and religious—should receive a sufficient livelihood and the social benefits provided by responsible employers in our nation. These obligations, however, cannot be met without the increased contributions of all the members of the Church. We call on all to recognize their responsibility to contribute monetarily to the support of those who carry out the public mission of the Church. Sacrificial giving or tithing by all the People of God would provide the funds necessary to pay these adequate salaries for religious and lay people; the lack of funds is the usual underlying cause for the lack of adequate salaries. The obligation to sustain the Church's institutions—education and health care, social service agencies, religious education programs, care of the elderly, youth ministry, and the like—falls on all the members of the community because of their baptism; the obligation is not just on the users or on those who staff them. Increased resources are also needed for the support of elderly members of religious communities. These dedicated women and men have not always asked for or received the stipends and pensions that would have assured their future. It would be a breach of our obligations to them to let them or their communities face retirement without adequate funds.

352. Many volunteers provide services to the Church and its mission which cannot be measured in dollars and cents. These services are

---

[10]*Justice in the World*, 40.
[11]*Dogmatic Constitution on the Church*, 8.

important to the life and vitality of the Church in the United States and carry on a practice that has marked the history of the Church in this country since its founding. In this tradition, we ask young people to make themselves available for a year or more of voluntary service before beginning their training for more specific vocations in life; we also recommend expanding voluntary service roles for retired persons; we encourage those who have accepted this challenge.

353. All church institutions must also fully recognize the rights of employees to organize and bargain collectively with the institution through whatever association or organization they freely choose.[12] In the light of new creative models of collaboration between labor and management described earlier in this letter, we challenge our church institutions to adopt new fruitful modes of cooperation. Although the Church has its own nature and mission that must be respected and fostered, we are pleased that many who are not of our faith, but who share similar hopes and aspirations for the human family, work for us and with us in achieving this vision. In seeking greater justice in wages, we recognize the need to be alert particularly to the continuing discrimination against women throughout Church and society, especially reflected in both the inequities of salaries between women and men and in the concentration of women in jobs at the lower end of the wage scale.

354. Individual Christians who are shareholders and those responsible within church institutions that own stocks in U.S. corporations must see to it that the invested funds are used responsibly. Although it is a moral and legal fiduciary responsibility of the trustees to ensure an adequate return on investment for the support of the work of the Church, their stewardship embraces broader moral concerns. As part-owners, they must cooperate in shaping the policies of those companies through dialogue with management, through votes at corporate meetings, through the introduction of resolutions, and through participation in investment decisions. We praise the efforts of dioceses and other religious and ecumenical bodies that work together toward these goals. We also praise efforts to develop alternative investment policies, especially those which support enterprises that promote economic development in depressed communities and which help the Church respond to local and regional needs.[13] When the decision to divest seems unavoidable, it should be done after prudent examination and with a clear explanation of the motives.

355. The use of church property demands special attention today. Changing demographic patterns have left many parishes and institutions with empty or partially used buildings. The decline in the

---

[12]National Conference of Catholic Bishops, *Health and Health Care* (Washington, D.C.: USCC Office of Publishing and Promotion Services, 1981), 50.
[13]See ch. IV of this pastoral letter.

number of religious who are teaching in the schools and the reduction of the number of clergy often result in large residences with few occupants. In this regard, the Church must be sensitive to the image the possession of such large facilities often projects, namely, that it is wealthy and extravagant in the use of its resources. This image can be overcome only by clear public accountability of its financial holdings, of its properties and their use, and of the services it renders to its members and to society at large. We support and encourage the creative use of these facilities by many parishes and dioceses to serve the needs of the poor.

356. The Church has a special call to be a servant of the poor, the sick, and the marginalized, thereby becoming a true sign of the Church's mission—a mission shared by every member of the Christian community. The Church now serves many such people through one of the largest private human services delivery systems in the country. The networks of agencies, institutions, and programs provide services to millions of persons of all faiths. Still we must be reminded that in our day our Christian concerns must increase and extend beyond our borders, because everyone in need is our neighbor. We must also be reminded that charity requires more than alleviating misery. It demands genuine love for the person in need. It should probe the meaning of suffering and provoke a response that seeks to remedy causes. True charity leads to advocacy.

357. Yet charity alone is not a corrective to all economic social ills. All citizens, working through various organizations of society and through government, bear the responsibility of caring for those who are in need. The Church, too, through all its members individually and through its agencies, must work to alleviate injustices that prevent some from participating fully in economic life. Our experience with the Campaign for Human Development confirms our judgment about the validity of self-help and empowerment of the poor. The campaign, which has received the positive support of American Catholics since it was launched in 1970, provides a model that we think sets a high standard for similar efforts. We bishops know of the many faithful in all walks of life who use their skills and their compassion to seek innovative ways to carry out the goals we are proposing in this letter. As they do this, they *are* the Church acting for economic justice. At the same time, we hope they will join together with us and their priests to influence our society so that even more steps can be taken to alleviate injustices. Grass-roots efforts by the poor themselves, helped by community support, are indispensable. The entire Christian community can learn much from the way our deprived brothers and sisters assist each other in their struggles.

358. In addition to being an economic actor, the Church is a significant cultural actor concerned about the deeper cultural roots of our economic problems. As we have proposed a new experiment in collaboration and participation in decision making by all those affected at all levels of U.S. society, so we also commit the Church to become a model of collaboration and participation.

C. The Road Ahead

359. The completion of a letter such as this one is but the beginning of a long process of education, discussion, and action; its contents must be brought to all members of the Church and of society.

360. In this respect we mentioned the twofold aim of this pastoral letter: to help Catholics form their consciences on the moral dimensions of economic decision making and to articulate a moral perspective in the general societal and political debate that surrounds these questions. These two purposes help us to reflect on the different ways the institutions and ministers of the Church can assist the laity in their vocation in the world. Renewed emphasis on Catholic social teaching in our schools, colleges, and universities; special seminars with corporate officials, union leaders, legislators, bankers, and the like; the organization of small groups composed of people from different ways of life to meditate together on the Gospel and ethical norms; speakers' bureaus; family programs; clearinghouses of available material; pulpit aids for priests; diocesan television and radio programs; research projects in our universities—all of these are appropriate means for continued discussion and action. Some of these are done best on the parish level, others by the state Catholic conferences, and others by the National Conference of Catholic Bishops. These same bodies can assist the laity in the many difficult decisions that deal with political options that affect economic decisions. Where many options are available, it must be the concern of all in such debates that we as Catholics do not become polarized. All must be challenged to show how the decisions they make and the policies they suggest flow from the ethical moral vision outlined here. As new problems arise, we hope through our continual reflection that we will be able to help refine Catholic social teaching and contribute to its further development.

361. We call upon our priests, in particular, to continue their study of these issues, so that they can proclaim the gospel message in a way that not only challenges the faithful but also sustains and encourages their vocation in and to the world. Priestly formation in our seminaries will also have to prepare candidates for this role.

362. We wish to emphasize the need to undertake research into many of the areas this document could not deal with in depth and to continue exploration of those we have dealt with. We encourage our Catholic universities, foundations, and other institutions to assist in these necessary projects. The following areas for further research are merely suggestive, not exhaustive: the impact of arms production and large military spending on the domestic economy and on culture; arms production and sales as they relate to Third World poverty; tax reforms to express the preferential option for the poor; the rights of women and minorities in the workforce; the development of communications technology and its global influences; robotics, automation, and reduction of defense industries as they will affect employment; the economy and the stability of the family; legitimate profit versus greed; securing economic rights; environmental and ecological questions; future roles of labor and unions; international financial institutions and Third World debt; our national deficit; world food problems; "full employment" and its implementation; plant closings and dealing with the human costs of an evolving economy; cooperatives and new modes of sharing; welfare reform and national eligibility standards; income support systems; concentration of land ownership; assistance to Third World nations; migration and its effects; population policies and development; the effects of increased inequality of incomes in society.

D. *Commitment to a Kingdom of Love and Justice*

363. Confronted by this economic complexity and seeking clarity for the future, we can rightly ask ourselves one single question: How does our economic system affect the lives of people—*all* people? Part of the American dream has been to make this world a better place for people to live in; at this moment of history that dream must include everyone on this globe. Since we profess to be members of a "catholic" or universal Church, we all must raise our sights to a concern for the well-being of everyone in the world. Third World debt becomes our problem. Famine and starvation in sub-Saharan Africa become our concern. Rising military expenditures everywhere in the world become part of our fears for the future of this planet. We cannot be content if we see ecological neglect or the squandering of natural resources. In this letter, we bishops have spoken often of economic interdependence; now is the moment when all of us must confront the reality of such economic bonding and its consequences and see it as a moment of grace—a *kairos*—that can unit all of us in a common community of the human family. We commit ourselves to this global vision.

364. We cannot be frightened by the magnitude and complexity of these problems. We must not be discouraged. In the midst of this struggle, it is inevitable that we become aware of greed, laziness, and envy. No utopia is possible on this earth; but as believers in the redemptive love of God and as those who have experienced God's forgiving mercy, we know that God's providence is not and will not be lacking to us today.

365. The fulfillment of human needs, we know, is not the final purpose of the creation of the human person. We have been created to share in the divine life through a destiny that goes far beyond our human capabilities and before which we must in all humility stand in awe. Like Mary in proclaiming her *Magnificat*, we marvel at the wonders God has done for us, how God has raised up the poor and the lowly and promised great things for them in the kingdom. God now asks of us sacrifices and reflection on our reverence for human dignity—in ourselves and in others—and on our service and discipleship, so that the divine goal for the human family and this earth can be fulfilled. Communion with God, sharing God's life, involves a mutual bonding with all on this globe. Jesus taught us to love God and one another and that the concept of neighbor is without limit. We know that we are called on to be members of a new covenant of love. We have to move from our devotion to independence, through an understanding of interdependence, to a commitment to human solidarity. That challenge must find its realization in the kind of community we build among us. Love implies concern for all—especially the poor—and a continued search for those social and economic structures that permit everyone to share in a community that is a part of a redeemed creation (Rom 8:21-23).

Testimony on Welfare Reform

*Written Testimony Submitted to the
Senate Finance Committee's Subcommittee on
Social Security and Family Policy
by Rev. J. Bryan Hehir on Behalf of the
United States Catholic Conference*

February 2, 1987

Good Morning, Mr. Chairman:

1. I am pleased to be here this morning to represent the views of the U.S. Catholic Conference, the public-policy arm of the Roman Catholic bishops of the United States.

2. The topic of this morning's hearing, the Aid to Families with Dependent Children program, is of deep concern to the bishops. Our views on this subject are shaped by two perspectives. The first is the principle that human dignity is the fundamental criterion against which public policy must be measured. Second, and more specifically, is the conviction that in a society as rich as ours there is no excuse for the extremes of deprivation and poverty that leave millions without even the basic necessities of life.

3. Throughout this century the Church has been actively involved in working with and for the poor. By means of our ongoing pastoral work, our extensive network of charitable agencies, our efforts to organize and empower the poor, and our advocacy work to improve public policies, we have had extensive contact with the problems of the poor. This experience has led the Catholic bishops to work for improvements in the AFDC program. Throughout its history, the Catholic Conference has consistently called for adequate benefit levels, a comprehensive full-employment strategy, rejection of welfare rules that weaken families, and administration of the program in a manner that supports dignity, equity, and self-determination.

4. That is still our message, Mr. Chairman. Before discussing in detail the specific topic of this morning's hearing, it is necessary to point out that the median benefit for a family of three that receives both AFDC and food stamps and has no other income is less than three-fourths of the government's official poverty line. This despite increases in benefits that have been approved in some states in the past year. In Virginia, where I serve in a parish, the maximum combined AFDC and food-stamp benefit for a family consisting of a mother and two children is only 74 percent of the poverty line. That's $354.00 a month in cash and $175.00 in food stamps. In your state of New York they do a little better. There the *maximum* combined AFDC energy-assistance and food-stamp benefit for a mother with two children is about 90 percent of the poverty line. Of course, the inadequacy of even that benefit is alarmingly clear from the statistics on homeless families lodged in "fleabag" hotels. It is clear that welfare benefits are woefully inadequate in this country and do not provide sufficient income for the necessities of life. As we have stated on other occasions, we believe that the federal government should establish a national minimum standard benefit to cover those basic human needs.

5.   AFDC benefits should also be adjusted annually to reflect increases in the cost of living. As you know, AFDC benefits, which are primarily for children, are not automatically indexed for inflation as are benefits for the elderly, so their value has dropped by one-third since 1970. Poor children are entitled to the same federal protection as the elderly.

6.   Federal rules also discourage states from raising AFDC benefits on their own. States that are inclined to substantially increase their AFDC payment levels are stymied by the federal food-stamp rules that reduce food stamp benefits by 30 cents for every dollar of increased welfare income. To increase a welfare family's income by $30.00 a month, the state has to raise AFDC benefits by $45.00. A state such as New York with a 50 percent federal matching rate would spend $21.60 for each $30.00 increase in the family's income while the federal government would spend only $8.40. This interaction between AFDC and food stamps is a powerful disincentive for states to raise AFDC levels. A 100 percent federally funded minimum benefit could help to counteract this problem.

7.   In addition to a federal benefit floor, there are three other major questions under consideration in this year's welfare debate:

- Should we permit states to deny aid to otherwise eligible needy children solely because they live with both their parents?
- What should we do about unmarried teenage mothers who do not live with their own families?
- How should we go about trying to prevent welfare dependency?

8.   The way we look at these questions and the ways we try to answer them are intimately connected to our views about family life and the role of government in upholding human dignity.

---

1. Benefits for Two-Parent Families

9.   On the question of benefits for two-parent families, our views are shaped by a long tradition of Catholic social teaching about human dignity, human rights, and the family, as well as our practical expe-

rience in working with families devastated by poverty, conflict, disabilities, and despair. Both our moral vision and our direct experience tell us that government should not be in the business of dividing families, yet that is precisely what the AFDC program does. In half of the states, two-parent families with children can get no welfare aid no matter how poor they are. A family gets nothing from the AFDC program unless one parent, usually the father, abandons the children. Such a policy is flagrantly unjust. In our judgment, such a policy is not morally defensible.

10. Even in those states that offer the AFDC for Unemployed Parents program, federal rules are so strict that only a handful of two-parent families can qualify. Most are ineligible because the father is just entering the work force and has not worked enough quarters or because he has been unemployed for over a year. Still others are not eligible even though the family income is well below the state eligibility limit, because one of the parents is working too much—more than 100 hours a month. These rules have never made sense in the past. Now, with less than one-third of the unemployed receiving unemployment benefits and with a totally inadequate minimum wage, they are even more cruel and destructive.

11. Last week I testified before the Banking Committee about growing homelessness among two-parent families, even those with a parent working. Staffs at our social agencies are helpless in the face of these situations. There are virtually no subsidized apartments for such families and no cash assistance. Imagine how our Catholic social agency workers feel when they have to explain that families must separate to survive. The state statistics bear out our experience—when states have terminated their two-parent programs, there have been immediate increases in the single-parent programs, as fathers left home and mothers reapplied for benefits for themselves and their families.

12. Perhaps even worse in some ways are the effects on unmarried parents in communities ravaged by high rates of long-term unemployment and poverty. How many marriages are never performed because the couple recognizes that the father will not be able to support the family and that his very presence would deny government aid to the wife and children?

13. For the past three years, the USCC has supported a House-passed intiative by Rep. Harold Ford that would require all states to implement the AFDC Unemployed-Parent program and would make the work-history rules a bit more rational. Each year the Senate has acquiesced to administration opposition to the House provision—most notably last year after a dramatic telegram from the president when he was in Reykjavik. We urge the Finance Committee to exercise strong leadership this year and to insist that the current blatant discrimination against marriage be eliminated in the AFDC program.

2. Teen-age Mothers

14. While the AFDC program requires many parents to leave home before the children can get help, some policy-makers want to require unmarried teen parents to stay at home. On the face of it, this proposal has a lot of appeal. It is obvious that, in general, most young mothers would do best with the supervision, help, and support of their own parents. Unfortunately, the issue is not so simple.

15. The Church has a long history of work with young unmarried mothers from residential maternity homes to adoption and foster-care services to community-based services to pregnant and new mothers. We know only too well how difficult it is for teen mothers to manage on their own. We try, whenever possible, to unite pregnant teens with their own parents. However, we have residential and nonresidential programs filled with young mothers who simply cannot live with their own families. Sometimes the best solution is to find apartments for them and to continue to provide support services. Some of the teenagers in our programs have been pressured by their parents to have abortions. Others come from homes with persistent or intermittent substance abuse, violence, or neglect. Even where the problems are less dramatic, new mothers are sometimes emotionally rejected by their parents, who fear disgrace or influence on younger sisters. We simply cannot withhold AFDC from these new mothers who, for very legitimate reasons, need to leave their parents' homes.

16. We also think it would be unwise to give state and local welfare departments new authority to decide in advance which young mothers should remain at home and which are justified in trying to establish separate households. Welfare departments are not adequately funded or staffed to make such sensitive decisions in addition to their many other responsibilities. Think of the welfare departments that are so often in the news because of failure to act promptly in reported cases of child abuse and neglect. Think of the frequent accounts of the inability of welfare departments to aid homeless families or to find adequate foster homes for abused and abandoned infants and children. I do not mean to attack welfare department employees who are trying to meet their responsibilities in the face of impossible demands. But we must be realistic about their ability to take on new assignments when workers already have caseloads far in excess of manageable limits. It would be unfair and even dangerous to subject very young mothers to a bureaucratic process of proving their own parents unfit. Those who are able to find other living arrangements through private agencies or on their own should not face this additional burden. Welfare departments already have authority to step in when they discover that young mothers are neglecting or abusing their children. Additional discretion is not necessary.

17. A more positive approach would be to make funding available for nonprofit agencies to counsel young parents and their families and to reconcile those who could really benefit by reunification. It would also make sense to repeal the 1981 federal legislation that reduced or eliminated AFDC payments to families with a teen parent residing at home. The grandparent-deeming and single filing-unit rules substantially reduce aid to young mothers who live with their own families. Why not create incentives for families rather than requirements that could endanger young mothers and their children?

---

3. Preventing Long-Term Dependency

18. In their new pastoral letter *Economic Justice for All*, the bishops stress their conviction that decent job opportunities are the best solution for most welfare recipients. They call for job creation programs that incorporate training, placement, and subsidized child care to supplement the limited number of jobs available in the private sector.
19. In our view, government programs should reward rather than punish welfare recipients who try to become self-supporting. However, the way the programs work now, there are few incentives and many disincentives for welfare mothers to find or keep jobs. This situation had been true for many years, but worsened following the 1981 Reconciliation Act, which removed many of the previous work incentives in AFDC. If AFDC is to be reformed or replaced, the key to success would be enough supplemental benefits in cash, medical assistance, and child care so that working parents can have the basic necessities required for human dignity.
20. While we strongly support proposals to increase work and training opportunities for welfare recipients, we are troubled by the way that the question has been framed. The vast majority of welfare recipients are on the rolls for between one and two years. Only a very small group of families remains on welfare for a long period of time. Recently, much of the discussion has focused on these families, and the question has become how to get mothers, especially young mothers, off the welfare rolls and into the labor force as quickly as possible. Most people assume that these mothers and their children as well as society as a whole would be better off if the children were put in day care at the earliest possible age so that the mothers could be placed in jobs or be given work assignments so as to "earn" their welfare checks. Some states want to require mothers to leave their babies in child care when they are as young as six months so that the mothers can get jobs.
21. Let me mention several of our concerns about these proposals. First, we believe that human work has a special dignity and is a key

to achieving justice in society. But, as Pope John Paul II reminded us in several papal encyclicals—namely, *On Human Work* and *On the Family*—caring for one's own children is work that is just as important and valuable to society as paid employment. While the trend is clearly toward mothers of young children working at least part time, we question whether the government should degrade the value of maternal care by a policy that *requires* mothers of young children to take jobs outside the home. Do we really want federal policy to enshrine the notion that the family is only an economic unit and that parents' primary responsibility is to provide for material needs rather than emotional, intellectual, or spiritual needs?

22. Second, we do not agree that mandatory work programs for mothers of young children are necessary or wise. It is clear from the Employment Training program in Massachusetts and other experiments that well-managed voluntary programs that offer good education and training opportunities and real jobs are the answer. Of course, low unemployment, above-average wages, and a booming economy also contribute to a high rate of success. When good jobs are available, there is little problem in persuading welfare recipients to take them.

23. Child-care and health benefits are also essential. Mothers who find satisfactory, affordable day-care arrangements and have private health coverage or Medicaid (or have extraordinary luck) can usually manage to keep their jobs. When society fails to provide one or both of these essentials, either the mother can't hold her job or the children are neglected. Either result is unsatisfactory, but the latter should not be tolerated.

24. We also need to look carefully at the real costs of adequate child care in light of anticipated earnings of welfare mothers. How much are we willing to spend on day care so that mothers can get off welfare rolls and on to work rolls? Since adult welfare recipients are nearly all women and newcomers to the labor force, we have to be cautious about what they can be expected to earn. Unless they have an employer or family member willing to provide child care, they will need government subsidies. In many states, the cost of good child care for one child will be more than the current maximum AFDC payment for a mother and one child. In nearly all states, good child care for two children will cost more than the current maximum AFDC grant for a mother and two children. Because nearly all of these women will have very low earnings for at least several years, they will continue to be eligible for food stamps and the earned-income tax credit. The total combined cost of the day care, food stamps, and earned-income tax credit would be higher than the combined current benefits for mothers staying at home with their own preschoolers.

25. Of course, we know that most state proposals for work programs assume much lower costs for child care than are reasonable. State administrators have approached church-sponsored child-care centers

with proposals to expand capacity—but at the same time accept much lower reimbursement rates. Some states expect nonprofit child-care programs to subsidize their jobs programs rather than the other way around.

26. There is an absolute shortage of child care in this country, and the shortage of good care is really alarming. The Archdiocese of Washington has a very good center here in this city, but it generally has a waiting list of six months to a year. The center charges $420.00 a month to care for children six months old to one year, and $312.00 a month for children between one and five. In Washington, D.C., the maximum AFDC benefit is $257.00 a month for a mother and one child, and $327.00 for a mother with two children. The District can contract to care for a child and pay $312.00-$420.00 a month to our center or provide $257.00 a month for the mother to stay home with her own child. If the mother has a three-year-old and a four-year-old, the District can pay the center $624.00 a month or pay the mother $327.00.

27. Of course, cheaper care is available but much of it is of very poor quality, unregulated, and usually unsupervised. Economizing on poor quality day care is risky and incurs long-term costs for children and society. Unless the states expect to find jobs for welfare mothers as bricklayers, electricians, computer technicians, or other well-paid jobs that are usually held by men, the states will have to pay for the day-care costs of the preschoolers. Thus, except for states with a significant growth in jobs with above-average wages, the projected cost savings of work programs for mothers of preschool children are largely illusory.

28. Like other mothers, most welfare mothers have entered the work force by the time that their youngest children enter school. With provision for afterschool supervision, it is not unreasonable to expect welfare mothers to work at least part time if decent jobs are available. Because of the much lower costs of care for school-aged children, the AFDC program could realize significant savings by helping these mothers find jobs. The AFDC program has not made this goal a priority, and it is disappointing to hear policy-makers argue for mandatory programs for mothers of preschoolers without a real effort to help mothers of older children.

29. Before closing, I also want to mention briefly our interest in two bills you have introduced to aid homeless AFDC families.

30. Last Thursday, the USCC testified on homelessness before the Subcommittee on Housing. In that testimony, we urged consideration of S.37, a bill that would permit use of AFDC Emergency Assistance funds to be used for construction and rehabilitation of low-cost housing for AFDC families that would otherwise be homeless. The real problem is that the federal government has all but abandoned direct funding for low-income housing, and states and localities have to find other ways to get access to federal funds. This bill would permit use

of AFDC funds for cost-effective housing development. This is a very creative solution but should be part of a much broader attack on the primary cause of homelessness: a shortage of low-cost housing.

31. We also hope that the Agriculture Committee will take swift action on S.36, the chairman's bill that would make sure that homeless families lodged in welfare hotels are not denied food stamps.

Conclusion

32. Of course, there are many other issues that could be addressed concerning AFDC and related programs, but my testimony today is based largely on the pastoral on the economy in which the bishops stressed the need for:

- a national eligibility standard and a national minimum-benefit level to ensure adequate levels of support;
- a requirement for all states to provide welfare benefits to otherwise eligible two-parent families with a working or unemployed parent; and
- a redesign of AFDC so as to give recipients a real chance to escape poverty and to become self-supporting through gainful employment.

33. As the new pastoral points out, the search for a more human and effective way to deal with poverty should not be limited to the short-term reform measures we present here. While we have no blueprint, the agenda should include serious discussion of more fundamental alternatives to the existing welfare system.

34. We urge the committee to begin an examination of a family-allowance or children's-allowance system that would supplement other income to ensure a floor of support for all children. We agree with the chairman that the issue of child support from absent parents needs more attention. States are just beginning to implement the new Child Support Enforcement Act, with varying degrees of success, and it is too early for broad conclusions. However, the committee should carefully study the effects of the new act and consider the need for additional refinements.

35. Mr. Chairman, thank you for this opportunity to testify today on behalf of the Catholic bishops.

Testimony on International Debt

Testimony Presented before the
House Subcommittee on Foreign Operations
by Archbishop Rembert Weakland, OSB
on Behalf of the United States Catholic Conference

March 4, 1987

Mr. Chairman:

1. I testify today on behalf of the U.S. Catholic Conference, the public-policy arm of the Catholic bishops of the United States. I express the appreciation of the USCC for the invitation to appear before this committee. I welcome the opportunity to offer some remarks on behalf of the USCC on the increasingly serious and urgent problem of the debt of the Third World countries, which now stands at $1.035 trillion, according to the World Bank.

2. I am sure you are aware that last November the U.S. Catholic bishops approved a pastoral letter on the U.S. economy titled *Economic Justice for All.* I had the privilege of chairing the five-man ad hoc committee of bishops who spent five years preparing the draft of that document. During those five years, the committee members were exposed to a broad range of opinion on the economic policy issues we had chosen to address—one of which, "the U.S. economy and the developing nations," included the subject of this hearing.

3. As I have pointed out to other congressional bodies, our Catholic tradition recognizes the crucial importance of the kind of empirical analysis and technical competence on issues of public policy that we have just heard; these are clear prerequisites for reaching fair and effective decisions on these complex issues.

4. During the preparation of our letter, we conducted a series of hearings at which many professional economists provided us with valuable insights into how the system works and how it might be improved. But we believe that the economic analysis must be complemented by a moral perspective that reflects the human needs, the real people, the human problems behind the statistics and the economic indicators. Economic decisions affect human persons and are therefore fundamentally moral.

5. The argument of our pastoral letter rests on three premises: First, the dignity of the human person created in the image of God is the measure against which every economic decision, policy, and institution must be judged; second, because this human dignity can be realized only in community, every person has a right to participate

501

in the economic life of the society; third, all members of the society have a special obligation to the poor and the disadvantaged. For us, the ultimate test of justice is how the economic policy choice affects the poor.

6.   We find ourselves, therefore, at the intersection of empirical economic analysis and the normative questions of value and human purpose. While we acknowledge that our three perspectives do not lead directly to specific conclusions about policy—that is, that there can be no purely moral approach to economic choices—we nevertheless insist that purely empirical economic analyses cannot produce by themselves an adequate policy either.

7.   The formulation and implementation of economic policies cannot be left solely to technicians, special interest groups, and market forces; it must also centrally involve ethical values and moral priorities. We also believe that the perspective of Catholic teaching provides a point of entry and an angle of vision distinct from, and an indispensable supplement for, that of the professional economist.

8.   We decided to treat the Third World debt situation, at least briefly, in our letter partly because the dynamic of our process and the thinking I have just summarized led us in that direction and partly too because our discussions with our fellow bishops from Latin America and the many communications we have received from American missionaries serving in the Third World added a note of personal urgency to the more detached conclusions of our analysis.

9.   We believe very strongly that a debt burden which resulted in a net transfer of nearly $30 billion in 1986 to the industrialized countries (principally the United States) from countries in which upward of 800 million people live in poverty so miserable that it is "beneath any rational definition of human decency"; in which hundreds of millions of people are chronically hungry; in which 40,000 children die every day from malnutrition and disease; in which two-thirds of the world's people live at an economic level that is increasingly below that of the industrialized world is much more than a set of problems calling for a technical solution. It is a scandal; it calls for a moral solution that should entail significant sacrifices on the part of those who benefit materially from this situation.

10.   In the international section of our pastoral letter, we acknowledge in the first place, what we term "the complexity of economic relations in an interdependent world." We say that these economic relations constitute "the framework in which the solidarity we seek on a national level finds its international expression." Although we recognize that the United States has economic relations with a whole spectrum of other nations, "our emphasis on the preferential option for the poor moves us to focus our attention mainly on U.S. relations with the Third World " Among those relations, we give considerable prominence to international finance: "The debtor-creditor relationship

exemplifies both the interdependence of the international economic order and its asymmetrical character, (i.e., the dependence of the developing countries)."

11. Although I am sure you are as aware as we are of the nature, dimensions, and causes of the present Third World debt situation, I believe it would be useful anyway to indicate to you how we see this matter from the angle of vision noted above.

12. The total aggregate debt of the developing countries has now gone beyond the $1 trillion we cited in our letter. The servicing of this enormous debt (the largest part of which is interest) entails an outflow of capital so huge that for all practical purposes it inhibits those countries' development—whether development is viewed as economic growth or as improvement of the quality of life of poor people (which would be our preferred definition).

13. One might think from accounts in the media that the so-called debt crisis burst full-blown and unexpectedly on the world in August 1982, when Mexico announced that it could not meet its debt-servicing requirements. In fact, however, as you know, it had been accumulating throughout the 1970s at least, as food and energy prices rose sharply and newly rich oil-exporting countries invested their profits in the banks of the industrialized countries. Developing countries borrowed these funds to pay their increased energy and other import bills—and then borrowed again when oil prices doubled once more at the end of the decade and falling prices for their commodity exports reduced their ability to service the debts incurred earlier.

14. Already at the beginning of the 1980s, before commercial lending began to decline and nearly three years before the Mexican announcement, the Brandt Commission noted that the borrowing needs of even the better-off developing countries were likely to rise considerably during the ensuing decade, at least partly because they would need to borrow more in order to service the debt already accrued. The commission went on to observe that "the debtor economies and the entire international credit structure are now very vulnerable to any disruptions in the flows of capital." "The heart of the debt problem," it said, "is that a very large proportion of the funds are lent on terms which are onerous for borrowers from the point of view of both the repayment capacity of the projects they finance and the time debtor countries need to correct structural imbalances in their external accounts."

15. What is not always recognized is that developing-country borrowing saved the industrialized countries from the full impact of the oil price rise. "Over the last few years," the commission continued, "economic activity in the industrialized countries has been sustained by a major recycling of financial surpluses through the commercial banks." The commission quoted an Organization for Economic Cooperation and Development report that says, "Had developing countries followed the example of industrialized countries after 1973, by cutting back both their growth and imports to adjust to the oil price increase, the recession in the industrialized world would have been far more serious."

16. In other words, these countries of the South bailed out the industrialized countries of the North by quadruplinig their own external debt in the decade of the 1970s. When oil prices doubled again in 1979, they were unable to repeat that performance, especially during the recession that ensued and as the terms of trade worsened for their exports. At the end of 1979, their debt was about $300 billion; the Brandt Commission estimated that another $500 billion might have to be added by 1985 unless the oil-importing countries checked their imports and their growth—"provided the funds could be found." As is manifest in the $1 trillion total, those funds were not found until recently.

17. The Brandt Commission's prescription for relief was "massive transfers" of resources through concessional foreign aid and commercial lending, which would require "intermediation" by public institutions like the World Bank and the International Monetary Fund, since "private commercial banks . . . can no longer be counted on to conduct the recycling process unassisted." "All countries must share the burden," the commission said and called for, among other things, a system of universal international taxation.

18. As we all know, all countries have not shared the burden; commercial lending has dwindled to a trickle; there is a large and growing net transfer of financial resources (nearly $30 billion last year) from poor people and poor countries to relatively rich countries and relatively rich people; the catch phrases of the day are "policy reform," "structural adjustment," "conditionality," and"austerity."

19. This, in our summary view, is the historical record. The prescriptions of the Brandt Commission—and most others being considered now—are either macroeconomic solutions which do not take the human element adequately into consideration or Band-Aids (some of them quite large) which treat only the symptoms or efforts to lighten the debt burden so that these countries can buy our exports. As we wrote in our pastoral letter, however, the Third World debt crisis reveals a more fundamental systemic problem. What happened in the 1980s, like what happened in the decade before it, resulted not only from policy but from structure.

20. The broad outline of the post-World War II international financial system was established at the Bretton Woods Conference of 1944, which created the World Bank and the IMF and laid the foundation for the General Agreement on Tariffs and Trade. The purpose of these arrangements was to prevent the kind of economic actions that were perceived to have led to the war. In the system that emerged, the dollar was the dominant currency, much as the British pound sterling had been in the interwar period; and its role as the basic medium of exchange led to nearly three decades of unprecedented economic growth and prosperity. Even after the United States terminated payment in gold, the dollar remained the dominant currency—throughout the period and to the present day. As the dollar appreciated in price and dollar-denominated loans were rescheduled at higher interest rates (and with high rescheduling fees for the banks), the burden on the debtor countries grew steadily to its present dimensions.

21. Especially after the Mexican crisis of 1982, the rather limited number of major lenders (twenty in the United States) began to worry about the high proportions of their portfolios that were in Third World loans; the particular fear was that a major debtor might default, wipe out an important bank, and trigger a damaging process in the international financial system. From the debtor's side of the table (the perspective we emphasize in this testimony) the continuing payments are seen as threatening social stability in debtor countries, slowing down economic growth, and hindering efforts to improve the standard of living of the poor.

22. For many of us who are concerned with this problem of Third World debt, there is the further complication of how at least some of the borrowed money was spent. It is documented, for example, that capital flight from Third World countries has increased, as ruling and economic elites transferred funds into high-interest-paying accounts and investments in the industrialized countries. (I do not need to bore you with examples, since they are only too obvious.) The very banks that are paying interest on the foreign accounts of those elites are obtaining much of the money to do so by further penalizing and taxing workers and farmers in developing countries that are meeting their debt-service burden. Then when, as in 1982, a major country gets into difficulty, the banks either cease lending (but continue to insist on payment and therefore earn profits) or are cajoled into rescheduling loans, for which they increase the spread between the interest they pay on deposits and the interest they collect on the loans (and charge high fees for doing it).

23. It seems to us that the injustice in these circumstances is rather clear: First, poor people in poor countries are forced to pay back debts pushed on their not uneager but often unrepresentative governments by profit-seeking banks in the industrialized world; second, poor countries which shored up the industrialized world after the first oil shock, but could not do so after the second, are now required to continue—and in fact, increase—the net transfer of resources to the relatively rich North; third, workers and farmers in countries like the United States are losing jobs, income, and assets because their former customers either cannot afford to buy their products in view of the required debt repayments or are competing in those very markets in order to earn foreign exchange to pay back the debts; fourth, the bulk

of this debt is interest, not principal. (Some, particularly in the Third World, ask whether the front loading of interest in these circumstances could be considered usury.)

24. A Joint Economic Committee report of last May, for example, estimated that U.S. agricultural exports to Latin America declined one-third, prices of exported farm commodities fell about 20 percent, and competing grain exports from Latin America more than doubled — all because of the debt crisis of that region. The Brandt Commission was quite right to say all countries must share the burden. We would take it one step further: the creditor institutions in particular must share the burden.

25. In the midst of this malfunctioning system, the IMF rose to quick and unexpected prominence in 1982. Originally established to provide short-term credit to countries that were having difficulties with their balance of payments, the IMF found its time frame unexpectedly lengthened because of the systemic problems that were emerging — and thus was pushed into the role of a development agency. But the IMF's standard formula for meeting the short-term liquidity problems did not change: Devalue the currency to encourage exports by lowering their price and thus earn foreign exchange; hold the line on wage increases to reduce the incentive to consume (and thus compete with exports); and cut consumer subsidies and public services to reduce inflation and the budget deficit.

26. These are the "austerity" measures associated with the IMF's standby agreements; the IMF insists that it does not "impose" these conditions. Moreover, former IMF Managing Director Jacques de Larosiere, at the World Bank/IMF meeting last fall expressed concern about "the most pernicious human costs" of the debt problem after having told ECOSOC last summer that a successful strategy must also "pay attention to the health, nutritional, and educational requirements of the most vulnerable groups. . . . For example, safeguarding human needs may imply that employment in overstaffed and loss-making public enterprises or defense spending be reduced in preference to cutting an accelerated immunization and health care program for children." There is little evidence, however, that this approach has yet carried over consistently into IMF practice.

27. In fact, the Third World debt problem up to now has been handled on an ad hoc basis by the IMF, the World Bank, the Federal Reserve Board, the Treasury, and, with considerable reluctance, the commercial banks. Notwithstanding de Larosiere's statements, the solutions have therefore been bankers' solutions; they have treated the matter solely as a macroeconomic problem and have emphasized economic growth, generally ignoring equity considerations altogether. The question has been posed this way: How can the indebted countries achieve sustainable growth while continuing to make progress toward the restoration of normal debtor-creditor relationships? The result of operating from this angle of vision has been that in order to sustain bank profitability (not just the soundness of the financial system), the IMF and its collaborators have insisted that foreign creditors of these debtor countries be paid in full and on time, even at the cost of reduced living standards and declining incomes for the poor, increasing unemployment, steep price rises for food staples, and, in some cases, repression of fundamental human rights.

28. We fully agree with de Larosiere that "further progress on the debt problem depends critically on each of the major parties pulling his weight. Co-responsibility [used in his November 21 speech somewhat before it appeared in the recent Vatican document on debt] must therefore remain the cornerstone of the strategy. Second, a satisfactory solution to the problem . . . is feasible only in the context of durable growth in the debtor countries." We would add that such growth is unlikely and certainly undesirable without an at least commensurately equitable sharing of benefits and the decisions about them by the poor majorities in those countries. The international financial system should not be saved by the two groups least responsible for the current crisis—the poor in the Third World and the taxpayers of industrialized countries like the United States (who will pay the bill if governments must shore up improvident banks).

29. We are pleased to see that pundits, politicians, and even some bankers are beginning to recognize that the creditors must accept a share of the sacrifices needed to resolve the Third World debt crisis. We believe, however, that it is reasonable to look carefully at two kinds of debt problems at least. The first is that of mainly Latin American countries, which account for "roughly 40 percent of the total external debt of all capital-importing countries." Between 1981 and 1983, according to the IMF, net commercial lending to Latin America dropped from $55 billion to $1 billion, import volume decreased by 40 percent, unemployment rose, and for all practical purposes growth stopped. More recently, we have noted the dramatic announcements and actions by Mexico, Brazil, and Argentina. These events seem to us to be one more set of clear indications that the policies followed up to this point, in addition to being unfair, are also ineffective.

30. The debt of sub-Saharan Africa poses a quite different problem. The bulk of it is owed not to commercial banks, but to governments or to the multilateral institutions created by governments—the World Bank, the regional banks, and the IMF. As we pointed out in our pastoral letter, "although their aggregate debt of about $100 billion is only a quarter that of Latin America, their collateral (oil, minerals, manufactures, grain, etc.) is much less adequate, their ability to service external debt much weaker, and the possibility of their rescheduling it very small." In this case, we believe that "forgiveness," perhaps in the guise of converting this official debt to a local-currency obligation to be paid into a development bank in the country, would be an

appropriate and effective solution. Criteria for such conversion would, of course, have to be very carefully studied.

31. As we noted at the beginning, moral principles and doctrinal positions do not yield specific policies. They do not tell us, for example, how to choose among the score or more solutions proposed for this problem. But they do offer some general benchmarks against which to judge those proposals. We would look with great skeptcism, for example, on solutions whose main objective and anticipated result would be to assure the creditors payment in full, or on proposals that consider the present problem one of temporary liquidity rather than incipient insolvency, or those that would create a new international institution to buy up bad debts from banks in exchange for newly issued bonds or that would convert debt into equity at some kind of discount, etc.

32. In our view, none of these measures, as currently described, would improve the lot of the poor, since all of them are designed more to tinker with the system than to diagnose it in depth. The people least able to pay these debts and most burdened by them would not be helped by any of these proposals—except perhaps in the now discredited sense of "trickle-down."

33. A new contribution to the debt debate is the recent publication of the Pontifical Commission for Justice and Peace, *At the Service of the Human Community: An Ethical Approach to the International Debt Question.* In his introductory presentation, Cardinal Roger Etchegaray, president of the commission, after summarizing the history of the crisis in much the same terms the U.S. bishops used, writes:

> When credit agencies consider the situation solely from the economic and monetary angle, they often impose on the debtor countries terms, in exchange for accrued credit, that can contribute, at least in the short term, to unemployment, recession and a drastic reduction in the standard of living. This causes suffering, first of all for the poorest as well as for certain sectors of the middle class. In brief, it is a situation that is intolerable and, in the medium term, disastrous for the creditors themselves. Debt servicing cannot be met at the price of the asphyxiation of a country's economy, and no government can morally demand of its people privations incompatible with human dignity. . . . Economic structures and financial mechanisms are at the service of the human person and not vice versa.

34. The first of the ethical principles enunciated by the Vatican document is the very term used by the managing director of the IMF in his speech quoted above: co-responsibility. Both the U.S. bishops' letter and the Vatican document emphasize that

> in order to be just, interdependence should give rise to new and broader expressions of solidarity which respect the equal dignity of all peoples. . . . Solidarity implies an awareness and acceptance of co-responsibility for the causes and the solutions relative to international debt. . . . The various partners must agree on an equitable

sharing of the adjustment efforts and the necessary sacrifices, taking into account the priority to be given to the needs of the most deprived peoples. It is the responsibility of the countries that are better off to assure a larger share (*An Ethical Approach*).

35. The pontifical commission's document spreads this co-responsibility rather widely: "Due to their greater economic power, the industrialized countries bear a heavier responsibility, which they must acknowledge and accept." (Politicians are called on specifically to form public opinion in this area.)

36. Groups in authority in indebted countries must be willing "to explain their own actions, errors and even abuses" and avoid the temptation to "shift full responsibility to other countries" so that they will not have "to propose any changes which would affect them directly." They must also "accept having their actions and any responsibilities they may have in their countries' indebtedness scrutinized [and must] . . . promote sustained economic growth . . . in order to ensure a broader, and more just distribution among all."

37. Though "creditors have rights, acknowledged by the debtors . . ., creditor states have to find reimbursement conditions which are compatible with each debtor state's ability to meet its basic needs."

38. Commercial banks are urged to finance "projects on the basis of their impact on growth in preference to 'safer' projects with more immediate investment returns," even though this approach "goes beyond the traditional function of commercial banks insofar as it invites them to undertake a type of discernment which transcends the ordinary criteria of profitability."

39. "Multinational companies have extensive economic, financial and technological power. . . . As economic and financial actors on the international stage, they are called to co-responsibility and solidarity which is above and beyond their own vested interests."

40. Finally, the multilateral financial organizations "are faced with new and urgent responsibilities: to help solve the debt crisis of the developing countries; to avoid a generalized collapse of the international financial system; to help all peoples, especially those in greatest need, to bring about their own development; to combat the spread of poverty under all its various forms and thereby promote peace by eliminating the threats of conflicts."

41. The link which the Vatican document establishes between a just solution of the debt problem and social peace is crucially important. Although the debt crisis has coincided with—or perhaps even partially caused—considerable democratization in Latin America during the last few years as mismanagement by authoritarian ruling groups was revealed, there is a danger that the austerity associated with IMF standby agreements and commercial bank pressure for full repayment may push these fledgling democracies to adopt unpopular policies that could lead to a revival of authoritarianism to enforce the austerity programs. Thus the banks may be pitting themselves unwittingly against the very forces in the debtor countries that could provide a democratic growth-with-equity alternative.

42. Our discussion here today, as well as much of the analytical material in our pastoral letter, has a dispassionate, even clinical, tone. We hear a different voice in letters from American missionaries overseas, like one that came in recently describing the missionary's return to the mission country after some period of time: "Today I rode the bus downtown, for which I paid 250,000 pesos. . . . When I was here ten years ago, I could have bought the bus for that price."

43. We also hear a different voice when we meet with Latin American bishops on these issues as we did a year ago in Miami. The "cool" analysis of the debt problem became immediate, personal, passionate, and urgent when we heard a Brazilian bishop say, for example: "Your debt is an iron ring around the necks of my people." These bishops had two major financial problems on their minds—the debt and capital flight. They were very hard on their own political and economic leaders for pushing money out of the country into those attractive overseas investments, but almost equally hard on the industrialized countries for placing those profit temptations in the paths of the elites.

44. I worry a little about the almost exclusive focus on the debt problem in hearings like this, as well as about the tendency to view it in tandem with the trade problem—as if to suggest that the main or only reason for relieving the debt burden is to make it possible for the debtor countries to buy our exports. We do not believe the Third World debt problem can be solved without addressing all aspects of the international order. We said in our pastoral letter on the economy that "we believe that U.S. policy toward the developing world should reflect our traditional regard for human rights and our concern for social progress. In economic policy, as we noted in our pastoral letter on nuclear war, the major international economic relationships of aid, trade, finance, and investment are interdependent among themselves and illustrate the range of interdependence issues facing U.S. policy. . . . Each relationship offers us the possibility of substantial positive movement toward increasing social justice in the developing world."

45. In the debt area as with the other three—trade, aid, and investment—the problem goes beyond even the system itself.

> It afflicts and oppresses large numbers of people who are already severely disadvantaged. That is the scandal: It is the poorest people who suffer most from the austerity measures required when a country seeks the IMF "seal of approval," which establishes its creditworthiness for a commercial loan (or perhaps an external aid program). It is these same people who suffer most when commodity prices fall, when food cannot be imported or they cannot buy it, and

when natural disasters occur. Our commitment to the preferential option for the poor does not permit us to remain silent in these circumstances.

46. We are aware that neither of our two pastoral letters prescribes a policy solution to the problems they focus on. We think that is proper. The virtue of prudence enters the equation as soon as one moves beyond the realm of principle. We see these two letters as inextricably linked; peace is, after all, the fruit of justice. We know that just as what the peace pastoral recommended in a general sense would call for a very different policy than the United States is following today, so would the economic pastoral. But just as one effect of the peace pastoral was to identify the Roman Catholic community with the effort to reverse the arms race and stem the dangerous drift toward nuclear war, one effect of the economic pastoral will, we hope, be to identify the Roman Catholic community with the cause of economic justice—especially for the poor, both in the United States and in the Third World.

47. How that objective is to be achieved is, of course, a matter of debate on many issues. One of them—possibly the most urgent and intransigent—is the question we are discussing today.

48. Even though we don't have a formula to propose to you, we would like to suggest several principles which we and many other religious groups believe should underlie a normative approach to a solution to the problem of Third World debt:

- Responsibility for the solution must be shared in an equitable fashion by both creditors and debtor countries, and the burden must be lifted from the poor.
- The primary objective of any approach must be to improve the quality of life of the poorest people through restored and equitably shared economic growth, not to preserve the profitability of banks.
- Criteria for adjustment of each country's debt situation should take into account, among other things, what the money was borrowed for, how it was used, what efforts the debtor country has already made or begun to repay it, and how the debtor nation proposes to stop capital flight.
- Efforts to resolve the short-term debt problems should be undertaken in close association with a very basic look at the entire international financial system, with a view to systemic changes designed to establish more equitable arrangements that can prevent the recurrence of this kind of crisis.
- Any structural adjustment or other debt-solution package must

preserve the basic human rights of the citizens of the debtor country and the integrity of its government.

- Any viable solution must recognize and relieve external factors beyond the control of the debtor country that tend to aggravate and perpetuate the burden—interest rates, commodity prices, trade barriers, budget deficits, etc.

49. Thank you for your attention.

A Pastoral Statement for Catholics on Biblical Fundamentalism

*A Statement Issued by the Ad Hoc Committee
on Biblical Fundamentalism and Authorized
by the Administrative Committee of the
National Conference of Catholic Bishops*

March 26, 1987

1.   This is a statement of concern to our Catholic brothers and sisters who may be attracted to Biblical Fundamentalism without realizing its serious weaknesses. We Catholic bishops, speaking as a special committee of the National Conference of Catholic Bishops, desire to remind our faithful of the fullness of Christianity that God has provided in the Catholic Church.

2.   Fundamentalism indicates a person's general approach to life which is typified by unyielding adherence to rigid doctrinal and ideological positions — an approach that affects the individual's social and political attitudes as well as religious ones. Fundamentalism in this sense is found in non-Christian religions and can be doctrinal as well as biblical. But in this statement we are speaking only of Biblical Fundamentalism, presently attractive to some Christians, including some Catholics.

3.   Biblical Fundamentalists are those who present the Bible, God's inspired Word, as the only necessary source for teaching about Christ and Christian living. This insistence on the teaching Bible is usually accompanied by a spirit that is warm, friendly, and pious. Such a spirit attracts many (especially idealistic young) converts. With ecumenical respect for these communities, we acknowledge their proper emphasis on religion as influencing family life and workplace. The immediate attractions are the ardor of the Christian community and the promises of certitude and of a personal conversion experience to the person of Jesus Christ without the need of church. As Catholic pastors, however, we note its presentation of the Bible as a single rule for living. According to Fundamentalism, the Bible alone is sufficient. There is no place for the universal teaching Church — including its wisdom; its teachings, creeds, and other doctrinal formulations; its liturgical and devotional traditions. There is simply no claim to a visible, audible, living, teaching authority binding the individual or congregations.

4.   A further characteristic of Biblical Fundamentalism is that it tends to interpret the Bible as being always without error, or as literally true, in a way quite different from the Catholic Church's teaching on

the inerrancy of the Bible. For some Biblical Fundamentalists, inerrancy extends even to scientific and historical matters. The Bible is presented without regard for its historical context and development.

5.   In 1943, Pope Pius XII encouraged the Church to promote biblical study and renewal, making use of textual criticism. The Catholic Church continued to study the Bible as a valuable guide for Christian living. In 1965, the Second Vatican Council, in its *Constitution on Divine Revelation*, gave specific teaching on the Bible. Catholics are taught to see the Bible as God's book—and also as a collection of books, written under divine inspiration by many human beings. The Bible is true— and to discover its inspired truth we should study the patterns of thinking and writing used in ancient biblical times. With Vatican II, we believe that "the books of Scripture must be acknowledged as teaching firmly, faithfully, and without error that truth which God wanted put into the sacred writings for the sake of our salvation" (*Constitution on Divine Revelation*, no. 11). We do not look upon the Bible as an authority for science or history. We see truth in the Bible as not to be reduced solely to literal truth, but also to include salvation truths expressed in varied literary forms.

6.   We observed in Biblical Fundamentalism an effort to try to find in the Bible all the direct answers for living—though the Bible itself nowhere claims such authority. The appeal of such an approach is understandable. Our world is one of war, violence, dishonesty, and personal and sexual irresponsibility. It is a world in which people are frightened by the power of the nuclear bomb and the insanity of the arms race, where the only news seems to be bad news. People of all ages yearn for answers. They look for sure, definite rules for living. And they are given answers—in a confident and enthusiastic way, in Fundamentalist Bible groups.

7.   The appeal is evident for the Catholic young adult or teenager— one whose family background may be troubled; who is struggling with life, morality, and religion; whose Catholic education may have been seriously inadequate in the fundamentals of doctrine, the Bible, prayer life, and sacramental living; whose catechetical formation may have been inadequate in presenting the full Catholic traditions and teaching authority. For such a person, the appeal of finding the *the answer* in a devout, studious, prayerful, warm, Bible-quoting class is easy to understand. But the ultimate problem with such Fundamentalism is that it can give only a limited number of answers and cannot present those answers on balance, because it does not have Christ's teaching Church, nor even an understanding of how the Bible originally came to be written and collected in the sacred canon or official list of inspired books.

8.   Our Catholic belief is that we know God's revelation in the total gospel. The gospel comes to us through the Spirit-guided Tradition of the Church and the inspired books: "This sacred Tradition, there-

fore, and Sacred Scripture of both the Old and New Testament are like a mirror in which the pilgrim Church on earth looks at God" (*Constitution on Divine Revelation*, no. 7).

9.   A key question for any Christian is: Does the community of faith which is the Lord's Church have a living Tradition which presents God's Word across the centuries until the Lord comes again? The Catholic answer to this question is an unqualified "yes." That answer was expressed most recently in the *Constitution on Divine Revelation* of the Second Vatican Council. We look to both the Church's official teaching and Scripture for guidance in addressing life's problems. It is the official teaching or *magisterium* that in a special way guides us in matters of belief and morality that have developed after the last word of Scripture was written. The Church of Christ teaches in the name of Christ and teaches us concerning the Bible itself.

10.   The basic characteristic of Biblical Fundamentalism is that it eliminates from Christianity the Church as the Lord Jesus founded it. That Church is a community of faith, worldwide, with pastoral and teaching authority. This nonchurch characteristic of Biblical Fundamentalism, which sees the Church as only spiritual, may not at first be clear to some Catholics. From some Fundamentalists, they will hear nothing offensive to their beliefs, and much of what they hear seems compatible with Catholic Christianity. The difference is often not in what is said—but in what is not said. There is no mention of the historic, authoritative Church in continuity with Peter and the other apostles. There is no vision of the Church as our mother—a mother who is not just spiritual, but who is visibly ours to teach and guide us in the way of Christ.

11.   Unfortunately, a minority of Fundamentalist churches and sects not only put down the Catholic Church as a "man-made organization" with "man-made rules," but indulge in crude anti-Catholic bigotry with which Catholics have long been familiar.

12.   We believe that no Catholic properly catechized in the faith can long live the Christian life without those elements that are had only in the fullness of Christianity: the Eucharist and the other six sacraments, the celebration of the Word in the liturgical cycle, the veneration of the Blessed Mother and the saints, teaching authority and history linked to Christ, and the demanding social doctrine of the Church based on the sacredness of all human life.

13.   It is important for every Catholic to realize that the Church produced the New Testament, not vice-versa. The Bible did not come down from heaven, whole and intact, given by the Holy Spirit. Just as the experience and faith of Israel developed its sacred books, so was the early Christian Church the matrix of the New Testament. The Catholic Church has authoritatively told us which books are inspired by the Holy Spirit and are, therefore, canonical. The Bible, then, is the Church's book. The New Testament did not come before the

Church, but from the Church. Peter and the other apostles were given special authority to teach and govern before the New Testament was written. The first generation of Christians had no New Testament at all—but they were the Church then, just as we are the Church today.

14. A study of the New Testament, in fact, shows that discipleship is to be a community experience with liturgy and headship and demonstrates the importance of belonging to the Church started by Jesus Christ. Christ chose Peter and the other apostles as foundations of his Church, made Simon Peter its rock foundation, and gave a teaching authority to Peter and the other apostles. This is most clear in the Gospel of Matthew, the only Gospel to use the word *church*. The history of twenty Christian centuries confirms our belief that Peter and the other apostles have been succeeded by the Bishop of Rome and the other bishops, and that the flock of Christ still has, under Christ, a universal shepherd.

15. For historical reasons, the Catholic Church in the past did not encourage bible studies as much as she could have. True, printing (the Latin Bible was the first work printed) was not invented until the mid-fifteenth century, and few people were literate during the first sixteen centuries of Christianity. But in the scriptural renewal, the Church strongly encourages her sons and daughters to read, study, and live the Bible. The proclamation of the Scriptures in the liturgical assembly is to be prepared for by private bible study and prayer. At the present time, two decades after Vatican II, we Catholics have all the tools needed to become Christians who know, love, and live the Holy Bible. We have a well-ordered lectionary that opens for us the treasures of all the books of the Bible in a three-year cycle for Sunday and holy day Masses, and a more complete two-year cycle for weekday Masses. Through the lectionary, the Catholic becomes familiar with the Bible according to the rhythm of the liturgical seasons and the Church's experience and use of the Bible at Mass. We have excellent translations (with notes) in *The New American Bible* and *The Jerusalem Bible*. We have other accurate translations with an *imprimatur*. We have an abundance of commentaries, tapes, charts, and bible societies.

16. We Catholics have excellent bible resources and scholars of international repute. Our challenge now is to get this knowledge into the minds, hearts, and lives of all our Catholic people. We need a Pastoral Plan for the Word of God that will place the Sacred Scriptures at the heart of the parish and individual life. Pastoral creativity can develop approaches such as weekly bible study groups and yearly bible schools in every parish. We need to have the introduction to each bible reading prepared and presented by the lector in a way that shows familiarity with and love for the sacred text (cf. Foreword to the *Lectionary*; Introduction: nos. 15, 155, 313, 320). In areas where there is a special problem with Fundamentalism, the pastor may consider a Mass to which people bring their own Bibles and in which qualified lectors present a carefully prepared introduction and read the text—without, however, making the liturgy of the Word a bible study class. We need better homilies, since the homily is the most effective way of applying biblical texts to daily living. We need a familiar quoting of the Bible by every catechist, lector, and minister. We have not done enough in this area. The neglect of parents in catechetics and the weakness of our adult education efforts are now producing a grim harvest. We need to educate—to reeducate—our people knowingly in the Bible so as to counteract the simplicities of Biblical Fundamentalism.

17. In addition to that, we Catholics need to redouble our efforts to make our parish Masses an expression of worship in which all—parishioners, visitors, and strangers—feel the warmth and the welcome and know that here the Bible is clearly reverenced and preached. The current trend toward smaller faith-sharing and bible-studying groups within a parish family is strongly to be encouraged.

18. We call for further research on this entire question. We note that the U.S. Center for the Catholic Biblical Apostolate (3211 Fourth Street, N.E., Washington, D.C. 20017) will maintain an updated listing of available resources for Catholic bible study. Any individual Catholic or parish representative may write to learn the many available helps for developing bible study and bible teaching in accord with our long and rich Catholic tradition.

Statement on the Ku Klux Klan

*A Statement Issued by the
Administrative Board of the
United States Catholic Conference*

March 27, 1987

1.   We are deeply troubled by the visible and recurring signs of racism in our society. Individual incidents of racial confrontation and violence in various parts of the nation suggest the extent to which racial divisions and prejudice continue to exist in our social, economic, and cultural life. The persistent presence of this evil in our midst compels us to restate with added urgency what we said in 1979:

> Racism is a sin: a sin that divides the human family, blots out the image of God among specific members of that family, and violates the fundamental human dignity of those called to be children of the same Father. Racism is the sin that says some human beings are inherently superior and others essentially inferior because of race. It is the sin that makes racial characteristics the determining factor for the exercise of human rights. It mocks the words of Jesus: "Treat others the way you would have them treat you" (Mt 7:12). Indeed, racism is more than a disregard for the words of Jesus; it is a denial of the truth of the dignity of each human being revealed by the mystery of the incarnation.

2.   As moral teachers, we are not only responsible for articulating the dignity and equality of all persons; we also must speak out against specific violations of that dignity. In recent months, there has been significant activity by and publicity about the Ku Klux Klan and several other racist organizations. We state unequivocally that Catholics who join the Ku Klux Klan or any organizations that actively promote racism act in violation of Catholic teaching. These organizations are a scandalous contradiction to all that we hold sacred and teach in the name of Jesus Christ.

3.   As Catholic bishops, we reaffirm that every person and every institution that bears the name Catholic should proclaim to all that the sin of racism defiles the image of God and degrades the sacred dignity of humankind. We challenge our people to respect the fundamental dignity of the human person and the solidarity of the human family. We repeat the appeal we made in our pastoral letter on racism:

> Let all know that it is a terrible sin that mocks the cross of Christ and ridicules the incarnation. For the brother and sister of our brother Jesus Christ are brother and sister to us. . . .
> Racism is not merely one sin among many; it is a radical evil that

divides the human family and denies the new creation of a redeemed world. To struggle against it demands an equally radical transformation, in our own minds and hearts as well as in the structure of our society.

Testimony on the
Fair Housing Amendments Act of 1987

Testimony Presented before the
Senate Subcommittee on the Constitution
by Bishop James W. Malone on Behalf of the
United States Catholic Conference

April 9, 1987

Mr. Chairman:

1.   I am pleased to appear before this subcommittee today to represent the United States Catholic Conference and to express our strong support for the Fair Housing Amendments Act of 1987 (S. 558). Legislation to provide an effective enforcement mechanism against unjust discrimination in housing is long overdue; and therefore, I hope Congress will take prompt action on S. 558. I commend you, Mr. Chairman, for beginning the process, and I pledge the support of the United States Catholic Conference in working to see that this legislation is approved.

2.   This legislation is needed precisely because the Fair Housing Act of 1968 is not working. There is extensive evidence that unjust housing discrimination continues to exist in our nation. Indeed, it is widespread. A recent survey commissioned by the Department of Housing and Urban Development estimated that black families looking for homes in metropolitan areas are likely to encounter discrimination almost half the time. Blacks looking for a place to rent have a 72 percent chance of encountering discrimination. Similar evidence of discrimination against other racial minorities is also extensive.

3.   While the most blatant forms of housing discrimination, such as restrictive covenants, have been largely eliminated, other forms of exclusion and segregation are still commonplace practice in our society. Racial steering, redlining, discriminatory mortgage and lease restrictions, and providing false information to minority buyers or renters are among the techniques that are still often used against blacks, Hispanics, and other minorities in communities across the nation.

4.   This kind of discrimination is personally offensive to those involved and socially harmful for many different reasons. Ultimately, however, our opposition to such discrimination rests on the fact that it is morally wrong.

5.   In the Catholic tradition, our moral vision begins with the dignity of the human person. All persons are deserving of a special reverence

because they are made in the image and likeness of God. To offend that human dignity is, therefore, in a very real way, to offend against God.

6.   Unjust discrimination on the basis of race is clearly a violation of the dignity of the human person and the basic rights which protect this dignity. Since discrimination in housing is an evident form of this kind of racism, it must be labeled as morally wrong at both the personal and the social level.

7.   In 1979, our conference of bishops issued a pastoral letter on racism, in which we described it as a sin. I believe it is appropriate to apply to discrimination in housing the same words we used to describe racism in general:

> Racism is a sin: a sin that divides the human family, blots out the image of God among specific members of that family, and violates the fundamental human dignity of those called to be children of the same Father. Racism is the sin that says some human beings are inherently superior and others essentially inferior because of race. It is the sin that makes racial characteristics the determining factor for the exercise of human rights. It mocks the words of Jesus: "Treat others the way you would have them treat you" (Mt, 7:12).

8.   It is on the basis of this vision of human dignity and equality that we must condemn discrimination in housing and work to help create effective legal and institutional mechanisms to prevent it. This is precisely what S. 558 is intended to accomplish — to create an effective and efficient enforcement mechanism against housing discrimination.

9.   It is widely recognized that the current law fails to provide adequate enforcement. Victims of housing discrimination can report violations to the Department of Housing and Urban Development, but HUD can do little to stop the violations. While the department has the authority to attempt to bring the two parties together for conciliation, this is clearly inadequate, as evidenced by the extensive discrimination that continues to exist in this field.

10.   It is true that under present law, a victim of housing discrimination can hire an attorney and bring a private law suit. However, this is clearly not a realistic option for most individuals. The time and money involved are simply too great an obstacle for them to pursue this course.

11.   The bottom line in this discussion is effectiveness. Since the present enforcement mechanisms are clearly not adequate, the goal must be to establish a procedure that will assure prompt and effective redress for victims of housing discrimination. In our judgment, the Fair Housing Amendments Act of 1987 would do a great deal to meet this goal. The Department of Housing and Urban Development would be able to investigate, initiate, and process complaints alleging discriminatory housing practices in a much more prompt and efficient manner. This legislation would provide a number of options for vic-

tims of discrimination—including conciliation by the parties involved, referral to a certified state or local agency, a hearing before an administrative law judge with rights of judicial review, and commencement of private civil actions as under present law.

12. In the end, the legislation would ensure more prompt and effective action. It would put teeth into the law by speeding up the process and by providing tough but reasonable penalties in the case of violations.

13. I am pleased to note that S. 558 includes provisions that will make it unlawful to discriminate against handicapped persons. Discrimination by landlords prevents many such individuals from finding housing in which they can live independently. As a result, they are forced to move into nursing homes or extended rehabilitation centers, or to live with their parents. Including persons with disabilities under the coverage of the Fair Housing Law will improve the chances for many such persons to live with the independence and dignity that they seek. In this regard, I am pleased to point out that the National Catholic Office for Persons with Disabilities has also endorsed S. 558.

14. One of the most significicnat features of this legislation is that it would make it unlawful to refuse to rent or sell a housing unit to a family solely because of the presence of children. This is a distinct but very serious form of housing discrimination. It is appropriate that it be included under the provisions of the Fair Housing Law, because it is not only a personal and family hardship for those involved, it is also a social injustice. For the good of both individuals and society, it should be made illegal.

15. To limit the housing choices available to families with children places an unjust burden on these families. It places a particularly severe hardship on single-parent families. This kind of discrimination artificially inflates the price of housing for families and may even contribute to the growing homelessness among families with children. Such housing bias constitutes a threat to the most basic unit of social organization.

16. In our recent pastoral letter *Economic Justice for All*, we listed several key priorities by which all social policies should be governed. One of these deals specifically with family life. In the words of the pastoral letter: "Economic and social policies . . . should be continually evaluated in light of their impact on the strength and stability of family life. The long-range future of this nation is intimately linked with the well-being of families, for the family is the most basic form of human community" (no. 93).

17. If we are to apply this principle, then surely we must find a remedy that will effectively prohibit discrimination against families with children.

18. In closing, I would emphasize that, while housing bias is only one form of discrimination, it is clearly linked to many of the continuing civil rights problems in our nation today. Where a person lives impacts on education, employment, voting, and other civic and social relations. To the extent that the rights of individuals and families are violated in the area of housing opportunities, they are affected across the full range of civil rights.

19. The passage of these Fair Housing Amendments will contribute in a very real way to the good of individuals and to the common good as well. It will be a necessary and appropriate reflection of our nation's constitutional heritage that recognizes the equality, dignity, and inalienable rights of all its citizens.

Statement on Waldheim

*A Statement Issued by the President of the
National Conference of Catholic Bishops*

June 22, 1987

1. In view of the current controversy over the proposed visit of Austrian President Kurt Waldheim to Pope John Paul II, I believe that it might be helpful for me to make the following statement as president of the National Conference of Catholic Bishops. Obviously, I have no competence to speak of Vatican diplomacy. However, I do want to express my hope that plans for the September 11, 1987, meeting in Miami between Jewish leaders and the Holy Father will continue despite the serious concern raised by some that the intention of the Holy Father to receive President Kurt Waldheim will impact negatively on the Miami meeting.

2. Preparations for the meeting in Miami have been under way for more than a year, carried forward by Jewish and Catholic representatives working together. The National Conference of Catholic Bishops is proud of the dialogue which has taken place concerning this event. In fact, we see it as a concrete result of the excellent relations we maintain with our Jewish brothers and sisters. The bishops are pleased that the Miami meeting will include a significant statement addressed to the Holy Father by a representative of the Jewish community and a response by the pope.

3. As the Holy See has stated publicly, the Holy Father did not initiate the meeting with President Waldheim. Moreover, such a meeting is in keeping with the standard practice of the Holy See to receive duly elected political leaders. It can also be noted that to be received by the pope does not mean that the Holy See is making a statement on the personal character of the one being received. It is the pope's practice to maintain dialogue with many of the world's political leaders, a duty he exercises frequently as he fulfills his diplomatic and pastoral responsibilities.

4. I am aware of the sensitivity of this and related issues for the Jewish community in the United States and throughout the world. I see the wisdom of considering further dialogue at some appropriate level with a representative international Jewish agency. How this may be done is beyond my particular competence to determine.

5. I pray that the good relations the conference of bishops has with our Jewish brothers and sisters in this country will be strong enough

to overcome any specific difficulty of the moment. I look forward to being present with the Holy Father when he meets with Jewish leaders at one of the first events in his second pastoral visit to the United States next September.

Political Responsibility
Choices for the Future

A Statement Issued by the
Administrative Board of the
United States Catholic Conference

September 1987

I. Introduction

1. A notable characteristic in the 1980s has been the increasing visibility of religious questions and themes in the political life of the United States. *Religion* and *politics*, once thought to be topics never joined in polite conversation or public debate, have become part of our daily discourse at every level of society.

2. In one sense, the role of religion in public life is neither new nor surprising. From the inaugural addresses of Washington and Lincoln, to the public opinion polls of the 1980s, Americans affirm, in diverse ways, that religious conviction is woven through our national history and heritage. In our Constitution, whose 200th anniversary we commemorate this year, as well as in our courts and legislatures, we have set forth the disestablishment principle to govern relations between church and state. The purpose of this principle has been to distinguish key elements in our heritage, not to silence or suppress religious witness or influence. Indeed, such suppression of religion would violate an equally important element of our heritage — the free exercise of religion. These constitutional precepts serve a useful function in keeping the religious community free to speak and act without the need for government endorsement or the fear of retaliation.

3. The role of religion in our public life has been visible and constant. But the 1980s have brought a new edge to this topic. Many reasons are offered to explain the role of religious themes. In our view, a primary feature is the centrality of moral questions for a broad range of public policy choices which we face as a nation. From medical technology to military technology, from economic policy to foreign policy, the choices before the country are laden with moral content. The moral dimension arises from the human significance of these choices, the possibility of either enhancing human dignity or eroding it by the policies we pursue as a people. Precisely because the moral content of public choice is so central today, the religious communities are inevitably drawn more deeply into the public life of the nation. These communities possess long and systematically developed moral traditions which can serve as a crucial resource in shaping the moral vision needed for the future.

II. The Church and the Political Order

4.   It is appropriate in this context to offer our own reflections on the role of the Church in the political order. Christians believe that Jesus' commandment to love one's neighbor should extend beyond individual relationships to infuse and transform all human relations from the family to the entire human community. Jesus came to "bring glad tidings to the poor . . . to proclaim liberty to captives and recovery of sight to the blind, . . . and to let the oppressed go free . . ." (Lk 4:18). He called us to feed the hungry, clothe the naked, care for the sick and afflicted, and comfort the victims of injustice (cf. Mt 25:35-41). His example and words require individual acts of charity and concern from each of us. Yet they also require understanding and action on a broader scale in pursuit of peace and in opposition to poverty, hunger, and injustice. Such action necessarily involves the institutions and structures of society, the economy, and politics.

5.   The Church, the People of God, is itself an expression of this love and is required by the gospel and its long tradition to promote and defend human rights and human dignity.[1] In his encyclical *Redemptor Hominis*, Pope John Paul II declares that the Church "must be aware of the threats to [humanity] and of all that seems to oppose the endeavor 'to make life ever more human' and make every element of life correspond to humanity's true dignity — in a word, [the Church] must be aware of all that is opposed to that process."[2] This view of the Church's ministry and mission requires it to relate positively to the political order, since social injustice and the denial of human rights can often be remedied only through governmental action. In today's world, concern for social justice and human development necessarily requires persons and organizations to participate in the political process in accordance with their own responsibilities and roles.

6.   Christian responsibility in the area of human rights includes two complementary pastoral actions: the affirmation and promotion of human rights and the denunciation and condemnation of violations of these rights. In addition, it is the Church's role as a community of faith to call attention to the moral and religious dimension of secular issues, to keep alive the values of the gospel as a norm for social and political life, and to point out the demands of the Christian faith for

---

[1]*Human Rights and Reconciliation*, 1974 Synod of Bishops.
[2]*Redemptor Hominis*, 14.

a just transformation of society. Such a ministry on the part of every individual as well as the organizational Church inevitably involves political consequences and touches upon public affairs.

The Responsibility of All Members of the Church

7.   The Church's responsibility in this area falls on all its members. As citizens, we are all called to become informed, active, and responsible participants in the political process. It is the laity who are primarily responsible for activity in political affairs, for it is they who have the major responsibility for renewal of the temporal order. In the words of the Second Vatican Council:

> . . . the laity, by their very vocation, seek the kingdom of God by engaging in temporal affairs and by ordering them according to the plan of God. . . . They live in the ordinary circumstances of family and social life, from which the very web of their existence is woven.
> They are called there by God so that by exercising their proper function and being led by the spirit of the gospel, they can work for the sanctification of the world from within, in the manner of leaven.[3]

8.   The hierarchy also has a distinct and weighty responsibility in this area. As teachers and pastors, they must provide norms for the formation of conscience of the faithful, support efforts to gain greater peace and justice, and provide guidance and even leadership on occasions when human rights are in jeopardy. Drawing on their own experience and exercising their distinctive roles within the Christian community, bishops, clergy, religious, and laity should join together in common witness and effective action to bring about Pope John Paul II's vision of a well-ordered society based on truth, justice, charity, and freedom.[4]

The Distinct Role of the Church

9.   The Church's role in the political order includes the following:

- education regarding the teachings of the Church and the responsibilities of the faithful;
- analysis of issues for their social and moral dimensions;
- measuring public policy against gospel values;
- participating with other concerned parties in debate over public policy; and
- speaking out with courage, skill, and concern on public issues

---

[3]*Lumen Gentium*, 31.
[4]*Familiaris Consortio*.

involving human rights, social justice, and the life of the Church in society.

10. Unfortunately, our efforts in this area are sometimes misunderstood. The Church's participation in public affairs is not a threat to the political process or to genuine pluralism, but an affirmation of their importance. The Church recognizes the legitimate autonomy of government and the right of all, including the Church itself, to be heard in the formulation of public policy. As Vatican II declared:

> By preaching the truth of the gospel and shedding light on all areas of human activity through her teaching and the example of the faithful, she [the Church] shows respect for the political freedom and responsibility of citizens and fosters these values.
> . . . She also has the right to pass moral judgments, even on matters touching the political order, whenever basic personal rights or the salvation of souls make such judgments necessary.[5]

11. A proper understanding of the role of the Church will not confuse its mission with that of government but, rather, see its ministry as advocating the critical values of human rights and social justice.

12. It is the role of Christian communities to analyze the situation in their own country, to reflect upon the meaning of the gospel, and to draw norms of judgment and plans of action from the teaching of the Church and their own experience.[6] In carrying out this pastoral activity in the social arena, we are confronted with complexity. As the 1971 Synod of Bishops pointed out: "It does not belong to the Church, insofar as she is a religious and hierarchical community, to offer concrete solutions in the social, economic, and political spheres for justice in the world."[7] At the same time, it is essential to recall the words of Pope John XXIII: "It must not be forgotten that the Church has the right and duty not only to safeguard the principles of ethics and religion, but also to intervene authoritatively with her children in the temporal sphere when there is a question of judging the application of these principles to concrete cases."[8]

13. The application of gospel values to real situations is an essential work of the Christian community. Christians believe the gospel is the measure of human realities. However, specific political proposals do not in themselves constitute the gospel. Christians and Christian organizations must certainly participate in public debate over alternative policies and legislative proposals, yet it is critical that the nature of their participation not be misunderstood.

---

[5]*Gaudium et Spes*, 76.
[6]*A Call to Action*, 4.
[7]*Justice in the World*, 37. 1971 Synod of Bishops.
[8]*Pacem in Terris*, 160.

14. We bishops specifically do not seek the formation of a religious voting bloc; nor do we wish to instruct persons on how they should vote by endorsing or opposing candidates. We do, however, have a right and a responsibility as teachers to analyze the moral dimensions of the major issues of our day. We urge citizens to avoid choosing candidates simply on the basis of narrow self-interest. We hope that voters will examine the positions of candidates on the full range of issues, as well as their personal integrity, philosophy, and performance. We are convinced that a consistent ethic of life should be the moral framework from which we address all issues in the political arena. In this consistent ethic, we address a spectrum of issues, seeking to protect human life and promote human dignity from the inception of life to its final moment.

15. As bishops, we seek to promote a greater understanding of the important link between faith and politics and to express our belief that our nation is enriched when its citizens and social groups approach public affairs from positions grounded in moral conviction and religious belief. Our view is expressed very well by Pope John Paul II when he said: "Christians know from the Church's luminous teachings that without any need to follow a one-sided or partisan political formula, they ought to contribute to forming a more worthy society, one more respectful of the rights of man, based on the principles of justice and peace."[9]

16. As religious leaders and pastors, our intention is to reflect our concern that politics receive its rightful importance and attention and that it become an effective forum for the achievement of the common good. For, in the words of John Paul II, "[Humanity's] situation in the modern world seems indeed to be far removed from the objective demands of the moral order, from the requirements of justice, and even more of social love. . . . We have before us here a great drama that can leave nobody indifferent."[10]

III. Issues

17. Without reference to political candidates, parties, or platforms, we wish to offer a listing of some issues which we believe are important in the national debate during 1988. These brief summaries are not intended to indicate in any depth the details of our positions in these matters. We refer the reader to fuller discussions of our point of view in the documents listed in the summaries that appear below. We wish to point out that these issues are not the concerns of Catholics alone; in every case, we have joined with others to advocate these positions.

---

[9]Pope John Paul II, "Papal Address in Spain," *Origins* 11:29, pp. 389ff.
[10]Ibid., 16.

They represent a broad range of topics on which the bishops of the United States have already expressed themselves and are recalled here in alphabetical order to emphasize their relevance in a period of national debate and decision.

A. Abortion

18. The right to life is the most basic human right, and it demands the protection of law.

19. Abortion is the deliberate destruction of an unborn human being and therefore violates this right. We do not accept the concept that anyone has the right to choose an abortion. We reject the 1973 Supreme Court decisions on abortion, which refuse appropriate legal protection to the unborn child. We support the passage of a constitutional amendment to restore the basic constitutional protection of the right to life of the unborn child. We reject the public funding of abortion. (*Documentation on the Right to Life and Abortion*, 1974, 1976, 1981; *Pastoral Plan for Pro-Life Activities: A Reaffirmation*, 1985.)

B. Arms Control and Disarmament

20. The pastoral letter *The Challenge of Peace: God's Promise and Our Response* (1983) gave "strictly conditional moral acceptance" to the policy of nuclear deterrence. The strict conditions include: (1) a condemnation of counter-city or counter-population uses of nuclear weapons; (2) support for a policy of "no first-use" of nuclear weapons; and (3) an endorsement of a series of arms control measures. The arms control provisions included support for a comprehensive test-ban treaty, support for ratification of the Threshold Test-Ban Treaty and the Treaty on Nuclear Explosions for Peaceful Purposes, and support for specific initiatives which the United States could take to restrain the quantitative and qualitative developments of the arms race. (*The Challenge of Peace*, 1983.)

C. Capital Punishment

21. In view of our commitment to the value and dignity of human life, we oppose the use of capital punishment. We believe that a return to the use of the death penalty is leading to—indeed, can only lead to—further erosion of respect for life in our society. We do not question society's right to punish the offender, but we believe that there are better approaches to protecting our people from violent crimes than resorting to executions. In its application, the death penalty has been discriminatory toward the poor, the indigent, and racial minorities. Our society should reject the death penalty and seek methods of dealing with violent crime that are more consistent with the gospel vision of respect for life and Christ's message of healing love. (*Community and Crime*, Statement of Bishops' Committee on Social Development and World Peace, 1978; U.S. Bishops' *Statement on Capital Punishment*, 1980.)

D. Civil Rights

22. Discrimination based on sex, race, ethnicity, or age continues to exist in our nation. Such discrimination constitutes a grave injustice and an affront to human dignity. It must be aggressively resisted by every individual and rooted out of every social institution and structure.

23. Racism is a particularly serious form of discrimination. Despite significant strides in eliminating racial prejudices in our country, there remains an urgent need for continued reconciliation in this area. Racism is not merely one sin among many; it is a radical evil dividing the human family. The struggle against it demands an equally radical transformation in our own minds and hearts as well as in the structures of our society. (*Brothers and Sisters to Us: U.S. Bishops' Pastoral Letter on Racism in Our Day*, 1979; *The Hispanic Presence: Challenge and Commitment*, 1983.)

E. The Economy

24. The pastoral letter *Economic Justice for All* presents the basic moral principles that should guide economic life. For example:

- Every economic decision and institution should be judged in light of whether it protects or undermines the dignity of the human person. The economy must be at the service of all people, especially the poor.
- Human dignity can be realized and protected only in community.
- Human rights are the minimum conditions for life in community. All people have a right to life, food, clothing, shelter, rest, medical care, education, and employment. Society as a whole, acting through private and government institutions, has the moral responsibility to enhance human dignity and protect human rights.

25. The most urgent priority for domestic economic policy is to create jobs with adequate pay and decent working conditions. High levels of unemployment and underemployment are morally unacceptable in a nation with our economic capacity. The minimum wage, which has not been adjusted since 1981, should be raised. We reaffirm the

Church's traditional teaching in support of the right of all workers to organize and bargain collectively.

26. The fact that so many people are poor in a nation as wealthy as ours is a social and moral scandal that must not be ignored. Dealing with poverty is not a luxury to which our nation can attend when it finds the time and resources. Rather, it is a moral imperative of the highest priority.

27. In view of the increasing importance of U.S. international economic relations, especially relations within the developing countries, it is essential that all aspects of international economic policy—trade, aid, finance, investment—reflect basic moral principles. America's role in the international economy must be reevaluated and concern for the poor made a policy priority. We have a moral obligation to take the lead in helping to reduce poverty in the Third World. (*Economic Justice for All: Pastoral Letter on Catholic Social Teaching and the U.S. Economy*, 1986.)

F. Education

28. All persons of whatever race, sex, condition, or age, by virtue of their dignity as human beings, have an inalienable right to education. We advocate:

- sufficient public and private funding to make an adequate education available for all citizens and residents of the United States of America and to provide assistance for education in our nation's program of foreign aid;
- governmental and voluntary action to reduce inequalities of educational opportunity by improving the opportunities available to economically disadvantaged persons;
- orderly compliance with legal requirements for racially integrated schools;
- voluntary efforts to increase racial and ethnic integration in public and nonpublic schools; and
- equitable tax support for the education of pupils in public and nonpublic schools to implement parental freedom in the education of their children.

(*To Teach as Jesus Did*, A Pastoral Message on Catholic Education, 1972; *Sharing the Light of Faith: National Catechetical Directory for Catholics of the United States*, 1979.)

G. Family Life

29. The well-being of society is intimately linked to the health and vitality of family life. The family is the most basic unit of social organ-

ization and is instrumental in humanizing and personalizing society. This nation's institutions, laws, and policies must support and positively defend the rights and duties of the family. All programs, policies, and services must be evaluated in light of their impact on the life and stability of the family. (*Character of the Rights of the Family*, presented by the Holy See, 1983; *Plan of Pastoral Action for Family Ministry*; and *Familiaris Consortio*, Apostolic Exhortation of Pope John Paul II, 1981.)

H. Food and Agricultural Policy

30. The right to eat flows directly from the right to life. We support a national policy aimed at securing the right to eat for all the world's people. This policy is promoted through our policies on agricultural production and domestic and international food assistance.

31. The United States, through its income support programs, its credit and research programs, its tax and trade policies, it strategies for rural development, and its foreign aid, should support the maintenance of an agricultural system based on small- and moderate-sized family farms both at home and abroad. The preservation and conservation of our natural resource base should also be a key element of U.S. national agricultural policy.

32. We support legislation to protect the rights of farm workers, and we call for measures to improve the working conditions and the general welfare of farm-worker families.

33. Domestically, nutrition programs should help meet the needs of hungry and malnourished Americans, especially children, the poor, the unemployed, and the elderly. It is essential that the food stamp program, the school lunch and child nutrition programs be funded at adequate levels.

34. Internationally, U.S. food aid should be given to the poorest countries and neediest people without regard to political considerations, principally in emergency situations to combat global hunger and malnutrition. Development assistance should emphasize equitable distribution of benefits and help other nations move toward food self-reliance. (*Food Policy and the Church: Specific Proposals*, Statement of the USCC Administrative Board, 1975; *Economic Justice for All*, 1986.)

I. Health

35. Adequate health care is a basic human right. Access to appropriate health care must be guaranteed for all people without regard to economic, social, or legal status. Special efforts should be made to remove barriers to prompt personalized and comprehensive care for the poor.

36. Government also has a responsibility to remove or alleviate environmental, social, and economic conditions that cause much ill health and suffering for its citizens. Greater emphasis is required on programs of health promotion and disease prevention.

37. We support the adoption of a national health insurance program as the best means of ensuring access to high quality health care for all. Until a comprehensive and universal program can be enacted, we urge the following:

- requiring employers to provide a minimum health insurance benefit to employees;
- strengthening existing programs for the poor, the elderly, and disabled people;
- expanding Medicaid coverage to all people with poverty level incomes; and
- special aid to hospitals that provide disproportionate amounts of charity care to the poor.

(*Health and Health Care: A Pastoral Letter to the American Catholic Bishops*, 1981.)

J. Housing

38. Decent housing is a basic human right. A greater commitment of will and resources is required to meet our national housing goal of a decent home for every American family. To meet this housing need, the government must continue to fund adequately housing assistance programs that will assist people to obtain affordable housing. Continuation of housing production and preservation programs is vital to maintaining the stock of affordable housing. Housing policy must better meet the needs of low- and middle-income families, the elderly, rural families, and minorities. It should also promote reinvestment in central cities and equal housing opportunity. Preservation of existing housing stock and a renewed concern for neighborhoods are required. (*The Right to a Decent Home: A Pastoral Response to the Crisis in Housing*, 1975.)

K. Human Rights

39. Human dignity requires the defense and promotion of human rights in global and domestic affairs. With respect to international human rights, there is a pressing need for the United States to pursue a double task: (1) to strengthen and expand international mechanisms by which human rights can be protected and promoted; and (2) to take seriously the human rights dimensions of U.S. foreign policy. Therefore, we support U.S. ratification of the International Covenants on Civil and Political Rights and on Economic, Social, and Cultural Rights. Further, we support a policy that gives greater weight to the

protection of human rights in the conduct of U.S. affairs. The pervasive presence of U.S. power creates a responsibility to use that power in the service of human rights. (*U.S. Foreign Policy: A Critique from Catholic Tradition*, Congressional Testimony, January 1976.)

L. Immigration and Refugee Policy

40. A number of unresolved issues remain in the immigration policy area. They include the fate of the residual population of undocumented aliens who did not qualify under the ongoing legalization program and the matter of indiscriminate firings and discrimination in hiring decisions resulting from employer sanctions. Another area of fundamental concern is improving the working and living conditions for all workers in the migrant-labor stream and discouraging agricultural employers from continuing to rely on temporary foreign agricultural labor.

41. A third area of concern is the maintenance of the principle that has governed legal immigration to the United States for most of this century. That principle is rooted in the concept of family reunification and recognizes that legal immigration is a source of cultural, social, and economic enrichment for the United States. A fourth area of concern is refugees. The 1980 Refugee Act considered 50,000 refugees as the "normal flow." As we are approaching this figure, we must not forget that "special humanitarian concern" implies a spirit of generosity belied by the constantly contracting size of refugee admissions to the United States. Our final concern is about people who are in temporary need of special consideration. A safe-haven policy would meet the immediate needs of foreign nationals stranded here or fleeing to the United States from countries beset by civil strife, war, or natural calamity. (Bishops' *Resolution* of November 1985; *Policy Statements* by the USCC General Secretary and *Testimony* on behalf of the USCC on all of the above concerns.)

M. Mass Media

42. The philosophy of marketplace economics, as applied to telecommunications industries during the past decade, has led to the relaxation or elimination of policies that protect the public's access to modern means of sending and receiving messages and exchanging ideas. We are concerned that these changes are adversely affecting the free flow of information required in a democratic society and increasing the gap between the information rich and information poor in our society and the world. We urge legislative initiatives in the Congress which restore the public accountability of broadcasters, cable operators, and others who use the public resource of the airwaves. Specifically, we support passage of legislation to require broadcasters to cover controversial issues and to provide balance in such discussions (the Federal Communications Commission policy known as the Fairness Doctrine); to prohibit the rapid buying and selling of broadcast stations (which amounts to speculating in a public resource); and to require the Federal Communications Commission to hold broadcast licensees strictly accountable under the public interest standard.

43. We support the concept of universal and affordable telephone service for all Americans and the provision of so-called lifelines or subsidized telephone rates for the poor.

44. We support reasonable and constitutionally acceptable regulations to limit the distribution of indecent, pornographic, or sexually explicit materials through the electronic media, including the telephone, so that they are not accessible to minors.

45. We oppose advertisements or public service announcements concerning contraceptives, since such presentations infringe on the right of parents to teach their children about responsible sexuality. (*Statements* and *Testimony* by the USCC Department of Communication before the Congress and the Federal Communications Commission.)

N. Regional Conflict in the World

46. Three situations of regional conflict that are of significance for the whole international system, and where U.S. policy has a substantial, indeed a decisive influence, are Central America, the Middle East, and Southern Africa.

47. Central America has for some time been the most visible focus of our attention to regional conflicts. Our position concerning the indigenous roots of the conflicts, the imperative need for fundamental social change, the futility and immorality of proposed military solutions has been stated often and is well known. As the dominant external actor, our government should join with our hemispheric allies to advance realistic proposals of dialogue, leading to negotiated settlements and guaranteed processes of political and social reform. Direct military intervention by any outside power, including the United States, and military aid to irregular forces in the area cannot be justified under any foreseeable circumstances. Substantial and sustained levels of U.S. economic assistance to the region, rigidly monitored to assure maximum benefit to the people, especially the poorest, should replace the excessively high levels of military assistance. We express continued concern over the militarization of the region; the still present danger of a more generalized conflict; the violations of human rights; the inadequate judicial systems; and the wrenching tragedy of countless refugees and displaced persons. We urge special consideration by our government for all Central American refugees living here who have fled the violence of their homelands. (USCC *Testimony* on Central America, 1983, 1984, and 1985.)

48. In the Middle East, the quest for peace continues and the relevant parties bear distinct yet interdependent responsibilities. First, the international community, especially its principal diplomatic actors, inevitably influences the future of the Middle East. Second, the United Nations is a vital element in any Middle East negotiations, and its diplomatic and peacekeeping role will undoubtedly be crucial to a long-term resolution of the conflict. Third, the regional parties, whose conflicting claims of justice are the essence of the political and moral problem in the Middle East, are the key to peace. Finally, the religious communities with roots in the Middle East must reflect the best of our traditions in supporting the movement for peace with justice for all the people of the region. We have a continuing concern for the protection of the basic rights, both civil and religious, of the Christian minorities in the Middle East, and we encourage the local churches there to continue their steadfast witness to the faith. (*Statement on the Middle East: The Pursuit of Peace with Justice*, NCCB, 1978.)

49. The position of South Africa has long been of grave moral concern to the world because of its internal racial policies and its occupation of Namibia/South West Africa. In recent years, it has become a threat to the entire area of Southern Africa because of its military incursions into the territories of several of its neighbors and its effort to destabilize them by economic pressure and the support of guerrilla movements.

50. The bishops of South Africa and many others have repeatedly pointed out the path to justice and peace. U.S. foreign policy, corporate activity, and even private initiatives can influence what happens inside that country and South Africa's relations with neighboring states. (*Statement on South Africa*, USCC Administrative Board, September 11, 1985; and *Divestment, Disinvestment, and South Africa: A Policy Statement*, USCC Administrative Board, September 10, 1986.)

51. This is not an exclusive listing of the issues that concern us. As Pope John Paul II has said, "The Church cannot remain insensible to whatever serves true human welfare any more than she can remain indifferent to whatever threatens it. . . ."[11] Thus, we are advocates on many other social justice concerns such as welfare reform, the civil and political rights of the elderly and the handicapped, the reform of our criminal justice system, and the protection of the land and the environment. We are also concerned about the growing crisis of AIDS and the need for compassionate and effective policies in dealing with this serious disease.

---

[11] *Redemptor Hominis*, 13.

IV. Conclusion

52. In summary, we believe that the Church has a proper role and responsibility in public affairs flowing from its gospel mandate and its respect for the dignity of the human person. We hope these reflections will contribute to a renewed political vitality in our land, both in terms of citizen participation in the electoral process and the integrity and accountability of those who seek and hold public office.

53. We urge all citizens to use their franchise by registering to vote and going to the polls. We encourage them to demand information from the campaigns themselves as well as from the media coverage of those campaigns and to take stands on the candidates and the issues. If the campaign year is to engage the values of the American people, the campaigners and voters alike must share the responsibility for making it happen. All are urged to become involved in the campaign or party of their choice, to learn about the issues, and to inform their conscience.

54. We pray that Christians will provide courageous leadership in promoting a spirit of responsible political involvement. May they follow the example of Jesus in giving special concern for the poor, and may all their actions be guided by a deep love of God and neighbor.

Value and Virtue
Moral Education in the Public School

A Statement Issued by the
Administrative Board of the
United States Catholic Conference

September 1987

1. Children and young people are the future of our country, our civilization, and our world. They eventually will be responsible for the home, the church, the state, and the world at large. However, before entrusting our institutions and world to them, we must encourage in them a basic value system whereby they will respect, cherish, and care for themselves and other creatures. We need to help the young to develop into generous men and women of high and noble ideals.

2. High expectations challenge us, as adults, to provide the best for all youth as we call forth the best in them. This is no easy task. Children and young people experience difficulties as they pursue maturity and responsibility. The tragedies of teenage suicide, teenage pregnancy, teenage alcohol and drug abuse are but some of the signs of their struggle to mature. These troubling signs are often rooted more deeply in the sense of aimlessness and hopelessness that leads our youth to choose such negative options, options that divest them personally, and all of us, of their potential contributions.

3. We, as bishops, have a responsibility to provide guidance for the members of our own Church as they seek to form their consciences in making moral choices. We, as American citizens concerned for children and young people, would like to add our voice to the public debate on the issue of moral education in the pubilc schools of this nation. We do not wish to impose a religious viewpoint on our fellow citizens, but we do wish to provide our reasoned reflection on what we perceive to be a national concern. We are thoroughly convinced that it is through shared human reasoning that we can arrive at a common understanding of what is most promising for children and young people of this nation.

4. In our pastoral letter on the economy, we acknowledged that "sustaining a common culture and a common commitment to moral virtues is not easy in our world." The fact that it is not easy does not mean that it is impossible.

5. We state our belief, as Father John Courtney Murray wrote some years ago: "Pluralism . . . implies disagreement and dissension within the community. But it also implies a community within which there must be agreement and consensus."

6.   We were reminded of this during the recent centennial celebration of the Statue of Liberty. We were inspired by the bestowal of citizenship on "[the] tired, [the] poor, [the] masses yearning to breathe free" from different races, creeds, and nationalities. Their acceptance of our invitation and their presence among us have broadened the pluralism within our country. Their oath of citizenship demonstrates the ongoing ability of men and women to accept the shared vision that undergirds this nation—found in such documents as the Declaration of Independence, the Constitution, and the Bill of Rights. An explicit shared public moral vision within our schools is also possible.

7.   Four important and basic institutions have traditionally had a great impact on the total education of children and young people: the family, the church, the school, and the government. Historically, moral education has long had an honored place in the public schools of the United States. But, in recent years, the public philosophy, the shared moral vision that binds us together as a people, diverse yet one, has been significantly diluted and this development has adversely affected moral education in the public schools. Consequently, to the extent that there is a problem with moral education in the United States today, it fuels the "values problem" in the public schools.

8.   A decline of our public philosophy has provided for a lively discussion—which we genuinely welcome—concerning moral education for children and young people in the public schools. This discussion has sometimes been marred by conflict, the questioning of motives, and dire warnings on all sides. We affirm a need in our nation for the present debate. We support efforts to find proper means of teaching moral values and truth in the public schools, and we do this as expressions both of our concern for the children and young people served by the public schools and for the future of our country.

9.   Therefore, we would like to affirm the following points as part of the national discussion:

a) We maintain that a renewed shared moral vision within the public schools is possible. It must be grounded in the common bond of humanity that links people of every race, creed, and color. This country was established out of the respect and desire for human dignity. It remains for us today to spell out anew the ingredients of that shared humanity for our children and young people.

b) We maintain that schooling is an essential and unique part of the education process. Schools should enable the human person to become the best possible person, which necessarily includes being an authentically moral person. Anything less is to be satisfied with good technicians who cannot intelligently and reasonably deal with moral issues in their personal or societal lives.

c) We hold that the values, virtues, moral ideals, and truth of our heritage should be infused into the curriculum like threads woven into a fabric. Explicit and authentic education in critical moral thinking is necessary for quality education.

d) We regard teachers as transmitters of our cultural legacy and heritage. We strongly encourage teachers to be aware of themselves as models for the young in the pursuit of moral excellence. We also encourage them to lead the way in helping the public realize that schooling without moral education is poor schooling.

e) We maintain that students must be made aware of the moral impact they exert on one another in the course of their school time together. Peer pressure among students need not be solely for ill, but can be a great support in the pursuit of moral excellence.

f) We maintain that school communities as a whole must see themselves as moral communities that involve students, parents, teachers, administrators, and support staff.

10. We are encouraged in our concern for public schooling by the recent phenomenon of the school reform movement. Initiatives have engaged a broad spectrum of the community at the local, state, and national levels.

11. We call upon those responsible for schooling at the local, state, and national levels to convene the administrators, teachers, parents, and citizenry to address the moral needs of children and young people. On our part, we pledge our support and involvement. The Catholic community at the national, diocesan, and parish levels should enter into dialogue with their brothers and sisters across this land to address the national concern in a spirit that preserves everyone's integrity and dignity, while renewing a national moral vision.

12. Finally, we express our gratitude to those educators and parents who are already working conscientiously to provide children and young people with a solid grounding in moral values. We likewise express appreciation to the educators, parents, and many others who are parties to the present national discussion about moral education in public schools.

13. All groups in society, including public officials and legislators, have a stake in this discussion and a right and responsibility to contribute to it. The discussion, futhermore, should be carried on in a spirit and manner that express co-responsibility, cooperation, and a commitment to the common good. Ideological partisanship and unwillingness to hear what others are saying have no part here.

14. The goal is distinctly practical: to define and implement a form of moral education, integrated into the total curriculum, that corresponds to student needs and community consensus. Such a goal enriches the individual student and the nation.

The Many Faces of AIDS
A Gospel Response

A Statement Issued by the
Administrative Board of the
United States Catholic Conference

November 14, 1987

Introduction

Dear Sisters and Brothers in the Lord, and All People of Good Will:

1. In the life of society, as in the lives of individuals, there are events of significance and moments of decision. Today our society is experiencing a significant event and a decisive moment: the ominous presence of the disease known as AIDS (Acquired Immunodeficiency Syndrome).

2. Whether this infection exists as an unrecognized HIV virus in a pregnant woman or in a small child; whether it weakens the body of a person with ARC (AIDS-Related Complex); or whether it comes as the likelihood of a more imminent death from the disease itself, AIDS is a reality that we all must face.

3. The Church confronts in this disease a significant pastoral issue. The etiology of this deadly epidemic, its prevention, and the care of those stricken present society with serious moral decisions. How are we to relate to those who have been exposed to the virus or to those who have the disease? What are our responsibilities as members of the Church and society with regard to their care and support? What can and ought we to do in order to prevent the further spread of the disease? How we make these choices with their moral implications will affect both the present generation and, most likely, future ones as well.

4. In order to help make these and similar choices, we have decided to issue this statement, *The Many Faces of AIDS: A Gospel Response*. We invite you to read it with care and attend to its recommendations.

5. Our reflections may be summarized in this way:

- As with all other diseases, AIDS is a human illness to which we must respond in a manner consistent with the best medical and scientific information available.
- As members of the Church and society, we have a responsibility to stand in solidarity with and reach out with compassion and understanding to those exposed to or experiencing this disease.

We must provide spiritual and pastoral care as well as medical and social services for them and support for their families and friends.

- As members of the Church, we must offer a clear presentation of Catholic moral teaching with respect to human intimacy and sexuality.
- Discrimination or violence directed against persons with AIDS is unjust and immoral.
- As a society, we must develop educational and other programs to prevent the spread of the disease. Such programs should include an authentic understanding of human intimacy and sexuality as well as an understanding of the pluralism of values and attitudes in our society.
- Those who have been exposed to the virus are expected to live in a way that does not bring injury or potential harm to others.

6.   Faithful to the Lord's gospel and to the best of our American heritage, we are confident that our society will make wise decisions as, together, we face this significant moment.

The Many Faces of AIDS
A Gospel Response[1]

7.   One of the distinctive aspects of Jesus' ministry was the manner in which he took the common and not so common events of human life and revealed a meaning or a potentiality that most, if not all, of his contemporaries had not discovered: that human love is revelatory of divine love, that death can disclose the possibility of new life. The challenge facing today's followers of the risen Lord is to do the same with contemporary experiences, whether of joy or sorrow, to discover the deeper meaning that might otherwise remain hidden.

8.   One such experience is the presence of AIDS in our country and other parts of the world. During the last few years, as bishops, we have encountered persons with AIDS in our pastoral ministry. We would like to share some of "the many faces of AIDS" that we have met.

9.   Mary and Phil are in their mid-thirties. Both are successful career professionals. After many years of searching, they found each other and are very much in love. They were married three years ago and

---

[1]AIDS is an acronym for "Acquired Immunodeficiency Syndrome." According to current medical information, the source of the disease is a retrovirus that, in this statement, will be referred to as the HIV virus or the AIDS virus. Currently, only about 10 to 15 percent of those infected with the virus meet the AIDS case definition established by the Centers for Disease Control. In this statement, we include those who have the syndrome itself, those who have ARC (AIDS-Related Complex), and those infected by the AIDS virus.

are eager to have a child. Mary's friend, who is about to have major surgery, has asked her to donate blood. In keeping with today's blood bank policies and practices, Mary's blood has been tested for exposure to AIDS. The results are positive; she has been infected with the AIDS virus from a previous partner. She feels as if her life has been brought to a sudden, tragic end.

10. John is a young man who was raised in the inner city by a loving single-parent mother. Despite his mother's best efforts, he found his environment to be like a prison and sought escape by turning to drugs. Now after six months of intermittent illness, he has been admitted to a public hospital. The diagnosis is AIDS. He feels as if he has been victimized from the beginning by forces beyond his control.

11. Peter is in his late-twenties and successful in his career. His life journey to this point has not always been easy. He has been aware of his homosexual orientation since his teens, but the reactions of others to this have often left him feeling alone or rejected. Over the years, he has been sexually active, and recently, when his employer discovered that Peter has AIDS, he was fired. He feels frightened and angry as he tries to live without medical insurance.

12. Lilly is fifteen months old. Her mother, a drug addict, was exposed to the AIDS virus before Lilly's conception, and Lilly was born with AIDS. Her mother abandoned her. Because few will adopt a child with AIDS, Lilly is being cared for in a public hospital. She will know no other home, for it is expected that she will die soon.

13. What does the gospel tell us about these representatives faces of AIDS?[2]

14. First, Jesus has revealed to us that God is compassionate, not vengeful. Made in God's image and likeness, every human person is of inestimable worth. All human life is sacred, and its dignity must be respected and protected. The teaching of Jesus about human sexuality and the moral norms taught by the Church are not arbitrary impositions on human life but disclosures of its depth.

15. Second, the gospel acknowledges that disease and suffering are not restricted to one group or social class. Rather, the mystery of the human condition is such that, in one way or another, all will face pain, reversal, and, ultimately, the mystery of death itself. Seen through the eyes of faith, however, this mystery is not closed in upon itself. Through sharing in the cross of Christ, human suffering and pain have a redemptive meaning and goal. They have the potential of opening a person to new life. They also present an opportunity and a challenge to all, calling us to respond to suffering just as Jesus did — with love and care.

---

[2]Many diocesan bishops have issued statements about AIDS as well as guidelines in regard to the employment and education of persons with AIDS. These contributed greatly to the development of this statement.

16. Third, while preaching a gospel of compassion and conversion, Jesus also proclaimed to those most in need the good news of forgiveness. The father in the parable of the prodigal son did not wait for his son to come to him. Rather, he took the initiative and ran out to his son with generosity, forgiveness, and compassion. This spirit of forgiveness Jesus handed on to his followers.

17. For Christians, then, stories, of persons with AIDS must not become occasions for stereotyping or prejudice, for anger or recrimination, for rejection or isolation, for injustice or condemnation. They provide us with an opportunity to walk with those who are suffering, to be compassionate toward those whom we might otherwise fear, to bring strength and courage both to those who face the prospect of dying as well as to their loved ones.

18. In this gospel perspective, we address this statement to our sisters and brothers in the Roman Catholic community of faith and to all people of good will in our society. We speak as pastors who strive to be faithful to the gospel and the Church's teaching. We also speak as representatives of a religious tradition in a pluralistic society as, together with all persons of good will, we face the new and distinctive challenge of AIDS.

19. Our reflections are threefold. First, we present some facts about AIDS and comment on what they say to us. Then we address issues associated with the prevention of the disease. Finally, we explore appropriate care for persons with AIDS. At various points throughout this statement, we indicate the responsibilities and obligations of all the members of the Church and society. In an Appendix, we address certain significant related questions. All that we say in this statement is not intended to be the last word on AIDS, but rather our contribution to the current dialogue.

The Facts about AIDS and a Commentary

20. The AIDS phenomenon is complex. We do not intend to review all of the pertinent facts. The Surgeon General of the United States and others have provided careful analyses of the causes of AIDS, the ways in which it is transmitted, and the various dangers or risks of contracting the disease. Some of those facts are simply highlighted here.

- At the present time, AIDS is an incurable disease. Not restricted to the United States, it is found throughout the world. Currently, two-thirds of the persons afflicted with AIDS in the United States are homosexual or bisexual men. Some estimate that the number of heterosexual persons with AIDS will increase significantly in the next five years. At present, nearly one out of four persons with AIDS is a drug user who used contaminated intravenous needles or other drug paraphernalia infected with the AIDS virus. Four hundred and twenty-three hemophiliacs and people with blood-coagulating disorders and two thousand nine hundred and fifty-five women have been diagnosed as having AIDS.[3]

- AIDS is a disease that cuts across all racial and ethnic lines.[4]
- AIDS is not merely an "adult disease" in the United States. As of October 12, 1987, five hundred and ninety-five children have been reported as having contracted the disease.
- At this time, after extensive research, there is no evidence that AIDS can be contracted through ordinary, casual contact.[5]
- AIDS can be contracted through certain forms of intimate sexual contact and encounters with tainted blood. It can also be transmitted from a mother to her child during pregnancy as well as through artificial insemination and by organ transplants.

AIDS, in other words, is a human disease whose spread, according to the best available scientific knowledge, is limited to identifiable modes of communication and contact.

21. Because reasonable actions and attitudes are based on facts, not fiction, we mention these facts as a background for some important observations about the AIDS phenomenon. They also apply to those suffering from ARC (AIDS-Related Complex).

22. First, while it is understandable that there is fear and uncertainty about a disease as new and deadly as AIDS, we encourage all members of our society to relate to its victims with compassion and understanding, as they would to those suffering from any other fatal disease.

23. Second, we are alarmed by the increase of negative attitudes as well as acts of violence directed against gay and lesbian people since AIDS has become a national issue. We strongly condemn such vio-

---

[3]The statistics about this disease are continually updated. This statement relies on the most recent figures issued by the Centers for Disease Control on October 12, 1987.

[4]One of the most sensitive issues faced in the preparation of this statement is the fact that disproportionate numbers of blacks and Hispanics have been infected by the AIDS virus. Raising this issue could be perceived as motivated by racism, which is contrary to the very gospel spirit that informs this statement. On the other hand, to ignore the pertinent statistics could contribute to the spread of the disease among some of the most vulnerable and marginalized members of our society. For example, current statistics issued by the Centers for Disease Control on October 12, 1987, indicate that 25% of people with AIDS are black, while blacks constitute 12% of the United States population. Similarly, 14% are classified as Hispanic, while those who are considered to be Hispanic are 7.9% of our population. Recently, programs have been developed within the black and Hispanic communities to educate their members about the danger of AIDS. Programs such as these might be the most appropriate way to begin addressing this complex situation.

[5]*AIDS: Information/Education Plan to Prevent and Control AIDS in the United States*, U.S. Department of Health and Human Services (March 1987), p. 9.

lence. Those who are gay or lesbian or suffering from AIDS should not be the objects of discrimination, injustice, or violence. All of God's sons and daughters, all members of our society, are entitled to the recognition of their full human dignity.

24. Third, because there is presently no positive or sound medical justification for the indiscriminate quarantining of persons infected with the AIDS virus, we oppose the enactment of quarantine legislation or other laws that are not supported by medical data or informed by the expertise of those in the health-care or public-health professions. The best of our civic heritage of extreme caution and restraint in restricting human and civil rights should be the norm in this situation, as in all others. We urge legislators to act judiciously rather than to react out of a sense of hysteria or latent prejudice. Especially acute is the problem of health insurance. We decry the exclusion of certain groups of persons from health insurance coverage. At the same time, we recognize the problems faced by the insurance industry as well as those who pay premiums because of the cost of treatment. This exemplifies the weakness of our health-care delivery system. This problem must be addressed in a way that will provide adequate and accessible health care for all.

25. Fourth, we oppose the use of the HIV antibody test for strictly discriminatory purposes. However, if safeguards are provided to prevent such discrimination and to maintain the needed degree of confidentiality, such tests may play an important role in basing patient care on facts rather than fear or stereotypes. Testing for the AIDS virus, with appropriate counseling beforehand and afterwards, should be readily available to all who request it. Those who undergo such testing and receive a negative report can be reassured and educated on risk factors for contracting the virus. Those who receive a positive test result can be promptly offered counseling and care. There may be sound public health reasons for recommending the use of the HIV antibody test in certain situations, either because some persons have a heightened risk of becoming infected or because precautions may have to be taken by others (e.g., prospective spouses, hospital staffs) if the test results are positive. Nevertheless, we agree with many public-health authorities who question the appropriateness and effectiveness of more sweeping proposals, such as widespread mandatory testing.

26. Fifth, we are greatly concerned that some in the health-care professions or working in health-care institutions refuse to provide medical or dental care for persons exposed to the AIDS virus or presumed to be "at risk." We call upon all in the health-care and support professions to be mindful of their general moral obligation, while following accepted medical standards and procedures, to provide care for all persons, including those exposed to the AIDS virus. Similarly, although funeral directors may find it necessary to take appropriate precautions, they are not justified in refusing to accept or prepare for burial the bodies of deceased persons with AIDS. Nor are they justified in unnecessarily charging more for the funerals of persons with AIDS.

27. Sixth, to the extent possible, persons with AIDS should be encouraged to continue to lead productive lives in their community and place of work. They also have the right to decent housing, and landlords are not justified in denying them this right merely because of their illness.

28. Seventh, we support collaborative efforts by governmental bodies, health providers, and human service agencies to provide adequate funding and care for persons with AIDS. We also encourage the development of hospice-like programs that will afford persons with AIDS dignified and effective care and treatment. We call for the development of programs to care for infants and children with AIDS, especially those facing life and death without parental care.

29. Eighth, because of the virtually epidemic proportions of AIDS, we acknowledge the need for cooperative efforts by private and public entities to discover ways to treat and cure this disease and to commit adequate funding for basic research, applied research, and general education.

30. Ninth, we call on the federal government to provide additional funding for the care of those infected with the HIV virus who do not have health insurance as well as expanded income support for those impoverished by illness related to the AIDS virus. We also ask the federal government to take the lead in funding the necessary research and educational efforts as well as ensuring protection for those exposed to the AIDS virus against discrimination in insurance, employment, health care, education, and housing. The federal government should also provide funding for voluntary testing and ensure the confidentiality of such testing.

31. Tenth, current programs and services need to be expanded to assist the families of those with AIDS while they are alive and also to support them in their bereavement. In addition, new programs, services, and support systems need to be developed to deal with unmet and poorly met needs. To accomplish this, parishes and Catholic health-care providers and agencies are encouraged to collaborate with others to ensure that there is continuity of health care and pastoral services to families and persons with AIDS in response to the unique set of psychological, social, and spiritual issues that may arise during the illness.

32. Eleventh, hospitals, because of their responsibility to care for the sick, and Catholic hospitals, because of their special mission and philosophy, have a unique call and role in caring for persons with AIDS. Hospitals have the responsibility and obligation to ensure that persons with AIDS and their families are cared for compassionately. Hospital personnel and church personnel also ought to go beyond

their institutions to become facilitators, advocates, educators, and conveners to ensure that currently unmet and poorly met needs will be addressed in their communities by collaboration and networking with others in developing programs, services, and funding.

33. Twelfth, as a society, we need effective educational media programs to help reduce fear, prejudice, and discrimination against persons with AIDS, ARC, antibody-positive persons, and those perceived to be in high-risk groups.

The Prevention of AIDS

34. Within the health care professions, it is customary to make a distinction between the prevention of a disease and its treatment. While treatment is a response after the disease has been contracted, prevention strives to eliminate the conditions and circumstances that give rise to the disease. Because the prospects for the treatment of AIDS have been so dismal, emphasis — and hope — has focused more on its prevention, and this is where the greatest controversy has emerged.

35. These are sensitive issues. In a brief statement like this, we cannot apply the Church's teaching to all possible human behavior. Instead, in accord with the Church's traditional wisdom and moral teaching, we will offer some general principles and concrete guidelines. We speak to an entire nation whose pluralism we recognize and respect.

36. These observations come from our profound care for those who place themselves or might be placed in danger of contracting AIDS: intravenous drug users and their partners; children born and unborn; and persons involved in sexual contact that is physically dangerous or morally wrong. In other words, the primary concern of our observations is people's moral and physical well-being, not their condemnation, however much we might disagree with their actions.

37. Consistent with the insights and values found in the Scriptures, our religious tradition, and a philosophy of the human person that is consonant with both, we believe that the best source of prevention for individuals and society can only come from an authentic and fully integrated understanding of human personhood and sexuality, and from efforts to address and eliminate the causes of intravenous drug abuse. We are convinced that the only measures that will effectively prevent this disease at present are those designed to educate and to change behavior.

38. We view the human person as one reality with several dimensions: truly to be human means to be open to the world of the spiritual, the world of meaning and truth. Nonetheless, one's participation in the spiritual dimension of life can be inhibited by such social realities as

poverty and oppression, by loneliness and alienation, and by other such social and psychological factors.

39. If, then, we are to address the prevention of AIDS in an effective way, we must deal with those human and societal factors that reduce or limit the quality of human life. When people think their lives devoid of meaning, or when they find themselves in oppressive and despair-inducing poverty, they may turn to drugs or reach out for short-term physical intimacy in a mindless effort to escape the harsh conditions in which they live.

40. The Church and society need to address these realities. We have a responsibility first of all to help people realize that, whatever their circumstances, God's gift of life is precious, and there is more to life than its sometimes depressing or superficial dimensions. We must also attend to issues of economic well-being, as we did in our pastoral letter *Economic Justice for All*. The pastoral demonstrates, at length, poverty's impact upon people's lives. It also emphasizes our obligation to win respect for the true meaning of life as we seek to eradicate those things that debase the quality of life.

41. Second, in our society, we must offer everyone a fully integrated understanding of human sexuality. Every person, made in God's image and likeness, has both the potential and the desire to experience interpersonal intimacy that reflects the intimacy of God's triune love. This reflection in human love of the divine love gives special meaning and purpose to human sexuality. Human sexuality is essentially related to permanent commitment in love and openness to new life. It is most fully realized when it is expressed in a manner that is as loving, faithful, and committed as is divine love itself. That is why we call upon all people to live in accord with the authentic meaning of love and sexuality. Human sexuality, as we understand this gift from God, is to be genitally expressed only in a monogamous, heterosexual relationship of lasting fidelity in marriage.

42. In light of this understanding of the human person, we are convinced that unless, as a society, we live in accord with an authentic human sexuality, on which our Catholic moral teaching is based, we will not address a major source of the spread of AIDS. Any other solution will be merely short-term, ultimately ineffective, and will contribute to the trivialization of human sexuality that is already so prevalent in our society.

43. That is why we oppose the approach to AIDS prevention often popularly called "safe sex." This avenue compromises human sexuality—making it "safe" to be promiscuous—and, in fact, is quite misleading. As the National Academy of Sciences has noted in its study of AIDS, "many have argued that it is more accurate to speak in terms of 'safer' sex because the unknowns are still such that it would be irresponsible to certify any particular activity as absolutely safe.'"[6]

44. What kind of approach *will* we support?

45. As pastors of dioceses throughout the United States, we commit ourselves and our resources, within our moral restraints and prudent judgment, to provide education to limit the spread of AIDS and to offer support for persons with AIDS.

46. We will also support legislation and educational programs that seek to provide accurate information about AIDS. This is both legitimate and necessary. Pertinent biological data and basic information about the nature of the disease are essential for understanding the biological and pathological consequences of one's personal choices, both to oneself and others.

47. Nonetheless, as we have intimated above, we also have a responsibility as religious leaders to bring analysis to bear upon the moral dimensions of public policy. In our view, any discussion of AIDS must be situated within a broader context that affirms the dignity and destiny of the human person, the morality of human actions, and considers the consequences of individual choices for the whole of society.

48. Since AIDS is transmitted through intravenous drug use, we support and urge increased public support for drug treatment programs, the elimination of the importation of illicit drugs, and every effort to eliminate the causes of addiction in all communities, especially those of the poor.

49. Since AIDS is also transmitted through sexual practices, legislation and public guidelines should encourage private and public institutions to go beyond mere biological education. Such legislation or guidelines must respect, however, the inalienable right of parents to be the first educators of their children regarding the meaning and purpose of human sexuality.

50. While we advocate the provision of more than mere biological information in sex education, we recognize that this raises important questions because of existing constitutional restraints or interpretations of the separation of church and state. We are willing to join other people of good will in dialogue about how such a fuller understanding of human sexuality might be communicated in our public schools and elsewhere. We believe that there are certain basic values present in our society that transcend religious or sectarian boundaries and that can constitute a common basis for these social efforts.

51. Because we live in a pluralistic society, we acknowledge that some will not agree with our understanding of human sexuality. We rec-

---

[6]Institute of Medicine of the National Academy of Sciences, *Confronting AIDS: Directions for Public Health, Health Care and Research* (Washington, D.C.: National Academy Press, 1986), p. 97.

ognize that public educational programs addressed to a wide audience will reflect the fact that some people will not act as they can and should; that they will not refrain from the type of sexual or drug-abuse behavior that can transmit AIDS. In such situations, educational efforts, if grounded in the broader moral vision outlined above, could include accurate information about prophylactic devices or other practices proposed by some medical experts as potential means of preventing AIDS. We are not promoting the use of prophylactics, but merely providing information that is part of the factual picture. Such a factual presentation should indicate that abstinence outside of marriage and fidelity within marriage as well as the avoidance of intravenous drug abuse are the only morally correct and medically sure ways to prevent the spread of AIDS. So-called safe sex practices are at best only partially effective. They do not take into account either the real values that are at stake or the fundamental good of the human person.

52. With regard to educational programs for those who have already been exposed to the disease, the situation is somewhat different. For such individuals, without compromising the values outlined above, as a society, we have to face difficult and complex issues of public policy.

53. The teaching of classical theologians might provide assistance as we search for a way to bring into balance the need for a full and authentic understanding of human sexuality in our society and the issues of the common good associated with the spread of disease.[7] As noted above, at the level of public programming, we must clearly articulate the meaning of a truly authentic human sexuality as well as communicate the relevant health information.

---

[7] Augustine, *de Ordine* ii. 4. 12. Thomas Aquinas, *De regimine principum* iv. 14; *Summa theologiae* I-II. 96.2; 101.1, ad 2; II-II.10.11: "Humanum regimen derivatur a divino regimine, et ipsum debet imitari. Deus, autem, quamvis omnipotens et summe bonus, permittit tamen aliqua mala fieri in universo, quae prohibere posset, ne, eis sublatis, majora bona tollerentur, vel etiam pejora mala sequerentur. Sic igitur et in regimine humano illi qui praesunt recte aliqua mala tolerant, ne aliqua bona impediantur, vel etiam ne aliqua mala pejora incurrantur, sicut Augustinus dicit in II *de Ordine*." (Unofficial Translation: "Human governance is derived from divine governance, and it ought to imitate this divine governance. Although God is omnipotent and good in the highest degree, nevertheless he permits certain evil things to develop in the universe, which he would be able to prevent except that, if these things were taken away greater goods would be eliminated or even greater evils would follow as a consequence. So also in human governance, those who govern rightly tolerate certain evils lest certain goods be impeded or also lest some greater evil obtain, as Augustine said in the second book of his *de Ordine*.") For a reading of this tradition of the toleration of the lesser evil, see Adelard Dugre, "La tolerance du vice d'apres saint Augustin et saint Thomas," *Gregorianum* VI (1925), pp. 442-446. The classic articulation of this principle by the modern papal magisterium can be found in *Ci riesce* of Pius XII, December 6, 1953, *AAS*. Annus xxxv, series ii, vol. xx, pp. 798-801. For an example of the typical discussions and application of this among the subsequent moralists, cf. Marcellino Zalba, *Theologiae moralis summa* II (second edition, 1957), no. 118, para. 1-2, p. 47.

54. In the forum of a doctor-patient or a similar relationship, it is also necessary to address the question of how best to serve the common good in an individual case. This is what we meant earlier when we said that concrete responses must be made in specific contexts. Historically, this has been an appropriate forum for such advice because the health-care profession is concerned with both the well-being of the individual patient and public health. The same is true today.

55. In sum, it is our judgment that the best approach to the prevention of AIDS ought to be based on the communication of a value-centered understanding of the meaning of human personhood. Such a perspective provides a suitable context for the consideration of legislation or educational policy.

56. In light of this position, as participants in the public life of this nation, we are willing to commit the best efforts of the United States Catholic Conference to work on such programs. We also wish to assure legislators and public officials that we are willing to collaborate with them in the development of an informed and enlightened public policy for the prevention of AIDS.

57. We also encourage our Catholic elementary schools, high schools, colleges and universities, and religious education programs to develop curricular guidelines and educational materials to educate their students about the prevention of AIDS. All guidelines and educational materials should stress the importance of chastity and the power of God's love which enables us to live a chaste life. Of course, such guidelines and materials must be developed in collaboration and consultation with parents as much as possible.

58. Similarly, we ask every diocese to provide priests, deacons, religious, and lay leaders with a complete education about the medical, psychosocial, and pastoral issues related to AIDS and ARC so that they may communicate such information in a manner best suited to their respective communities. This information should include a list of resources and support systems available to persons with AIDS and ARC, seropositive persons, their families, and friends.

59. We also wish to say a word about the responsibilities of those who find themselves "at risk" of having been exposed to the AIDS virus. Earlier we stated something of the meaning and purpose of human sexuality. If a person chooses not to live in accord with this meaning or has misused drugs, he or she still has the serious responsibility not to bring injury to another person. Consequently, anyone who is considered to be "at risk" of having been exposed to the AIDS virus has a grave moral responsibility to ensure that he or she does not expose anyone else to it. This means that such a person who is considering marriage; engaging in intimate sexual contact; or planning to donate blood, organs, or semen has a moral responsibility to be tested for exposure to the AIDS virus and should act in such a way that it will not bring possible harm to another.

Care for Persons with AIDS and ARC

60. In the section on the facts about AIDS, we addressed several areas of concern about the care of persons with the disease and their families and friends. Here we will expand on those themes.

61. We commend those who have done so much to bring care and comfort to persons with AIDS and their loved ones. Much can be learned from what has already been done.

62. Persons with AIDS, their families, and their friends need solidarity, comfort, and support. As with others facing imminent death, they may experience anger towards and alienation from God and the Church, as they face the inevitability of dying. It is important that someone stand with them in their pain and help them, in accord with their religious tradition, to discover meaning in what appears so meaningless. Offering or ensuring this human companionship is especially important lest those who would diminish respect for life by encouraging euthanasia or suicide determine how to "care" for persons with AIDS.

63. We stand together with every person because all of us face eventual death. We reach out in a spirit of solidarity to those who are approaching death more rapidly and prematurely because of AIDS.

64. We seek to overcome fear and prejudice and to support hospitals, care centers, and other community institutions that provide the necessary physical, psychological, and spiritual care to persons with AIDS.

65. We pledge that we will work with public, private, and other religious groups to achieve the objectives we outlined earlier. We will support interfaith efforts to provide ministry to persons with AIDS and their families and friends. We will assist in finding temporary housing for families and friends who are visiting people with AIDS and unable to find accommodations on their own, as well as make counseling available when they return home.

66. It is critical that persons with AIDS continue to be employed as long as it is appropriate. The Catholic Church in the United States accepts its responsibility to give good example in this matter. We ask each diocese to develop, if it has not already done so, a general employment policy for all employees with life-threatening illnesses, including AIDS.

67. We call upon each diocese to appoint, where appropriate, a person responsible for coordinating its ministry to persons with AIDS and their loved ones.

68. We also encourage the development of training programs for those who minister to people affected by AIDS or ARC (e.g., hospital eucharistic ministers, visitors to the sick, confessors). Similarly, we also urge that people be trained to counsel persons before and after they are tested for the AIDS virus.

69. In order to coordinate and enhance these diocesan efforts and to collaborate with other national bodies, we have expanded the responsibilities of the appropriate entities within the bishops' conference to help us respond to the AIDS challenge and to develop appropriate recommendations for consideration by the Administrative Committee of the National Conference of Catholic Bishops.

70. In sum, by collaborating with other agencies and programs, we hope that the Church will provide an appropriate example about the manner in which those suffering from AIDS, and their families and friends, are cared for as well as the nature of that care. Through this collaboration, we will help provide the kind of care and services that place persons with AIDS in appropriate settings that best meet their needs. In addition, we encourage the use of church facilities as sites for providing various levels and kinds of care.

Conclusion

71. We began these reflections by looking at four of the many faces of persons with AIDS. We saw in them the call and the challenge of the risen Lord to become a people of care, compassion, and action on behalf of those who have AIDS or ARC or related conditions, as well as their loved ones. More profoundly, we saw the challenge of which Pope John Paul II recently reminded us, to love as God loves us: "without distinction, without limit." For "He loves those of you who are sick, those who are suffering from AIDS and from AIDS-related complex."

72. We have heard the invitation of that same Lord, spoken to all members of the human family, to express their sexuality in a truly human manner. We have sensed the challenged of providing for the prevention of AIDS in a complex, pluralistic society. We have recognized our own ecclesial responsibilities in the area of prevention and care, and of the need to collaborate with others.

73. The stories of Mary, John, Peter, and Lilly are not mere examples. They reveal our real, flesh-and-blood sisters and brothers. Our response to their needs, and the needs of other persons with AIDS, will be judged to be truly effective both when we discover God in them and when they, through their encounter with us, are able to say: "In my pain, fear, and alienation, I have felt in your presence a God of strength, hope, and solidarity."

74. By the grace of God, may this happen soon!

Appendix
Some Serious Questions —
and Responses

75. In the preceding pages, we have articulated a theoretical framework for responding to the challenge of the spread of AIDS in our society and made some specific observations and directives. The application of this guidance will be the responsibility of each diocesan bishop.

76. During recent months, several critical questions have arisen. While these questions are not entirely new, they are being asked in a new context: the fact that AIDS is considered by some a disease of pandemic proportions. We offer the following guidance in these matters. It is our prudential judgment that this guidance is faithful to the authentic teaching of the magisterium and to the Church's traditional moral wisdom.

a) *Should there be educational programs about AIDS in our schools, religious education programs, and adult education programs?*

77. While we recognize, above all, the inalienable rights of parents as the primary educators of their children and their importance in this area, we also affirm that there ought to be educational programs about AIDS at *every* appropriate level of Catholic schools and religious education programs. Adapted to the maturity of the learners, these programs should communicate the biological facts about AIDS as well as the values which should form their consciences. Several dioceses in the United States and Canada have developed guidelines for these educational efforts. The guidelines of the Diocese of Cleveland provide an example of one approach to developing an initial pastoral response. Essential to these efforts are programs to assist parents in their responsibility to be the primary educators of their children.

b) *When should these programs begin?*

78. The answer to this question will depend, in part, on the particular situation of the respective diocese and/or school. In areas where it is known that young people in the fifth and sixth grades (or younger) are being influenced by a drug culture or by social acceptance of promiscuous sex, formal education should begin as early as possible.

c) *In light of the medical evidence and the guidance offered in the statement, how should the Church relate to people who have been infected by the AIDS virus and are being served by its educational or social service programs or who are employees?*

79. The Church is called to model for the larger society the loving concern and compassion of Jesus for the sick and the suffering. This is not a ministry just for our health-care institutions or for a few dedicated individuals, but for the whole Church. All diocesan agencies and parishes have roles to play in ensuring dignity, acceptance, care, and justice for people with HIV infection and their families.

80. We recommend that dioceses draw up, as soon as possible, their own policy on the responsibility of the Church as pastoral minister, employer, educator, and social service provider and clarify the application of state and local public policy to the diocesan guidelines.

Pastoral Ministry

81. We encourage dioceses to identify the following:

- those responsible for the design and implementation of a diocesan plan for pastoral care of persons with AIDS;
- those responsible for training and support of pastoral ministers; and
- the ways in which the human, civil, and canonical rights of the person with AIDS will be respected, especially in the matter of confidentiality.

Employment

82. Many people with AIDS infection are able to continue working for long periods without further risk to themselves or others. Such persons are entitled to the same treatment with regard to employment as other persons. Those unable to continue working because of their physical deterioration should continue to receive health and other benefits available to other employees.

83. Church agencies should carry on employee education programs designed to dispel irrational fears about the dangers of contracting AIDS through casual contact in the workplace. Employees, such as health-care and child-care workers, who may come in contact with the body fluids of persons with AIDS, should receive continuing comprehensive and thorough education in infection control procedures. Special efforts must be made to have adequate personnel, equipment, and supplies on hand to prevent needless exposure to the virus by such employees.

Education

84. Infection with AIDS in and of itself should not be a reason to exclude students from any Catholic elementary or secondary school, religious education program, or institution of higher learning. However, alternate educational and catechetical arrangements may be made for infected children whose behavior has been shown to be a danger to others. Infected preschool children and neurologically damaged children who lack control over their body functions or who have a history of biting others will need special consideration. Catholic day-care and foster-care providers should seek to provide programs and procedures to make available assistance to such children and their families. Church agencies serving pregnant women have a special responsibility to provide practical help and support to AIDS-infected women during pregnancy, delivery, and the postpartum period.

Social Services

85. Catholic social service and health agencies are called to work together to ensure the availability of medical care and support services to persons with AIDS infection. No client, patient, or applicant for services from a Catholic agency or facility should be denied assistance, and employees should be held accountable for compliance with this policy. Diocesan agencies should also advocate for the development and funding of community-based services for persons with AIDS.

Confidentiality

86. Every precaution should be taken to protect the confidentiality of records, files, and other information about the HIV status of employ-ees, students, applicants, clients, and patients.

d) *How are Catholic hospitals to respond to the desire of health-care professionals who feel that it is their responsibility to provide "safe-sex" information in order to reduce the spread of disease?*

87. As we indicated above, we must be clear about our position: An integrated understanding of human sexuality provides the basis for any truly adequate program to prevent the sexual transmission of AIDS. Catholic health-care institutions and those who serve in them should be unequivocal about the moral teaching of the Church in their programs and personal counseling. It is important that Catholic health-care institutions provide educational programs about AIDS for their staffs and the public at large. It would be contradictory for these institutions to advocate a "safe-sex" approach to the prevention of the disease. It would be permissible, in accord with what has been said earlier about not promoting "safe-sex" practices, to speak about the practices recommended by public-health officials for limiting the spread of AIDS in the context of a clear advocacy of Catholic moral teaching.

88. On the more personal level of the health-care professional, the first course of action should be to invite a patient at risk, or one who already has been exposed to the disease, to live a chaste life. If it is obvious that the person will not act without bringing harm to others, then the traditional Catholic wisdom with regard to one's responsibility to avoid inflicting greater harm may be appropriately applied.

89. These are not all of the questions and issues which we face. There are other concerns about such matters as patient confidentiality, contact tracing, and the relationship between individual and societal rights. We encourage theologians and others to continue discussing them in light of the insights of our tradition and the Church's teaching.

National Pastoral Plan for Hispanic Ministry

A Statement Issued by the
National Conference of Catholic Bishops

November 18, 1987
(Revised 1989)

1. This pastoral plan is addressed to the entire Church in the United States. It focuses on the pastoral needs of the Hispanic Catholic, but it challenges all Catholics as members of the Body of Christ.[1]

We urge that the plan be studied carefully and taken seriously. The result of years of work involving thousands of people who participated in the III Encuentro, it is a strategic elaboration based on the conclusions of that Encuentro.

2. We, the bishops of the United States, adopt the objectives of this plan and endorse the specific means of reaching them, as provided herein. We encourage dioceses and parishes to incorporate this plan with due regard for local adaptation. We do so with a sense of urgency and in response to the enormous challenge associated with the ever-growing presence of the Hispanic people in the United States. Not only do we accept this presence in our midst as our pastoral responsibility, conscious of the mission entrusted to us by Christ,[2] we do so with joy and gratitude. For, as we stated in the pastoral letter of 1983, "At this moment of grace we recognize the Hispanic community among us as a blessing from God."[3]

We present this plan in a spirit of faith — faith in God, that he will provide the strength and the resources to carry out his divine plan on earth; faith in all the People of God, that all will collaborate in the awesome task before us; faith in Hispanic Catholics, that they will join hands with the rest of the Church to build up the entire Body of Christ. We dedicate this plan to the honor and glory of God and, in this Marian Year, invoke the intercession of the Blessed Virgin Mary under the title of Our Lady of Guadalupe.

---

[1] 1 Corinthians 12:12-13.

[2] Matthew 28:18-20.

[3] National Conference of Catholic Bishops, *The Hispanic Presence: Challenge and Commitment* (= HP), pastoral letter of the U.S. Bishops (Washington, D.C.: USCC Office of Publishing and Promotion Services, 1983), no. 1.

I. Introduction

3. This *National Pastoral Plan* is a result of the commitment expressed in our pastoral letter on Hispanic ministry, *The Hispanic Presence: Challenge and Commitment*: "We look forward to reviewing the conclusions of the *III Encuentro* as a basis for drafting a National Pastoral Plan for Hispanic Ministry to be considered in our general meeting at the earliest possible date after the *Encuentro*."[4] This plan is a pastoral response to the reality and needs of the Hispanic people in their efforts to achieve integration and participation in the life of our Church and in the building of the kingdom of God.

4. Integration is not to be confused with assimilation. Through the policy of assimilation, new immigrants are forced to give up their language, culture, values, and traditions and adopt a form of life and worship foreign to them in order to be accepted as parish members. This attitude alienates new Catholic immigrants from the Church and makes them vulnerable to sects and other denominations.

By integration we mean that our Hispanic people are to be welcomed to our church institutions at all levels. They are to be served in their language when possible, and their cultural values and religious traditions are to be respected. Beyond that, we must work toward mutual enrichment through interaction among all our cultures. Our physical facilities are to be made accessible to the Hispanic community. Hispanic participation in the institutions, programs, and activities of the Church is to be constantly encouraged and appreciated. This plan attempts to organize and direct how best to accomplish this integration.

5. The plan has its origins in our pastoral letter, and it is based on the working document of the III Encuentro and the Encuentro conclusions. It takes seriously the content of these documents and seeks to implement them.

It takes into account the sociocultural reality of our Hispanic people and suggests a style of pastoral ministry and model of Church in harmony with their faith and culture. For this reason, it requires an explicit affirmation of the concept of cultural pluralism in our Church within a fundamental unity of doctrine as expressed so many times by the Church's magisterium.[5]

---

[4]Ibid., no. 19.

[5]Pope Paul VI, *Evangelii Nuntiandi* (= EN), apostolic exhortation *On Evangelization in the Modern World* (Washington, D.C.: USCC Office of Publishing and Promotion Services, 1975), no. 20; Cf. Second Vatican Council, *Gaudium et Spes* (= GS) *Pastoral Constitution on the Chruch in the Modern World*, no. 153; National Conference of Catholic Bishops, *Cultural Pluralism in the United States* (= CP), statement by the USCC Committee on Social Development and World Peace (Washington, D.C.: USCC Office of Publishing and Promotion Services, 1981), 8.

This plan employs the methodology of a *Pastoral de Conjunto* where all the elements of pastoral ministry, all the structures, and all of the activities of pastoral agents—both Hispanic and non-Hispanic—are coordinated with a common objective in view. To integrate this plan into the process of church organization, departments, and agencies at all levels (national, regional, diocesan, parish) will require local adaptation so that all elements of pastoral ministry are operating in unison.

The plan's general objective is a synthesis of the prophetic pastoral guidelines approved at the III Encuentro. It provides the vision and orientation for all pastoral activity.[6]

This document is also a response to the proselytism of the sects. Its effectiveness requires the renewal of our parish structures, active participation by pastors and administrators, and a renewed missionary attitude at all levels of our Church.[7]

6. Pastoral planning is the effective organization of the total process of the life of the Church in fulfilling her mission of being a leaven of the kingdom of God in this world. Pastoral planning includes the following elements:

- analysis of the reality wherein the Church must carry out her mission;
- reflection on this reality in light of the gospel and the teachings of the Church;
- commitment to action resulting from this reflection;
- pastoral theological reflection on this process;
- development of a pastoral plan;
- implementation;
- ongoing evaluation of what is being done;
- and, the celebration of the accomplishment of this life experience, always within the context of prayer and its relationship to life.

Pastoral de Conjunto is a coresponsible, collaborative ministry involving coordination among pastoral agents of all of the elements of pastoral life and the structures of the same in view of a common goal: the kingdom of God.

This pastoral plan is a technical instrument which organizes, facilitates, and coordinates activities of the Church in the fulfillment of her evangelizing mission. It is at the service of the *Pastoral de Conjunto*.

---

[6]III Encuentro Nacional Hispano de Pastoral, *Prophetic Voices: The Document on the Process of the III Encuentro Nacional Hispano de Pastoral* (= PV) (Washington, D.C.: USCC Office of Publishing and Promotion Services 1987).

[7]Vatican Secretariat for Promoting Christian Unity, *Sects or New Religious Movements: Pastoral Challenge* (Washington, D.C.: USCC Office of Publishing and Promotion Services, 1986), p. 15, nos. 5.3-5.4.

It is not only a methodology, but an expression of the essence and mission of the Church, which is communion.

II. Framework of Hispanic Reality

A. History

7.   The Hispanic presence in the Americas began immediately with Christopher Columbus' first voyage of discovery in 1492, and the first Christian evangelization began in 1493 with the Spanish settlements on Hispaniola. The event was more encounter than discovery because Europeans rapidly intermingled with native Americans of high and sophisticated cultures, thus launching a new age and a new people — a true *mestizaje*.

In search of land and labor, Spaniards soon encountered the region that would one day become the United States. In 1513, Ponce de León probed the coasts of La Florida; then, Panfilo de Narvaez attempted the settlement of Florida in 1527, while Nuno de Guzman at the same time pressed overland north of Mexico. Survivors of Narvaez' failed expedition brought word of many tribes and great wealth. Fray Marcos de Niza responded in 1539 by preceding the great expedition of Francisco Vasquez de Coronado into the flanks of the Rockies. A year later Fray Juan Padilla gave his life as a martyr on the Kansas plains. Padre Luis Cancer, a Dominican missionary, poured out his life in Florida in 1549. Despite the setbacks in conversion, Pedro Menendez de Aviles forged ahead by founding the city of San Agustin in 1565. Jesuit missionaries moved into Chesapeake Bay only to vanish long before Roanoke. A map of 1529 illustrated by the royal Spanish cartographer Diego Ribero shows that missionaries and explorers arrived as far north as present-day Maryland, New York, and New England and gave Spanish names to the rivers and mountains they saw. Far to the west, adventurers probed into New Mexico, where missionaries lost their lives in futile attempts at evangelization; not until Juan de Onate arrived in 1598 with scores of new settlers did stability finally come. Generations before the Pilgrims tenuously built their colonies, Spanish missionaries struggled to bring the Americas into the fold of Christ.

8.   In the 17th century, Franciscan missionaries raised elegant churches in the Pueblo towns of New Mexico; Jesuits along the western slopes of New Spain wove scattered Indian rancherias into efficient social systems that raised the standard of living in arid America. But the primacy of evangelization as a cornerstone of Spanish royal policy was swept away by political ambitions in the 18th century; the missions fell victim to secularism. First, the Jesuits were exiled and the order suppressed; Franciscans and Dominicans tried valiantly to stem

the tide of absolutism, but their numbers dwindled rapidly and the Church's service to the poor crumpled.

Independence swept Mexico, and the northern provinces of New Spain, now the states of a new republic, fell to the invading armies of the United States. Under the provisions of the Treaty of Guadalupe Hidalgo in 1848, the old mission territories were annexed to the burgeoning United States. Spanish Florida and Louisiana, for a while French, were stars in the blue field of conquest; and from the Mississippi to the Pacific shores the frontiers of *mestizaje* were put under Anglo law and custom.

9. The 19th century was characterized by decades of neglect and adjustment. Hispanic and native American populations were ill served and overlooked. The people of the mainland continued to move north as they had for more than a millennium; only now they encountered a new tide of empire which was inundating old familiar places and families.

Political and social conditions in the 20th century have only enhanced the northern migration. New avenues of immigration opened from the island nations; Puerto Ricans, Cubans, and Dominicans poured into the Eastern Seaboard. Mexicans continued to trek north to find work and opportunities. And the worsening conditions of Central and South America have added thousands to the stream of immigrants who speak a language once dominant in North America and now scorned by all too many who remain ignorant of the deep cultural power it exercises throughout the world.

The United States of America is not all America. We speak of the Americas to describe a hemisphere of many cultures and three dominant languages — two from the Iberian peninsula and one from a North Atlantic island. Since the Church is the guardian of the mission of Jesus Christ, it must forever accommodate the changing populations and shifting cultures of mankind. To the extent the Church is impregnated with cultural norms, to that extent it divides and separates; to the extent it replaces cultural norms with the primacy of love, it unites the many into the Body of Christ without dissolving difference or destroying identity.

B. Culture

10. The historical reality of the Southwest, the proximity of countries of origin, and continuing immigration, all contribute to the maintenance of Hispanic culture and language within the United States. This cultural presence expresses itself in a variety of ways: from the immigrant who experiences "culture shock," to the Hispanic whose roots in the United States go back several generations and who struggles with questions of identity while often being made to feel an alien in his own country.

Despite these differences, certain cultural similarities identify Hispanics as a people. Culture primarily expresses how people live and perceive the world, one another, and God. Culture is the set of values by which a people judge, accept, and live what is considered important within the community.

Some values that make up the Hispanic culture are a "profound respect for the dignity of each *person* . . . deep and reverential love for *family life* . . . a marvelous sense of *community* . . . a loving appreciation of God's gift of *life* . . . and an authentic and consistent *devotion* to Mary. . . ."[8]

Culture for Hispanic Catholics has become a way of living out and transmitting their faith. Many local practices of popular religiosity have become widely accepted cultural expressions. Yet the Hispanic culture, like any other, must continue to be evangelized.[9]

C. Social Reality

11. The median age among Hispanic people is twenty-five. This plus the continuous flow of immigrants ensures a constant increase in population.

Lack of education and professional training contribute to high unemployment. Neither public nor private education has responded to the urgent needs of this young population. Only 8 percent of Hispanics graduate at the college level.[10]

Families face a variety of problems. Twenty-five percent of the families live below the poverty level, and 28 percent are single-parent families.[11]

Frequent mobility, poor education, a limited economic life, and racial prejudice are some of the factors that result in low participation in political activities.

As a whole, Hispanics are a religious people. Eighty-three percent consider religion important. There is an interest in knowing more about the Bible and a strong presence of popular religious practices.[12]

Despite this, 88 percent are not active in their parishes. On the other hand, the Jehovah's Witnesses, pentecostal groups, and other sects are increasing within the Hispanic community. According to recent studies, the poor, men, and second-generation Hispanics are those who least participate in the life of the Church.[13]

---

[8] HP, no. 3.

[9] EN, no. 20.

[10] Census Bureau, December 1985.

[11] Ibid.

[12] Roberto Gonzalez and Michael LaVelle, *The Hispanic Catholic in the United States: A Socio-Cultural and Religious Profile* (Northeast Catholic Pastoral Center for Hispanics, Inc., 1985).

[13] Ibid.

Assessment

12. 1. The Catholic heritage and cultural identity of Hispanics are threatened by the prevailing secular values of the American society. They have marginal participation in the Church and in society; they suffer the consequences of poverty and marginalization.

2. This same people, due to its great sense of religion, family, and community, is a prophetic presence in the face of the materialism and individualism of society. Since the majority of Hispanics are Catholic, their presence can be a source of renewal within the Catholic Church in North America. Because of its youth and growth, this community will continue to be a significant presence in the future.

3. The current pastoral process offers some exciting possibilities on both social and religious levels: more active participation in the Church, a critique of society from the perspective of the poor, and a commitment to social justice.

4. As the year 1992 approaches celebrating the five-hundreth anniversary of the evangelization of the Americas, it is more important than ever that Hispanics in the United States rediscover their identity as well as their Catholicity, be reevangelized by the Word of God, and forge a much needed unit among all Hispanics who have come from the entire spectrum of the Spanish-speaking world.

III. Doctrinal Framework

13. The mission of the Church is the continuation of Jesus' work: to announce the kingdom of God and the means for entering it.[14] It is the proclamation of what is to come and also an anticipation of that plenitude here and now in the process of history. The kingdom which Jesus proclaims and initiates is so important that, in relation to it, all else is relative.[15]

The Church, as community, carries out the work of Jesus by entering into the cultural, religious, and social reality of the people, becoming incarnate in and with the people, "in virtue of her mission and nature she is bound to no particular form of human culture, nor to any political, economic, or social system."[16] Therefore, she is able to preach the need for conversion of everyone, to affirm the dignity of the human person, and to seek ways to eradicate personal sin, oppressive structures, and forms of injustice.

14. The Church in its prophetic voice denounces sin and announces

---

[14]Matthew 28:18-20.

[15]PV, *A Pastoral Theological Reflection.*

[16]GS, no. 42.

hope and in this way continues the historic and tangible presence of Jesus. Since Jesus proclaimed Good News to the poor and liberty to captives,[17] the Church continues to make an option for the poor and the marginalized.

The Church likewise identifies with the risen Christ, who reveals himself as the new creation, as the proclamation and realization of new values of solidarity among all: through his simplicity, in peace, through the proclamation of his kingdom which implies a new social order; through a new style of Church as leaven; and above all, through his gift to us of his Spirit.

15. This Spirit unites the members of the community of Jesus intimately one with another, all in Christ with God. Our solidarity comes from this indwelling Spirit of Christ. The Spirit impels the community to accomplish in life a prophetic commitment to justice and love and helps it to live, within an experience of missionary faith, its union with the Father.

This responsibility falls on the whole Church—the People of God: the pope and bishops, priests, religious, and laity, who with a sense of coresponsibility must accomplish Jesus' work. All this is expressed in a singular way in the Eucharist. It is here that Jesus offers himself as victim for the salvation of all and challenges the entire People of God to live out the commitment of love and service.

16. The spirituality or *mistica* of the Hispanic people springs from their faith and relationship with God. *Spirituality is understood to be the way of life of a people, a movement by the Spirit of God, and the grounding of one's identity as a Christian in every circumstance of life.* It is the struggle to live the totality of one's personal and communitarian life in keeping with the gospel; spirituality is the orientation and perspective of all the dimensions of a person's life in the following of Jesus and in continuous dialogue with the Father.

Since spirituality penetrates the totality of life, it is likewise made manifest in a multitude of expressions. At this particular moment of their journey, Hispanic Catholics are revealing their spirituality through the nine prophetic pastoral guidelines of the III Encuentro, which have been summarized in the *General Objective* and *Specific Dimensions* of this plan. The pastoral plan is thus not only a series of goals and objectives, but also a contribution to the development, growth, and fruition of the people's life of faith as discerned in the Spirit of God and incarnated in our time.

---

[17]Luke 4:18-19.

V. General Objectives

17. TO LIVE AND PROMOTE . . . by means of a *Pastoral de Conjunto* a MODEL OF CHURCH that is: communitarian, evangelizing, and missionary, incarnate in the reality of the Hispanic people and open to the diversity of cultures, a promoter and example of justice . . . that develops leadership through integral education . . . THAT IS LEAVEN FOR THE KINGDOM OF GOD IN SOCIETY.

VI. Specific Dimensions

18. The four specific dimensions wherein the general objective is made explicit are:

    A. *Pastoral de Conjunto: From Fragmentation to Coordination*
    B. Evangelization: *From a Place to a Home*
    C. Missionary Option: *From Pews to Shoes*
    D. Formation: *From Good Will to Skills*

A. *Pastoral de Conjunto: From Fragmentation to Coordination*

1. Background

19. The Hispanic Catholic experiences a lack of unity and communion in the Church's pastoral ministry.

There is a lack of union and coordination in criteria, vision, goals, and common actions, as well as a lack of fraternity, communion, and teamwork in the various aspects of pastoral ministry. The challenge here is for the laity, religious, and clergy to work together.

The process of III Encuentro emphasized certain key elements of the *Pastoral de Conjunto*: broad participation by the people, small communities, small groups; teamwork; integration of different pastoral areas; a common vision; interrelating among the dioceses, regions, and the national level; openness to the needs of the people and to the universality of the Church. These key elements are to be joined to already existing efforts in Hispanic pastoral ministry throughout the country. Many dioceses are already providing offices and resources for Hispanic ministry. Although much has been done, the needs are still great.

20. These experiences help the Hispanic people to live the Church as communion. The *Pastoral de Conjunto* manifests that communion to which the Church is called in its fullest dimension. The Hispanic people wish to live this communion of the Church not only among themselves but also with the different cultures which make the Church universal here in the United States.

Greater participation by Hispanic Catholics in the total life of the Church will make possible their authentic integration and help the Church to become an even greater presence and leaven of communion in our society.

2. Specific Objective

21. To develop a *Pastoral de Conjunto* which, through pastoral agents and structures, manifests communion in integration, coordination, in-servicing, and communication of the Church's pastoral action, in keeping with the general objective of this plan.

3. Programs and Projects

a) *Pastoral Integration*

22. (1) To integrate the common vision of this *National Pastoral Plan* in all the structures of the NCCB/USCC, which are responsible for pastoral action and education.

How: The Secretariat for Hispanic Affairs will meet with the directors of the departments of the NCCB/USCC to seek to integrate Hispanic pastoral activity within the existing structures.

When: In accordance with the normal channels for plans and programs and budget procedures of the respective entities involved (NCCB/USCC).

Responsible Agent: Secretariat for Hispanic Affairs.

23. (2) To share the common vision of the *National Pastoral Plan* at different levels; diocese, area (e.g. deaneries, vicariates, etc.), parish, apostolic movements and organizations, so that they may respond to this missionary thrust in evangelization.

How: On the diocesan or area level—convocation of priests and diocesan personnel by the diocesan bishop; on the area or parish level—gathering by the area Hispanic center or groups, the pastor of parish organizations and pastoral ministries; on the level of apostolic movements and organizations—gatherings with national leaders of movements to seek the best way to implement the *National Pastoral Plan*.

When: In accordance with the normal channels for plans and programs and budget procedures of the respective entities involved.

Responsible Agents: Diocesan level: the diocesan bishop, the vicar, Hispanic office, area coordinator; Parish: pastor; Organizations and apostolic movements: national directors, Secretariat for Hispanic Affairs.

24. (3) To ensure Hispanic leadership in pastoral decision making at all levels.

How: Priority funding for leadership competency; hiring Hispanics for pastoral decision-making positions at all levels.

When: In accordance with the normal channels for plans and programs and budget procedures of the respective entities involved.   ˗

Responsible Agents: NCCB/USCC, the diocesan bishop, vicars, pastors, and other personnel directors.

25. (4) Promote understanding, communion, solidarity, and multicultural experiences with other cultural minorities.

How: Sharing the common vision and plan with existing church organizations.

When: In accordance with the normal channels for plans and programs and budget procedures of the respective entities involved (NCCB/USCC).

Responsible Agents: NCCB Committee for Hispanic Affairs and the Secretariat for Hispanic Affairs.

b) Coordination of Hispanic Pastoral Action

26. (1) Maintain or create structures on the national, regional, and diocesan levels to ensure effective coordination of Hispanic pastoral life according to this plan. The secretariat, the regional and diocesan offices and institutes are indispensable in carrying out the coordination and continuity of this plan, as well as the formation of pastoral ministers with this common vision. The creation of pastoral centers and offices is advised in those dioceses where they do not exist and are needed, as is the coordination of those in existence.

How: Economically ensuring the existence of these offices and institutes; through the creation of coordinating teams at the national, regional, and diocesan levels to carry out this *Pastoral de Conjunto*.

When: In accordance with the normal channels for plans and programs and budget procedures of the respective entities involved (NCCB/USCC).

Responsible Agents: NCCB Committee for Hispanic Affairs, Secretariat for Hispanic Affairs, regional offices, and diocesan offices.

27. (2) Promote the *Pastoral de Conjunto* at the diocesan level through the creation of a diocesan pastoral plan in order to adopt and implement this *National Pastoral Plan* in each diocese according to its own reality.

How: Creating a diocesan pastoral team or council made up of vicar, priests, deacons, religious, and laity representing parishes, communities, and movements, who will carry out the necessary steps for total pastoral planning.

When: In accordance with the normal channels for plans and programs and budget procedures of the respective entities involved.

Responsible Agents: The diocesan bishops, vicars, diocesan directors for Hispanic affairs and diocesan promotion teams (EPDs), with the assistance of the regional offices.

28. (3) Promote the area and the parish *Pastoral de Conjunto* through the creation of an area or parish pastoral plan in order to adapt and implement the diocesan plan in each parish.

How: Gatherings of the area coordinator and/or the pastor and the pastoral team with representatives of the small ecclesial communities and the pastoral council in order to carry out the necessary steps of total pastoral planning.

When: In accordance with the normal channels for plans and programs and budget procedures of the respective entities involved.

Responsible Agents: The area coordinator, the pastor, and parish team or pastoral team or pastoral council.

29. (4) To develop diocesan and area coordination among small ecclesial communities in the areas and the parishes.

How: Periodic meetings with the coordinators or facilitators of the areas and of the small ecclesial communities to foster a common vision of missionary evangelization.

When: In accordance with the normal channels for plans and programs and budget procedures of the respective entities involved.

Responsible Agents: Diocesan offices for Hispanic affairs, diocesan promotion teams (EPDs), area centers and pastors, in collaboration with diocesan offices of adult religious education and of lay ministry.

c) In-Service Training for Hispanic Pastoral Action

30. (1) That pastoral institutes, pastoral centers, and schools of ministries provide the formation and training of pastoral agents for Hispanic ministry at the national, regional, diocesan, and parish levels, according to the common vision of the pastoral plan.

How: Through the creation of programs, courses, materials and other necessary resources, mobile teams, etc.

When: In accordance with the normal channels for plans and programs and budget procedures of the respective entities involved.

Responsible Agents: National Federation of Pastoral Institutes and directors of other pastoral centers.

31. (2) Develop the theological-pastoral growth of Hispanics in the United States.

How: Facilitating *encuentros* for Hispanic pastoral ministers; publishing theological pastoral reflections of Hispanics; organizing opportunities for practical experience in different pastoral areas; assisting with scholarships for advanced studies in different pastoral areas; celebrating liturgies which incorporate the wealth of Hispanic cultural expressions.

When: In accordance with the normal channels for plans and programs and budget procedures of the respective entities involved.

Responsible Agents: National Federation of Pastoral Institutes and other centers of pastoral formation (e.g., *Instituto de Liturgia Hispana*).
32. (3) Employ the formational resources and personnel of the NCCB/USCC for the integral development of Hispanic leadership.

How: Ensuring that Hispanics be included in the priorities of the NCCB/USCC as an integral part of the Church of the United States, in coordination with the existing entities of Hispanic pastoral activity.

When: In accordance with the normal channels for plans and programs and budget procedures of the respective entities involved (NCCB/USCC).

Responsible Agent: Secretariat for Hispanic Affairs.

d) Pastoral Communication

33. (1) Promote dialogue and cooperation among diverse groups, apostolic movements, and small ecclesial communities in order to achieve mutual understanding, sharing, and support that will lead to communion, common vision, and unity of criteria for pastoral action.

How: Periodic gatherings and *encuentros* between representatives of different entities; exchange of newsletters or information items; organization of common projects.

When: In accordance with the normal channels for plans and programs and budget procedures of the respective entities involved.

Responsible Agents: Vicar, diocesan director for Hispanic affairs, area coordinators, clergy, leaders of small ecclesial communities, and directors of apostolic movements.
34. (2) Use the mass media as an instrument of evangelization in denouncing violence in all its forms and the injustices suffered by families, youth, women, the undocumented, migrants, refugees, farmworkers, prisoners, and all other marginalized in society.

How: Inform and train personnel in charge of the Church's mass communications media in order that they incorporate the concerns and needs of Hispanics into the total ministry of their office according to the vision of the pastoral plan.

When: In accordance with the normal channels for plans and programs and budget procedures of the respective entities involved.

Responsible Agents: Communication departments of various church organizations.
35. (3) Train and raise the consciousness of pastoral ministers to specialize in the use of mass communications media.

How: By means of regional workshops, where training and technical skills and critical awareness can take place.

When: In accordance with the normal channels for plans and programs and budget procedures of the respective entities involved.

Responsible Agents: Diocesan communications offices in collaboration with the regional offices and pastoral institutes, with the assistance of the USCC Committee on Communications.

36. (4) To make available the Secretariat for Hispanic Affairs' newsletter, *En Marcha*, to the grass roots as an instrument of information and formation for Hispanic pastoral ministers.

How: Using the existing channels of communication of regional and diocesan offices and their lists of leaders in order to enlarge its circulation.

When: In accordance with the normal channels for plans and programs and budget procedures of the respective entities involved.

Responsible Agent: Secretariat for Hispanic Affairs.

B. Evangelization: From a Place to a Home

1. Background

37. The great majority of our Hispanic people feel distant or marginated from the Catholic Church. Evangelization has been limited in many cases to Sunday liturgies and a sacramental prepration which has often not stressed a profound conversion that integrates the dimensions of faith, spiritual growth, and justice for the transformation of society. The Hispanic community recognizes that the parish is, ecclesiastically and historically speaking, the basic organizational unit of the Church in the United States, and it will continue to be so; at the same time, it is affirmed that conversion and a sense of being Church are often best lived out in smaller communities within the parish which are more personal and offer a greater sense of belonging.

38. Many apostolic movements and church organizations have traditionally served to unite our church people in small communities for various purposes. We encourage the continuance of these organizations and their development as viable and effective means for evangelization.

Within the pastoral process of Hispanic ministry other efforts have been made to recognize small groups for analysis, reflection, and action; to respond to the needs of the people. By means of mobile teams and reflection groups, the III Encuentro also facilitated the evangelization process through the formation of small ecclesial communities.

These small ecclesial communities promote experiences of faith and conversion as well as concern for each person and an evangelization process of prayer, reflection, action, and celebration.

39. The objective of the programs that follow is to continue, support, and extend the evangelization process to all Hispanic people. In this way we will have a viable response by the Catholic community to the proselytism of fundamentalist groups and the attraction they exercise on our people. In addition, we will be more sensitive to our responsibility to reach out in a welcoming way to newcomers and to the inactive and unchurched.

2. Specific Objective

40. To recognize, develop, accompany, and support small ecclesial communities and other Church groups (e.g., *Cursillos de Cristiandad*, *Movimiento Familiar Cristiano*, RENEW, Charismatic Movement, prayer groups, etc.), which in union with the bishop are effective instruments of evangelization for the Hispanic people. These small ecclesial communities and other groups within the parish framework promote experiences of faith and conversion, prayer life, missionary outreach and evangelization, interpersonal relations and fraternal love, prophetic questioning and actions for justice. They are a prophetic challenge for the renewal of our Church and humanization of our society.

3. Programs and Projects

a) *Elaboration of Criteria and Training for the Creation, Development, and Support of Small Ecclesial Communities*

41. (1) To bring together a "think tank" of pastoral agents with experience in small ecclesial communities, to prepare a workbook of guidelines which spells out the constitutive elements of small ecclesial communities, and the criteria and practical helps for their development and coordination in the light of the Pastoral Prophetic Guidelines of the III Encuentro.

How: Organize a national "think tank" of people experienced in various styles of small ecclesial communities.

When: In accordance with the normal channels for plans and programs and budget procedures of the respective entities involved.

Responsible Agents: Coordinated by the Secretariat for Hispanic Affairs with the assistance of the National Advisory Committee to the Secretariat (NAC), in collaboration with the regional offices, National Federation of Pastoral Institutes, and the diocesan offices for Hispanic affairs.

42. (2) To organize a national training session for teams representing each region, with the help of the workbook and other church documents, so as to develop a common vision and methodology in the formation and support of small ecclesial communities. These teams are then to conduct training sessions at the regional and diocesan levels.

How: By way of a national training session to spearhead regional and diocesan workshops.

When: In accordance with the normal channels for plans and programs and budget procedures of the respective entities involved.

Responsible Agents: Coordinated by the Secretariat for Hispanic Affairs, in collaboration with the regional diocesan offices.

43. (3) To invite the diocesan directors of apostolic movements and pastors to a pastoral theological reflection on integral evangelization and small ecclesial communities. This will facilitate a joint evaluation and discernment which will produce an integration of objectives and collaboration in the development of programs of evangelization.

How: By inviting the diocesan directors by way of workshops and courses organized in the different dioceses of the country.

When: In accordance with the normal channels for plans and programs and budget procedures of the respective entities involved.

Responsible Agent: Diocesan offices for Hispanic affairs.

b) Parish Renewal for Community Development and Missionary Outreach

44. Part of the process of III Encuentro was the organization of mobile teams to visit and bring closer to the Church those who feel distant and marginalized. This made us more aware of the strong campaign of proselytism which confronts the Hispanic people. It is imperative to offer dynamic alternatives to what fundamentalist groups and sects offer. The framework for such alternatives is a missionary parish which forms small ecclesial communities to promote integral evangelization in which faith is shared and justice is lived out.

The following projects of parish renewal are suggested for adaptation and implementation at the local level to evangelize the unchurched and marginalized.

45. (1) Create a welcoming and inclusive atmosphere that is culturally sensitive to the marginalized.

How: Emphasizing a missionary and community focus in the Sunday Masses, homilies, parish schools, programs of catechesis, sacramental preparation and celebrations, bulletins, and other parish programs (e.g., RCIA); directing liturgical and catechetical programs to include and motivate them to participate in small ecclesial communities; organizing in each parish and by areas, consciousness-raising activities with a missionary and community focus.

When: In accordance with the normal channels for plans and programs and budget procedures of the respective entities involved.

Responsible Agents: Pastor and parish groups, pastoral council, in collaboration with the diocesan offices and area centers.

46. (2) Accompany the existing movements and groups in the parish so that their evangelizing purposes can be enhanced in accordance with the vision of the pastoral plan.

How: Ongoing formation on the original purpose of the various movements and groups and the evangelizing mission of the Church and the pastoral plan.

When: In accordance with the normal channels for plans and programs and budget procedures of the respective entities involved.

Responsible Agents: Diocesan offices and the directors of the apostolic movements and groups.

47. (3) To promote the parish as a "community of communities," especially through small area groups or through small ecclesial communities integrating families and existing groups and especially preparing these communities to receive those who are marginalized from the Church.

How: Organize workshops on the diocesan level for pastors and the members of pastoral councils to study and plan the organization of small ecclesial communities in accord with the general objective of this plan; from a Hispanic team or integrate Hispanics into the pastoral council with the pastor and other parish ministers.

When: In accordance with the normal channels for plans and programs and budget procedures of the respective entities involved.

Responsible Agents: The diocesan bishop, vicar, and the diocesan office for Hispanic affairs, in coordination with the regional offices.

48. (4) Train teams of visitors to be proclaimers of the Word and the love of God and to form communities with the visited families, thus acting as a "bridge" between the marginalized and the Church.

How: Parish training workshops to develop skills to analyze the local reality; respond to the needs of marginalized families; form communities of acceptance, love, and justice; facilitate a process of conversion, formation, and ecclesial commitment; appreciate popular religiosity; teach the Bible and its Catholic interpretation; acquire basic knowledge of the liturgy and its relationship to private prayer.

When: In accordance with the normal channels for plans and programs and budget procedures of the respective entities involved.

Responsible Agents: The diocesan office for Hispanic affairs, area centers, and the diocesan promotion teams (EPDs), in coordination with the pastor and pastoral council.

49. (5) Organize a pastoral visitation plan to the homes of the marginalized through a process of listening/responding to needs and then inviting these families to form part of small ecclesial communities.

How: Organize a systematic plan of visitations for each parish.

When: In accordance with the normal channels for plans and programs and budget procedures of the respective entities involved.

Responsible Agents: The pastor and the pastoral council.

50. (6) Promote integration between faith and the transformation of unjust social structures.

How: Develop a form of conscientization and commitment to justice, which is an integral part of evangelization in small ecclesial communities and all parish programs; work together to respond to the needs of the most marginalized from a faith commitment based on a continued analysis of the local reality; by integrating the Church's social teachings and commitment to justice as an integral part of evangelization in the formation of small ecclesial communities, and by reviewing and evaluating existing programs from this perspective and making the necessary changes in them.

When: In accordance with the normal channels for plans and programs and budget procedures of the respective entities involved.

Responsible Agents: The pastor, Hispanic parish leaders, the pastoral council in collaboration with the diocesan offices, the regional office, the pastoral institutes, and the *Instituto de Liturgia Hispana*.

C. Missionary Option: From Pews to Shoes

1. Background

51. Throughout the process of the III Encuentro, the Hispanic people made a preferential missionary option for the poor and marginalized, the family, women, and youth. These priority groups are not only the recipients but also the subjects of the Hispanic pastoral ministry.
52. The *poor* and *marginalized* have limited participation in the political, social, economic, and religious process. This is due to underdevelopment and isolation from both church and societal structures through which decisions are made and services offered. The following problems stand out:

- lack of opportunities for education and advancement; and
- poor health, hygiene, and living conditions.
- Migrant farmworkers, in addition, suffer instability of life and work, which aggravates the aforementioned problems.

53. Hispanic *families*, most of them urban, poor, and larger than non-Hispanic families, face a series of difficulties involving such things as:

- communication between spouses and between parents and children;
- divorce and separation;
- unwed mothers;
- abortion;
- alcoholism and drugs;
- lack of formation for educating children sexually and morally;
- isolation in both the Hispanic and non-Hispanic environment;
- lack of church contact, especially with the parish structure; and
- undocumented status and resulting family tensions.

54. Within this reality, women suffer a triple discrimination:

- social (*machismo*, sexual and emotional abuse, lack of self-esteem, exploitation by the media);
- economic (forced to work without proper emotional and technical preparation, exploited in regard to wages and kinds of work, bearing full responsibility for the family, lacking self-identity); and
- religious (her importance in the preservation of faith is not taken into account, she is not involved in decision making yet bears the burden for pastoral ministry).

55. Youth—both male and female:

- a large number is alienated from the Church;
- generally lack adequate attention and pastoral care;
- victims of the materialism and consumerism of society; experience difficulty in finding their own identity as they exist between different languages and cultures;
- suffer the consequences of family disintegration; and
- feel strong peer and other pressures toward drugs, crime, gangs, and dropping out of school.

2. Specific Objective

56. To promote faith and effective participation in church and societal structures on the part of these priority groups (the poor, women, families, youth) so that they may be agents of their own destiny (self-determination) and capable of progressing and becoming organized.

3. Programs and Projects

a) *Organization and Assistance for Farmworkers (Migrants)*

57. One full-time person at the national level in the Office of the Pastoral Care of Migrants and Refugees who will plan and evaluate the pastoral ministry with farmworkers (migrants) through two annual meetings with one person from each region.

How: Consult regional offices about representatives and about adequate structures for that region.

When: In accordance with the normal channels for plans and programs and budget procedures of the respective entities involved.

Responsible Agent: NCCB Committee on Migration.

b) Conscientization on Christian Social Responsibility and Leadership Development

58. To develop social justice ministries and leadership development by means of specific contacts with sociocivic entities that respond to the conditions of the poor and the marginalized. These ministries should state the influence and the concrete collaboration of the Church with these entities.

How: Community organizing efforts at the national, regional, diocesan, and parish levels.

When: In accordance with the normal channels for plans and programs and budget procedures of the respective entities involved.

Responsible Agents: USCC Committee on Social Development and World Peace and the Campaign for Human Development.

c) Hispanics in the Military

59. Meetings of military chaplains according to areas, where there is Hispanic personnel. The objective is to:

- integrate the process of the III Encuentro in their specific ministry;
- reflect together on the situation of Hispanics in the military, especially women, given the difficulties and pressures which they frequently encounter; and
- elaborate a program of conscientization and evangelization for Hispanics in the military.

How: A committee of military chaplains for Hispanic ministry organized in areas where there are military bases with large numbers of Hispanics.

When: In accordance with the normal channels for plans and programs and budget procedures of the respective entities involved.

Responsible Agents: Archdiocese for the Military Services, in collaboration with the National Federation of Pastoral Institutes.

d) Promotion of Family Life Ministry

60. (1) To analyze the variety of family expressions and specific pastoral issues; discover and design models of participation and organization for the integration of the family in the Church and society; establish common goals for family life ministry.

How: By organizing a national forum or forums on Hispanic family life ministry in cooperation with dioceasan leaders of Hispanic family life.

When: In accordance with the normal channels for plans and programs and budget procedures of the respective entities involved.

Responsible Agents: NCCB Committee on Marriage and Family Life, in collaboration with the Secretariat for Hispanic Affairs.

61. (2) Publish results of the national forum or forums in a pedagogical format for use in small ecclesial communities.

How: Through a committee of the participants in the national forum or forums on family life ministry.

When: In accordance with the normal channels for plans and programs and budget procedures of the respective entities involved.

Responsible Agent: NCCB Committee on Marriage and Family Life, in cooperation with the Secretariat for Hispanic Affairs.

62. (3) Disseminate material prepared and encourage its use at the local level.

How: Through diocesan offices for family life, Hispanic ministry, regional pastoral institutes, and diocesan pastoral centers.

When: In accordance with the normal channels for plans and programs and budget procedures of the respective entities involved.

Responsible Agent: NCCB Committee on Marriage and Family Life, in cooperation with the Secretariat for Hispanic Affairs.

e) The Woman and Her Role in the Church

63. To provide forums for women who offer different services or ministries in Hispanic pastoral ministry, in order to:

- analyze the situation of Hispanic women to manifest more clearly their gifts of intelligence and compassion, which they share with the Church;
- identify a model of Church that nourishes and fosters ministries by women;
- value the role of the small ecclesial community in the promotion of women; and
- examine, in light of the process of the III Encuentro, the reality of the Hispanic woman and consider which ministries should be maintained and which should be created.

How: Regional gatherings.

When: In accordance with the normal channels for plans and programs and budget procedures of the respective entities involved.

Responsible Agents: National Federation of Pastoral Institutes, in collaboration with the Secretariat for Hispanic Affairs and the NCCB Committee on Women in Society and the Church.

f) Youth Ministry

64. (1) Organization: to guarantee the participation of Hispanic youth in the life and mission of the Church.

How: By encouraging the creation of organisms of coordination at the national, regional, diocesan, and parish levels; and by providing opportunities for Hispanic youth to discern religious and priestly vocations.

When: In accordance with the normal channels for plans and programs and budget procedures of the respective entities involved.

Responsible Agents: The Secretariat for Hispanic Affairs, in collaboration with the NCCB Committee for Hispanic Affairs and the USCC Youth Desk.

65. (2) Networking Hispanic Youth Ministry: to identify existing, effective programs which can serve as models for reaching the most alienated youth and to assist in multiplying these programs in different dioceses and parishes.

How: Share programs and methodologies with other dioceses; use existing centers, regional *encuentros*, mobile teams, organizations, small ecclesial communities, and storefronts on diocesan and parish levels so that Hispanic youth can experience the Church welcoming them and offering them opportunities for formation and service.

When: In accordance with the normal channels for plans and programs and budget procedures of the respective entities involved.

Responsible Agents: Diocesan Youth Offices and *Comite Nacional Hispano de Pastoral Juvenil* (CNH de PJ), in collaboration with the Secretariat for Hispanic Affairs and the USCC Youth Desk.

66. (3) National Encuentro of Hispanic Youth Regional Representatives—Topics for consideration for the National Encuentro should include:

- statistics on Hispanic youth and pertinent data on the reality of youth;
- existing models of youth pastoral ministry;
- training seminars for ministers of youth evangelization; and
- strategies for family involvement.

How: Through diocesan and regional *encuentros*.

When: In accordance with the normal channels for plans and programs and budget procedures of the respective entities involved.

Responsible Agents: Hispanic youth in collaboration with the NCCB Committee for Hispanic Affairs and the National Committee for Hispanic Youth/Young Adult Ministry (CNH de PJ), in collaboration with the Secretariat for Hispanic Affairs.

D. *Formation: From Good Will to Skills*

1. Background

67. Throughout the process and in the conclusions of the III Encuentro, we have found the following to be true of Hispanic people with respect to formation.

There is an appreciation for the great efforts being made to form pastoral ministers on the part of the institutes, centers of pastoral ministry, schools of ministry, parishes, and others that have brought about a greater conscientization, sense of responsibility, and desire for participation.

There is a lack of pastoral ministers, which makes uncertain the survival of the Catholic faith among Hispanics. Pastoral ministers, especially the laity, have not always found support, interest, recognition, or acceptance in church structures such as the parish and diocesan offices.

68. There is need for the creation of centers and programs of formation, spirituality, and catechesis that can respond to the needs of Hispanics, especially at the parish level.

It is important that the projects of formation/spirituality that are developed have an integral and missionary dimension and bring about a commitment to justice. Integral leadership formation must include basic catechetical training.

2. Specific Objective

69. To provide leadership formation adapted to the Hispanic culture in the United States that will help people to live and promote a style of Church which will be a leaven of the kingdom of God in society.

3. Programs and Projects

a) *Program of Reflection and Conscientization*

70. Facilitate the continuation of the theological-pastoral reflection at all levels as an integral part of pastoral ministry and a way of discerning the journey of the people.

(1) To foster theological-pastoral reflection for pastoral ministers at the grass-roots level who accompany the people in the pastoral process.

How: Local workshops; a workbook of guidelines to assist ministers in facilitating such reflection in small ecclesial communities.

When: In accordance with the normal channels for plans and programs and budget procedures of the respective entities involved.

Responsible Agents: Pastor and parish leaders assisted by the diocesan offices for Hispanic affairs, other diocesan offices, the National
Federation of Pastoral Institutes, in collaboration with the Secretariat
for Hispanic Affairs and the NCCB Committee on the Laity.

71. (2) Organize seminars/study sessions of reflection for pastoral
specialists in the different areas of liturgy, catechesis, theology, and
evangelization.

How: Regional seminars/study sessions, in collaboration with the
pastoral institutes.

When: In accordance with the normal channels for plans and programs and budget procedures of the respective entities involved.

Responsible Agent: National Federation of Pastoral Institutes and
the *Instituto de Liturgia Hispana*.

b) Research Projects

72. To study scientifically the Hispanic reality in its socioeconomic,
cultural, religious, and psychological aspects; especially concentrate
on:

- the family;
- popular religiosity;
- poor and marginalized (migrants, barrio, urban poor);
- youth; and
- women.

How: Procure scholarships for research on the graduate level.

When: In accordance with the normal channels for plans and programs and budget procedures of the respective entities involved.

Responsible Agents: NCCB Committee for Hispanic Affairs and other
appropriate NCCB/USCC committees (in cooperation with Catholic
universities and colleges, and seminaries, with the collaboration of
the National Federation of Pastoral Institutes).

c) Programs to Identify Candidates for Ordained Ministry and the Vowed Life

73. To design, support, and implement vocation programs sensitive
to Hispanic cultural and religious perspectives.

(1) Prepare lay Hispanic men and women to become vocation
recruiters.

How: Develop training programs for Hispanic laity in collaboration
with diocesan and religious vocation directors.

When: In accordance with the normal channels for plans and programs and budget procedures of the respective entities involved.

Responsible Agents: Bishops' Committee on Vocations, National Conference of Diocesan Vocation Directors, and the National Religious Vocation Conference.

74. (2) Place Hispanic vocations as a priority on the agenda of Hispanic lay organizations.

How: Develop vocation-awareness training sessions for leadership of Hispanic lay organizations.

When: In accordance with the normal channels for plans and programs and budget procedures of the respective entities involved.

Responsible Agents: Bishops' Committee on Vocations, in collaboration with regional and diocesan offices of Hispanic affairs.

75. (3) Prepare vocation directors to recruit, more effectively, Hispanic candidates.

How: Sponsor training workshops such as *In My Father's House*.

When: In accordance with the normal channels for plans and programs and budget procedures of the respective entities involved.

Responsible Agents: Bishops' Committee on Vocations, National Conference of Diocesan Vocation Directors, and the National Religious Vocation Conference.

76. (4) Involve Hispanic parishioners in identifying potential candidates for priesthood and religious life.

How: Implement the CALLED BY NAME parish-based program.

When: In accordance with the normal channels for plans and programs and budget procedures of the respective entities involved.

Responsible Agents: Bishops' Committee on Vocations, in collaboration with diocesan vocation directors.

d) *Programs of Formation and Training*

77. To organize courses for training of leaders at different places and levels, with emphasis on the participation of the priority groups according to the content and experience of the III Encuentro.

(1) Train leaders from the people to create, encourage, and coordinate small ecclesial communities and represent the voice of the people in civic and social institutions. Provide guidelines for liturgical celebrations which will facilitate the spiritual growth of these gatherings.

How: Training sessions, courses on the local level, and mobile teams of formation.

When: In accordance with the normal channels for plans and programs and budget procedures of the respective entities involved.

Responsible Agents: Pastors and parish leaders in coordination with diocesan offices for Hispanic affairs, other diocesan offices, regional pastoral institutes, and the *Instituto de Liturgia Hispana*.

78. (2) Elaborate a program on the importance of the role of women in the history of Hispanics and in the Church to look deeply at feminine and masculine dimensions of the human person; to value the place of women within the Hispanic context and in relation to other cultures. Train leaders to be able to apply this program at the level of the small ecclesial communities.

How: Through seminars and courses conducted by the regional institutes.

When: In accordance with the normal channels for plans and programs and budget procedures of the respective entities involved.

Responsible Agents: National Federation of Pastoral Institutes, in collaboration with the Secretariat for Hispanic Affairs and NCCB Committee on Women in Society and the Church.

79. (3) To elaborate a program of youth pastoral ministry for youth leaders and adult advisors that contains elements of culture, politics, socioeconomics, pastoral life, vision of the Church, and youth pastoral techniques.

How: Naming a task force to design such a program; training teams in use of the program.

When: In accordance with the normal channels for plans and programs and budget procedures of the respective entities involved.

Responsible Agents: *Comite Nacional Hispano de Pastoral Juvenil* (CNH de PJ) in collaboration with the NCCB Committee for Hispanic Affairs and the Secretariat for Hispanic Affairs.

80. (4) To collaborate with seminaries, permanent diaconate centers, and houses of formation of religious men and women so that their formation programs for persons preparing for ministry with the Hispanic people will correspond to the vision of the process of the III Encuentro, as spelled out in the *National Pastoral Plan*.

How: Establish channels of communication and cooperation between these centers of formation and Hispanic pastoral institutes; formation programs for persons preparing for ministry with the Hispanic people.

When: In accordance with the normal channels for plans and programs and budget procedures of the respective entities involved.

Responsible Agents: National Federation of Pastoral Institutes, in collaboration with the NCCB Committees on Vocations, Priestly Formation, and the Permanent Diaconate, and the Conference of Major Superiors of Men (CMSM) and the Leadership Conference of Women Religious (LCWR).

81. (5) Encourage the use of programs of formation for Hispanic and non-Hispanic directors and personnel of diocesan offices involved in education and pastoral ministry in order to help them learn about the history, culture, needs, and pastoral principles of Hispanics.

How: Periodic study seminars for diocesan personnel, pastors, and parish personnel.

When: In accordance with the normal channels for plans and programs and budget procedures of the respective entities involved.

Responsible Agents: The diocesan bishop, in collaboration with the vicar or diocesan offices for Hispanic affairs; the area team, with the assistance of pastoral institutes.

82. (6) Invite those centers of Bible studies and materials production to produce programs and materials to assist Hispanics in the use and understanding of the Bible.

How: Communicate with the appropriate Bible centers.

When: In accordance with the normal channels for plans and programs and budget procedures of the respective entities involved.

Responsible Agents: NCCB Committee for Hispanic Affairs and Secretariat for Hispanic Affairs.

83. (7) Convoke different pastoral ministers in the nation to: study the program of proselytism among Hispanics; assess this reality; and prepare materials and mobile teams to train other pastoral agents on the local and diocesan level.

How: Through a national meeting.

When: In accordance with the normal channels for plans and programs and budget procedures of the respective entities involved.

Responsible Agent: NCCB Committee for Ecumenical and Interreligious Affairs.

e) Program of Elaboration of Materials

84. That the pastoral institutes promote and form a team responsible for producing materials popularly accessible to the people at the grass-roots level. Special recommendation for the production of:

(1) Materials that help our leaders achieve a more profound understanding of their Catholic faith and a living spirituality as committed laity.

(2) Biblical materials at the leadership and grass-roots levels that assist Catholics in understanding and living the Word in order to avoid ignorance and fundamentalism.

(3) A workbook or manual in popular language for a continuous analysis of reality in the light of the gospel and the teachings of the Church as a basis for pastoral action and its evaluation.

(4) Simple materials for pastoral ministers, for use in training workshops and courses, so they can use these materials easily in the small ecclesial communities.

(5) Resources for information on immigration. This includes the development of information materials on immigration, directed to a popular audience to provide orientation on rights of the undocumented and laws pertaining to legalization and naturalization.

(6) A handbook of guidelines on political rights and responsibilities as part of a program of conscientization on Christian responsibility to accompany a national campaign for voter registration through the involvement of parishes.

(7) A simple and practical pamphlet of orientation on parent-children relations, which keeps in mind characteristics of the Hispanic family, including production and dissemination of it for use in family gatherings or small ecclesial communities.

(8) A pamphlet on popular religiosity, its values and basis, accessible to the small ecclesial communities.

(9) Elaboration of materials in the areas of liturgy and spirituality, including liturgical catechesis with distinction of roles.

(10) Practical materials on natural family planning.

How: Formation of a production committee for the elaboration of materials.

When: In accordance with the normal channels for plans and programs and budget procedures of the respective entities involved.

Responsible Agents: National Federation of Pastoral Institutes, in collaboration with diocesan pastoral centers and the *Instituto de Liturgia Hispana*.

VII. Evaluation

A. Orientation

85. Evaluation is an integral part of pastoral planning. It is the process that keeps us in constant personal conversion as ministers and in constant communitarian conversion as a people.

It is not a matter of looking back in a purely technical way to guarantee that what has been planned has been done; rather, it must be an expression of what the Church is and does in relation to the kingdom.

With the help of evaluation, new horizons can be seen, as well as possibilities and alternatives to the efforts that have not produced results in attaining the goal. An effective evaluation should also provide the opportunity of reshaping the plan in the light of ongoing pastoral experiences.

86. Since it is not a matter of a purely technical analysis, the atmosphere in which pastoral evaluation takes place is of the greatest importance. The whole process of the III Encuentro has been accompanied by reflection and prayer, that is to say, with a *mistica*. Pastoral evaluation demands an atmosphere of reflection, trust, freedom, mutual collaboration, and communion, for what is involved is the life of the total community in its journey to the kingdom.

This demands participation by the people in the evaluation, since they have participated in the planning and decision making.

Coordination, as a central element and goal of pastoral planning, calls for periodic evaluations and not just evaluation at the end. This creates a continuous process of discerning and assessing an ever-changing reality, the totality of pastoral ministry, and the priorities involved in action.

B. Specific Objective

87. To determine if the general objective of the plan is being attained and whether the process faithfully reflects what the Church is and does in relation to the kingdom.

C. Programs and Projects

88. Carry out a continuous evaluation of the whole pastoral process according to the *National Pastoral Plan*.

1. Coordinate from the national level the total process of evaluation.

How: BEFORE: Appoint the National Advisory Committee (NAC) to design the appropriate instruments in line with the orientation and objective of the evaluation. There should be a uniform system for evaluation at the various levels; develop a training process for the use of the instruments at the regional and diocesan levels.

AFTER: Compile the data of diocesan and regional evaluation reports and the national report; employ the resources needed to interpret the reports according to the specific objective of the evaluation process; disseminate the results of the evaluation to the different levels in order to revitalize the process of pastoral planning.

When: In accordance with the normal channels for plans and programs and budget procedures of the respective entities involved.

Responsible Agents: NCCB Committee for Hispanic Affairs and the Secretariat for Hispanic Affairs, in collaboration with the National Advisory Committee (NAC).

2. Provide training and formation for the evaluation process at the regional and diocesan levels.

89. *How*: Organize a training workshop for the regional directors concerning the pastoral value, orientation, and objectives of the evaluation and the use of the instruments for the region and diocese; organize training workshops for diocesan directors at the regional level to provide orientation on the evaluation and on the use of the instrument for the diocese.

When: In accordance with the normal channels for plans and programs and budget procedures of the respective entities involved.

Responsible Agents: National Advisory Committee (NAC), in collaboration with the Secretariat for Hispanic Affairs.

3. Evaluate the pastoral plan at the diocesan level.

90. *How*: Convoke representatives of the parishes and the small ecclesial communities to use the appropriate instrument to carry out the evaluation; prepare a written report of the results of the evaluation to send to the regional office.

When: In accordance with the normal channels for plans and programs and budget procedures of the respective entities involved.

Responsible Agents: The ordinary, the vicar, and diocesan office for Hispanic affairs.

4. Evaluate the pastoral plan at the regional level.

91. *How*: Convoke representatives of the dioceses and use the appropriate instrument to carry out the evaluation; prepare a written report of the results of the evalution to send to the national office.

When: In accordance with the normal channels for plans and programs and budget procedures of the respective entities involved.

Responsible Agents: Regional offices.

5. Evaluate the pastoral plan at the national level.

92. *How*: Convoke representatives of all the regions and use the appropriate instrument to carry out the evaluation; prepare a written report of the results of the evaluation to be incorporated into the regional and diocesan evaluations for a complete interpretation of the evaluation.

When: In accordance with the normal channels for plans and programs and budget procedures of the respective entities involved.

Responsible Agents: NCCB Committee for Hispanic Affairs and the National Advisory Committee (NAC), in collaboration with the Secretariat for Hispanic Affairs.

VIII. Spirituality and *Mistica*

93. This pastoral plan is a gospel reflection of the spirituality of the Hispanic people. It is a manifestation and response of faith.

When we look at this spirituality, we find that one of the most important aspects of its content is a sense of the presence of God, which serves as a stimulus for living out one's daily commitments.

In this sense, the transcendent God is nevertheless present in human affairs and human lives. Indeed, one might go so far as to speak of God as a member of the family, with whom one converses and to whom one has recourse, not only in moments of fervent prayer, but also in one's daily living. Thus, God never fails us. He is Emmanuel, God-with-Us.

94. The Hispanic people find God in the arms of the Virgin Mary. That is why Mary, the Mother of God, as goodness, compassion, protection, inspiration, example . . . is at the heart of the Hispanic spirituality.

The saints—our brothers and sisters who have already fulfilled their lives in the following of Jesus—are examples and instruments of the revelation of God's goodness through their intercession and help.

All this makes Hispanic spirituality a home of living relationships, a family, a community. It will find expression and consequence more in ordinary life than in theory.

95. Hispanic spirituality has as one of its sources the "seeds of the Word" in the pre-Hispanic cultures, which considered their relationships with the gods and nature to be an integral part of life. In some cases, the missionaries adopted these customs and attitudes; they enriched and illuminated them so as to incarnate the Divine Word of Sacred Scripture and the Christian faith to make them come alive in religious art and drama. All this has taken shape in popular devotions which preserve and nourish the peoples' spirituality. At the same time, Christian principles have been expressed in attitudes and daily behavior which reveal divine values in the experience of the Hispanic people. This spirituality has been kept alive in the home and has become a profound tradition within the family.

96. The spirituality of the Hispanic people, a living reality throughout its journey, finds expression in numerous ways. At times it takes the form of prayer, novenas, songs, and sacred gestures. It is found in personal relationships and hospitality. At other times, it surfaces as endurance, patience, strength, and hope in the midst of suffering and difficulties. Their spirituality can also inspire a struggle for freedom, justice, and peace. Frequently it is expressed as commitment and forgiveness as well as in celebration, dance, sacred images, and symbols. Small altars in the home, statues, and candles are sacramentals of God's presence. The *pastorelas, posadas, nacimientos, via crucis,* pilgrimages; processions; and the blessings offered by mothers, fathers, and grandparents are all expressions of this faith and profound spirituality.

97. At various times through the centuries, these devotions have gone astray or have been impoverished due to the lack of a clear and enriching catechesis. This pastoral plan with its evangelizing, community-building, and formative emphasis can be a source of evangelization for these popular devotions and an encouragement for enriching liturgical celebrations with cultural expressions of faith. It seeks to free the Spirit who is alive in the gatherings of our people.

98. The III Encuentro process was yet one more step in the devel-

opment and growth of their spirituality. Many participants appeared
to have moved from a personal and family spirituality to one that is
communitarian and ecclesial. They moved from a sense of individual
and family injustices to a recognition of general injustice to all people.
This growth was sensed also in their awareness and experience of
being Church, in their familiarity with ecclesial documents, in their
active participation in liturgies and prayers.

99. For people who celebrate life and death with great intensity and
meaning, the eucharistic liturgy has a special place. The liturgy and
sacraments offer to a people imbued with a profound religious sense
the elements of community, the assurance of grace, the embodiment
of the paschal mystery, in the dying and rising of the Lord in his
people. This is especially true of what happens in the celebration of
the Eucharist—the source of our unity. Numerous possibilities are
found for artistic elements that enrich the sacramental celebrations
with originality and joyfulness. These sacramental moments capture
the spirituality and *mistica*, which overflow from the living of their
Christian vocation and their Hispanic identity.

100. In the gathering around a simple, common table, Jesus told his
disciples to "do this in memory of me." It was to this gathering that
Jesus revealed his mission, his life, his innermost prayer to his friends
and then asked them to do the same in his memory. He mandated
them to do all that he had done, had lived for, in their lives. The
consistent stopping to share a common meal has nourished the Hispanic people throughout history. As Jesus' disciples, they reserve a
place for him at the table.

101. Throughout the process of the III Encuentro, many Hispanic
Catholics have sought to live in dialogue with their God, who inspires
and motivates; with Mary, who accompanies Jesus' disciples. The
pastoral plan takes its source out of the gathering and sharing of the
Hispanic people. It is an expression of his presence in us. The pastoral
plan provides a way for this People of God to express their life with
the Spirit, a life deeply rooted in the gospel.

Resolution on Korea

A Resolution Passed by the
National Conference of Catholic Bishops

November 18, 1987

1. The peoples of Korea and the United States have had a long and cordial relationship forged by common sacrifice in war and nurtured by a shared, if at times frustrated, respect for democratic traditions. Our respective Catholic communities have long worked together to propagate our common faith and spiritual values. At the present time, some 127 American missioners and religious are serving the Church in Korea. In view of this long-standing political and religious friendship, it is natural that, as the Catholic bishops in the United States, we view the events now unfolding in Korea with great and sympathetic interests.

2. This is especially so because of the significant role played by Cardinal Kim and his fellow bishops in supporting their people's desire for political and economic justice and democratic rule. We express our admiration and respect for the leadership, the courage, and the wisdom demonstrated by our brother bishops in Korea, as well as that of the priests, religious, and laity, in their peaceful and principled contributions to the struggle for human rights.

3. The episcopal conference of the United States and the Korean episcopal conference have developed a sustained pattern of cooperation. A specific reason for this collaboration is the understanding of both conferences that the policies of the U.S. government and U.S. corporations have long had a significant impact on Korean political and economic life. From security policy to trade policy to human rights, the content of U.S. policy directly affects the lives of the Korean people. In this delicate and historic moment in the history of South Korea, we express our ecclesial solidarity and support for the bishops of Korea and the people they serve.

4. We urge the continuing dialogue and peaceful cooperation of all Koreans in seeking the goal of a tranquil society dedicated to justice, humanity, and the rule of law.

5. We call upon the U.S. government to recognize the Korean national desire for representative democracy and the importance of the Korean people's being the sole architects of their own political, economic, and security institutions.

6. Finally, we call upon the American people to support with sym-

pathy and understanding the Korean people as they struggle to establish a community that will revere both spiritual values and human rights.

Resolution on Lebanon

A Resolution Passed by the
National Conference of Catholic Bishops

November 18, 1987

1. As the Catholic bishops of the United States we have repeatedly addressed messages of solidarity and support to the Christians of Lebanon and to all the people of Lebanon in their long agony of a terrible war which has now lasted over a decade.

2. Again, this year we want to speak of Lebanon, to say to the Lebanese that their plight remains in our prayers and in our hearts; to offer whatever material or moral support that we can to alleviate their suffering and to hasten the advent of peace and justice in their homeland.

3. In the evolution of this conflict, it has always been clear that outside forces have exceedingly complicated the resolution of issues among the Lebanese. It has always been clear that settlement of the conflict will require not only courage and wisdom within Lebanon, but a disinterested and honorable concern by major outside actors, not least the United States.

4. It is too easy to say Lebanon is simply a Lebanese problem. It has always been larger than the borders of Lebanon. At a diplomatic level, we urge all the external powers affecting Lebanon to recognize the right of the Lebanese people to a future that is not subordinated to the interests of other nations, but which is conceived and realized for the welfare of the Lebanese themselves.

5. The most urgent need of the moment is economic assistance for Lebanon. The war has taken its toll not only of individual lives but of the nation's economic and social system. The Lebanese need food, medicines, and other basic humanitarian aid. We urge the executive and legislative branches of the U.S. government to take a fresh look at the emergency needs of the Lebanese people and to respond with generosity required by these needs.

6. As bishops, we pledge an increased effort by our Catholic agencies to meet the needs of the Christian community in Lebanon and the needs of the wider Lebanese population. We also pledge to the bishops of Lebanon and their people our continued interest, support, and availability to respond to their requests of us.

Norms for Priests and Their Third Age

A Statement Issued by the
National Conference of Catholic Bishops

November 18, 1987

1. The senior years of a priest's ordained ministry, especially the retirement years, are important for the proper completion and perfection of the priestly vocation. These norms, in accord with the *Code of Canon Law*, are intended to promote both the value and the dignity of the person as well as the ministry and mission of the Church. These norms, in accord with the *Code of Canon Law*, suggest that retirement from a diocesan appointment does not imply an end to ministry. Rather, they speak of an entry into a third age where the Spirit is calling us to reflect upon, to integrate, and to complete the ministry to which we were called.

2. The bishop normally should allow any priest to retire when he has reached the age of seventy-five. The diocesan bishop, in consultation with the presbyteral council, can adopt a diocesan policy that allows priests, for pastoral or personal reasons, to retire from diocesan assignment at an earlier age. Pastors are asked to submit their letters of resignation by the age of seventy-five.

> Canon 538,3: When a pastor has completed his seventy-fifth year of age he is asked to submit his resignation from office to the diocesan bishop, who, after considering all the circumstances of person and place, is to decide whether to accept or defer the resignation; the diocesan bishop, taking into account the norms determined by the conference of bishops, is to provide for the suitable support and housing of the resigned pastor (*Code of Canon Law*, Washington, D.C., Canon Law Society of America, 1983).

3. Diocesan policy should specify the age when every priest will enter into a process of discernment with the diocesan bishop regarding when and how he will retire from diocesan appointment. Further, all dioceses should provide for those who, through disability, have to retire prior to the age determined by diocesan policy.

4. The diocesan bishop, in consultation with the presbyteral council, might wish to consider the naming of a retirement committee for the purpose of discerning with each given priest his proper time for resigning his diocesan appointment. While retaining to himself the right to make the final decision with any given priest, the diocesan bishop will be assisted and guided by the report and the reflections which such a committee will offer him.

5. Each diocese should maintain its own index of senior priests.

Thus, retired from their own diocesan appointments, these men could indicate the kinds of ministry they want to continue to offer. The pastors of the diocese would thus be able to contact those priests easily in times of special need.

6. Diocesan bishops should develop plans and programs to assist priests with preparation for their third age. This will enhance the value of this third age both for the individual priest and for the local church whose ministry will continue to be a central focus of his life.

7. Diocesan bishops should appoint a priest whose duties include assisting senior priests with their third-age planning as well as being an advocate for their concerns. The diocese also is encouraged to provide options for third-age ministry.

8. Diocesan bishops should strongly promote a program that encourages the physical, emotional, and spiritual health of all priests. Senior priests must be included in such programs; and, efforts to provide sufficient medical insurance for them are essential.

9. The diocese should provide various options for the housing of third-age priests, according to diocesan policy. Normally, the retiring priest should be given a choice in regard to his retirement housing.

10. Diocesan bishops should provide as a norm special arrangements for those who are physically or emotionally in need of such care.

11. Each diocese should guarantee that priests be given adequate support through a long-range, financially independent, and professionally managed pension fund. In addition, the priest should bear in mind responsible stewardship of his own resources. Participation in the social security system, as well as IRAs or other forms of savings, is considered an essential element of this stewardship. He should also be mindful of the needs of the local church in his last will and testament.

12. The diocesan bishops should normally ensure that diocesan programs give specific consideration to the spiritual growth of third-age priests. Thus the diocesan program of retreats, conferences, mentoring, spiritual direction, and support groups all should consider the senior priests.

13. Diocesan bishops and priests should develop a special sensitivity to the needs and the inclusion of the senior priests in diocesan life.

14. Dioceses, in their efforts to provide effective retirement policies and procedures, should be aware of the resources and expertise provided by national organizations both within and outside the Church.

Statement on School-based Clinics

A Statement Issued by the
National Conference of Catholic Bishops

November 18, 1987

Always be prepared to make a defense to any one who calls you to account for the hope that is in you.

Peter 3:15

1.   With these words, Pope John Paul II greeted the young people of the world in 1985, when he issued his apostolic letter celebrating International Youth Year. The Holy Father focused on youth as a time of hope, reminding young people not only that "the future belongs to you" but also that "the future depends on you"—that the youth of today must be prepared to take moral responsibility for the plans and actions that will build or endanger the world of tomorrow.[1]

2.   In what follows, we address a specific issue affecting the physical, emotional, and moral health of young people in the United States, within this context articulated by the Holy Father. With him, we see youth as a special stage of development when each human individual begins making his or her own truly personal decisions—decisions of great social as well as personal importance. Youth is also a fragile time, when the spark of hope in the future must be nurtured, harmonized with intellectual development, and channeled toward service to others in love. Whether this occurs in an individual case will depend to an incalculable degree on the ways in which parents, schools, churches, and society at large are willing and able to challenge young people to live up to their God-given human dignity.

3.   To forget the need for this challenge—or to set it aside to pursue short-sighted agendas that are unworthy of the dignity of human persons—is to do a disservice to young people themselves and to everyone whose hope for the future rests on them. This is why we invite not only Catholics but all people of good will to reflect on the concerns expressed in this statement. We ask parents, pastors, and teachers who directly deal with young people, to give them special attention.

---

[1]John Paul II, *Apostolic Letter to the Youth of the World on the Occasion of International Youth Year* (Washington, D.C.: USCC Office of Publishing and Promotion Services, 1985), n. 1.

Teen Pregnancy and the
School-based Clinic

4. Our nation prides itself on its ability to confront, analyze, and solve difficult problems. Yet continuing high pregnancy rates among unwed teenagers seem to many Americans to present a hopeless situation. And the problem has worsened since the federal government and other public and private agencies began spending many millions of dollars annually on family planning services.

5. The sobering reality is this: A dramatic increase in sexual activity has given rise to a similar increase in teenage pregnancy; access to contraceptives has also greatly increased, but this has not led to reductions in pregnancy rates among teenagers. In fact, such access may have helped to confirm teenagers in their sexually active behavior. In recent years, birthrates among sexually active teenagers have dropped, but chiefly because of a massive increase in abortions performed on teenage girls.[2]

6. Confronted with two decades of disappointing results, some family planning advocates have declared this to be a "time for new thinking about teenage pregnancy." A landmark editorial with this title, published in a prominent medical journal in 1985, urged that family planning clinics' current emphasis on voluntariness and "nondirective" counseling be discarded when dealing with teenagers. A more aggressive approach was recommended in which counselors would give "authoritative guidance," stressing "the critical importance of compliance" with a contraceptive regimen.[3]

---

[2]"Between 1971 and 1976 the proportion of white teenagers who had ever been pregnant increased in rough proportion to their increased rates of sexual activity. . . . During this same period, there was reported an impressive improvement in contraceptive use, regularity of use and use of the more effective methods. Why this improvement did not result in a pregnancy decline requires more detailed analysis" in Zelnik and Kantner, "First Pregnancies to Women Aged 15-19: 1976 and 1971," *Teenage Sexuality, Pregnancy, and Childbearing*, Furstenberg, Lincoln and Menken, eds. (Philadelphia: University of Pennsylvania Press, 1981), p. 106. The same trends are apparent in more recent surveys by the federal government: U.S. Centers for Disease Control, "Teenage Pregnancy and Fertility in the United States, 1970, 1974, and 1980," *CDC Surveillance Summaries*, February 1987 (*Morbidity and Mortality Weekly Report* 1987, 36 pp. 1SS-10SS). New tentative data indicate a slight decrease in the teen pregnancy rate between 1980 and 1983. Maciak, Spitz, Strauss et al., "Pregnancy and Birth Rates Among Sexually Experienced Teenagers—1974, 1980, and 1983," *Journal of the American Medical Association* 258 (1987): 2069-2071. The authors suggest without evidence that this decrease may be partly due to "increased use of contraception," but their data indicate another factor: The percentage of teenagers becoming sexually active leveled off during these years. This study is therefore consistent with the suggestion that reductions in pregnancy rates are best sought by addressing the deeper problem of premature sexual activity.

[3]Dryfoos, "A Time for New Thinking about Teenage Pregnancy," *American Journal of Public Health* 75 (January 1985): 13-14. This editorial's author went on to become a leading advocate of school-based clinics (see footnote 4) and now serves on the Board of Directors of the Center for Population Options, which coordinates strategy for their establishment nationwide.

7.   In this context, a nationwide campaign has been launched to provide contraceptive services on or adjacent to public school property. The basic concept of school-based clinics is not new and is not necessarily associated with the provision of contraceptive services to unmarried minors. Yet a new campaign to garner support and funding for nationwide establishment of such clinics seems motivated in large part by an interest in using the schools for these services, based on a realization that past pregnancy reduction efforts have been unsuccessful. It is this aspect of the school-based clinic campaign that has deservedly provoked opposition and controversy. Some advocates of school-based contraceptive clinics claim they offer certain advantages:

- They provide direct access to students during the school day, facilitating "follow-up" visits and supportive counseling on consistent use of contraceptives.
- They promote "confidentiality" by obviating the need for follow-up calls to parents' homes.
- They can offer other health services to attract students in the early stages of a sexually active lifestyle and to reduce any "stigma" that young people may associate with visiting a birth control clinic.
- They can utilize a school's system of rewards and punishments to encourage contraceptive use (as in one administrator's plan to have students earn points toward school trips and other perquisites by keeping their clinic appointments).[4]

8.   We object to the campaign to provide contraceptive services through school-based clinics on both moral and practical grounds. We will address the moral dimension first, then discuss briefly whether this campaign seems likely to be effective even on its own pragmatic terms.

Questions of Principle

9.   From the viewpoint of moral principle, this approach to teenage pregnancy is misguided because it fails to respect the dignity of teenagers, their parents, and their teachers.

10.   *The Human Dignity of Young People.* We maintain that every human person is of inestimable worth as a child of God made in his image and likeness. Sexuality is an integral aspect of human dignity; it is not merely physical in nature, for it is capable of expressing and confirming the deepest possible form of human intimacy. Through their sexuality, human beings are called to reflect the intimacy and

---

[4]Dryfoos, "School-based Health Clinics: A New Approach to Preventing Adolescent Pregnancy?" *Family Planning Perspectives* 17 (March/April 1985): 70-75.

permanency of the divine love and to exercise responsibly the awesome power to become co-creators of new human life.

11. The genital expression of human sexuality is ordered to a total giving of oneself to another person in marriage. Because premarital sexual activity divorces sexual intimacy from the total personal commitment, which is its only adequate context, such activity fails to live up to the truth of the human person.[5] This is why we counsel young people to respect God's law, which calls for sexual abstinence before marriage. Unmarried teenagers who fall into sexual relationships often end in exploiting each other, and the inevitable failure of such relationships can seriously harm the self-esteem and openness to others of those involved. Educational programs that ignore these realities and treat sex as a purely physiological reality or implicitly condone it as a form of recreation distort human sexuality and thereby do an injustice to students.[6]

12. A school-based program for providing contraceptives to unmarried teenagers fails to respect teenagers themselves because it takes a promiscuous lifestyle for granted and resorts to the deception that premarital sexual activity is without adverse consequences so long as pregnancy is avoided. This message makes light of the serious medical, emotional, moral, and spiritual consequences of premature sexual experimentation. Teenagers are taught to deal with their sexuality by suppressing their fertility with drugs and devices, instead of learning the self-control needed to live in harmony with the precious gift of sexuality and its power to create new life. The adverse consequences may include impairment of the ability later in life to form a lasting and satisfying commitment in marriage.[7] A school-based clinic for providing contraceptives to unmarried teenagers contributes to the illusion that it is always possible to have sexual intercourse without being prepared to assume the responsibility of parenthood. It does teenagers a disservice by deceiving them about the physical and emotional realities of sexual intimacy and by failing to teach them the highest standards of responsibility.

---

[5]In addition to the dignity of the human person, as such, for the Christian man and woman this sexual experimentation fails to live up to the fundamental call to holiness as expressed in 1 Thes 4:2-5 and 1 Cor 6:13-15,17-20.

[6]See Second Vatican Council, *Pastoral Constitution on the Church in the Modern World*, nn. 49-50; National Conference of Catholic Bishops, *To Live in Christ Jesus: A Pastoral Reflection on the Moral Life* (November 11, 1976), nn. 50-51; Sacred Congregation for the Doctrine of the Faith, *Declaration on Certain Questions concerning Sexual Ethics* (December 29, 1975); Idem., *Educational Guidance in Human Love* (November 1, 1983); Pope John Paul II, *Familiaris Consortio: The Apostolic Exhortation on the Family* (November 22, 1981), n. 11.

[7]See *To Live in Christ Jesus*, n. 51. Recent data suggest that even stable premarital cohabitation arrangements may be associated with lower degrees of marital communication and satisfaction later in life. See DeMaris and Leslie, "Cohabitation with the Future Spouse: Its Influence upon Marital Satisfaction and Communication," *Journal of Marriage and the Family* 46 (February 1984): 77-85.

13. Many school-based clinics do even greater harm by facilitating abortion in cases when a teenage girl becomes pregnant. Some clinics refer directly for abortion; others have arrangements with outside agencies that advocate and refer for abortions.[8] Such arrangements are not only unjust and destructive to the unborn child—they also show little concern for the well-being of the teenage girl who is persuaded to eliminate her child. We deplore this tragic destruction of human life and its awful consequences for young women. In these instances, the school-based clinic becomes yet another influence teaching young people that expedient violence is an acceptable means for solving problems. Moreover, by facilitating abortion as a last resort for resolving contraceptive failure, they create a further incentive to irresponsible sexual behavior.

14. The Rights of Parents. Because they have conferred life on their children, parents have an original, primary, and inalienable right to guide their education and socialization. They also have a right and responsibility to guide their children's health care. Such rights are not delegated by the state, but are inherent in the parent-child relationship; hence, even government may not override parents in this regard unless failure to do so will seriously endanger the well-being of a particular child.[9]

15. The threat posed to parents' rights by school-based contraceptive clinics seems evident, since one reason for locating these clinics in schools is to gain access to teenagers without their parents' involvement. Although many school-based clinics provide for some form of parental consultation, this often consists of a signature approving unlimited clinic visits of an unspecified nature for an entire school year or even for an entire term of study. Confidentiality is invoked to bar parents from reviewing their children's records and from learning of specific visits, services, or prescriptions.[10]

16. Such policies are in stark and ironic contrast with numerous laws and policies requiring parental consent for the simplest of procedures affecting a child's health. There is no justification for a double standard that requires schools to obtain parental consent before a school nurse can dispense an aspirin for a headache, but provides for access to contraceptive drugs and devices without parental consultation. Mindful that millions of Catholic parents have children in the public schools,

---

[8]Dryfoos, "School-based Health Clinics," p. 73.

[9]See Vatican, *Charter of the Rights of the Family* (October 22, 1983), art. 5. On parents' right to determine medical treatment for their children, and the limits of that right, see Bryce, "The Treatment of Infants Born with Handicapping Conditions," Statement on Behalf of the NCCB Committee for Pro-Life Activities before the U.S. House Education and Labor Subcommittee on Select Education, October 1982.

[10]Dryfoos, "School-based Health Clinics," p. 73.

we particularly object to contraceptive programs, which undermine the moral and religious values that parents try to impart to their children. Moreover, we note that many non-Catholic parents and religious leaders have raised objections similar to our own.

17. *The Role of the School.* People of every race, condition, and age, by virtue of their dignity as human persons, have an inalienable right to education—an education that will promote moral as well as physical and intellectual maturity. The school is of outstanding importance in helping parents prepare their children to assume adult responsibilities.[11] Society has an obligation to ensure that schools are not diverted from this vital and difficult task of promoting intellectual and moral development.

18. School-based contraceptive clinics pose a threat to the public school system because they render the schools more controversial, divert them from their traditional role of imparting knowledge and building character, and raise new problems of legal liability. To the extent that schools become involved in providing or prescribing contraceptives, their admonitions to "say no" to irresponsible and destructive behavior will be drained of moral authority, and the schools will lose the effectiveness they might have had in helping parents to impart healthy values to their children.

The Question of Effectiveness

19. These concerns would be valid even if it could be demonstrated that school-based clinics will substantially reduce teenage pregnancy rates. But this approach may fail even by its own pragmatic standards, just as previous efforts to promote contraception and abortion in our society have failed to provide the benefits promised by their advocates.

20. It is now well established that knowledge of and access to contraceptives do not ensure prevention of pregnancy among teenagers. Some studies even claim that access to family planning clinics is associated with an increase in sexual activity, pregnancies, and abortions.[12] Others indicate that special counseling and aggressive promotion of contraceptives, of the kind that school-based contraceptive clinics supposedly make possible, may have little lasting effect in either increas-

---

[11]Second Vatican Council, *Decree on Christian Education*, nn. 1, 5.

[12]Weed and Olsen, "Effects of Family-Planning Programs for Teenagers on Adolescent Birth and Pregnancy Rates" and "Effects of Family-Planning Programs on Teenage Pregnancy—Replication and Extension," *Family Perspective* 20 (1986): 153-170, 173-195. See Raspberry, "Some Questions on Birth Control and Teenagers," the *Washington Post* (October 17, 1986).

ing or decreasing pregnancy rates.[13] Some advocates of school-based contraceptive programs, while claiming significant reductions in the "fertility rate" among students, have had to admit that this signifies a decrease in live *births* which may be attributable to an increase in abortions rather than to a decrease in pregnancies.[14]

21. One recent study has been described in some of the popular media as showing that school-based clinics reduce both sexual activity and pregnancies. But in fact the study dealt with a program in which several different services coexisted, including access to a family planning clinic as well as counseling designed to counter peer pressure to engage in sexual activity. Apparently, the counseling led to a slight *delay* in the *onset* of sexual activity among teenagers. The researchers did not investigate whether this delay would have been greater, or its results more lasting, if the teenagers had not received a mixed message from the simultaneous promotion of abstinence and contraception.[15]

22. Even as a short-term solution to teen pregnancy, then, school-based contraceptive services have not been shown to deliver what they promise. They will certainly fail as a long-term solution because they ignore the root causes of the teen pregnancy problem and fail to mobilize the inner resources of teenagers, parents, and teachers to address those causes in a responsible manner.

23. Particularly disturbing are some recent proposals for rendering contraceptive programs more effective in reducing teenage pregnancy. Family planning advocates have often argued that contraceptive-

---

[13]Brief descriptions of some of the most recent studies can be found in: "Birth Control Access Not Factor in Teen Repeat Pregnancy Rate," *Ob.Gyn. News* (January 1-14, 1986); Teltsch, "Teen-age Mothers Get Aid in Study: Program Succeeds in Curbing Pregnancies, but its Effect Wears Off after a Year," the *New York Times* (May 19, 1985); "Contraceptive Counseling for Abortion Patients," *Ob.Gyn. News* (February 15-28, 1986); Herveg-Baron, Furstenberg, Shea and Harris, "Supporting Teenagers' Use of Contraceptives: A Comparison of Clinic Services," *Family Planning Perspectives* 18 (March/April 1986): 61; Archdiocese of Boston, *Report on School-based Health Clinics* (Boston: Daughters of St. Paul, 1986), pp. 37-40.

[14]See Kenney, "School-based Clinics: A National Conference," in *Family Planning Perspectives* 18 (January/February 1986): 45; Mosbacker, *Teen Pregnancy and School-based Health Clinics* (Washington D.C.: Family Research Council of America, 1986), pp. 4-5.

[15]Some newspapers mistakenly reported that the contraceptive clinic adjacent to the school was determined to be responsible for the delay in onset of sexual activity — see for example "Counseling by School Clinics Said to Aid Sexual Restraint," in the *Washington Post* (October 16, 1986). What originally prompted the provision of special services was an enormous increase in rates of sexual activity in Baltimore inner-city high schools after introduction of a state-mandated sex education course. The claim that the special services markedly reduced pregnancy rates among the sexually active has been questioned because of the small sample population and the absence of data on changes in the abortion rate. Regarding the study and its critics see: Zabin, Hirsch, Smith, Streett and Hardy, "Evaluation of a Pregnancy Prevention Program for Urban Teenagers," *Family Planning Perspectives* 18 (May/June 1986): 119-126; Weed, "Curbing Births, Not Pregnancies," in the *Wall Street Journal* (October 14, 1986); Schevtchuk, "School Sexuality Program Criticized," *National Catholic News Service* (July 16, 1986.)

oriented sex education does not encourage premarital sex, and that contraceptive services are directed to teenagers who are already sexually active. Increasingly, this approach is now rejected as inadequate because it is believed that teenagers must be reached and trained in contraceptive use before they have begun having sexual intercourse. Moreover, the argument is now heard that "ambivalence" about teenage sexuality, specifically moral and religious qualms about premarital sexual experimentation, should be combatted because this ambivalence prevents teenagers from wholeheartedly embracing a contraceptive regimen.[16] With such arguments, the debate has already moved beyond the question of whether family planning clinics may *inadvertently* encourage premarital sex among teenagers—such encouragement is suggested as a necessary element of the solution. We object to such proposals on moral grounds, while also noting that explicit promotion of a promiscuous lifestyle is likely to *aggravate* the problems of teenage pregnancy and abortion.

Meeting Health-Care Needs

24. It is often said that school-based clinics are necessary to meet the general health care needs of students in the public schools. We agree that the basic health needs of young people, particularly in low-income areas, are not being adequately addressed in our nation. The question whether school-based health clinics offer the best solution to this problem is distinguishable from the question of contraceptive and abortion services and deserves consideration on its own merits.
25. In this regard, we wish to place in perspective the benefits that school-based health services can realistically be expected to provide. We believe basic health care must be improved for all low-income Americans—especially for the very young and the very old, who are most vulnerable—and not only for the school-age population. Among teenagers, those most in need of improved care may be those who have already dropped out of school. Also needed is more adequate funding of existing local, state, and federal health care programs such as WIC and Medicaid; without adequate funding, improved access to

---

[16]In most school-based clinics, teenagers' initial clinic visits are for nonsexual matters but they "are asked at their initial visit if they are sexually active. If they are *or plan to be soon*, they are encouraged to practice contraception" (Dryfoos, "School-based Health Clinics," p. 72; emphasis added). For the claim that contraceptive training must be inculcated in teenagers *before* they become sexually active see: Finkel and Finkel, "Sexual and Contraceptive Knowledge, Attitudes and Behavior of Male Adolescents," in Herveg-Baron et al., p. 334. The authors dismiss the argument that this approach may encourage premarital sex because they take as a given that "no program or policy decision can hope to prevent premarital coitus" in any event. For the claim that contraceptive effectiveness is reduced by ambivalent attitudes toward premarital sex, see the statements by Wulf and Lincoln (p. 52), Jones, et al. (pp. 59, 61), and Kisker (pp. 83-84) *Family Planning Perspectives* 17 (March/April 1985).

clinics will mean little. In a given case, the establishment of a new clinic in a public school may actually divert funds from more cost-effective initiatives.[17]

26. Furthermore, the most serious threats to the life and health of our nation's students are not primarily "health care" problems in a narrow sense. They involve self-destructive behavior patterns associated with problems of attitude and character, frequently aggravated by oppressive poverty and by a real or perceived lack of meaningful opportunities for the future. The most prominent killers of teenagers today are drugs and alcohol, automobile accidents, homicide, and suicide.[18] Schools and other institutions must work with parents to combat these threats, but that response may not lie primarily in the area of medical practice.

27. Finally, if school-based health clinics are to make a positive contribution to students' health, school officials must be wary of proposed "medical" solutions that may be counterproductive. For example, most parents and teachers would presumably oppose the distribution in the schools of sterile intravenous needles to prevent transmission of AIDS, since this gesture would undermine efforts to teach students to "say no" to drugs. The distribution of condoms to prevent pregnancy and the sexual transmission of AIDS deserves similar skepticism. The possible long-term physical complications of some contraceptive drugs and devices should raise questions about their inclusion among clinic services on public health grounds alone.[19] And at a time when the teenage suicide rate is frighteningly high, and by some reports even higher among the sexually active, it would be gravely

[17]See Archdiocese of Boston, "Report on School-based Health Clinics," pp. 17-18.

[18]U.S. Bureau of the Census, *Statistical Abstract of the United States 1987* (Washington D.C., 1986), pp. 76, 79. According to Dr. Robert L. Johnson of the New Jersey Medical School, "each year nearly 55,000 American adolescents die as the result of some form of violence (accidents 24,000; suicide 5,000-6,000; homicide 6,000). These occurrences are often associated with some form of risk taking and the adolescents' belief in their own indestructibility; they may also be the result of drug and alcohol use or unrecognized or untreated depression" (Testimony to the U.S. House Energy and Commerce Subcommittee on Health and the Environment, June 5, 1987). For young black males in the U.S., homicide is now the leading cause of death. See U.S. Centers for Disease Control, "Annual Summary 1984: Reported Morbidity and Mortality in the United States," *Morbidity and Mortality Weekly Report* 32:54 (1986): 91-93.

[19]The adverse effects of DES and intrauterine devices are now well known. At present, most teenage clients at family planning clinics are given oral contraceptives for pregnancy prevention. The U.S. Food and Drug Administration requires oral contraceptive manufacturers to include the following warning in their package inserts: "The use of oral contraceptives is associated with increased risk of several serious conditions including thromboembolism, stroke, myocardial infarction, liver tumor, gall bladder disease, visual disturbances, fetal abnormalities, and hypertension." These contraceptives, of course, provide no protection against sexually transmitted diseases and may actually increase the likelihood of chlamydia infections: Williams (ed.), *Contraceptive Technology 1986-1987* (New York: Irvington, 1986), p. 139. Women who begin using the pill at a very young age, or who use it before their first pregnancy, are among those who may be at heightened risk of breast cancer (ibid., p. 159). While ordinarily physicians advise

irresponsible to prescribe for teenage girls contraceptive drugs whose side effects include severe depression — and particularly irresponsible to do so while keeping parents in the dark.[20]

28. In short, school-based health clinics — *not* contraceptive clinics — may be a partial solution to the health needs of young people. This is a complex issue which may be resolved differently in different areas depending on local social and economic factors and the kinds of services offered. But any legitimate role such clinics might play in providing health services will be undermined by inclusion of contraception and abortion-related services.

29. Unfortunately, major organizations supporting and funding establishment of school-based clinics have announced a policy that such services must be included in any "comprehensive health care" agenda.[21] In some cases, clinic advocates have agreed initially not to provide these services, only to reintroduce them after establishment of a school-based clinic.[22] Skepticism regarding the overall agenda of the school-based clinic campaign is therefore warranted. A given clinic will not merit support unless it clearly separates itself from the campaign to facilitate contraception and abortion for unmarried minors.

A Positive Approach

30. Despite considerable controversy regarding family planning clinics, there is a remarkable degree of consensus among social and behavioral scientists regarding the basic causes of high teenage pregnancy

---

that teenagers should have six to twelve regular periods before oral contraceptives are prescribed, they prescribe them for sexually active teenagers who have not begun menstruating on the grounds that "the medical and social risks of pregnancy probably exceed the risks of taking oral contraceptives" (ibid., p. 156). In light of high contraceptive failure rates among young teenagers, and the high discontinuance rate for oral contraceptives in this age group due to unpleasant side-effects, one cannot treat realistically contraceptives and pregnancy as *mutually exclusive* risk factors.

[20]See "Youth Suicide — United States, 1970-1980," in U.S. Centers for Disease Control, *Morbidity and Mortality Weekly Report* 36 (February 20, 1987): 87-89. Particularly alarming is a recent finding that students receiving reproductive health services such as family planning from school-based clinics in New York City were twice as likely to have experienced severe depression and three times as likely to have attempted suicide compared with students receiving general health care. Welfare Research, Inc., *Health Services for High School Students: Assessment of the New York City (High) School-based Clinics Funded by the New York State Department of Health* (Short-Term Assessment) (New York, June 3, 1987), p. 79. Depression and even suicidal impulses have long been recognized as possible side-effects of oral contraceptives: *Contraceptive Technology*, p. 167; Seaman, *The Doctors' Case against the Pill* (New York: Doubleday, 1980), pp. 129-137; Mintz, *The Pill: An Alarming Report* (Boston: Beacon Press, 1970), pp. 109-110.

[21]See Dryfoos, "School-based Health Clinics," p. 71; Archdiocese of Boston, "Report on School-based Health Clinics," pp. 9-10.

[22]"Most school-based clinics began by offering comprehensive health care, then added family planning services later, at least partly in order to avoid local controversy" (Dryfoos, "School-based Health Clinics," p. 71).

rates. That consensus was recently affirmed by a panel of the National Academy of Sciences (NAS) in a major report on adolescent sexuality, pregnancy, and childbearing.[23]

31. NAS researchers recognize, as anyone must, that rising teen pregnancy rates are due to an increase in premarital sexual activity. They further recognize that decisions about whether or not to become sexually active are rooted in social, economic, and psychological factors affecting teenagers' ability to act responsibly in their own best interests. But they conclude that "we currently know very little about how to discourage effectively unmarried teenagers from initiating intercourse," and so reason that society must take a high rate of teen sexual activity for granted while adopting the purely symptomatic solution promised by programs of contraception and abortion for minors.[24]

32. We part from the NAS regarding this final counsel of despair. To despair of improving teenagers' self-discipline and their hope for the future is to abandon hope not only with regard to the teen pregnancy problem but with regard to teenagers themselves.

33. Specifically, we question the NAS report's suggestion that efforts to teach sexual abstinence to teenagers will be ineffective. In fact, it is the family planning movement's agenda that has been implemented for almost two decades and proven ineffective. Teaching self-control and moral responsibility and creating an environment in which this teaching can become meaningful and be acted upon have not been attempted on an adequate scale during this time. In recent decades, our public schools have moved directly from comparative silence regarding sexuality to a "value-neutral" informational approach, without pausing to consider a different approach to sex education: one that places biological facts in a context of moral responsibility to oneself and others.

34. Admittedly, such an approach cannot succeed in a vacuum. What is needed is something quite radical, in the original sense of the word: an approach that rejects mere alleviation of superficial symptoms and reaches the root of the problem. This approach must have at least four components.

35. First, schools must be encouraged to do their job of imparting basic knowledge and skills. If part of the teen pregnancy problem is a lack of discipline and maturity among young people, schools can contribute to a solution by teaching responsible habits of thinking and living. Campaigns to persuade young people to delay sexual activity and childbearing are more likely to touch a responsive chord if students have skills which they feel will help them play a significant role in society after they leave school.

---

[23]National Research Council, *Risking the Future: Adolescent Sexuality, Pregnancy, and Childbearing* (Washington D.C.: National Academy Press, 1987).

[24]Ibid., p. 262; on abortion, see pp. 264–65.

36. Pregnancy rates have reportedly decreased in communities where young people are involved in meaningful job preparation and in athletic and creative activities. Some data indicate that early childhood education programs reduce the chances that a child will experience an unwed pregnancy and other serious problems later in life.[25] Thus, some of the most effective responses to teenage pregnancy, as well as to problems such as drug abuse, may not specifically concern sexuality as such and may not always be conducted during the teen years. It is important for schools to maintain and improve their vital and irreplaceable role as training grounds for future workers, leaders, and citizens; support and funding for this difficult task should not be diverted to questionable agendas such as that of the family planning movement.

37. Second, young people need reasons for hope. They will have little motivation to develop the character and skills needed to plan for the future unless they can see a future for themselves that is worth the effort. Making the future possible requires more than education and counseling—it requires a concerted effort to change the social and economic circumstances that make a productive future seem a fantasy beyond the reach of so many of our nation's young people. In many low-income areas this means addressing the hopelessness and fatalism that often result from circumstances of oppressive poverty.[26] Genuine opportunities for further education and employment, for participation in community life, and for stable family life must be offered to students as real and achievable possibilities. Special attention should be given to factors such as unemployment, which can have devastating effects on the integrity of families and hence a significant impact on children's ability to avoid harmful patterns of behavior in sexuality as well as other areas of life.[27]

38. Improved health care is necessarily part of such a program for enhancing opportunities for young people. Among the immediate needs in this area are health benefits for the 37 million Americans who lack health insurance and expanded funding for welfare programs, combined with reforms to end discrimination in these programs against intact families. Priority should be given to improved prenatal care and other support for teenagers who do become preg-

---

[25]See Brozan, "Success in Preventing Teen-Age Pregnancy," the *New York Times* (March 14, 1987); Raspberry, "The Best Preventive: Education," in the *Washington Post* (September 22, 1986).

[26]National Research Council, pp. 266-267; Robbins, Kaplan and Martin, "Antecedents of Pregnancy Among Unmarried Adolescents," in *Journal of Marriage and the Family* 47 (August 1985): 567-583.

[27]National Conference of Catholic Bishops, *Economic Justice for All: Pastoral Letter on Catholic Social Teaching and the U.S. Economy* (Washington, D.C.: USCC Office of Publishing and Promotion Services, 1986), nn. 136, 141; Newcomer and Udry, "Parental Marital Status Effects on Adolescent Sexual Behavior," in *Journal of Marriage and the Family* 49 (May 1987): 235-240.

nant, because this can alleviate some of the problems for mother and child which have sometimes wrongly been attributed to teenage child-bearing as such.[28]

39. Third, the adults who shape teenagers' environment outside the school must commit themselves to support the value of chastity and marital commitment. We cannot expect to resolve the problems of teenage sexuality and pregnancy unless we take a close look at how we adults are setting an example. This example must come first of all from parents. Parents who exemplify traditional family values, who work to communicate these values to their children, and who establish clear expectations and standards for their children's behavior can reasonably expect to have a substantial impact on whether their sons and daughters engage in premarital sexual activity.[29] Moreover, parents have a right to expect that the means of social communication will not undermine this impact. Relevant to this concern are community efforts to discourage public distribution of pornographic materials, efforts by government to enforce existing laws against legally obscene materials, and intensified scrutiny of the ways in which sexually promiscuous behavior is presented in popular entertainment as an accepted norm.[30] On this final point a major family planning organization recently launched an advertising campaign arguing that American television presents a distorted picture of human sexuality.[31] We accept the validity of that argument, but we reject the suggestion that such presentations will be rendered less distorted or less destructive by simultaneous promotion or advertising of contraceptives. On the contrary, a realistic portrayal of human sexuality will draw young people's attention to the emptiness of a lifestyle that involves exploit-

---

[28]*Economic Justice for All*, n. 177; Children's Defense Fund, *Maternal and Child Health Data Book: The Health of America's Children* (1986): 1-16.

[29]The National Research Council reports mixed results on whether parents' traditional family values or their willingness to discuss sex with their children reduce the likelihood of premarital sexual activity (*Risking the Future*, pp. 102-104). Three researchers have recently presented evidence that premarital sex is much less likely for girls whose parents *combine* both factors (that is, traditional values and a willingness to communicate them). They note that the same impact is not seen among boys, apparently because "the topic of sex is raised with sons in traditional families only after sons become sexually active." Moore, Peterson and Furstenberg, "Parental Attitudes and the Occurrence of Early Sexual Activity," in *Journal of Marriage and the Family* 48 (November 1986): 777-782. Also see Miller, McCoy, Olson and Wallace, "Parental Discipline and Control Attempts in Relation to Adolescent Sexual Attitudes and Behavior," in *Journal of Marriage and the Family* 48 (August 1986): 503-512. (Sexual permissiveness and genital experience were lowest among adolescents who reported that their parents were "moderately strict" in supervising their behavior.)

[30]Vatican, *Charter of the Rights of the Family*, art. 5 (f); Pope John Paul II, *Familiaris Consortio*, n. 76.

[31]See full-page ads from Planned Parenthood Federation of America: "Why a Million Teens Will Get Pregnant This Year," in the *New York Times* and the *Washington Post* (November 18, 1986); "They Did It 20,000 Times on Television Last Year," *USA Today* (December 8, 1986).

ing others and the nobility of human beings who respect the bodily dignity of themselves and other people.

40. Finally, within the supportive context of these educational, economic, and social initiatives, programs of education in human sexuality which respect parental rights and the need for moral responsibility can have a significant impact on young people's lives. Such programs should emphasize the same kind of self-discipline and personal responsibility in the area of sexuality that are already exemplified in traditional educational programs, as well as in current programs dealing with such matters as drug and alcohol abuse. They should present human sexuality as it truly is—as an integral aspect of the human personality which is ordered toward permanent commitment in marriage and the creation of new life. The adverse physical, emotional, and moral consequences of premarital sexual experimentation among teenagers should be clearly and honestly presented.[32]

41. Ours is a pluralistic society with a diversity of moral and religious views. But the moral case against premarital sex for minors is not simply a matter of denominational dogma. Such moral formation can and should be a task for public schools, as well as for parents who are the primary educators of their children. Indeed, as the U.S. Surgeon General's report on AIDS recently emphasized, a strong case can be made in favor of sexual abstinence and monogamous commitment simply on public health grounds.[33] Our public schools should not evade their obligation in this regard on the grounds that they cannot teach morality.

42. We recognize that because our society is pluralistic, many individuals and organizations will continue to offer contraception and abortion as solutions to the problems of teenage sexuality. We agree that ignorance about the biological facts of sexuality is not desirable. But pluralism should not be used as a pretext for giving a diluted message or a double message about moral responsibility to teenagers. Rather, schools should build on a consensus among the American people that is even confirmed by many family planning advocates: that sexual self-restraint is a positive good to be promoted among unmarried minors. A school's efforts to inculcate in its students the strength of character needed to avoid premature sexual activity will be rendered both hypocritical and ineffectual if contraceptives are simultaneously recommended or prescribed under its aegis. Programs that promote contraceptives in the cause of "safe" or "safer" sex or place such practices on the same level as marital fidelity, abstinence,

---

[32]See Bennett, "Sex and the Education of Our Children," in *America* (February 14, 1987): 120-125.

[33]Koop, *Surgeon General's Report on AIDS* (Washington D.C.: U.S. Department of Health and Human Services 1986), pp. 16, 18. Any assessment of the effectiveness of condoms in preventing transmission of AIDS and other diseases must take into account such measures' greatly increased contraceptive failure rates among unmarried minors.

and the avoidance of promiscuous sexual behavior will inevitably weaken and distort the message that teenagers urgently need to hear.

43. Moreover, just as teachers do not assume individual teenagers are unreachable on subjects such as drug and alcohol abuse simply because they have experimented with these harmful practices, they should not assume that contraceptive programs are the only workable solution for certain teenagers simply because they have been sexually active in the past. We uphold the ability of people to change for the better, to open themselves to a morally responsible way of life.

44. We are committed to setting an example in this area. To this end, we will assist Catholic schools in improving and expanding their programs of education in sexuality and family life.[34] By their example of dedication to a celibate life, priests and religious in particular should help teach young people the value of chastity and the role it can play in reaching psychological and spiritual maturity. Moreover, many nondenominationl programs for education in chastity have already been developed and tested in public schools; programs like these merit greatly expanded private and public support.[35]

Policy Implications

45. In light of the foregoing analysis, we have come to the following policy conclusion regarding the issues raised by school-based health clinics:

- The provision of contraceptive and abortion services through school-based clinics is morally objectionable and is open to question, even on practical grounds, as a response to the problem of teenage pregnancy. Federal and state laws as well as local school board policies should be amended to exclude such services from the public schools. Because so many of these decisions are made at the local level, we urge Catholics to work effectively with other concerned taxpayers in their local com-

---

[34]See National Committee for Human Sexuality, USCC Department of Education, *Education in Human Sexuality for Christians: Guidelines for Discussion and Planning* (Washington D.C.: USCC Office of Publishing and Promotion Services, 1981).

[35]Current examples of such programs and materials (and their authors) include: *Sex Respect* (Coleen Kelly Mast); *Parents and Children Talk About Sexuality* (PACTS) (Ann Marie Kalloz, R.N., and Maureen Malone, B.S.W.); *Teen Star* (Hanna Klaus, M.D., Natural Family Planning Center of Washington, D.C.). Also note the common-sense approach of the 1986 government brochure "Many Teens Are Saying 'No'" (U.S. Department of Health and Human Services, Office of Population Affairs). Since 1981 the federal government has supported development of educational programs in sexual abstinence through the Adolescent Family Life program (Title XX of the Public Health Service Act), but the available funding for such approaches is a tiny fraction of the amount spent annually on contraceptives for teenagers.

munities to promote a morally responsible approach to this issue.

- School-based health clinics that clearly separate themselves from the agenda of contraceptive advocates may provide part of an effective response to the health needs of young people. This question deserves discussion in its own merits and may legitimately be answered differently in different areas of the country.
- A comprehensive response to the problem of teenage sexual activity and pregnancy must include efforts to strengthen the traditional character-forming task of the schools, to improve social and economic opportunities for young people in low-income areas, to support parents in their difficult task of passing on healthy values to their children, and to establish programs of education promoting the values of chastity and fidelity.

46. This is an ambitious agenda, and to some it will seem unrealistic. But we invite those who would disagree with some elements of our moral message to reflect on the alternatives. Regarding the tragic problems of teenage sexuality and teenage pregnancy, our society can take only three paths: We can continue on the same road of ambivalence as at present, whose results according to most observers will continue to be disappointing; we can explicitly decide to eliminate moral and religious qualms about teenage sexual promiscuity in order to indoctrinate more wholeheartedly all our young people in a contraceptive mentality; or we can work together to build a society in which family values can become meaningful and effective in young people's lives. We believe the first avenue abandons millions of young people in our nation to needless tragedy, while the second would cheapen our very humanity by promoting a coarse and hedonistic approach to human sexuality. Only the third avenue offers a ray of hope—if we only have the will to work together for its realization.

47. The enormous task of creating a supportive climate for healthy attitudes toward sexuality will demand the cooperation of the media and of many private and public agencies, both religious and secular. We invite all Americans to contribute to this effort, so that we may face this and other challenges to our society's children in ways that fully respect their dignity.

Statement on Central America

A Statement Issued by the
United States Catholic Conference

November 19, 1987

I. Introduction

1. We meet at a time of unprecedented hope for peace in Central America. We celebrate the wisdom and courage of those who made at least more probable what was deemed almost impossible brief months ago. Meeting in Guatemala on the feast of the Lord's Transfiguration, El Salvador's patronal feast, the five presidents of Central America committed their governments to a process of peace and reconciliation for each of their countries and for the region. We pray they will succeed, with divine guidance, in bringing it to a successful end.
2. We are fully sensitive to the delicacy of these present weeks in which the schedule for compliance moves forward. We wish our words here to be seen both as a further expression of our strong support for the unfolding peace process as well as the expression of our continual effort to reflect critically on the moral issues at stake. We have addressed matters of our country's relations with Central America for over a decade. We have joined with our Central American brothers in the episcopate in urging the adoption of sincere dialogue and negotiation among contending parties. And with them we have insisted, as we continue to insist, that true peace can come about only when the fundamental causes of the conflicts, especially the historic denials of social justice, are sincerely faced.
3. Peace, as the cessation of hostilities, may truly be at hand, for which all must give fervent thanks. But genuine peace, a gift from God and the fruit of justice, will continue to elude us until men and women of good will, here and throughout the hemisphere, resolve to construct together the civilization of love to which we are called.
4. "Central America has lately become a focus of attention and concern for the entire world." So wrote the bishops of Central America and Panama three years ago in their major document on the regional crisis, *Our Salvation Is Christ*. Central America has clearly been a focus of great attention and concern here in the United States, as we ourselves noted in our *Statement on Central America* in 1981, and it is of very special concern for us in the Church.
5. Over the years, we have prayed and preached and worked in varied ways for peace and justice in that troubled region. We have

expressed our solidarity with our brother bishops and their local churches, whose pilgrimage is marked with great suffering. We have spoken out publicly, numerous times, seeking to direct the policies of our country into ever more constructive ways.

6.   All of these and more—our prayer, our expressions of ecclesial solidarity, our efforts to influence public policy—are distinct and proper elements of our pastoral mission today. As the Holy Father noted last spring in Santiago:

> The Church, as is clearly stated in the Second Vatican Council, "is not identified with any political community nor bound by ties to any political system" (*Gaudium et Spes*, 76). But it is also true that, as an imperative of the mission it received from Jesus Christ, the Church must cast the light of the Gospel on all temporal situations, including political activity, so that society will increasingly manifest those moral and ethical values that reveal the transcendental character of the person and the need to protect his inalienable rights.

7.   This year marks a decade of sustained attention by our episcopal conference to the issues of Central America. In this period, we can note certain welcome developments in one or another country—advances in a democratic polity, election of civilian presidents, diminution of some of the most heinous human rights violations. Overall, however, the decade has witnessed a deterioration in the social, political, and economic life of the region. It is this situation of crisis and the role of our own government in affecting it to which we direct our attention here.

8.   It is our impression that the crises that today afflict Central America, indeed Latin America in general, are inadequately grasped by policymakers and citizens alike; that the policy focus has been distorted by an almost exclusive attention to one country; and that the broad public discussion that should inform our policy has become falsely constricted. It is in an effort to help stimulate fresh, and one hopes deeper, thinking about our government's policy toward the region that these reflections are offered.

II. Central America Today

9.   Over the course of this decade, the standard and quality of life of the great majority of Central Americans has declined. Untold suffering and misery have increased dramatically, and the region has been brought to the very brink of devastation.

10.   In part, this is true for much of the hemisphere, where the 1980s have been termed a *lost decade* for the economies of most Latin American countries. Unemployment and underemployment have soared; inflation in some countries has reached previously unimagined heights;

almost every country is saddled with heavy external debt, the total indebtedness of Latin America now approaching $400 billion. It is this tragedy that the Holy Father addressed when he met with the UN Economic Commission for Latin America and the Caribbean last April, noting that the crisis experienced by the region as a whole was the most serious of the past half century. It is this "perspective of pain" that moved him to issue in Chile

> . . . an appeal to the public authorities, to private enterprise, to whatever persons or institutions in the entire region within sound of my voice and, naturally, to the developed nations, summoning them to meet this formidable moral challenge which was described a year ago in the *Instruction on Christian Freedom and Liberation* in the following terms: "The aim of this in-depth reflection is to work out and set in motion ambitious programs aimed at the socioeconomic liberation of millions of men and women caught in an intolerable situation of economic, social and political oppression" (81).

Central America's Specific Problems

11. The current crises of Latin America, especially the economic crises of growth, inflation, unemployment, and debt, are fully reflected in the small and poor countries that make up the Central American isthmus. But these countries have also experienced their own special suffering in recent years.

12. Poverty, injustice, and violence; excessive militarism and rampant corruption; a deterioration of family life and of cultural values; widespread religious and ideological confusion; and bitter internal wars that in the decade have taken over 150,000 lives, displaced nearly 2 million more, and caused hundreds of millions of dollars of damage — these are some of the core realities of much of today's Central America.

13. In the recent public debates in our country over U.S. policy toward the region, these realities seem to be relegated to positions of secondary importance, when they are not ignored altogether. A near exclusive focus of attention on Nicaragua and a policy debate reduced to the question of U.S. support for an armed opposition reflect, in our view, a skewed and inadequate approach.

Voices from Central America

14. A more complete view can be found in the joint messages of the Central American episcopates issued at their regular biennial assemblies. At both their 1986 and 1984 assemblies, speaking as bishops and pastors, they identified the same five problem areas of greatest concern to their local churches. We would do well to consider them.

15. At the top, unsurprisingly, is the problem of *armed violence* — the violation of human rights, the existing armed conflicts, and the danger of their expansion. Next is the related issue of *militarism,* of the exaggerated role assumed by the armed forces in most of those societies, due in part to generous subsidies provided by outside powers. Third is the matter of rampant *corruption,* both public and private. Fourth, what may seem an unlikely public policy issue but which is of great concern to the bishops of Central America, the *manipulation of Catholic faith* and of popular religiosity by three distinct groups: the aggressively proselytizing fundamentalist sects, many with financial ties to the U.S.; the politically more radical Catholic sectors identified as the "popular church"; and the intransigent conservative sectors who try to put the gospel at the service of their own interests. And fifth, the *attacks on the institutions of marriage and the family* from several quarters but including, according to the bishops, campaigns financed by foreign governments imposing values hostile to the existing culture.

16. We consider it worth restating what our brother bishops of Central America have to say about the fundamental issue which most directly relates to the policy of our own government, that of the problem of violence, of war, and of peace:

> Armed violence has come to several of our Republics, and with it the danger of turning into a regional conflict. This violence continues to bear down on our countries, causing forced displacement of people within each country, the painful drama of refugees, widows and orphans whose numbers grow constantly, the abandonment of farms, the increasing unemployment, hunger and illness, the lack of doctors and medicines.
>
> And though the causes of conflicts were internal, two outside forces have come into play; the ideological, generally Marxist, on the part of the revolutionary groups, and the other, that of national security, which generally issues in repression by the military and the intervention of superpowers seeking to maintain spheres of influence; in their quest for a perilous balance of power, they feed the arms race, foment militarization and place the peace of the region at permanent risk.
>
> We can do no less than condemn the war and the consequent sending of arms to Central America and we issue a fervent invitation to the dialogue for peace.
>
> In this connection, we offer our encouragement to our sister Church of El Salvador, which has struggled to bring about a dialogue and has been accepted as mediator by both sides. We support as well those efforts of other nations to seek effective ways of ending armed intervention in our countries, the removal of outside forces from the region, and the freedom for Central Americans peacefully to settle their differences. At the same time, we implore the great powers to resolve their differences in peace and not continue the useless shedding of blood in our region (*Message from the XXI Plenary Meeting of SEDAC,* Tegucigalpa, November 29, 1984).

17. In these few lines, the bishops of Central America and Panama have encapsulated much of the real problem of Central America and its only acceptable solution; namely, that the devastation of war affects disproportionately the most vulnerable, the poorest, and sets back already weakened economies; that while the conflicts have indigenous roots in the long-standing patterns of injustice, superpower interference has added the geopolitical dimension, threatening the expansion into a still wider war; that the answer lies in effective dialogue among the contending parties, facilitated by sister nations of Latin America, with the superpowers resolving to deal with one another outside the Central American arena.

III. Central America and U.S. Policy

18. With this panoramic view in mind, let us look briefly at each of the countries, examining features that relate to aspects of U.S. policy. **19.** *El Salvador*, once the center of attention, has all but disappeared from the policy discussion. The costly war, now in its eighth year, may have left our newspapers but not the lives of the people of El Salvador. People are still being killed—in armed confrontations, in aerial bombardments, from land mines. Both sets of combatants commit serious violations of commonly accepted human rights. Killings and disappearances by so-called death squads still continue, although not, to be sure, at the appalling levels of a few years ago. The criminal justice system barely functions; there is no single known instance of military personnel being criminally punished for human rights abuses against Salvadoran citizens. The earthquake of October 1986 caused such destruction, leaving 300,000 people homeless, that it was comparable, in the words of Archbishop Rivera Damas, to a second war. **20.** Refugees and displaced persons are still prominent aspects of the Salvadoran reality. Many of the *internal refugees*, people who had fled to church-run centers as far back as 1980, have been helped to relocate, but people continue to flock to the city from conflict areas, and many continue to seek refuge in the United States. Whatever their individual and personal motivations, most of these people have escaped from truly desperate circumstances, from a country torn by war and devastated by natural disaster, and should be allowed—once having made the difficult journey here—to remain at least until conditions in El Salvador genuinely improve. A civilian presidency is the beginning, not the end, of necessary reforms and improvements. **21.** Many refugees as well continue to live in camps in Honduras and should be enabled, but not forced against their will, to return when their safe passage and security in their homeland can be assured. We urge the UN High Commission for Refugees to continue its role in providing for and protecting these persons. **22.** The recently enacted Immigration Reform and Control Act has caused great concern among many in El Salvador, including the nation's bishops, who fear that it may result in the forced repatriation of large numbers of Salvadorans. There are reports that some Salvadorans are already returning, partly because employers have fired or refused to hire undocumented Salvadorans in the sometimes mistaken fear of incurring sanctions. The return of many thousands would have repercussions far beyond the obvious economic ones, almost certainly increasing the civil strife and violence that have for too long wracked that tiny country.

23. The dialogue for peace between the government and the opposition, which the Church and especially Archbishop Rivera Damas have tirelessly pursued, had, until lately, largely broken down. The new Central American Peace Process, the most hopeful development in years, calls for internal dialogue in El Salvador and may succeed in reviving the necessary talks. We continue to urge our government to provide every possible encouragement to this process.

24. Finally, the question of military aid to El Salvador. This was the central issue before us in 1981 as we discussed and voted on our *Statement on Central America*. We concluded then, as Archbishop Romero had pleaded just before his assassination, that the United States should not provide arms to the then military-civilian junta. We acknowledge changes since that time, including the election of a civilian president. And while we also acknowledge the right in principle of a sovereign state to seek abroad the means for its own defense, we cannot accept that outside powers, essentially our country and the Soviet Union, vie with one another in adding fuel to the flames of an already burning house. In the sense in which it applies to both powers, we join with the Central American bishops when they say, as cited above, "We can do no less than condemn the war and the consequent sending of arms to Central America."

25. We have further concerns about our military aid to El Salvador, which fairly represents a still larger problem. Over the last five years, El Salvador has received substantial military aid, starting with the 1980 allocation that Archbishop Romero opposed of less than $6 million, through the high point in 1984 of over $200 million, to the present levels of over $100 million.

26. At some point, one must ask what these expenditures have resulted in. The government has not fallen nor has the insurgency been defeated; that is clear. But have we in fact, while intending to support the emergence of civilian and democratic rule, created a situation which makes it more difficult for the civilian sectors to exercise the necessary control over the military? And is this not of a piece with the problem noted over recent years of ever higher percentages of our bilateral aid being consigned to military and strategic, rather than to development purposes? When, as in this present year, two-thirds of all bilateral aid is so committed, while in 1973 it was but a quarter, we must

strongly question the military emphasis of our foreign aid program.
27. *Nicaragua* is the one country of the region not receiving economic or military assistance from the United States government; it has become increasingly dependent on such aid from the Soviet Union and its allies, an issue of growing concern to the democracies of the region. The war of attrition waged by irregular forces of Nicaraguan dissidents (the *contras*), funded largely by entities, both public and private, of this country has been the dominant fact of Nicaragua's life today and the overriding policy issue. Tensions between the United States and Nicaragua were aggravated by the breakdown in bilateral relations between the two countries.

28. Significant human rights violations have been reliably attributed to both sides. *Contra* attacks against noncombatants, forced recruitment and kidnappings, and extensive use of land mines have been widely noted. So have Sandinista abusive treatment of prisoners and detainees; the excessive restrictions on trade union activities, on freedom of expression, and on other civil liberties; and the reported violation of due process associated with the special tribunals. Nicaragua's record in this regard is not, according to the principal international human rights monitors, the worst in the region, but it is sufficiently bad to concern all who favor the growth of democratic institutions.

29. One area of special concern to us as bishops has been the deeply disturbing conflict that has developed between the government and the leaders of the Catholic Church, with the government on several occasions marshalling the exceptional powers of the state to deprive the Church of personnel, property, and the free exercise of ministry. The expulsion of a bishop, the expatriation of a key aide to the archbishop, the closing of the bishops' radio station and the archdiocesan newspaper, all in the last two years, as well as the prior expulsion of several foreign clergy and religious have been matters of deep concern, whose resolution we have repeatedly urged. We welcome the steps already taken to redress these concerns within the framework of the peace process, specifically the reopening of Radio Católica and permission for three of the clerics to return. We urge that the remaining obstacles be swiftly addressed. We stand with the Church in Nicaragua in the defense of their right to preach the gospel without harassment or interference.

30. The war has been the central issue and the unfortunate, almost exclusive, focus of the policy debate in this country. There is no issue of U.S. hemispheric policy that has so sharply and bitterly divided the American people as has the policy of our government to arm and train that part of the Nicaraguan opposition generally referred to as the *contras*.

31. Some of our fellow citizens, indeed some of our faithful, seem genuinely convinced that so evil is the Sandinista regime, or so inevitable an eventual Soviet-Cuban aggression through Managua, that they countenance few restrictions on what the U.S. may do to prevent such an outcome.

32. We have long argued that a significant U.S.-Nicaragua problem exists but only a political solution can finally be successful in Nicaragua, as in Central America generally; there is no politically or morally acceptable military solution. Further intensification of the military conflict must be avoided and the tide turned decisively in a new direction.

33. We have argued that direct military aid to forces seeking the overthrow of a government with which we are not at war and with which we maintain diplomatic relations is at least legally doubtful and morally wrong. U.S. mining of Nicaraguan harbors, training and supplying of irregular forces, and otherwise aggressing against another sovereign nation seem clearly to violate treaty obligations under the UN and OAS charters and the Rio Treaty and to violate as well the principles of customary international law. The finding by the International Court of Justice that our government was guilty of nine different violations of international law is at least persuasive. But it is not ours to argue the law, nor is our objective to present policy based on the legal issues.

34. We do believe the policy of support for the *contras* to be flawed morally; however sincere the intentions of the persons who have crafted and implemented it. Our Catholic teaching demands that several stringent criteria be met before one can discard the overriding "presumption in favor of peace and against war" (*The Challenge of Peace: God's Promise and Our Response*, 83).

35. Some would argue that the condition of sufficient cause was well met. As troubled as we have been by aspects of today's Nicaragua, it seems to us far from clear that Sandinista abuses could merit such lethal response. Still less do the criteria of likelihood of success, proportionality, and even proper authority seem to have been met. Without formally judging any of these criteria, we do hold that the criterion of last resort has truly been disregarded, and it is on this matter that we consider the U.S. *contra* policy to be most seriously in error.

36. As the Central American Peace Process is beginning to demonstrate, there *are* alternatives to a war policy; there *are* available structures — the Central American governments themselves, newly united by the peace accord signed in Guatemala last August, the now-forming regional parliament, the Contadora Group — all committed to the peaceful resolution of the conflicts and the protection of basic rights and freedoms. It is these profoundly hopeful efforts to construct peace with justice that we are called to encourage and support. The peaceful means, far from having been exhausted, have just begun to be explored.

37. *Guatemala* inaugurated its first civilian president in twenty years

in January 1986, and some important changes have clearly taken place. For two decades of military rule, Guatemala had endured the most sustained and pervasive political violence in the Americas. Estimates of the numbers killed in just the past decade vary, but all agree the victims, many of them Indians, numbered in the tens of thousands. The now familiar term *disappearance* first entered the human rights vocabulary because of Guatemala, and for years arbitrary arrest, torture, disappearance, and political killings were everyday occurrences.

38. Although military violence against civilians in the countryside has been sharply reduced, it nevertheless still continues. The so-called model villages and the conscripted civil patrols, both highly controversial programs of former governments, continue in many areas, effectively preventing the desired repatriation of thousands of refugees from nearby Mexico. A *self-amnesty* law promulgated by the previous government just days before President Cerezo's inauguration, eliminating any possible punishment from crimes committed during previous terms of office, is a source of deep discord among many Guatemalans. According to the major human rights organizations, the rule of law has yet to be established in Guatemala, and the overall human rights situation, while improved, remains very bad, particularly for the indigenous populations.

39. Still, there have been noteworthy advances. There appears to be no state-sponsored violence; the kidnappings and killings are believed to be the work of individual members of the security forces, not responsive to civil authority as before. There is a freely elected congress; the president has succeeded in dissolving the much feared Technical Investigation Department (DIT); he has sponsored the important regional initiative of a Central American parliament and has pursued a policy toward Nicaragua known as *active neutrality*. He has also apparently sought to keep U.S. assistance to the Guatemalan military at minimal levels.

40. Guatemala, as the traditionally most prominent nation of Central America, may well be able to play a key role in the regional quest for peace. We trust that our government will do all possible to encourage President Cerezo's independent role, including his active neutrality policy, and will make aid to the Guatemalan military contingent on genuine accountability and elimination of human rights abuses.

41. *Honduras*, the second poorest country in the hemisphere, has been triply burdened by the wars waged in the three countries on its borders. It has become the host of thousands of Salvadoran, Nicaraguan, and Guatemalan refugees. It has become the staging area for the principal *contra* forces attacking Nicaragua. And it has become the site of very large and repeated U.S. military exercises. Although it acquired an elected civilian government earlier in this decade than its neighbors,

Honduras has ironically undergone greater militarization in these years than during the time of military rule.

42. Honduran citizens, some say as many as 16,000, have been displaced from areas of *contra* activities. There have been numerous reports of Hondurans abused by *contras* and victimized by Nicaraguan cross-border attacks; the presence of large numbers of U.S. troops creates a particular set of problems. Whatever the truth of these reports, it seems abundantly clear that Honduras has become a pawn in conflicts not of its own making and deserves to be freed at least of the excessive attentions of our military. We do not see a justification for expending so much capital and effort in developing temporary military installations and conducting repeated and costly military exercises when the Honduran people so clearly need a different kind of assistance.

43. *Costa Rica* has been spared many of the social and political upheavals that plague the region, although its grave economic crises and the large influx of undocumented aliens from neighboring countries pose daunting challenges. Fortunately, Costa Rica has long maintained a democratic and socially responsive form of government and is justly famous for having abolished its armed forces in 1949. The growing militarization of the region that the Central American bishops so lament should in no way be allowed to erode Costa Rica's exemplary non-militaristic tradition.

44. The country's most recent source of pride, the awarding of the 1987 Nobel Peace Prize to President Oscar Arias Sanchez, both acknowledges this tradition of peacemaking and symbolizes the universal acclaim for the Arias-led Central American Peace Process. With the bishops of Central America, we join in fervent gratitude for this magnificent initiative of President Arias and the other four presidents of Central America and pledge our prayers and fullest support for the success of the Esquipulas II accords.

45. *Panama*, often viewed as marginal to Central America, shares many of its problems. Recent internal conflicts there have highlighted the excessive military control and intervention in the civil area of government. We commend the recent and repeated calls of the Panamanian bishops for full and effective protection of civil rights and the democratic process, and for the socioeconomic promotion of those large sectors of the poor who remain outside the nation's progress.

46. We urge that our government devise one consistent policy toward Panama, fully respectful of Panama's national sovereignty and the 1977 Torrijos-Carter treaties, while stressing respect for and promotion of human and social rights and the democratic process as essential for national and regional peace.

IV. Summary Recommendations

47. We conclude by summarizing some of the concerns we have expressed over the years and again in this statement, which we commend to the community of the Church and to all our fellow citizens. We pray that a renewed, more informed, public discussion may develop around these issues that so affect the future well-being of the hemisphere.

Central America in Context

48. Central America is but a part, a small but integral part, of Latin America. We urge our government to expand its policy vision beyond the immediate crises of Central America to the whole of the hemisphere. The problems and needs and dangers facing the rest of Latin America are far greater than those confronting the isthmus and, if left unattended, will overwhelm and cancel out any progress made in the Central American area.

Priority of Economic Justice

49. The most urgent policy issues facing Latin America today are economic. U.S. policy, both public and private, should give highest priority to addressing the problems of Latin America's staggering external debt, fragile economies, and concentration of productive agricultural land. The return to democracy in the major countries of South America, as well as the advances of democratic rule in Central America, are put at greatest risk by the hemispheric crisis of growth and the external debt problem.

The Superpowers and the Region

50. The issues of geopolitics, which have so dominated the U.S. public discourse on Central America in recent years, should be taken up directly with the principal sources of U.S. concern, the Soviet Union and Cuba. While the U.S.-Soviet competition is a concern to parties in the region, the task of preventing the introduction of Soviet bases or strategic weapons or combat forces into our border region should be dealt with as any other major issue threatening world peace, by direct negotiation between the United States and the Soviet Union. We should not use Central American lives as pawns in a superpower struggle.

The Peace Process

51. Of the interlocking scourges of poverty, injustice, and violence that beset Central America today, the violence of war may, ironically, be the easiest to contain. Its end is, in any case, a precondition for dealing with the others. We make our own the repeated urgings of the bishops of Central America that governments and insurgents alike pursue with vigor the dialogue and reconciliation process called for by the Central American peace accord.

52. Today, the essential framework for negotiations is the Esquipulas II Peace Process initiated by President Arias. It is not a perfect instrument; it involves risk, and it cannot satisfy every legitimate concern at once; but it is the most reasonable and hopeful plan yet devised and must be given every chance. We pray that the active participation of bishops in each of the national reconciliation commissions will help assure a reconciling peace based on truth.

The Necessary U.S. Support for the Peace Process

53. Our own government, which has historically exercised exceptional influence in the region, is in a particularly favored position today to further the incipient peace process. We urge U.S. policy to match in deed what has been repeatedly stated in principle; namely, that the United States is truly committed to a peaceful resolution of the conflicts through the political processes of the dialogue and negotiations.

The Supportive Role of Other American States

54. The Central American bishops have often decried the unhelpful involvement of powers external to Latin America and have praised the peacemaking efforts of neighboring countries, essentially the four states that border Central America—the Contadora Group of Mexico, Panama, Colombia, and Venezuela—together with the *new democracies* of South America—Peru, Brazil, Argentina, and Uruguay. The new Central America peace accord, itself "encouraged by the visionary and permanent will of the Contadora and Support Group," also calls upon those Latin republics to assist in verifying compliance with the process.

55. These countries are as concerned as we are for the peaceful resolution of Central American conflicts and are well suited to assure its success. It is vital that our government maintain explicit support for and cooperate with the provisions of the Arias peace plan, and encourage the contributions of these other American states.

Refugees

56. The flight of so many hundreds of thousands of Central Americans from their homelands over this decade, including the desperate efforts of unprecedented numbers to seek refuge in this country, is the clearest sign of the human tragedy that besets the region. We have urged that their plight be given the high attention it deserves and that the needs of these persons be generously responded to by all the countries of the region and by our own.

57. Specifically, we urge our parishes, religious communities, and social service agencies to increase their already commendable assistance to all refugees, asylum seekers, and displaced persons in need. We are conscious, in a special way at this time, of those who may not fulfill the legal requirements of the present legislation on legalization. We urge our government to interpret the conditions for granting political asylum as broadly and generously as possible, and we strongly urge that even those Central Americans who are not able to make a *prima facie* claim to refugee status under the law be allowed, on humanitarian grounds, to remain here temporarily under the conditions of what is known as extended voluntary departure status.

Our Need for Reconciliation

58. Finally, just as we recognize the need for internal reconciliation within the sharply divided societies of Central America if peace and progress are to be achieved, so we must acknowledge that our own social fabric has been damaged in recent years precisely over the Central American issues. Our society, indeed our Catholic community, has been divided, we believe unnecessarily so, in these last years because of divergent views about Central America, and we acknowledge our need for reconciliation.

59. We urge the leaders of both our national parties to use the period leading up to the 1988 elections to construct a national consensus around the real challenges facing us in the hemisphere, not allowing deeper polarization to develop over issues of less central importance. We urge our fellow Catholics, whatever their political views, to consider how they might best bring moral perspectives to bear on the human anguish of today's Central America. We encourage their efforts to support the poor of Central America with humanitarian aid and development funds.

V. Conclusion

60. We offer these reflections as bishops, seeking to view these issues of public policy from the perspective of our faith and the social teachings of the Church. We offer them as citizens, conscious of our responsibility to contribute according to our abilities to the formulation of ever more just and humane policies.

61. We renew our long-standing call for the pursuit of negotiation, peace, and reconciliation at a time of great opportunity and danger for the region. There are signs of significant progress in the extraordinary efforts of the nations of Central America to fashion a regional peace accord and begin to carry it out. We especially applaud the efforts of Cardinal Obando y Bravo, Archbishop Rivera Damas, and the other bishops of the region to mediate and advance the process of negotiations. But these efforts need to be actively supported, built upon, and enlarged. They need the strong and persistent support of the United States. We ask our government to do everything possible to support regional efforts to turn from war to negotiations, from violations of human rights to respect for human freedom. Let us turn our energies and resources in the region from supplying weapons of war to building instruments of peace, from armed conflict to constructive negotiations on how peace might be established and freedom and democracy might be strengthened. Let us also together work to overcome the economic injustices which are still at the heart of so much conflict in this troubled region.

62. This year marks the twentieth anniversary of the great development encyclical of Paul VI, *Populorum Progressio*. In commenting on that letter of his predecessor, Pope John Paul II devoted this year's World Day of Peace message to the themes of development and solidarity, the keys for peace, and highlighted several of the same principles we have raised in our statement.

63. "The spirit of solidarity," John Paul insists, "is a spirit that is open to dialogue," one fruit of which can be regional agreements "to promote the common good and encourage bilateral negotiations. . . ." Nations must be free to grow and develop as equal partners. "Seeking economic, military, or political superiority at the expense of the rights of other nations places in jeopardy any prospects for true development or true peace." Among the great problems facing us today, the pope mentions the developing world's external debt and the crucial problem of disarmament, noting the serious threats to world peace presented by "current East-West tensions and North-South inequalities." "All states have responsibility for world peace and this peace cannot be ensured until a security based on arms is gradually replaced with a security based on the solidarity of the human family."

64. We believe that peace is possible, that peace in Central America can and must be built up through dialogue and the processes of political, rather than military activities, and that it must be sustained by the solidarity of the other nations, including the needed economic assistance that the wealthier countries can provide.

65. We ask God's blessings on the suffering people of Central America, especially those most affected by the years of crisis, the refugees, the wounded, the bereaved. In this year of Mary, we ask Our Lady of the Americas to watch over all who suffer for, and who work for, peace in Central America.

Testimony on Emergency Hunger Policy

Testimony Presented before the
House Subcommittee on
Domestic Marketing, Consumer Relations and Nutrition
by Bishop John Ricard on Behalf of the
United States Catholic Conference

February 24, 1988

Mr. Chairman:

1. I am Bishop John Ricard of the Archdiocese of Baltimore. I am pleased to appear before you today on behalf of the United States Catholic Conference, which is the public policy arm of the U.S. Catholic bishops. I thank you for the invitation to come here today to share our deep concern about the continuing reality of hunger in our midst and to share some recommendations to improve the food stamp and child nutrition programs. We hope that these modest improvements can help to combat hunger as we develop the political will and broader measures to eliminate hunger in our land.

2. I come here today not as a nutrition expert but rather as a pastor who has seen firsthand the suffering that comes from hunger, poor nutrition, and poverty. I come today out of a sense of compassion and urgency for the many children and their parents, the elderly, the unemployed, and the homeless who literally run out of food at some time each month. I also come out of a moral conviction that hunger undermines the lives, dignity, and rights of those who suffer from it. My experience convinces me that the problem of hunger in our nation is one that requires urgent and strong action.

3. Various reports issued during the last several years clearly document the presence and ravages of hunger in our land. The Physicians Task Force on Hunger in America and the U.S. Conference of Mayors both have detailed the extent of hunger and the many gaps in services. Those who suffer the most are children, women, and minorities — the most vulnerable among us. Especially disturbing is the harm done to unborn children and infants who are the innocent victims of hunger. A recent report by the Children's Defense Fund confirms that this country still has a high rate of infant mortality, one of the clearest symptoms of hunger, which is a disgrace to a rich and caring nation.

4. While disagreements may arise over the actual statistics of hunger and malnutrition or the meaning of changing rates of poverty and infant mortality, no one can legitimately claim that this nation does not face a serious problem of hunger. The real difficulty is in providing hungry people with a diet adequate enough to maintain their physical, mental, and spiritual health through our federal food programs.

5.   The most recent survey by the U.S. Conference of Mayors on hunger and homelessness, entitled *The Continuing Growth of Hunger, Homelessness and Poverty in America's Cities: 1987,* shows that the demand for emergency food assistance increased over the previous year surveyed in all but two cities. What is worse is that all but one of the cities expect the demand for emergency food assistance to increase during the coming year. The report points out too many cases where hungry people are turned away for lack of adequate emergency food supplies.

6.   Sadly, I can only confirm these reports in our efforts in Catholic dioceses across the country. What we have learned from individual bishops, Catholic Charities agencies, pastors in inner cities, those working with farmers, and volunteers on the soup lines is essentially the same message — that there are significant numbers of hungry people and families; that the "economic recovery" of the last several years has passed them by; and that the cutbacks in the federal food assistance programs have hurt the poor severely.

7.   Let me briefly share with you our experience in Baltimore. Seven years aso, the Archdiocese of Baltimore founded a soup kitchen called Our Daily Bread. At that time, we were serving some 150 people a day. Our Daily Bread was one of only four soup kitchens at that time. Today, there are twenty-three soup kitchens in Baltimore and Our Daily Bread serves 450 people a day. It has served over 1 million meals since it opened. Obviously, the need has grown.

8.   We also established three years ago a wholesale food purchasing operation called Bread on the Water. We are able to provide over a million dollars a year in nutritious foods to some 350 local agencies, who are then able to feed poor families at a cheaper cost than is otherwise available. This amounts to over 1 million tons of food annually that Bread on the Water is able to provide hungry people. We even supply food through this program to agencies in Pennsylvania. Recently, we have started giving out bags of groceries to people who come to our Catholic Center in downtown Baltimore. We have been providing this service to over 400 families for the past two years.

9.   Despite all of this we feel we cannot meet the demand. Our resources are being stretched to the breaking point. More and more people are running out of food earlier each month and they turn to us for additional help. I assure you that we will continue to try to do what we can, but we cannot possibly hope to meet the need. Our efforts cannot and should not substitute for just public policies and effective programs to meet the needs of the hungry.

10.   I am aware of similar experiences in other cities and communities across the nation. Catholic Charities USA reports that in 1985 their affiliated local agencies served 1,175,000 people. This included food

banks, soup kitchens, and other parish services. In 1986, they served 3,173,000 people. In the Archdiocese of New York, St. Francis Xavier Welcome Table served 700 to 800 people every Sunday in 1986. Last year, they served over 1,200 every Sunday. The archdiocese also participates in an wider emergency food assistance program which serves some 1.2 million people monthly, 70 percent of whom are families. In Davenport, Iowa the diocese there reports that the River Bend Food Bank, which it helped form and through whom many of its parishes feed the hungry, added twenty-five new food pantries just last year.

11. Here in Washington, less than a mile away, So Others Might Eat served 254,703 meals in the last year and Catholic Charities distributed more than 340 tons of food to hungry families in our nation's capital.

12. These reports are all the more discouraging because in the 1970s major progress had been made against hunger and malnutrition through the establishment or expansion of food stamps, child nutrition programs, and other special supplemental food programs. However, the economic recession of the early 1980s coupled with the cutbacks in basic food assistance programs has eroded our national commitment to the poor and hungry and weakened the effectiveness of our efforts to combat hunger. This neglect cannot be allowed to continue.

13. Hunger is a fundamentally moral issue. In traditional Catholic social teaching, the right to a sufficient amount of food to sustain life is a human right, one linked to the right to life itself. Pope John XXIII, in his encyclical *Pacem in Terris*, listed the right to food as one of the most important human rights. We cannot permit the human dignity of so many of our fellow citizens to be undermined because they are too poor to feed themselves and their families.

14. Therefore, when we address the question of public policy to combat hunger, we are not speaking of feeding people simply out of our charity or as a matter of privilege. Rather, it is a matter of social justice and basic human rights. This concept of rights implies an obligation on the part of the larger society and our government. When the normal workings of the economy and society cannot provide for the basic nutritional needs of some citizens, then the government has the responsibility to act. It has the duty to see that no one goes without adequate food or other basic necessities. We believe that the federal government has the ultimate responsibility to see that the people of this nation are properly fed. Certainly, all levels of government and a wide range of private groups can and must do more to help those who are left at the margins of society, but our national government has a responsibility that cannot be neglected.

15. We have listened carefully to the suggestion that the voluntary sector, and the churches in particular, ought to be able to take up the slack caused by the cutback in the federal food assistance programs. This suggestion, that private charity can make up for gaps in public services, ignores both reality and history. Our experience teaches us

that it is not possible for the private voluntary sector to replace government programs. Our experience was recently confirmed in testimony before the House Select Committee on Hunger where so many witnesses testified to the inability of the private voluntary agencies to fill the gap. Certainly, the churches have and will continue to increase their efforts and resources to assist the hungry and the poor. However, the churches cannot and should not substitute for the essential responsibility that just public policy and government programs must play in meeting basic human needs. We can be effective partners; we cannot go it alone.

16. The increase in basic food assistance and financial aid by churches and other private agencies in recent years should not be misread as a sign of success for voluntarism, but rather should be seen for what it is—a desperate attempt to feed hungry people when others have abandoned their responsibility. While we are very proud of our efforts to feed and shelter the poor, we cannot pretend that soup kitchens and shelters represent a truly humane and effective response to hunger. They cannot substitute for a national commitment to end hunger and invest our common resources to feed the hungry.

17. Viewed from the perspective of the Catholic social teaching, the failure of our economy to provide adequate employment for so many of the poor and the cutbacks in federal food assistance over the last seven years are intolerable. New initiatives are needed to begin to recommit ourselves to eliminating hunger. We urge you to support a number of modest measures that we believe will strengthen existing federal food assistance programs, including:

- An increase in the basic food stamp benefit level. Many food stamp recipients are running out of food each month because benefit levels are too low. Current levels also do not provide for an adequate diet. It is our hope that over time benefit levels can more closely approximate USDA's Low Cost Food Plan.
- An elimination or lifting of the food stamp shelter cost deduction. Housing costs continue to rise often forcing many low-income people to choose between housing and adequate diets. A phaseout of this deduction will increase food assistance and also help to relieve the problem of homelessness.
- A change in the household definition to allow relatives who have to double up to receive their full entitlement to food stamps. The shortage of available housing forces many to move in with relatives to avoid homelessness. Cutting back on benefit levels because relatives must double up intensifies both the problem of homelessness and hunger. We also wish to ensure that benefits are not reduced when relatives pay rent to other family members with whom they have doubled up.
- A reduction in the prorating of initial allotments of food stamps.

Recipients ought to be eligible to receive full benefits if they apply during the first half of the month and at least half their benefits if they apply in the second half of the month. This will help recipients in stretching limited food dollars.

- An exclusion of the first $50.00 of child support as income in determining benefit levels. Childcare is a costly item for low-income families. The adoption of this measure would bring the Food Stamp Program into conformity with AFDC rules and provide more food assistance to these families, as well as providing an incentive for absent parents to pay child support.
- A raise in dependent care deductions to the level allowed by AFDC rules.
- An extension of food stamp benefits to household members who are otherwise eligible when one of the members is on strike. Denying food stamp benefits to other family members, particularly children, who have no say in the decision about whether a wage earner goes on strike, is an unjust penalty.
- A permanent authorization for food stamp eligibility of homeless persons in shelters.
- The resumption of the requirement that those eligible for food stamps be made aware of the availability of the benefits. An information outreach program is critical if this nation is going to close the gap between eligibility and participation.

18. We are particularly concerned with the effects of inadequate nutrition on children. They are our future and are especially vulnerable to the harmful effects of inadequate nutrition. Therefore, we urge you to support several changes that could strengthen the child nutrition programs. Some of these changes include:

- An increase in the reimbursement rate to schools for the school breakfast program. Since only about a quarter of the eligible children who currently participate in the school lunch program also participate in the school breakfast program, it is necessary to expand the program and improve the nutritional level of the program itself.
- A restoration of one more meal or snack in the Child Care Food Program for those children in daycare centers. Many parents must work more than eight hours or have long commutes. It is helpful in these situations for young children to be able to receive additional meals or snacks.
- A restoration of the participation of nonprofit organizations in the Summer Food Program. Children need adequate nutrition all year long. Allowing nonprofits to participate will help provide sufficient numbers of feeding centers to meet the need.
- An allowance for low-income families to adopt or take in foster

children without having their food stamps reduced. Low-income families should not have their federal and state adoption assistance and foster care payments counted as income in determining food stamp benefit levels. This will help to ensure better care for these children and cut down on institutionalization.

19. Finally, we urge you to support an extension of the authorization of the Temporary Emergency Food Assistance Program (TEFAP) at its current $50 million level and increase the share of TEFAP administrative funds that must go to emergency feeding organizations. TEFAP has been of great assistance to many local community feeding centers. However, because of the uncertainty caused by the disruption in the distribution of certain commodities, we are concerned that the distribution network will also be disrupted and in some cases shut down. The establishment of an emergency feeding network has not been an easy task. It would be unwise and ultimately self-defeating in our efforts to eradicate hunger if we did not help to maintain this system until commodities are once again available.

20. Hunger is a symptom of the disease of poverty. The long-term solution to poverty and hunger will only come about with adequate employment for those who can work and income support programs for those who cannot. The Catholic bishops of the United States said in their recent pastoral on the economy, *Economic Justice for All*, that ". . . private charity and voluntary action are not sufficient. We also carry out our moral responsibility to assist and empower the poor by working collectively through government to establish just and effective policies." We hope that some of these proposals we support will move us toward establishing these just and effective policies.

21. In closing, I would like to emphasize that the debate over federal food assistance programs is not just a debate about statistics or budget numbers. Rather, we are talking about human beings—their pain and joy, their hopes and fears. Is it too much to ask that the richest society on earth act to ensure that no American goes hungry, that all our sisters and brothers have a sufficient amount of food for their families? This debate is ultimately about what kind of country we want to be, whether we will find the will and the ways to protect human life and human dignity by eliminating hunger in our nation.

Statement on Civil Rights

A Statement Issued by the
General Secretary of the
United States Catholic Conference

March 22, 1988

1. The U.S. Catholic Conference welcomes and applauds the votes today in Congress to override the president's veto of the Civil Rights Restoration Act. We strongly support this legislation for what it does to strengthen significantly our national commitment to combat discrimination while safeguarding our vital concerns about human life and religious liberty.

2. The U.S. Catholic Conference believes government has a fundamental duty to protect the life, dignity, and rights of the human person, regardless of race, gender, age, nationality, or disabling condition. This is why we supported the goals of the act, successfully urged its modification in several important respects, supported final passage in both houses of Congress, and urged an override of the president's unfortunate veto.

3. We are particularly pleased that this new law ensures that no institution will be required to provide abortion services or benefits as a condition of receiving federal funds. We also believe the new law as interpreted by the committee report and floor debate adequately accommodates our legitimate concerns in the area of religious liberty.

4. Today's votes are important steps forward in strengthening federal civil rights protection. After years of debate and improvement, the Civil Rights Restoration Act represents a significant victory for civil rights and for our nation. It is also an important step forward in ensuring that our nation's civil rights laws do not require any institution to violate fundamental convictions on human life.

5. We now hope that Congress will build on this significant civil rights victory by strengthening federal fair-housing laws to combat more effectively housing discrimination in our land.

Statement to Youth on School-based Clinics

A Statement Issued by the
Administrative Committee of the
National Conference of Catholic Bishops

March 23, 1988

1. We are writing to you, the youth of our country, about a very important concern that touches your life.

2. Human sexuality is a gift from God and an important part of your total personality. Integrating your sexuality with all the facets of your life is a lifelong process that can be most difficult in the teen years when you face so many changes and challenges.

3. Human sexuality is also a gift that is designed for the total union of a man and woman in marriage. This union expresses the deepest form of human intimacy and is meant to enrich the life-giving love and commitment of married couples.

4. We know the pressures you face every day to become involved in sexual activity. We know that some young people do become sexually involved and that a number of teenage girls become pregnant each year.

5. You may also be aware of an effort to set up clinics in your schools to provide contraceptive services as a solution to teenage pregnancies. This is something that is happening all over the country. Many people think that the only way to help you cope with your sexuality is to provide you with contraceptives. They assume that young people will be involved in sexual activity and cannot achieve the self-control that will lead to healthy physical and spiritual growth.

6. We know that there are better solutions. Because we care about you and your growth and development, we would like to help you develop healthy attitudes about sexuality. We want you to understand that school-based clinics will present *real* dilemmas that you must face. We want to support you in living in a way that will lead to true and lasting happiness for you.

7. Let's look at some of the claims made by supporters of school-based clinics.

Claim 1: School-based clinics assume that you will be sexually active and cannot learn how to make wise and responsible choices about sexuality. Their solution is to give you contraceptives.

Response: We do not believe that sexual activity among young people is inevitable. In fact, clinics may even promote the attitude that everyone is sexually active. This is certainly not true. We believe in your ability to choose another way of living—to learn the positive values of honesty, responsibility, promise-keeping, self-control, commitment, and respect for the other person that will help you to reserve your sexual activity for marriage.

Claim 2: School-based clinics claim that making contraceptives available to you will reduce teenage pregnancy.

Response: Even though contraceptives are widely promoted in our society, especially through commercials and advertisements, they have *not* led to fewer teenage pregnancies. We believe that the wide availability of contraceptives confirms teenagers in their harmful sexual behavior. You are being told to deal with your sexuality by using pills and devices, instead of learning about the beauty of sexuality in God's plan and the responsible values that will help you grow as a sexual person. The only 100 percent safe way to avoid an unwed pregnancy is to reserve sexual activity for marriage.

Claim 3: School-based clinics lead you to believe that contraceptives can prevent all of the negative consequences of teenage sexual activity.

Response: Premarital sexual activity *has* adverse consequences for you. There *are* serious medical, emotional, moral, and spiritual consequences of premature sexual activity. Clinics deceive you by not telling you about the physical and emotional realities of sexuality and by failing to teach you about the responsibilities of sexual intimacy. Please remember: for unmarried teenagers, the *only* sure way to avoid the sexual transmission of AIDS or any other sexually transmitted disease is to refrain from sexual activity.

Claim 4: School-based clinics say they must give young people information about abortion and refer them to abortion clinics in order to provide a comprehensive answer to teenage pregnancy.

Response: Abortion is not the answer! Abortion not only destroys the unborn child, but it also has severe emotional and physical consequences for the teenage mother and may have emotional consequences for the father as well. In a society that already contains far too much violence, adults should be helping young people to deal with the problems of pregnancy without promoting the violent solution of abortion.

Claim 5: School-based clinics lead you to believe that once you have become sexually active you will always be sexually active.

Response: Teachers and counselors do not assume that teenagers cannot understand the harm of drugs and alcohol simply because they have experimented with them. In fact, people are encouraged to "Say No to Drugs!" and are helped to overcome drug and alcohol abuse. The same is true for teenagers who have been sexually active.

They can learn responsible values and change their behavior. We believe in your ability to change for the better, to open yourself to a morally responsible way of life.

8.   Premarital sexual intercourse is a risky venture, a behavior that will violate your moral principles and your hopes for happiness. We know that pressures from our society to become sexually active are great. We encourage you to resist these pressures — to say NO to premarital sexual activity.

9.   We challenge local communities across the country to drop the idea of school-based clinics. In their place, we encourage schools, parents, and churches to:

- provide you with the best information about human sexuality — how it is a marvelous gift from God that should not be abused;
- help you to think critically about the sexual messages you find on television, in songs, in music videos, in advertisements and to compare these messages with the positive understanding of human sexuality that you are learning;
- teach you honesty, moral responsiblity, promise-keeping, self-control, commitment, and respect for other persons to help you reserve sexual activity for marriage;
- support you in living these positive, healthy values.

10.   We the Catholic bishops of the United States pledge our energies in working with you, your families, and your schools to help build a society in which the positive values of human sexuality will be lived and appreciated.

Homelessness and Housing
A Human Tragedy, A Moral Challenge

A Statement Issued by the
Administrative Board of the
United States Catholic Conference

March 24, 1988

The Church, "sharing the joy and hope, the grief and anguish of
the people of our time, especially those who are poor or affected in
any way," feels it has a serious obligation to join with those who
are working, without self-interest and with dedication, to find concrete and urgent solutions to the housing problem and to see that
the homeless receive the necessary attention and concern on the part
of public authorities.[1]

John Paul II

1.   These recent words of our Holy Father pose a special challenge
for American Catholics. They call us to renewed reflection and effective action on the national disgrace of widespread homelessness in
our midst and the broader housing crisis that undermines the life and
dignity of so many of our sisters and brothers who lack a decent place
to live.

2.   In these brief reflections, we seek to call attention to the moral
and human dimensions of the housing issue, to review the teaching
of the Church in this area, to reflect on our own experience, and to
suggest some future directions for national housing policy.

Our Purpose/Our Experience

3.   We come to this issue as pastors, not policy-makers, as teachers,
not housing technicians. But we know from our own pastoral experience and the work of our dioceses and parishes across the nation
that homelessness and poor housing are destroying lives, undermining families, hurting communities, and weakening the social fabric of
our nation. Homeless people and those without adequate housing
frequently turn to the Church for help. We see their suffering. We
feel their pain. Across this nation, the Church is reaching out in an
unprecedented way to provide shelter to tens of thousands of men,
women, and children. We help millions of families avoid eviction and

---

[1]Pope Paul II, Letter to Pontifical Commission Justitia et Pax (December 8, 1987).

obtain other needed assistance. Dioceses, Catholic Charities, and parishes have built and continue to serve in thousands of affordable housing units. Through the Campaign for Human Development, we have assisted a wide variety of local self-help groups working to improve housing for the poor and powerless. We are deeply involved in housing. But our efforts cannot and should not substitute for effective and just public policies to deal with the crisis of homelessness and the urgent need for decent housing in our communities and country.

Our Social Teaching

4.   We bring to this discussion more than our experience in sheltering the homeless or providing housing. We bring our faith and our traditional teaching about housing and the human person. This is not a new concern for us. For decades, the Catholic Church in the United States has been an advocate for more effective national housing policy. In 1975, we issued a major statement on housing. Our recent pastoral letter on economic justice raised a number of values and principles with clear implications for housing. Other Catholic groups have addressed this issue with urgency and wisdom.[2] Recently, the Pontifical Commission Justitia et Pax released a major document on housing and homelessness, *What Have You Done to Your Homeless Brother?*, examining the worldwide dimensions of this problem, sharing the universal teaching of the Church, and calling for public action to provide decent, adequate housing, especially for the poor and vulnerable.

5.   The Church has traditionally viewed housing, not as a commodity, but as a basic human right. This conviction is grounded in our view of the human person and the reponsibility of society to protect the life and dignity of every person by providing the conditions where human life and human dignity are not undermined, but enhanced. As Pope John Paul II said in introducing the recent Vatican document, "A house is much more than a roof over one's head." It is "a place where a person creates and lives out his or her life." The right to housing is a consistent theme in our teaching and is found in the Church's *Charter of the Rights of the Family*.[3] We believe society has the

---

[2]United States Catholic Conference, *The Right to a Decent Home: A Pastoral Response to the Crisis in Housing* (Washington, D.C.: USCC Office of Publishing and Promotion Services, 1975). *1985 Policy Statement: Housing* (Catholic Charities USA). *Housing: The Third Human Right* (Washington, D.C.: USCC Campaign for Human Development, 1985). National Conference of Catholic Bishops, *Economic Justice for All: Pastoral Letter on Catholic Social Teaching and the U.S. Economy* (Washington, D.C.: USCC Office of Publishing and Promotion Services, 1986), nos. 61-95.

[3]Holy See, *Charter of the Rights of the Family* (Washington, D.C.: USCC Office of Publishing and Promotion Services, 1983).

responsibility to protect these rights, and the denial of housing to so many constitutes a terrible injustice.

6.   We also bring to this discussion other important values drawn from our social teaching: principles of stewardship, participation, and a preferential option for the poor and vulnerable. *Stewardship* calls us to use the gifts of God's creation for the benefit of all and raises basic questions of equality, fairness, and justice. *Participation* suggests that we measure our progress by whether people are able to shape their own destiny and meet their own basic needs by a broader participation in economic, civic, and social life. The *preferential option for the poor* restates the biblical lesson that we shall be judged by our response to "the least among us," that the quality of justice is best measured by how the poor and most vulnerable are faring. The Church needs to share this teaching more broadly and educate about the reality of homelessness and poor housing in our midst.

7.   These principles are not new in Catholic teaching, but they offer a sharp contrast to much of the recent discussion about housing policy. This nation appears to be walking away from its commitment, expressed in 1949, to provide a decent home for all Americans. Housing is being seriously neglected as a priority of national concern, government action, and federal investment. We have witnessed the increasing abandonment of the national role in housing. Federal resources for subsidized housing, for example, have dropped more than 80 percent in the last six years. In both the executive and legislative branches of government, we have lacked the consensus and commitment for constructive action.

8.   The human and social consequences of this neglect are all around us:

- One of every four American households (almost 20 million) had a significant housing problem in 1983, according to government figures. The problems were physical inadequacy, crowding, and heavy cost burden.
- The number of families seeking emergency shelter has increased by 31 percent in the past two years.
- There are 44,000 persons on the public housing waiting list in Chicago; 60,000 in Miami; 200,000 in New York City; 23,000 in Philadelphia; and 13,000 in Washington, D.C. In many cities, the waiting lists are closed because there is no reasonable hope of obtaining housing.
- Housing costs have accelerated almost three times faster than incomes in the past fifteen years.
- In New York, 16,000 children live in shelters or "welfare" hotels.
- Homeownership in this country has declined annually since 1981, following thirty-five years of steady increase. In most cases, it takes two good salaries to purchase a home.

- In 1949, the average thirty-year-old home buyer needed to spend 14 percent of his paycheck to afford a typical home. By 1985, this figure had risen to 44 percent.
- Each year, 70,000 units of public housing are abandoned, the victims of neglect and reduced rehabilitation budgets.
- Between now and the year 2000, most of the 1.9 million publicly assisted units may be lost as subsidies or use restrictions expire.
- Half of all renter households with incomes below $7,000 a year spend at least 60 percent of their meager incomes on rent and utilities.[4]

9. Beyond the numbers are the human dimensions of this crisis. Many young families are being forced to double up with relatives as the price of housing is beyond their reach. Senior citizens who thought themselves secure, face dramatic rent increases that cut deeply into their pensions. In too many of our cities, we see houses without people, while we see so many people without houses. In rural areas and small towns, the housing delivery system is woefully inadequate and people struggle to provide their families with decent housing. For too many, the great American dream of a decent home has been shattered. It is slowly turning into a nightmare full of fear and frustration for too many poor and middle-income Americans. As the Vatican document on housing reminds us: "This situation is not simply a fact to which those with responsibility in the field and indeed all people are called to react. Rather, from an ethical point of view, it is a *scandal. . . .*"[5]

Future Directions

10. Our nation, our leaders, and our people need a new understanding of how vitally important housing is to the well-being of our families and our communities. We need a new commitment to find creative ways to work together to shelter the homeless and provide decent, affordable housing for everyone. Those who serve the homeless in

---

[4]Based on Reports from the U.S. Department of Housing and Urban Development; the U.S. Senate Subcommittee on Housing and Urban Affairs; U.S. House of Representatives Subcommittee on Housing and Community Development; U.S. Conference of Mayors, *Recommendations for a National Housing Policy* (October 5, 1987); Philip L. Clay, *A Risk of Loss: The Endangered Future of Low-Income Rental Housing Resources* (National Reinvestment Corp., May 1987).

[5]Pontificial Commission Justitia et Pax, *What Have You Done to Your Homeless Brothers? The Church and the Housing Problem* (Washington, D.C.: USCC Office of Publishing and Promotion Services, 1988), p. 12.

our shelters tell us the numbers are growing; the pressures are increasing; our resources are being stretched to the breaking point. Our shelter activities, by themselves, are an inadequate response to the need. We fear we are developing a new and often dehumanizing way of caring for the poorest among us, a strategy of isolating homeless people in often primitive shelters.

11. We do not want to be misunderstood. We are very proud of our efforts to feed and shelter the poor. We are trying to ensure that no one goes without these absolute necessities. We continue to insist that government must help provide these basic necessities. Every effort must be made within existing programs to uphold and enhance the dignity of homeless persons. Yet, we cannot pretend that soup kitchens and shelters represent a truly humane and effective response to poverty and homelessness. Charitable efforts cannot substitute for public policies that offer real opportunities and dignity for the poor. Shelters cannot substitute for real housing for low-income families and poor individuals. We owe our sisters and brothers more than a cot and a blanket for the night; we owe them a chance for a better life, an opportunity to live a life of dignity in decent housing.

12. It is not our role or our expertise to describe the specific policies and programs to meet these needs. But we can suggest some directions and criteria for a renewed commitment to decent housing. We believe that the major goals for national housing policy should include the following:

- *Preservation:* Effective policies to help preserve, maintain, and improve what low-cost, decent housing we already have.
- *Production:* Creative, cost-effective, and flexible programs that will increase the supply of quality housing for low-income families, the elderly, and others in great need.
- *Participation:* Encouraging the active and sustained involvement and empowerment of the homeless, tenants, neighborhood residents, and housing consumers. We need to build on the American traditions of homeownership, self-help, and neighborhood participation.
- *Partnership:* Ongoing support for effective and creative partnerships among nonprofit community groups, churches, private developers, government at all levels, and financial institutions to build and preserve affordable housing.
- *Affordability:* Efforts to help families obtain decent housing at costs that do not require neglect of other basic necessities.
- *Opportunity:* Stronger efforts to combat discrimination in housing against racial and ethnic minorities, women, those with handicapping conditions, and families with children.

Conclusion

13. Churches, community groups, the private sector, and state and local governments must all do more to meet our common responsibilities for housing. We must recognize the homeless person as part of the human family, as part of us. However, there is no substitute for an involved, competent, and committed federal government providing resources, leadership, and direction for a broad and flexible attack on homelessness and poor housing. A recent survey makes clear that there is broad public support for such action.[6] What is missing are leadership and commitment. We invite those who seek to lead this nation; those who represent us at all levels in government; those involved in housing construction, finance, and development; leaders of neighborhood groups, unions, businesses, and human service agencies to join with us in a determined search for how this richly blessed nation can eliminate homelessness and take concrete steps to provide decent, affordable housing for those in need. As the Pontifical Commission Justitia et Pax declared:

> Political authorities, religious leaders and, in general, public opinion all recognize that a situation in which millions of human beings lack adequate housing is a serious problem. . . . A fundamental human right is, in reality, being violated. An adequate response to such a large-scale problem calls for the shaping of a consistent political will, as well as increased awareness of the collective responsibilty of all, and particularly of Christians, for the future of society.[7]

14. As believers, we find our reason and direction for action in the life of Jesus and the teaching of his Church. We are reminded by the gospel that the first human problem Jesus faced on earth was a lack of shelter. There was "no room in the inn" for the Holy Family in Bethlehem. Today, we see in the faces of homeless men, women, and children, the face of Christ. We know that in reaching out to them, standing with them in defending their rights, in working with them and their families for decent housing, we serve the Lord.

15. As Americans and believers, we are haunted by the tragic reality of so many without decent housing in our land. It is a sign of serious social neglect and moral failure. We ask everyone to join us in a sustained and urgent effort to find creative and effective responses to this national tragedy. A great and good nation cannot turn away as people wander our streets looking for a decent home.

---

[6]Mellman and Lazarus Research, "A Survey of Attitudes toward Hunger and Homelessness in America" (Washington, D.C.: Mellman and Lazarus Research, January 1988).

[7]*What Have You Done to Your Homeless Brother?*, p. 8

Testimony to Democratic and Republican Platform Committees

*Testimony Presented by the
Director of the USCC Government Liaison Office
on Behalf of the Bishops of the United States*

May 10, 1988

1. The Catholic community is deeply involved in the life of this country. We are working to meet the spiritual, pastoral, and educational needs of millions of people. We also feed the hungry, shelter the homelsss, care for the elderly and the immigrant. Through our recent pastoral letters on nuclear arms and economic justice and advocacy on behalf of the unborn and the poor, we seek to contribute to a broad national debate on the values and visions that ought to guide our nation in the years ahead.

2. We join in the public debate not to impose some sectarian doctrine, but to speak for those who cannot speak for themselves, to share our experience in serving the poor and vulnerable, and to voice our hope that our nation might be an effective force for true justice and genuine peace in our own country and around the world.

3. We believe our nation is enriched, our traditions of pluralism enhanced, when religious and other groups share their convictions about how our nation can best achieve our national goals of life, liberty, and the pursuit of happiness.

4. Last November the Administrative Board of the U.S. Catholic Conference said in its statement *Political Responsibility: Choices for the 1980s*:

> We bishops specifically do not seek the formation of a religious voting bloc; nor do we wish to instruct persons on how they should vote by endorsing or opposing candidates. We do, however, have a right and a responsibility as teachers to analyze the moral dimensions of the issues of our day.
>
> We hope that voters will examine the positions of candidates on the full range of issues as well as their personal integrity, philosophy, and performance. We are convinced that a consistent ethic of life should be the moral framework from which we address all issues in the political arena.

5. Although we come before you today to share our views on a wide variety of issues, we come with a single message. We urge you to measure every policy and proposal before you for how it touches the human person and whether it enhances or diminishes human life, human dignity, and human rights.

Abortion and the Right to Life

6. A legal system that permits the destruction of unborn human beings by abortion contradicts the principle that human rights are inherent and inalienable. Thus, the 1973 Supreme Court decisions on abortion and subsequent decisions which rely on them must be reversed, and society's resources should be redirected to solving the problems for which abortion is mistakenly proposed as a solution. Especially for our nation's young people, those resources should be placed at the service of efforts to reduce the premature sexual activity that leads to high unintended pregnancy rates as well as other adverse consequences.

7. Unless there is action by the Supreme Court, restoration of legal protection of the lives of the unborn will require an amendment to the Constitution. We specifically urge the platform committee to support such an amendment.

8. Meanwhile, legislators should seek ways to affirm the dignity of unborn human life. Laws protecting individuals and organizations which conscientiously object to abortion should be maintained and strengthened, and public-funding policies should continue to encourage childbirth over abortion. Specifically, we oppose all public funding of abortion in programs for medical care and other services.

9. Although we strongly support legal equity for women, we vehemently reject efforts to link abortion "rights" to this objective. Women have been at the forefront of the drive to secure legal protection for the unborn and are generally more opposed to abortion than men are. The legitimate and important goal of equity for women should not be exploited as a vehicle for abortion and abortion funding.

10. We are deeply concerned at the evidence that, after more than a decade of denying the right to life before birth, the law's protection of the right after birth has also begun to erode. This has become clear in efforts to discriminate against infants born with physical or mental disabilities by denying them sustenance and basic lifesaving medical care. In recent years the dignity of life has been further threatened by public campaigns to authorize active euthanasia or assisted suicide for terminally ill patients, seriously disabled adults, and other vulnerable citizens.

Arms Control and Disarmament

11. In the last several years, we have addressed a broad range of national security policies that depend on the possession and planned use of nuclear weapons.

12. Our pastoral letter *The Challenge of Peace: God's Promise and Our Response* condemns the countercity and counterpopulation use of nuclear weapons; rejects the notion of waging limited nuclear war because of the risk of escalation to all-out nuclear war; and questions the moral acceptability of policies that contemplate the initiation of nuclear war to repel a conventional attack, as is the case in NATO strategy. The pastoral letter also concluded that nuclear deterrence was morally acceptable, but only under strict conditions. This conditional acceptance requires that the components of the deterrent be limited to those sufficient to deter and that the arms race be reversed through mutual, verifiable arms control agreements.

13. The Intermediate-Range Nuclear Forces Treaty is a modest but important first step toward meeting these conditions. It must be a point of departure to mutual, verifiable arms control measures that make deep cuts in strategic weapons, along the lines of the proposed Strategic Arms Reduction Talks agreement, that ban all testing of nuclear weapons, that outlaw chemical weapons, and that reduce conventional forces to a new balance at the lowest levels possible. While progress is being made on these arms control initiatives, we strongly recommend that the integrity of existing arms control agreements, especially the Anti-Ballistic Missile Treaty and Strategic Arms Limitation Talks II, not be undermined or eroded. Finally, we oppose the addition of new weapons, such as the MX missile, that are destabilizing and excessively costly.

Civil Rights

14. Discrimination continues to haunt our nation. Whether based on race, ethnicity, sex, age, or disability, discrimination is a grave injustice and an affront to human dignity. Millions of our people continue to be deprived of the civil rights. Government must continue and strengthen its efforts to erase unjust discrimination in all its forms so that all Americans can exercise their basic human rights.

15. Racism is a particularly serious and ugly form of discrimination. A radical evil dividing the human family, racism must be resisted by every individual and eradicated from every social institution and structure.

16. The enactment of the revised 1988 Civil Rights Restoration Act was a significant step forward in strengthening federal civil rights protection while safeguarding vital concerns about human life and religious liberty. Now, new and effective remedies must be developed to combat housing discrimination, including discrimination against families with children.

Crime and Criminal Justice

17. Crime and violence are major and legitimate concerns for many. We support strong and effective action to control handguns, leading to their eventual elimination from our society. We advocate greater utilization of community-based correctional facilities, effective programs of education, rehabilitation, and job training for offenders, and the compensation of victims and crime.

18. We oppose the use of the death penalty. The return to the use of the death penalty can only lead to further erosion of respect for life. Our nation should reject the death penalty and seek means of dealing with violent crime which are more consistent with human dignity.

Economic Policy and International Relations

19. In the 1986 pastoral letter *Economic Justice for All*, the U.S. bishops applied the principles of Catholic social teaching to the four major areas of international economic relations: aid, trade, finance, and investment. In each area, we found and continue to find significant gaps between principles of social and economic justice and prevailing U.S. economic policy.

20. We continue to support foreign assistance by the U.S. government, but we do not support the heavy emphasis on military assistance. We continue to support multilateral aid via the World Bank and the International Monetary Fund, but with growing concern about the development model ("structural adjustment," meaning export-led economic growth) these institutions prefer. We continue to support food aid in emergencies, but are increasingly concerned about the tendency to lengthen the emergency period and thus risk creating both dependency on foreign food imports and disincentives to local food production. We believe the United States should adopt a different stance from the current one regarding international trade, but we are concerned about those aspects of trade legislation that attempt to punish our competitors and ignore social injustices inflicted on workers by some economic decisions of business. We are particularly concerned about the burgeoning sales of arms to Third World countries by many countries including the United States.

21. We also have had a particular concern that countries receiving foreign assistance not be forced to adopt population methods which violate basic human rights or deeply held cultural values.

22. The beginning of a new administration of either major party seems to us an appropriate time to pause and take stock of the realities of economic life in the broadest possible measure. As we underline in our pastoral letter, "We call for a U.S. international economic policy designed to empower people everywhere and enable them to continue to develop a sense of their own worth, improve the quality of their lives, and ensure that the benefits of economic growth are shared equitably."

Education

23. We support public policy that guarantees the rights of all persons to an adequate education regardless of race, sex, national origin, economic status, or personal disability. In particular, we advocate policies to improve the educational opportunities available to economically disadvantaged persons and minorities, including bilingual education, as well as compliance in schools with the legal requirements of all civil rights statutes regarding race, sex, age, and handicap conditions.
24. There should be special recognition given to the contribution made to this nation by private elementary and secondary schools. Catholic school parents alone account for a savings of $14 billion to the country's taxpayers, while at the same time contributing their share of taxes for public education.
25. We also support—and urge the platform committee to support— public means to enhance the education of children in private schools; the choice that parents make to educate their children in private schools should not be penalized by denying them equal educational opportunities for their children. We therefore urge support for the inclusion of provisions to guarantee equitable participation by private school students in all present and future federal education and education-related legislation.
26. We call your special attention to the need to rectify the devastating repercussions from the *Aguilar* vs. *Felton* decision. As a result of the court's decision, federal compensatory educational programs for eligible disadvantaged students attending private schools have been significantly reduced as to numbers of children served and the quality of instructional services. In many cases, services have been eliminated outright. New alternative programs have proven to be more costly, less effective educationally, and more disruptive to the regular academic programs of these children.
27. We likewise encourage support for sufficient federal financial assistance to help both public and private schools address the increasing mandates of environmental regulations imposed upon them.
28. We encourage the promotion of policies that will provide financial assistance to students in need to enable them to attend the higher educational institutions of their choice as well as initiate federal tax

advantages for middle-income parents to promote savings for the college costs of their children. We ask you to address the nation's need for quality and affordable childcare services for the working poor. Public and private agencies should be encouraged and provided with federal financial assistance to establish centers offering early childhood services, family services, and extended daycare for school-age children.

29. Our recommendations in the area of language and literacy include the development of a national literacy program to provide services to every needy adult and aggressive enforcement of laws which ensure every limited-English child's right to an equal education.

Employment and Income

30. As a nation, we must make it possible for everyone who wants a job to find employment in a reasonable amount of time. For those who are unable to work or cannot find a job, we should provide a decent income. Current policies fall short of creating new jobs with adequate pay and decent working conditions, which are necessary to meet a goal of full employment.

31. Joblessness and underemployment are still too widespread. The human and economic costs of this joblessness are morally unaccept-able and cannot be tolerated. Policy efforts must be made to expand employment opportunities in both the private and public sectors. Effective action against joblessness and unemployment will require a careful mix of general economic policies and targeted employment programs.

32. The federal minimum wage should be a livable wage that allows a full-time worker to maintain a family. We also reaffirm the Church's teaching regarding the responsibility of government to protect the right of workers to organize and bargain collectively.

33. The lack of affordable quality childcare for the children of employed parents is a growing urgent problem, especially for low-income fam-ilies. Federal policy should enhance and support the efforts of employ-ers, local government, nonprofit agencies, and churches to meet this need.

34. We urge a guarantee of a decent income for those who cannot work and adequate assistance for those in need. To achieve these goals, we support a comprehensive reform of the welfare system, which will provide an adequate income base for all Americans and replace the present system of fragmented programs. Current federal policy, which permits states to discriminate against married couples with children, is anti-family and should be abandoned. While welfare-assistance policies should encourage and support people's efforts to become self-supporting, mandatory workfare programs are an unacceptable alternative to training and real jobs with fair compensation. **35.** Federal welfare policy should ensure that adequate health coverage and childcare are available to poor families who leave welfare when the parents secure employment.

Food and Agricultural Policy

36. Hunger is a growing national scandal that this nation should not tolerate. Everyone has a right to a sufficient amount of food to live his or her life in dignity. This right follows directly from the right to life. Therefore, we call for a national policy aimed at securing this right and making the elimination of hunger a national priority. We support the necessary increases and changes in the food stamp program; child nutrition; Women, Infants and Children Program; and the Temporary Food Assistance Program to meet more effectively the nutritional needs of hungry, malnourished Americans.

37. The goal of our agricultural policy should be adequate supplies of nutritious and healthy food, both domestically and overseas, and just remuneration for producers. We support an agricultural system based on small and moderate-sized family-owned and -operated farms, at home and abroad, as the best guarantee of a just food system. The United States should support such a system through its income and price-support programs, its credit and research programs, its tax policies, its supply-management programs, its strategies for rural development, and its foreign trade and aid policies.

38. We support legislation to protect the rights of farm workers, and we call for measures to improve the working conditions and general welfare of farm-worker families, including expanding minimum wages and unemployment compensation, improved housing and health care, and special protection from the harmful effects of pesticides.

Health Care

39. Health care is a basic human right that flows from the sanctity of human life. It falls to government to assure all people of adequate access to health care regardless of their economic, social, or legal status.

40. We face a health care crisis in this country which is fueled by the erosion of Medicaid and Medicare benefits, spiraling health care costs, and the burgeoning ranks of the uninsured. These factors conspire to deprive millions of Americans of adequate preventive and acute care.

41. While our goal remains a comprehensive national health insurance program, immediate attention must be given to the needs of the rural and urban poor. Priority should be given to the guarantee of quality prenatal and pediatric care to low-income mothers and children. Federal policies must encourage public- and private-sector cooperation in developing a coordinated health care system which serves the poor and provides protection of conscience in health care delivery.

Housing

42. Housing is not just a commodity. Decent housing is a basic human right. This nation has all but abandoned its responsibility to ensure every citizen an adequate place to stay. We must recognize the terrible injustice people suffer as a result of this housing crisis. Public policy must give direction and set basic criteria that will establish a commitment to decent housing.
43. This policy should:

- preserve, maintain, and improve the existing private and public low-cost, decent housing;
- develop programs that are cost-effective and flexible to increase the supply of quality housing for low-income people;
- encourage wide participation of tenants, community groups, and consumers in the housing decisions that affect their communities;
- support effective and creative partnerships among nonprofit organizations, private developers, financial institutions, and all levels of government to build and maintain affordable housing; and
- combat discrimination in housing based on race, ethnicity, sex, disability, or families with children.

Human Rights

44. The dignity of the human person requires the defense and promotion of human rights in global and domestic affairs. With respect to human rights internationally, there is a pressing need for the United States to pursue a double task: to strengthen and expand international mechanisms by which human rights can be protected and promoted; and to take seriously the human rights dimensions of our foreign policy.
45. Therefore, we support ratification of the international covenants on civil and political rights; on economic, social, and cultural rights; and on the elimination of torture. We also support a policy that gives greater weight to the protection of human rights in the conduct on U.S. affairs. The pervasive presence of U.S. power in many parts of

the world creates a responsibility to use that power in the service of human rights.

Immigration

46. For over seventy years, we have been conducting major national and local programs helping migrants and refugees find their way in American society. We have also actively participated in the legislative and advocacy processes that help shape this nation's immigration policy. Our concerns regarding the future of immigration legislation in this country are threefold.

47. First, we are deeply troubled by the plight of undocumented aliens untouched by the legalization program that was part of the Immigration Reform and Control Act of 1986. We fear that these people will become a new underclass facing greater privation, exploitation, and fear than they have in the past. At the same time, we are deeply concerned that the law's employer-sanction provisions prohibiting the employment of undocumented aliens have the potential for adversely affecting U.S. citizens and legal aliens of Hispanic origin. It is our sincere hope that the anti-discrimination provisions of the bill will adequately bar such negative impacts.

48. Second, while we appreciate recent attempts to reform U.S. legal immigration policy, such efforts are entirely too premature. Further, it is our belief that when the time comes to modify this aspect of immigration law, the following principles, recently enunciated by the National Conference of Catholic Bishops' Committee on Migration, should shape future legislative efforts.

- Family reunification must be affirmed as the fundamental precept driving a just immigration system. Our fundamental tradition is fair treatment of all nations and their emigrants.
- Temporary labor programs should be gradually excised wherever necessary; permanent workers should receive full rights and those temporary-worker categories that are necessary ought to offer full labor market rights.
- Every effort should be made to discourage illegal immigration by promoting just immigration law.
- The endangerment of any nation's valuable human resources must be avoided, especially in the case of Third World countries.

49. Finally, the United States must reaffirm its role as the world's principal "safe haven." We urge that U.S. immigration law and policy retain the process whereby the number and funding for refugees to be admitted annually are determined by refugee needs. We also support expeditious handling and due consideration for the requests of aliens who seek asylum here. We further support a compassionate policy designed to provide temporary status for those whose journeys here are brought about by violent political upheaval or by natural calamities in their countries of origin.

Mass Media

50. Communications media should be both responsive and responsible to the public interest. Laws regarding electronic media should seek to make the benefits arising from new technologies available to all. We reject the application of "marketplace" economic thinking to the telecommunications industry, for this has the effect of widening the gap between the information-rich and the information-poor in society. For this reason, we support legislative initiatives to restore the accountability of broadcasters and the owners of cable systems to the communities they are licensed or franchised to serve. The public interest must be the guiding principle behind regulatory activities at the Federal Communications Commission.

51. We call for the restoration of the Fairness Doctrine through legislative or administrative action. We support legislative or administrative action that would restore the accountability of cable operators and broadcast licensees to the needs and interests of all elements of society, especially children, minorities, the elderly, and the poor. We support the concept of universal telephone service at a cost that all Americans can afford. While we oppose government control of the content of mass media, we support common-carrier regulations to restrict the use of the telephone to make available indecent or pornographic materials—many of them an affront not only to religiously based moral values, but to any standard of decency in a civilized society.

Regional Conflicts in the World

52. *Central America*. The Central American Peace Plan (Esquipulas II) is the most helpful development in years and requires every possible support. We urge U.S. policy to take into full consideration the legitimate concerns of the countries of the region, seeking regional solutions to regional problems whenever possible. We believe this applies as much to the current crisis in Panama as to the rest of Central America.

53. The Guatemala Accords signed in August are but the first essential step in a process leading to genuine peace, reconciliation, and development in each of the wartorn countries. We favor a continual and significant reduction in U.S. military aid to Central America and a concomitant diplomatic effort to persuade other nations also to refrain from adding to the disastrous military buildup in the region.

54. Economic assistance, especially development aid, should be extended to all the Central American countries, including Nicaragua, willing to comply with established human rights criteria. Until conditions in El Salvador, Guatemala, and Nicaragua are significantly improved, including the end of state or insurgent terrorism, we continue to support the right of refugees from those counties to seek and find temporary safe haven in the United States.

55. *Middle East.* Among the regional conflicts in the world, none is more complex or more significant for global peace than the Middle East. The continuing carnage of the Iran-Iraq war, the persistent violence and economic devastation in Lebanon, and the Palestinian protest in the West Bank and Gaza all illustrate the need for fundamental political measures needed to address the questions of justice and peace in the Middle East.

56. The basic policy of the U.S. Catholic Conference has focused upon the Arab-Israeli issues and the war in Lebanon. We continue to believe that UN Resolution 242 sets the framework for a Middle East peace, which should provide for secure recognized borders for Israel and should also provide for a homeland for Palestinians, along with their participation in negotiations affecting their destiny. The special significance of Jerusalem should be protected by an internationally recognized judicial safeguard which takes account of the historic and religious status of the city in the eyes of the three monotheistic faiths.

57. The issues of protecting human and civil rights, particularly the rights of religious liberty, are a primary concern throughout the Middle East, where religion is closely tied to the political life of the region.

58. In Lebanon, the violence and devastation continue in a fashion that requires the concentrated attention and action of the international community. The fundamental goals must be to protect the sovereign integrity and territory of Lebanon. The Lebanese should have the possibility of determining their own destiny, free from the intervention of outside powers. While this political objective should be a primary concern of the U.S. policy, it clearly will take time to achieve it. In the interim, the United States, through public and private agencies, should provide the humanitarian and economic assistance that the Lebanese people so sorely need.

59. *Southern Africa.* South Africa has long been of grave moral concern to the world because of its internal racial policies and its occupation of Namibia-South West Africa. In recent years, it has become a threat to the entire area of southern Africa because of its military incursions into the territories of several of its neighbors; indeed, it has virtually occupied a large portion of Angola.

60. The United States is South Africa's largest trading partner and second-largest foreign investor. U.S. foreign policy and its influence on corporate activity in South Africa should be directed toward needed change in South Africa and in its relations with neighboring states. To this end, we support more intensive economic sanctions against South Africa as one of the few remaining nonviolent pressures for the dismantling of the immoral system of apartheid.

Conclusion

61. American Catholics have a dual heritage. As believers, we are heirs of a tradition that calls us to measure our society by how it touches the least, the lost, and the left-out among us. As citizens, we are part of a remarkable democratic tradition that sets before us the pledge of "liberty and justice for all." Today, as both believers and citizens, we urge this great political party to shape its platform first and foremost by how it touches each human person. We especially ask you to fashion a platform which respects the life, enhances the dignity, and protects the rights of all our sisters and brothers, especially the poor and most vulnerable.

Building Peace: A Pastoral Reflection on the Response to *The Challenge of Peace*

A Statement Issued by the
National Conference of Catholic Bishops

and

A Report on *The Challenge of Peace* and Policy Developments 1983-1988

A Report of the Ad Hoc Committee on the
Moral Evaluation of Deterrence

June 25, 1988

> For her part, the Church recognizes her responsibility in building peace. Not only does she recall the principles drawn from the Gospel, but she also seeks to form people capable of being true artisans of peace in the places where they live.[1]
>
> John Paul II

Introduction

1. Five years ago, we bishops of the United States adopted our pastoral letter on nuclear arms, *The Challenge of Peace*. As pastors, we sought to say a word of hope in a time of fear, to challenge believers to become artisans of peace in the nuclear age. As teachers, we sought to share the Church's wisdom on nuclear arms and apply it in one of the world's nuclear superpowers. We shared both the complexity and urgency of these matters, calling for prayer, reflection, and action to reduce the moral and physical dangers of the nuclear age.

2. Five years later, we offer this brief reflection on how *The Challenge of Peace* has challenged our Church. We also offer it as an introduction to the report of the Ad Hoc Committee on the Moral Evaluation of Deterrence. We look back with gratitude to the efforts to share the letter and we look ahead with commitment to the continuing challenge of building peace in a world still threatened by nuclear arms.

---

[1]Pope John Paul II, "Address to Diplomatic Corps" (Rome, January 9, 1988), *L'Osservatore Romano*, English weekly edition (January 25, 1988): no. 12, p. 8.

The Response Was Extraordinary

3.   When we began to write our letter, we had no idea of the attention and activity it would generate. Among the bishops of the United States, we found great concern and consensus. Our efforts within the bishops' conference to articulate and apply the Church's teaching on nuclear arms gave rise to considerable debate and remarkable unity in our common efforts to share the gospel message of peace and justice.

4.   In dioceses and parishes, the letter launched an unprecedented process of prayer, preaching, education, reflection, discussion, and action. Countless Catholics have gathered in conferences and workshops, in homes and parishes to pray for peace and to reflect on the challenges of the letter.

5.   In many of our own schools, colleges, and universities the message of the letter has been integrated into courses, conferences, and curricula. In secular colleges and universities, in research institutes, and in the specialized literature on nuclear issues, *The Challenge of Peace* is used on a frequent basis.

6.   In terms of the broader public debate and decision making on nuclear policy, the pastoral letter has been both a catalyst and a resource in the discussion of the moral dimensions of nuclear arms and strategy. We have learned from and been strengthened by the efforts of other religious groups who have developed and shared their own reflections on the moral dimensions of nuclear arms.

7.   *The Challenge of Peace* has strengthened our Church, enriched its life, and engaged many of its people. But too many still remain unaware of the letter and the teaching of the Church in this area. Much more needs to be done to share the gospel message of peace founded on justice and to bring this message more clearly into the public arena. We know we have a long way to go, but we are grateful and encouraged by the significant activity that emerged as a result of the pastoral letter. We hope these brief reflections will give new impetus to efforts to share the letter and act on its implications.

The Continuing Challenge

8.   The peace pastoral was not some passing preoccupation or brief phase in the Church's life. It represents an ongoing commitment to weave concern for these matters into the fabric of Catholic life. As the letter said: "Peacemaking is not an optional commitment. It is a requirement of our faith. We are called to be peacemakers, not by some movement of the moment, but by our Lord Jesus."[2]

9. Nuclear policy remains a central moral dilemma for believers. We still live in a world torn by divisions and threatened by the nuclear arsenals of East and West. In our 1986 pastoral letter, *Economic Justice for All*, we reiterated our concern that the extraordinary amount of resources allocated to arms were depriving our society of the resources necessary to meet the just needs of the poor. As Pope John Paul II said in January of 1988: "The stockpiling of these weapons in itself constitutes a threat to peace, as well as a provocation to the peoples that lack the essentials for survival and development."[3] In his powerful encyclical *On Social Concern (Sollicitudo Rei Socialis)*, the Holy Father pointed out that the rivalry between the superpowers, the arms trade, and the worldwide investment in weapons of war have disastrous effects on the lives of the poor in the developing countries.[4]

10. We stand at a moment of genuine crisis and unavoidable choices. The fate of the human family, perhaps even of the earth itself, may well depend upon the choices made in the months and years ahead. As human beings, we cannot be indifferent to this crisis. As American citizens, we have the freedom and responsibility to influence our own nation's policies. As Catholics, we are called to be peacemakers shaped by our traditional teaching on nuclear arms.

The Deterrence Report

11. *A Report on "The Challenge of Peace" and Policy Developments 1983-1988* seeks to assess the facts of the nuclear problem in 1988 in light of the principles of our pastoral letter. We believe it faithfully reflects and applies Catholic teaching on nuclear arms. In our report, we renew the judgment of the pastoral letter that we can offer only "strictly conditioned moral acceptance" of nuclear deterrence. We cannot simply condemn or embrace deterrence. Rather, we call for urgent and persistent efforts to move more decisively toward effective arms control and mutual disarmament, to fashion a more secure and lasting basis for peace, and to put in place nuclear policies which reflect more

---

[2]National Conference of Catholic Bishops, *The Challenge of Peace: God's Promise and Our Response* (Washington, D.C.: USCC Office of Publishing and Promotion Services, 1983), no. 333.

[3]Pope John Paul II, "Address to Diplomatic Corps," no. 3, p. 6.

[4]Pope John Paul II, *On Social Concern (Sollicitudo Rei Socialis)* (Washington, D.C.: USCC Office of Publishing and Promotion Services, 1988), nos. 20-24.

clearly the moral principles and values of *The Challenge of Peace*. This report will guide the efforts of our conference in this area and will strengthen our work for effective arms control, mutual disarmament, and genuine peace in our divided world. We hope Catholics and all those of goodwill will read it, reflect upon its basic principles and prudential judgments, and act on its call to shape policies to reduce the moral and physical dangers of this nuclear age.

Becoming a Peacemaking Church

12. As pastors and believers, we are required by the Gospel to do far more than to develop a pastoral letter and initiate efforts to begin to educate and act on the Church's teaching. We also need to do more than to assess current developments for their moral implications. We must work to broaden, deepen, and strengthen the Church's work for peace. The whole Church is called to become a *peacemaking church*, to "form people capable of being true artisans of peace," in the words of Pope John Paul II.[5] In this task, we are united with our Holy Father and the Universal Church. It was in Coventry that Pope John Paul said: "Like a cathedral, peace must be constructed patiently and with unshakable faith."[6] Five years after the adoption of our letter, we recommit ourselves to that task. We are called to seek practical ways to make the peace and justice of the kingdom, more visible in a world torn by fear, hatred, and violence.

13. A *peacemaking church* needs to pray constantly for peace. As we share God's word and celebrate the Eucharist, there will be many opportunities to reflect and pray on the biblical basis for peacemaking and church teaching on nuclear arms. Every worshiping community should regularly include the cause of peace in its prayers of petition. It is in prayer that we encounter Jesus who is our peace and learn from him the way to peace. It is in prayer we find the hope and perseverance which sustain us as instruments of Christ's peace in the world. In this Marian Year, we call on Mary, the Queen of Peace, to intercede for us and for the people of the world that we may walk in the ways of peace.

14. A *church of peacemaking* is also a community which regularly shares the Church's teaching on peace in its schools, religious education efforts, and other parish activities. A special effort is necessary in our institutions of higher education where research, teaching, and scholarship can be put at the service of peace. Much has been done to integrate fully and faithfully the Church's teaching in our educational

---

[5]Pope John Paul II, "Address to Diplomatic Corps," no. 12, p. 8.
[6]Pope John Paul II, "Homily at Bagington Airport" (Coventry, May 30, 1982), *Origins* 12:4 (June 10, 1982): 55, cited in *The Challenge of Peace*, no. 200.

efforts. We urge that the teacher of the letter be presented in its totality, including the principles governing a nation's right and obligation of self-defense and an individual's right of conscientious objection.

15. Much more needs to be done to integrate fully the Church's teaching in our educational efforts. We especially need to work toward a more fully developed theology of peace. As the pastoral letter said: "A theology of peace should ground the task of peacemaking solidly in the biblical vision of the Kingdom of God, then place it centrally in the ministry of the Church."[7] We need continued theological reflection in colleges, universities, seminaries, and other centers of thought and learning on peacemaking, on the complex question of deterrence, and on how the Church can provide clear teaching and strong witness for peace grounded in our Christian faith.

16. A *church of peacemaking* is a community which speaks and acts for peace, a community which consistently raises fundamental moral questions about the policies that guide the arsenals of the world. As believers and citizens, we are called to use our voices and votes to support effective efforts to reverse the arms race and move toward genuine peace with justice. The Deterrence Report focuses on the ethical dimensions of nuclear issues. Our conference will be actively sharing these principles and policy directions with those who shape the policies of our nation as part of our continuing commitment to defend human life whenever it is threatened. The U.S. Catholic Conference and our Department of Social Development and World Peace have a special responsibility in this area, but it is also a task for the whole Church. Each of us is called to participate in the debate over how our nation and world can best move toward mutual disarmament and genuine peace with justice.

17. We serve a diverse Church with legitimate differences on how best to apply principles to policies. The pastoral and other church teaching are best shared in respectful dialogue. The voice of a *peacemaking church* must reflect the facts, rest on competent analysis, and understand that persons of goodwill sometimes differ on specific questions. We cannot just proclaim positions. We must argue our case for peace, not only with conviction and competence, but also with civility and charity. We need to bring special pastoral skill and sensitivity to the important task of helping our people become builders of peace in their own situations. For many of our people, these are personal and professional concerns as well as public issues. They deserve personal support and creative pastoral care as they try to live the values of the Gospel in their own demanding roles and responsibilities and as they wrestle with the ethical dimensions of their own work and citizenship.

18. Finally, a *peacemaking church* is a community which keeps hope alive. We sometimes find ourselves suspended between hope and

---

[7]*The Challenge of Peace*, no. 25.

fear. Surrounded by weapons of mass destruction, we try to imagine and to bring about a future without them. Our faith does not insulate us from problems; it calls us to confront them and to a constant effort to build a better, more lasting basis for peace, knowing that God's grace will never fail us.

Conclusions

19. Five years after our letter, we are still at a beginning, not an end. We are grateful for all that has been done to share the message of the letter. We affirm the efforts to act faithfully on its implications. We call for a renewed commitment to pray, educate, and work for peace at every level of the Church's life.

20. We pray that the leaders of our nation and world will find the wisdom, the will, and the ways to move toward genuine peace and mutual disarmament. We pray that believers will become more effective witnesses and workers for peace, helping our world say "no" to the violence of war, "no" to nuclear destruction, "no" to an arms race that robs the poor and endangers us all.

21. As bishops, we recommit ourselves to our pastoral letter of five years ago and to the task of sharing and acting on its message. Our commitment to this task cannot be diminished by the passage of time, the press of other priorities, or the frustrations of the moment. Now is a time to build on the activities of the past five years, to renew our efforts to educate and advocate for peace, to help make our Church a truly peacemaking community, and to work with all people of good-will to help shape a world of peace and justice.

22. In renewing this commitment, we must remember who calls us to this task and why. It was Jesus who said: "Blessed are the peace-makers, for they will be called children of God" (Mt 5:9). As his followers, we take up again the urgent and continuing priority of "building peace" in the nuclear age.[8]

---

[8]Pope John Paul II, "Address to Diplomatic Corps," no. 12, p. 8.

A Report on *The Challenge of Peace* and Policy Developments 1983-1988

Introduction

1. *The Challenge of Peace*[1] was the product of many influences and many ideas. No single resource was more evident in the document than the teaching of Pope John Paul II; the basic theme of the pastoral letter was an effort to develop the Holy Father's statement at Hiroshima in 1981: "From now on it is only through a conscious choice and through a deliberate policy that humanity can survive."[2]

A. The Moral Meaning of the Nuclear Age

2. The pastoral letter of 1983 sought to define the moral choices of the nuclear age. Using religious, moral, political, and strategic ideas, *The Challenge of Peace* analyzed the political context and the strategic content of the policy choices and the personal choices of conscience which stand before nations and citizens in the nuclear age. The document was the product of the Catholic religious-moral tradition, but it was addressed to both the community of the Church and the wider civil community. Part of the content of the pastoral letter was a statement of religious values and moral principles which are not limited by time or changing conditions. Other parts of the letter involved descriptions of problems and proposals for policy which were contingent in nature and in need of continuing revision. A basic moral judgment of *The Challenge of Peace*, a "strictly conditional moral acceptance" of deterrence, requires a continuing political-moral analysis of the elements of deterrence policy as that policy is defined and implemented by the United States and the Soviet Union.

3. In order to contribute to this necessary moral analysis, the general meeting of the NCCB/USCC voted in November 1985 to commission an explicit public review of how the "conditions" of *The Challenge of Peace* were being observed in the nuclear arms competition. Following this action Bishop James Malone, then president of NCCB/USCC, appointed this ad hoc committee and gave it the following mandate:

> The basis of the study will be the moral principles and the moral judgments of the pastoral letter. The task of the committee will be to assess all the relevant [facts] and moral principles needed to pre-

---

[1]National Conference of Catholic Bishops, *The Challenge of Peace: God's Promise and Our Response* (Washington, D.C.: USCC Office of Publishing and Promotion Services, 1983).

[2]John Paul II, "Address to Scientists and Scholars" (Hiroshima, February 25, 1981), *Origins* 10:39 (March 12, 1981): no. 4, p. 621.

sent to the NCCB membership a judgment on the moral status of deterrence.[3]

4. This *Report on "The Challenge of Peace" and Policy Developments 1983-1988* is a logical extension of the position the National Conference of Catholic Bishops adopted in the pastoral letter. In writing this report, we presuppose the biblical, theologial, and moral teaching of *The Challenge of Peace*; our task is to assess a series of events, policy choices, and technical trends not fully explored in the pastoral letter. We write this report to remain faithful to our own commitment of 1983, and because of the continuing urgency of the situation posed by nuclear weapons for our nation, for other nations, and for the global community.

5. The moral dimension of the problem created by nuclear weapons cannot be understood solely in terms of the weapons themselves. It is the political context in which nuclear weapons exist, joined with the technological nature of the weaponry, which creates the qualitatively new issues of the nuclear age. Essentially, the nuclear age has been shaped by a quantum leap in the development of military arsenals and no corresponding change in our form of political organization. Politically, the world is a community of independent sovereign states each of which retains the capability of resorting to force to resolve political, territorial, and economic disputes. Hence, in this political configuration the perennial problems which have faced states for centuries persist:

- how to prevent aggression;
- how to shape relationships on the basis of justice and freedom;
- how to protect human rights within states and among states; and
- how to protect the small states from designs of larger nations.

6. These questions, in their empirical and ethical dimensions, are the classical issues of international politics. It is because of these questions that states with differing ideologies and competing interests contend with each other daily and all too frequently clash militarily. This century has witnessed two wars of global dimensions. Since the end of the Second World War, there have been over 150 recorded military conflicts. Quite apart from the existence of nuclear weapons, the classical problems of war and peace are still with us. The first goal of politics and morality should be to avoid all resort to force as a means of settling differences. But we do not live apart from nuclear weapons;

---

[3]NCCB Ad Hoc Committee on the Moral Evaluation of Deterrence, *Origins* 15:24 (November 28, 1985): p. 400.

they exist and they have changed radically the way the classical questions are understood.

7. The moral problem of the nuclear age arises when the classical political questions are joined to the contemporary technological prospects of a nuclear war. There is a moral mandate to protect the values of justice, freedom, and order in the international arena. There is an absolute moral norm which protects the right to life of innocent persons. There is also a moral imperative to avoid nuclear war or anything which could lead toward or increase the possibility of nuclear conflict. The moral problem of the nuclear age is how to keep the peace and how to ensure that it is a just peace, one which preserves the freedom of nations, their right to development, and the human rights of persons.

8. The particular theme which *The Challenge of Peace* focused upon and to which we return in this report is the unique dangers posed by the nuclear arsenals. The uniqueness arises from the scope and degree of devastation these weapons can wreak. In the nuclear debate of the 1980s the kind of destruction which the arsenals of the superpowers can cause has been brought home to the public with new urgency and great specificity. Rather than repeat these statistics and predictions here, it is more pertinent to state the widely shared conclusion which flows from an understanding of the meaning of nuclear war. Nuclear war remains a possibility, but it is increasingly seen as devoid of the rational political purpose and moral limits which have made war a justifiable activity in the past. Nuclear weapons threaten to destroy the very objectives which once provided the political and moral justification for using force. To state the case in the categories of our pastoral letter: Traditional just-war theory requires that just causes exist for nations to assert a right of self-defense or defense of others, but nuclear war challenges the basic idea of what constitutes a just means. Reason, morality, and faith combine today in opposition to the idea that nuclear war fits our traditional understanding of justifiable use of force.

9. It is easier to draw this conclusion than it is to pursue its consequences. For living in the nuclear age means that we can condemn nuclear war, but we will still have to live with nuclear weapons. There are several dimensions to the nuclear dilemma:

- *the scientific community* unlocked the mystery of nuclear power— we will never return to an age when the knowledge of how to build nuclear weapons is absent;
- *military strategists* are commanded to prepare for nuclear war, but to do so in a fashion which reduces the possibilities that it will ever occur;
- *political leaders* threaten to resort to nuclear weapons if necessary, and simultaneously proclaim that their use is unthinkable;

- *the general public* fluctuates between moments of great fear of nuclear holocaust, great hope that negotiations will solve the nuclear dilemma, and the normal instinct of suppressing any thought about this perplexing and frightening reality.

10. How do we live with nuclear weapons, politically, strategically, and morally, until the day when we can live without them? Some believe such a day is a distinct possibility; others are equally convinced such a goal is a delusion or at least a dangerous distraction from more modest objectives of living with nuclear weapons more safely. In *The Challenge of Peace*, we held out the hope of a world freed of the nuclear threat, but we addressed in much greater detail the issues of how to move toward a world with less nuclear danger and greater political control and how to maintain a clear sense of the moral imperatives which are older than the nuclear age and must be related to it.

11. This report is designed to continue the quest for a world rid of the nuclear danger and to continue the process of defining the political and moral direction which should guide national policy and personal choice in the nuclear age.

B. The Church and the Nuclear Age

12. It will take the wisdom and courage of many individuals and institutions to dispel the nuclear paradox: scientists and strategists, politicians and poets, citizens and educators. The Catholic Church is called by its own doctrine—by the Gospel of Christ and the tradition of the centuries—to be a participant in the pursuit of peace.

13. The papal teaching of the nuclear age, from Pius XII to John Paul II, has been the leading voice in the Church, seeking to adapt and to apply the classical moral teaching on war to the dramatically new situation created by weapons of mass destruction. The papal teaching has been consistently realistic about the problems of peace, but it has been insistently prophetic in its assertion that a "moral aboutface" is needed to make progress toward disarmament. Other voices in the Church, from episcopal conferences to organized efforts among laity and religious, have responded to papal leadership and the call of Vatican II to face this "moment of supreme crisis" in which we live. The complexity of the crisis assures a diversity of views within the Church about the best means to address it. But the moral tradition of the Church establishes a set of common values to guide our efforts.

14. The principal value threatened by the nuclear age is one which stands at the center of the Church's ministry of peace: the defense of human life. Each life is sacred and all life is a gift from God. The resources of our faith, the Sacred Scriptures and Catholic tradition, teach us that we are entrusted with life—we neither own it nor control it; human life is sacred because it originates with God and because we are destined for eternal communion with God. Each person carries his or her life as a sacred trust, and we believe that the lives of others are to be treated with awe and reverence. Respect for human life as sacred is at the core of the Catholic moral doctrine. In this century the sacredness of human life has been violated by totalitarian political systems of left and right and by the scourge of war at the global and local levels. In our time the paradoxical fact is that life is sometimes threatened by discoveries which attest to the genius of the human spirit, but which stand in need of moral guidance. This has been the case since the beginning of the nuclear age. Unlocking the power of atomic energy was a unique watershed in human history; yet its development as an instrument of warfare poses an unprecedented threat to human welfare. Pope John Paul II repeatedly has placed his moral teaching on the nuclear age in this broad context of the relationship of technology, politics, and ethics. The challenge of the nuclear age, according to the Holy Father, is not to condemn scientific discovery nor the technology which flows from it, but to develop the moral vision and political wisdom to set a direction for and place restraints upon the power placed in human hands by splitting the atom.

15. Protecting human life from nuclear destruction must be pursued in tandem with promoting those values necessary for life to be lived with dignity. Pope John XXIII in *Pacem in Terris* set forth the values in which national and international society must be built: truth, justice, freedom, and love. A lasting peace must reside in these values; sometimes peace requires the use of force, domestically or internationally, to defend these values. But the challenge of the nuclear age is to protect life, promote basic values, and prevent recourse to nuclear weapons in any form.

16. Catholic teaching on war and peace has a positive conception of peace. It is not simply the absence of violence, but the product of an order built into human relationships at every level of life. Peace is the fruit of order; a morally justified social order is shaped by truth, justice, freedom, and love. The paradox of the nuclear age is that vast amounts of intellectual and political energy must be expended to assure that something does not occur: nuclear war. But this is an insufficient conception of the political-moral challenge of our time. An equal amount of human effort must be invested in shaping a just relationship among states and within states. We must build the peace and keep the peace if we are to be true to the Gospel of Christ and the moral tradition of his Church.

C. The U.S. Bishops and the Nuclear Dilemma

17. As bishops in the United States, we are teachers in our time of the universal teaching of the Church on war and peace. As citizens of the United States we experience in concrete fashion the responsibility and the apprehension of living in a nuclear nation. Both of these legacies were at the root of our decision in 1980 to prepare the pastoral letter, *The Challenge of Peace*.

18. In *The Challenge of Peace* we asserted that "as a people, we must refuse to legitimate the idea of nuclear war" (no. 131). And we also pointed out that to do this would require of us "not only new ideas and new vision, but what the gospel calls conversion of the heart" (no. 131). Clearly, it was as pastoral leaders and moral guides that we entered into the public policy debate on war and peace, and more specifically on nuclear weapons and strategies for their use.

19. In publishing this report, on the fifth anniversary of our 1983 pastoral letter, we once more join the public policy debate from our particular religious and moral perspective. We do not lay claim to any special grasp of military or political realities beyond that of any carefully informed citizens. But we do bring to the debate a special awareness of spiritual/religious realities that we are convinced must help to guide us as a people concerned to act in a morally acceptable way. We invite all who read this report to do it in the spirit in which we wrote it, the spirit of the psalmist who prayed:

> I will hear what God proclaims;
>   the Lord — for he proclaims peace.
> To his people, and to his faithful ones,
>   and to those who put in him their hope.
>   (Psalm 85:9)

20. As we issue this report, we assert again that we are teachers, not technicians. We cannot avoid our responsibility to lift up the moral dimensions of the choices before our world and nation. But even as we point out these hard choices, we are filled with a spirit of hope that learning God's ways and walking in his path will bring us to peace. We claim as our own

> . . . what Isaiah, son of Amoz, saw concerning Judah and Jerusalem.
>   In days to come,
> The mountain of the Lord's house
>   shall be established as the highest mountain
>   and raised above the hills.
> All nations shall stream toward it;
>   many peoples shall come and say:
> "Come, let us climb the Lord's mountain,
>   to the house of the God of Jacob,
> That he may instruct us in his ways,
>   and we may walk in his paths."
> For from Zion shall go forth instruction,
>   and the word of the Lord from Jerusalem.
> He shall judge between nations,
>   and impose terms on many peoples.
> They shall beat their swords into plowshares
>   and their spears into pruning hooks;

One nation shall not raise the sword against another,
  nor shall they train for war again.
O house of Jacob, come,
  let us walk in the light of the Lord!

(Isaiah 2:1-5)

21. In *The Challenge of Peace* and now in this report we write as pastors and teachers. We are convinced that ideas matter, that the way we understand and think about policies and personal choices is, in the end, a more potent force than the material elements of power and technology which are the external elements of the nuclear competition. We are equally convinced that values matter, that both knowledge and power require direction, guidance, inspiration, and restraint.

22. The contribution of a religious-moral vision to the nuclear age is precisely to offer a method of evaluating the choices posed by politics, war, and peace in our time. The reception given *The Challenge of Peace* and the continuing dangers and possibilities of nuclear politics move us to address the moral issues once again.

23. *The Challenge of Peace* concluded its assessment of nuclear deterrence policy with the following judgment:

> These considerations of concrete elements of nuclear deterrence policy, made in light of John Paul II's evaluation, but applying it through our own prudential judgments, lead us to a strictly conditioned moral acceptance of nuclear deterrence. We cannot consider it adequate as a long-term basis for peace (no. 186).

24. The logic of a "strictly conditioned moral acceptance" of deterrence requires that the "conditions" be examined to see if the policy decisions and programs undertaken in the name of deterrence should be supported, modified, or rejected. The pastoral letter recognized this responsibility for a continuing evaluation of the nuclear question. After setting forth the criteria and policy judgments which constitute "the conditions" of the pastoral, the bishops state:

> Clearly, these criteria demonstrate that we cannot approve of every weapons system, strategic doctrine, or policy initiative advanced in the name of strengthening deterrence. On the contrary, these criteria require continual public scrutiny of what our government proposes to do with the deterrent (no. 187).

25. In the normal policy and legislative work of our episcopal conference, as well as in the teaching we do in our own dioceses, we have tried as bishops to carry on this task of public scrutiny of deterrence policy. While these daily tasks of education and advocacy are indispensable, the urgency, complexity, and changing character of the nuclear challenge require periodic efforts to assess the problem more comprehensively and to sharpen the sense of moral responsibility which nations possessing nuclear arsenals must accept.

D. The Significance of the Present Moment

26. The moral responsibility remains constant, but the conditions in which it is fulfilled change. When *The Challenge of Peace* was written in the early 1980s, there was virtually no serious discussion between the superpowers, there were no prospects for serious arms control, and the defense expenditures of both the Soviet Union and the United States were rising sharply. To some degree the situation of the late 1980s must be defined in light of these earlier developments. But there are other characteristics of our present situation which may be more important in the long-run. The December 1987 and May 1988 summit meetings between President Reagan and General Secretary Gorbachev, following upon the Geneva (1985) and Reykjavik (1986) summits, signal a systematic approach to nuclear diplomacy which was barely evident in 1983. The words and deeds of the 1988 summit and subsequent events have raised cautious hopes among the most seasoned observers of superpower relations that an authentically new opportunity for redefining the political relationship of the world's two major military powers may be at hand.

27. The precise definition of the new situation is that it is an opportunity not yet a certainty. For both superpowers, there are internal reasons and international pressures which demand an effort to restructure their political and military competition. For different reasons, the United States and the Soviet Union find the pressure of military spending a debilitating drain on their domestic economic and social progress. Both face sustained international criticism for failures to place restraints on their strategic competition. To use the words of Pope John Paul II's recent address on the nuclear arms race: "The stockpiling of these weapons in itself constitutes a threat to peace, as well as a provocation to the peoples that lack the essentials for survival and development."[4] In both countries strategic experts recognize that the development of new technologies in the arms race raises the specter of a more dangerous nuclear relationship.

28. The new opportunity which many sense at hand requires a more responsible arms control policy, but it goes beyond a fixation on weapons systems and warhead tabulations. Whether the opportunity to address the deeper political dynamics of the superpower competition can be grasped depends upon the vision, skill, tactics, and judgment of two governments. But it also involves the general public in both societies. Our political systems differ radically; the very notion of public opinion is difficult to apply to the two nations. But our publics share a certain tragic destiny: we are both targets; the possibility of a future for our children is always an open question because

---

[4]John Paul II, "Address to Diplomatic Corps" (Rome, January 9, 1988), *L'Osservatore Romano*, English weekly edition (January 25, 1988): no. 3, p. 6.

the weapons that threaten both nations are "absolute weapons." The expression of public opinion bears little similarity because of our differing political systems. But it is not naive to presume that in the face of the common danger of nuclear war the citizens of the United States and the Soviet Union share the same fears and sustain the same hopes. Publics can hope, but governments must act. The new dialogue between the superpowers and the first steps taken in 1987 and 1988 to renew the arms control process are the beginning of responsible statesmanship. To grasp the new opportunity will require building carefully but persistently on the foundation of the recent summits.

29. This report is written in response to the charge of Bishop Malone and in light of the charged political climate for arms control. The report is divided into three sections: (1) a review of the moral teaching of *The Challenge of Peace*, (2) an assessment of certain policy developments related to the teaching of the pastoral letter, and (3) a judgment on the moral status of deterrence in 1988.

I. *The Challenge of Peace* A Summary Statement

30. The distinctive characteristic of *The Challenge of Peace* is that it is a religious-moral evaluation of the political, strategic, and technological dimensions of the nuclear age. While the letter is pervaded by a stream of empirical facts and technical distinctions, the reason for the pastoral letter was to submit these data to moral judgment.

31. The moral tradition of the letter is the Catholic ethic on the use or nonuse of force, a tradition which runs from the Sermon on the Mount through the statements of Pope John Paul II. In the pastoral letter, particular weight is given to the papal teaching from Pope Pius XII to Pope John Paul II. It is in recent papal teaching and in the document *Gaudium et Spes* (*Pastoral Constitution on the Church in the Modern World*) of Vatican II that the classical tradition of legitimating and limiting the use of force confronts the reality of the nuclear revolution. This confrontation was dramatically symbolized in John Paul II's statement at Hiroshima in 1981: "In the past it was possible to destroy a village, a town, a region, even a country. Now it is the whole planet that has come under threat."[5] This assessment, specifying the qualitatively new destructive potential introduced by nuclear weapons, served as a premise of the more detailed analysis of the pastoral letter.

32. Starting from this premise *The Challenge of Peace* both echoes the papal and conciliar teaching and also expands beyond it, using the resources of biblical and theological scholarship. The pastoral letter contains a series of prudential judgments encompassing both the application of moral principles and the assessment of empirical data.

---

[5]John Paul II, "Address to Scientists and Scholars," no. 4, p. 621.

A fundamental teaching characteristic of the pastoral letter is the distinction it repeatedly makes between its affirmation of *moral principles* drawn from the philosophical and theological tradition of the Church and its *specific judgments* of policy and practice:

> In this pastoral letter . . . we address many concrete questions concerning the arms race, contemporary warfare, weapons systems, and negotiating strategies. We do not intend that our treatment of each of these issues carry the same moral authority as our statement of universal moral principles and formal church teaching (no. 9).

33. The pastoral letter refuses either to remain at the level of principle or to disguise the fact that moral conclusions about social policy are inevitably dependent on contingent data. It is precisely in the policy section of the pastoral letter that it engages specific issues not addressed in the papal and conciliar teaching. The policy section had three components: moral evaluation of the *use* of nuclear weapons, the strategy of *deterrence,* and then a set of policy *prescriptions.*

A. Use of Nuclear Weapons

34. The Challenge of Peace made three distinct judgments on the use of nuclear weapons. The judgments comprise a spectrum, moving from absolute prohibition through a prudential prescription to a presumption against use.

35. The absolute prohibition is the pastoral letter's categorical rejection of countercity or countercivilian bombing of any kind: "Under no circumstances may nuclear weapons or other instruments of mass slaughter be used for the purpose of destroying population centers or other predominantly civilian targets" (no. 147).

36. The reaffirmation of one of the core principles of the just-war ethic is specified in the pastoral letter in two ways. First, the principle holds even if our cities have been struck by an adversary. Second, the bishops apply the principle to individual cases in the chain of command: "No Christian can rightfully carry out orders or policies deliberately aimed at killing noncombatants" (no. 148).

37. A different kind of moral judgment is rendered on the initiation of nuclear war. The absolute categorical character of the first case is replaced by a complex form of reasoning blending moral principles with empirical assessments of the chances of escalation, the possibilities of limiting the effects of using nuclear weapons, and the degree of risk involved in taking the world into the nuclear arena. The conclusion of this process of evaluation is the judgment that: "We do not perceive any situation in which the deliberate initiation of nuclear warfare, on however restricted a scale, can be morally justified" (no. 150). This "no first use" conclusion is joined with a broader theme of the pastoral: ". . . [W]e seek to reinforce the barrier against any use of nuclear weapons" (no. 153). The nature of this conclusion against *first use*, contingent as it is on a series of empirical judgments, demands further moral examination in the Church and in the wider society.

38. The third case of use, retaliatory (or second) use in a "limited exchange," typically refers to the kind of nuclear war-fighting envisioned in Central Europe. Here the pastoral letter is less categorical than its opposition to civilian bombing and it is less clear than its opposition to first use. The basic argument of this section is to establish a presumption against second use by raising a series of questions about the possibility of limiting the effects of nuclear weapons. The presumption is not a prohibition; the effect of the presumption, however, is to place the burden of proof on those who assert that "limited use" is politically and morally possible. The logic of the letter is to make the burden of proof a very heavy one. Essentially, the "just-war" or "limited war" ethic asserts that one should have moral certainty that weapons to be used can be employed within the limits of the twin moral principles of discrimination and proportionality.

39. The questions raised about the possibilities of maintaining a "limited use" of nuclear weapons highlight the multiple pressures which make limitation very unlikely. The dynamic of technological warfare, the normal range of human error, the lack of experience with nuclear warfighting which all powers fortunately share, all create a tone of radical skepticism in *The Challenge of Peace* about the language of limited war as applied to nuclear conflict. To repeat the judgment of the pastoral letter:

> In the face of this frightening and highly speculative debate on a matter involving millions of human lives, we believe the most effective contribution or moral judgment is to introduce perspectives by which we can assess the empirical debate. Moral perspective should be sensitive not only to the quantitative dimensions of a question but to its psychological, human, and religious characteristics as well. The issue of limited war is not simply the size of weapons contemplated or the strategies projected. The debate should include the psychological and political significance of crossing the boundary from the conventional to the nuclear arena in any form. To cross this divide is to enter a world where we have no experience of control, much testimony against its possibility, and therefore no moral justification for submitting the human community to this risk.[6] We

---

[6]"Undoubtedly aware of the long and detailed technical debate on limited war, Pope John Paul II highlighted the unacceptable moral risk of crossing the threshold to nuclear war in his "Angelus Message" of December 13, 1981: 'I have, in fact, the deep conviction that, in the light of a nuclear war's effects, which can be scientifically foreseen as certain, the only choice that is morally and humanly valid is represented by the reduction of nuclear armaments, while waiting for their future complete elimination, carried out simultaneously by all the parties, by means of explicit agreements and with the commitment of accepting effective controls.'" *The Challenge of Peace*, footnote 70, quoting *Peace and Disarmament: Documents of the World Council of Churches and the Roman Catholic Church* (Geneva and Rome: World Council of Churches and Vatican, 1982), p. 240.

therefore express our view that the first imperative is to prevent any use of nuclear weapons and our hope that leaders will resist the notion that nuclear conflict can be limited, contained, or won in any traditional sense (no. 161).

40. Nonetheless, at the conclusion of its assessment of nuclear use, *The Challenge of Peace* has neither advocated any form of use nor has it condemned every conceivable use of nuclear weapons *a priori*. There is in the letter a narrow margin where use has been considered, not condemned, but hardly commended. From this narrow margin the pastoral moves to an evaluation of deterrence.

B. The Strategy of Deterrence

41. *The Challenge of Peace* based its evaluation of deterrence on the just-war ethic, guided by *Gaudium et Spes* (1965) and by Pope John Paul II's *Message to the United Nations* (1982). The conciliar text had described the moral dilemma of deterrence, but had not entered into a detailed moral judgment. Pope John Paul II had gone beyond the Council: "In current conditions 'deterrence' based on balance, certainly not as an end in itself but as a step on the way toward a progressive disarmament, may still be judged morally acceptable."[7] *The Challenge of Peace* went beyond the papal judgment to probe the logic of conditional approval and to specify the meaning of "conditional." The letter examined theories of deterrence, the arguments about nuclear "warfighting" as a strategy and the debate which has surrounded plans for nuclear targeting. Without repeating the full argument here, we call attention to the detailed assessment of these questions found in paragraphs 178-185 of *The Challenge of Peace*.

42. The "dilemma of deterrence" cited above is the problem of how to sustain a credible deterrent (to prevent nuclear attack while refraining from any intent to target civilians or to violate the limits of proportionality). Anyone who has tried theoretically or practically to reconcile these objectives knows the inherent tension between them. In *The Challenge of Peace* we acknowledged the need for a deterrence strategy but also asserted that "not all forms of deterrence are morally acceptable" (no. 178).

43. The principal limit defining a justifiable deterrent is the prohibition against directly targeting or striking civilians. The pastoral letter asserts the prohibition, which we reaffirm here, and summarizes an exchange of the NCCB and the U.S. Government about the U.S. position on targeting doctrine.[8]

44. The second limit placed on justifiable deterrence is the principle

---

[7]John Paul II, "Message to UN Special Session on Disarmament 1982," no. 8, cited in *The Challenge of Peace*, no. 173.

[8]See *The Challenge of Peace*, no. 179, footnote 81.

of proportionality. It is particularly needed to address two questions analyzed in the pastoral letter. The first is the damage done by attacks on "military or industrial" targets located near civilian centers. Second is the damage envisioned in various forms of nuclear war-fighting strategies.

45. The first problem is inherent in the existing deterrence strategies of both superpowers, since each targets the industrial capacity of the other. There will inevitably be continuing arguments about what constitutes a "proportionate threat" to deter or what is "proportionate damage," but we remain convinced that

> . . . there are actions which can be decisively judged to be disporportionate. A narrow adherence exclusively to the principle of noncombatant immunity as a criterion for policy is an inadequate moral posture, for it ignores some evil and unacceptable consequences. Hence, we cannot be satisfied that the assertion of an intention not to strike civilians directly, or even the most honest effort to implement that intention by itself constitutes a "moral policy" for the use of nuclear weapons (no. 181).

46. The second problem, war-fighting strategies, arises from the quest for a coherent connection between "deterrence and use" policies and from the search for "discriminate deterence." While acknowledging the concerns which drive both of these endeavors and welcoming any effort to guarantee the immunity of the civilian population, we remain convinced that such proposals should not be understood as an assurance that nuclear war is subject to precise or rational limits. The "dilemma of deterrence" is not ameliorated by notions that nuclear weapons are "normal," "controlled" instruments of military policy. The logic of the pastoral letter, reasserted here, is to build a barrier against nuclear use and to confine the role of deterrence to "the specific objective of preventing the use of nuclear weapons . . ." (no. 185).[9]

47. The conclusion of *The Challenge of Peace* on deterrence was cited earlier in this report, but it deserves repetition here:

> These considerations of concrete elements of nuclear deterrence policy, made in light of John Paul II's evaluation, but applying it through our own prudential judgments, lead us to a strictly conditioned moral acceptance of nuclear deterrence. We cannot consider it adequate as a long-term basis for peace (no. 186).

48. The "strict conditions" which the pastoral imposed on deterrence involved two kinds of restraints. The first involved a "temporal" dimension; in the language of the pastoral, deterrence is not a "long-term" answer to the nuclear question. The temporal aspect of con ditionality was not intended to place a moral straightjacket on policy. It did not, for example, set an exact timetable after which the moral

---

[9] Cf. ibid., nos. 140, 153.

acceptance would be exhausted. This is too simple an instrument of assessment for the deterrence relationship which is dynamic in character and dependent upon the choices of other actors besides the United States. Such a mechanistic view also fails to consider that the policy of deterrence is comprised by several elements, some of which can be acceptable while others stand in need of criticism and change.

49. The "temporal condition" contained in *The Challenge of Peace* is an attempt to reflect and specify the meaning of the papal dictum that deterrence should be seen as part of a complex process leading to a new political relationship. In this sense, the temporal condition is meant to test "the direction" of the deterrence relationship and the policies which sustain it. Are these policies moving toward progressive disarmament? In the short term, are these policies moving in the direction of reducing the likelihood of nuclear use, enhancing the stability of the superpower relationship, and making possible quantitative and qualitative reductions in the arms race?

50. The second condition placed on deterrence policy by the pastoral letter is designed to test the "character" or the "component elements" of the deterrent. The test applied is rooted in moral categories, using the principles of proportionality, noncombatant immunity, last resort, and the risks implied in different forms of deterrence policy. Testing the character of weapons, forms of deployment, and declaratory policy in this way corresponds to the classical concerns of arms control, which stress less the numbers of weapons in the deterrence relationship than the impact certain weapons have on the stability of the nuclear balance.

51. The intent to test both the "direction" of deterrence policy and the "character" of specific weapons in the deterrent led *The Challenge of Peace* to set forth specific criteria and conditions for moral judgment about deterrence.

C. Criteria and Conditions for Policy Evaluation

52. These criteria and conditions should be used together as a framework for assessing several aspects of nuclear strategy.

Criteria for Conditional Acceptance of Deterrence:

> 1) If nuclear deterrence exists only to prevent the *use* of nuclear weapons by others, then proposals to go beyond this to planning for prolonged periods of repeated nuclear strikes and counterstrikes, or "prevailing" in nuclear war, are not acceptable. They encourage notions that nuclear war can be engaged in with tolerable human and moral consequences. Rather, we must continually say "no" to the idea of nuclear war.
> 2) If nuclear deterrence is our goal, "sufficiency" to deter is an adequate strategy; the quest for nuclear superiority must be rejected.

3) Nuclear deterrence should be used as a step on the way toward progressive disarmament. Each proposed addition to our strategic system or change in strategic doctrine must be assessed precisely in light of whether it will render steps toward "progressive disarmament" more or less likely (no. 188).

Conditions for Conditional Acceptance of Deterrence:

In light of the criteria we opposed the following proposals:

1) The addition of weapons which are likely to be vulnerable to attack, yet also possess a "prompt hard-target kill" capability that threatens to make the other side's retaliatory forces vulnerable. Such weapons may seem to be useful primarily in a first strike; we resist such weapons for this reason and we oppose Soviet deployment of such weapons which generate fear of a first strike against U.S. forces.
2) The willingness to foster strategic planning which seeks a nuclear war-fighting capability that goes beyond the limited function of deterrence outlined in this letter.
3) Proposals which have the effect of lowering the nuclear threshold and blurring the difference between nuclear and conventional weapons (no. 190).

In support of the concept of "sufficiency" as an adequate deterrent, and in light of the existing size and composition of both the U.S. and Soviet strategic arsenals, we recommended:

1) Support for immediate, bilateral, verifiable agreements to halt the testing, production, and deployment of new nuclear weapons systems.
2) Support for negotiated bilateral deep cuts in the arsenals of both superpowers, particularly those weapons systems which have destabilizing characteristics. . . .
3) Support for early and successful conclusion of negotiations of a comprehensive test ban treaty.
4) Removal by all parties of short-range nuclear weapons which multiply dangers disproportionate to their deterrent value.
5) Removal by all parties of nuclear weapons from areas where they are likely to be overrun in the early stages of war, thus forcing rapid and uncontrollable decisions on their use.
6) Strengthening of command and control over nuclear weapons to prevent inadvertent and unauthorized use (no. 191).

53. In congressional testimony of 1984, Cardinal Bernardin and Archbishop O'Connor returned to the theme of setting forth additional criteria by which proposed changes in the deterrent arsenal should be judged. Against the background of debates concerning the wisdom of deploying the MX missile or proceeding toward defensive systems, they offered the following guideline:

If a particular system is found to be of dubious strategic value (i.e., not absolutely necessary to preserve our deterrence posture) and yet is certain to cost large sums of money, then these two criteria lead us to recommend against the system in question.[10]

54. The application and refinement of these criteria and conditions to a range of policy questions is the task of the rest of this report. As we begin the process of evaluating policy choices and technological trends, we reaffirm a key guideline for interpreting our position as bishops on these complex questions. The guideline is found in *The Challenge of Peace*, but applies with equal force to this report:

> In this pastoral letter, . . . we address many concrete questions concerning the arms race, contemporary warfare, weapons systems, and negotiating strategies. We do not intend that our treatment of each of these issues carry the same moral authority as our statement of universal moral principles and formal church teaching. . . . When making applications of these principles we realize—and we wish readers to recognize—that prudential judgments are involved based on specific circumstances which can change or which can be interpreted differently by people of good will . . . (nos. 9-10).

II. Policy Developments
Assessment and Recommendations

55. Three areas of nuclear policy are directly relevant to the conditions set by *The Challenge of Peace*: (1) the politics and strategy of arms control policy, (2) technological developments and the arms race, and (3) the economic impact of defense spending.

A. Arms Control Policy

56. Arms control is fundamentally a political process which Catholic teaching sees as a step toward disarmament. Arms control should be viewed, therefore, in light of the political relationship which has prevailed between the superpowers and the new opportunity, noted above, which presents fundamental choices to the Soviet Union and the United States.

57. The new opportunity, even if utilized, should not be expected to dissipate or dissolve the basic realities of U.S.-Soviet relations. As *The Challenge of Peace* observed, the two nations are divided by history, philosophy, polity, and conflicting interests. The possibility which may be open is not to transcend these fundamental differences, but to regulate the competitive relationships with new criteria. The superpowers confront each other directly, through their European allies, and in a variety of ways in the southern hemisphere.

58. The capabilities of both nuclear giants to create a nuclear crisis or

---

[10]Cardinal Bernardin and Archbishop O'Connor, Testimony for the U.S. Catholic Conference on U.S. Arms Control Policy before the Committee on Foreign Affairs, U.S. House of Representatives (June 26, 1984), p. 150, *Origins* 14:10 (August 9, 1984): 157.

a nuclear catastrophe for the rest of the world is the most threatening way in which their relationship affects others. But beyond the nuclear question, the political role of the Soviet Union and the United States remains decisive for the safety, stability, and welfare of the international community. In the European theater one effect of the Intermediate-Range Nuclear Forces (INF) Treaty is to increase the significance of the political questions both within the alliances and between the superpowers directly. The most intractable issues between the superpowers for much of the last fifteen years have been their involvement in regional conflicts from the Horn of Africa to Afghanistan and the Persian Gulf to Nicaragua and Central America. This report focuses upon the specifically nuclear relationship, but it would be a narrow view of the challenge of the present moment if the wider political context of the superpower relationship were ignored. Arms control can be a catalyst to an improved political relationship, and changes in the political context of superpower relations can open the road to new steps in controlling weaponry. This reciprocal relationship of politics and strategy means, in part, that a failure to move forward on the arms control front will very likely make progress in other areas of U.S.-Soviet relations more difficult.

59. Essentially the task of testing the new opportunity in superpower relations will require both political vision and strategic wisdom. The latter is needed to restrain the nuclear competition and to reduce its component elements. The former is required to set limits on the political competition which will be in the interests of the major powers, but will also decrease the hold of bipolar politics on others in the international community.

60. Turning specifically to arms control, both Pope John Paul II's statements linking acceptance of deterrence with movement toward disarmament and the pastoral letter's endorsement of a series of arms control measures give this topic a central place in evaluating events since 1983. The following developments stand out.

1. The INF Treaty

61. The INF Treaty, signed by Mr. Reagan and Mr. Gorbachev on December 8, 1987, represents the first bilateral arms control accomplishment since the SALT I Treaty (1972). The treaty provides for abolition of two classes of nuclear delivery systems (intermediate-range and shorter-range missiles). Although these weapons constitute a small percentage of the strategic arsenals of the superpowers, the dual significance of reconstituting the arms control process with a treaty and of achieving actual reductions in nuclear weaponry constitutes steps in accord with the criteria of *The Challenge of Peace*, and we have supported ratification of the treaty in congressional testimony.

The INF Treaty, in the view of its supporters and its critics, inevitably points beyond itself to other larger arms control questions. It was also depicted in this light in the statement of Pope John Paul II, who devoted much of his annual *Address to the Diplomatic Corps* to the INF Treaty and to the issue of nuclear disarmament:

> Nuclear disengagement, which for the time being still involves only a very limited proportion of the respective arsenals, may now be pursued without the global military balance being called into question, to the point of reaching the lowest level compatible with mutual security. . . . According to the protagonists, the agreement on intermediate nuclear weapons is more a point of departure than an end in itself. It was the occasion for the two signatories to affirm their determination to accelerate the negotiations taking place on ballistic nuclear weapons, which are the most menacing of all. It is important not only to mitigate but to remove definitively the threat of a nuclear catastrophe. It is certainly the wish of the entire international community that such talks succeed as soon as possible, inspired by the same principles.[11]

2. *The Nuclear and Space Talks (NST)*

62. The negotiations on strategic forces and space-based defenses are the next step beyond the INF Treaty. In line with the criteria of *The Challenge of Peace*, we support the "deep cuts" formula (1,600 launchers and 6,000 warheads) which is being used in these negotiations. We welcome these proposed reductions even while noting the accepted fact that the *kinds* of weapons which are constrained or reduced are the more important criterion than the *number* reduced. In the NST, there are important quantitative (number) and qualitative (kind) reductions which are being negotiated. These negotiations deserve and have our strong support.

3. *Existing Treaties*

63. While NST proceed, we find it imprudent and counterproductive to erode or dismantle fragile restraints on an arms competition vigorously in progress. Hence, we support maintaining the limits established in the SALT I-ABM Treaty on defensive systems, and we oppose the U.S. decision not to abide by the SALT II limits on offensive forces. Finally, we reaffirm the recommendation of the 1983 pastoral that negotiation should be vigorously pursued on a comprehensive test ban treaty.

4. *New Deployments*

64. The INF Treaty and the NST must be seen within the context of

---

[11]John Paul II, "Address to Diplomatic Corps," nos. 3, 4, p. 7.

other developments in the 1980s. Even as the superpowers have carried on nuclear negotiations, they have also proceeded with nuclear modernization programs (i.e., the development of new weapons) which are the product of decisions taken in the 1970s and early 1980s. Since the 1970s, the Soviet Union has deployed four new strategic systems and several thousand warheads. The United States is carrying forward new deployments on every leg of the strategic triad (land-based missiles — ICBMs, submarine-launched missiles — SLBMs, and bombers). Both the Soviet Union and the United States, therefore, are deploying weapons which, in both number and kind, run contrary to the conditions of *The Challenge of Peace*. The pastoral letter specifically cited weapons which increase the incentive "to preempt" (strike first) in a crisis as particularly undesirable. The Soviet Union's deployment of the SS-18s and its plan to deploy SS-24s, along with the U.S. deployment of the MX run directly counter to this recommendation. The U.S. planned deployment of the D-5 submarine-launched missile (Trident II) involves a more complex judgment; its range and relative invulnerability can add stability in a crisis, but its accuracy and yield run counter to the criteria of the pastoral letter.

5. Independent Initiatives

65. During the 1980s, both the United States and the Soviet Union have taken steps which fit the category of "independent initiatives" found in *The Challenge of Peace*, but in each case the initiative was not reciprocated. The NATO alliance made decisions in 1980 and again in 1983 to withdraw a total of 2,400 battlefield nuclear weapons from the European theater. In August 1985, the Soviet Union announced a unilateral moratorium on nuclear testing which it extended through 1986; the Soviets have now resumed nuclear testing.

6. Conventional Arms Control

66. This assessment of certain major trends in superpower relations does not capture all the pertinent dimensions of the arms control picture. Two major areas which will have an increasing importance in the 1990s are conventional arms control and nonproliferation policies. The legitimate concern paid to the unique qualities of the nuclear danger should not distract needed attention from the control of conventional armaments. This is a global problem, going far beyond the bounds of direct superpower relations and beyond the interaction of NATO and the Warsaw Pact. The more than 150 conflicts since World War II have all used conventional weapons, many of them supplied by the industrialized nations to parties in the developing world. The "North-South" dimension of conventional arms trade and the need for regional restraints in the arms competition would require a separate report. In the encyclical *On Social Concern*,[12] Pope John Paul II identified the conventional arms trade as one of the principal ways in which the East-West superpower competition distorts and corrupts the quest for authentic development in the Third World:

> If arms production is a serious disorder in the present world with regard to true human needs and the employment of the means capable of satisfying those needs, *the arms trade* is equally to blame. Indeed, with reference to the latter it must be added that the *moral judgment is even more severe*. As we all know, this is a trade without frontiers, capable of crossing even the barriers of the blocs. It knows how to overcome the division between East and West, and above all the one between North and South, to the point—and this is more serious—of pushing its way into the *different sections* which make up the southern hemisphere. We are thus confronted with a strange phenomenon: while economic aid and development plans meet with the obstacle of insuperable ideological barriers and with tariff and trade barriers, *arms* of whatever origin circulate with almost total freedom all over the world. And as the recent document of the Pontifical Commission "Justitia et Pax" on the international debt points out, everyone knows that in certain cases the capital lent by the developed world has been used in the underdeveloped world to buy weapons (no. 24).

67. In the East-West framework the relationship between nuclear and conventional arms control will be increasingly important. Precisely if it is possible to proceed with "deep cuts" of 30 to 50 percent in strategic arsenals will the need to evaluate a corresponding move on the conventional front become clear. In *The Challenge of Peace*, we said that our emphasis on controlling the nuclear arms race was not intended to make the world safe for conventional war. To address this concern, the future of arms control negotiations will have to pay greater attention to relating progress on the nuclear front to steps on conventional arms control. In his assessment of the INF Treaty, Pope John Paul II made two points relevant to conventional arms control. First, the objective of negotiations should aim at ensuring security at the lowest possible level of conventional arms which is compatible with "reasonable requirements for defense."[13] Second, even granting the first criterion, the pope still warned that "there is need to avoid at all cost a new form of escalation in conventional weapons which would be hazardous and ruinous."[14]

68. If both stable deterrence is to be maintained and a new round of conventional escalation to be avoided, the proposed new negotiations for NATO and the Warsaw Pact on conventional arms will have to be pursued with a clearer policy focus and much greater political

---

[12]John Paul II, *On Social Concern* (*Sollicitudo Rei Socialis*) (Washington, D.C.: USCC Office of Publishing and Promotion Services, 1988).

[13]John Paul II, "Address to Diplomatic Corps," no. 4, p. 7.

[14]Ibid.

urgency than has marked much of the now moribund negotiations on Mutual Balanced Force Reductions. In the West, particularly, these conventional negotiations will require particular attention to the political dimensions of the alliance relationship.

7. Nuclear Nonproliferation

69. The second neglected area of the 1980s has been the problem of nuclear proliferation. Since the Non-Proliferation Treaty (NPT) came into force (1970), a framework for controlling the proliferation of nuclear weapons has existed. The nonproliferation negotiations and the nonproliferation order established by the treaty essentially constituted a compact between the major nuclear states and the nonnuclear powers. Essential to the compact was the commitment of the superpowers to restrain and reverse the "vertical" arms race in return for a pledge from nonnuclear states to refrain from "horizontal" proliferation.

70. In 1995 the NPT is due for renewal; it is clear that several key nonnuclear states are dissatisfied with the present regime and the role of the nuclear powers in it. This is not the only, or perhaps not even the principal, threat to nonproliferation. Local and regional problems may in the final analysis be the decisive determinant in a proliferation decision. But the status of the compact on vertical and horizontal proliferation is directly under the control of the Soviet Union and the United States. The imperative to renew progress on arms control before the NPT is due for renewal is a primary consideration in the arms control picture.

71. Finally, the assessment of specific aspects of U.S.-Soviet policies on arms control does not adequately convey the critical character of the present moment. In *The Challenge of Peace*, we noted that one of the distinguishing elements of the nuclear age is that we cannot afford one serious mistake. The consequences would be catastrophic—probably beyond our capacity to imagine. In the United States we have known the fear generated by Three Mile Island, and the Soviet and European populations have experienced the reality of Chernobyl, but these events are mere shadows compared to the devastation and terror which even a "limited" nuclear exchange would produce.

72. The nuclear debate of the 1980s has resulted in a higher level of public sensitivity to the fragile hold we have on our common nuclear future and an increased awareness of the moral dangers of the nuclear age. Even those in the expert community who stress that deterrence is "robust" or "stable" acknowledge that we cannot simply presume that deterrence which "has worked" for forty years will surely continue "to work." The possibilities of technical accident, human miscalculation, or diplomatic crisis—taken singly or together—pose permanent threats to the system which the superpowers now rely upon for "security."

73. These possibilities of failure exist in the very nature of nuclear deterrence. The more troubling fact is that recent trends in the character of weapons being deployed accentuate the dangers of deterrence. Large, MIRVed, very accurate missiles, often deployed as vulnerable targets, tilt the nuclear balance toward a preemptive posture on both sides. In the technical literature on the nuclear balance, analysts of quite different policy persuasions agree that present trends are not conducive to deterrence stability. From this analysis the question arises whether it is possible and useful to conceive of "going beyond deterrence." *The Challenge of Peace* asserted that deterrence is not a long-term solution to a sound security system. Recently Pope John Paul II returned to this theme himself:

> Such a strategy, applied in a context of detente and cooperation, must lead to a progressive search for a new balance, at the lowest possible level of weapons, so as to arrive eventually at the elimination of the atomic weapon itself. In this matter one must move towards total disarmament. May the protagonists understand that their mutual security is always furthered by an interpenetration of interests and vital relations![15]

74. All commentators, whether they are political analysts, strategists, or moralists, find it easier to propose going beyond deterrence than to prescribe the steps for accomplishing this task. One direction involves trying to realize some of the potential of the U.S.-Soviet political relationship described above. As long as nuclear weapons exist, deterrence will be an inherent fact of the superpower relationship. But improvement in the political atmosphere can, over time, reduce the significance of nuclear deterrence in the total relationship.

75. This political approach will have to be joined with a strategy of arms control. The objectives of arms control are more modest than disarmament, but the latter is impossible within the former. Moreover, arms control which is not yet disarmament still can contribute to a safer world by stressing the objectives of survivable forces with clearly verifiable limits. Arms control can channel the superpower competition in the interim while other, more profound efforts seek to transform the political relationship. The fundamental importance of arms control needs to be reaffirmed in this evaluation. It is one way we take hold of our common nuclear future with the Soviet Union.

76. In light of this assessment, our evaluation of the last five years does not produce a single simple conclusion. The INF Treaty has been signed and some other possibilities are now on the negotiating table, which, if completed, would fulfill some key criteria of the pastoral letter. But in the face of this still uncertain promise, there stands the historical fact of major additions to the strategic arsenals of both super-

---

[15]Ibid., no. 5, p. 7.

powers, weapons whose character and numbers decidedly increase the danger of nuclear war occurring. This pattern of policy is not adequate to the moral danger of the age that these arsenals, by miscalculation or mistake, will escape human control and destroy in an hour what humanity has taken centuries to build and shape.

77. The "conditional acceptance" of deterrence found in *The Challenge of Peace* is directly tied to the pursuit of arms control and, ultimately, disarmament. The arms control successes cited in this report should be welcomed. But the opportunities missed when arms control was shunted aside for years at a time deserve equal attention. To some degree the arms control successes of the present are compensating for lost opportunities in the past decade. Failure to pursue arms control systematically erodes support for deterrence. In the coming decade the moral legitimacy of deterrence policy will be tested precisely by the linkage of deterrence, arms control, and disarmament.

B. Technological Developments

78. Technology acts as a two-edged sword in the nuclear competition; some technological changes (e.g., Permissive Action Links) contribute to increasing control of nuclear weapons; other developments (e.g., MIRVing) have had a long-term destablizing impact. Since 1983, developments in missile accuracy, anti-satellite weapons, and stealth technology have continued the bivalent influence of technology on the arms race. The dilemmas of command, control, and communications systems (C3) illustrate this well. Some improvements in C3 are dangerous if they enhance "war-fighting" capabilities and feed the illusion of surviving an extended nuclear exchange. Other improvements would decrease reliance on strategies of launch under attack or launch on warning, and so enhance the stability of deterrence in crisis. These latter improvements are at present hardly keeping up with the expansion and evolution of weaponry; they require vigorous attention at the level of technology and at the level of superpower political understanding.

79. But the most significant change by far in the area of technology and policy has been the proposal of President Reagan to pursue a defense against ballistic missiles. Technically described as the Strategic Defense Initiative (SDI), it originated on March 23, 1983, in a presidential address to the nation. The key passages of the address are well known:

> Let me share with you a vision of the future which offers hope. It is that we embark on a program to counter the awesome Soviet missile threat with measures that are defensive. . . . What if free people could live secure in the knowledge that their security did not rest upon the threat of instant U.S. retaliation to deter a Soviet attack,

that we could intercept and destroy strategic ballistic missiles before they reached our own soil or that of our allies?[16]

80. The proposal, described as "radical" by both then Secretary of Defense Weinberger and critics of the SDI, holds particular importance in any review of *The Challenge of Peace* for three reasons. First, the proposal was made only weeks before publication of the pastoral, so there is no treatment of defensive systems in the letter. Second, the defensive proposal now premeates the debate about nuclear policy. A recent group of the Aspen Institute Strategy Group observed: "Virtually all issues related to arms control, alliance security, and Soviet-American strategic relations are now linked to SDI in one way or another."[17] Third, the proponents of SDI, from the president to the secretary of defense to supporters in the public debate, all have made the claim that SDI constitutes a superior moral policy to that of deterrence as we have known it in the nuclear age. Individually and collectively these reasons point toward the need to address the SDI proposal. Here, we seek to outline the character of the SDI debate, using representative public positions, and then to comment on it in light of relevant moral principles.

1. SDI: What Is It?

81. In simple terms, SDI is a research program charged with investigating the technological possibilities of defense against ballistic missiles. But the description cannot remain simple, for even within the Reagan Administration there is a certain pluralism in describing the scope and purpose of SDI. The president's address described the goal of the program in terms of rendering nuclear weapons "impotent and obsolete." Mr. Weinberger described the meaning of the SDI proposal as a "radical rejection of benign acquiescence in reliance upon the threat of mutual destruction."[18] Taken at face value these descriptions depict a program designed *to transcend* a policy of deterrence based on the threat of nuclear retaliation.

82. Almost from the beginning of the SDI program, however, official statements have included a more modest goal, not to transcend deterrence but *to enhance* deterrence. In 1986, Mr. Weinberger spoke of three justifications for the SDI program: to hedge against a Soviet breakthrough on defensive technologies, to guard against a Soviet

---

[16]President Reagan, "Launching the SDI," cited in Z. Brzezinski, ed., *Promise or Peril: The Strategic Defense Initiative* (Washington, D.C.: Ethics and Public Policy Center, 1986), pp. 48-49.

[17]Aspen Strategy Group Report, *The Strategic Defense Initiative and American Security* (Lanham, Md.: University Press of America, 1987), p. ix.

[18]C. W. Weinberger, Secretary of Defense, *Annual Report to the Congress Fiscal Year 1987* (Washington, D.C.: U.S. Government Printing Office, 1986), p. 73.

breakout of the ABM Treaty, and, finally, "the very real possibility that American science and technology will achieve what appears to some to be an impossible dream."[19] The first two reasons do not transcend deterrence, the third looks to that goal.

83. Enhancing deterrence means using defensive systems in a mode which will complicate Soviet planning for a preemptive strike against American land-based ICBMs. The administration case is neither a pure instance of area defense (of population) nor point defense (of missiles) but a mix of partial area and partial point defense designed to forestall Soviet confidence in resorting to a nuclear attack.[20]

84. These two descriptions of the SDI (transcending and enhancing deterrence) have created a certain confusion in the public debate, since the technological challenge and strategic rationale for the two are substantially different. In spite of a less than clear policy focus, the administration has been quite successful in securing congressional support for SDI. A recent congressional staff report records the growth of SDI appropriations:

> In FY 1985 the Administration requested $1.78 billion for SDI, a 79 percent nominal increase over the previous year's funding level. Congress approved $1.40 billion for FY 1985, a 41 percent increase. In FY 1986, the Administration requested $3.72 billion for SDI, a 166 percent increase over FY 1985. Congress approved $2.76 billion, a 97 percent increase. And in FY 1987, the Administration requested $4.8 billion for SDI, a 74 percent increase. Congress approved $3.2 billion, a 16 percent increase.[21]

85. While these statistics indicate a certain congressional reserve about the program, the significant increases should not be overlooked; spending rose by 41 percent, 97 percent, and 16 percent in nominal terms over a three year period. The congressional study specifies the meaning of these expenditures: "The SDI program's budget has more than tripled since its inception, it has become the largest military research program in DOD—the department's top strategic priority—and its funding level now surpasses the combined technology base funding for the Army, Navy, and Air Force."[22]

86. In addition to an aggressive legislative program, the administra-

---

[19]C. W. Weinberger, "U.S. Defense Strategy," *Foreign Affairs* 64:4 (1986): p. 682. For the Reagan Administration's evaluation of Soviet activities on defensive systems, see, e.g., *Soviet Strategic Defense Programs* (Washington, D.C.: Department of State and Department of Defense, 1985).

[20]K. Adelman, Director of U.S. Arms Control and Disarmament Agency, Testimony before NCCB Ad Hoc Committee on the Moral Evaluation of Deterrence, March 27, 1987.

[21]*SDI: Progress and Challenges—Part Two: Staff Report Submitted to Senator Proxmire and Senator Johnston* (March 19, 1987), p. 3. (Since the staff report was published, the Congress decided to fund SDI at $3.9 billion for FY 1988.)

[22]Ibid.

tion has expanded the policy framework in its presentation of the SDI. Two speeches by senior State Department officials set the policy rationale and criteria for SDI. In January 1985, then Under Secretary of State Kenneth Dam set forth the "strategic concept" which the administration is using to link its SDI program with its arms control philosophy:

> For the next ten years, we should seek a radical reduction in the number and power of existing and planned offensive and defensive nuclear arms, whether landbased, spacebased, or otherwise. We should even now be looking forward to a period of transition, beginning possibly ten years from now, to effective nonnuclear defensive forces, including defenses against offensive nuclear arms. This period of transition should lead to the eventual elimination of nuclear arms, both offensive and defensive. A nuclear-free world is an ultimate objective to which we, the Soviet Union, and all other nations can agree.[23]

87. In February 1985, Ambassador Paul H. Nitze moved the SDI debate forward by establishing criteria which any deployment would have to satisfy. The Nitze criteria have become a canonical reference in the SDI debate, with both critics and supporters of the proposal appealing to them. Nitze reiterated Dam's argument that the objective of the SDI was "a cooperative effort with the Soviet Union, hopefully leading to an agreed transition toward effective nonnuclear defenses that might make possible the eventual elimination of nuclear weapons."[24] Movement toward this goal involves three stages: the near-term, a transition period, and an ultimate phase. In the near-term, deterrence based on nuclear retaliation will continue to structure the nuclear relationship, but research in defensive technologies and arms control aimed at "radical reductions" in offensive forces would both be pushed vigorously.

88. In the transitional period—the key moment—greater reliance will be placed on defensive systems. The criteria which must be met in any deployment are technological feasibility, survivability, and cost-effectiveness.[25] If defensive systems cannot be deployed in a survivable manner, they become tempting targets and increase strategic instability. If these systems are not "cost-effective at the margin," then it will be cheaper for the adversary to build countermeasures. The transition period would be, in Nitze's words, "tricky"; it would require progress in controlling offensive weapons, and it would have to be executed in cooperation with the Soviets. Provided the conditions of the first two periods are met, the ultimate phase of the new strategic

---

[23]K. W. Dam, "Geneva and Beyond: New Arms Control Negotiations," *Department of State Bulletin* 85:2096 (March 1985): 39.

[24]P. H. Nitze, "On the Road to a More Stable Peace," *Department of State Bulletin* 85:2097 (April 1985): 27.

[25]Ibid., p. 28.

concept could, in Nitze's view, lead to "the reduction of nuclear weapons down to zero."[26]

89. Both the specific proposal of the SDI—a multilayered defense designed to attack ballistic missiles in the four stages of their trajectory (boost phase, post-boost phase, midcourse flight, and terminal phase)— and the strategic concept sustaining it have come under criticism. The public debate has focused on the technological feasibility of SDI and its impact on strategic stability and arms control.

2. SDI: Technology, Strategy, and Arms Control

90. The nuclear debate has always had a forbiddingly technical character, but the SDI controversy has raised the technical discussion to a new plateau of complexity. Both the density of the technological data and the diversity of expert opinions make the debate about the feasibility of the system a crucial point in the policy arena. Diversity of opinion should not be taken to mean the experts are equally divided; there seems to be substantially more doubters in the scientific community than advocates of SDI.

91. Yet the administration has continued to be optimistic in its assessment of the feasibility of SDI—at least the SDI designed *to enhance* deterrence. Paul H. Nitze spoke in March 1986 of "impressive advances" in the investigation of SDI technology. The progress is such that "the United States has good reason to believe that SDI technologies hold the promise for feasible, survivable, and cost-effective defenses."[27] Dr. George Keyworth, science adviser to President Reagan when SDI was proposed, spoke to the NCCB ad hoc committee in terms which seemed to reach beyond Nitze's cautious "promise" to a tangible product. describing the technological progress made since 1983, Keyworth said:

> That progress meant that by the time of the Geneva Summit in 1985 we could, with some confidence, picture a boost-phase defense system driven by any of several *different* technologies. . . . These numbers describe an awesome defensive capability; a battery of perhaps a dozen such weapons would so overwhelm the offensive forces that countering them by proliferation would be out of the question. So if in March of 1983 we were asking IF we could develop SDI, we can now ask *how* best to choose from those that are emerging.[28]

92. The evaluations of feasibility coming from other voices in the scientific and strategic community have often been notably more cau-

---

[26]Ibid.

[27]P. H. Nitze, "The Promise of SDI," *Department of State Bulletin* 86:2110 (May 1986): 55.

[28]G. A. Keyworth, II, "SDI and Arms Control," Testimony to NCCB Ad Hoc Committee on the Moral Evaluation of Deterrence, December 5, 1986, pp. 12-13.

tious. Perhaps the preeminent critical contribution to the technical debate from outside the administration has been the report commissioned by the American Physical Society (APS). The APS convened a study group "to evaluate the status of the science and technology of directed energy weapons (DEW)."[29] The group was established because of "the divergence of views within the scientific community"[30] on SDI. The 400-page study is devoted exclusively to directed energy weapons (only one possible SDI technology), but its detailed assessment lends weight to its cautious prediction:

> Although substantial progress has been made in many technologies of DEW over the last two decades, the Study Group finds significant gaps in the scientific and engineering understanding of many issues associated with the development of these technologies. Successful resolution of these issues is critical for the extrapolation to performance levels that would be required in an effective ballistic missile defense system. At present, there is insufficient information to decide whether the required extrapolations can or cannot be achieved. Most crucial elements required for a DEW system need improvements of several orders of magnitude. Because the elements are interrelated, the improvements must be achieved in a mutually consistent manner. We estimate that even in the best of circumstances, a decade or more of intensive research would be required to provide the technical knowledge needed for an informed decision about the potential effectiveness and survivability of directed energy weapon systems. In addition, the important issues of overall system integration and effectiveness depend critically upon information that, to our knowledge, does not yet exist.[31]

93. The APS Study Group eschewed the policy issues of arms control, strategic stability, and cost. Two other recent studies are more policy-oriented, joining their judgments on the feasibility of SDI to arms control concerns. The Aspen Strategy Group Report argues that meeting the administration's own criteria of survivability and cost-effectiveness would effectively rule out any deployment of space-based defenses until well into the 1990s. The strategy group specifies three challenges facing SDI:

- many innovations which assist the defense also enhance offensive capabilities;
- effective boost-phase defense "seems problematic"; and
- iterminal phase defense seems unlikely using SDI's nonnuclear technology.

---

[29] N. Bloembergen (Harvard University), C. K. Patel (AT&T Bell Laboratories), co-chairs, et al. *Report to the American Physical Society of the Study Group on Science and Technology of Directed Energy Weapons*, p. 1. (Published in *Reviews of Modern Physics* 59:3 Part II [July 1987].)

[30] Ibid.

[31] Ibid., p. 2

The Aspen Group advocates an SDI research program, but one carried out within the limits of the ABM Treaty (strictly interpreted) and joined with an arms control policy pursuing deep cuts in offensive weapons. Changing the commonly used metaphor, the Aspen Report sees SDI not as a "bargaining chip" but a "lever": "SDI will not likely drive the Soviets to accept offensive reductions that leave asymmetries in our favor. . . . But what SDI can do—and, arguably, has done in light of the Reykjavik summit—is to prompt the Soviets to offer reductions of a magnitude that eluded U.S. negotiators throughout the 1970s and early 1980s."[32] The wise use of the lever, argues the report, is to strike *The Grand Compromise* of Soviet cuts in their most menacing offensive systems for U.S. restraints—within the ABM Treaty—on defensive technologies.

94. Similar policy perspectives to the Aspen Study are found in the 1985 report of the Stanford Center for International Security and Arms Control, *Strategic Missile Defense: Necessities, Prospects and Dangers in the Near Term.*[33] The report is signed by scientists with a wide variety of views on the policy issues of SDI. But supporters and critics of SDI join in recommending research conducted within the parameters of the ABM Treaty, and research which is not pushed by political objectives, but governed by scientific criteria.

95. The purpose in setting forth administration positions and these reports is not to count or even to weigh authorities on the feasibility and arms control issues, but to illustrate how the SDI debate is being joined.

3. SDI: The Moral Argument

96. One of the characteristics of the nuclear debate of the 1980s, fostered in part by *The Challenge of Peace*, has been a growing dissatisfaction with the theory and policy of deterrence. The standard doctrine has come under critique from the left and the right of the political spectrum and both have resorted to moral as well as political-strategic arguments to stress the shortcomings of deterrence. The moral case propounded for defensive systems fits into this wider atmosphere of dissatisfaction with deterrence. Both President Reagan and former Secretary Weinberger regularly appeal to the moral motivation and moral quality of the SDI. Supporters of the SDI pick up on this theme, joining a critique of Mutual Assured Destruction theories to an argument about the moral stability which will accompany a defense dominated nuclear relationship.

---

[32] Aspen Strategy Group Report, p. 45.

[33] Center for International Security and Arms Control, *Strategic Missile Defense: Necessities, Prospects and Dangers in the Near Term* (Stanford: Stanford University, 1985).

97. As bishops, we are interested in the scientific and strategic dimensions of the SDI policy debate, but we are not in a position to contribute to them. It is precisely the visible role which the moral argument has assumed in the policy arena which draws us into more specific commentary here. The SDI is proposed by some of its supporters as a superior moral answer to the moral dilemmas of the nuclear age analyzed in *The Challenge of Peace*. We seek here to probe the relationship of the moral claims made for SDI and other dimensions of the policy debate.

98. The case made for the moral superiority of SDI is primarily an ethic of intention; using the just-war ethic, supporters of SDI review the nuclear age, pointing out how classical deterrence doctrine has been willing to abide or endorse threats against innocent populations. In contrast to this posture, a case is made describing the *intended objectives* of SDI: either the transition to a world where the nuclear threat has been negated or at least to a world where the principal targets shift from populations to weapons. Stated at the level of intentionality, the SDI case seeks to capture the moral high ground, undoubtedly contributing to the popularity of the program with the general public.

99. But the complexity and the stakes of the policy debate on SDI require that the moral argument be pressed beyond its intended objectives. The SDI debate is less a dispute about objectives or motives than it is about means and consequences. To probe the moral content of the effects of pursuing SDI is to raise issues about its risks, costs, and benefits.

100. Giving proper weight to the effects of pursuing SDI moves the focus of the moral argument back from the desirability of freeing the world from the *factual condition* of an assured destruction posture (an objective commended by everyone) to the *technological feasibility* of fulfilling this intention, to the potential risks for *strategic stability* of an offensive-defensive arms competition, and to the *economic costs* and *tradeoffs* which pursuit of SDI will require in a deficit-ridden federal budget. These categories of feasibility, stability, and cost are already prominent in the SDI debate. The point here is to assert that the moral character of SDI cannot be determined apart from these other elements precisely because consequences count in a moral assessment.

101. First, while the feasibility argument is primarily a scientific-technological question, there are risks associated with pursuing some technological paths:

- risks to the existing arms control regime;
- risks of introducing dimensions of uncertainty into the already delicate political-psychological fabric of deterrence;
- risks that defensive systems can have real or perceived offensive uses;

- finally, risks that some forms of SDI would be ineffective against an adversary's first-strike, but more effective against a retaliatory second-strike, thereby eroding crisis stability.

Assessing these risks—evaluating which are prudent to pursue, which are too high to tolerate—involves a moral as well as a technological judgment. Precisely because of the number and quality of scientific judgments which have warned against precipitous movement toward SDI, it is necessary to stress the need for continued technological scrutiny and moral restraint concerning a decision which might later be regretted.

102. The second question concerns the impact of the defensive option on strategic stability. The critics of deterrence (*The Challenge of Peace* included) detail several negative factors in the deterrence regime, but the judgments of Vatican II, Pope John Paul II, and the pastoral letter also posit a role for deterrence in a world of sovereign states armed with nuclear weapons. While the need to move "beyond deterrence" is asserted by both Pope John Paul II and the U.S. bishops, there is also found in their statements the logic of the 1976 Vatican statement at the United Nations: that a move beyond deterrence should not place the world in a more dangerous condition than our present plight.[34] Hence, moves beyond deterrence are open to scrutiny. They must be assessed in light of their impact on the basic purpose of deterrence—its role in preventing the use of nuclear weapons.

103. Assessment of SDI in light of its impact on strategic stability will force the moral argument onto the path of examining the contrasting views of whether the "transition" from assured destruction to common security can be carried off with acceptable risk. Supporters of the SDI argue from the moral and the strategic perspective about the opportunities it provides to transform the nuclear dilemma—to end the mutual threats which constitute the present delicate deterrence balance.[35] These arguments stress the goal of the transition.

104. While this goal is undoubtedly attractive, the more compelling moral case presently rests with those who specify the likely risks of an aggressive SDI program at this time:

- the obstacle it poses to effective movement on arms control;
- the possible shift toward offensive use of the defensive system;
- the further "tilt" of the deterrence relationship toward preemptive strategies during the transition period.

---

[34]"Statement of the Holy See to the United Nations General Assembly," *L'Osservatore Romano,* English weekly edition (June 17, 1976): 9.

[35]Cf. K. B. Payne and C. Gray, "Nuclear Policy and the Defensive Transition," *Foreign Affairs* 62:4 (1984): 820-842; G. Weigel, "Breaking the Doctrinal Gridlock: Common Security and the Strategic Defensive Initiative," *This World* 16 (Winter 1987): 3-22.

No one of these results is a certain consequence of pursuing SDI deployment but the collective danger they pose to the dynamic of deterrence leaves us unconvinced of the merits of proceeding toward deployment of the system. The combination of the technological and the strategic evaluations of the present status of SDI appear to us to promise serious risks and very hypothetical benefits this time.

105. The feasibility and strategic stability arguments are central to the policy debate about SDI. Third, the economic argument—the escalating cost of SDI in a time of continuing budget deficits and in a decade which has seen deep cuts in programs for the poor at home and abroad—has particular moral relevance. While *The Challenge of Peace* recognized the need for and moral legitimacy of defense spending, it followed recent papal and conciliar teaching in pressing for limits on military spending. The deep divisions in the technological community about the feasibility of SDI, the arguments cited above about the negative impact on strategic stability, and the certainty of the costs of SDI bring it within the framework of the Bernardin-O'Connor criteria cited earlier in this report. Specifically, their judgment is that a program which fails to attract a clear consensus on technological-strategic grounds should not be allowed to command resources at a time when other human needs go unfulfilled.

106. In summary, our primary purpose in this section has been to dispel the notion that the moral character of SDI can be decided simply by examining it in terms of the objectives (or ends that it intends). These are not the only morally relevant factors that need to be taken into account in rendering a moral judgment about SDI. Judged within an adequate moral framework, one that takes into account the relevant moral circumstances surrounding this policy, it is our prudential judgment that proposals to press deployment of SDI do not measure up to the moral criteria outlined in this report. Our judgment about SDI can be summarized in the following statements:

- Some of the officially stated objectives of the SDI program, to move away from a long-term reliance on deterrence and to protect civilians and society as a whole, correspond to key themes of the pastoral letter.
- The pursuit of these objectives must be carried out within limits which protect other principles of the pastoral letter:

  –that the framework of arms control agreements and negotiations not be eroded or made more difficult;
  –that a new surge of offensive competition not be stimulated as a consequence of introducing defensive proposals;
  –that the stability of deterrence not be weakened in an untested attempt to transcend or enhance it;

–that defense spending as a whole not absorb a morally disproportionate percentage of the federal budget.

- Observing these limits in the immediate future requires that:

  –SDI be maintained as a research and development program, within the restraints of the ABM Treaty, not pressed to deployment;
  –the ABM Treaty should not be cast aside or overridden;
  –a specific test of each new step in SDI be an assessment of its effects on the offensive-defensive interaction of the arms competition;
  –clear criteria be established about spending for SDI in relationship to other needs in legitimate defense expenditures (e.g., conventional forces) and particularly in relationship to the basic human needs of the poor in our country and in other nations.

C. The Economy and Military Spending

107. The last criterion for SDI actually must be applied to the entire range of military spending. A persistent theme in the papal and conciliar teaching on peace is the need to redirect national and global resources from arms to human and social development objectives. From the classic statement of Vatican II — "the arms race is an utterly treacherous trap for humanity, and one which injures the poor to an intolerable degree"[36] — to the repeated statements of John Paul II on the same theme, the imperative to contain military spending and increase aid to the poor is stated with utter clarity. The same utter clarity marks the record of recent military spending — the moral imperative is being ignored or violated. A 1986 UN Declaration on Disarmament and Development by a panel of distinguished experts tells the sorry story: "In over four decades since the establishment of the United Nations, the worldwide military spending has rarely fallen in real terms during any period of time. The current military expenditures represent well over 5 percent of total world output and are over twenty-five times as large as all official development assistance to developing countries."[37]

---

[36]*Gaudium et Spes (Pastoral Constitution on the Church in the Modern World)*, no. 81. Published in W. M. Abbott, SJ, ed., *The Documents of Vatican II* (New York: The America Press, 1966).

[37]Abdel-Rahman, et al., *Disarmament and Development: Joint Declaration by the Panel of Eminent Personalities in the Field of Disarmament and Development* (New York, United Nations, 1986), p. 1.

108. While many nations, including developing countries, drive the trend of military spending, the UN Declaration correctly observes that "[t]he bulk of global military spending remains concentrated among the industrialized countries. . . ."[38] Among the industrialized nations, the superpowers lead the way. This pattern of increasing investment in the arms competition in light of the global disparities of wealth and poverty was criticized in both the peace and economic pastoral letters. The pattern is morally unacceptable. No one has more persistently argued the moral case for reallocation of global resources than Pope John Paul II. In *On Social Concern*, he reiterated a theme which has characterized his pontificate:

> The first consideration of the striking content of the Encyclical's historic phrase may be supplemented by a second consideration to which the document itself alludes: how can one justify the fact that *huge sums of money*, which could and should be used for increasing the development of peoples, are instead utilized for the enrichment of individuals or groups, or assigned to the increase of stockpiles of weapons, both in developed countries and in the developing ones, thereby upsetting the real priorities? This is even more serious given the difficulties which often hinder the direct transfer of capital set aside for helping needy countries. If "development is the new name for peace," war and military preparations are the major enemy of the integral development of peoples (no. 10).

109. The 1980s version of defense versus social spending took on new dimensions of tension within the United States as social programs for the poor were cut and as federal budget deficits (the product to a great extent of high military spending and tax cuts) grew to destabilizing proportions. Since the publication of *The Challenge of Peace*, the pastoral on the economy, *Economic Justice for All*,[39] has focused attention on the persistence of poverty within the United States. The budget debate each year makes clear that a direct and unyielding competition exists between defense and social spending. Social spending covers federal expenditures for health care, housing, food and nutrition, and income security for children and families classified as poor. These specific areas of health, nutrition, and housing for the poor were precisely the concerns of *Economic Justice for All*.[40]

110. We do not think the determination of a just level of defense expenditures is a simple task. We know the cheapest defense is often an increasingly nuclear defense. To avoid that trend, we stated in 1983 that we would consider raising expenditures for conventional forces if this decreased the nuclear danger. We still are prepared, in

---

[38]Ibid.

[39]National Conference of Catholic Bishops, *Economic Justice for All: Pastoral Letter on Catholic Social Teaching and the U.S. Economy* (Washington, D.C.: USCC Office of Publishing and Promotion Services, 1986).

[40]Cf. ibid., nos. 136–292.

light of the pastoral letter and the Bernardin-O'Connor criteria, to assess programs on their merits. But it is clear that our two pastoral letters point toward the need to reduce defense spending in the 1980s as a percentage of our national budget, to test scrupulously programs certain to consume large revenues, and to recognize that national and international security can be threatened by causes other than military forces.

III. The Status of Deterrence—An Evaluation

111. The judgment of "strictly conditioned moral acceptance" of deterrence in 1983 was meant to convey the strategic paradox and moral problem we encountered in evaluating nuclear policy. The essential moral question, defined above, remains: Can credible deterrence be reconciled with right intention, proportionality, and discrimination?

112. In 1983, we were not persuaded to condemn deterrence, nor were we prepared simply to endorse it. Its contribution to peace is the paradoxical role it plays in restraining the use of nuclear weapons. We could not disprove this claim, and we found some reasons to be convinced by it. At the same time, the negative dimensions of the deterrence relationship—its danger, its costs, its capacity to perpetuate divisions in international affairs—were there for all to see. Hence, the *most* we could say in support of deterrence was "conditional acceptance."

113. Since *The Challenge of Peace* was published, the ethical commentary on it and on the problem of nuclear deterrence has been voluminous. The statements of other episcopal conferences, the declarations of other churches and religious organizations, the writings of philosophers, statesmen, and political analysts have all grappled with the moral status of deterrence policy.

114. It is possible to sketch the broad outlines of this commentary. Some, using the principles of discrimination and proportionality, as we did, believe that emerging technology in the nuclear field (increasing accuracy and miniaturization of warheads) will provide a deterrent force which is both strategically credible and morally justifiable. When this technological faith is combined with a certain definition of the threat facing the West, it seems to provide for its supporters a coherent moral theory of deterrence. Nuclear threat and even use are a proportionate response to the political threat faced by the West, and the new technology provides a legitimate means to use if deterrence fails.[41]

115. A very different analysis of the nuclear relationship finds jus-

---

[41]See, e.g., A. Wohlstetter, "Bishops, Statesmen, and Other Strategists on the Bombing of Innocents," *Commentary* (June 1983): 15-35; report of the Commission on Integrated Long-Term Strategy, *Discriminate Deterrence* (Washington, D.C.: January 1988).

tification of deterrence policy—even conditional acceptance—a mistaken view of what exists. In this moral assessment, deterrence policy is inherently tied to a willingness to go to countersociety warfare, bursting all the moral bonds needed to keep warfare within the moral universe. This reading of the nuclear reality finds no grounds for any acceptance of the existing strategy of deterrence.[42]

116. These choices, and variants of them, were before us when we wrote *The Challenge of Peace*. Our answer to the moral dilemma of deterrence policy, then and now, is less clear-cut than either of these positions. In trying to address all the factors of the deterrence relationship—including the values served by it and those threatened by it—it has seemed to us a problem where absolute clarity in one answer often sacrifices part of the problem to be solved. Our judgment is not as confident about technology as the first view, or as convinced about the intrinsic evil of nuclear deterrence, taken as a whole, as the second view.

117. Deterrence, of course, is not an entity but a policy. It is a policy involving several component elements: weapons systems, force posture, declaratory policy, targeting doctrine, and the relationship of these to the objectives of security policy and—an aspect of it—arms control policy. As others have noted, when one looks back on the evolution of the nuclear age, it is highly unlikely that anyone would have chosen to have our present situation result. The deterrence relationship has been shaped by many forces, not all of them coherently related to each other.

118. Yet, any assessment of the policy of deterrence will be hard-put not to acknowledge that in a world of widespread nuclear knowledge and at least six nuclear powers, deterrence has been a significant factor in preventing the use of nuclear weapons. This attribute of deterrence weighed heavily with us in the writing of *The Challenge of Peace* and it does so now. Beyond this fundamental function, nuclear deterrence most likely has contributed to a more cautious posture of the two nuclear powers in world affairs.

119. But this side of the nuclear equation must be balanced against the various costs of nuclear deterrence. The political cost of two powers holding the fate of the northern hemisphere (and probably much of the south too) hostage is clearly an unacceptable way to structure international relations. Even the caution of superpowers is not immune from criticism, since they have found ways to engage each other through proxy forces in other nations, often at the expense of the latter. Pope John Paul II spoke directly to this reality in *On Social Concern:*

---

[42]See, e.g., J. Finnis, J. M. Boyle, Jr. and G. Grisez, *Nuclear Deterrence, Morality and Realism* (Oxford: Clarendon Press, 1987).

International relations, in turn, could not fail to feel the effects of this "logic of the blocs" and of the respective "spheres of influence." The tension between the two blocs which began at the end of the Second World War has dominated the whole of the subsequent forty years. . . . In light of these considerations, we easily arrive at a clearer picture of the last twenty years and a better understanding of the conflicts in the northern hemisphere, namely between East and West, as an important cause of the retardation or stagnation of the South (nos. 20, 22).

120. Psychologically, the costs of living with the nuclear threat have been documented in both East and West. Economically, the diversion of resources over the long-term to the nuclear competition has merited the critique and condemnation of secular and religious leadership. Finally, as we have analyzed above, the deterrence relationship is not static. The technological drive in recent years has moved the competition in directions which erode the stability of deterrence and increase the chance of nuclear use.

121. We remain convinced that the policy of nuclear deterrence is not a stable long-term method of keeping the peace among sovereign states. This is still the foundation of our evaluation of deterrence policy. We are also convinced that in the short-term and midterm assessment of our future the best moral evaluation is neither to condemn deterrence outright nor to accept it as self-regulating or "normal."

122. More precisely, we are persuaded to renew the judgment of *The Challenge of Peace*: that nuclear deterrence merits only strictly conditioned acceptance. In a dangerous world, a world of both widespread nuclear knowledge and extensive nuclear arsenals, we find condemning nuclear deterrence too drastic a solution and embracing it too simple a response. With Pope John Paul II we hope

that all countries, and especially the great powers, will perceive more and more that the fear of "assured mutual destruction," which is at the heart of the doctrine of nuclear deterrence, cannot be a reliable basis for security and peace in the long term.[43]

123. This assessment of various elements of deterrence policy is less dramatic than a single univocal judgment, but we believe it is more adequate to the complex pattern of U.S.-Soviet relations which exists today and is most appropriate for us as we call on our own country and other nations to pursue more effectively bilateral and multilateral arms control and to move decisively toward progressive disarmament.

124. Our purpose in writing this report has been to test whether "conditional acceptance" of deterrence continues to define the moral significance of the deterrence relationship. Specifically, we have meas-

---

[43]John Paul II, "Address to Diplomatic Corps," no. 5, p. 7.

ured the conditions set forth in 1983 against the empirical trends and developments of the past five years. In this examination, we have found some steps commendable and other trends eroding both strategic stability and the legitimacy of deterrence policy. The lack of clear movement in the direction of a more stable deterrent and ultimately disarmament causes us profound concern. We are not satisfied with the progress on these fronts in recent years.

125. Some who follow the judgment of the pastoral letter on the policy of deterrence may conscientiously conclude that present U.S. policy does not meet the strict conditions set forth and that there is no reasonable expectation of significant change in the future. Such persons will obviously oppose that policy. They believe such opposition is the logical consequent of a judgment which gives conditioned moral acceptance to deterrence.

126. Our committee's response is not to drop "conditional acceptance," but to advocate more actively a series of measures which still very much need to be undertaken to meet the conditions of *The Challenge of Peace*. Our "conditional acceptance" is not an endorsement of a status quo that we find inadequate and dangerous. It is a position that requires us to work for genuine and far-reaching changes in the policies that guide nuclear arsenals of the world. More particularly it requires us to continue to pursue and advocate a more secure and morally justifiable basis for peace based on the following criteria:

- Deterrence based on the direct targeting of urban populations is morally unacceptable. We oppose it in all cases.
- Deterrence policy implemented by weapons which combine size, accuracy, and multiple warheads in a credible "first-strike" posture adds unacceptable risk to the deterrence relationship. We, therefore, oppose existing trends and will oppose future policies, which push the deterrence posture of both superpowers in this direction.
- The dynamic of the existing policies of both superpowers enhances the risk of the preemptive use of nuclear weapons. We advocate reversal of this process as the first goal of arms control policy.
- The levels of strategic armaments far exceed the requirements of survivable second-strike deterrence — the only posture to which conditional acceptance can be given. We support "deep cuts" in strategic forces as the second goal of arms control policy.
- The risks of provoking an offensive and defensive competition between the superpowers and the existing disparity of views about the nature, purpose, and feasibility of space-based defense are more compelling to us than the promises made about the program. We oppose anything beyond a well-defined research and development program clearly within the restraints of the ABM Treaty.

- Our acceptance of deterrence is conditioned upon serious efforts at restraining proliferation. Existing policies of the superpowers are clearly inadequate on this question. We urge a renewed effort in the coming decade to halt the spread of nuclear weapons.
- The first major nuclear arms control treaty was a partial ban on testing. Twenty-five years later the U.S. and Soviet Union, along with the other nuclear states, have failed to fulfill the promise of that first step. We call for a renewed effort, pursued with much greater purpose and conviction, to complete negotiations on a comprehensive test ban treaty. We call for ratification of both the Threshold Test Ban Treaty and the Peaceful Nuclear Explosions Treaty.
- The competition in nonnuclear arms must also be addressed. We urge more concerted efforts to outlaw the production, possession, and use of chemical and biological weapons and to reduce conventional forces to a new balance compatible with reasonable requirements for defense.
- The cost of the arms competition is a continuing indictment of its role in international politics. The distortions in resource allocation by the superpowers and other nations—large and small, rich and poor—fit Pope John Paul II's description of "a structure of sin." He rightly describes present global patterns of military spending as a process leading toward death rather than development.[44] We will support efforts to redirect budgetary choices in the United States toward greater attention to the poor at home and abroad.

127. The conditions just specified are aimed at containing the nuclear competition, reducing its risks, enhancing chances for arms reduction, and ultimately using arms control as a step toward nuclear disarmament. These measures were central to *The Challenge of Peace*, and this report seeks to update and refine our recommendations for reducing dangers of the nuclear age. The challenge was stated clearly and urgently in the message of Pope John Paul II delivered by Cardinal Casaroli to the United Nations Third Special Session on Disarmament:

> Disarmament is not an end in itself. The end is peace, and security is one of its essential elements. The evolution of international relations today reveals that disarmament is a necessary condition, if not the primary condition, for security. . . . [T]he type of security on which our planet has depended for the last several decades—a balance of terror based on nuclear deterrence—is a security with a far

---

[44]*On Social Concern*, no. 24. For the most recent statistics on military spending and social spending see, e.g., R. L. Sivard, *World Military and Social Expenditures 1987-88* (Washington, D.C.: 1988), 12th edition.

too high risk level. This awareness should encourage Nations to enter into a new phase in their relations with all due urgency.[45]

128. This report is written at a time when a complementary strategy must be pressed. We are skeptical about escaping the strategic and moral dilemmas of the nuclear age through technology (either in space or by more accurate weapons). The complementary strategy which needs to be pressed is a creative and sustained effort to reshape the political dimension of U.S.-Soviet relations. Such an effort should seek to relativize the nuclear component of this relationship. This is an enormously complex process—tried often before with few positive results. But it is worth another effort, not only to lessen the danger of a superpower confrontation but also to limit the ways in which present East-West competition is injected into the conflicts of others, transforming them into ever more intractable problems.

129. To contain the nuclear danger of our time is itself an awesome undertaking. To reshape the political fabric of an increasingly interdependent world is an even larger and more complicated challenge. But it is precisely this possibility which engages the interest of both political analysts and religious and moral thinkers in our day. It is this question of fashioning the future of relationships among states and peoples that Pope John Paul II addressed in *On Social Concern*. The call of the encyclical to go beyond "the logic of the blocs" is addressed in a particular fashion to the U.S. and the Soviet Union, but the concern of the letter reaches beyond the superpower competition to the needs of the vast majority of the globe who are affected by the superpower competition but are not capable of influencing it:

> Surmounting every type of *imperialism* and determination to preserve their *own hegemony*, the stronger and richer nations must have a sense of moral *responsibility* for the other nations, so that a *real international system* may be established which will rest on the foundation of the *equality* of all peoples and on the necessary respect for their legitimate differences. The economically weaker countries, or those still at subsistence level, must be enabled, with the assistance of other peoples and of the international community, to make a contribution of their own to the common good with their treasures of *humanity* and *culture*, which otherwise would be lost for ever (no. 39).

130. This is a call to fundamental change in the pattern of international politics. Such fundamental changes do not occur easily or quickly in the life of states and nations. They are the product of both deep historical forces and intelligent, courageous human choices. Success in these endeavors is never assured, and progress is maintained only by continual effort and initiative. But changes do occur. In the West

---

[45]John Paul II, "Message to Third UN Special Session on Disarmament" (New York, June 2, 1988), *Origins* 18:5 (June 16, 1988): no. 2, p. 67.

the seventeenth century marked the end of large-scale religious wars and the twentieth century—after two major wars—has a record of sustained peace among the democracies.

131. The cosmic challenge of the papal encyclical to go beyond "the logic of the blocs" in the name of both keeping the nuclear peace and building the peace through just relations with the poor of the world is larger in scope and more complex in substance than either of the successes noted above. But nothing less than this kind of vision—joining the East-West issues and the North-South issues in a coherent plan—is equal to the world in which we live.

132. We are convinced that the present time is better served by those willing to risk falling short of a large vision than the alternative risk of being satisfied with small achievements which fail to address the dangers or the opportunities of the moment. In that spirit, we submit this report on the meaning of *The Challenge of Peace* in 1988.

Statement on Federal Funding of *in vitro* Fertilization Experiments

*A Statement Issued by the
General Secretary of the
United States Catholic Conference*

July 15, 1988

1. The Catholic bishops of the United States have long opposed federal funding of *in vitro* fertilization in humans for a number of reasons, not the least of which is the abortifacient character of this procedure. In 1979 the U.S. Department of Health, Education and Welfare received comments from over 13,000 citizens and 80 members of Congress, the overwhelming majority of which opposed federal support for IVF. Since that time, the government has maintained a *de facto* moratorium on funding of such research by refraining from appointment of the ethics advisory board necessary for review and approval of specific experiments.

2. I therefore view with grave concern yesterday's decision by the Secretary of Health and Human Services to appoint a new ethics advisory board to review and approve IVF experiments in humans. Only last year, congressional testimony on behalf of the NCCB Committee for Pro-Life Activities stated that "recent developments have only heightened the concerns that led us" to oppose federal funding in 1979. Recent studies suggest that over 95 percent of the embryos produced by IVF die before birth. The production of human life outside a mother's body has made possible the deliberate discarding, freezing, and experimental manipulation of human beings at their earliest stage of development. I conclude from congressional testimony by IVF researchers that much of the research they wish to pursue using laboratory-generated embryos is not only unethical in itself, but also intended to render more efficient the elimination of prenatal lives considered genetically imperfect.

3. For all these reasons, I urge Health and Human Services Secretary Bowen to reconsider his decision to pursue this kind of research, which does not conform to the administration's stated policy of respect for human life from the moment of conception.

Statement on Principles for Legal Immigration Policy

A Statement Passed by the
Administrative Board of the
United States Catholic Conference

September 13, 1988

1. The Catholic Church in the United States has long maintained a strong concern for immigrants. That commitment stems directly from the Church's belief in the dignity of labor systematically articulated by Pope Leo XIII in his 1891 encyclical *Rerum Novarum*. Since then, a substantial body of church documents, including the encyclicals *Exsul Familia, Mater et Magistra, Pacem in Terris, Octogesima Adveniens, Laborem Exercens,* and *Sollicitudo Rei Socialis,* have all affirmed the right to work. The right of individuals and families to migrate in order to secure work can be viewed as a necessary corollary. This right to migrate for work should never be displaced by the exercise of a nation's sovereign right to control its own borders. Protecting the public interests of our own society and recognizing the right to immigrate are determinations that should be made in the context of the universal common good.
2. The Church's traditional position was clearly expressed by the Vatican in the 1969 *Instruction on the Pastoral Care of People Who Migrate*:

> Public authorities unjustly deny the rights of human persons if they block or impede emigration or immigration except where grave requirements of the common good, considered objectively, demand it.[1]

3. Over the years, the Church's position—often balancing the demands of the common good with the right to migrate—has been stated many times by the U.S. bishops in response to changes in immigration policy and law.
4. Currently, major new proposals to reform the U.S. legal immigration system are under discussion. We recognize that there is a need to reshape our immigration system, but we strongly encourage Congress to engage in extensive, thoughtful, and public debate before any new immigration law is enacted.
5. As a contributor to this debate, the Church draws on her long experience in protecting the rights of immigrants. From that experi-

---

[1]Sacred Congregation of Bishops, *Instruction on the Pastoral Care of People Who Migrate,* Vatican City, 1969, no. 7.

ence, we offer the following principles to guide the development of any legal immigration policy.

- *First,* family reunification must be affirmed as the basic precept driving a just immigration system.
- *Second,* our fundamental tradition is fair treatment to all nations and their emigrants.
- *Third,* temporary labor programs should be gradually eliminated. Permanent workers should receive full rights. Those temporary worker categories that are necessary ought to offer full labor market rights.
- *Fourth,* every effort should be made to discourage illegal immigration by promoting just immigration law.
- *Fifth,* the endangerment of any nation's valuable human resources must be avoided; this is especially true in the case of developing countries.

Report of the Ad Hoc Task Force on Food, Agriculture, and Rural Concerns

*A Report Issued by the
United States Catholic Conference,
National Conference of Catholic Bishops*

November 15, 1988

I. Ethical Framework and Issues of Concern

A. Introduction

1. In their 1986 pastoral letter on the U.S. economy, *Economic Justice for All: Pastoral Letter on Catholic Social Teaching and the U.S. Economy,* the Catholic bishops summarized Catholic social teaching on the global economic order in a series of moral principles and applied them to four areas of public policy — one of which was food and agriculture. In this connection they said:

> We are concerned that this food system may be in jeopardy as increasing numbers of farm bankruptcies and foreclosures result in increased concentration of land ownership. We are likewise concerned about the increasing damage to natural resources resulting from many modern agricultural practices: the overconsumption of water, the depletion of topsoil, and the pollution of land and water. Finally, we are concerned about the stark reality of world hunger in spite of food surpluses. Our food production system is clearly in need of evaluation and reform (*Economic Justice for All*, no. 217).

2. The present crisis in the food system is but one aspect of a profound transformation taking place in the social and economic structures of the global community. This transformation has many causes, among which are technological changes, government farm programs, general economic policies (monetary, trade, and fiscal), inadequate educational and other services to rural people, and some practices of farmers themselves. But underlying all these contributing factors are the changing structure of ownership; greater concentration and control of food production and distribution and of the agricultural resource base; and the deteriorating condition of land, water, and air. As in other economic sectors, the basic questions are: Who effectively controls the system? Who makes the crucial decisions? These basic questions lead to others, e.g.: Who benefits from the system? Does it enable people to participate effectively in it? Are the major actors in the food sector—producers, input suppliers, processors, and retailers— responsive to the needs of society?

3. In September 1986, the National Conference of Catholic Bishops/ United States Catholic Conference established this task force to deal with these questions representing one major and specific segment of the pastoral letter's concerns. The task force was asked to reflect upon the difficulties faced by so many rural people both here in America and in other countries and to suggest ways in which the Church can respond to these problems and to their deeper causes. Our concern embraces the various components and related problems of a food and agriculture system that produces abundantly but is plagued by many serious and growing deficiencies. Among these are increased hunger in both urban and rural areas; growing numbers of hungry people in poor countries abroad; persistent poverty on farms and in rural communities; the increased migration of poor rural people to the cities; increasing concentration of ownership and control in food processing and marketing; overproduction of food and fiber leading to mounting costs for subsidies to producers; severe tensions with our food-trading partners; massive Third World debt; misery and destitution among farmworkers in the United States; environmental damage; and the rising concern of consumers about the safety and quality of the food they eat.

4. The recent drought is a vivid example of many of these problems and dramatizes rural and urban interdependence as well as the conflicting interests plaguing our food and farm system. The media has made us graphically aware of the destruction wrought by the drought upon so many farms in our nation. This destruction has reduced supplies of some grains leading to real tragedy for many families and higher food prices for consumers. It has also intensified trade tensions in a competition for global markets. It could also threaten hard won improvements in land conservation. The swift passage of drought relief legislation this past summer will buffer some of the worst effects faced by farmers, but many farmworkers who are among those most devastated by the drought will not have the help they need. The drought demonstrates our vulnerability and links to one another in facing these issues.

5. As pastors, we are concerned with ministry, particularly to those who feel the crisis most directly. Rural people have pastoral needs unique to their situation; they look to their bishops, pastors, pastoral ministers, and fellow parishioners for help and support in meeting these needs. In their economic pastoral the bishops committed themselves to provide the pastoral services needed by rural people. Those who are suffering because of the rural crisis are especially vulnerable to depression, marriage and family problems, alcohol and drug dependency, and other human ills. We feel an urgent need to develop the means to help these people both spiritually and materially through the many resources available in parish communities. Care needs to be taken so that rural communities will not suffer disproportionately from any shortage of priests and other pastoral workers.

6.   We cannot stress strongly enough however that, while rural people are the primary focus of this report, urban people are intimately bound to the lives of their rural sisters and brothers. It is easy to see the connection in many less developed countries where so many landless rural poor are driven to seek a safe haven in the cities only to find in too many cases unemployment, squalor, and destitution. But the connections are also evident in the industrialized countries where urban people dependent on rural communities for the food that sustains them express concern about poisoned streams and rivers, food contaminated by pesticides, and the social and economic costs of environmental damage from toxic chemicals and nuclear waste. Moreover, in a world economy growing ever more linked, both urban and rural communities are affected by the common economic realities of trade, debt, and monetary policies. The purpose of this report then is not only to express our compassion and support for rural people but also to stimulate and encourage the people of our cities to join the struggle actively and work for justice in rural communities.

7.   As a task force we have concluded that while pastoral ministry is firmly grounded in gospel values, it must also be supported by sound policy analysis and formulation and supplemented by systematic and effective education and advocacy. In order to enable the U.S. Catholic Conference and individual bishops to deal responsibly with these four functions — *policy analysis and formulation, education, advocacy, and pastoral ministry* — we propose the following ethical framework, policy priorities, and structure (including organizational relationships).

B. Ethical Framework

8.   An ethical framework derived from Scripture and Catholic social teaching provides the Church, as a community and an actor in shaping societal views, with an angle of vision from which to assess present conditions and their causes and to suggest directions for public policy.

1. Human Dignity — the Right to Food

9.   Each of us is created in the image and likeness of God. The human person is sacred and is the clearest reflection of God among us. Our human dignity comes from God, not from nationality, race, sex, economic status, or any human accomplishment. The fundamental principle of respect for the dignity of the human person is at the core of Catholic social teaching.

10.   It is central to the Church's teaching on human dignity that every-

one has a legitimate claim to the goods and services required to live a truly human life. This central element underpins a set of specific personal rights which constitute the baseline against which we access society's ability to secure them. The right to a truly human life implies the right to a diet that will sustain that kind of life. This means people need the amount and quality of food required for normal physical and human activity and development, not just for survival. People must also have access to that food through either cultivation or purchase. They must be able to grow it, secure it from the waters, or buy it. This right is at the basis of our concern about policies related to agriculture and fishing in this country, food assistance for low-income people here and abroad, and agricultural development in poor, food-deficit countries in the Third World.

2. Social Nature of the Person—Participation

11. The human person is not only sacred but also social. Catholic tradition recognizes the value of individuality, but it also insists that we are all radically social; we grow and develop fully only in community. Therefore, the way society is organized economically, politically, legally, etc., has direct impact on human persons and their dignity. This concern for the social nature of the person leads Catholic social teaching to put a great deal of emphasis upon community, solidarity, and cooperation and on the need for people to participate effectively in the decisions that affect their lives. The emphasis upon the social nature of the person sets Catholic social thought apart from a strain of contemporary thought that emphasizes individualism and unbridled competition.

12. Basic justice demands that people be assured a minimum level of participation as the way to carry forward God's creative activity in society. For farmers, participation means ownership of land and equipment and reasonable access to the external resources required to produce food. Without more widespread dispersal of land ownership and increased diversification of products produced, there is little likelihood of relieving the present crisis or securing the right to food.

13. Farmers—grain and poultry producers, dairy farmers, ranchers, fruit growers, cotton, wool, and vegetable producers—however, have responsibilities in producing and growing food and fiber. They must produce enough food of good quality to meet consumers' needs and they must exercise care for the land and consideration for those who eat the food. Likewise, producers of cotton contribute to the building up of society by the production of fiber for clothing and of food derivatives from the cotton seed. Cotton farming is an important part of the American agricultural system.

14. Fishermen, who harvest the riches of inland waters and the sea, make a significant contribution to an adequate and varied supply of food; they share the social responsibility and should also be enabled to participate fully in the food system. Concentration has also adversely affected this segment of our food system. Like many other segments of agriculture, the fishing industry is also experiencing increased tensions over trade matters. Society in turn must make it possible for all of these producers to fulfill their roles in a farm and food system which enhances their human dignity and yet recognizes the social responsibility that goes with private ownership.

15. Other segments of the economy such as timber and mining, whose workers are dependent on corporate owners for employment, also affect rural areas. The well-being of these workers and their communities is dependent upon both general economic factors and the specific decisions of their employers in such matters as wage scales and working conditions. One need only look as far as central Appalachia (or, in a different but related context, Central America) to see the enormous inequities in power and decision making which arise when resources become highly concentrated. Special care must be taken to preserve the rights of the labor force in these industries, as well as the quality of life in their communities.

16. The bishops' emphasis on participation, cooperation, and the need of people to work to exercise their creativity leads them to be concerned about the increasing concentration of ownership of land and farms, the trend away from diversification and toward increasing specialization in a few crops, and the strong individualism of farmers that leaves them easy prey to exploitation by outside economic forces. The bishops view with particular concern the growing concentration of economic power that accompanies the consolidation of land ownership and the vertical integration of the food and agriculture system — with the possible consequent loss of responsiveness to public need in this crucial sector of our economy:

> The Catholic tradition has long defended the right to private ownership of productive property. This right is an important element in a just economic policy. It enlarges our capacity for creativity and initiative. Small and medium-sized farms, businesses, and entrepreneurial enterprises are among the most creative and efficient sectors of our economy. They should be highly valued by the people of the United States, as are land ownership and home ownership. Widespread distribution of property can help avoid excessive concentration of economic and political power. For these reasons ownership should be made possible for a broad sector of our population.
>
> The common good may sometimes demand that the right to own be limited by public involvement in the planning or ownership of certain sectors of the economy. Support of private ownership does not mean that anyone has the right to unlimited accumulation of wealth. "Private property does not constitute for anyone an absolute or unconditioned right. No one is justified in keeping for his exclusive

use what he does not need, when others lack necessities" (*On the Development of Peoples*, 23). Pope John Paul II has referred to limits placed on ownership by the duty to serve the common good as a "social mortgage" on private property (*Economic Justice for All*, nos. 114, 115).

17. It would be a mistake, however, to seek solutions only from government, many of whose programs have contributed to the crisis in rural areas; the principle of subsidiary applies here as in other sectors. Food and fiber producers must also take individual and cooperative initiatives to resolve their own problems. We suggest that they create or join cooperatives as a means of self-development. This also applies to other rural residents who seek to improve their social and economic conditions. The principle of solidarity, leading to common concern and cooperative action, needs to be brought into play in the formation of cooperatives or other self-development community ventures.

3. Option for the Poor

18. Catholic social teaching is concerned about the whole society — about the common good. The Scriptures — and that tradition — have also taught us to have a particular concern for the poor. It is not an either-or proposition, but we must give special attention to the poor, because without that attention the human community cannot become whole and the common good is not pursued. This theme, commonly referred to now as the *option for the poor*, is a basic and consistent one throughout Catholic social teaching. The biblical concept of justice underlines the notion that in God's eyes the justice of a community is measured by how it treats the powerless and the vulnerable. Like the prophets of the Old Testament, Jesus consistently took the side of the powerless and those on the margins of society. In his description of the final judgment he says that we will be judged on how we treated him when he was hungry, thirsty, a homeless stranger, naked, sick, and imprisoned.

19. The option for the poor also emphasizes that attention to conventional economics is not satisfactory; the question is not only how we produce but also how we share. This theme of social justice is a major thread running through the pastoral on the economy. In rural America it is especially pertinent to farmworkers, especially migrants, and the rural poor — farmers and nonfarmers — who constitute a disproportionate number of the Americans who live at or below the poverty line.

20. There is much other evidence that rural people in both industrialized and developing countries face very serious — though often very diverse — problems. In addition to the hunger and malnutrition which continue to afflict hundreds of millions of rural (and urban) people, there is a continued migration of these people to already overcrowded cities. Massive debt and the unbalanced trade inflict intractable poverty upon multitudes of people particularly in the developing nations. Misery and destitution are the lot, especially of millions of landless farmworkers. Overproduction in the agricultural sector resulting in part from unwise production incentives leads to rising budgetary outlays for price supports and subsidies and to severe agricultural trade tensions among the industrialized exporting nations, as well as between industrialized and developing countries. Global environmental problems of increasing variety and severity challenge both ingenuity and resources.

4. Respect for Creation — Stewardship

21. Scripture, as well as the Church's teachings, emphasizes that God is present to creation and that creative engagement in God's handiwork is itself reverence for God. All creation is a gift; we share creaturehood with the rest of animate and inanimate nature. We have to be faithful stewards of these God-given resources of the earth. The Church has repeatedly stressed that their misuse or appropriation by a minority of the world's population for their own benefit betrays the gift of creation, for what God has chosen to give are gifts for the entire human family.

22. Because rural communities and those where fishing supports families are so obviously and uniquely involved with and dependent on the life systems of land, water, and weather, respect for nature and the requirements of stewardship should serve as special guiding principles in questions related to food, agriculture, and rural development. There is also reason to be concerned about land ownership: an owner-operator living on the land has the best reason to be a good steward. Corporate owners of mines and timberlands have a similar obligation of stewardship, which is also shared by workers in these industries.

23. The challenges and problems associated with the care of our natural resources apply most directly and immediately to rural residents. It is they who utilize these resources on behalf of the rest of society to provide food, industrial raw materials, and recreational opportunities. However, the economic pastoral also points out that stewardship is a responsibility of the whole society. The resources created by God are for the benefit of all — rural residents have trusteeship in relationship to the land, not unrestricted ownership; there is a social mortgage on land, Pope John Paul II has said. Consequently, economies must be organized in such a way that those who have the primary responsibility for caring for the resource base are enabled to discharge that responsibility.

> All people on this globe share a common ecological environment that is under increasing pressure. Depletion of soil, water, and other

natural resources endangers the future. Pollution of air and water threatens the delicate balance of the biosphere on which future generations will depend. The resources of the earth have been created by God for the benefit of all, and we who are alive today hold them in trust (*Economic Justice for All*, no. 12).

24. We are concerned at the disproportionate use—and even abuse— of these gifts of creation by the wealthier countries—an exploitation now extending to and accelerating in the developing countries. New efforts must be made to care for our common ecological environment, both to ensure its sustainability for future generations and to facilitate a more just distribution of these resources today.

C. Matters of Concern in Public Policy

25. The Church's role in public policy is to help to define the ethical content of major issues of public concern. This role should be expressed in criteria applied to issues and decisions:

- relevance to the ethical framework sketched above and its basis in Catholic teaching;
- current or likely future cogency;
- the Church's history of involvement in the particular issue area;
- the extent and salience of the Church's contribution or role;
- the personnel and monetary resources required to make a significant and appropriate impact; and
- the consensus in the Catholic community on the matter.

26. Each of these concerns manifests at least one aspect of the complex global food and agriculture system. The linkage among the issues should be stressed rather than any priority ranking. The need for public policy action and the relevance of Catholic social teaching to the policy options will influence the emphasis to be given to any one issue.

1. Land Ownership—Control of Resources

27. The bishops favor a system of small and moderate-sized family-owned and operated farms in all types of farming as the primary structural component of a just food system. Such a system would ensure more participation and serve as a buffer against the types of abuses that tend to accompany excessive concentration of the ownership of productive resources. Our current farm system reflects a high concentration of production: the very large farms that produce half of U.S. food and fiber and receive a disproportionate share of direct government payment represent a small numerical fraction of all farms.

28. Participation in the economic, political, and social life of society is a way to join in carrying forward God's creative activity. How people participate in the economy is one of the basic questions the economic pastoral says must shape our human, moral, and Christian economic perspective. Concentration of ownership of economically productive resources effectively inhibits participation. For this reason, Catholic social teaching urges greater dispersion of ownership and management than we now have in most sectors of the economy including agriculture.

29. The classic principle of subsidiary in Catholic social teaching calls for communities as small as the family and as large as the global society (and all levels in between) to engage actively in the pursuit of economic justice. The founders and early leaders of our nation took steps to foster such participation and ensure broad distribution of political power. Greater dispersion of ownership and management helps to expand economic participation and makes economic decisions more accountable to the common good. Wider dispersion of land ownership has been reflected in U.S. public policy several times in our history, e.g.: the Preemption Acts of the early nineteenth century, the Homestead Act of 1862, the Reclamation Act of 1902, and more recently, changes in national tax and credit policies.

30. Closely associated with the question of land ownership and control are such issues as property rights, zoning, taxes, credit, technology, targeting of government farm-income and price-support programs, as well as vertical integration—control of the processing, marketing, distribution, and sometimes production of food by a single company or group of companies. Moreover, alternative forms of food production—especially organic and low-input agriculture—would be helped by crop diversification and dispersed ownership.

31. In many food-deficit developing countries, the problem of access to and control of natural resources, especially land and water, is the central issue. The particular characteristics and solutions will vary from region to region. What will not vary is the fact that in many poor countries, social and economic justice is neither conceivable nor achievable without genuine land reform or reform of systems where other resources such as fishing are controlled by a few powerful interests.

2. Hunger—Food Security

32. The presence of increasing numbers of hungry people in the United States and in the developing countries points to the need for a renewed and highly visible campaign to end hunger not only by feeding hungry people in the United States and elsewhere, but also by helping them prevent future hunger. As the bishops' economic pastoral points out:

> A world with nearly half a billion hungry people is not one in which food security has been achieved. . . . The gospel imperative takes on new urgency in a world of abundant harvests where hundreds of millions of people face starvation . . . (*Economic Justice for All*, no. 282)

and where forty thousand children die every day from the effects of malnutrition and the accompanying diseases to which it makes them vulnerable.

33. Only poor people are hungry. Therefore, it is important that steps to increase employment (and decrease unemployment) be reinforced. These efforts must include opportunities for skills training and upgrading of elementary and secondary education systems.

34. The larger economic questions include not only food aid and increased agricultural production in the food-deficit regions of the developing world, but also the impact of other economic policies of the industrialized nations—especially in agricultural trade and in the financial arrangement that has contributed to the mounting debt burden of these poor countries. In our own country, too, increased support needs to be given to national and local food assistance programs.

3. Rural Poverty

35. Hunger is a symptom of poverty, and poverty is a distinctive characteristic of many rural communities in the United States and abroad. The rural poor suffer high rates of hunger and malnutrition, inadequate housing, and a lack of decent health care and education. Many rural communities lag behind urban areas economically, adding to the persistence of problems of widespread and intractable rural poverty. The lack of access to services compounds the misery and makes the task of eliminating rural poverty even more difficult.

36. The task force wants to highlight the plight of racial and ethnic minorities in rural communities. Recent USCC testimony calls special attention to the fact that

> black farmers in the South too often continue to be largely ignored. The continued loss of black-owned farmland, as pointed out by the U.S. Civil Rights Commission "can only serve to further diminish the state of blacks in the social order and reinforce their skepticism regarding the concept of equality under the law." While many of these farms are small, they provide a source of identity and economic stability for many black people. The eventual loss of black-owned farmland will only serve to further alienate and marginalize many black people. Many farm laborers and migrant workers are of Hispanic origin and are among the most poorly paid workers, too often living in squalor and working under unsafe conditions (*Testimony on Rural Development Policy*, May 27, 1988).

37. Regarding the plight of farmworkers, the bishops' pastoral on the economy is explicit:

> . . . they are not as well protected by law and public policy as other groups of workers; and their efforts to organize and bargain collectively have been systematically and vehemently resisted, usually by farmers themselves. Migratory field workers are particularly susceptible to exploitation. This is reflected not only in their characteristically low wages but also in the low standards of housing, health care, and education made available to these workers and their families (*Economic Justice for All*, no. 230).

38. Services to the rural poor must be accompanied by efforts to change unjust social structures that lead to disproportionate rural poverty in the U.S. and in the developing countries, which, by and large, are poor by definition. The key areas of concern in this respect are rural development (education, economic development, employment, housing, and health and welfare for the domestic poor) and special areas of advocacy including the treatment of farmworkers (particularly migrants) and minority farmers. In the international arena that concern extends to agricultural development, trade, debt, and the distribution of wealth and income. Education, in particular, should be aimed at helping people to lead productive and satisfying lives in rural areas, as well as adapt to urban environments in the event that they move away from rural communities.

4. Preservation of Natural Resources — Stewardship

39. The primary issues of concern in this category are protection of soil, water, and air; the development and use of technology (especially biotechnology); the protection of producers, farmworkers, and fishermen from toxic chemicals; and the production of nutritious, safe, and healthy food for consumers. The growing concern over environmental issues and the U.S. role in global food production make the protection of soil, water, and air a leading concern as the third millennium approaches. Technology, which serves as one of the dominant factors in shaping our food system, confronts our society with new moral choices. The emerging field of biotechnology dramatizes this moral dilemma and offers the Church an opportunity to contribute to shaping the values which will guide the research and application of this technology to food production. Rural America has become a major dumping ground for toxic chemicals and nuclear waste, and the continued use of petrochemicals in agriculture threatens both food safety and the quality of our water and soil.

40. Stewardship is more likely to be enhanced by the diversification

in agricultural production that might accompany more dispersed ownership of farmland. Continuous cultivation of a single crop exhausts
the resource base; weakens crop resistance to disease, blight, and
pests; heightens farmers' dependence on increasingly expensive pesticides, herbicides, fertilizers, irrigation water, and fossil fuel energy;
and tempts producers to abandon proven conserving practices. Reduction of purchased inputs, through more diversified and regenerative
agriculture would reduce farmers' costs; enhance rather than deplete
the natural resources; and result in the production of safer, healthier,
and more nutritious food (and, not incidentally, greatly-reduce government outlays for agricultural programs). Stewardship demands
that we live within the ecological limits of the planet, consuming in
modest quantities and producing in ways that sustain us in the present
and preserve resources for future generations.

5. Food, Trade, and Aid

41. The United States plays a leading role in an international economic
system that is becoming ever more interdependent, especially as regards
food. Increased tensions over agricultural trade between the U.S. and
its allies and the dominance of the industrialized countries over the
economies of the developing countries are of particular concern. Intensified efforts must be made, particularly through meaningful trade
negotiations, to reduce the heightened economic tensions among the
industrialized and major agricultural exporting nations. The Church
itself should devote some resources to policy analysis and development of policy positions on trade issues taking into account the special
trade needs of the less developed countries. The issues of land reform,
hunger, rural poverty, and protection of natural resources have particular relevance to the relationship between the United States and
the less developed countries.

42. In summary, we note that general support for the developing
countries has been a long-term commitment of the bishops' conference, and special attention has been given to questions of food aid
and development. However, the *new* questions of debt and trade,
increasingly recognized as central to development and food security,
have come upon the scene with an unanticipated urgency. As the
economic pastoral points out in the section on international matters:

> *The World Food Problem—A Special Urgency:* These four resource trans-
> fer channels—aid, trade, finance, and investment—intersect and
> overlap in all economic areas, but in none more clearly than in the
> international food system. The largest single segment of develop-
> ment assistance support goes to the agricultural sector and to food
> aid for short-term emergencies and vulnerable groups; food consti-
> tutes one of the most critical trade sectors; developing countries have
> borrowed extensively in the international capital markets to finance
> food imports; and a substantial portion of direct private investment
> flows into the agricultural sector (*Economic Justice for All,* no. 281).

II. Organizational Relationships

43. Our direct experience and the experience of those to whom we minister convince us that the issues of land control, hunger, rural poverty, and natural resource use need to be addressed with a sense of greater urgency and visibility. It is our judgment that a more effective discharge of the four functions — pastoral ministry, policy analysis and formulation, public advocacy, and education — would provide more tangible evidence of the Church's engagement in these issues and help create the commitment necessary to evoke a deepened response and involvement in the food and agricultural sector on the part of the Church and others of good will.

44. The Church in this country has been involved in rural affairs and food policy for a very long time. In this century, the Catholic Church in the United States has spoken out frequently on world hunger and on the responsibilities of a country that is richly endowed with food-growing resources. Groups of bishops have published letters on regional problems of rural life including *This Land Is Home to Me* in 1974 and *Strangers and Guests* in 1980. In 1923 the National Catholic Rural Life Conference was established to mark the Church's special interest in rural people. Other Catholic organizations such as state Catholic conferences, the Rural Life Directors' Association, Catholic Charities, Catholic Relief Services, and the Campaign for Human Development have also been active on these central concerns.

45. Our review of the activities of the major Catholic agencies involved leads us to the conclusion that strict compartmentation of their functions is neither wise nor feasible. Rather, since several agencies are engaged one way or another in all four of these functions, the relationship as it is eventually worked out will be largely a matter of different emphases by different organizations.

46. Nevertheless, in the judgment of the task force, there is a need to

- delineate more precisely how these agencies can conduct their activities in a fashion that will avoid unnecessary duplication and will enhance the Church's overall ministry to rural people;
- clarify and strengthen communication and coordination among the key organizations; and
- increase the resources the Church allocates to these issues.

We stress, however, that the effectiveness of these measures ultimately depends on the strength of our ministry at the local, state, and regional levels. We urge that the modifications the task force proposes be adopted to enhance the Church's service to rural people and witness in these matters both at home and abroad. Against this background the task force recommends the following.

A. USCC

47. The USCC should continue to exercise primary responsibility for *policy analysis and development* and *public policy advocacy* in dealing with national and international aspects of food and agriculture. The USCC is the U.S. Church's most visible agency at the national and international levels and has become the primary vehicle through which the bishops speak on public policy matters. It has the responsibility and the capability to conduct policy development and analysis and undertake the government liaison necessary to advocate particular public policies. Rural concerns — particularly those related to food, agriculture, and natural resources — link with unusual intimacy the domestic and international dimensions of these questions. The USCC is in a position to relate and coordinate the two aspects operationally and to represent the Church's interests in international policy questions with other bishops' conferences and with multilateral agencies.
48. Therefore, the task force recommends the establishment of a joint subcommittee of the International Policy Committee and the Domestic Policy Committee of the USCC. The subcommittee could enhance the visibility, coordination, and direction for this set of issues. It is further recommended that the membership of this subcommittee include representatives of other appropriate organizations and groups as well as bishops.

B. NCRLC

49. The board of the National Catholic Rural Life Conference (NCRLC) should consider accepting as its major responsibilities the *education* of its members, the *development* of support services for rural pastoral ministers, and the *enhancement* of its role as a catalyst and convener for social justice in food, agriculture, and rural issues.
50. Addressing the education and ministry needs of rural people and diocesan rural life directors has been an historical contribution of the NCRLC, whereas the USCC is designed primarily to address public policy. Moreover, the NCRLC has been an advocate in a variety of issues for grass-roots rural people and even a prophetic voice for them and the Church in general. Collectively, these contributions are vital elements of the Church's ministry in response to the rural crisis and necessary for the Church to be faithful to its mission.
51. For more than a half-century, the NCRLC has given a voice and moral support to rural people. The conference has built a network of diocesan pesonnel and grass-roots rural people. It has paid attention to the spiritual dimension of people struggling for survival on the land. It continues to call rural and urban people alike to work for greater justice in our food system and for the long-term care of land, water, and air.

52. Although for many decades the NCRLC was almost the lone voice of the Church regarding food, agriculture, and rural issues, its voice and its network in recent years have not been strong enough at a time when the crisis has deepened in the rural communities of this country. It is for this reason that the task force makes the following recommendations:

53. First, the NCRLC should develop an expanded, organized, and coordinated network of diocesan rural life directors and rural concerns advocates, as well as of grass-roots rural people in order to

- assist the local church to understand and be present to and caring of people in rural communities affected by the rural crisis;
- advise the USCC in its selection and the development of public policy issues in this area;
- participate in the dissemination of the policy positions and analyses of the USCC on relevant issues; and
- advocate for or respond to legislation related to those policy positions.

54. Second, the NCRLC should continue its educational effort through its magazine, newsletter, and other publications and services. The number of people who receive these publications and services should be increased. Thought should be given to a cooperative effort between the NCRLC and the USCC whereby the latter would make use of the *Catholic Rural Life* magazine and some of its other shorter publications in its mailing lists, thus widening their circulation and avoiding duplication.

55. Third, the NCRLC should contribute to the spiritual growth of rural people through the development of liturgy aids, seasonal prayer services, and reflection pieces for parish ministers and others in rural communities.

56. Fourth, the NCRLC should develop a close working relationship with other organizations in the Church which have developed programs for rural people, in order to build on one another's strengths, share resources, and avoid duplication, e.g., The Edwin V. O'Hara Institute for Rural Ministry Education, Catholic Charities, the Campaign for Human Development, diocesan agencies, state Catholic conferences, etc.

57. Fifth, the NCRLC should find ways to continue to advocate greater justice in our food system and the intergenerational care of land, water, and air.

58. Sixth, the NCRLC Board should expand to include three to five bishops from a variety of regions in the United States.

59. In order that the National Catholic Rural Life Conference be able to accomplish these goals, the task force further recommends that adequate staff be supported through annual diocesan contributions, membership growth, and grants from individuals and foundations.

C. Diocesan Rural Life Directors

60. Dioceses need to strengthen the role and contribution of diocesan rural life directors to *education and pastoral ministry* by providing additional resources and training and by integrating their activities into the ongoing program of the NCRLC. Pastoral ministry should be recognized as the key service rendered by diocesan personnel dealing with rural matters at the local level; education should be a close second. NCRLC can be of great help to these efforts through training programs, educational services, research, and publications. Bishops will need to expand financial and staff resources in order to provide adequate rural ministry. In dioceses where there are no designated rural life directors, a staffed rural life office should be established, or, in cases where this is not possible, the social action office should be strengthened in order to enhance its service to rural people.

61. Special emphasis should be placed on preparation for those ministering in rural communities. Continuing education of clergy and other rural ministers should include a familiarization with the particular rural culture, as well as workshops and programs to assist in more effective ministry to rural people. Liturgies must be developed that are sensitive to rural conditions and appropriate to the experience of people on the land. Homilies, healing services, and other spiritual resources of the Church may be offered. Counseling, support-group formation, and the active presence of priests, women religious, and other ministers and friends working in solidarity with the rural community have made a significant difference to many people caught in the rural crisis. Collaboration with other churches, farm organizations, and community groups for ongoing analysis and education of the broader issues as they relate to the local community is also encouraged. Both rural and urban people should be brought into the dialogue for mutual understanding and cooperative action.

D. State Catholic Conferences

62. The state Catholic conferences should continue to exercise primary responsibility for *policy development* and *legislative advocacy* at the state and local levels. Formal linkages already exist between the USCC and the directors of the state conferences — particularly through the USCC Offices of Social Development and World Peace, Government Liaison, and General Counsel. This relationship should be augmented through more regular reporting and exchange of information and analysis by the new joint subcommittee and Social Development and World Peace staff, particularly on legislative matters. The rural life agenda should also be strengthened by increased attention to these matters at the state level by the state Catholic conferences and through the state

Catholic conference directors' national association. To strengthen communications between the rural communities and state Catholic conferences, we urge that diocesan rural life directors serve on appropriate state Catholic conference committees.

E. Catholic Relief Services, Campaign for Human Development, and Catholic Charities USA and Other Agencies

63. Other Catholic agencies should review their current activities with the intent of achieving a greater integration of the rural life agenda in ways that fit their particular missions. CRS and CHD, for example, have significant *educational* support activities. Both agencies have education staffs whose purpose is to produce and disseminate educational material, and both conduct and support *operations* (overseas in the case of CRS, domestic for CHD) to reduce rural poverty and improve the quality of rural life. We encourage closer collaborative efforts among USCC, NCRLC, CRS, and CHD to strengthen the complementary nature of their educational work. We also encourage CHD to continue to be sensitive to the varied needs of the rural poor in its grants program.

64. Catholic Charities USA articulates a threefold mission to provide direct services, stimulate direct action for social change, and convene with others to effect a transformation of society. Three priorities follow the application of the mission of Catholic Charities USA to the needs of rural areas:

- continued provision of accessible direct services;
- direct action involving rural communities; and
- participation in transforming communities/society, both by its own convenings and as part of the network of agencies described here.

In all its functions, Catholic Charities should continue to develop greater awareness of rural issues building on its past and current service of rural needs. Its parish social ministry project is a particular resource that can be offered to rural churches at the diocesan level. Greater involvement in rural concerns should be initiated at the regional convening level. As a result of the emphasis on rural policy at the regional convenings, the annual congress of Catholic Charities USA will be able to address these issues in a more focused and informed way. The NCRLC could be a particularly valuable resource to Catholic Charities as the organization increases its emphasis on rural issues.

65. Other associations of departments, offices, and institutions such as the Catholic Health Association and the National Catholic Educational Association also have constituencies in rural areas. The priorities and allocation of resources by these agencies of the Church are governed by the same principles we have outlined and relate directly to many of the issues discussed in sections II and III; their activities also need to reflect the commitment of the Church to ministry in rural areas and advocacy on rural matters.

III. Conclusion

66. The task force recognizes that the Church in the United States is very diverse — urban, suburban, and rural. Therefore, it is essential to highlight the links between us on issues of food and agriculture. What happens in rural America directly affects the quality of life for the rest of the United States and the world. Without increased emphasis, a legitimate expression of solidarity may be too easily crowded out by other pressing concerns and even indifference. Food security, rural poverty, food trade, and environmental concerns need to be shared concerns. Food and agriculture is an agenda that can build solidarity among urban and rural people. These problems know no borders and do not stop at the city gate. We are in this together. Our nation's food and agricultural policies will enrich or diminish all of us wherever we live.

67. The task force believes that the ethical framework, the public policy issues, the advocacy, and pastoral ministry concerns outlined in this report accurately reflect the priorities of the variety of church organizations involved in the areas of food and agriculture and rural life. It is our judgment that they constitute a genuine and logical implementation of the concerns outlined in the pastoral letter on the U.S. economy. The task force also believes that the organizational relationships proposed in this report will enable the Catholic Church in the United States to improve its pastoral ministry in rural America, build networks for ministry, help empower rural communities for self-development, reach policy positions on relevant problems, and implement these policies in the public arena. The problems of rural life, local and global, are critically important, and we are anxious to have a structure in place that will enable the bishops to tackle them effectively.

Resolution on the Tenth Anniversary of the NCCB Pastoral Statement on Handicapped People

A Resolution Issued by the
National Conference of Catholic Bishops

November 15, 1988

1. The *Pastoral Statement of U.S. Catholic Bishops on Handicapped People* was issued on November 16, 1978. It offered great hope to persons with disabilities, opening the Church to their full membership.

2. In the decade since we issued this pastoral statement, many parish and diocesan buildings, programs, and services have been made accessible, and more and more persons with mental and physical disabilities are participating in church life. Diocesan staff are also commonly available to assist parishes in becoming more welcoming.

3. On the occasion of this tenth anniversary, we the Catholic bishops of the United States of America, reaffirm and recommit ourselves to the guidelines, principles, and practices set forth in our pastoral statement. We challenge the Church in the United States to go beyond physical access to buildings and the provision of religious and social services. We draw attention to the many persons with disabilities who recognize their own leadership abilities and who experience a call to pastoral ministry, to ordained priesthood, to membership in a religious community, or to employment within the Church.

4. We acknowledge persons with mental retardation who provide, along with their presence and some pastoral services within the Church, their gifts of simplicity of heart. We affirm those persons with disabilities who dared to be the first in a given area of ministry, and we call all persons with disabilities to the fullness of their baptismal commitment.

5. We proclaim that if any member is prevented from active participation, the church community is incomplete. We call upon church leadership throughout the country to promote accessibility of mind and heart, so that all persons with disabilities may be welcomed at worship and at every level of service as full members of the Body of Christ.

Policy Statement on Employer Sanctions

A Statement Issued by the
National Conference of Catholic Bishops

November 16, 1988

1. The Gospel of Christ challenges us to care for the less fortunate. The Catholic Church in the United States has repeatedly expressed its concern for a segment of our population that must be counted among the least fortunate: undocumented aliens. The Church's attention today must focus now on the imposition of employer sanctions which is causing so much suffering for these undocumented workers.

Our Past Position

2. The United States Catholic Conference (USCC) opposed employer sanctions from the beginning. From 1971 to 1977, the U.S. House of Representatives considered a series of employer sanctions bills. It was not until 1976, following a presidential commission's recommendation that sanctions be tied to a legalization program, that the U.S. Senate initiated immigration reform. In that year, on behalf of the National Conference of Catholic Bishops, Archbishop Robert F. Sanchez of Santa Fe testified against employer sanctions before the Senate Subcommittee on Immigration and Refugee Policy. Since that time, the USCC has refined and reiterated this opposition.

3. In a 1985 statement to the Senate Subcommittee on Immigration and Refugee Policy, Archbishop Anthony J. Bevilacqua, then bishop of Pittsburgh and chairman of the Bishops' Ad Hoc Committee on Migration and Tourism, presented the USCC position:

> One must consider the relationship of sanctions to the overall questions of immigration reform. If indeed sanctions become a precondition for a fair and generous legalization program, the USCC will consider supporting them. Unless these conditions are satisfied, the Church must oppose sanctions.[1]

4. One of the Church's conditions for a "fair and generous" program was an eligibility date that would allow as many people as possible

---

[1] Most Reverend Anthony J. Bevilacqua, "Statement on behalf of the United States Catholic Conference before the Senate Subcommittee on Immigration and Refugee Policy" (June 18, 1985).

to apply for legalization. The final version of the Immigration Reform and Control Act of 1986 (IRCA) offered legalized status only to individuals who had resided continuously in the United States since before January 1, 1982. This 1982 cutoff date was too restrictive. It left an ineligible population of post-1982 arrivals that many estimate is as large as the eligible population.

5. The USCC has been encouraging an expansion of the legalization program to post-1982 entrants. In addition, the USCC supported efforts to extend the legalization program for six months beyond its initial application period. The Senate thwarted these efforts by voting down an extension bill which had passed the House.

6. Because of the failure of IRCA to meet minimum standards of generosity and because of its negative effects on the residual undocumented population, we must, once again, underscore our opposition to employer sanctions. This concern goes beyond the negative effects of sanctions on the residual undocumented population. We are also disturbed by the potential for more widespread discrimination. As General Secretary Monsignor Daniel F. Hoye stated in the final USCC letter to Congress before IRCA was passed in 1986:

> Sanctions . . . will probably exacerbate discrimination against foreign-looking and foreign-sounding individuals. . . . Employer sanctions are unbalanced, and essential guarantees against workplace discrimination have become almost unrecognizable.[2]

7. There is no doubt that the impact of employer sanctions can be severe. Jobless, undocumented people form a subculture that by choice or by necessity fails to be integrated into the mainstream of life in the United States. They may face a lack of food, housing, and health care. As their number increases, they could cause division and major social problems in this country. Undocumented and unemployed persons may be tempted to commit crimes in order to survive or to provide sustenance for their families. They are vulnerable to exploitation by unscrupulous employers who violate the law and hire unauthorized noncitizens willing to work long hours for the lowest wages. These employees may be too intimidated to ask for compliance with basic health and safety laws. Far from eliminating this easily exploited group of people, IRCA has driven them deeper into the underground of our society. In fact, even those whom the law explicitly protects — individuals whose employment began before IRCA became law — have suffered. Many have been fired by employers ignorant of the law. They cannot now legally obtain new jobs.

---

[2]Monsignor Daniel F. Hoye, "Letter to Congress regarding the Conference Report on H.R. 3810 and S. 1200" (October 15, 1986), pp. 3, 4.

The Moral Roots of Our Concern

8.   Catholic social teaching explicitly supports the human rights of aliens outside their home countries. These rights, by their very nature, extend to the rights of the undocumented aliens. The 1969 Vatican *Instruction on the Pastoral Care of People Who Migrate* speaks of the "right to seek conditions of life worthy of man" that include humane working conditions, decent housing, and the education of children.[3] In addition, Pope John Paul II states in his encyclical *On Human Work*:

> Emigration in search of work must in no way become an opportunity for financial or social exploitation.
>   The most important thing is that the person working away from his native land . . . should not be placed at a disadvantage in comparison with the other workers in that society in the matter of working rights.[4]

9.   The right to migrate for work cannot be simply ignored in the exercise of a nation's sovereign right to control its own borders. In this regard, Catholic social teaching sets a higher ethical standard for guarding the rights of the undocumented within our borders than do current United States law and policy. The Church must necessarily concern herself with the universal common good and the human rights of all persons, no matter what borders they cross.

10.   Catholic tradition defends the right to migrate as a basic right in accord with the common good, with one exception: migration based on excessively selfish interests. Catholic social teaching also recognizes that political and economic pressures often combine to compel people to become refugees and leave their homelands.

11.   The Church's obligation to work for change in United States immigration policies derives from our moral duty to seek an increasingly just immigration system. The Church especially must encourage a spirit of justice and generosity. Nowhere is this needed more in our society than in the case of undocumented persons. A spirit of justice and generosity to the undocumented enriches the moral life of this country. It anchors in fact our professed national concern for the human rights of all people.

---

[3]Sacred Congregation for Bishops, Vatican City, August 22, 1969, *Instruction on the Pastoral Care of People Who Migrate* (Washington, D.C.: USCC Office of Publishing and Promotion Services, 1969), ch. I, no. 7.

[4]John Paul II, *On Human Work* (*Laborem Exercens*) (Washington, D.C.: USCC Office of Publishing and Promotion Services, 1981), part IV, no. 23.

Our Plan of Action

12. How best can we work toward ensuring the rights and needs of the undocumented? First, it must be said that many strategies are possible for social actions that follow the light of Catholic teachings. People of good will and good faith can differ on their approaches. In our judgment effective opposition to employer sanctions does not require that we break the law. Defying legal sanctions must be viewed as an exceptional act justified only by clear moral necessity to prevent a greater evil for which all other remedies have been exhausted.[5] The common good requires all persons to uphold the law and, where the law is deficient, to change it.

13. As leaders of the Catholic community, we urge the following actions for helping the undocumented:

- Work to change the employer sanctions law. If enough cases of discrimination can be reported through the Government Accounting Office, Congress must revisit the law. It is important that we document and report any instances of discrimination. The USCC is compiling a record of these cases.
- Promote legislation that provides legalization opportunities for people who arrived after January 1, 1982.
- Educate employers. It is essential to alert employers to the exact compliance requirements in order to mitigate employment discrimination.[6]
- Support legislation that provides effective safe haven for those fleeing economic and political upheavals. Aside from country-

---

[5]The Second Vatican Council stated in the *Pastoral Constitution on the Church in the Modern World (Gaudium et spes)*, ch. I, no. 16: "For man has in his heart a law written by God. To obey it is the very dignity of man; according to it he will be judged." [Published in Walter M. Abbott, SJ, *The Documents of Vatican II* (New York: America Press, 1966), p. 213.]

[6]a) Many employers do not realize that employees hired before *November 6, 1986* are *grandfathered* by the law. These employees should not be dismissed or asked to show documents demonstrating their immigration status and employers cannot be sanctioned for failing to do so.

   b) Under the current interpretation of the law employees who are only sporadically employed (e.g., freelance or irregular domestic workers in private homes) are not affected by employer sanctions and they need not be asked to complete the form (I-9) verifying employment eligibility.

   c) An employer must make a reasonable, good faith effort to ensure that the documents provided are valid, but employers are not required to authenticate documents.

   d) Employers should be careful to see that INS inspections for possible violation of the employer sanctions law do not also involve random searches to arrest or detect undocumented workers.

   e) Employers should use the three-days notice provided by the law to prepare for an inspection, and the I-9 files should be kept separate from personnel files.

specific legislation, this may require a new standard of humanitarian admissions under U.S. law.
- Strive to provide housing, food, and clothing to newcomers
  and unemployed workers and their families. Document the
  social service needs of the nonlegalized families and individuals
  in dioceses across the country.
- Provide education on the socioeconomic conditions in the countries of origin which generate migration. As the bishops' pastoral letter on the economy suggested, we can press for a U.S.
  international economic policy designed to empower people
  everywhere and ensure that the benefits of economic growth
  are shared equitably.[7]

Conclusion

14. As we continue to explore more creative pastoral and governmental responses to employer sanctions, let us think together and
share our ideas across the country without any unnecessary polarization. In the midst of difficult social policy debates, the Church has
an obligation to promote an atmosphere of civility.
15. We must concentrate not on ourselves and on our differences,
but on the needs of those we seek to serve. Through our direct service
we make it clear that newcomers can always turn to the Church as a
friend. We will protect them, support them, and love them as full
members of our family in Christ. In the name of Jesus Christ, the
Church must be the first to insist that love knows no borders.

---

[7]National Conference of Catholic Bishops, *Economic Justice for All: Pastoral Letter on Catholic Social Teaching and the U.S. Economy* (Washington, D.C.: USCC Office of Publishing and Promotion Services, 1986), no. 292.

A Word of Solidarity, A Call for Justice
A Statement on Religious Freedom in
Eastern Europe and the Soviet Union

A Statement Issued by the
United States Catholic Conference

November 17, 1988

Introduction

1.   The Church in Eastern Europe and the Soviet Union today is a church of many realities. There is the particularly tragic memory of Bishop Ernest Coba of Albania, murdered by prison authorities for celebrating a Mass with a few other inmates in his cell, in contravention of prison regulations, on Easter Day, 1979. In Czechoslovakia in 1988, there is the case of Augustin Navratil, a Catholic layman and father of nine, who has been involuntarily committed to a psychiatric clinic for responding to newspaper criticisms of his widely supported 31-point petition for religious rights. Then, there is the young believer in the German Democratic Republic ([GDR] East Germany) who was denied admission to medical school because of her open profession of her faith.

2.   But there are also other, more hopeful, realities. There is the triumphant return of Pope John Paul II to his native Poland in 1979, the first visit by a pope to that country in its thousand-year history and the first papal visit to any communist country. There is the image of 300,000 people gathered at the national eucharistic congress in Marija Bistrica, Yugoslavia in 1984, the largest religious gathering in Eastern Europe outside Poland since World War II; and there is the crowded weekday Mass in one of any number of parishes in Czechoslovakia, filled with believers practicing their faith despite the threat of discrimination in education and employment and innumerable other obstacles imposed by the present government.

3.   All of these realities and images—and many, many more—make up the complex picture of religious life in Eastern Europe and the Soviet Union today. They form a picture of a church that has suffered and continues to suffer much from repression and restrictions, a modern reminder that "[t]he Church was born on the Cross and grew up

in the midst of persecutions."[1] They also present a picture of a vibrant church, with a long and rich heritage, which our Holy Father has attested "bears special witness to the *fruitfulness of the meeting of the human spirit with the Christian mysteries* [and] continues to exercise a salutary influence on the mind of the whole Church."[2]

4. In writing this statement at this time, we seek to focus attention upon the situation of religion in these communist countries by reviewing, in some detail, the current situation of one religious body: the Catholic Church. We look at the situation of the Catholic Church within the framework of our concern for the protection of the religious liberty of all and our support for fundamental human rights and genuine peace in our own country and throughout the world. The Holy Father recently described this framework in this way:

> In the first place, religious freedom, an essential requirement of the dignity of every person, is a cornerstone of the structure of human rights, and for this reason is an irreplaceable factor in the good of individuals and of the whole of society, as well as of the personal fulfillment of each individual. It follows that the freedom of individuals and of communities to profess and practice their religion is an essential element for peaceful human coexistence. Peace, which is built up and consolidated at all levels of human association, puts down it roots in the freedom and openness of consciences to truth.[3]

5. In recent years, we have spoken often on the moral imperative of safeguarding the fundamental right to religious liberty. We addressed the issue from a theoretical perspective in our 1980 pastoral letter on Marxist communism,[4] and we specifically addressed the situation of the churches in Eastern Europe in our 1977 statement *Religious Liberty in Eastern Europe: A Test Case for Human Rights*,[5] and in various other public statements.[6] Equally important, we have expressed our ecclesial solidarity with our brothers and sisters in Eastern Europe through personal visits, prayers, and witness on their behalf.

---

[1] Pope John Paul II, "Address at Lourdes" (August 14, 1983).

[2] Pope John Paul II, *Go into All the World* (*Euntes in Mundum*), apostolic letter "On the Occasion of the Millennium of the Baptism of Kievan Rus'" (Washington, D.C.: USCC Office of Publishing and Promotion Services, 1988), p. 22.

[3] Pope John Paul II, "1988 World Day of Peace Message," *Origins* 17:28 (December 24, 1987): 493.

[4] National Conference of Catholic Bishops, *Pastoral Letter on Marxist Communism* (Washington, D.C.: USCC Office of Publishing and Promotion Services, 1980).

[5] United States Catholic Conference, "Religious Liberty in Eastern Europe: A Test Case for Human Rights" (May 4, 1977), in *Quest for Justice*, J. Brian Benestad and Frank Butler, eds. (Washington, D.C.: USCC Office of Publishing and Promotion Services, 1981), p. 136.

[6] Testimony of Rev. J. Bryan Hehir, "Religious Freedom as a Human Right," U.S. Congress: Hearings before the Subcommittee on Human Rights and International Organizations, House Foreign Affairs Committee (February 10, 1982); Testimony of Rev. J. Bryan Hehir, "Religious Liberty in Eastern Europe and the Soviet Union," U.S. Congress: Hearings before the Senate Foreign Relations Committee (July 20, 1984).

6.   In 1988, we feel compelled once again to address the situation of believers in the communist countries of Eastern Europe and the Soviet Union. It is appropriate as a final commemoration of several important anniversaries that have been observed in the past three years: the 11th centenary of the evangelization of the Slavs settled in Great Moravia and Pannonia by Saints Cyril and Methodius (1985); the 800th anniversary of the Christianization of Latvia (1986); the 600th anniversary of the Baptism of Lithuania (1987); the 950th anniversary of the death of Hungary's founder and first king, St. Stephen; and the millennium of the adoption of Christianity in Kievan Rus' (1988).[7] The very fact that these anniversaries have been celebrated throughout the world—including in Slovakia, Lithuania, and Ukraine—despite government interferences is a tribute to the persistence, strength, and dynamism of the churches in these regions.

7.   In addition to paying tribute to the rich traditions of the churches, it is particularly appropriate that we address their current status in light of recent developments in many of these communist countries. Much has happened in the past decade that has changed the dynamic of the situation in Eastern Europe, including the elevation of a Slavic pope, the emergence of independent movements, and the rise to power of new leadership in the Soviet Union and elsewhere. Yet, much remains the same. The situation of the churches varies considerably from country to country—reflecting the depth and variety of religious conviction among the people and the degree of tenacity and pragmatism of the communist party leadership—but a general pattern of intolerance of religion remains clearly evident.

8.   Therefore, as bishops, we feel an urgent need to focus attention once again on what the Holy Father has called the "radical injustice" of the violation of religious freedom; to express our solidarity with our suffering brothers and sisters in Eastern Europe and the Soviet Union; to urge the structural reforms necessary for greater religious freedom for these brothers and sisters; and to highlight the urgency and efficacy of more concerted action by all Catholics, the governments of the world, and others of good will in defending and promoting religious freedom in these countries.

9.   We focus here primarily on the situation of Catholics in Eastern Europe and the Soviet Union, but religious repression and intolerance are by no means directed only at Catholics or confined only to the countries examined in this statement. The difficulties faced by non-

---

[7]For Pope John Paul II's commemoration of these anniversaries, see: *The Apostles of the Slavs* (*Slavorum Apostoli*), papal encyclical (Washington, D.C.: USCC Office of Publishing and Promotion Services, 1985); "On the Sixth Centenary of the 'Baptism' of Lithuania" in *Origins* 17:8 (July 16, 1987): 128; *Go into All the World* (*Euntes in Mundum*), apostolic letter "On the Occasion of the Millennium of the Baptism of Kievan Rus'" (Washington, D.C.: USCC Office of Publishing and Promotion Services, 1988); "Message to Ukrainian Catholics" (*Magnum Baptismi Donum*) in *Origins* (May 5, 1988): 816.

Catholics in Eastern Europe and the Soviet Union and by some or all religions in Vietnam, Cambodia, Cuba, Iran, Turkey, Sudan, and elsewhere also demand serious attention. This statement, while limited in scope, is meant to provide a case study of the continuing restrictions and sometimes outright repression that confront all religions, in varying ways and degrees, not only in Eastern Europe and the Soviet Union but also in many countries throughout the world. We cannot overemphasize that the denial of religious liberty to one faith group or in one country is a threat to all faiths in all countries and must be the concern of all who value human rights. When Soviet Jews, Bulgarian Muslims, Vietnamese Buddhists, or innumerable others suffer for their beliefs, we all suffer. As American Catholics, we share their suffering just as we share the duty to protect and promote, through our words and actions, religious freedom and tolerance wherever and whenever they are lacking. For this reason, we will continue to speak consistently on behalf of the rights of these groups and individuals and those of all faiths who suffer in their beliefs.

I. Background: Principles and Practices

A. Components of the Right of Religious Liberty Catholic Teaching

10. We seek to evaluate the extent of religious freedom in Eastern Europe and the Soviet Union in light of the many dimensions of this fundamental human right.[8]

11. "In the first place," according to Pope John Paul II, "religious freedom [is] an essential requirement of the dignity of every person [and] . . . a cornerstone of the structure of human rights."[9] Religious liberty is unique among the many essential requirements of human dignity because its object is an individual's relationship with God, the ultimate end of the human person. As a social and civil right, it has both a personal dimension—the freedom of conscience—and a social dimension—the free exercise of religion.

12. *Freedom of conscience* is the aspect of the right of religious liberty that requires that each person be free from all external coercion in his or her search for God, religious truth, and faith. It is the freedom to make a personal religious decision. It requires, among other things, that believers be treated equally with other citizens and not be dis-

---

[8]See "1988 World Day of Peace Message"; Vatican Council II, *Declaration on Religious Freedom (Dignitatis Humanae)* (1965); John Courtney Murray, *The Problem of Religious Freedom* (Westminster, Md.: Newman Press, 1965).
[9]"1988 World Day of Peace Message," p. 493.

criminated against in economic, social, political, or cultural life; and that educational programs, the media, and government policies respect religious beliefs and not attempt to undermine or destroy them. Because human nature is both personal and social, religious faith is expressed in outward acts and within a community of faith. Hence, freedom of conscience is directly tied to the social dimension of religious liberty: the free exercise of religion.

13. *The free exercise of religion* involves a twofold immunity. In the words of the Second Vatican Council, this means that all "are to be immune from coercion on the part of individuals or of social groups and of any human power, in such wise that in matters religious no one is to be forced to act in a manner contrary to his own beliefs. Nor is anyone to be restrained from acting in accordance with his own beliefs, whether privately or publicly, whether alone or in association with others, within due limits."[10] There are three distinct but interrelated aspects to this freedom to exercise one's religion: freedom of religious expression and evangelization, ecclesial freedom, and freedom of religious association.

a) *Freedom of religious expression and evangelization* affirms that individuals and religious bodies are to be free from coercion in public worship and public religious observances and practices. It also requires freedom to publish and import Bibles and other religious literature; the freedom to have social communications media and access to public communications; the freedom to teach publicly and witness to the faith; and the freedom to address the religious and moral dimensions of social, economic, and political questions. It also includes the rights of parents to determine the kind of religious education that their children are to receive and to avoid education for their children that is not in conformity with their religious beliefs.

b) *Ecclesial or institutional freedom* is the corporate right of religious organizations to internal autonomy, that is, to control the many dimensions of church life. This autonomy requires the freedom to develop and teach doctrine; the freedom to choose and train ministers in their own institutions and to appoint and transfer these ministers without external inteference; and the freedom to construct and use buildings for religious needs and to obtain other materials necessary for the church's life.

c) *Freedom of religious association* affirms the freedom of a person to enter or leave a community of faith; the freedom to form religious groups for educational, cultural, charitable, or social purposes; the freedom to assemble to engage in religious pilgrimages; and the freedom to communicate freely with co-religionists at home and abroad.

14. This brief summary of the many essential components of religious liberty provides the *criteria* by which we seek to judge the current

---

[10]*Declaration on Religious Freedom*, no. 2.

situation in Eastern Europe and the Soviet Union. The claims of some governments notwithstanding, it is clear from this summary that freedom of conscience and freedom of worship *alone* do not constitute freedom of religion.

15. It is also clear from this summary that the right to religious liberty is inextricably connected to other legal rights and protections, most notably, freedom of conscience, association, and speech; equality before the law; and legal recognition of independent entities. If a state limits or denies the right to full religious freedom, it almost certainly will limit or deny these other rights as well. In this sense, the civil and social right to religious liberty is a point of reference and a measure of other fundamental rights.[11] In fact, Pope John Paul II reminds us in his recent encyclical *On Social Concern (Sollicitudo Rei Socialis)* that the lack of religious liberty is one index of poverty and underdevelopment:

> The denial or limitation of human rights—as for example the *right to religious freedom*, the right to share in the building of society, the freedom to organize and to form unions or to take initiatives in economic matters—do these not impoverish the human person as much as, if not more than, the deprivation of material goods? And is development which does not take into account the full affirmation of these rights really development on the human level?[12] (Emphasis added.)

16. Given the fundamental importance of the right involved, we are specially committed to those whose religious freedom is suppressed or limited, not for the purpose of being polemical or adversarial, but in order to enable *all* persons to share in and contribute to the common good. Human dignity and the common good demand religious liberty.

B. Religious Repression and Intolerance in Eastern Europe and the USSR: An Overview

17. The present situation of religious liberty in Eastern Europe can only be understood in light of complex historical, cultural, religious, and political factors unique to each country. Most Eastern European states have suffered many centuries of foreign domination, and few have a recent tradition of religious or political freedom or tolerance. The Latin Catholic and Orthodox churches have been dominant— except in the German Democratic Republic (where the Protestant Church has been in the majority) and Albania (where Islam predominates)—and often were closely aligned with the state. Moreover,

---

[11]"1988 World Day of Peace Message," p. 495.

[12]Pope John Paul II, *On Social Concern (Sollicitudo Rei Socialis)*, papal encyclical (Washington, D.C.: USCC Office of Publishing and Promotion Services, 1987), p. 25.

nationalism and religion have long been closely linked in Eastern Europe, sometimes creating divisions among Christians, but in other cases engendering a vital sense of cultural, social, and political identity that continues to have far-reaching consequences.

18. Clearly, some of these factors have facilitated the communist persecution of religion; others help to explain the widely divergent situation of the churches in the Soviet-bloc countries. However, it is the abiding ideological hostility to religion common to all communist regimes that has most significantly defined the present situation. In our 1980 pastoral letter on Marxist communism, we noted certain variants in Marxist theory and practice, which include questions of religion.[13] Despite these variants, all communist movements are grounded in a "scientific atheism" that rejects, not only the Christian vision of the person, society, history, and morality, but also the very idea of religion itself. The scientific atheism of Marxism-Leninism regards religion as a distortion of reality, an illusion that manifests social and economic conditions that impede the realization of a socialist society. Lenin regarded religion as a poison, deliberately administered for sinister social purposes by the bourgeois class. As an antidote to this poison, he advocated indoctrination in scientific atheism, in conjunction with severe restrictions on religion, until it inevitably withered away under new social and economic conditions.

19. This ideological antagonism toward religion has translated into a long history of persecution of religion by communist governments, first in the Soviet Union and later throughout Eastern Europe. The scale of persecution has been and remains sustained and comprehensive, and its roster of victims all inclusive: Catholics, Protestants, Orthodox, Jews, Muslims, Jehovah's Witnesses, and many others.

20. As sustained and comprehensive as this persecution of religion has been and is, its particular form has varied widely over time and place, depending upon the strength of the churches, strategic considerations of the governments, and other factors. In general, the policies of communist governments have followed three approaches, reflecting differing judgments as to the methods by and pace at which religion can or should be suppressed: (1) an all-out assault on religion; (2) a containment of religion through strict administrative controls; and (3) a form of coexistence with religion, which accommodates religious institutions—within well-defined limits—for the sake of national interests.[14]

---

[13]*Pastoral Letter on Marxist Communism*, pp. 13-15.

[14]For similar categories applied specifically to the Soviet Union, see Trevor Beeson, *Discretion and Valour: Religious Conditions in Russia and Eastern Europe* (Philadelphia: Fortress Press, 1982), pp. 48-49.

1. Outright Repression

21. The first approach to religion — which was most prevalent during the Stalin period but continues in some areas today — calls for an all-out assault on religion as a reactionary threat to the communist state and an obstacle to social and economic progress. This all-out assault includes, in its most severe form, the outright prohibition of all religious activities — as is found in Albania — or entire denominations — as is the case with the Eastern Catholic Church in Ukraine and Romania, and the Jehovah's Witnesses in Czechoslovakia and the Soviet Union.[15] It includes the confiscation of church property and the exile, imprisonment, or murder of bishops, priests, and lay leaders. These repressive measures are augmented by intensive atheistic indoctrination, bitter anti-religious propaganda campaigns, and official sanctioned discrimination against religious believers.

2. Containment through Administrative Measures

22. Under this second approach — which is the most typical today in the Soviet bloc — religion is seen as a deeply rooted historical, cultural, social, and political force that must be tolerated, at least in the short term, but only within strictly defined limits. Through law and administrative norms and practices, the government attempts to limit religious liberty, in all relevant respects, to freedom of worship. The Soviet Constitution is typical, It states:

> Citizens of the U.S.S.R. are guaranteed freedom of conscience, that is, the right to profess or not to profess any religion, and to conduct religious worship or atheist propaganda. Incitement of hostility or hatred on religious grounds is prohibited. In the U.S.S.R. the church is separate from the State, and the school from the church.[16]

23. This and other constitutional and statutory provisions are combined with extensive administrative regulations of "religious cults" to constrain severely religious activity. State registration of all religious groups is used to deny legal status to some groups. Once registered, churches face strict regulations that, in most cases, prohibit formal religious education for children, parish associations or study groups, charitable activities, most or all religious publications, religious orders, and evangelization.

---

[15]In other cases, the government authorities systematically have attempted to discourage and eliminate religious belief and practice by prohibiting virtually all essential activities. For example, the small number of synagogues that are allowed to function in the Soviet Union are severely hampered by the fact that rabbinical ordination, the teaching of Hebrew, and many other basic practices are illegal or officially discouraged.

[16]1977 Constitution, Article 52. English Translation from *Moscow News* supplement to issue no. 42 (October 1977).

24. The few aspects of religious life that are not banned are often subverted through state control or co-optation of all important aspects of church organization, including appointments, finances, training of clergy, publishing, opening or closing of churches, and the like. All but the most ordinary day-to-day activities of the religious communities require state approval, and the decisions of government authorities are often arbitrary, guided by political expediency, or based on regulations that are not even published. Those who actively oppose or circumvent these administrative controls or are involved in religious activities deemed to be "anti-state" are subject to fines, searches, arrest, imprisonment, intimidation, harassment, and beatings.

25. As in the first model, these strict controls are reinforced by active discrimination against believers in education and employment, persistent anti-religious propaganda, and pervasive atheistic indoctrination through the schools, the media, and various other means, not the least of which are the state-sponsored ceremonies, such as the *Jugendweihe* (Youth Dedication) in the German Democratic Republic, which are designed as atheistic substitutes for confirmation and other religious rites.

3. Coexistence and Limited Accommodation

26. This third approach is more accepting of religion as a fact of life that must be tolerated and that can have, within certain limits, a positive role in furthering national interests. This model suggests the possibility of a more open relationship between church and state than the other two models.

27. What distinguishes this approach is that it allows considerably more religious activity than just freedom of worship. The churches—most notably in Yugoslavia and Poland—are relatively free to manage their internal affairs without significant state interference and control, and they have a certain degree of freedom of religious association and expression. The Church is able to choose its own bishops and clergy and to run its seminaries without significant government interference, and religious orders are permitted. The religious press is more likely to offer a credible independent voice; Bibles and other religious literature are generally available; contacts with co-religionists abroad are extensive and unhindered; and large-scale religious gatherings are permitted. The churches are permitted to operate secondary schools—and, in Poland, a university—and formal religious education of children is allowed at the parish level and in the home. The churches also maintain rather extensive charitable activities, although they are limited in scope, for the most part, to work in hospitals, orphanages, and senior citizen centers.

28. The churches still suffer under this approach from some of the significant restrictions found in the second model, however, including the prohibition of church-affiliated primary schools; state- and self-censorship (though usually to a lesser extent) of religious publications; government-imposed limits on newsprint and printing equipment; and, with few exceptions, a lack of access to radio or television. Perhaps most important, religious believers face discrimination, anti-religious propaganda, and atheistic indoctrination similar to that found in the previous two models. Finally, with certain exceptions, the churches are limited in their ability to criticize publicly government policies and face considerable pressure to endorse strongly these policies.

29. Clearly, no Eastern European government's policy toward religion fits neatly into one of these three categories. The policies of these governments have changed over time and often depend on which denomination or national group is involved. Most governments follow a combination of these approaches, though one approach often dominates policy and practice at a particular time. Recognizing these important qualifications, some general observations about the approach to the Catholic Church are possible: Albanian policy and the Soviet and Romanian policies toward the Eastern Catholic Church most closely represent the first model; the general religious policies of the Soviet Union, Czechoslovakia, Bulgaria, and Romania fall under the second model; the Hungarian approach is a hybrid of the second and third models; and the German Democratic Republic, Polish, and Yugoslav policies roughly correspond to the third approach.

30. These distinctions, while not always clear-cut, are important because the approach that is followed has enormous significance for the degree of religious freedom the churches retain. But, except for Albania — which is unique in that it prohibits all religion — the differences, however significant, are differences of degree not quality. The extent of denial of religious liberty may vary widely between countries, but the fact remains that the policies of all these governments are rooted in an ideological hostility toward religion and are designed to restrict religious freedom in morally unacceptable ways.

31. The churches have defended themselves against this hostility and these restrictions in a variety of ways, which reflect ecclesiological, cultural, and political differences. In some cases, prohibited activities have been continued in secret; in others, believers have directly confronted the government, usually with harsh consequences. Many religious bodies have pursued a nonconfrontational approach, seeking a practical compromise with the state in an effort to prevent further limitations on their activities. In a relatively few cases, some individuals have collaborated with or become virtually subservient to the state. Since Pope John XXIII, the Holy See has pursued political agreements with various Eastern European governments as part of a long-range strategy to win, by small steps, at least a measure of religious freedom for the Church. While some might disagree with the particular response of individuals or churches to religious persecution, those of us who are not directly confronted with their difficult choices should be slow to judge the many different ways that believers have chosen to respond in faith to a very difficult situation.

32. In order to illustrate the spectrum of church-state relations in Eastern Europe and the Soviet Union, it might be useful to look briefly at the situation in each of the nine countries. We do not attempt an exhaustive analysis of the complex factors at work here, but simply offer an overview of the present situation of the Catholic Church, as a modest case study of church-state relations in these countries.[17]

II. Religious Repression and Intolerance: A Closer Look

Soviet Union

33. As with many other government policies, the Soviet Union's approach to religion has served as the model for the whole of Eastern Europe. This approach has alternated between attempts to destroy religious institutions through outright persecution and the more subtle, but still very damaging, efforts to constrain religion to worship alone through strict administrative controls.

34. After years of oppression under the Czars, the Catholic Church in the Soviet Union has been repressed systematically under communist rule.[18] The majority Russian Orthodox Church and all religious institutions have also suffered greatly under communism. The government has been especially hostile to the Catholic Church because it has served as a focus for the development of a distinct national and

---

[17]Numerous books, articles, and periodicals provide an overview of the religious situation in these countries from various perspectives. See, for example, Pedro Ramet, *Cross and Commissar: The Politics of Religion in Eastern Europe and the USSR* (Bloomington: Indiana University Press, 1987); Trevor Beeson, *Discretion and Valour: Religious Conditions in Russia and Eastern Europe* (Philadelphia: Fortress Press, 1982); Bohdan Bociurkiw and John Strong, eds., *Religion and Atheism in the U.S.S.R. and Eastern Europe* (Toronto: University of Toronto Press, 1975); *Occasional Papers on Religion in Eastern Europe* (Easton, Pa.: Christians Associated for Relationships with Eastern Europe); *Religion in Communist Dominated Areas* (New York: Research Center for Religion and Human Rights in Closed Societies); *Religion in Communist Lands* (Framingham, Mass.: Keston College; see also Keston News Service [biweekly]); U.S. Department of State, "Country Reports on Human Rights Practices for 1988," report submitted to the House Committee on Foreign Affairs and the Senate Committee on Foreign Relations (February 1988).

[18]On the Catholic Church in the Soviet Union, see Roman Solchanyk and Ivan Hvat, "Catholicism in the Soviet Union," in Pedro Ramet, ed., *Christianity under Stress*, 3 vols. (Durham, N.C.: Duke University Press, forthcoming [1989]); on religion, in general, in the Soviet Union, see, for example, Ludmilla Alexeyeva, *Soviet Dissent: Contemporary Movements for National, Religious, and Human Rights* (Middletown, Conn.: Wesleyan University Press, 1985); Richard Marshall, Jr., ed., *Aspects of Religion in the Soviet Union*, 1917-1967 (Chicago: University of Chicago Press, 1971).

cultural identity, especially in the Baltic States, western Ukraine, and western Byelorussia.

The Baltic States

35. After a period of independence between the world wars, the Baltic States—Lithuania, Latvia, and Estonia—were forcibly annexed by the Soviet Union in 1940, an action not recognized by the Vatican, the United States, and thirty-two other states to this day.[19]

36. Lithuania is the only republic in the Soviet Union that is predominantly Latin Catholic;[20] after forty-four years of continuous Soviet occupation, some three-fourths of the 3.3 million people remain practicing Catholics.[21] During these years, the Catholic Church has been a bulwark against Soviet attempts to repress and eradicate the religious, cultural, and political expression of Lithuanian identity. Six centuries after the Christianization of Lithuania, the Church remains relatively strong and unified despite over a century of oppression under the Czars and almost five decades of overt attacks, strict controls, and pervasive atheistic propaganda under Soviet communism.

37. The Church's situation has improved slightly in recent years with progress towards regularizing and strengthening the Church's hierarchy, including the recent appointment of Cardinal Vincentas Sladkevicius of Kaisiadorys, the first known Lithuanian cardinal in modern times; with a threefold increase since 1973 in the number of students allowed to enroll at the lone seminary in Kaunas; with the publication, in token quantities, of the documents of Vatican II, a new translation of the New Testament, portions of the Latin Catholic Sacramentary and Lectionary, a few prayer books and catechisms, a modest Catholic almanac, and one or two other publications; and with the promise to return the Cathedral and the Church of St. Casimir in the capital city of Vilnius and the Queen of Peace Church in Klaipeda.

38. Since 1972, an organized protest movement—with its own underground journals, the most notable being the *Chronicle of the Catholic Church in Lithuania*—has helped galvanize widespread opposition to religious repression in Lithuania and has focused international attention on the Church's plight. The Soviet authorities have reacted harshly to the growth of this movement by harassing, intimidating, impris-

---

[19]The tradition of Lithuanian self-rule dates back to 1236 when King Mindaugas founded a Lithuanian state that, over the next two centuries, emerged as one of the leading powers in Central Europe.

[20]The Soviet Union is made up of fifteen republics with quite diverse national, cultural, religious, and political characteristics.

[21]Much has been written on the Catholic Church in Lithuania, see, for example, Stanley Vardys, *The Catholic Church, Dissent and Nationality in Soviet Lithuania* (New York: Columbia University Press/distributor, 1978); *The Chronicle of the Catholic Church in Lithuania* (Brooklyn, N.Y.: Lithuanian Catholic Religious Aid).

oning, and confining to psychiatric hospitals leaders—including several priests—of the *Chronicle*, the Lithuanian Helsinki Group, the Catholic Committee for the Defense of Believers' Rights, and other groups concerned with basic human rights. Others have been assaulted or have died under suspicious circumstances.

39. This harsh reaction to religious protests may have diminished somewhat with the emergence of *glasnost* and *perestroika*, but surveillance and intimidation of religious dissenters continue, as do the more subtle but no less damaging restrictions on the Church. A state-induced shortage of priests; the government's refusal to allow Bishop Julijonas Steponavicius to function as apostolic administrator of the Archdiocese of Vilnius; the ban on religious education of children, charitable activities, all religious orders, and most religious publications; and increasingly sophisticated anti-religious propaganda prevent the Church from exercising even its most basic religious functions.

40. In sum, the situation of the Church brings to mind "the image of the Hill of Crosses which has grown up in [Lithuania]: thousands of crosses, witnessing the suffering and the hope of the entire nation, which has been able to preserve its faith even in the most painful hours of trial."[22]

41. Unlike the Church in Lithuania, the Catholic Church in Latvia is a minority church (about 20 percent of the population), but it is stable and has been growing in strength and influence in the last few years, buttressed by the naming of the first known cardinal in the Soviet Union, Cardinal Julijans Vaivods, in 1983. The Latvian Church faces the same constraints as its counterpart in Lithuania but, as in Lithuania, some minor concessions have been won in recent years: the number of seminarians at the seminary in Riga—one of only two Catholic seminaries in the Soviet Union—has more than doubled (to about sixty-five) in the past decade; a lectionary and catechism have been published; and two new bishops have been named since 1982.

Ukraine

42. The celebration of the millennium of the conversion of St. Vladimir and the introduction of Christianity into Kievan Rus' is seriously marred by the fact that the Eastern Catholic Church in Ukraine remains illegal.[23] Since it was abolished and forcibly merged with the Russian

---

[22]Pope John Paul II, "Address to Bishops and Administrators of Lithuanian Dioceses" (Rome, April 27, 1988).

[23]See Bohdan R. Bociurkiw, *Ukrainian Churches under Soviet Rule: Two Case Studies* (Cambridge, Mass.: Ukrainian Studies Fund, 1984); Ukranian Press Service (Ontario, Canada: St. Sophia Religious Association).

Orthodox Church in 1946, a large underground church (estimates range from 3 to 6 million faithful) has developed — though its existence and legitimacy are denied by Soviet authorities. Although verifiable statistics are unavailable, there are as many as eighteen bishops and, perhaps, a thousand priests functioning without government permission in Ukraine. Inspired by the election of Pope John Paul II, the advent of *glasnost,* and the millennium, an organized human rights movement has emerged among believers since 1982, and the underground church has become more visible in its call for legalization. The Soviet authorities have responded by denying all requests for recognition, arresting or harassing numerous priests, and embarking on a massive propaganda campaign against "religious nationalism" in Ukraine.

43. We are encouraged by the start of formal discussions between the Catholic Church and the Orthodox Church on the status of Ukrainian Catholics (as well as other Eastern Catholics). We join with Pope John Paul II in urging that the great numbers of faithful of this repressed Church be permitted to "enjoy true freedom of conscience and respect for their religious right to give public worship to God according to many different traditions in their own rite and with their own pastors."[24] As our Holy Father has said, "Membership in the Catholic Church should not be considered by some as incompatible with the good of one's own earthly country and with the inheritance of St. Vladimir."[25]

44. In addition to the Latin Catholics in Lithuania and Latvia, and the Eastern Catholics in Ukraine, at least 4 million Latin Catholics are found in western parts of Byelorussia and Ukraine (i.e., in the former Polish territories that, after World War II, passed under the control of the Soviet Union) and other Soviet Republics.[26] The Church in these areas is forced to operate with relatively few parishes, fewer priests, and no resident bishops.

Perestroika, Glasnost, and Religion

45. There is little doubt that General Secretary Gorbachev's *perestroika* (restructuring) and *glasnost* (openness) have ushered in a new political climate and a process of reform that, if successful, would bring about significant and necessary change in Soviet economic, political, and

---

[24]Pope John Paul II, "Message to Ukrainian Catholics," pp. 816, 818.

[25]Pope John Paul II, "Homily Marking the Millennium of the Baptism of Kievan Rus'" (Rome, July 10, 1988).

[26]The Byelorussian and Ukrainian republics retain seats in the United Nations, giving the USSR a total of three.

cultural life.[27] It is much less clear whether there also would be significant improvement in the government's approach to religion. We welcome the tentative moves toward a relaxation of the strict controls on religion. More Bibles are being printed and imported; some church buildings have been returned; a number of religious prisoners have been released or allowed to emigrate; steps have been taken to improve dialogue between religious leaders and state officials; there has been a fuller and more frank treatment of religion in the official media; there have been official admissions of past and present abuses of the rights of believers; a few experiments in establishing religious charities have been allowed; and some previously illegal religious bodies have been registered. Believers have also benefited from the greater freedom of expression and association brought about by *glasnost*.

46. It remains to be seen, however, whether General Secretary Gorbachev's reforms will include fundamental changes in religious policies comparable to those announced for other areas of Soviet life. The promises to release all prisoners of conscience; to reopen more churches; and, most important, to revise the 1929 law regulating religious bodies and other laws affecting believers have raised hopes and expectations that the current process of reform, in fact, will include greater tolerance of religion. The fulfillment of these promises would be cause for hope. Other necessary signs of true improvements in the state's policy toward religion would include:

- legalization of the Eastern Catholic Church in Ukraine and other churches that have been banned and restoration of their property;
- recognition of religious bodies as legal entities;
- an end to the anti-religious campaign in the official press, discrimination against believers, and interference in the selection of bishops and the training and appointment of priests;
- a lifting of the ban on educational, charitable, cultural, and social activities, and on formal religious education of children, youth, and adults;
- a guarantee of the right to travel abroad and to emigrate; and
- publication and public review of all decrees and instructions governing the regulation of religious bodies.

---

[27] There is burgeoning literature on the Soviet reforms: see, for example, Seweryn Bialer, *The Soviet Paradox: External Expansion, Internal Decline* (New York: Vintage Books, 1986); Timothy J. Colton, *The Dilemma of Reform in the Soviet Union* (New York: Council on Foreign Relations, 1986); S. Frederick Starr, "Soviet Union: A Civil Society," *Foreign Policy* 70 (Spring 1988): 26; Robert Tucker, "Gorbachev and the Fight for Soviet Reform," *World Policy Journal* (Spring 1987): 179.

Structural reforms of this type would be important indicators of the nature and direction of *glasnost* and *perestroika*.[28]

47. It is still less clear whether other communist governments in Eastern Europe will reform their religious policies. The significant differences between these countries' policies regarding atheistic propaganda and the regulation of religion indicate that religious policy in this region is not monolithic. While the Soviet model has been applied throughout Eastern Europe, countries such as Poland and Yugoslavia have adapted it to their own situations in ways that allow the churches considerably more latitude than in the Soviet Union. In countries such as Albania, on the other hand, the Soviet model has assumed an unprecedented severity. Differences in the strength and approach of the communist party leadership, historical and cultural factors, and the vitality of religion help account for these varied approaches; they do not, however, justify the ideological and structural intolerance of religion, which is at the heart of the policies of all of these governments.

Albania

48. Christianity in Albania dates from the first century preaching of Saints Paul and Andrew. Today, this ancient Church suffers from religious persecution unprecedented in modern times.[29] After years of religious persecution, all religion was formally abolished by government decree in 1967, when 2,200 mosques, churches, and other religious buildings were closed and religious leaders were imprisoned or executed, leading dictator Enver Hoxha to boast that Albania was "the first atheist state in the world." Albania is the only country in the world where the suppression of all religious belief and practice is constitutionally mandated. Since 1979, any religious activity is punishable by imprisonment without trial. Albania is also the only country in Eastern Europe that has not signed the Helsinki Accords or any other international human rights convention. Albania remains a member of the United Nations, however, despite its explicit rejection of the principles of the UN Charter.

49. All three religious traditions—Muslim (68 percent), Orthodox (19 percent), Catholic (13 percent)—have been devastated by the communist persecution, but the harshest repression has been directed

---

[28]For a more detailed list of necessary reforms of religious policies, see, "An Appeal for Religious Freedom in the Soviet Union on the Occasion of the Millennium of Christianity in Kievan Rus'" (Washington, D.C.: James Madison Foundation, 1988).

[29]Pope John Paul II has appealed frequently for religious freedom for Albanians. See, for example, "Address to Albanian Pilgrims" (May 6, 1988); for the fullest account to date of the Catholic Church in communist Albania, see Gjon Sinishta, *The Fulfilled Promise* (1976). See also, the *Albanian Catholic Bulletin* (Santa Clara, Calif.: Albanian Information Service); and Bernard Tonnes, "Religious Persecution in Albania," *Religion in Communist Lands* 10:3 (Winter 1982): 242-255.

against the Catholic Church. Between 1945 and 1981, 137 Catholic clergy were executed or died in prison. The persecution continues unabated. Bishop Ernest Coba was killed in 1979 for saying Mass in secret. The one remaining prelate, Bishop Nikoll Troshani, is detained in a labor camp, as are the few remaining priests. In recent years, priests have been executed for baptizing children and believers have been given jail sentences of twelve years for possessing Bibles and eight years for having a child baptized. Despite these hardships, even the government has admitted that religion endures, as people continue to follow religious rituals, pray, and read the Scriptures secretly. **50.** We pledge our solidarity with this Church, which continues to suffer in silence, and we pray that the Albanian government soon will realize that faith cannot be eliminated by government decree and that religious persecution must come to an end.

Bulgaria

51. The situation of the Church in Bulgaria is also very serious.[30] Religious activity is at a far lower ebb than in any other Eastern European country except Albania. Bulgaria experienced especially severe repression of religion in the early 1950s. Since the 1970s, government policy toward religion in general has been relaxed somewhat, but Muslims have been singled out for severe repression because of their beliefs and their Turkish roots.

52. The majority Orthodox Church is the only religious group that is free to train its clergy in its own seminary, print books, and own land. Religious education and evangelization by any church are banned, and young people are discouraged from attending worship services. The state even has gone so far as to offer cash incentives to those who participate in substitute secular ceremonies. Bibles and other religious literature remain almost impossible to obtain.

53. The Catholic Church in Bulgaria consists of Latin (two dioceses) and Eastern (one diocese) Catholics; about sixty thousand faithful, served by about thirty priests. The Church was severely persecuted between 1948 and 1952. It continues to experience difficulties with the appointment of bishops (the Sofia-Plovdiv See was vacant from 1983-1988) and the training of priests (Catholic seminaries remain closed; only recently did the government sanction the ordination of three priests annually). The government also has renewed efforts to prevent religious education of children under age sixteen. One of the few positive developments has been a partial lifting of the virtual isolation of Bulgarian Catholics from the outside world. Since 1978,

---

[30]See, for example, Janice Broun, "The Church in Bulgaria," *Pro Mundi Vita: Dossiers* 34 (March 1986); "Religious Survival in Bulgaria," *America* 15:3 (November 16, 1985): 323-327.

a small number of Catholics has been allowed to make religious pilgrimages and study abroad.

54. The Bulgarian Church seeks the freedom to appoint bishops and to train priests without state interference, and to provide religious instruction to Catholics of all ages. Such freedom would threaten no one and would contribute to revitalizing this venerable church.

Czechoslovakia

55. In 1987, Pope John Paul II described the Church's status in Czechoslovakia as a "sad situation with no analogy in countries of Christian tradition."[31] While most Eastern European countries have refrained from overt attacks on the churches since the 1950s, the Czechoslovak government has, since 1968, reintroduced an increasingly harsh policy toward religion that remains in place—and may have intensified—in the 1980s.[32]

56. In a country with a large Catholic majority, ten of the thirteen dioceses have been without a resident bishop for decades due to the state's refusal to accept the Vatican's appointments (three Vatican appointments—two auxiliaries and an apostolic administrator—were finally accepted in 1988, the first in fifteen years). State restrictions on admissions at the two remaining seminaries (there were thirteen in 1945) and state control over ministerial licenses (more than five hundred priests have been deprived of their licenses) have left one-quarter of the parishes without a priest. A government-sponsored priests' association, *Pacem in Terris*, has been condemned by the Vatican and Cardinal Frantisek Tomasek of Prague for its pro-government political activities. Religious orders of men have been illegal since 1950, while orders of women have been prohibited from accepting new novices since 1971 and, with a few recent exceptions, are allowed to work only in homes for senior citizens and centers for the incurably sick and handicapped. The government also has made it virtually impossible to build new churches and has restricted severely contacts with the Church outside Czechoslovakia. As in the Soviet Union and Bulgaria, believers suffer from prohibition of most religious activity and face sustained atheistic propaganda and serious discrimination in education and employment as a result of worshiping openly.

57. These government policies have been applied with particular severity against Eastern Catholics, who have borne the heavy cross of oppression. The Eastern Catholic Church was forcibly incorporated

---

[31]Pope John Paul II, meeting with Cardinal Frantisek Tomasek at Vatican, October 1, 1987.

[32]See, for example, International League for Human Rights, "Human Rights in Czechoslovakia" (February 1987); "Christians and the Ideological Struggle in Czechoslovakia," *Pro Mundi Vita: Dossiers* (April 1982).

into the Orthodox Church after World War II. In the portion of Czecho-slovakia that was annexed to the Soviet Union (Carpatho-Ruthenia), the Church continues to operate underground with priests and bish-ops. The remaining diocese in Slovakia was restored in 1968 but remains without bishops and continues to be oppressed in countless ways.

58. Despite these and similar policies, the 1980s have brought a strong religious revival in Czechoslovakia, especially among the young, in some of the traditionally more secularized urban areas and in heavily Catholic Slovakia.[33] This revival is evidenced by several large pilgrim-ages in recent years and high levels of daily Mass attendance. In 1987 and 1988, this revitalized Church, led by Cardinal Tomasek and some other bishops, has been clear and unified in its articulation of the pressing need for new, more open policies toward religion. We sup-port the aspirations of the Catholics in Czechoslovakia, as outlined in their 31-point Charter of Believers, for an end to discrimination against believers and state interference with Catholic seminaries and the appointment of priests. In demanding restoration of the religious orders, construction of new churches, ordination of new bishops, freedom to receive and publish religious materials, and the right to form Catholic associations, Czech and Slovak Catholics seek no priv-ileges but only the ability to live their faith and contribute to the common good. The recognition of these legitimate demands combined with the success of the recently announced ten-year plan for spiritual renewal would do much to heal the scars of the past, bring about reconciliation, and strengthen the moral fabric of society.

German Democratic Republic

59. The religious situation in the GDR differs from that of the Soviet Union, Albania, Bulgaria, and Czechoslovakia insofar as the major religious bodies retain a greater degree of independence in internal church affairs.[34] The crass anti-religious propaganda and harassment campaigns against clergy and church leaders that aggravate church-state tensions in these other countries have been abandoned, for the most part, in the GDR. The Socialist Unity Party (SED) has sought a relationship based on dialogue, while allowing the churches a certain limited freedom of action.

60. Given its minority status (about 8 percent of the population) and a desire to maintain its distance from the communist government, the Catholic Church's relationship with the state has been somewhat strained. The Church has criticized discrimination against Christian

---

[33]Czechoslovakia consists of two republics, the Czech and Slovak, each with different religious profiles.

[34]See, for example, Pedro Ramet, "East Germany: Strategies of Church-State Coexis-tence," *Religion in Communist Dominated Areas* 24:2 (Spring 1985): 37-41.

youth in education and employment (including the "youth dedication" ritual for fourteen-year-olds); protested the introduction of
premilitary training in the schools and the militarization of society
generally; and, most significant, has condemned the continuing atheistic education that has accelerated the secularization of society. Only
in 1987 was the Church allowed to hold a national convocation—the
first since World War II and a most significant event for the Church.
61. It is the state's monopolization of youth, its ideological threat,
and the virtual impossibility for practicing Christians to have access
to higher studies and public offices, rather than the direct attacks and
subversion of the church common in some other Eastern European
countries, that impede improvement in church-state relations in the
GDR. As Cardinal Joachim Meisner has said, Christians seek only the
ability to live their faith and to "assume their social responsibility, in
full accord with their conscience oriented by the faith of the church."[35]
Christians desire to lend their talents to society "without thereby
following any star other than that of Bethlehem."[36]

Hungary

62. The Hungarian government's willingness to compromise, on a
limited basis, regarding church-state questions and a generally nonconfrontational approach by the Catholic Church (about 60 percent
of the population) and the Reformed and Lutheran churches (about
20 percent of the population) have combined to ensure believers in
Hungary a degree of religious freedom in certain areas of church life
that is not found in some other Eastern European countries.[37]
63. Hungary is distinguished from the more repressive regimes by
the limited number of Catholic religious orders that are permitted to
operate eight secondary schools; the filling of vacancies in episcopal
sees with less rigid state interference; the general availability of Bibles
and other religious materials; and the broadcast of religious programs
by the state radio every Sunday. In the past decade, private religious
meetings have been largely tolerated; the study of the Bible as literature has been introduced into state secondary schools; a retreat house
for lay people has been opened; and the state has permitted the
establishment of a religious women's community dedicated to medical
and social services.
64. No doubt the Church has benefited from some loosening of restric-

---

[35]Cardinal Joachim Meisner, letter to diocesan clergy, cited in *National Catholic News Service* (February 10, 1988).
[36]Cardinal Joachim Meisner, "Homily at Convention of Catholics in Dresden" (July 11, 1987).
[37]See, for example, Emeric Andras and Julius Morel, eds., *Church in Transition: Hungary's Catholic Church from 1945 to 1982* (Vienna: Hungarian Institute for Sociology of Religion, 1983).

tions on it, but, as certain Hungarian bishops have indicated, more fundamental changes are necessary. It has been suggested that it is necessary to rethink the present legal framework for church-state relations, in a spirit of cooperation and out of a desire to contribute to Hungarian society.[38] Specifically, the bishops have requested an end to the bureaucratic restrictions on religious instruction; a free hand for involvement with young people; rehabilitation of the religious orders, associations, and publications that were dissolved during the Stalin era; an expansion of the eight high schools to accommodate unmet demand; greater access to the media; the right for priests to visit freely hospitals, prisons, and schools; and a reconsideration of the government's policy toward Catholic conscientious objectors. These kinds of reforms could contribute to the creation of a new structure for church-state relations in Hungary.

Poland

65. Since the consolidation of communist rule in Eastern Europe after World War II, the Catholic Church in Poland has been the strongest and one of the most dynamic in the region—in part because of its size, its identification with Polish national aspirations, its strong moral leadership, and its role as the major independent institution in the country.[39] The election of Pope John Paul II in 1978 seems to have only increased the strength of an already vital Church.

66. The Church's remarkable resilience is most evident in its success in maintaining a significant degree of religious freedom, despite the government's persistent efforts to suppress it. Both in law and in fact, Polish citizens enjoy considerable freedom to practice their religion. Although the Church still lacks legal status, the government has had to respect, for the most part, her institutional integrity. Unlike many other Eastern European countries, Polish law allows religious education in the home and in the churches. The Catholic Church operates the only independent university in Eastern Europe, numerous independent theological institutes and seminaries, several high schools, and an extensive catechetical program. Church publications and the Catholic press offer a credible independent voice. The Church also is allowed limited charitable activities, and some lay organizations and

---

[38]The government has promised a new law to regulate religious affairs in 1990. Debate is now taking place within the communist party and the churches about the underlying principles of the proposed legislation.

[39]Pope John Paul II has addressed the Polish situation many times: see, for example, the Holy Father's addresses during his 1987 visit to Poland in *Origins* 17:6 (June 25, 1987). For a history of the Polish Catholic Church, see Ronald C. Monticone, *The Catholic Church in Communist Poland, 1945-1985* (New York: Columbia University Press/distributor, 1986); Eric O. Hanson, *The Catholic Church in World Politics* (Princeton, N.J.: Princeton University Press, 1987), ch. 6.

movements, such as the Catholic Intellectuals' Club and Oases, are permitted to operate at the local level.[40] The Church has retained ownership of much of its property and has embarked, in the past few years, on a vigorous building program. Finally, the number of clergy and religious has more than doubled since 1945, and Poland remains one of the few countries in Europe where religious vocations are on the increase.

67. This relative freedom should not obscure the need, often expressed by the Polish bishops, for important changes in state policies. State officials intimidate parents and their children who want to enroll in the optional catechetical programs. More important, the religious education of children and young people is threatened by secular programs and what the Polish bishops in 1986 termed a campaign of "intense atheistic propaganda" in the state schools.[41] Religious publications, though relatively independent, have limited circulation and are subject to governmental censorship; and churches have no access to state-controlled radio and television other than the weekly radio broadcasts of religious services. The state continues to refuse legal status to the Church and lay Catholic associations, and the government consistently has encouraged anti-Church propaganda.

68. Perhaps, the most distinctive feature of the Polish case is the way in which the Church's strength and relative freedom have enabled it to serve as a defender of and advocate for other human rights and to contribute positively to the common good. It has played a courageous and pivotal role in the crisis brought about by the government's imposition of martial law and its attempt to crush Solidarity, and in subsequent efforts to stabilize the social, economic, and political situation. It has supported the human and social ideals expressed by Solidarity, opposed martial law, and demanded legal recognition of various civil, cultural, and political rights as part of its call for farsighted transformations in the economic and political system. At the same time that it has spoken on behalf of social justice, the Church has assumed the role of mediator, encouraging steady, nonviolent change in an effort to foster national unity.

Romania

69. As in Poland, religious practice is very strong in Romania and has similarly close ties to nationalistic feelings and culture, but the gov-

---

[40]In 1988, after the government had blocked the Church's original plan for an agricultural foundation, a unique — but much less extensive — Church-sponsored agricultural program was established to provide equipment and improved water supplies for the largely private agricultural sector in Poland.

[41]Statement of Polish Bishops' Conference, March 13, 1986.

ernment's religious policies are much harsher.[42] As in the Soviet Union, Bulgaria, and Czechoslovakia, most religious activities other than worship are virtually banned, and the state exercises strict control over the churches. The government has settled, by necessity, for a form of coexistence with the majority Orthodox Church. But it has severely suppressed the Eastern Catholic Church (1.8 million adherents), which was banned and forcibly integrated into the Orthodox Church in 1948. Latin Catholics (1.2 million) have also suffered because the government has considered them a threat to national unity due to their primarily German and Hungarian origins and their loyalty to Rome. The five Latin Catholic dioceses have been effectively reduced to two due to difficulties in appointing bishops; the orders and religious congregations have been suppressed; the training of priests is highly restricted; and the Church, as such, is not recognized by the state. Appeals by believers seeking the most basic of religious freedoms have been ignored or suppressed. Discrimination against believers, especially ethnic Hungarians and members of other minority groups, is increasing, and the state frequently attacks religion through the media and the schools.

70. In recent years, the Church has won small concessions from the government. The Bucharest Archdiocese has a bishop for the first time since 1954, and pilgrims have traveled to Rome for the first time since World War II. The very modest nature of these concessions is indicative of the difficulties faced by our Romanian brothers and sisters and the urgency and legitimacy of their desire for greater freedom to live fully their faith.

Yugoslavia

71. Since the Belgrade Protocol of 1966, which formalized relations between the Holy See and the Yugoslav government (Yugoslavia is the only Eastern European country with which the Holy See maintains formal diplomatic relations), the Catholic Church has maintained a considerable degree of freedom from state interference in internal church administration and has taken an active role in national life, despite continued strong pressure from the government.[43]

72. The almost 7 million Catholics in Yugoslavia (found mostly in Croatia and Slovenia) are less restricted than in many other communist countries in Eastern Europe. They benefit from a vigorous Catholic

---

[42]See, for example, P. Delvoy, "The Church in Romania," *Pro Mundi Vita: Dossiers* 4 (November-December 1978).

[43]See, for example, Stella Alexander, *Church and State in Yugoslavia Since 1945* (Cambridge: Cambridge University Press, 1979); Pedro Ramet, "Yugoslavia: The Catholic Church, 1945-1985," *Religion in Communist Dominated Areas* 25:3 (Summer 1986): 109-119.

press, extensive religious education programs, and some charities. Problems remain, however. The Church must guard against atheistic and Marxist indoctrination in state schools; some anti-religious media propaganda regarding the church's alleged misuse of religion for nationalistic and political ends; employment discrimination against Catholics; and efforts to divide the Church. Also of concern are a lack of access to radio and television; restrictions on religious practice for those in the military; and limitations on certain pastoral activities, such as prison and hospital ministry.

73. Yugoslavia's economic and political crisis since President Tito's death in 1980 has provoked divisions and disagreements within the communist party and exacerbated tensions among Yugoslavia's nationalities, notably between the Orthodox Serbs and the Muslim Albanians. These tensions have adversely affected church-state relations. The Church is not in a position to play the same role in helping to resolve these tensions as the Polish Church, but, as in Poland, the Church is a leader in promoting human rights and, with the Serbian Orthodox Church, in encouraging unity in a quite diverse Yugoslav society.

III. A Program of Action

A. A New Framework for Church-State Relations

74. In speaking to the current dynamic of church-state relations in some detail, we seek to highlight the fact of the continuing denial of fundamental religious freedoms and the urgent need for fundamental reform in this area by the communist governments of Eastern Europe and the Soviet Union. In doing so, we seek to avoid the tendency of those, on the one hand, who believe that the whole story of the Church in these countries is told by the despicable murder of Bishop Coba and the unjustified confinement of Augustin Navratil; as well as those, on the other hand, who would deny or ignore the reality of these and other continuing attacks on basic human rights and mistake full churches for full religious freedom.

75. This review of church-state relations in these nine countries shows important differences in the extent that religious practices are tolerated by the state. The context in which the Polish Church functions is very different than that in neighboring Czechosolvakia or Lithuania, and the situation in Albania has no analog in Eastern Europe. But important as these differences are, it is evident to us that all governments in Eastern Europe and the Soviet Union share a common hostility — expressed in different ways — toward religion, and this hostility is reflected in repressive or restrictive state policies.

76. It is also clear to us that the churches throughout this region desire and deserve the freedom fully to profess and practice their faith and fully to participate in the building of a just and free society, in conformity with the interests of the nation and the demands of the common good. As Pope John Paul II noted in April of this year, "That freedom which [our fellow believers] demand is rooted in the human heart . . . enriching the lives of [the] nation with the contribution of a sober, well-formed conscience, living by the values of the highest truth, justice, brotherhood, and peace."[44] Expanded religious freedom, then, would benefit both believers and society; it is necessary for integral human development, and it would contribute to the development and maturation of these societies in ways commensurate with their long and rich traditions.

77. We are encouraged by the breezes of renewal that are beginning to blow across the Soviet Union and parts of Eastern Europe and pray that they will bring positive and far-reaching political, economic, and cultural reforms. Such reforms must not be confined to these spheres, however, but must extend to religion as well. Progress in these other areas will be measured, in part, by the extent to which institutional guarantees of greater religious freedom are put into place.

78. Greater religious freedom would mean a new framework of church-state relations that allows more than freedom of worship alone. This new framework would allow for the widespread dissemination of uncensored religious materials and would provide greater access to the media. It would mean new policies that protect parents' rights to provide formal religious education to their children; that end discrimination and atheistic and anti-religious propaganda; and that allow the formation of church groups for educational, charitable, cultural, and social purposes. Moreover, it would allow religious bodies the freedom to choose, train, and appoint ministers without state interference; to construct church buildings; to run their own schools; to form religious orders; and to control the many other dimensions of their corporate life.

79. Such a new framework would go far in implementing the principles enshrined in the Universal Declaration of Human Rights, the Helsinki Final Act, and other international agreements signed by the Soviet Union and all of the countries of Eastern Europe except Albania. These and other just demands have been expressed frequently by believers of all faiths in Eastern Europe and the Soviet Union for many years. With our Holy Father, our "hope wells up that—at least in [these] matters which are essential—the longings of our . . . brothers and sisters who sincerely confess their religious faith will not be disappointed."[45]

---

[44] Pope John Paul II, "Address to Bishops and Administrators of Lithuanian Dioceses" (April 27, 1988).
[45] Ibid.

B. A Response of Solidarity by Churches, Groups, and Individuals

80. The fact of repression of and restrictions on religious practice in Eastern Europe and the Soviet Union creates in us a responsibility and an opportunity. We must, as Pope John Paul II has said, "endeavor to assume an attitude of Christian solidarity with our brothers in the faith who are undergoing discrimination and persecution. It is also necessary to seek forms in which this solidarity can be expressed."[46]

81. In the spirit of Christian solidarity, we cannot succumb to indifference, complacency, or despair in the face of a seemingly intractable problem of religious liberty in certain countries and under certain political systems. What we said in *The Challenge of Peace* is apt:

> Soviet behavior in some cases merits the adjective reprehensible, but the Soviet people and their leaders are human beings created in the image and likeness of God. To believe we are condemned in the future only to what has been the past of U.S.-Soviet relations is to underestimate both our human potential for creative diplomacy and God's action in our midst which can open the way to changes we could barely imagine.[47]

82. Without trivializing or ignoring the deep ideological antagonism toward religion that has been variously manifested in the Soviet Union since the 1917 revolution and throughout Eastern Europe in the past forty years, we are convinced that real progress is both possible and necessary. We recognize that significant progress toward religious freedom will be the result of changes in the internal dynamics of these countries, but we can play a role in encouraging the process of change. Therefore, we pledge ourselves and urge others concerned with promoting justice, freedom, and peace to take the following actions.

83. Because the promotion of human rights is required by the gospel and is central to the Church's ministry, we must pursue the cause of religious liberty as an essential component of our defense of human dignity, our option for the poor and vulnerable, and our pursuit of peace and justice. In doing so, we cannot forget that the lack of religious liberty is not a concern of Catholics or Christians only, but also of Jews, Muslims, and members of all faiths. The ability of religious communities to voice a united advocacy for freedom, based on the principle that the lack of religious freedom for one is a lack of

---

[46]Pope John Paul II, General Audience (April 4, 1979).

[47]National Conference of Catholic Bishops, *The Challenge of Peace: God's Promise and Our Response* (Washington, D.C.: USCC Office of Publishing and Promotion Services, 1983), no. 258.

religious freedom for all, would be a prophetic statement and one in keeping with the ecumenical spirit of our times.

84. The starting point for action on behalf of religious liberty is to *inform* ourselves of the situation of believers in Eastern Europe and the Soviet Union. We must respond to the dire need for education about the complex realities of the situation. This education should take seriously the differences in the treatment of religion between communist countries as well as the common problems, and it should avoid the polemics, oversimplifications, and self-righteousness, which are so tempting in this area.

85. Education must lead to *action* and *advocacy* for greater religious freedom in Eastern Europe and the Soviet Union, and in the many other areas of the world where it remains unrealized. Among the many steps that can be taken, we commit ourselves to and recommend the following:

    a) wherever possible, more East-West *contacts and exchanges*, especially between churches and believers, but also between professionals, scientists, cultural groups, unions, and others. These exchanges can be invaluable means of sharing information, improving understanding, and developing trust;

    b) the *introduction of the issue of religious liberty* and other human rights concerns into these contacts and exchanges. The need to raise these issues frankly and constructively becomes especially urgent precisely when these relationships are pursued as small steps toward improved understanding, trust, and peace;

    c) application to businesses operating in Eastern Europe and the Soviet Union of the same *norms of corporate responsibility* that are used to evaluate the appropriateness of U.S. business presence and activities in other parts of the world;

    d) wherever possible and to the extent feasible, *financial support* for the churches in Eastern Europe and the Soviet Union and for the many private organizations that provide direct aid, such as Bibles, religious literature, and other materials, to these churches; and

    e) public and private *protest* against violations of religious liberty, whether directed against individual believers or religion in general.

86. Finally, and most important, we should continue to *pray* for those who suffer for their beliefs, recognizing our own deeply felt need for their prayers as well. We should pray with the confidence that Jesus has been sent "to proclaim liberty to captives and . . . to set the downtrodden free" (Lk 4:18), and with the assurance that those who are persecuted for Christ's sake will be greatly rewarded in heaven (cf. Lk 6:22-23).

C. Policy Proposals

87. These individual and corporate efforts are, perhaps, the most important ways in which we can act in solidarity with our brothers and sisters in Eastern Europe and the Soviet Union. But, as concerned citizens, we cannot ignore the positive ways in which U.S. policy can play a role, however limited, in encouraging the expansion of religious liberty in these countries.

88. A constant theme of our statements on matters of international justice and peace has been that human rights — as a matter of principle and as a matter of integrity — should play a prominent role in U.S. foreign policy. In giving human rights this prominence, the United States respects the sovereignty of other nations at the same time that it exercises its legitimate concern for violations of basic human dignity. We are encouraged by efforts to make religious liberty and human rights concerns a more integral part of U.S. relations with the Soviet Union and Easten Europe in the past decade. Three dimensions of this policy of integrating human rights into U.S. foreign policy deserve more detailed attention.

1. International Agreements and Institutions

89. The Helsinki review process has provided a primary mechanism for dealing with these human rights concerns.[48] The accords bind the signatories, which include all countries of Eastern Europe except Albania, to respect human rights and fundamental freedoms, including the freedom of religious belief and practice. Since the signing of the accords in 1975, follow-up meetings have been held in Belgrade, Madrid, and Vienna. This review mechanism has encouraged the formation of independent human rights monitoring groups throughout the Soviet bloc, has focused international attention on human rights issues, has legitimized the efforts of governmental and nongovernmental organizations to raise human rights concerns directly with signatory governments, and has directly linked issues of human rights and security in Europe.

90. This dynamic, ongoing process has coincided with some improvements in religious liberty, but the overall results have been disappointing. Despite important differences noted above, it is clear that none of the countries examined in this statement have upheld fully their obligations under the religious liberty provisions of the Helsinki

---

[48]For an overview of the Helsinki process, see, for example, Vojtech Mastny, *Helsinki, Human Rights, and European Security* (Durham, N.C.: Duke University Press, 1986); CSCE Commission Report, "Basket III: Implementation of the Final Act of the Conference on Security and Cooperation in Europe: Findings 11 Years After Helsinki" (March 1987).

Accords. Rather than despair of the usefulness of international agreements such as the Helsinki Accords, however, the United States should continue to insist on full compliance with such agreements and seek to strengthen them.

91. In addition to support for the Helsinki Accords, it is necessary to implement more fully the UN Declaration on Human Rights; the 1981 UN Declaration on the Elimination of All Forms of Intolerance and of Discrimination Based on Religion or Belief; and other international instruments and to continue to support and to strengthen international mechanisms charged with monitoring and protecting human rights, especially the United Nations. In this regard, we welcome the establishment, in 1986, of a special rapporteur on religious intolerance under the auspices of the UN Human Rights Commission and support his efforts to report objectively on intolerance and discrimination wherever they exist.[49]

2. Bilateral Relations

92. A second aspect of U.S. policy concerns its bilateral relations with the countries of Eastern Europe. This statement has tried to avoid suggesting that church-state relations are uniformly bad and that there is no hope for improvement. The cases of Poland, the German Democratic Republic, and Yugoslavia show the possibility of a measured and differentiated use of the United States' influence, however limited, for improvements in religious liberty. It is too early to tell whether proposed reforms in the Soviet Union and throughout the Soviet bloc will become a reality and will include greater religious freedom. It is clear, however, that General Secretary Gorbachev's policies offer potentially significant changes in thought and practice that deserve to be taken seriously and encouraged—not as the answer to radically different political philosophies and moralities and continuing East-West conflict, but as a potential basis for gradual expansion of freedoms in the Soviet bloc and improvements in East-West relations. The liberalization and the desire for improved East-West relations and trade in countries such as the Soviet Union, the GDR, Yugoslavia, and Hungary point to the desirability of a new assessment of U.S. policy via-à-vis these countries.

93. Such an assessment should consider the possibility of using affirmative measures to influence human rights policies and practices, including developing closer relations, extending credits, and encouraging cultural and educational exchanges and tourism. Such initiatives have the potential to contribute to incremental improvements in human

---

[49]Angelo d'Almeida Ribeiro, the special rapporteur, has submitted two important reports on implementation of the declaration; see UN Doc. E/CN.4/1987/35 and UN Doc. E/CN.4/1988/45.

rights in some East European countries. In all such initiatives, U.S. diplomacy should make it clear that continued improvement in relations will depend, in part, on continued improvement with regard to religious liberty and human rights.

3. Religious Liberty and Peace

94. A third aspect of U.S. foreign policy involves the Soviet Union in particular and concerns the relationship between peace and human rights, specifically religious liberty. Pope John XXIII, in his encyclical *Pacem in Terris*, put forward freedom as one of the "four pillars that support the house of peace."[50] As Pope John Paul II has so often emphasized, the guarantee of religious freedom, in particular, is essential for the proper development of the human person; helps bring moral cohesion and the common good to individual societies; and contributes to the climate of mutual trust, which is an indispensable condition for and primary expression of true social and international peace.[51] Conversely, religious repression, like every form of injustice, creates deep social divisions and mistrust that endanger and sap the energies for peace. Moreover, it negates the positive contribution to the work of peace and justice that inspires all of the great religious traditions.

95. Clearly, fuller protection of religious freedoms and other human rights in the Soviet bloc is one of *many* prerequisites to the more stable, peaceful relationship between East and West that should be our goal. Until this basic fact is taken seriously, dialogue with Soviet bloc governments often will be difficult and sterile. As we said, in our 1983 pastoral letter *The Challenge of Peace*, U.S. relations with these governments should be guided by this "cold realism" about the obstacles to fruitful dialogue. But this realism must be "combined with the conviction that political dialogue and negotiations must be pursued. . . . Acknowledging all the differences between the two philosophies and political systems, the irreducible truth is that objective mutual interests do exist between the superpowers."[52]

96. Therefore, we must work tirelessly, as individuals, as a Church, and as a nation for greater freedom and justice in countries where these are not respected. But we cannot ignore the necessity for continued dialogue with the governments of these countries in order to create possibilities for agreement in areas where concrete if limited convergence of interest can be found. This dialogue has led recently to progress in disarmament and U.S.-Soviet relations. We hope and expect that it will lead to similar progress on religious liberty and

---

[50]"1981 World Day of Peace Message," p. 465, citing Pope John XXIII, *Pacem in Terris*.
[51]"1988 World Day of Peace Message," p. 495.
[52]*The Challenge of Peace*, no. 225.

human rights. We must pursue disarmament and improved relations *in tandem with* religious liberty and human rights. Because each has its own distinct dynamic and rationale, they should not be held hostage to one another, but neither should one be pursued with indifference to the other. *Both* must be pursued with vigor and perseverance, for both share a common aim: a more authentic and lasting peace.

IV. Conclusion

97. We have spoken here in considerable detail about infringements on religious liberty in Eastern Europe and the Soviet Union, which are a continuing injustice and threat to peace, and which all too often are hidden, ignored, or dismissed. We have spoken as teachers and pastors who seek to educate about these unjust restrictions and to inspire Catholics and the wider society to take concrete steps of solidarity to assist the millions of believers in these countries who long for greater religious freedom. As preachers of the gospel, who have spoken consistently on behalf of justice, peace, and freedom in our own country and throughout the world, we have implored the governments of Eastern Europe and the Soviet Union to live up to their commitments under international covenants and to initiate a new framework for church-state relations so as to promote authentic human development, social progress, and peace.

98. By speaking in these ways, we ally ourselves with the bishops of Eastern Europe in their suffering and in their ministry to their oppressed peoples. They and their fellow Christians celebrate centuries of Christianity in their nations, complete in the knowledge that their faith not only has not diminished but thrives. The celebration of these anniversaries and the continuing vitality of the Eastern and Western forms of Christianity are, as Pope John Paul II has reminded us, "above all, an incentive to turn our pastoral and ecumenical sensibilities from the past towards the future, to strengthen our longing for unity and to intensify our prayer."[53]

99. We pray fervently for Christian unity, and we pray especially that all believers of all faiths soon will see the day when religious persecution and intolerance have become unvenerated relics of an unhappy past, anachronisms with no place in modern societies. Until this day dawns, we remain strengthened by the faithful witness of our brothers and sisters in Eastern Europe and the Soviet Union, and we will work and pray that they soon will be liberated from the structures of sin

---

[53]*Go into All the World,* p. 26.

that bind them. With the Holy Father we pray that "these brothers and sisters of ours [will] feel our spiritual closeness, our solidarity, and the comfort of our prayer. We know that their sacrifice, to the extent that it is joined to Christ's, bears fruits of true peace."[54]

---

[54]"1988 World Day of Peace Message," p. 496.

Appendix

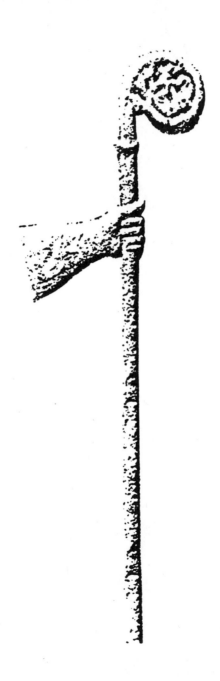

Chronological Table of Important Events in the History of the Church in the United States from 1983-1988

1983: President Ronald Reagan, in the State of the Union Address, reiterated his support for a constitutional amendment on school prayer and for tuition tax credits for parents with children in private and parochial schools. He repeated these stances January 31 at the National Religious Broadcasters' Convention, where he also condemned abortion. Archbishop Joseph L. Bernardin of Chicago was elevated to the College of Cardinals. In addition, he was named the 1982 South Carolinian of the Year for "dedicated service to mankind and superior accomplishments." Archbishop John R. Quinn of San Francisco was named to help guide developments in religious life in America. Cardinal Humberto Medeiros, archbishop of Boston, died. Cardinal Terrence Cooke, archbishop of New York, died. U.S. Supreme Court allowed bus transportation for children attending parochial as well as public schools. Seattle Archbishop Raymond G. Hunthausen's administration was investigated. Philadelphia became the last archdiocese in the country to have Saturday evening Masses for fulfillment of the Sunday Mass obligation.

1984: Full diplomatic relations were established between the United States and the Vatican. William A. Wilson was named first U.S. ambassador to the Holy See. Bernard F. Law was named archbishop of Boston. John J. O'Connor was appointed archbishop of New York. Monsignor John Tracy Ellis received the Theodore M. Hesburgh Award for his outstanding contribution to Catholic higher education. The New York U.S. District Court ruled that government funding for military chaplains does not violate the U.S. Constitution. "A Chorus Line," the longest running Broadway show, won the Christopher Award. Professional basketball star Julius Irving received the Father Flanagan Award for service to youth. The U.S. Senate rejected a proposed constitutional amendment to allow organized, spoken prayer in the public school. As papal pro-nuncio, Archbishop Pio Laghi presented his diplomatic credentials to President Reagan. Newark Father Richard Hynes was elected president of the National Federation of Priest Councils. Sister Frances A. Mlocek, IHM, was appointed director of finance for the National Conference of Catholic Bishops and the United States Catholic Conference. The John Courtney Murray Award was presented to Monika Hellwig of the Georgetown University faculty. The bicentennial of California missionary Father Junipero

Serra's death was commemorated. Also noted was the 100th anniversary of the Third Council of Baltimore.

1985: Boston Archbishop Bernard F. Law and New York Archbishop John J. O'Connor were elevated to the College of Cardinals. Catholic Relief Services, in a cooperative relief program, distributed $471 million in relief aid to African nations. Sixteen Sanctuary workers, including two priests and three nuns, were indicted for smuggling illegal aliens. Seven black Catholic bishops joined the anti-apartheid protest in Washington, D.C. President Reagan spoke encouragingly to the 71,000 pro-life marchers in the nation's capital. The number of U.S. permanent deacons increased to 7,102. Cardinal O'Connor and four U.S. bishops discussed peace with Nicaragua's President Ortega. Catholic Near-East Welfare Association contributed more than $750,000 famine relief to Ethiopian bishops. U.S. Catholics contributed more than $43.6 million to the Society for the Propagation of the Faith. The U.S. Catholic Conference opposed military aid to the *contras*. Franciscan Father Junipero Serra was declared venerable. Over 40,000 attended Youth Rally in New York. Mother Teresa of Calcutta was awarded the Presidential Medal of Freedom. Jesuit Father Alvaro Corrada del Rio, SJ, was ordained first Hispanic auxiliary bishop of Washington, D.C. The Catholic Church Extension Society celebrated its eightieth anniversary. Cardinal O'Connor received the first Cardinal Bea Interfaith Award from the Anti-Defamation League of B'nai B'rith. Knights of Columbus donated more the $66 million and logged more than 23 million volunteer hours for charity.

1986: Catholics honored Rev. Dr. Martin Luther King, Jr., on the first federal holiday commemorating his birthday. Federal Court permitted resumption of federal remedial education programs in Pennsylvania private schools. Catholic Medical Mission Board shipped more than $13.5 million worth of medicine to the poor. U.S. Catholics contributed $46.5 million to the Society for the Propagation of the Faith, an increase of 6.7 percent over the previous year. Seattle Archbishop Raymond G. Hunthausen received the President's Award of the National Federation of Priest's Councils. Bishop Donald R. Pelotte, SSS, was ordained as the first Native American bishop. Catholic Relief Services provided $6 million to Polish children endangered by the Chernobyl nuclear accident. Cardinal John Carberry received the first *Pro Fidelitate et Virtute* Award of the Institute of Religious Life. Maryknoll missioners celebrated their seventy-fifth anniversary. The Catholic University of America professor William May named to International Theological Commission by Pope John Paul II. Hostage Father Lawrence M. Jenco was freed by Shiite Moslems. Sisters of St. Joseph celebrated the 150th anniversary of their arrival in the United States. For her anti-drug activities, The Catholic University of America's Cardinal Gibbons Medal was awarded to First Lady Nancy Reagan. Frank Shakespeare was named second U.S. ambassador to the Vatican. The U.S. Bishops' Campaign for Human Development allocated $634 million to self-help projects. Father Theodore Hesburgh retired after thirty-five years as president of the University of Notre Dame. U.S. Bishops' Committee for the Church in Latin America allocated $4 million for pastoral projects in Latin America. New Jersey bishops denounced surrogate motherhood as "a legal outrage and moral disaster." Sister Jane Coyle was the first nun named as administrator of a Baltimore archdiocesan parish.

1987: On Pentecost Sunday, the Marian Year began. Los Angeles Archbishop Roger M. Mahoney was named to U.S. Commission on Agricultural Workers. Franciscan Father Bruce Ritter was presented with an award by President Reagan. The Catholic University of America celebrated its 100th anniversary. St. George Martyr Eparchy for Romanian Catholics in the United States was established by the Vatican. *Our Sunday Visitor* marked its seventy-fifth anniversary. Detroit Auxiliary Bishop Thomas J. Gumbleton and retired Bishop Charles A. Buswell of Pueblo, Colorado were arrested at nuclear test site. Seton Hall University professor Father Stanley L. Jaki, OSB, was awarded the $330,000 Templeton Prize for Progress in Religion. New York Cardinal O'Connor was named by President Reagan to National Commission of Care for AIDS Victims. San Francisco Archbishop John R. Quinn defended John Paul II's meeting with Austrian President Kurt Waldheim against Jewish opposition. Cardinal Patrick O'Boyle, first resident archbishop of Washington, D.C., died. Representatives of all religious faiths took part in an interfaith commemoration of the bicentennial anniversary of the U.S. Constitution. *A Shepherd's Care: Reflections on the Changing Role of Pastor* was issued by the USCC. Buffalo Father Nelson Baker's cause for canonization was introduced. The total number of students for the priesthood in the United States dropped below 10,000 for the first time in decades to 9,410. The Covenant House for runaways received more than 2,500 calls the first day its hot line opened. Miami Auxiliary Bishop Augustin A. Roman played a major role in terminating siege at federal detention center in Oakdale, Louisiana. "Moment of Silence" in public schools was rejected by the U.S. Supreme Court. Pope John Paul II visited the United States.

1988: Archbishop James Hickey of Washington, D.C. and Archbishop Edmond Szoka of Detroit were elevated to the College of Cardinals. Francis B. Schulte was appointed archbishop of New Orleans. President Reagan designated January 17 as "National Sanctity of Human Life Day." By January 19, there were 8,443 permanent deacons and 1,885 candidates. Anthony M. Kennedy was sworn in as justice of the U.S. Supreme Court. Archbishop Eugene A. Marino became the nation's first black archbishop. Paulist Fathers issued first edition of their magazine, *Catholic Evangelization in the United States of America*. Trustees of The Catholic University of America stripped Father Charles E. Curran of his church license to teach theology. Two hundred and forty U.S. religious and political leaders signed the document, *An Appeal for Religious Freedom in the Soviet Union on the Occasion of the Millennium of Christianity in Kievan Rus'*. New York Cardinal O'Connor participated in Cuban ceremonies marking the 200th anniversary of the birth of Father Feliz Varela, an exiled Cuban hero who served in the Archdiocese of New York. The second Native American bishop, Charles J. Chaput, was named to head the Diocese of Rapid City. First American National Congress was held. Mother Teresa addressed more than 20,000 at the National Blue Army Shrine. New York Auxiliary Bishop Austin Vaughan and 850 others were arrested at Valley Forge, Pennsylvania, during Operation Rescue on July 4. Bishop Ignatius Kung Pin-Mel of Shanghai was released after thirty years of imprisonment. Marist Brother Sean Sammon was elected president of the Conference of Major Superiors of Men. Glenmary Home Missionaries celebrated the fiftieth anniversary of their society. President Reagan nominated Hispanic Catholic Lauro Cavazos for the position of Secretary of Education. Cardinal John Dearden, former archbishop of Detroit, died.

Growth of the Church in the United States

*1983-1985**

Categories	1983	1985
Population	52,392,934	52,654,908
Archdioceses	33	34
Dioceses	146	150
Priests	57,891	57,183
Seminarians	11,262	10,440
Parishes	19,118	19,313

*1986-1988***

Categories	1986	1988
Population	52,893,217	54,918,989
Archdioceses	34	34
Dioceses	152	155
Priests	53,382	52,948
Seminarians	8,556	5,646
Parishes	19,546	19,705

*These statistics are taken from the 1984 and 1986 editions of *The Official Catholic Directory*, published by P. J. Kenedy & Sons, New York, N.Y.

The most alarming fact of this set of statistics is the decrease of 5,516 seminarians in such a brief period, very close to a drop of 50 percent in the number of students for the priesthood.

**These statistics are taken from the 1985 and 1989 editions of *The Official Catholic Directory*.

Organization and Purpose of the NCCB/USCC

The National Conference of Catholic Bishops (NCCB) and the United States Catholic Conference (USCC) are the organizations of the American Catholic hierarchy. Through these distinct but closely related conferences—one a canonical entity, the other a civil corporation—the bishops fulfill their responsibilities of leadership and service to Church and nation.

The voting membership of the NCCB consists of approximately 300 active Catholic bishops of the United States, who meet at least once a year in a plenary session. Although they do not have voting status, retired bishops— numbering around ninety-three—also are invited to all general meetings and may take part in discussions. The elected officers of the NCCB include a president, a vice president, a treasurer, and a secretary; all serve three-year terms. The conference functions through a general assembly, an administrative committee of fifty bishop members, four executive-level committees, and some forty-three standing and ad hoc committees. NCCB committees deal with pastoral issues that are important to the Church as a whole. The NCCB enables the bishops to exchange ideas and information, deliberate on the Church's broad concerns, and respond as a body. In some cases, their response is a document; in others, it is a program.

The United States Catholic Conference is the public policy agency of the Catholic bishops of America. It provides an organizational structure and the resources needed to ensure coordination, cooperation, and assistance in the public, educational, and social concerns of the Church at the national or interdiocesan level. Unlike the NCCB, whose members are bishops, exclusively, the USCC's policy-making entities include priests, men and women religious, and lay people. The USCC shares several structures with the NCCB: its administrative board is the same body as the NCCB administrative committee, and the same executive-level committees serve both conferences.

The General Secretariat, located in Washington, D.C., is staffed principally by the general secretary—elected by the administrative committee or board for a five-year term—and three associate general secretaries. It provides day-to-day administration and direction for the work of both the NCCB and the USCC. Indeed, while most staff are assigned to one conference or the other, a significant number work for both. NCCB/USCC committees and their staffs help the bishops establish and implement policy on many matters intimately connected with Catholic life such as doctrine, worship, the parish, evangelization, and canon law. The conferences also carry on the work of sanctification by offering a multitude of informational and consultative services to diocesan offices and other church agencies and institutions.

Index

About the Editor

REVEREND HUGH J. NOLAN, Professor Emeritus at Immaculata College, was ordained a priest of the Archdiocese of Philadelphia in 1941 and obtained his doctorate in American Church History with distinction in 1944. He established the master's program in American Church History at St. Paul Seminary (St. Paul, Minnesota) and has taught at La Salle, Rosemont, and Cabrini Colleges, as well as at Villanova University and The Catholic University of America. He was head of the Theology Department at Immaculata College for twenty-one years and was elected a member of the Academy of American Franciscan History.

Father Nolan is the author of *Francis Patrick Kenrick, Third Bishop of Philadelphia, 1830-1851*. In addition, he also wrote "Francis Patrick Kenrick, 1830-1851" and "Dennis Cardinal Dougherty, 1918-1951" for the recent *History of the Archdiocese of Philadelphia*. He edited the *Pastoral Letters of the American Hierarchy, 1792-1983* and has contributed to the *New Catholic Encyclopedia, Minnesota History, America, Ave Maria*, and the *Catholic Historical Review*. He was editor in chief of the *Records of the American Catholic Historical Society* for twelve years. He has recently returned, after a brief absence, as a columnist for the *Catholic Standard and Times*, the Philadelphia archdiocesan newspaper and contributes to the *Boston Pilot*, the *Voice*, and the *Florida Catholic*. Presently, Father Nolan is pastor of St. Isaac Jogues Parish, Valley Forge, Pennsylvania.

Credits

Dust Jacket Design: OPPS Production Staff

Dust Jacket Photo: Detail of a bishop's crosier from the ruins of the Cistercian Abbey, Boyle, Country Roscommon, Ireland, by Dan Juday

Text Design: Mack Rowe Visual Communications, Ltd.; Alexandria, Virginia

Production

Typeface: Palatino and Palatino Semi-bold

Typography: VIP Systems, Inc.; Alexandria, Virginia